A. L. Gilman

November 1948

*The Pleasure of Their Company*

# THE PLEASURE OF THEIR COMPANY

*An Anthology of Civilized Writing*

EDITED, AND WITH AN INTRODUCTION, BY

Louis Kronenberger

MACDONALD & CO. (Publishers) LTD.
LONDON

*First published* 1947

# *Table of Contents*

# INTRODUCTION

No one word or phrase quite sums up the contents of this anthology; yet the things it contains have decided points in common. What you will find here are examples of that large literature inspired by worldly experience, or the comic sense of life, or the civilized point of view; that literature in which urbanity, irony, elegance, skepticism, sophistication, wit—or the contemplation of those who possessed such qualities—play a leading part. This is the literature of men and women who have noted and understood, exposed or embellished, the way of the world. They themselves, we might add, have been well enough versed in it always to observe its forms while impaling its foibles.

Such a literature has, beyond its fascination and allure, a real and abiding value. It has not, to be sure, the highest value. Anyone at all capable of responding to the urbane has the right to be spared the obvious, so that I shall not labor the point that the comedy of the human spectacle is surpassed by the drama of the human spirit; that there is nothing here to set against the dark, luminous, passionate, multiform world of a Shakespeare or a Dostoevsky. Indeed, it is part of the genius of such men, and a mere fraction of their powers, to be as worldly or witty on occasion as any Lucian or Voltaire. But there is little danger that any of us will tend to claim too much for urbane literature. It is the way of the world to pay lip service or conscience money to "earnestness," and even to depreciate the charms of sophistication while delighting in them. For at their worst there is something trivial about them and perhaps, even at their best, something faintly tarnishing. With the philosophers, after all, solitude is allotted the highest social position, and contemplation outranks the most dazzling talk. There is no divine mystery, and little human poetry, in worldliness; there is notably less virtue than vice, and possibly less decency than decorum. But there is all the same an immense amount of good sense, of wit, of brilliance, of insight, of grace, and of what is best called style: if the deepest things in life seem foreign to it, all but the deepest things are fish into its net.

There is a spurious or vulgar kind of worldliness, and hence of worldly literature, that has helped get the true kind a bad name; and it may be useful, at the outset, to brand this black sheep of the family. The word *sophistication*, which there is no way for me to avoid using from time to time, is itself an unhappy word; one sprung from low beginnings and still given to shabby connotations and uses. It has come to stand for what is both too knowing and too chic, and we associate it with people who think it a crime to be dowdy and a disgrace to be duped. There is even a kind of shady literature that borrows its name, though the name, there, is hardly more than a synonym for sex. "Sophistication" in this popularized and déclassé sense is a word and a thing that largely came out of the twenties, trailing with it their flashiness, their cynicism, their smug nonconformities, their lickerish tastes, their refusal to be shocked but desire to be shocking. There was a whole literature of this kind of thing, in which all ten of the commandments were painstakingly, if often rather languidly, broken. Frequently the style was more purple than the sins were scarlet, and epigrams were scattered about like broken glass, and with just that kind of sharpness. But much oftener the style and the tone were hard. Nobody believed in anything; and nobody had any wish to believe in anything, which is the point where doubt becomes decadence. Most of these writers were quite unconventional in a highly conventional way; and they were haunted by fashions in feeling and thought, though endowed very little with style. One could easily name names and quote passages, but it seems kinder to stroll through the cemetery than to muss up particular graves.

There was nothing new about this literary phase of the twenties. There are always milieus, and writers emerging from them, that, while making life add up to very little, make it add up wrong. But periodically in the history of society—and almost always as a reaction against stuffy and too repressive eras—there come real outbursts of defiantly amoral behavior, when the fashion is to be cynical and "emancipated," when in the name of frankness social codes are all but reversed, when the baby gets thrown out with the bath water, and virtue is scouted that gentility may be crushed. For our purposes it is not so much whether these movements constitute an evil as that they culminate in excess. There is something, even taking the worldly view, very excessive about the callousness and knowingness of the Restoration literature; there is something very excessive about the orchids and hashish of the nineties in England. The sophistication of these and other eras is either unripe or overripe; it is something, moreover, that takes an arrogant pride in itself—and not least in its faults. The impulse behind it will sometimes, as with Restoration comedy and verse, be in large part genuine. But it will oftener be self-conscious, artificial and outré, as it was—over and above its revolt against Victorianism—in the literature that ended (for it did not begin) in the nineties. Either way, it manages after a time to bore and even irritate us; there is always something too flamboyant and emphatic about its methods. Seeming to stand at the opposite pole from the tract, it shares with the tract a desire to assert, espouse, propagandize something, and it has some of a tract's relentlessness in driving home its point.

As for the sophistication that is largely a euphemism for sex, only a German professor would feel any compulsion to discourse on it. We are all familiar with it, and with its prime desire to titillate or shock. What we possibly overlook is that it has a much wider and less adolescent appeal than we might imagine. There is nothing surprising in that; sex, as the German professor would point out, is the least common denominator of literature no less than of life, and the basis for almost everybody's standards of worldliness. We shall eventually note how large a part sex plays in civilized literature, as, among other things, a theme for social comedy. The trouble with it at the merely concupiscent or exhibitionistic level, beyond what may be crude in treatment, is that it is made to exist without an exhilarating enough context, without reference to temperament or recourse to wit; and that after a time a lively mind finds its repetitions tiresome. Some guides to gallantry, some scandalous chronicles, manage to go on diverting us, and so to save themselves, by their concurrent portrayal of manners. Generally speaking, however, sex purveyed as a commodity rather than as a key to behavior falls outside the bounds of civilized writing.

There still remains to be blackballed that portion of literature which is no more than fashionable or foppish. Most of it, to be sure, does not live long; and if it is unearthed after two or three generations, proves so insipid that we need look no further to discredit it. But in one's own age a good deal of such writing gets published and praised, is *not* dull, and in a passing way is extremely engaging. Its very merit lies, however, in its contemporaneousness; in its timing no less than its texture it is a soufflé, and what once made, say, a *Peter Whiffle* so diverting now conspires to date it.

How good fashionable literature—as such—will be depends largely on how good its age is. The trivia of an age that achieves real style and wit will very likely catch—and for a long time keep—some of their fragrance. The minor Caroline poets, the minor eighteenth-century composers, the minor Georgian letter-writers, the minor French aphorists, have somewhere an affinity with Marvell, with Mozart, with Horace Walpole, with La Rochefoucauld because, in each case, a whole society was penetrated with the same traditions and even, up to a point, endowed with the same temperament. The present age—to view it only from the standpoint of worldliness and not of world events—is not too happy a one for civilized writing. In spite of mounting evidence, ours is by no means the most vulgar era in history. But it is at the very least the age that from the direst necessity found words like *phony* and *chichi*. It is not less the age whose most celebrated hostess is Miss Elsa Maxwell. The result, in terms of urbane literature, is obvious—and yet a little complicated. Ours is a time when those born to create that literature have been for the most part diverted into writing satire. The difference is not simply one of tone, the suave and smiling frequently becoming the savage and farcical; it is equally one of subject-matter. For the burden of the most lasting civilized writing, of our classics of wit and urbanity, is what never changes in human nature: its foibles and illusions and vanities, the absurdity in the lover, the childishness of the artist, the inconsistencies of the philosopher, the wise man's self-deceptions, the strong man's weaknesses; and beneath all that, the endless recurrence of folly, the everlasting repetition of failure, hence the ruefulness that deepens the comedy of the human scene. Such sophistication is very much a matter of stance and perspective and attitude, which somehow does not particularize but universalizes. (A satiric study of a moment in the history of manners does just the opposite.) And always with such sophistication, it is the cream of the jest that the observer is not exempted from what he observes, and knows it.

But the satire of our age, whether born of moral fervor or cynical amusement or frivolity or frustration, has a much more immediate target and a much more concentrated aim. It is some of it very funny and some of it very sharp. But, essentially, it is concerned with abuses that call for remedy, with conditions that cry out for change; or as an exposé of foolish and garish and boorish manners, it takes rather too smug a pleasure in laughing at them. Ours is, besides, a peculiarly neurotic age whose outward urbanity, where it exists, reflects little inward composure, and whose sophisticates sometimes seem as atrophied in feeling as they are over-delicate in sensibility. It may well be that we cannot judge the age in terms of worldliness alone, but must judge it—even here—in terms of world events. For this is an age that has come very close to chaos; and a period with the grim commitments of this one cannot do much about maintaining tone. And yet the old, old insistence that amid violent uproars the note of civilization needs more than ever to be struck, the forms of civilization need more than ever to be upheld, does very strictly obtain. Culture *is*, if not the vanquisher of anarchy, at least its eternal foe. Irony makes no frontal attack, but like conscience slaps us between the eyes, unexpectedly, at midnight. Urbanity is a very real form of self-discipline; and the one that, because it lends them distinction, men have the greatest incentive to acquire.

Though it has been easy enough to recognize the kind of thing that is too great for this book and the kind of thing that is too small, I have yet been at something of a loss to fix its exact limits. But I have chosen to make them rather narrow than broad. At the risk of a certain want of variety, it has seemed desirable that this book should be dedicated to one great field of literature. My principle was, along with reflecting his milieu and manner, not to exceed the most characteristic *interests* of the cultivated *homme du monde*. Swift is ironic, Joyce is witty, Flaubert is sophisticated, Pindar is elegant, Plato is urbane; yet these men are essentially part of other and weightier traditions. Obviously, these men are in every cultivated worldling's library and even very often on his lips. Obviously Bach's music and Sophocles' dramas and Giotto's paintings are a definite part of his cultural life. But it is Mozart's *Figaro* and Congreve's *Way of the World* and Lautrec's Paris that lie closest to his heart.

In another direction, too, it has been necessary to distinguish. If the Swifts are, among other things, too angry for this book, the Addisons are too amiable. I have ruled out whatever seemed to me to belong to the genteel tradition, however rich it might be in a certain kind of urbanity or elegance. There are a great many gentlemen and ladies scattered throughout the pages of this anthology; but I hope there are no gentlemen and ladies who are not equally men and women. Some of our present companions may affect a monocle; but none of them, I think, make use of rose-colored glasses. If they are arbiters of taste, they are nowhere the mere victims of tastefulness. If they refuse to raise their voices, they equally refuse to lower their eyes.

But the field, however limited, is not exactly narrow. It still reconciles the flirt of a fan with a large, clear-eyed view of the universe. It has a place for a Max Beerbohm who carried dandyism past an attitude into an art, no less than for a Montaigne who made of himself a supreme lesson in anatomy for all ages. It even has a place for those who fired a volley in the cause of humanity—for a Diderot or Voltaire—because, fighting with wit, they annihilated with laughter.

The field, to be sure, is a distinct one—as distinct as civilization is from life. But what is special about it flows out of, and back into, something universal. We are inclined to divide people on the basis of their natures and say with Horace Walpole that life is a comedy to him who thinks, a tragedy to him who feels. We might better divide them on the basis of their temperaments, saying with Figaro in *The Barber of Seville*: "I force myself to laugh at everything, for fear of having to weep." For in so dividing men, we also in a way unite them; we distinguish, not those natural feelings which are everywhere pretty much alike, but men's cultivated as opposed to their spontaneous reactions. The truth, in spite of Walpole, is that to most people life is no more tragedy than comedy, no more comedy than tragedy. It is not only something that mingles both; it is also something that they have never taken the pains to formulate. It is only a relative handful of human beings who gather up their experiences and their observations and turn them into an attitude toward the world, a kind of art-form for existence. Nor is this something that in any way explains existence; it is only something that makes it harmonious and expressive while remaining unexplained. It has become with some people what we designate as the tragic sense of life, and with others what we designate as the comic sense of life. One or the other permeates—may, indeed, be said to have produced—many of the masterpieces of art.

The tragic sense, the comic sense of life are not "philosophies," like pessimism and optimism. They are not centripetal or essentially self-interested, not ways of adapting or addressing oneself to the world, but a form of vibration, a kind of vision. The tragic sense has nothing to do with personal suffering or despair, but is manifest rather in the resignation of Shakespeare's

> Men must endure
> Their going hence even as their coming hither;

in the moral intensity of Wordsworth's

> Suffering is permanent, obscure and dark
> And has the nature of infinity.

It is something apprehended as a quality of life rather than a condition of living. Men may have the tragic sense and be personally very happy, or have the comic sense and be—as so often they prove to be—profoundly melancholy.

If the comic sense of life has not the grandeur of the tragic sense, it is quite possibly more unifying. For, all the more because it robs existence of any godlike sense of design, it reduces it to some workable kind of perspective. Assuming a world of misapprehensions and cross-purposes, it is driven from affirmation to irony, and saved by amusement from anger. From a glimpse of things *sub specie æternitatis* it is moved to conclude that man himself is vain, and deluded, and sometimes a little mad; from a view of perfection, that man cannot achieve it and would find it hampering if he could. It sees Icarus destroyed not so much by his vast pretensions as by his fatal ignorance. It encounters Canutes who have never been near the sea. It observes Squire Western abandoning the hunt for his daughter to hunt the fox that crosses his path. It sees the philosopher forfeiting all his serenity to obtain a smile from a barmaid, or the conqueror of empires in a panic for having offended his wife. It notes the vanity in man's benevolence, the egotism in his aspiration, the queer accidents of fame, the strange antecedents of glory. Selfishness, it observes, often confers blessings, and self-sacrifice will sometimes cause pain; virtue can be a thistle and vice a flowering shrub. But this comic sense, confronted by all these paradoxes and ironies, is not gloating or malevolent: there is something humane rather than harsh in its laughter. If it discourages humanity from being too easily impressed or illuded, it saves it from being shocked, from being self-righteous, from being intolerant. In its way, it *creates* what is civilized from the realization that life itself is not.

The comic sense penetrates and lights up such a classic work as *Candide;* everywhere twists the tail of human credulousness and ignorance and nebulous idealism. This brief chronicle, fuller of woes than Æneas' wanderings, than Job's long ordeal, proceeds at breakneck speed, relentless in its horror, relentless in its hilarity. It is an extravaganza of suffering in which sympathy could not possibly keep pace with misfortune. It is hardly less a directory of outrages, villainies, and crimes—the evidence that Voltaire obligingly offers in support of the thesis that this is the best of all possible worlds. It is, finally, a testimonial to man's own inability to recognize happiness when he finds it; witness Candide rejecting El Dorado to pursue his illusion of Cunegonde. But however wickedly it enjoys its own satire, *Candide*, by being something more than satire, somehow rounds a point of human wisdom, even writes a prescription for human happiness. The prescription, to be sure, has been conspicuously ignored: small-scale gardening has never become the rage. It never will; to most men, it smacks of the sort of advice they reserve for poor relations. Idealism and egotism—and who, inquires the comic spirit, shall quite separate the two?—idealism and egotism ask a great deal more of life. And even the comic sense, so absorbed by the vanity of man's illusions, is bound to admit that his illusions sweeten life even more, perhaps, than their loss embitters it.

The great world is necessarily the scene and subject-matter of a large part of civilized literature. There, if in any milieu, we shall find elegance, urbanity, sophistication, all the *leniores virtutes*, the established forms, the high amenities of living. There we shall find existence aspiring to the level of an art—if only the art of pleasing. Pleasure itself, though forever sought there, is suavely policed by breeding and taste. It is a world of overtones and obliquities, where shoulders and eyebrows are eloquent, where wit must justify malice, and an insult be conveyed with as much style as a compliment. Its thousand artifices are designed to create an illusion of something delightfully natural; its thousand complexities aim at an effect of something supremely simple—the *simplex munditiis* of Horace.

This, to be sure, is a large claim on its part, and a great act of faith on ours. The world of high society has been known to fall short of such perfection. Not all its enjoyments are embossed with style. Not all its members are entirely well-bred, let alone witty. More often than not, it is apt to provide a spectacle of the bored at the mercy of the boring. On the one hand, its forms can be asphyxiating; on the other, the neglect of them can be scandalous. So much so, that the disparity between what the great world pretends to be and what it really is, is one of the oldest and safest of all forms of satire. The supposed charm of great ladies, the reputed dash and *désinvolture* of grand seigneurs, the traditional glitter of ballrooms and brilliance of dinner parties—these, for centuries, have been the spent rockets and burst balloons of satirists. And all this is to be concerned with only the manners of the great world; a far harsher pen has gone to work on its morals. The selfishness, the rancor, the treachery, the heartlessness, the vice have packed so many volumes that we, with no thought of being a whit more lenient, may here restrict them to one sentence.

And yet it is in the great world alone that we shall sometimes find a perfect flowering of the amenities. There *have* been courts at which true elegance was prized, great houses in which true urbanity was practiced; there have been salons where, as nowhere else, conversation was turned into an art and personalities were harmonized like colors. The chimaera, on occasion, has become a reality. But even as a chimaera it continues to be fascinating. It may engage the snob in us, but snobbishness is perhaps a little more interesting than it seems. We are not speaking of the cruel or parvenu kind; of country-club notions of "the best people"; of the stockbroker's daughter snubbing the clothing-manufacturer's niece. We are speaking of society, and hence of snobbery, on the really grand scale. We are speaking of the duchesses that servant girls are sneered at for wanting to read about but whom, actually, almost everybody wants to read about—though conceivably not all in the same books. Whether or not duchesses lead glittering lives or possess a distinguished manner, they remain the symbols of such things. Furthermore, they are examples of rarity. There are very few duchesses, just as there are very few geniuses or sword-swallowers or saints, and it is natural to want to know how they function. Not to feel an interest in society at their level is almost not to have any imagination, for at that level the snob is a romantic. He is in love with the aristocratic ideal. A name like Valois, a great house like Chatsworth, a palace like Schönbrunn conjures up, almost with the force of poetry, something in the history of civilization. On no one, surely, has the great world—for better or worse—exerted a stronger spell than on the literary man. From Shakespeare to Congreve and Pope, Gibbon and Sterne, Balzac and Goethe, Proust and Henry James, writers—personally no less than professionally—have been beguiled by rank. No doubt their ambitions were quite crassly involved; and long ago, in the days of patronage, their livelihoods as well. No doubt, too—so strange a thing is vanity—it pleases them to attain through mere merit to a level conferred on others by birth. But beyond that, beyond even the writer's natural response to distinction and style, I think it is his romantic imagination, his confusing the glamorous symbol with the all-too-tarnished reality, that makes a peculiar snob of him. Max Beerbohm has neatly spoofed the literary man's snobbishness—and his competitiveness as well—in *Maltby and Braxton.* Yet out of the fascinations of high society has come much distinguished literature; and equally, much merciless dissection.

But, spite of our Thackerays and Balzacs and Prousts, perhaps the most minute and elaborate picture of the great world that we possess has come from inside. The Duc de Saint-Simon's *Memoirs* are concerned with what our untutored imaginations might visualize as the most lustrous court life of modern history—the world of Louis XIV. Here, indeed, is all the paraphernalia of a sovereign great world—palaces at Marly, at Fontainebleau, at Versailles, at Meudon, at Sceaux, at Saint-Cloud; dinners and balls; musicales and masquerades, ladies with "an incomparable grace," wits to people an age, and a king who for kingliness, in the way he moved or bowed or sat at supper, has perhaps never been surpassed. Here is a gilded world if ever there was one. But here, as the gilt peels off, is something else; and not merely profligacy and self-indulgence, or sumptuousness without taste, or a vanity-ridden monarch who prescribes forms that shackle his court and indulges in whims that terrify it. Here are the comedy and drama and melodrama of a whole society, the absurd side of it jostling the outrageous, the bland look gainsaying the deep betrayal, the thirst for power, the jockeying for favor, the courtier turned conspirator, the prince become outcast—the way of the world enacted with the most deadly seriousness by a group of consummate worldlings. Here, though the scene is a generation or so later, is the crushing evidence on which that other duke of genius, La Rochefoucauld, based his appalling verdict on mankind.

Saint-Simon was not, like La Rochefoucauld, a searching theorist of human behavior. He had an eye, not a mind; and an eye, in particular, for the eloquent detail. Nor was he, like La Rochefoucauld, at all disinterested or enlightened. His whole career, in a sense, was a crusade to assert the dignity and restore the eminence (lowered by Louis XIV's setting his bastards above them) of the dukes. Details of etiquette, minutiæ of precedence, obsessed him; so that, along with much else, his *Memoirs* are a kind of solemn farce in which a ducal trifle assumes all the importance of a European crisis. But if Saint-Simon was partly a great fool, he was partly a real genius. If his prejudices, his dislikes, his medieval cast of mind obscured the meaning of much that went on, they never obscured the methods. In addition, he could set forth scenes of court life with wonderful spaciousness, and could paint and sometimes probe human beings with the brilliance of a great novelist. His style, at the farthest remove from the point and polish of La Rochefoucauld's, is the most unaristocratic thing imaginable. Yet it includes a gift for the compressed phrase and explosive epithet that has often and understandably been called Tacitean. Though the *Memoirs* are of staggering length, mere extracts from them destroy one of their finest achievements—the *narrative* they provide of court life, with characters entering and exiting, re-entering and re-exiting, over thousands of pages; with cabals and intrigues, shifts of loyalty and changes of fortune, rolling up an imperishable document of worldly existence. Yet even an extract, I think, will convey Saint-Simon's power, and suggest how no novelist, not even Proust, has dealt comparably with his subject. Proust, one might add, pored continually over the *Memoirs*, and it was in them, perhaps, that he fixed on such names as Mirepoix and Charlus.

In literature, as in life, only the self plays a more dominating role than sex. There are as many ways of treating sex as there are human philosophies or literary moods; and each—lyric, tragic, romantic, realistic, naturalistic, puritanical, hedonist, comic, satiric, farcical—possesses its own kind of truth. Some of these moods will, indeed, call sex by another name—love or passion or ecstasy, for example; or they will call it madness; or they will call it sin. They will hail it as a blessing, discourse on it as an art, accept it as a need, mutter over it as a nuisance; remark with any peasant that all cats are gray in the dark, and again with Pascal that "Cleopatra's nose, had it been shorter the whole aspect of the world would have been altered." They will tell of kings who gave up their thrones for love, and of little men who kept their seats in the street-car while their wives swayed adoringly on a strap. They will show the ego exulting in its worldliness, as when Emma Bovary cries out with bourgeois rapture: "I have a lover!" They will show the ego exulting again, in that unforgettable line of Racine's: "I loved the very tears I was causing to flow." They will remember that though Dido killed herself for love, Théophile Gautier was so bored by sexual intercourse that he was ready to work out arithmetic problems in the midst of it. They see in the passion of Albert and Annie Jones something that links them with Tristan and Isolde; but they also see what links both pairs with the cow and the bull.

I have jumbled together all these varieties of love, all these attitudes toward sex, not to produce something cynical in its incongruousness, but the more quickly and clearly to indicate the basis for the civilized point of view. For from observation and experience it tends to distrust all absolutes about sex, and from temperament to deprecate all extremes.

It knows there is enough truth in each of these moods for there to be no final truth in any of them. Love, it observes, keeps men faithful; but so, just as effectively, does lack of temptation. One man quickly tires of the most seductive of wives; another sees his wife, grown old, with all the beauty she possessed when young, or retaining a beauty she never had at all. Or the ego or the world's opinion guides man's amatory conduct. He so much wants what he cannot have that he will feverishly pursue what he really does not want; or he courts out of competitiveness and persists out of wounded vanity.

Thus the civilized point of view is aware of all the rules and risks, along with the rewards, of love-making. But this does not mean that sex then simply becomes a game or even an art, that it cannot be treated with the greatest seriousness. On the contrary, it may be played with the whole mind and being, rather than with just the lips and the heart. What is perhaps the most worldly and adult of all love affairs in fiction—that between Count Mosca and the Duchess of Sanseverina in *The Charterhouse of Parma*—is quite without levity. But it is also quite without illusions.

There is finally that central fact, which can have such dramatic possibilities and such comic overtones—that War Between the Sexes that Mr. Thurber has portrayed, in our day, as a sort of surrealist pandemonium. Outright war or not, it is clearly a real and eternal contest; and perhaps no phase of it brings so much into play as the classic one of courtship. Whether, as Shaw insists, it is woman who really does the pursuing or whether, as most men are pleased to think, it is themselves, does not greatly matter. Either way, if the courtship involves people of spirit, and is conducted with any skill, it offers a great deal of civilized fun to those on the sidelines; indeed, without necessarily being shorn of romance, it becomes saturated with comedy. So much so that the most mettlesome courtship in the English language forms the basis for the finest stage comedy in English literature. *The Way of the World* may be limited by its artifices and weakened by its plot; but it is quite unrivaled in its tone—a tone of pure comedy that aerates both what is realistic in the play and what could be romantic. Thus the "chase and surrender" of Millamant acquires in Congreve's telling an air supremely urbane and yet quite buoyant, playful, and gay. Somehow—in her sensibilities no less than her charms—Millamant is exactly the right heroine for such a role. Had she a warmer heart, she could not mock at her suitor so lightly or so long; had she no heart at all, we should not acquiesce in his winning her. But she remains a consummate coquette without being a mere unprincipled trifler. She is too spoiled and too ungirlish to be lovable; but she is captivating, and a splendid figure from her wonderful first entrance:

> Here she comes, i'faith, full sail, with her fan spread and her streamers out, and a shoal of fools for tender.

Yet *The Way of the World* offers more than a lively duel between the sexes. If only Millamant raises it, as a *play*, above the usual level of Restoration comedy, the dialogue almost everywhere glorifies it as a piece of writing.

For our present purposes it is unfortunate that the most perfect high comedies, the most sophisticated studies, of sex and courtship and marriage exist in exceedingly long novels, in *The Charterhouse* (which is so much else besides), in *The Egoist*, in *Emma*. The temptation to use mere passages has been a great one, but I have resisted it from a conviction that novels—and certainly distinguished novels—ought never to be tampered with. Nothing better remained than to fall back on such stories as *The Matron of Ephesus* and *The Jewels*, which involve situation rather than interplay of character, and are a little cold and it may be a little facile in their irony. For the rest, there are Don Juan and his Julia, the Boccaccian tale given the Byronic twist.

The civilized and skeptical mind is frequently moved, from its distrust of all absolutes, to defend the *opposite* of what passes in the world for truth or morality. At its lowest level this procedure may be no more than a clever parlor game or a tricky show of dialectics; yet even there it can uncover a startling half-truth or an opposed kind of truth. Consider, for example, some of Chesterton's paradoxes, or the hackneyed counter-definition of a gentleman as "a man who is never *un*intentionally rude," or Wilde's "When the gods wish to punish us, they answer our prayers." And at its highest level this deliberate reversal of accepted values becomes, far from something frivolous, a real weapon of enlightenment and even of morality itself. They misjudge Fielding who regard his *Jonathan Wild* as no more than a kind of photographic negative in which all black things become white, and white things black. In propounding his thesis that true greatness is hostile to goodness, and in illustrating it by acclaiming as truly great the most blackhearted criminal of his day, Fielding is simply overstating one proposition in order to discredit its opposite. If he first shocks us by eulogizing the base methods through which Wild prospers, he soon makes us recall how many men that the world really tends to honor followed methods not very different. And they need not even have been conscious villains, these plundering politicos and captains of industry; they may have quite sincerely believed that "This is a hard world" where dog eats dog, a world of every-man-for-himself and the survival of the fittest. Fielding's ironic thesis exactly squares, moreover, with Lord Acton's famous blunt verdict that "All great men are bad men."

Of the large literature that turns traditional values inside out, *The Praise of Folly* is, of course, a classic example. Erasmus's celebrated satire is, taken at one level, simply an ingenious and rather too protracted piece of dialectics that, often through mere word-juggling, makes out a handsome case for Folly. But in another sense the book is much more than either playful or disingenuous, and becomes a plea for judging humanity on a human basis, for disinfecting men's minds of the idea that things not wholly good must be wholly bad, for showing how, at times, wisdom can be a blight and foolishness a blessing. It becomes, as its present translator observes in his preface, a plea for tolerance. Such a plea has its value in any age; in the moral Bronze Age of Erasmus it was as needed as it was dangerous.

Diderot's *Le Neveu de Rameau* is not quite so clear-cut a reversal of values; concerned with many things at once, it can be interpreted in many ways. Carlyle considered it "decidedly the best of all Diderot's compositions"; Sainte-Beuve, while finding in it "a thousand bold and profound ideas," thought that it quite lacked "connectedness" and left a final impression that was "equivocal." It *is* disconnected, to the extent that it is polythematic; and the final impression is in certain respects ambiguous, though I think it was meant to be. Indeed, that is perhaps the point of the piece, in which almost everything—as so often in life—is double-edged and given to turning in upon itself. But Diderot's "farce-tragedy" is, for all that, clearly a major assault upon conventional values: in his heterodoxy Diderot's parasite is something of a devil's advocate at the canonization of Virtue. Or perhaps—frankly acknowledging, as he does, so much that the rest of us struggle to conceal—he is a brutal retort upon human hypocrisy; the accuser, while ostensibly the defender, of the self-interest that governs the world. Again, in his mockery of his "betters," Diderot's parasite is a sort of forerunner of Figaro, and as such in the main stream of eighteenth-century French social criticism.* For in exposing his parasite, Diderot is also arraigning a world that made possible the man's career. No one, at any rate, can doubt how much seriousness underlies Diderot's wit, or what method there is in his flippancy. And beyond all that, *Rameau's Nephew* has high and unambiguous virtues of another kind. To mention two, there is Diderot's brilliant characterization of young Rameau (who actually existed) and his thorough mastery of the dialogue form.

We have been looking at the world through the eyes of the civilized man; what only remains is to look directly at the man himself. Let us take him from real life, and in his own words; let us take Gibbon. His

* *Rameau's Nephew* itself, however, was not published until early—and not published in its most authentic form until late—in the nineteenth century.

*Autobiography* is a serene adagio, the record of a man who had indeed schooled himself to meet life and master it, to take the best counsel, to keep the best company, to enjoy distinguished pleasures and write, in the *Decline and Fall*, an immortal book. In Gibbon's *Autobiography* we find the classical ideal almost, for once, attained; we encounter, in the purest eighteenth-century way, the scholar and the gentleman. But the *Autobiography* is twice blessed: it perfectly reflects the civilized point of view, and it is also, without meaning to be, wonderful high comedy. To repeat the famous comment once again, Gibbon did mistake himself at times for the Roman Empire. He virtually cast himself in marble; and in marble he, even as lesser men, looked a little pretentious and absurd. He reduced his whole love life to a single antithesis, if it is not better called an epitaph—"I sighed as a lover, I obeyed as a son"; and you feel that to be so perfectly controlled as that, one must also be a trifle inhuman. One cannot, at any rate, be quite so smug or rich in self-esteem as Gibbon without somewhere making the reader temper his admiration with amusement. Yet, however much amused, he never quite leaves off admiring.

Obviously, this anthology is a mere selection from an immense field. The selection itself is no larger if only because civilized man is never very comfortable—even propped up in bed—grasping too many pounds of reading-matter. As for what went into the book that might have been left out, or vice versa, that was largely the result of personal taste, though a little the result of principle. On one head the two coincided: I both dislike and disapprove of anthologies that go in overwhelmingly for snippets and fragments, on the theory (it would seem) that mutilating many writers is better than properly representing a relative few; and though I have here and there offered extracts, for the most part this book has aimed at complete works. It has also aimed, within the limits of its space, at not favoring the very short over the fairly long. I have tried, too, not to succumb to the temptation of featuring the unusual or esoteric at the expense of the really good. Here, for example, you will find *Candide*, famous though it is, for the plain reason that it is not famous by accident, that it is clearly one of the masterpieces of literature.

I have my regrets for many things left out, but I won't be tedious about them. Certain writers who qualified perfectly, like Horace and La Fontaine, lose too much in translation. Other writers who qualified perfectly, like Jane Austen and Meredith, had nothing of the right length that I liked well enough. (It was only after a good deal of mulling over, however, that I put aside *Lady Susan.*) Still other writers have been omitted because they were largely subsumed in greater writers: Anatole France in Voltaire, Sheridan in Congreve, Edith Wharton in Henry James. Once or twice, as with Harold Nicolson's *Some People*, permission was refused. Space problems, again, worked against things like *The Importance of Being Earnest*, *The Marriage of Figaro*, *Crotchet Castle*, a host of letter-writers, a proper section of satiric and society verse, something from . . . but, after all, this is an anthology, not a library; and for that matter, a preface, not a dissertation.

Louis Kronenberger

Norwich, Connecticut, August 1945

*The Pleasure of Their Company*

# APHORISMS

## I

LA ROCHEFOUCAULD:

VANITY is the greatest of all flatterers.

To establish oneself in the world, one does all one can to seem established there.

IT is a form of coquetry to emphasize the fact that you do not indulge in it.

WE refuse praise from a desire to be praised twice.

HYPOCRISY is the homage that vice offers to virtue.

PRIDE does not wish to owe and vanity does not wish to pay.

WE often forgive those who bore us, but we cannot forgive those whom we bore.

WE sometimes imagine we hate flattery, but we only hate the way we are flattered.

VAUVENARGUES:

HABIT is everything—even in love.

VICE stirs up war: virtue fights.

No man is weak from choice.

SERVITUDE degrades men even to making them love it.

THE contempt of fools offends us less than the moderate esteem of the intelligent.

MAGNANIMITY owes no accounting to prudence for its motives.

WHOEVER is not a misanthropist at forty can never have loved mankind.

CHAMFORT

A MERE trifle consoles us, for a mere trifle distresses us.

PASCAL

HOWEVER fastidious we may be in love, we forgive more faults in love than in friendship.

LA BRUYERE

MARRIAGE is the only adventure open to the cowardly.

VOLTAIRE

A WISE woman never yields by appointment.

STENDHAL

THE law, in its majestic equality, forbids the rich as well as the poor to sleep under bridges.

ANATOLE FRANCE

# PETRONIUS

## *The Matron of Ephesus*

A MATRON in Ephesus was of such notable chastity that women came from miles around to gaze on her. So, naturally, when her husband was buried she was not satisfied by the popular fashion of following a corpse with streaming hair, and beating the naked breast in front of the crowd: she went with the dead man into his very tomb, an underground sepulchre in the Greek style, and settled down to watch and weep day and night. Her parents and her other relations could not divert her from tormenting herself, or from leaving herself to die of hunger; the government officials finally went away discouraged, and she dragged through her fifth day without food, mourned by every one as the unique example for womankind. A faithful maid sat beside the miserable lady, wept just the proper number of tears with her, and kept the light in the tomb burning. Only this one tale went the rounds in the city, and people of every class agreed that it was an unrivalled example of chastity and love.

In the meantime, the governor of the province ordered some thieves crucified behind the little house where the widow was weeping over this corpse which had so lately been a man. A soldier was ordered to guard the crosses so that the bodies should not be taken down and buried, and the next night he saw the light shining clearly among the trees, and heard the mourner's groans; he was as curious as other human beings, and he wanted to know who it was, and what was going on. So he went down into the vault; and when he saw a beautiful woman, he hesitated, as disturbed as if he had seen an omen or a spirit from the lower regions. But as soon as he noticed the prostrate body, the lady's tears, and her face torn by her own nails, he understood the reason—that she found her burning desire for the dead man unbearable. He brought his poor little supper into the tomb and began begging the weeping woman not to give herself up to useless grief, and not to break her heart with useless sobs: all men, he reminded her, came to the same end and the same last habitation. But she was annoyed by such plebeian condolences, and she struck her breast all the more violently, and tore off her hair to lay it on the body stretched before her. In spite of all that, the soldier did not go away; he tried to give the young woman some food, still with the same persuasion, until the maid was unable to resist the odour of the wine and put out her hand for the kindly offered supper. Then, restored by food and wine, she tried to overcome her mistress's resolution: "What good will you do," she asked, "if you do die of starvation, if you do bury yourself alive and die before Fate has asked for your soul? Do you think that your sorrow can please the body or the spirit of a man who is dead and buried? Why not begin life again? Why not shake off this mistaken idea of fidelity, which only women have, and enjoy the light of day as long as the gods permit? This very corpse should warn you to make the most of life." People usually listen when they are asked to eat or to live; the lady, hungry and thirsty from five days of starvation, let her resolution be broken down, and ate as greedily as the maid who had yielded before her.

Well, you know what generally tempts a well-fed human being. The soldier began attacking the lady's virtue with the same insinuating language that had persuaded her to live. The chaste creature saw that he was a personable youth, and not stupid. The maid was sympathetic and quoted to her, "Will you struggle even against a love that delights you? Do you never remember in whose country you live?"

Why delay the story? Having conquered one part of the lady's person, the victorious soldier won the rest. They lay together not only their nuptial night, but the second, and the third, with the doors of the tomb closed, so that any friend or stranger who came there would suppose that this superlatively virtuous lady had expired on her husband's body. The soldier was delighted with the lady's beauty and with the secrecy of their love; he bought all the delicate food that his pay would allow, and took it to the tomb as soon as darkness fell.

The parents of one of the crucified men saw that the guard was careless, and took the body down to bury it. The next morning, when the soldier saw one of the crosses without its corpse, he realized what the penalty would be, and told his lady what had happened: he would kill himself with his own sword rather than wait to be condemned by a court-martial, and she must make room for her dying lover to join her husband in that fatal place. But the lady was as compassionate as she was chaste. "The gods forbid," she said, "that at the same moment I should see the dead bodies of the two men who are most dear to me. Better to hang up a dead body than to kill a living man."

And in accordance with this speech, she told him that he must take her husband's body from its tomb and fasten it to the vacant cross. The soldier profited by the sagacious lady's ingenuity; and the following day, people wondered how the dead man had managed to crucify himself.

# CECIL

## *The Whig Aristocracy**

THE great Whig country houses of the eighteenth and early nineteenth centuries are among the most conspicuous monuments of English history. Ornate and massive, with their pedimented porticoes, their spreading balustraded wings, they dominate the landscape round them with a magnificent self-assurance. Nor are their interiors less imposing. Their colonnaded entrance halls, whence the Adam staircase sweeps up beneath a fluted dome; their cream and gilt libraries piled with sumptuous editions of the classics; their orangeries peopled with casts from the antique; their saloons hung with yellow silk, and with ceiling and doorways painted in delicate arabesque by Angelica Kauffmann, all combine to produce an extraordinary impression of culture and elegance and established power.

Yet, they are not palaces. There is something easy-going and unofficial about them. Between library and saloon one comes on little rooms, full of sporting prints and comfortable untidiness; the bedrooms upstairs are friendly with chintz and flowered wallpaper. Even the great rooms themselves, with their roomy writing tables, their armchairs, their tables piled with albums and commonplace books, seem designed less for state occasions than for private life: for leisure and lounging, for intimate talk, and desultory reading. And the portraits that glow down from the walls exhibit a similar character. The gentlemen lean back in their hunting coats, the ladies stroll in their parks with spaniels snapping at the ribbons that dangle from the garden hats, slung on their arms. In big and in detail these houses convey an effect of splendid naturalness. In this they are typical of the society which was their creator.

The Whig aristocracy was a unique product of English civilization. It was before all things a governing class. At a time when economic power was concentrated in the landed interest, the Whigs were among the biggest landowners: their party was in office for the greater part of the eighteenth century; during this period they possessed a large proportion of the seats in the House of Commons; they produced more ambassadors and officers of state than the rest of England put together. And they lived on a scale appropriate to their power. "A man," said

* From *The Young Melbourne*, by Lord David Cecil, copyright 1939. Used by special permission of the publishers, The Bobbs-Merrill Company.

one of their latest representatives, "can jog along on £40,000 a year." And jog very well they did. They possessed, most of them, a mansion in London and two or three in the country; they moved through the world attended by a vast retinue of servants, of secretaries and chaplains, of companions, librarians and general hangers-on; they never travelled but in their own carriages; they kept open house to a continuous stream of guests, whom they entertained in the baroque and lavish style approved by their contemporaries.

For the elaboration of their life was increased by the period they lived in. The eighteenth century, that accomplished age, did not believe in the artless and the austere. In its view the good man or, as they would have phrased it, "the man of sense and taste," was he whose every activity was regulated in the light of a trained judgment and the experience of the wise in his own and former ages. From his earliest years the Whig nobleman was subjected to a careful education. He was grounded in the classics first by a tutor, then at Eton, then at the University. After this he went abroad for two years' grand tour to learn French and good manners in the best society of the continent. His sisters learnt French and manners equally thoroughly at home; and their demeanour was further improved by a course of deportment. The Whigs' taste was in harmony with the ideal that guided their education. They learnt to admire the grand style in painting, the "correct" in letters, the Latin tradition in oratory. And in everything they paid strict attention to form. Since life to them was so secure and so pleasant, the Whig aristocrats tended to take its fundamental values very much for granted; they concentrated rather on how to live. And here again, their ideal was not an artless one. Their customs, their mode of speech, their taste in decoration, their stylish stiff clothes, are alike marked by a character at once polished and precise, disciplined and florid. If one of them writes a note it is rounded with a graceful phrase, their most extempore speeches are turned with a flourish of rotund rhetoric.

Yet—and here it is that it differs from those of similar societies on the continent—theirs was not an unreal life; no Watteau-like paradise of exquisite trifling and fastidious idleness. For one thing it had its roots in the earth. Founded as their position was on landed property, the Whig aristocracy was never urban. They passed at least half the year in their country seats; and there they occupied themselves in the ordinary avocations of country life. The ladies interested themselves in their children, and visited the poor; the gentlemen looked after their estates, rode to hounds, and administered from the local bench justice to poachers and pilferers. Their days went by, active, out-of-door, unceremonious; they wore riding-boots as often as silk stockings. Moreover, they were always in touch with the central and serious current of contemporary life. The fact that they were a governing class meant that they had to govern. The Whig lord was as often as not a minister, his eldest son an M.P., his second attached to a foreign embassy. So that their houses were alive with the effort and hurry of politics. Red Foreign Office boxes strewed the library tables; at any time of day or night a courier might come galloping up with critical news, and the minister must post off to London to attend a Cabinet meeting. He had his work in the country too. He was a landlord and magistrate, often a lord lieutenant. While every few years would come a general election when his sons, if not himself, might have to sally forth to stand on the hustings and be pelted with eggs and dead cats by the free and independent electors of the neighbouring borough. Indeed his was not a protected existence. The eighteenth century was the age of clubs; and Whig society itself was a sort of club, exclusive, but in which those who managed to achieve membership lived on equal terms; a rowdy, rough-and-tumble club, full of conflict and plain speaking, where people were expected to stand up for themselves and take and give hard knocks. At Eton the little dukes and earls cuffed and bullied each other like street urchins. As mature persons in their country homes, or in the pillared rooms of Brooks's Club, their intercourse continued more politely, yet with equal familiarity. While their House of Commons life passed in a robust atmosphere of combat and crisis and defeat. The Whigs despised the royal family; and there was certainly none of the hush and punctilio of court existence about them. Within the narrow limits of their world they were equalitarians.

Their life, in fact, was essentially a normal life, compounded of the same elements as those of general humanity, astir with the same clamour and clash and aspiration and competition as filled the streets round their august dwellings. Only, it was normal life played out on a colossal stage and with magnificent scenery and costumes. Their houses were homes, but homes with sixty bedrooms, set in grounds five miles round; they fought to keep their jobs, but the jobs were embassies and prime ministerships; their sons went to the same universities as humbler students, but were distinguished from them there by a nobleman's gold-tasselled mortarboard. When the Duke of Devonshire took up botany, he sent out a special expedition to the East Indies to search for rare plants; Lord Egremont liked pictures, so he filled a gallery with Claudes and Correggios; young Lord Palmerston was offered the Chancellorship of the Exchequer a year or two after entering Parliament.

This curiously-blended life produced a curiously blended type of character. With so many opportunities for action, its interests were predominantly active. Most of the men were engaged in politics. And the women—for they lived to please the men—were political too. They listened, they sympathized, they advised; through them two statesmen might make overtures to each other, or effect a reconciliation. But politics then were not the life sentence to hard labour that in our iron age they have become. Parliament only sat for a few months in the year; and even during the session, debates did not start till the late afternoon. The Whigs had the rest of their time to devote to other things. If they were sporting they raced and hunted; if interested in agriculture they farmed on an ambitious scale; if artistic they collected marbles and medals; if intellectual they read history and philosophy; if literary they composed compliments in verse and sonorous, platitudinous orations. But the chief of their spare time was given up to social life. They gave balls, they founded clubs, they played cards, they got up private theatricals: they cultivated friendship, and every variety, platonic and less platonic, of the art of love. Their ideal was the Renaissance ideal of the whole man, whose aspiration it is to make the most of every advantage, intellectual and sensual, that life has to offer.

In practice, of course, this ideal was not so broad as it sounds. The Whigs could not escape the limitations imposed by the splendour of their circumstances. Like all aristocrats they tended to be amateurs. When life is so free and so pleasant, a man is not likely to endure the drudgery necessary to make himself really expert in any one thing. Even in those affairs of state which took up most of the Whigs' time, they troubled little with the dry details of economic theory or administrative practice. Politics to them meant first of all personalities, and secondly general principles. And general principles to them were an occasion for expression rather than thought. They did not dream of questioning the fundamental canons of Whig orthodoxy. All believed in ordered liberty, low taxation and the enclosure of land; all disbelieved in despotism and democracy. Their only concern was to restate these indisputable truths in a fresh and effective fashion.

Again, their taste was a little philistine. Aristocratic taste nearly always is. Those whose ordinary course of life is splendid and satisfying, find it hard to recognize the deeper value of the exercises of the solitary imagination; art to them is not the fulfilment of the soul, but an ornamental appendage to existence. Moreover, the English nobility were too much occupied with practical affairs to achieve the fullest intellectual life. They admired what was elegant, sumptuous and easy to understand; portraits that were good likenesses and pleasing decorations; architecture which appropriately housed a stately life. In books, they appreciated acute, wittily phrased observation of human nature, or noble sentiments expressed in flowing periods; Cicero, Pope, Horace, Burke. The strange and the harsh they dismissed immediately. Among contemporary authors they appreciated Jane Austen, condemned

Crabbe, for the most part, as sordid and low; and neglected Blake almost entirely. If they had read him, they would not have liked him. For—it is another of their limitations—they were not spiritual. Their education did not encourage them to be; and, anyway, they found this world too absorbing to concern themselves much with the next. The bolder spirits among them were atheists. The average person accepted Christianity, but in a straightforward spirit, innocent alike of mysticism and theological exactitude.

Further, their circumstances did not encourage the virtues of self-control. Good living gave them zest; wealth gave them opportunity; and they threw themselves into their pleasures with an animal recklessness at once terrifying and exhilarating to a modern reader. The most respectable people often drank themselves under the table without shocking anyone. "Colonel Napier came in to-night as drunk as an owl," remarks Lady Sarah Napier, of the staid middle-aged gentleman who was her husband. And their drinking was nothing to their gambling. Night after night they played loo and faro from early evening till the candles guttered pale in the light of the risen sun. Lord Stavordale lamented he had not been playing higher, on a night when he won £11,000 in a single hand at hazard. Georgiana, Duchess of Devonshire, cost her husband nearly £1,000,000 in card debts. Rich as they were, they often ruined themselves. The letters of the time are loud with lamentations about the duns coming in and the furniture going out. Nor was their sexual life of a kind to commend them to an austere morality. "I was afraid I was going to have the gout the other day," writes Lord Carlisle to a friend, "I believe I live too chaste: it is not a common fault with me." It was not a common fault with any of them. In fact an unmarried man was thought unpleasantly queer, if he did not keep under his protection some sprightly full-bosomed Kitty Clive or Mrs. Bellamy, whose embraces he repaid with a house in Montpelier Square, a box at the opera, and a smart cabriolet in which to drive her down to Brighthelmstone for a week's amorous relaxation. Nor did he confine himself to professional ladies of pleasure. Even unmarried girls like Lady Hester Stanhope were suspected of having lovers; among married women the practice was too common to stir comment. The historian grows quite giddy as he tries to disentangle the complications of heredity consequent on the free and easy habits of the English aristocracy. The Harley family, children of the Countess of Oxford, were known as the Harleian Miscellany on account of the variety of fathers alleged to be responsible for their existence. The Duke of Devonshire had three children by the Duchess and two by Lady Elizabeth Foster, the Duchess one by Lord Grey; and most of them were brought up together in Devonshire House, each set of children with a surname of its own. "Emily, does it never strike you," writes Miss Pamela Fitzgerald in 1816, "the vices are wonderfully prolific among Whigs? There are such countless illegitimates, such a tribe of children of the mist." It is noteworthy that the author of this lively comment was a carefully brought up young lady of the highest breeding. The free habits of these days encouraged free speech. "Comfortable girls," remarks a middle-aged lady of her growing nieces, "who like a dirty joke." And the men, as can be imagined, were a great deal freer than the women. For all their polish the Whigs were not refined people in the Victorian sense of the word.

It appears in other aspects of their lives. They could be extremely arrogant; treating their inferiors with a patrician insolence which seems to us the reverse of good breeding. Lady Catherine de Bourgh was not the caricature that an ignorant person might suppose. Fashionable young men of refined upbringing amused themselves by watching fights where the Game Chicken battered the Tutbury Pet into unconsciousness with bare and bloodstained fists. And the pamphlets, the squibs, the appalling political cartoons that lay open in the most elegant drawing-rooms show that the ladies of the day were not squeamish either.

Still, unseemly as some of its manifestations were, one must admit that there is something extremely attractive in this earthy exuberance. And, as a matter of fact, it was the inevitable corollary of their virtues. English society had the merits of its defects. Its wide scope, its strong root in the earth, gave it an astounding, an irresistible vitality. For all their dissipation there was nothing decadent about these eighteenth century aristocrats. Their excesses came from too much life, not too little. And it was the same vitality that gave them their predominance in public life. They took on the task of directing England's destinies with the same self-confident vigour, that they drank and diced. It was this vigour that made Pitt Prime Minister at twenty-four years old,* that enabled the Foxites to keep the flag of liberty flying against the united public opinion of a panic-stricken nation. Nor did they let their pleasures interfere with these more serious activities. After eighteen hours of uninterrupted gambling, Charles Fox would arrive at the House of Commons to electrify his fellow members by a brilliant discourse on American taxation. Rakes and ladies of fashion intersperse their narratives of intrigue with discussions on politics, on literature, even on morals. For they were not unmoral. Their lapses came from passion not from principle; and they are liable at any time to break out in contrite acknowledgments of guilt, and artless resolutions for future improve-

* Pitt diverged from the Whigs in later life: but he was brought up among them; and is, so far, representative of the Whig tradition.

ment. Indeed it was one of the paradoxes created by their mixed composition that, though they were worldly, they were not sophisticated. Their elaborate manners masked simple reactions. Like their mode of life their characters were essentially natural; spontaneous, unintrospective, brimming over with normal feelings, love of home and family, loyalty, conviviality, desire for fame, hero-worship, patriotism. And they showed their feelings too. Happy creatures They lived before the days of the stiff upper lip and the inhibited public school Englishman. A manly tear stood in their eye at the story of a heroic deed: they declared their loves in a strain of flowery hyperbole. They were the more expressive from their very unself-consciousness. It never struck them that they needed to be inarticulate to appear sincere. They were equally frank about their less elevated sentiments. Eighteenth century rationalism combined with rural common sense to make them robustly ready to face unedifying facts. And they declared their impressions with a brusque honesty, outstandingly characteristic of them. From Sir Robert Walpole who encouraged coarse conversation on the ground that it was the only form of talk which everyone enjoyed, down to the Duke of Wellington who described the army of his triumphs as composed of "the scum of the earth, enlisted for drink," the Augustan aristocracy, Whig and Tory alike, said what they thought with a superb disregard for public opinion. For if they were not original they were independent-minded. The conventions which bounded their lives were conventions of form only. Since they had been kings of their world from birth they were free from the tiresome inhibitions that are induced by a sense of inferiority. Within the locked garden of their society, individuality flowered riotous and rampant. Their typical figures show up beside the muted introverts of to-day as clear-cut and idiosyncratic as characters in Dickens. They took for granted that you spoke your mind and followed your impulses. If these were odd they were amused but not disapproving. They enjoyed eccentrics; George Selwyn who never missed an execution, Beau Brummel who took three hours to tie his cravat. The firm English soil in which they were rooted, the spacious freedom afforded by their place in the world, allowed personality to flourish in as many bold and fantastic shapes as it pleased.

But it was always a garden plant, a civilized growth. Whatever their eccentricities, the Whig nobles were never provincial and never uncouth. They had that effortless knowledge of the world that comes only to those, who from childhood have been accustomed to move in a complex society; that delightful unassertive confidence possible only to people who have never had cause to doubt their social position. And they carried to the finest degree of cultivation those social arts which engaged so much of their time. Here we come to their outstanding distinction. They were the most agreeable society England has ever known. The character of their agreeability was of a piece with the rest of them; mundane, straightforward, a trifle philistine, largely concerned with gossip, not given to subtle analyses or flights of fancy. But it had all their vitality and all their sense of style. It was incomparably racy and spontaneous and accomplished; based solidly on a wide culture and experience, yet free to express itself in bursts of high spirits, in impulses of appreciation, in delicate movements of sentiment, in graceful compliments. For it had its grace; a virile classical grace like that of the Chippendale furniture which adorned its rooms, lending a glittering finish to its shrewd humour, its sharp-eyed observation, its vigorous disquisitions on men and things. Educated without pedantry, informal but not slipshod, polished but not precious, brilliant without fatigue, it combined in an easy perfection the charms of civilization and nature. Indeed the whole social life of the period shines down the perspective of history like some masterpiece of natural art; a prize bloom, nurtured in shelter and sunshine and the richest soil, the result of generations of breeding and blending, that spreads itself to the open sky in strength and beauty.

It was at its most characteristic in the middle of the century, it was at its most dazzling towards its close. By 1780 a new spirit was rising in the world. Ossian had taught people to admire ruins and ravines, Rousseau to examine the processes of the heart; with unpowdered heads and the ladies in simple muslin dresses, they paced the woods meditating, in Cowperlike mood, on the tender influences of nature. Though they kept the style and good sense of their fathers, their sympathies were wider. At the same time their feelings grew more refined. The hardness, which had marred the previous age, dwindled. Gainsborough, not Hogarth, mirrored the taste of the time; sensibility became a fashionable word. For a fleeting moment Whig society had a foot in two worlds and made the best of both of them. The lucid outline of eighteenth-century civilization was softened by the glow of the romantic dawn.

Dawn—but for them it was sunset. The same spirit that tinged them with their culminating glory was also an omen of their dissolution. For the days of aristocratic supremacy were numbered. By the iron laws which condition the social structure of man's existence, it could only last as long as it maintained an economic predominance. With the coming of the Industrial Revolution this predominance began to pass from the landlords to other ranks of the community. Already by the close of the century, go-ahead manufacturers in the north were talking of Parliamentary reform; already, in the upper rooms of obscure London alleys, working men met together to clamour for liberty, equality, and fraternity. Within forty years of its zenith, the Whig world was completely swept away. Only a few survivors lingered on to illustrate to an uncomprehending generation the charm of the past. Of these the most distinguished was William Lamb, second Viscount Melbourne.

## BEERBOHM

# *Maltby and Braxton*

PEOPLE still go on comparing Thackeray and Dickens, quite cheerfully. But the fashion of comparing Maltby and Braxton went out so long ago as 1795. No, I am wrong. But anything that happened in the bland old days before the war does seem to be a hundred more years ago than actually it is. The year I mean is the one in whose spring-time we all went bicycling (O thrill!) in Battersea Park, and ladies wore sleeves that billowed enormously out from their shoulders, and Lord Rosebery was Prime Minister.

In that Park, in that spring-time, in that sea of sleeves, there was almost as much talk about the respective merits of Braxton and Maltby as there was about those of Rudge and Humber. For the benefit of my younger readers, and perhaps, so feeble is human memory, for the benefit of their elders too, let me state that Rudge and Humber were rival makers of bicycles, that Hilary Maltby was the author of 'Ariel in Mayfair,' and Stephen Braxton of 'A Faun on the Cotswolds.'

'Which do you think is *really* the best—"Ariel" or "A Faun"?' Ladies were always asking one that question. 'Oh, well, you know, the two are so different. It's really very hard to compare them.' One was always giving that answer. One was not very brilliant perhaps.

The vogue of the two novels lasted throughout the summer. As both were 'firstlings,' and Great Britain had therefore nothing else of Braxton's or Maltby's to fall back on, the horizon was much scanned for what Maltby, and what Braxton, would give us next. In the autumn Braxton gave us his secondling. It was an instantaneous failure. No more was he compared with Maltby. In the spring of '96 came Maltby's secondling. Its failure was instantaneous. Maltby might once more have been compared with Braxton. But Braxton was now forgotten. So was Maltby.

This was not kind. This was not just. Maltby's first novel, and Braxton's, had brought delight into many thousands of homes. People should have paused to say of Braxton "Perhaps his third novel will be better than his second," and to say as much for Maltby. I blame people for having given no sign of wanting a third from either; and I blame them with the more zest because neither 'A Faun on the Cotswolds' nor 'Ariel in Mayfair' was a merely popular book: each, I maintain, was a good book. I don't go so far as to say that the one had 'more of natural magic, more of British woodland glamour, more of the sheer joy of life in it than anything since "As You Like It,"' though Higsby went so fai as this in the *Daily Chronicle;* nor can I allow the claim made for the other by Grigsby in the *Globe* that 'for pungency of satire there has been nothing like it since Swift laid down his pen, and for sheer sweetness and tenderness of feeling—*ex forti dulcedo*—nothing to be mentioned in the same breath with it since the lute fell from the tired hand of Theocritus.' These were foolish exaggerations. But one must not condemn a thing because it has been over-praised. Maltby's 'Ariel' was a delicate, brilliant work; and Braxton's 'Faun,' crude though it was in many ways, had yet a genuine power and beauty. This is not a mere impression remembered from early youth. It is the reasoned and seasoned judgment of middle age. Both books have been out of print for many years; but I secured a second-hand copy of each not long ago, and found them well worth reading again.

From the time of Nathaniel Hawthorne to the outbreak of the war, current literature did not suffer from any lack of fauns. But when Braxton's first book appeared fauns had still an air of novelty about them. We had not yet tired of them and their hoofs and their slanting eyes and their way of coming suddenly out of woods to wean quiet English villages from respectability. We did tire later. But Braxton's faun, even now, seems to me an admirable specimen of his class—wild and weird, earthy, goat-like, almost convincing. And I find myself convinced altogether by Braxton's rustics. I admit that I do not know much about rustics, except from novels. But I plead that the little I do know about them by personal observation does not confirm much of what the many novelists have taught me. I plead also that Braxton may well have been right about the rustics of Gloucestershire because he was (as so many interviewers recorded of him in his brief heyday) the son of a yeoman farmer at Far Oakridge, and his boyhood had been divided between that village and the Grammar School at Stroud. Not long ago I happened to be staying in the neighbourhood, and came across several villagers who might, I assure you, have stepped straight out of Braxton's pages. For that matter, Braxton himself, whom I met often in the spring of '95, might have stepped straight out of his own pages.

I am guilty of having wished he would step straight back into them. He was a very surly fellow, very rugged and gruff. He was the antithesis of pleasant little Maltby. I used to think that perhaps he would have been less unamiable if success had come to him earlier. He was thirty years old when his book was published, and had had a very hard time since coming to London at the age of sixteen. Little Maltby was a year older, and so had waited a year longer; but then, he had waited under a comfortable roof at Twickenham, emerging into the metropolis for no grimmer purpose than to sit and watch the fashionable riders and walkers in Rotten Row, and then going home to write a little, or to play lawn-tennis with the young ladies of Twickenham. He had been the only child of his parents (neither of whom, alas, survived to take pleasure in their darling's sudden fame). He had now migrated from Twickenham and taken rooms in Ryder Street. Had he ever shared with Braxton the bread of adversity—but no, I think he would in any case have been pleasant. And conversely I cannot imagine that Braxton would in any case have been so.

No one seeing the two rivals together, no one meeting them at Mr. Hookworth's famous luncheon parties in the Authors' Club, or at Mrs. Foster-Dugdale's not less famous garden parties in Greville Place, would have supposed off-hand that the pair had a single point in common. Dapper little Maltby—blond, bland, diminutive Maltby, with his monocle and his gardenia; big black Braxton, with his lanky hair and his square blue jaw and his square sallow forehead. Canary and crow. Maltby had a perpetual chirrup of amusing small-talk. Braxton was usually silent, but very well worth listening to whenever he did croak. He had distinction, I admit it; the distinction of one who steadfastly refuses to adapt himself to surroundings. He stood out. He awed Mr. Hookworth. Ladies were always asking one another, rather intently, what they thought of him. One could imagine that Mr. Foster-Dugdale, had he come home from the City to attend the garden parties, might have regarded him as one from whom Mrs. Foster-Dugdale should be shielded. But the casual observer of Braxton and Maltby at Mrs. Foster-Dugdale's or elsewhere was wrong in supposing that the two were totally unlike. He overlooked one simple and obvious point. This was that he had met them both at Mrs. Foster-Dugdale's or elsewhere. Wherever they were invited, there certainly, there punctually, they would be. They were both of them gluttons for the fruits and signs of their success.

Interviewers and photographers had as little reason as had hostesses to complain of two men so earnestly and assiduously 'on the make' as Maltby and Braxton. Maltby, for all his sparkle, was earnest; Braxton, for all his arrogance, assiduous.

'A Faun on the Cotswolds' had no more eager eulogist than the author of 'Ariel in Mayfair.' When any one praised his work, Maltby would lightly disparage it in comparison with Braxton's—'Ah, if I could write like *that!*' Maltby won golden opinions in this way. Braxton, on the other hand, would let slip no opportunity for sneering at Maltby's work—'gimcrack,' as he called it. This was not good for Maltby. Different men, different methods.

'The Rape of the Lock' was 'gimcrack,' if you care to call it so; but it was a delicate, brilliant work; and so, I repeat, was Maltby's 'Ariel.' Absurd to compare Maltby with Pope? I am not so sure. I have read 'Ariel,' but have never read 'The Rape of the Lock.' Braxton's opprobrious term for 'Ariel' may not, however, have been due to jealousy alone. Braxton had imagination, and his rival did not soar above fancy. But the point is that Maltby's fancifulness went far and well. In telling how Ariel re-embodied himself from thin air, leased a small house in Chesterfield Street, was presented at a Levée, played the part of good fairy in a matter of true love not running smooth, and worked meanwhile all manner of amusing changes among the aristocracy before he vanished again, Maltby showed a very pretty range of ingenuity. In one respect, his work was a more surprising achievement than Braxton's. For whereas Braxton had been born and bred among his rustics, Maltby knew his aristocrats only through Thackeray, through the photographs and paragraphs in the newspapers, and through those passionate excursions of his to Rotten Row. Yet I found his aristocrats as convincing as Braxton's rustics. It is true that I may have been convinced wrongly. That is a point which I could settle only by experience. I shift my ground, claiming for Maltby's aristocrats just this: that they pleased me very much.

Aristocrats, when they are presented solely through a novelist's sense of beauty, do not satisfy us. They may be as beautiful as all that, but, for fear of thinking ourselves snobbish, we won't believe it. We do believe it, however, and revel in it, when the novelist saves his face and ours by a pervading irony in the treatment of what he loves. The irony must, mark you, be pervading and obvious. Disraeli's great ladies and lords won't do, for his irony was but latent in his homage, and thus the reader feels himself called on to worship and in duty bound to scoff. All's well, though, when the homage is latent in the irony. Thackeray, inviting us to laugh and frown over the follies of Mayfair, enables us to reel with him in a secret orgy of veneration for those fools.

Maltby, too, in his measure, enabled us to reel thus. That is mainly why, before the end of April, his publisher was in a position to state that 'the Seventh Large Impression of "Ariel in Mayfair" is almost exhausted.' Let it be put to our credit, however, that at the same moment Braxton's publisher had 'the honour to inform the public that an Eighth Large Impression of "A Faun on the Cotswolds" is in instant preparation.'

Indeed, it seemed impossible for either author to outvie the other in success and glory. Week in, week out, you saw cancelled either's every momentary advantage. A neck-and-neck race. As thus: —Maltby appears as a Celebrity At Home in the *World* (Tuesday). Ha! No, *Vanity Fair* (Wednesday) has a perfect presentment of Braxton by 'Spy.' Neck-and-neck! No, *Vanity Fair* says 'the subject of next week's cartoon will be Mr. Hilary Maltby.' Maltby wins! No, next week Braxton's in the *World*.

Throughout May I kept, as it were, my eyes glued to my field-glasses. On the first Monday in June I saw that which drew from me a hoarse ejaculation.

Let me explain that always on Monday mornings at this time of year, when I opened my daily paper, I looked with respectful interest to see what bevy of the great world had been entertained since Saturday at Keeb Hall. The list was always august and inspiring. Statecraft and Diplomacy were well threaded there with mere Lineage and mere Beauty, with Royalty sometimes, with mere Wealth never, with privileged Genius now and then. A noble composition always. It was said that the Duke of Hertfordshire cared for nothing but his collection of birds' eggs, and that the collections of guests at Keeb were formed entirely by his young Duchess. It was said that he had climbed trees in every corner of every continent. The Duchess' hobby was easier. She sat aloft and beckoned desirable specimens up.

The list published on that first Monday in June began ordinarily enough, began with the Austro-Hungarian Ambassador and the Portuguese Minister. Then came the Duke and Duchess of Mull, followed by four lesser Peers (two of them Proconsuls, however) with their Peeresses, three Peers without their Peeresses, four Peeresses without their Peers, and a dozen bearers of courtesy-titles with or without their wives or husbands. The rear was brought up by 'Mr. A. J. Balfour, Mr. Henry Chaplin, and Mr. Hilary Maltby.'

Youth tends to look at the darker side of things. I confess that my first thought was for Braxton.

I forgave and forgot his faults of manner. Youth is generous. It does not criticise a strong man stricken.

And anon, so habituated was I to the parity of those two strivers, I conceived that there might be some mistake. Daily newspapers are printed in a hurry. Might not 'Henry Chaplin' be a typographical error for 'Stephen Braxton'? I went out and bought another newspaper. But Mr. Chaplin's name was in that too.

'Patience!' I said to myself. 'Braxton crouches only to spring. He will be at Keeb Hall on Saturday next.'

My mind was free now to dwell with pleasure on Maltby's great achievement. I thought of writing to congratulate him, but feared this might be in bad taste. I did, however, write asking him to lunch with me. He did not answer my letter. I was, therefore, all the more sorry, next Monday, at not finding 'and Mr. Stephen Braxton' in Keeb's week-end catalogue.

A few days later I met Mr. Hookworth. He mentioned that Stephen Braxton had left town. 'He has taken,' said Hookworth, 'a delightful bungalow on the east coast. He has gone there to *work*.' He added that he had a great liking for Braxton—'a man utterly *unspoilt*.' I inferred that he, too, had written to Maltby and received no answer.

That butterfly did not, however, appear to be hovering from flower to flower in the parterres of rank and fashion. In the daily lists of guests at dinners, receptions, dances, balls, the name of Maltby figured never. Maltby had not caught on.

Presently I heard that he, too, had left town. I gathered that he had gone quite early in June—quite soon after Keeb. Nobody seemed to know where he was. My own theory was that he had taken a delightful bungalow on the west coast, to balance Braxton. Anyhow, the parity of the two strivers was now somewhat re-established.

In point of fact, the disparity had been less than I supposed. While Maltby was at Keeb, there Braxton was also—in a sense. . . . It was a strange story. I did not hear it at the time. Nobody did. I heard it seventeen years later. I heard it in Lucca.

Little Lucca I found so enchanting that, though I had only a day or two to spare, I stayed there a whole month. I formed the habit of walking, every morning, round that high-pitched path which girdles Lucca, that wide and tree-shaded path from which one looks down over the city wall at the fertile plains beneath Lucca. There were never many people there; but the few who did come came daily, so that I grew to like seeing them and took a mild personal interest in them.

One of them was an old lady in a wheeled chair. She was not less than seventy years old, and might or might not have once been beautiful. Her chair was slowly propelled by an Italian woman. She herself was obviously Italian. Not so, however, the little gentleman who walked assiduously beside her. Him I guessed to be English. He was a very stout little gentleman, with gleaming spectacles and a full blond beard, and he seemed to radiate cheerfulness. I thought at first that he might be the old lady's resident physician; but no, there was something subtly un-professional about him: I became sure that his constancy was gratuitous, and his radiance real. And one day, I know not how, there dawned on me a suspicion that he was—who?—some one I had known—some writer—what's-his-name—something with an M—Maltby—Hilary Maltby of the long-ago!

At sight of him on the morrow this suspicion hardened almost to certainty. I wished I could meet him alone and ask him if I were not right, and what he had been doing all these years, and why he had left England. He was always with the old lady. It was only on my last day in Lucca that my chance came.

I had just lunched, and was seated on a comfortable bench outside my hotel, with a cup of coffee on the table before me, gazing across the faded old sunny piazza and wondering what to do with my last afternoon. It was then that I espied yonder the back of the putative Maltby. I hastened forth to him. He was buying some pink roses, a great bunch of them, from a market-woman under an umbrella. He looked very blank, he flushed greatly, when I ventured to accost him. He admitted that his name was Hilary Maltby. I told him my own name, and by degrees he remembered me. He apologised for his confusion. He explained that he had not talked English, had not talked to an Englishman, 'for—oh, hundreds of years.' He said that he had, in the course of his long residence in Lucca, seen two or three people whom he had known in England, but that none of them had recognised him. He accepted (but as though he were embarking on the oddest adventure in the world) my invitation that he should come and sit down and take coffee with me. He laughed with pleasure and surprise at finding that he could still speak his native tongue quite fluently and idiomatically. 'I know absolutely nothing,' he said, 'about England nowadays—except from stray references to it in the *Corriere della Sera*'; nor did he show the faintest desire that I should enlighten him. 'England,' he mused, '—how it all comes back to me!'

'But not you to it?'

'Ah, no indeed,' he said gravely, looking at the roses which he had laid carefully on the marble table. 'I am the happiest of men."

He sipped his coffee, and stared out across the piazza, out beyond it into the past.

'I am the happiest of men,' he repeated. I plied him with the spur of silence.

'And I owe it all to having once yielded to a bad impulse. Absurd, the threads our destinies hang on!'

Again I plied him with that spur. As it seemed not to prick him, I repeated the words he had last spoken. 'For instance?' I added.

'Take,' he said, 'a certain evening in the spring of '95. If, on that evening, the Duchess of Hertfordshire had had a bad cold; or if she had decided that it *wouldn't* be rather interesting to go on to that party—that Annual Soirée, I think it was—of the Inkwomen's Club; or again—to go a step further back—if she hadn't ever written that one little poem, and if it *hadn't* been printed in "The Gentlewoman," and if the Inkwomen's committee *hadn't* instantly and unanimously elected her an Honorary Vice-President because of that one little poem; or if—well, if a million-and-one utterly irrelevant things hadn't happened, don't-you-know, I shouldn't be here. . . . I might be *there*,' he smiled, with a vague gesture indicating England.

'Suppose,' he went on, 'I hadn't been invited to that Annual Soirée; or suppose that other fellow,—'

'Braxton?' I suggested. I had remembered Braxton at the moment of recognising Maltby.

'Suppose *he* hadn't been asked. . . . But of course we both were. It happened that I was the first to be presented to the Duchess. . . . It was a great moment. I hoped I should keep my head. She wore a tiara. I had often seen women in tiaras, at the Opera. But I had never talked to a woman in a tiara. Tiaras were symbols to me. Eyes are just a human feature. I fixed mine on the Duchess's. I kept my head by not looking at hers. I behaved as one human being to another. She seemed very intelligent. We got on very well. Presently she asked whether I should think her *very* bold if she said how *perfectly* divine she thought my book. I said something about doing my best, and asked with animation whether she had read "A Faun on the Cotswolds." She had. She said it was *too* wonderful, she said it was *too* great. If she hadn't been a Duchess, I might have thought her slightly hysterical. Her innate good-sense quickly reasserted itself. She used her great power. With a wave of her magic wand she turned into a fact the glittering possibility that had haunted me. She asked me down to Keeb.

'She seemed very pleased that I would come. Was I, by any chance, free on Saturday week? She hoped there would be some amusing people to meet me. Could I come by the 3.30? It was only an hour-and-a-quarter from Victoria. On Saturday there were always compartments reserved for people coming to Keeb by the 3.30. She hoped I would bring my bicycle with me. She hoped I wouldn't find it very dull. She hoped I wouldn't forget to come. She said how lovely it must be to spend one's life among clever people. She supposed I knew everybody here to-night. She asked me to tell her who everybody was. She asked who was the tall, dark man, over there. I told her it was Stephen Braxton. She said they had promised to introduce her to him. She added that he looked rather wonderful. "Oh, he is, very," I assured her. She turned to me with a sudden appeal: "*Do* you think, if I took my courage in both hands and asked him, he'd care to come to Keeb?"

'I hesitated. It would be easy to say that Satan answered *for* me; easy but untrue; it was I that babbled: "Well—as a matter of fact—since you ask me—if I were you—really I think you'd better not. He's very odd in some ways. He has an extraordinary hatred of sleeping out of London. He has the real Gloucestershire *love* of London. At the same time, he's very shy; and if you asked him he wouldn't very well know how to refuse. I think it would be *kinder* not to ask him."

'At that moment, Mrs. Wilpham—the President—loomed up to us, bringing Braxton. He bore himself well. Rough dignity with a touch of mellowness. I daresay you never saw him smile. He smiled gravely down at the Duchess, while she talked in her pretty little quick humble way. He made a great impression.

'What I had done was not merely base: it was very dangerous. I was in terror that she might rally him on his devotion to London. I didn't dare to move away. I was immensely relieved when at length she said she must be going.

'Braxton seemed loth to relax his grip on her hand at parting. I feared she wouldn't escape without uttering that invitation. But all was well. . . . In saying good night to me, she added in a murmur, "Don't forget Keeb—Saturday week—the 3.30." Merely an exquisite murmur. But Braxton heard it. I knew, by the diabolical look he gave me, that Braxton had heard it. . . . If he hadn't, I shouldn't be here.

'Was I a prey to remorse? Well, in the days between that Soirée and that Saturday, remorse often claimed me, but rapture wouldn't give me up. Arcady, Olympus, the right people, at last! I hadn't realised how good my book was—not till it got me this guerdon; not till I got it this huge advertisement. I foresaw how pleased my publisher would be. In some great houses, I knew, it was possible to stay without any one knowing you had been there. But the Duchess of Hertfordshire hid her light under no bushel. Exclusive she was, but not of publicity. Next to Windsor Castle, Keeb Hall was the most advertised house in all England.

'Meanwhile, I had plenty to do. I rather thought of engaging a valet, but decided that this wasn't necessary. On the other hand, I felt a need for three new summer suits, and a new evening suit, and some new white waistcoats. Also a smoking suit. And had any man ever stayed at Keeb without a dressing-case? Hitherto I had been content with a pair of wooden brushes, and so forth. I was afraid these would appal the footman who unpacked my things. I ordered, for his sake, a large dressing-case, with my initials engraved throughout it. It looked compromisingly new when it came to me from the shop. I had to kick it industriously, and throw it about and scratch it, so as to avert possible suspicion. The tailor did not send my things home till the Friday evening. I had to sit up late, wearing the new suits in rotation.

'Next day, at Victoria, I saw strolling on the platform many people, male and female, who looked as if they were going to Keeb—tall, cool, ornate people who hadn't packed their own things and had reached

Victoria in broughams. I was ornate, but not tall nor cool. My porter was rather off-hand in his manner as he wheeled my things along to the 3.30. I asked severely if there were any compartments reserved for people going to stay with the Duke of Hertfordshire. This worked an instant change in him. Having set me in one of those shrines, he seemed almost loth to accept a tip. A snob, I am afraid.

'A selection of the tall, the cool, the ornate, the intimately acquainted with one another, soon filled the compartment. There I was, and I think they felt they ought to try to bring me into the conversation. As they were all talking about a cotillion of the previous night, I shouldn't have been able to shine. I gazed out of the window, with middle-class aloofness. Presently the talk drifted on to the topic of bicycles. But by this time it was too late for me to come in.

'I gazed at the squalid outskirts of London as they flew by. I doubted, as I listened to my fellow-passengers, whether I should be able to shine at Keeb. I rather wished I were going to spend the week-end at one of those little houses with back-gardens beneath the railway-line. I was filled with fears.

'For shame! thought I. Was I nobody? Was the author of "Ariel in Mayfair" nobody?

'I reminded myself how glad Braxton would be if he knew of my faint-heartedness. I thought of Braxton sitting, at this moment, in his room in Clifford's Inn and glowering with envy of his hated rival in the 3.30. And after all, how enviable I was! My spirits rose. I would acquit myself well. . . .

'I much admired the scene at the little railway station where we alighted. It was like a *fête* by Lancret. I knew from the talk of my fellow-passengers that some people had been going down by an earlier train, and that others were coming by a later. But the 3.30 had brought a full score of us. Us! That was the final touch of beauty.

'Outside there were two broughams, a landau, dog-carts, a phaeton, a wagonette, I know not what. But almost everybody, it seemed, was going to bicycle. Lady Rodfitten said *she* was going to bicycle. Year after year, I had seen that famous Countess riding or driving in the Park. I had been told at fourth hand that she had a masculine intellect and could make and unmake Ministries. She was nearly sixty now, a trifle dyed and stout and weather-beaten, but still tremendously handsome, and hard as nails. One would not have said she had grown older, but merely that she belonged now to a rather later period of the Roman Empire. I had never dreamed of a time when one roof would shelter Lady Rodfitten and me. Somehow, she struck my imagination more than any of these others—more than Count Deym, more than Mr. Balfour, more than the lovely Lady Thisbe Crowborough.

'I might have had a ducal vehicle all to myself, and should have liked that; but it seemed more correct that I should use my bicycle. On the other hand, I didn't want to ride with all these people—a stranger in their midst. I lingered around the luggage till they were off, and then followed at a long distance.

'The sun had gone behind clouds. But I rode slowly, so as to be sure not to arrive hot. I passed, not without a thrill, through the massive open gates into the Duke's park. A massive man with a cockade saluted me—hearteningly—from the door of the lodge. The park seemed endless. I came, at length, to a long straight avenue of elms that were almost blatantly immemorial. At the end of it was—well, I felt like a gnat going to stay in a public building.

'If there had been turnstiles—IN and OUT—and a shilling to pay, I should have felt easier as I passed into that hall—that Palladio-Gargantuan hall. Some one, some butler or groom-of-the-chamber, murmured that her Grace was in the garden. I passed out through the great opposite doorway on to a wide spectacular terrace with lawns beyond. Tea was on the nearest of these lawns. In the central group of people—some standing, others sitting—I espied the Duchess. She sat pouring out tea, a deft and animated little figure. I advanced firmly down the steps from the terrace, feeling that all would be well so soon as I had reported myself to the Duchess.

'But I had a staggering surprise on my way to her. I espied in one of the smaller groups—whom d'you think? Braxton.

'I had no time to wonder how he had got there—time merely to grasp the black fact that he *was* there.

'The Duchess seemed really pleased to see me. She said it was *too* splendid of me to come. "You know Mr. Maltby?" she asked Lady Rodfitten, who exclaimed "Not Mr. *Hilary* Maltby?" with a vigorous grace that was overwhelming. Lady Rodfitten declared she was the greatest of my admirers; and I could well believe that in whatever she did she excelled all competitors. On the other hand, I found it hard to believe she was afraid of me. Yet I had her word for it that she was.

'Her womanly charm gave place now to her masculine grip. She eulogised me in the language of a seasoned reviewer on the staff of a long-established journal—wordy perhaps, but sound. I revered and loved her. I wished I could give her my undivided attention. But, whilst I sat there, teacup in hand, between her and the Duchess, part of my brain was fearfully concerned with that glimpse I had had of Braxton. It didn't so much matter that he was here to halve my triumph. But suppose he knew what I had told the Duchess! And suppose he had—no, surely if he *had* shown me up in all my meanness she wouldn't have received me so very cordially. I wondered where she could have met him since that evening of the Inkwomen. I heard Lady Rodfitten concluding her review of "Ariel" with two or three sentences that might have been framed specially to give the publisher an easy "quote." And then I heard myself asking mechanically whether she had read "A Faun on the Cotswolds." The Duchess heard me too. She turned from talking to other people and said "I did like Mr. Braxton so *very* much."

'"Yes," I threw out with a sickly smile, "I'm so glad you asked him to come."

'"But I didn't ask him. I didn't *dare*."

'"But—but—surely he wouldn't be—be *here* if—" We stared at each other blankly. "Here?" she echoed, glancing at the scattered little groups of people on the lawn. I glanced too. I was much embarrassed. I explained that I had seen Braxton "standing just over there" when I arrived, and had supposed he was one of the people who came by the earlier train. "Well," she said with a slightly irritated laugh, "you must have mistaken some one else for him." She dropped the subject, talked to other people, and presently moved away.

'Surely, thought I, she didn't suspect me of trying to make fun of her? On the other hand, surely she hadn't conspired with Braxton to make a fool of *me?* And yet, how could Braxton be here without an invitation, and without her knowledge? My brain whirled. One thing only was clear. I could *not* have mistaken anybody for Braxton. There Braxton had stood—Stephen Braxton, in that old pepper-and-salt suit of his, with his red tie all askew, and without a hat—his hair hanging over his forehead. All this I had seen sharp and clean-cut. There he had stood, just beside one of the women who travelled down in the same compartment as I; a very pretty woman in a pale blue dress; a tall woman—but I had noticed how small she looked beside Braxton. This woman was now walking to and fro, yonder, with M. de Soveral. I had seen Braxton beside her as clearly as I now saw M. de Soveral.

'Lady Rodfitten was talking about India to a recent Viceroy. She seemed to have as firm a grip of India as of "Ariel." I sat forgotten. I wanted to arise and wander off—in a vague search for Braxton. But I feared this might look as if I were angry at being ignored. Presently Lady Rodfitten herself arose, to have what she called her "annual look round." She bade me come too, and strode off between me and the recent Viceroy, noting improvements that had been made in the grounds, suggesting improvements that might be made, indicating improvements that *must* be made. She was great on landscape-gardening. The recent Viceroy was less great on it, but great enough. I don't say I walked forgotten: the eminent woman constantly asked my opinion; but my opinion, though of course it always coincided with hers, sounded quite worthless, somehow. I longed to shine. I could only bother about Braxton.

'Lady Rodfitten's voice sounded over-strong for the stillness of evening. The shadows lengthened. My spirits sank lower and lower, with the sun. I was a naturally cheerful person, but always, towards sunset, I had a vague sense of melancholy: I seemed always to have grown weaker; morbid misgivings would come to me. On this particular evening there was one such misgiving that crept in and out of me again and again . . . a very horrible misgiving as to the *nature* of what I had seen.

'Well, dressing for dinner is a great tonic. Especially if one shaves. My spirits rose as I lathered my face. I smiled to my reflection in the mirror. The afterglow of the sun came through the window behind the dressing-table, but I had switched on all the lights. My new silver-topped bottles and things made a fine array. To-night *I* was going to shine, too. I felt I might yet be the life and soul of the party. Anyway, my new evening suit was without a fault. And meanwhile this new razor was perfect. Having shaved "down," I lathered myself again and proceeded to shave "up." It was then that I uttered a sharp sound and swung round on my heel.

'No one was there. Yet this I knew: Stephen Braxton had just looked over my shoulder. I had seen the reflection of his face beside mine—craned forward to the mirror. I had met his eyes.

'He had been with me. This I knew.

'I turned to look again at that mirror. One of my cheeks was all covered with blood. I stanched it with a towel. Three long cuts where the razor had slipped and skipped. I plunged the towel into cold water and held it to my cheek. The bleeding went on—alarmingly. I rang the bell. No one came. I vowed I wouldn't bleed to death for Braxton. I rang again. At last a very tall powdered footman appeared—more reproachful-looking than sympathetic, as though I hadn't ordered that dressing-case specially on his behalf. He said he thought one of the housemaids would have some sticking-plaster. He was very sorry he was needed downstairs, but he would tell one of the housemaids. I continued to dab and to curse. The blood flowed less. I showed great spirit. I vowed Braxton should not prevent me from going down to dinner.

'But—a pretty sight I was when I did go down. Pale but determined, with three long strips of black sticking-plaster forming a sort of Z on my left cheek. Mr. Hilary Maltby at Keeb. Literature's Ambassador.

'I don't know how late I was. Dinner was in full swing. Some servant piloted me to my place. I sat down unobserved. The woman on either side of me was talking to her other neighbour. I was near the Duchess' end of the table. Soup was served to me—that dark-red soup that you pour cream into—Bortsch. I felt it would steady me. I raised the first spoonful to my lips, and—my hand gave a sudden jerk.

'I was aware of two separate horrors—a horror that had been, a horror that was. Braxton had vanished. Not for more than an instant had he stood scowling at me from behind the opposite diners. Not for more than the fraction of an instant. But he had left his mark on me. I gazed down with a frozen stare at my shirtfront, at my white waistcoat, both dark with Bortsch. I rubbed them with a napkin. I made them worse.

'I looked at my glass of champagne. I raised it carefully and drained it at one draught. It nerved me. But behind that shirtfront was a broken heart.

'The woman on my left was Lady Thisbe Crowborough. I don't know who was the woman on my right. She was the first to turn and see me. I thought it best to say something about my shirtfront at once. I said it to her sideways, without showing my left cheek. Her handsome eyes rested on the splashes. She said, after a moment's thought, that they looked "rather gay." She said she thought the eternal black and white of men's evening clothes was "so very dreary." She did her best. . . . Lady Thisbe Crowborough did her best, too, I suppose; but breeding isn't proof against all possible shocks: she visibly started at sight of me and my Z. I explained that I had cut myself shaving. I said, with an attempt at lightness, that shy men ought always to cut themselves shaving: it made such a good conversational opening. "But surely," she said after a pause, "you don't cut yourself on purpose?" She was an abysmal fool. I didn't think so at the time. She was Lady Thisbe Crowborough. This fact hallowed her. That we didn't get on at all well was a misfortune for which I blamed only myself and my repulsive appearance and—the unforgettable horror that distracted me. Nor did I blame Lady Thisbe for turning rather soon to the man on her other side.

'The woman on my right was talking to the man on *her* other side; so that I was left a prey to secret memory and dread. I wasn't wondering, wasn't attempting to explain; I was merely remembering—and dreading. And—how odd one is!—on the top-layer of my consciousness I hated to be seen talking to no one. Mr. Maltby at Keeb. I caught the Duchess' eye once or twice, and she nodded encouragingly, as who should say "You do look rather awful, and you do seem rather out of it, but I don't for a moment regret having asked you to come." Presently I had another chance of talking. I heard myself talk. My feverish anxiety to please rather touched *me*. But I noticed that the eyes of my listener wandered. And yet I was sorry when the ladies went away. I had a sense of greater exposure. Men who hadn't seen me saw me now.

The Duke, as he came round to the Duchess' end of the table, must have wondered who I was. But he shyly offered me his hand as he passed, and said it was so good of me to come. I had thought of slipping away to put on another shirt and waistcoat, but had decided that this would make me the more ridiculous. I sat drinking port—poison to me after champagne, but a lulling poison—and listened to noblemen with unstained shirtfronts talking about the Australian cricket match. . . .

'Is Rubicon Bezique still played in England? There was a mania for it at that time. The floor of Keeb's Palladio-Gargantuan hall was dotted with innumerable little tables. I didn't know how to play. My hostess told me I must "come and amuse the dear old Duke and Duchess of Mull," and led me to a remote sofa on which an old gentleman had just sat down beside an old lady. They looked at me with a dim kind interest. My hostess had set me and left me on a small gilt chair in front of them. Before going she had conveyed to them loudly—one of them was very deaf—that I was "the famous writer." It was a long time before they understood that I was not a political writer. The Duke asked me, after a troubled pause, whether I had known "old Mr. Abraham Hayward." The Duchess said I was too young to have known Mr. Hayward, and asked if I knew her "clever friend Mr. Mallock." I said I had just been reading Mr. Mallock's new novel. I heard myself shouting a confused précis of the plot. The place where we were sitting was near the foot of the great marble staircase. I said how beautiful the staircase was. The Duchess of Mull said she had never cared very much for that staircase. The Duke, after a pause, said he had "often heard old Mr. Abraham Hayward hold a whole dinner table." There were long and frequent pauses—between which I heard myself talking loudly, frantically, sinking lower and lower in the esteem of my small audience. I felt like a man drowning under the eyes of an elderly couple who sit on the bank regretting that they can offer *no* assistance. Presently the Duke looked at his watch and said to the Duchess that it was "time to be thinking of bed."

'They rose, as it were from the bank, and left me, so to speak, under water. I watched them as they passed slowly out of sight up the marble staircase which I had mispraised. I turned and surveyed the brilliant, silent scene presented by the card-players.

'I wondered what old Mr. Abraham Hayward would have done in my place. Would he have just darted in among those tables and "held" them? I presumed that he would not have stolen silently away, quickly and cravenly away, up the marble staircase—as *I* did.

'I don't know which was the greater, the relief or the humiliation of finding myself in my bedroom. Perhaps the humiliation was the greater.

There, on a chair, was my grand new smoking-suit, laid out for me—what a mockery! Once I had foreseen myself wearing it in the smoking-room at a late hour—the centre of a group of eminent men entranced by the brilliancy of my conversation. And now—! I was nothing but a small, dull, soup-stained, sticking-plastered, nerve-racked recluse. Nerves, yes. I assured myself that I had not seen—what I had seemed to see. All very odd, of course, and very unpleasant, but easily explained. Nerves. Excitement of coming to Keeb too much for me. A good night's rest: that was all I needed. To-morrow I should laugh at myself.

'I wondered that I wasn't tired physically. There my grand new silk pyjamas were, yet I felt no desire to go to bed . . . none while it was still possible for me to go. The little writing-table at the foot of my bed seemed to invite me. I had brought with me in my portmanteau a sheaf of letters, letters that I had purposely left unanswered in order that I might answer them on KEEB HALL note-paper. These the footman had neatly laid beside the blotting-pad on that little writing-table at the foot of the bed. I regretted that the note-paper stacked there had no ducal coronet on it. What matter? The address sufficed. If I hadn't yet made a good impression on the people who were staying here, I could at any rate make one on the people who weren't. I sat down. I set to work. I wrote a prodigious number of fluent and graceful notes.

'Some of these were to strangers who wanted my autograph. I was always delighted to send my autograph, and never perfunctory in the manner of sending it. . . . "Dear Madam," I remember writing to somebody that night, "were it not that you make your request for it so charmingly, I should hesitate to send you that which rarity alone can render valuable.—Yours truly, Hilary Maltby." I remember reading this over and wondering whether the word "render" looked rather commercial. It was in the act of wondering thus that I raised my eyes from the note-paper and saw, through the bars of the brass bedstead, the naked sole of a large human foot—saw beyond it the calf of a great leg; a nightshirt; and the face of Stephen Braxton. I did not move.

'I thought of making a dash for the door, dashing out into the corridor, shouting at the top of my voice for help. I sat quite still.

'What kept me to my chair was the fear that if I tried to reach the door Braxton would spring off the bed to intercept me. If I sat quite still perhaps he wouldn't move. I felt that if he moved I should collapse utterly.

'I watched him, and he watched me. He lay there with his body half-raised, one elbow propped on the pillow, his jaw sunk on his breast; and from under his black brows he watched me steadily.

'No question of mere nerves now. That hope was gone. No mere optical delusion, this abiding presence. Here Braxton was. He and I were together in the bright, silent room. How long would he be content to watch me?

'Eleven nights ago he had given me one horrible look. It was this look that I had to meet, in infinite prolongation, now, not daring to shift my eyes. He lay as motionless as I sat. I did not hear him breathing, but I knew, by the rise and fall of his chest under his nightshirt, that he was breathing heavily. Suddenly I started to my feet. For he had moved. He had raised one hand slowly. He was stroking his chin. And as he did so, and as he watched me, his mouth gradually slackened to a grin. It was worse, it was more malign, this grin, than the scowl that remained with it; and its immediate effect on me was an impulse that was as hard to resist as it was hateful. The window was open. It was nearer to me than the door. I could have reached it in time. . . .

'Well, I live to tell the tale. I stood my ground. And there dawned on me now a new fact in regard to my companion. I had all the while been conscious of something abnormal in his attitude—a lack of ease in his gross possessiveness. I saw now the reason for this effect. The pillow on which his elbow rested was still uniformly puffed and convex; like a pillow untouched. His elbow rested but on the very surface of it, not changing the shape of it at all. His body made not the least furrow along the bed. . . . He had no weight.

'I knew that if I leaned forward and thrust my hand between those brass rails, to clutch his foot, I should clutch—nothing. He wasn't tangible. He was realistic. He wasn't real. He was opaque. He wasn't solid.

'Odd as it may seem to you, these certainties took the edge off my horror. During that walk with Lady Rodfitten, I had been appalled by the doubt that haunted me. But now the very confirmation of that doubt gave me a sort of courage: I could cope better with anything to-night than with actual Braxton. And the measure of the relief I felt is that I sat down again on my chair.

'More than once there came to me a wild hope that the thing might be an optical delusion, after all. Then would I shut my eyes tightly, shaking my head sharply; but, when I looked again, there the presence was, of course. It—he—not actual Braxton but, roughly speaking, Braxton—had come to stay. I was conscious of intense fatigue, taut and alert though every particle of me was; so that I became, in the course of that ghastly night, conscious of a great envy also. For some time before the dawn came in through the window, Braxton's eyes had been closed; little by little now his head drooped sideways, then fell on his forearm and rested there. He was asleep.

'Cut off from sleep, I had a great longing for smoke. I had cigarettes on me, I had matches on me. But I didn't dare to strike a match. The sound might have waked Braxton up. In slumber he was less terrible, though perhaps more odious. I wasn't so much afraid now as indignant. "It's intolerable," I sat saying to myself, "utterly intolerable!"

'I had to bear it, nevertheless. I was aware that I had, in some degree, brought it on myself. If I hadn't interfered and lied, actual Braxton would have been here at Keeb, and I at this moment sleeping soundly. But this was no excuse for Braxton. Braxton didn't know what I had done. He was merely envious of me. And—wanly I puzzled it out in the dawn—by very force of the envy, hatred, and malice in him he had projected hither into my presence this simulacrum of himself. I had known that he would be thinking of me. I had known that the thought of me at Keeb Hall would be of the last bitterness to his most sacred feelings. But—I had reckoned without the passionate force and intensity of the man's nature.

'If by this same strength and intensity he had merely projected himself as an invisible guest under the Duchess' roof—if his feat had been wholly, as perhaps it was in part, a feat of mere wistfulness and longing—then I should have felt really sorry for him; and my conscience would have soundly rated me in his behalf. But no; if the wretched creature *had* been invisible to me, I shouldn't have thought of Braxton at all—except with gladness that he wasn't here. That he was visible to me, and to me alone, wasn't any sign of proper remorse within me. It was but the gauge of his incredible ill-will.

'Well, it seemed to me that he was avenged—with a vengeance. There I sat, hot-browed from sleeplessness, cold in the feet, stiff in the legs, cowed and indignant all through—sat there in the broadening daylight, and in that new evening suit of mine with the Braxtonised shirt-front and waistcoat that by day were more than ever loathsome. Literature's Ambassador at Keeb. . . . I rose gingerly from my chair, and caught sight of my face, of my Braxtonised cheek, in the mirror. I heard the twittering of birds in distant trees. I saw through my window the elaborate landscape of the Duke's grounds, all soft in the grey bloom of early morning. I think I was nearer to tears than I had ever been since I was a child. But the weakness passed. I turned towards the personage on my bed, and, summoning all such power as was in me, *willed* him to be gone. My effort was not without result—an inadequate result. Braxton turned in his sleep.

'I resumed my seat, and . . . and . . . sat up staring and blinking at a tall man with red hair. "I must have fallen asleep," I said. "Yessir," he replied; and his toneless voice touched in me one or two springs of memory: I was at Keeb; this was the footman who looked after me. But—why wasn't I in bed? Had I—no, surely it had been no nightmare. Surely I had *seen* Braxton on that white bed.

'The footman was impassively putting away my smoking-suit. I was too dazed to wonder what he thought of me. Nor did I attempt to stifle a cry when, a moment later, turning in my chair, I beheld Braxton leaning moodily against the mantelpiece. "Are you unwellsir?" asked the footman. "No," I said faintly, "I'm quite well."—"Yessir. Will you wear the blue suit or the grey?"—"The grey."—"Yessir."—It seemed almost incredible that *he* didn't see Braxton; *he* didn't appear to me one whit more solid than the night-shirted brute who stood against the mantel-piece and watched him lay out my things.—"Shall I let your bath-water run nowsir?"—"Please, yes."—"Your bathroom's the second door to the left sir."—He went out with my bath-towel and sponge, leaving me alone with Braxton.

'I rose to my feet, mustering once more all the strength that was in me. Hoping against hope, with set teeth and clenched hands, I faced him, thrust forth my will at him, with everything but words commanded him to vanish—to cease to be.

'Suddenly, utterly, he vanished. And you can imagine the truly exquisite sense of triumph that thrilled me and continued to thrill me till I went into the bathroom and found him in my bath.

'Quivering with rage, I returned to my bedroom. "Intolerable," I heard myself repeating like a parrot that knew no other word. A bath was just what I had needed. Could I have lain for a long time basking in very hot water, and then have sponged myself with cold water, I should have emerged calm and brave; comparatively so, at any rate. I should have looked less ghastly, and have had less of a headache, and something of an appetite, when I went down to breakfast. Also, I shouldn't have been the very first guest to appear on the scene. There were five or six round tables, instead of last night's long table. At the further end of the room the butler and two other servants were lighting the little lamps under the hot dishes. I didn't like to make myself ridiculous by running away. On the other hand, was it right for me to begin breakfast all by myself at one of these round tables? I supposed it was. But I dreaded to be found eating, alone in that vast room, by the first downcomer. I sat dallying with dry toast and watching the door. It occurred to me that Braxton might occur at any moment. Should I be able to ignore him?

'Some man and wife—a very handsome couple—were the first to appear. They nodded and said "good morning" when they noticed me on their way to the hot dishes. I rose—uncomfortably, guiltily—and sat down again. I rose again when the wife drifted to my table, followed by the husband with two steaming plates. She asked me if it wasn't a heavenly morning, and I replied with nervous enthusiasm that it was. She then ate kedgeree in silence. "You just finishing, what?" the husband asked, looking at my plate. "Oh, no—no—only just beginning," I assured him, and helped myself to butter. He then ate kedgeree in silence. He looked like some splendid bull, and she like some splendid cow, grazing. I envied them their eupeptic calm. I surmised that ten thousand Braxtons would not have prevented *them* from sleeping soundly by night and grazing steadily by day. Perhaps their stolidity infected me a little. Or perhaps what braced me was the great quantity of strong tea that I consumed. Anyhow I had begun to feel that if Braxton came in now I shouldn't blench nor falter.

'Well, I wasn't put to the test. Plenty of people drifted in, but Braxton wasn't one of them. Lady Rodfitten—no, she didn't drift, she marched, in; and presently, at an adjacent table, she was drawing a comparison, in clarion tones, between Jean and Edouard de Reszke. It seemed to me that her own voice had much in common with Edouard's. Even more was it akin to a military band. I found myself beating time to it with my foot. Decidedly, my spirits had risen. I was in a mood to face and outface anything. When I rose from the table and made my way to the door, I walked with something of a swing—to the tune of Lady Rodfitten.

'My buoyancy didn't last long, though. There was no swing in my walk when, a little later, I passed out on to the spectacular terrace. I had seen my enemy again, and had beaten a furious retreat. No doubt I should see him yet again soon—here, perhaps, on this terrace. Two of the guests were bicycling slowly up and down the long paven expanse, both of them smiling with pride in the new delicious form of locomotion. There was a great array of bicycles propped neatly along the balustrade. I recognised my own among them. I wondered whether Braxton had projected from Clifford's Inn an image of his own bicycle. He may have done so; but I've no evidence that he did. I myself was bicycling when next I saw him; but he, I remember, was on foot.

'This was a few minutes later. I was bicycling with dear Lady Rodfitten. She seemed really to like me. She had come out and accosted me heartily on the terrace, asking me, because of my sticking-plaster, with whom I had fought a duel since yesterday. I did not tell her with whom, and she had already branched off on the subject of duelling in general. She regretted the extinction of duelling in England, and gave cogent reasons for her regret. Then she asked me what my next book was to be. I confided that I was writing a sort of sequel—"Ariel Returns to Mayfair." She shook her head, said with her usual soundness that sequels were very dangerous things, and asked me to tell her "briefly" the lines along which I was working. I did so. She pointed out two or three weak points in my scheme. She said she could judge better if I would let her see my manuscript. She asked me to come and lunch with her next Friday—"just our two selves"—at Rodfitten House, and to bring my manuscript with me. Need I say that I walked on air?

'"And now," she said strenuously, "let us take a turn on our bicycles." By this time there were a dozen riders on the terrace, all of them smiling with pride and rapture. We mounted and rode along together. The terrace ran round two sides of the house, and before we came to the end of it these words had provisionally marshalled themselves in my mind:

TO<br>ELEANOR<br>COUNTESS OF RODFITTEN<br>THIS BOOK WHICH OWES ALL<br>TO HER WISE COUNSEL<br>AND UNWEARYING SUPERVISION<br>IS GRATEFULLY DEDICATED<br>BY HER FRIEND<br>THE AUTHOR

'Smiled to masonically by the passing bicyclists, and smiling masonically to them in return, I began to feel that the rest of my visit would run smooth, if only—

'"Let's go a little faster. Let's race!" said Lady Rodfitten; and we did so—"just our two selves." I was on the side nearer to the balustrade, and it was on that side that Braxton suddenly appeared from nowhere, solid-looking as a rock, his arms akimbo, less than three yards ahead of me, so that I swerved involuntarily, sharply, striking broadside the front wheel of Lady Rodfitten and collapsing with her, and with a crash of machinery, to the ground.

'I wasn't hurt. She had broken my fall. I wished I was dead. She was furious. She sat speechless with fury. A crowd had quickly collected—just as in the case of a street accident. She accused me now to the crowd. She said I had done it on purpose. She said such terrible things of me that I think the crowd's sympathy must have veered towards me. She was assisted to her feet. I tried to be one of the assistants. "Don't let him come near me!" she thundered. I caught sight of Braxton on the fringe of the crowd, grinning at me. "It was all HIS fault," I madly cried, pointing at him. Everybody looked at Mr. Balfour, just behind whom Braxton was standing. There was a general murmur of surprise, in which I have no doubt Mr. Balfour joined. He gave a charming, blank, deprecating smile. "I mean—I can't explain what I mean," I groaned. Lady Rodfitten moved away, refusing support, limping terribly, towards the house. The crowd followed her, solicitous. I stood helplessly, desperately, where I was.

'I stood an outlaw, a speck on the now empty terrace. Mechanically I picked up my straw hat, and wheeled the two bent bicycles to the balustrade. I suppose Mr. Balfour has a charming nature. For he presently came out again—on purpose, I am sure, to alleviate my misery. He told me that Lady Rodfitten had suffered no harm. He took me for a stroll up and down the terrace, talking thoughtfully and enchantingly about things in general. Then, having done his deed of mercy, this Good Samaritan went back into the house. My eyes followed him with gratitude; but I was still bleeding from wounds beyond his skill. I escaped down into the gardens. I wanted to see no one. Still more did I want to be seen by no one. I dreaded in every nerve of me my reappearance among those people. I walked ever faster and faster, to stifle thought; but in vain. Why hadn't I simply ridden *through* Braxton? I was aware of being now in the park, among great trees and undulations of wild green ground. But Nature did not achieve the task that Mr. Balfour had attempted; and my anguish was unassuaged.

'I paused to lean against a tree in the huge avenue that led to the huge hateful house. I leaned wondering whether the thought of re-entering that house were the more hateful because I should have to face my fellow-guests or because I should probably have to face Braxton. A church bell began ringing somewhere. And anon I was aware of another sound—a twitter of voices. A consignment of hatted and parasoled ladies was coming fast adown the avenue. My first impulse was to dodge behind my tree. But I feared that I had been observed; so that what was left to me of self-respect compelled me to meet these ladies.

'The Duchess was among them. I had seen her from afar at breakfast, but not since. She carried a prayer-book, which she waved to me as I approached. I was a disastrous guest, but still a guest, and nothing could have been prettier than her smile. "Most of my men this week," she said, "are Pagans, and all the others have dispatch-boxes to go through—except the dear old Duke of Mull, who's a member of the Free Kirk. You're Pagan, of course?"

'I said—and indeed it was a heart-cry—that I should like very much to come to church. "If I shan't be in the way," I rather abjectly added. It didn't strike me that Braxton would try to intercept me. I don't know why, but it never occurred to me, as I walked briskly along beside the Duchess, that I should meet him so far from the house. The church was in a corner of the park, and the way to it was by a side path that branched off from the end of the avenue. A little way along, casting its shadow across the path, was a large oak. It was from behind this tree, when we came to it, that Braxton sprang suddenly forth and tripped me up with his foot.

'Absurd to be tripped up by the mere semblance of a foot? But remember, I was walking quickly, and the whole thing happened in a flash of time. It was inevitable that I should throw out my hands and come down headlong—just as though the obstacle had been as real as it looked. Down I came on palms and knee-caps, and up I scrambled, very much hurt and shaken and apologetic. "*Poor* Mr. Maltby! *Really—!*" the Duchess wailed for me in this latest of my mishaps. Some other lady chased my straw hat, which had bowled far ahead. Two others helped to brush me. They were all very kind, with a quaver of mirth in their concern for me. I looked furtively around for Braxton, but he was gone. The palms of my hands were abraded with gravel. The Duchess said I must on no account come to church *now*. I was utterly determined to reach that sanctuary. I marched firmly on with the Duchess. Come what might on the way, I wasn't going to be left out here. I was utterly bent on winning at least one respite.

'Well, I reached the little church without further molestation. To be there seemed almost too good to be true. The organ, just as we entered, sounded its first notes. The ladies rustled into the front pew. I, being the one male of the party, sat at the end of the pew, beside the Duchess. I couldn't help feeling that my position was a proud one. But I had gone through too much to take instant pleasure in it, and was beset by thoughts of what new horror might await me on the way back to the house. I hoped the Service would not be brief. The swelling and dwindling strains of the "voluntary" on the small organ were strangely soothing. I turned to give an almost feudal glance to the simple villagers in the pews behind, and saw a sight that cowed my soul.

'Braxton was coming up the aisle. He came slowly, casting a tourist's eye at the stained-glass windows on either side. Walking heavily, yet with no sound of boots on the pavement, he reached our pew. There, towering and glowering, he halted, as though demanding that we should make room for him. A moment later he edged sullenly into the pew. Instinctively I had sat tight back, drawing my knees aside, in a shudder of revulsion against contact. But Braxton did not push past me. What he did was to sit slowly and fully down on me.

'No, not down *on* me. Down *through* me—and around me. What befell me was not mere ghastly contact with the intangible. It was inclusion, envelopment, eclipse. What Braxton sat down on was not I, but the seat of the pew; and what he sat back against was not my face and chest, but the back of the pew. I didn't realise this at the moment. All I knew was a sudden black blotting-out of all things; an infinite and impenetrable darkness. I dimly conjectured that I was dead. What was wrong with me, in point of fact, was that my eyes, with the rest of me, were inside Braxton. You remember what a great hulking fellow Braxton was. I calculate that as we sat there my eyes were just beneath the roof of his mouth. Horrible!

'Out of the unfathomable depths of that pitch darkness, I could yet hear the "voluntary" swelling and dwindling, just as before. It was by this I knew now that I wasn't dead. And I suppose I must have craned my head forward, for I had a sudden glimpse of things—a close quick downward glimpse of a pepper-and-salt waistcoat and of two great hairy hands clasped across it. Then darkness again. Either I had drawn back my head, or Braxton had thrust his forward; I don't know which. "Are you all right?" the Duchess' voice whispered, and no doubt my face was ashen. "Quite," whispered my voice. But this pathetic monosyllable was the last gasp of the social instinct in me. Suddenly, as the "voluntary" swelled to its close, there was a great sharp shuffling noise. The congregation had risen to its feet, at the entry of choir and vicar. Braxton had risen, leaving me in daylight. I beheld his towering back. The Duchess, beside him, glanced round at me. But I could not, dared not, stand up into that presented back, into that great waiting darkness. I did but clutch my hat from beneath the seat and hurry distraught down the aisle, out through the porch, into the open air.

'Whither? To what goal? I didn't reason. I merely fled—like Orestes; fled like an automaton along the path we had come by. And was followed? Yes, yes. Glancing back across my shoulder, I saw that brute some twenty yards behind me, gaining on me. I broke into a sharper run. A few sickening moments later he was beside me, scowling down into my face.

'I swerved, dodged, doubled on my tracks, but he was always at me. Now and again, for lack of breath, I halted, and he halted with me. And then, when I had got my wind, I would start running again, in the insane hope of escaping him. We came, by what twisting and turning course I know not, to the great avenue, and as I stood there in an agony of panting I had a dazed vision of the distant Hall. Really I had quite forgotten I was staying at the Duke of Hertfordshire's. But Braxton hadn't forgotten. He planted himself in front of me. He stood between me and the house.

'Faint though I was, I could almost have laughed. Good heavens! was *that* all he wanted: that I shouldn't go back there? Did he suppose I wanted to go back there—with *him?* Was I the Duke's prisoner on parole? What was there to prevent me from just walking off to the railway station? I turned to do so.

'He accompanied me on my way. I thought that when once I had passed through the lodge gates he might vanish, satisfied. But no, he didn't vanish. It was as though he suspected that if he let me out of his sight I should sneak back to the house. He arrived with me, this quiet companion of mine, at the little railway station. Evidently he meant to see me off. I learned from an elderly and solitary porter that the next train to London was the 4.3.

'Well, Braxton saw me off by the 4.3. I reflected, as I stepped up into an empty compartment, that it wasn't yet twenty-four hours ago since I, or some one like me, had alighted at that station.

'The guard blew his whistle; the engine shrieked, and the train jolted forward and away; but I did not lean out of the window to see the last of my attentive friend.

'Really not twenty-four hours ago? Not twenty-four years?'

Maltby paused in his narrative. 'Well, well,' he said, 'I don't want you to think I overrate the ordeal of my visit to Keeb. A man of stronger nerve than mine, and of greater resourcefulness, might have coped successfully with Braxton from first to last—might have stayed on till Monday, making a very favourable impression on every one all the while. Even as it was, even after my manifold failures and sudden flight, I don't say my position was impossible. I only say it seemed so to me. A man less sensitive than I, and less vain, might have cheered up after writing a letter of apology to his hostess, and have resumed his normal existence as though nothing very terrible had happened, after all. I wrote a few lines to the Duchess that night; but I wrote amidst the preparations for my departure from England: I crossed the Channel next morning. Throughout that Sunday afternoon with Braxton at the Keeb railway station, pacing the desolate platform with him, waiting in the desolating waiting-room with him, I was numb to regrets, and was thinking of nothing but the 4.3. On the way to Victoria my brain worked and my soul wilted. Every incident in my stay at Keeb stood out clear to me; a dreadful, a hideous pattern. I had done for myself, so far as *those* people were concerned. And now that I had sampled *them*, what cared I for others? "Too low for a hawk, too high for a buzzard." That homely old saying seemed to sum me up. And suppose I *could* still take pleasure in the company of my own old upper-middle class, how would that class regard me now? Gossip percolates. Little by little, I was sure, the story of my Keeb fiasco would leak down into the drawing-room of Mrs. Foster-Dugdale. I felt I could never hold up my head in any company where anything of that story was known. Are you quite sure you never heard anything?'

I assured Maltby that all I had known was the great bare fact of his having stayed at Keeb Hall.

'It's curious,' he reflected. 'It's a fine illustration of the loyalty of those people to one another. I suppose there was a general agreement for the Duchess' sake that nothing should be said about her queer guest.

But even if I had dared hope to be so efficiently hushed up, I couldn't have not fled. I wanted to forget. I wanted to leap into some void, far away from all reminders. I leapt straight from Ryder Street into Vaule-la-Rochette, a place of which I had once heard that it was the least frequented seaside-resort in Europe. I leapt leaving no address —leapt telling my landlord that if a suit-case and a portmanteau arrived for me he could regard them, them and their contents, as his own for ever. I daresay the Duchess wrote me a kind little letter, forcing herself to express a vague hope that I would come again "some other time." I daresay Lady Rodfitten did *not* write reminding me of my promise to lunch on Friday and bring "Ariel Returns to Mayfair" with me. I left that manuscript at Ryder Street; in my bedroom grate; a shuffle of ashes. Not that I'd yet given up all thought of writing. But I certainly wasn't going to write now about the two things I most needed to forget. I wasn't going to write about the British aristocracy, nor about any kind of supernatural presence. . . . I did write a novel—my last—while I was at Vaule. "Mr. and Mrs. Robinson." Did you ever come across a copy of it?'

I nodded gravely.

'Ah; I wasn't sure,' said Maltby, 'whether it was ever published. A dreary affair, wasn't it? I knew a great deal about suburban life. But—well, I suppose one can't really understand what one doesn't love, and one can't make good fun without real understanding. Besides, what chance of virtue is there for a book written merely to distract the author's mind? I had hoped to be healed by sea and sunshine and solitude. These things were useless. The labour of "Mr. and Mrs. Robinson" did help, a little. When I had finished it, I thought I might as well send it off to my publisher. He had given me a large sum of money, down, after "Ariel," for my next book—so large that I was rather loth to disgorge. In the note I sent with the manuscript, I gave no address, and asked that the proofs should be read in the office. I didn't care whether the thing were published or not. I knew it would be a dead failure if it were. What mattered one more drop in the foaming cup of my humiliation? I knew Braxton would grin and gloat. I didn't mind even that.'

'Oh, well,' I said, 'Braxton was in no mood for grinning and gloating. "The Drones" had already appeared.'

Maltby had never heard of 'The Drones'—which I myself had remembered only in the course of his disclosures. I explained to him that it was Braxton's second novel, and was by way of being a savage indictment of the British aristocracy; that it was written in the worst possible taste, but was so very dull that it fell utterly flat; that Braxton had forthwith taken, with all of what Maltby had called 'the passionate force and intensity of his nature,' to drink, and had presently gone under and not re-emerged.

Maltby gave signs of genuine, though not deep, emotion, and cited two or three of the finest passages from 'A Faun on the Cotswolds.' He even expressed a conviction that 'The Drones' must have been misjudged. He said he blamed himself more than ever for yielding to that bad impulse at that Soirée.

'And yet,' he mused, 'and yet, honestly, I can't find it in my heart to regret that I did yield. I can only wish that all had turned out as well, in the end, for Braxton as for me. I wish he could have won out, as I did, into a great and lasting felicity. For about a year after I had finished "Mr. and Mrs. Robinson" I wandered from place to place, trying to kill memory, shunning all places frequented by the English. At last I found myself in Lucca. Here, if anywhere, I thought, might a bruised and tormented spirit find gradual peace. I determined to move out of my hotel into some permanent lodging. Not for felicity, not for any complete restoration of self-respect, was I hoping; only for peace. A "mezzano" conducted me to a noble and ancient house, of which, he told me, the owner was anxious to let the first floor. It was in much disrepair, but even so seemed to me very cheap. According to the simple Luccan standard, I am rich. I took that first floor for a year, had it repaired, and engaged two servants. My "padrona" inhabited the ground floor. From time to time she allowed me to visit her there. She was the Contessa Adriano-Rizzoli, the last of her line. She is the Contessa Adriano-Rizzoli-Maltby. We have been married fifteen years.'

Maltby looked at his watch. He rose and took tenderly from the table his great bunch of roses. 'She is a lineal descendant,' he said, 'of the Emperor Hadrian.'

# VOLTAIRE

# *Candide*

## I. HOW CANDIDE WAS BROUGHT UP IN A MAGNIFICENT CASTLE, AND HOW HE WAS EXPELLED THENCE.

IN a castle of Westphalia, belonging to the Baron of Thunder-ten-Tronckh, lived a youth, whom nature had endowed with the most gentle manners. His countenance was a true picture of his soul. He combined a true judgment with simplicity of spirit, which was the reason, I apprehend, of his being called Candide. The old servants of the family suspected him to have been the son of the Baron's sister, by a good, honest gentleman of the neighborhood, whom that young lady would never marry because he had been able to prove only seventy-one quarterings, the rest of his genealogical tree having been lost through the injuries of time.

The Baron was one of the most powerful lords in Westphalia, for his castle had not only a gate, but windows. His great hall, even, was hung with tapestry. All the dogs of his farmyards formed a pack of hounds at need; his grooms were his huntsmen; and the curate of the village was his grand almoner. They called him "My Lord," and laughed at all his stories.

The Baron's lady weighed about three hundred and fifty pounds, and was therefore a person of great consideration, and she did the honours of the house with a dignity that commanded still greater respect. Her daughter Cunegonde was seventeen years of age, fresh-coloured, comely, plump, and desirable. The Baron's son seemed to be in every respect worthy of his father. The Preceptor Pangloss was the oracle of the family, and little Candide heard his lessons with all the good faith of his age and character.

Pangloss was profesor of metaphysicotheologico-cosmolo-nigology. He proved admirably that there is no effect without a cause, and that, in this best of all possible worlds, the Baron's castle was the most magnificent of castles, and his lady the best of all possible Baronesses.

"It is demonstrable," said he, "that things cannot be otherwise than as they are; for all being created for an end, all is necesarily for the best end. Observe, that the nose has been formed to bear spectacles—thus we have spectacles. Legs are visibly designed for stockings—and we have stockings. Stones were made to be hewn, and to construct castles—therefore my lord has a magnificent castle; for the greatest baron in the province ought to be the best lodged. Pigs were made to be eaten—therefore we eat pork all the year round. Consequently they who assert that all is well have said a foolish thing, they should have said all is for the best."

Candide listened attentively and believed innocently; for he thought Miss Cunegonde extremely beautiful, though he never had the courage to tell her so. He concluded that after the happiness of being born of Baron of Thunder-ten-Tronckh, the second degree of happiness was to be Miss Cunegonde, the third that of seeing her every day, and the fourth that of hearing Master Pangloss, the greatest philosopher of the whole province, and consequently of the whole world.

One day Cunegonde, while walking near the castle, in a little wood which they called a park, saw between the bushes, Dr. Pangloss giving a lesson in experimental natural philosophy to her mother's chamber-maid, a little brown wench, very pretty and very docile. As Miss Cunegonde had a great disposition for the sciences, she breathlessly observed the repeated experiments of which she was a witness; she clearly perceived the force of the Doctor's reasons, the effects, and the causes; she turned back greatly flurried, quite pensive, and filled with the desire to be learned; dreaming that she might well be a *sufficient reason* for young Candide, and he for her.

She met Candide on reaching the castle and blushed; Candide blushed also; she wished him good morrow in a faltering tone, and Candide spoke to her without knowing what he said. The next day after dinner, as they went from table, Cunegonde and Candide found themselves behind a screen; Cunegonde let fall her handkerchief, Candide picked it up, she took him innocently by the hand, the youth as innocently kissed the young lady's hand with particular vivacity, sensibility, and grace; their lips met, their eyes sparkled, their knees trembled, their hands strayed. Baron Thunder-ten-Tronckh passed near the screen and beholding this cause and effect chased Candide from the castle with great kicks on the backside; Cunegonde fainted away; she was boxed on the ears by the Baroness, as soon as she came to herself; and all was consternation in this most magnificent and most agreeable of all possible castles.

## II. WHAT BECAME OF CANDIDE AMONG THE BULGARIANS

CANDIDE, driven from terrestrial paradise, walked a long while without knowing where, weeping, raising his eyes to heaven, turning them often towards the most magnificent of castles which imprisoned the purest of noble young ladies. He lay down to sleep without supper, in the middle of a field between two furrows. The snow fell in large flakes. Next day Candide, all benumbed, dragged himself towards the neighbouring town which was called Waldberghofftrarbk-dikdorff, having no money, dying of hunger and fatigue, he stopped sorrowfully at the door of an inn. Two men dressed in blue observed him.

"Comrade," said one, "here is a well-built young fellow, and of proper height."

They went up to Candide and very civilly invited him to dinner.

"Gentlemen," replied Candide, with a most engaging modesty, "you do me great honour, but I have not wherewithal to pay my share."

"Oh, sir," said one of the blues to him, "people of your appearance and of your merit never pay anything: are you not five feet five inches high?"

"Yes, sir, that is my height," answered he, making a low bow.

"Come, sir, seat yourself; not only will we pay your reckoning, but we will never suffer such a man as you to want money; men are only born to assist one another."

"You are right," said Candide; "this is what I was always taught by Mr. Pangloss, and I see plainly that all is for the best."

They begged of him to acept a few crowns. He took them, and wished to give them his note; they refused; they seated themselves at table.

"Love you not deeply?"

"Oh yes," answered he; "I deeply love Miss Cunegonde."

"No," said one of the gentlemen, "we ask you if you do not deeply love the King of the Bulgarians?"

"Not at all," said he; "for I have never seen him."

"What! he is the best of kings, and we must drink his health."

"Oh! very willingly, gentlemen," and he drank.

"That is enough," they tell him. "Now you are the help, the support, the defender, the hero of the Bulgarians. Your fortune is made, and your glory is assured."

Instantly they fettered him, and carried him away to the regiment. There he was made to wheel about to the right, and to the left, to draw his rammer, to return his rammer, to present, to fire, to march, and they gave him thirty blows with a cudgel. The next day he did his exercise a little less badly, and he received but twenty blows. The day following they gave him only ten, and he was regarded by his comrades as a prodigy.

Candide, all stupefied, could not yet very well realise how he was a hero. He resolved one fine day in spring to go for a walk, marching straight before him, believing that it was a privilege of the human as well as of the animal species to make use of their legs as they pleased. He had advanced two leagues when he was overtaken by four others, heroes of six feet, who bound him and carried him to a dungeon. He was asked which he would like the best, to be whipped six-and-thirty times through all the regiment, or to receive at once twelve balls of lead in his brain. He vainly said that human will is free, and that he chose neither the one nor the other. He was forced to make a choice; he determined, in virtue of that gift of God called liberty, to run the gauntlet six-and-thirty times. He bore this twice. The regiment was composed of two thousand men; that composed for him four thousand strokes, which laid bare all his muscles and nerves, from the nape of his neck quite down to his rump. As they were going to proceed to a third whipping, Candide, able to bear no more, begged as a favour that they would be so good as to shoot him. He obtained this favour; they bandaged his eyes, and bade him kneel down. The King of the Bulgarians passed at this moment and ascertained the nature of the crime. As he had great talent, he understood from all that he learnt of Candide that he was a young metaphysician, extremely ignorant of the things of this world, and he accorded him his pardon with a clemency which will bring him praise in all the journals, and throughout all ages.

An able surgeon cured Candide in three weeks by means of emollients taught by Dioscorides. He had already a little skin, and was able to march when the King of the Bulgarians gave battle to the King of the Abares.

## III. HOW CANDIDE MADE HIS ESCAPE FROM THE BULGARIANS, AND WHAT AFTERWARDS BECAME OF HIM.

THERE was never anything so gallant, so spruce, so brilliant, and so well disposed as the two armies. Trumpets, fifes, hautboys, drums, and cannon made music such as Hell itself had never heard. The cannons first of all laid flat about six thousand men on each side; the muskets swept away from this best of worlds nine or ten thousand ruffians who infested its surface. The bayonet was also a *sufficient reason* for the death of several thousands. The whole might amount to thirty thousand souls. Candide, who trembled like a philosopher, hid himself as well as he could during this heroic butchery.

At length, while the two kings were causing Te Deum to be sung each in his own camp, Candide resolved to go and reason elsewhere on effects and causes. He passed over heaps of dead and dying, and first reached a neighbouring village; it was in cinders, it was an Abare village which the Bulgarians had burnt according to the laws of war. Here, old men covered with wounds, beheld their wives, hugging their children to their bloody breasts, massacred before their faces; there, their daughters, disembowelled and breathing their last after having satisfied the natural wants of Bulgarian heroes; while others, half burnt in the flames, begged to be despatched. The earth was strewed with brains, arms, and legs.

Candide fled quickly to another village; it belonged to the Bulgarians; and the Abarian heroes had treated it in the same way. Candide, walking always over palpitating limbs or across ruins, arrived at last beyond the seat of war, with a few provisions in his knapsack, and Miss Cunegonde always in his heart. His provisions failed him when he arrived in Holland; but having heard that everybody was rich in that country, and that they were Christians, he did not doubt but he should meet with the same treatment from them as he had met with in the Baron's castle, before Miss Cunegonde's bright eyes were the cause of his expulsion thence.

He asked alms of several grave-looking people, who all answered him, that if he continued to follow this trade they would confine him to the house of correction, where he should be taught to get a living.

The next he addressed was a man who had been haranguing a large assembly for a whole hour on the subject of charity. But the orator, looking askew, said:

"What are you doing here? Are you for the good cause?"

"There can be no effect without a cause," modestly answered Candide; "the whole is necessarily concatenated and arranged for the best. It was necesary for me to have been banished from the presence of Miss Cunegonde, to have afterwards run the gauntlet, and now it is necesary I should beg my bread until I learn to earn it; all this cannot be otherwise."

"My friend," said the orator to him, "do you believe the Pope to be Anti-Christ?"

"I have not heard it," answered Candide; "but whether he be, or whether he be not, I want bread."

"Thou dost not deserve to eat," said the other. "Begone, rogue; begone, wretch; do not come near me again."

The orator's wife, putting her head out of the window, and spying a man that doubted whether the Pope was Anti-Christ, poured over him a full . . . Oh, heavens! to what excess does religious zeal carry the ladies.

A man who had never been christened, a good Anabaptist, named James, beheld the cruel and ignominious treatment shown to one of his brethren, an unfeathered biped with a rational soul, he took him home, cleaned him, gave him bread and beer, presented him with two florins, and even wished to teach him the manufacture of Persian stuffs which they make in Holland. Candide, almost prostrating himself before him, cried:

"Master Pangloss has well said that all is for the best in this world, for I am infinitely more touched by your extreme generosity than with the inhumanity of that gentleman in the black coat and his lady."

The next day, as he took a walk, he met a beggar all covered with scabs, his eyes diseased, the end of his nose eaten away, his mouth distorted, his teeth black, choking in his throat, tormented with a violent cough, and spitting out a tooth at each effort.

## IV. HOW CANDIDE FOUND HIS OLD MASTER PANGLOSS, AND WHAT HAPPENED TO THEM.

CANDIDE, yet more moved with compassion than with horror, gave to this shocking beggar the two florins which he had received from the honest Anabaptist James. The spectre looked at him very earnestly, dropped a few tears, and fell upon his neck. Candide recoiled in disgust.

"Alas!" said one wretch to the other, "do you no longer know your dear Pangloss?"

"What do I hear? You, my dear master! you in this terrible plight! What misfortune has happened to you? Why are you no longer in the most magnificent of castles? What has become of Miss Cunegonde, the pearl of girls, and nature's masterpiece?"

"I am so weak that I cannot stand," said Pangloss.

Upon which Candide carried him to the Anabaptist's stable, and gave him a crust of bread. As soon as Pangloss had refreshed himself a little:

"Well," said Candide, "Cunegonde?"

"She is dead," replied the other.

Candide fainted at this word; his friend recalled his senses with a little bad vinegar which he found by chance in the stable. Candide reopened his eyes.

"Cunegonde is dead! Ah, best of worlds, where art thou? But of what illness did she die? Was it not for grief, upon seeing her father kick me out of his magnificent castle?"

"No," said Pangloss, "she was ripped open by the Bulgarian soldiers, after having been violated by many; they broke the Baron's head for attempting to defend her; my lady, her mother, was cut in pieces; my poor pupil was served just in the same manner as his sister; and as for the castle, they have not left one stone upon another, not a barn, nor a sheep, nor a duck, nor a tree; but we have had our revenge, for the Abares have done the very same thing to a neighbouring barony, which belonged to a Bulgarian lord."

At this discourse Candide fainted again; but coming to himself, and having said all that it became him to say, inquired into the cause and effect, as well as into the *sufficient reason* that had reduced Pangloss to so miserable a plight.

"Alas!" said the other, "it was love; love, the comfort of the human species, the preserver of the universe, the soul of all sensible beings, love, tender love."

"Alas!" said Candide, "I know this love, that sovereign of hearts, that soul of our souls; yet it never cost me more than a kiss and twenty kicks on the backside. How could this beautiful cause produce in you an effect so abominable?"

Pangloss made answer in these terms: "Oh, my dear Candide, you remember Paquette, that pretty wench who waited on our noble Baroness; in her arms I tasted the delights of paradise, which produced in me those hell torments with which you see me devoured; she was infected with them, she is perhaps dead of them. This present Paquette received of a learned Grey Friar, who had traced it to its source; he had had it of an old countess, who had received it from a cavalry captain, who owed it to a marchioness, who took it from a page, who had received it from a Jesuit, who when a novice had it in a direct line from one of the companions of Christopher Columbus. For my part I shall give it to nobody, I am dying."

"Oh, Pangloss!" cried Candide, "what a strange genealogy! Is not the Devil the original stock of it?"

"Not at all," replied this great man, "it was a thing unavoidable, a necessary ingredient in the best of worlds; for if Columbus had not in an island of America caught this disease, which contaminates the source of life, frequently even hinders generation, and which is evidently opposed to the great end of nature, we should have neither chocolate nor cochineal. We are also to observe that upon our continent, this distemper is like religious controversy, confined to a particular spot. The Turks, the Indians, the Persians, the Chinese, the Siamese, the Japanese, know nothing of it; but there is a sufficient reason for believing that they will know it in their turn in a few centuries. In the meantime, it has made marvellous progress among us, especially in those great armies composed of honest well-disciplined hirelings, who decide the destiny of states; for we may safely affirm that when an army of thirty thousand men fights another of an equal number, there are about twenty thousand of them p–x–d on each side.

"Well, this is wonderful!" said Candide, "but you must get cured."

"Alas! how can I?" said Pangloss, "I have not a farthing, my friend, and all over the globe there is no letting of blood or taking a glister, without paying, or somebody paying for you."

These last words determined Candide; he went and flung himself at the feet of the charitable Anabaptist James, and gave him so touching a picture of the state to which his friend was reduced, that the good man did not scruple to take Dr. Pangloss into his house, and had him cured at his expense. In the cure Pangloss lost only an eye and an ear. He wrote well, and knew arithmetic perfectly. The Anabaptist James made him his bookkeeper. At the end of two months, being obliged to go to Lisbon about some merchantile affairs, he took the two philosophers with him in his ship. Pangloss explained to him how everything was so constituted that it could not be better. James was not of this opinion.

"It is more likely," said he, "mankind have a little corrupted nature, for they were not born wolves, and they have become wolves; God has given them neither cannon of four-and-twenty pounders, nor bayonets; and yet they have made cannon and bayonets to destroy one another. Into this account I might throw not only bankrupts, but Justice which seizes on the effects of bankrupts to cheat the creditors."

"All this was indispensable," replied the one-eyed doctor, "for private misfortunes make the general good, so that the more private misfortunes there are the greater is the general good."

While he reasoned, the sky darkened, the winds blew from the four quarters, and the ship was assailed by a most terrible tempest within sight of the port of Lisbon.

## V. TEMPEST, SHIPWRECK, EARTHQUAKE, AND WHAT BECAME OF DOCTOR PANGLOSS, CANDIDE, AND JAMES THE ANABAPTIST.

HALF dead of that inconceivable anguish which the rolling of a ship produces, one-half of the passengers were not even sensible of the danger. The other half shrieked and prayed. The sheets were rent, the masts broken, the vessel gaped. Work who would, no one heard, no one commanded. The Anabaptist being upon deck bore a hand; when a brutish sailor struck him roughly and laid him sprawling; but with the violence of the blow he himself tumbled head foremost overboard, and stuck upon a piece of the broken mast. Honest James ran to his assistance, hauled him up, and from the effort he made was precipitated into the sea in sight of the sailor, who left him to perish, without deigning to look at him. Candide drew near and saw his benefactor, who rose above the water one moment and was then swallowed up for ever. He was just going to jump after him, but was prevented by the philosopher Pangloss, who demonstrated to him that the Bay of Lisbon had been made on purpose for the Anabaptist to be drowned. While he was proving this *à priori*, the ship foundered; all perished except Pangloss, Candide and that brutal sailor who had drowned the good Anabaptist. The villain swam safely to the shore, while Pangloss and Candide were borne thither upon a plank.

As soon as they recovered themselves a little they walked toward Lisbon. They had some money left, with which they hoped to save themselves from starving, after they had escaped drowning. Scarcely had they reached the city, lamenting the death of their benefactor, when they felt the earth tremble under their feet. The sea swelled and foamed in the harbour, and beat to pieces the vessels riding at anchor. Whirlwinds of fire and ashes covered the streets and public places; houses fell, roofs were flung upon the pavements, and the pavements were scattered. Thirty thousand inhabitants of all ages and sexes were crushed under the ruins. The sailor, whistling and swearing, said there was booty to be gained here.

"What can be the *sufficient reason* of this phenomenon?" said Pangloss.

"This is the Last Day!" cried Candide.

The sailor ran among the ruins, facing death to find money; finding it, he took it, got drunk, and having slept himself sober, purchased the favours of the first good-natured wench whom he met on the ruins of the destroyed houses, and in the midst of the dying and the dead. Pangloss pulled him by the sleeve.

"My friend," said he, "this is not right. You sin against the *universal reason;* you choose your time badly."

"S'blood and fury!" answered the other; "I am a sailor and born at Batavia. Four times have I trampled upon the crucifix in four voyages to Japan; a fig for thy universal reason."

Some falling stones had wounded Candide. He lay stretched in the street covered with rubbish.

"Alas!" said he to Pangloss, "get me a little wine and oil; I am dying."

"This concussion of the earth is no new thing," answered Pangloss. "The city of Lima, in America, experienced the same convulsions last year; the same cause, the same effects; there is certainly a train of sulphur under ground from Lima to Lisbon."

"Nothing more probable," said Candide; "but for the love of God a little oil and wine."

"How, probable?" replied the philosopher. "I maintain that the point is capable of being demonstrated."

Candide fainted away, and Pangloss fetched him some water from a neighbouring fountain. The following day they rummaged among the ruins and found provisions, with which they repaired their exhausted strength. After this they joined with others in relieving those inhabitants who had escaped death. Some, whom they had succoured, gave them as good a dinner as they could in such disastrous circumstances; true, the repast was mournful, and the company moistened their bread with tears; but Pangloss consoled them, assuring them that things could not be otherwise.

"For," said he, "all that is is for the best. If there is a volcano at Lisbon it cannot be elsewhere. It is impossible that things should be other than they are; for everything is right."

A little man dressed in black, Familiar of the Inquisition, who sat by him, politely took up his word and said:

"Apparently, then, sir, you do not believe in original sin; for if all is for the best there has then been neither Fall nor punishment."

"I humbly ask your Excellency's pardon," answered Pangloss, still more politely; "for the Fall and curse of man necessarily entered into the system of the best of worlds."

"Sir," said the Familiar, "you do not then believe in liberty?"

"Your Excellency will excuse me," said Pangloss; "liberty is consistent with absolute necessity, for it was necessary we should be free; for, in short, the determinate will—"

Pangloss was in the middle of his sentence, when the Familiar beckoned to his footman, who gave him a glass of wine from Porto or Opporto.

## VI. HOW THE PORTUGUESE MADE A BEAUTIFUL AUTO-DA-FÉ, TO PREVENT ANY FURTHER EARTHQUAKES; AND HOW CANDIDE WAS PUBLICLY WHIPPED.

AFTER the earthquake had destroyed three-fourths of Lisbon, the sages of that country could think of no means more effectual to prevent utter ruin than to give the people a beautiful *auto-da-fé;* for it had been decided by the University of Coimbra, that the burning of a few people alive by a slow fire, and with great ceremony, is an infallible secret to hinder the earth from quaking.

In consequence hereof, they had seized on a Biscayner, convicted of having married his godmother, and on two Portuguese, for rejecting the bacon which larded a chicken they were eating; after dinner, they came and secured Dr. Pangloss, and his disciple Candide, the one for speaking his mind, the other for having listened with an air of approbation. They were conducted to separate apartments, extremely cold, as they were never incommoded by the sun. Eight days after they were dressed in *san-benitos* and their heads ornamented with paper mitres. The mitre and *san-benito* belonging to Candide were painted with reversed flames and with devils that had neither tails nor claws; but Pangloss's devils had claws and tails and the flames were upright. They marched in procession thus habited and heard a very pathetic sermon, followed by fine church music. Candide was whipped in cadence while they were singing; the Biscayner, and the two men who had refused to eat bacon, were burnt; and Pangloss was hanged, though that was not the custom. The same day the earth sustained a most violent concussion.

Candide, terrified, amazed, desperate, all bloody, all palpitating, said to himself:

"If this is the best of possible worlds, what then are the others? Well, if I had been only whipped I could put up with it, for I experienced that among the Bulgarians; but oh, my dear Pangloss! thou greatest of philosophers, that I should have seen you hanged, without knowing for what! Oh, my dear Anabaptist, thou best of men, that thou should'st have been drowned in the very harbour! Oh, Miss Cunegonde, thou pearl of girls! that thou should'st have had thy belly ripped open!"

Thus he was musing, scarce able to stand, preached at, whipped, absolved, and blessed, when an old woman accosted him saying:

"My son, take courage and follow me."

## VII. HOW THE OLD WOMAN TOOK CARE OF CANDIDE, AND HOW HE FOUND THE OBJECT HE LOVED.

CANDIDE did not take courage, but followed the old woman to a decayed house, where she gave him a pot of pomatum to anoint his sores, showed him a very neat little bed, with a suit of clothes hanging up, and left him something to eat and drink.

"Eat, drink, sleep," said she, "and may our lady of Atocha, the great St. Anthony of Padua, and the great St. James of Compostella, receive you under their protection. I shall be back to-morrow."

Candide, amazed at all he had suffered and still more with the charity of the old woman, wished to kiss her hand.

"It is not my hand you must kiss," said the old woman; "I shall be back to-morrow. Anoint yourself with the pomatum, eat and sleep."

Candide, notwithstanding so many disasters, ate and slept. The next morning the old woman brought him his breakfast, looked at his back, and rubbed it herself with another ointment: in like manner she brought him his dinner; and at night she returned with his supper. The day following she went through the very same ceremonies.

"Who are you?" said Candide; "who has inspired you with so much goodness? What return can I make you?"

The good woman made no answer; she returned in the evening, but brought no supper.

"Come with me," she said, "and say nothing."

She took him by the arm, and walked with him about a quarter of a mile into the country; they arrived at a lonely house, surrounded with gardens and canals. The old woman knocked at a little door, it opened, she led Candide up a private staircase into a small apartment richly furnished. She left him on a brocaded sofa, shut the door and went away. Candide thought himself in a dream; indeed, that he had been dreaming unluckily all his life, and that the present moment was the only agreeable part of it all.

The old woman returned very soon, supporting with difficulty a trembling woman of a majestic figure, brilliant with jewels, and covered with a veil.

"Take off that veil," said the old woman to Candide.

The young man approaches, he raises the veil with a timid hand. Oh! what a moment! what surprise! he believes he beholds Miss Cunegonde? he really sees her! it is herself! His strength fails him, he cannot utter a word, but drops at her feet. Cunegonde falls upon the sofa. The old woman supplies a smelling bottle; they come to themselves and recover their speech. As they began with broken accents, with questions and answers interchangeably interrupted with sighs, with tears, and cries. The old woman desired they would make less noise and then she left them to themselves.

"What, is it you?" said Candide, "you live? I find you again in Portugal? then you have not been ravished? then they did not rip open your belly as Doctor Pangloss informed me?"

"Yes, they did," said the beautiful Cunegonde; "but those two accidents are not always mortal."

"But were your father and mother killed?"

"It is but too true," answered Cunegonde, in tears.

"And your brother?"

"My brother also was killed."

"And why are you in Portugal? and how did you know of my being here? and by what strange adventure did you contrive to bring me to this house?"

"I will tell you all that," replied the lady, "but first of all let me know your history, since the innocent kiss you gave me and the kicks which you received."

Candide respectfully obeyed her, and though he was still in a surprise, though his voice was feeble and trembling, though his back still pained him, yet he gave her a most ingenuous account of everything that had befallen him since the moment of their separation. Cunegonde lifted up her eyes to heaven; shed tears upon hearing of the death of the good Anabaptist and of Pangloss; after which she spoke as follows to Candide, who did not lose a word and devoured her with his eyes.

## VIII. THE HISTORY OF CUNEGONDE.

"I WAS in bed and fast asleep when it pleased God to send the Bulgarians to our delightful castle of Thunder-ten-Tronckh; they slew my father and brother, and cut my mother to pieces. A tall Bulgarian, six feet high, perceiving that I had fainted away at this sight, began to ravish me; this made me recover; I regained my senses, I cried, I struggled, I bit, I scratched, I wanted to tear out the tall Bulgarian's eyes—not knowing that what happened at my father's house was the usual practice of war. The brute gave me a cut in the left side with his hanger, and the mark is still upon me."

"Ah! I hope I shall see it," said honest Candide.

"You shall," said Cunegonde, "but let us continue."

"Do so," replied Candide.

Thus she resumed the thread of her story:

"A Bulgarian captain came in, saw me all bleeding, and the soldier not in the least disconcerted. The captain flew into a passion at the disrespectful behaviour of the brute, and slew him on my body. He ordered my wounds to be dressed, and took me to his quarters as a prisoner of war. I washed the few shirts that he had, I did his cooking; he thought me very pretty—he avowed it; on the other hand, I must own he had a good shape, and a soft and white skin; but he had little or no mind or philosophy, and you might see plainly that he had never been instructed by Doctor Pangloss. In three months time, having lost all his money, and being grown tired of my company, he sold me to a Jew, named Don Issachar, who traded to Holland and Portugal, and had a strong passion for women. This Jew was much attached to my person, but could not triumph over it; I resisted him better than the Bulgarian soldier. A modest woman may be ravished once, but her virtue is strengthened by it. In order to render me more tractable, he brought me to this country house. Hitherto I had imagined that nothing could equal the beauty of Thunder-ten-Tronckh Castle; but I found I was mistaken.

"The Grand Inquisitor, seeing me one day at Mass, stared long at me, and sent to tell me that he wished to speak on private matters. I was conducted to his palace, where I acquainted him with the history of my family, and he represented to me how much it was beneath my rank to belong to an Israelite. A proposal was then made to Don Issachar that he should resign me to my lord. Don Issachar, being the court banker, and a man of credit, would hear nothing of it. The Inquisitor threatened him with an *auto-da-fé*. At last my Jew, intimidated, concluded a bargain, by which the house and myself should belong to both in common; the Jew should have for himself Monday, Wednesday, and Saturday, and the Inquisitor should have the rest of the week. It is now six months since this agreement was made. Quarrels have not been wanting, for they could not decide whether the night from Saturday to Sunday belonged to the old law or to the new. For my part, I have so far held out against both, and I verily believe that this is the reason why I am still beloved.

"At length, to avert the scourge of earthquakes, and to intimidate Don Issachar, my Lord Inquisitor was pleased to celebrate an *auto-da-fé*. He did me the honour to invite me to the ceremony. I had a very good seat, and the ladies were served with refreshments between Mass and the execution. I was in truth seized with horror at the burning of those two Jews, and of the honest Biscayner who had married his godmother; but what was my surprise, my fright, my trouble, when I saw in a *san-benito* and mitre a figure which resembled that of Pangloss! I rubbed my eyes, I looked at him attentively, I saw him hung; I fainted. Scarcely had I recovered my senses than I saw you stripped, stark naked, and this was the height of my horror, consternation, grief, and despair. I tell you, truthfully, that your skin is yet whiter and of a more perfect colour than that of my Bulgarian captain. This spectacle redoubled all the feelings which overwhelmed and devoured me. I screamed out, and would have said, 'Stop, barbarians!' but my voice failed me, and my cries would have been useless after you had been severely whipped. How is it possible, said I, that the beloved Candide and the wise Pangloss should both be at Lisbon, the one to receive a hundred lashes, and the other to be hanged by the Grand Inquisitor, of whom I am the well-beloved? Pangloss most cruelly deceived me when he said that everything in the world is for the best.

"Agitated, lost, sometimes beside myself, and sometimes ready to die of weakness, my mind was filled with the massacre of my father, mother, and brother, with the insolence of the ugly Bulgarian soldier, with the stab that he gave me, with my servitude under the Bulgarian captain, with my hideous Don Issachar, with my abominable Inquisitor, with the execution of Doctor Pangloss, with the grand Miserere to which they whipped you, and especially with the kiss I gave you behind the screen the day that I had last seen you. I praised God for bringing you back to me after so many trials, and I charged my old woman to take care of you, and to conduct you hither as soon as possible. She has executed her commission perfectly well; I have tasted the inexpressible pleasure of seeing you again, of hearing you, of speaking with you. But you must be hungry, for myself, I am famished; let us have supper."

They both sat down to table, and, when supper was over, they placed themselves once more on the sofa; where they were when Signor Don Issachar arrived. It was the Jewish Sabbath, and Issachar had come to enjoy his rights, and to explain his tender love.

## IX. WHAT BECAME OF CUNEGONDE, CANDIDE, THE GRAND INQUISITOR, AND THE JEW.

THIS Issachar was the most choleric Hebrew that had ever been seen in Israel since the Captivity in Babylon.

"What!" said he, "thou bitch of a Galilean, was not the Inquisitor enough for thee? Must this rascal also share with me?"

In saying this he drew a long poniard which he always carried about him; and not imagining that his adversary had any arms he threw himself upon Candide: but our honest Westphalian had received a handsome sword from the old woman along with the suit of clothes. He drew his rapier, despite his gentleness, and laid the Israelite stone dead upon the cushions at Cunegonde's feet.

"Holy Virgin!" cried she, "what will become of us? A man killed in my apartment! If the officers of justice come, we are lost!"

"Had not Pangloss been hanged," said Candide, "he would give us good counsel in this emergency, for he was a profound philosopher. Failing him let us consult the old woman."

She was very prudent and commenced to give her opinion when

suddenly another little door opened. It was an hour after midnight, it was the beginning of Sunday. This day belonged to my lord the Inquisitor. He entered, and saw the whipped Candide, sword in hand, a dead man upon the floor, Cunegonde aghast, and the old woman giving counsel.

At this moment, the following is what passed in the soul of Candide, and how he reasoned:

If this holy man call in assistance, he will surely have me burnt; and Cunegonde will perhaps be served in the same manner; he was the cause of my being cruelly whipped; he is my rival; and, as I have now begun to kill, I will kill away, for there is no time to hesitate. This reasoning was clear and instantaneous; so that without giving time to the Inquisitor to recover from his surprise, he pierced him through and through, and cast him beside the Jew.

"Yet again!" said Cunegonde, "now there is no mercy for us, we are excommunicated, our last hour has come. How could you do it? you, naturally so gentle, to slay a Jew and a prelate in two minutes!"

"My beautiful young lady," responded Candide, "when one is a lover, jealous and whipped by the Inquisition, one stops at nothing."

The old woman then put in her word, saying:

"There are three Andalusian horses in the stable with bridles and saddles, let the brave Candide get them ready; madame has money, jewels; let us therefore mount quickly on horseback, though I can sit only on one buttock; let us set out for Cadiz, it is the finest weather in the world, and there is great pleasure in travelling in the cool of the night."

Immediately Candide saddled the three horses, and Cunegonde, the old woman and he, travelled thirty miles at a stretch. While they were journeying, the Holy Brotherhood entered the house; my lord the Inquisitor was interred in a handsome church, and Issachar's body was thrown upon a dunghill.

Candide, Cunegonde, and the old woman, had now reached the little town of Avacena in the midst of the mountains of the Sierra Morena, and were speaking as follows in a public inn.

## X. IN WHAT DISTRESS CANDIDE, CUNEGONDE, AND THE OLD WOMAN ARRIVED AT CADIZ; AND OF THEIR EMBARKATION.

"WHO was it that robbed me of my money and jewels?" said Cunegonde, all bathed in tears. "How shall we live? What shall we do? Where find Inquisitors or Jews who will give me more?"

"Alas!" said the old woman, "I have a shrewd suspicion of a reverend

Grey Friar, who stayed last night in the same inn with us at Badajos. God preserve me from judging rashly, but he came into our room twice, and he set out upon his journey long before us."

"Alas!" said Candide, "dear Pangloss has often demonstrated to me that the goods of this world are common to all men, and that each has an equal right to them. But according to these principles the Grey Friar ought to have left us enough to carry us through our journey. Have you nothing at all left, my dear Cunegonde?"

"Not a farthing," said she.

"What then must we do?" said Candide.

"Sell one of the horses," replied the old woman. "I will ride behind Miss Cunegonde, though I can hold myself only on one buttock, and we shall reach Cadiz."

In the same inn there was a Benedictine prior who bought the horse for a cheap price. Candide, Cunegonde, and the old woman, having passed through Lucena, Chillas, and Lebrixa, arrived at length at Cadiz. A fleet was there getting ready, and troops assembling to bring to reason the reverend Jesuit Fathers of Paraguay, accused of having made one of the native tribes in the neighbourhood of San Sacrament revolt against the Kings of Spain and Portugal. Candide having been in the Bulgarian service, performed the military exercise before the general of this little army with so graceful an address, with so intrepid an air, and with such agility and expedition, that he was given the command of a company of foot. Now, he was a captain! He set sail with Miss Cunegonde, the old woman, two valets, and the two Andalusian horses, which had belonged to the grand Inquisitor of Portugal.

During their voyage they reasoned a good deal on the philosophy of poor Pangloss.

"We are going into another world," said Candide; "and surely it must be there that all is for the best. For I must confess there is reason to complain a little of what passeth in our world in regard to both natural and moral philosophy."

"I love you with all my heart," said Cunegonde; "but my soul is still full of fright at that which I have seen and experienced."

"All will be well," replied Candide; "the sea of this new world is already better than our European sea; it is calmer, the winds more regular. It is certainly the New World which is the best of all possible worlds."

"God grant it," said Cunegonde; "but I have been so horribly unhappy there that my heart is almost closed to hope."

"You complain," said the old woman; "alas! you have not known such misfortunes as mine."

Cunegonde almost broke out laughing, finding the good woman very amusing, for pretending to have been as unfortunate as she.

"Alas!" said Cunegonde, "my good mother, unless you have been ravished by two Bulgarians, have received two deep wounds in your belly, have had two castles demolished, have had two mothers cut to pieces before your eyes, and two of your lovers whipped at an *auto-da-fé*, I do not conceive how you could be more unfortunate than I. Add that I was born a baroness of seventy-two quarterings—and have been a cook!"

"Miss," replied the old woman, "you do not know my birth; and were I to show you my backside, you would not talk in that manner, but would suspend your judgment."

This speech having raised extreme curiosity in the minds of Cunegonde and Candide, the old woman spoke to them as follows.

## XI. HISTORY OF THE OLD WOMAN.

"I HAD not always bleared eyes and red eyelids; neither did my nose always touch my chin; nor was I always a servant. I am the daughter of Pope Urban X, and of the Princess of Palestrina. Until the age of fourteen I was brought up in a palace, to which all the castles of your German barons would scarcely have served for stables; and one of my robes was worth more than all the magnificence of Westphalia. As I grew up I improved in beauty, wit, and every graceful accomplishment, in the midst of pleasures, hopes, and respectful homage. Already I inspired love. My throat was formed, and such a throat! white, firm, and shaped like that of the Venus of Medici; and what eyes! what eyelids! what black eyebrows! such flames darted from my dark pupils that they eclipsed the scintillation of the stars—as I was told by the poets in our part of the world. My waiting women, when dressing and undressing me, used to fall into an ecstasy, whether they viewed me before or behind; how glad would the gentlemen have been to perform that office for them!

"I was affianced to the most excellent Prince of Massa Carara. Such a prince! as handsome as myself, sweet-tempered, agreeable, brilliantly witty, and sparkling with love. I loved him as one loves for the first time—with idolatry, with transport. The nuptials were prepared. There was surprising pomp and magnificence; there were *fêtes*, carousals, continual *opera bouffe;* and all Italy composed sonnets in my praise, though not one of them was passable. I was just upon the point of reaching the summit of bliss, when an old marchioness who had been mistress to the Prince, my husband, invited him to drink chocolate with her. He died in less than two hours of most terrible convulsions. But this is only a bagatelle. My mother, in despair, and scarcely less afflicted than myself, determined to absent herself for some time from so fatal a place. She had a very fine estate in the neighbourhood of Gaeta. We embarked on board a galley of the country which was gilded like the great altar of St. Peter's at Rome. A Sallee corsair swooped down and boarded us. Our men defended themselves like the Pope's soldiers; they flung themselves upon their knees, and threw down their arms, begging of the corsair an absolution *in articulo mortis.*

"Instantly they were stripped as bare as monkeys; my mother, our maids of honour, and myself were all served in the same manner. It is amazing with what expedition those gentry undress people. But what surprised me most was, that they thrust their fingers into the part of our bodies which the generality of women suffer no other instrument but—pipes to enter. It appeared to me a very strange kind of ceremony; but thus one judges of things when one has not seen the world. I afterwards learnt that it was to try whether we had concealed any diamonds. This is the practice established from time immemorial, among civilised nations that scour the seas. I was informed that the very religious Knights of Malta never fail to make this search when they take any Turkish prisoners of either sex. It is a law of nations from which they never deviate.

"I need not tell *you* how great a hardship it was for a young princess and her mother to be made slaves and carried to Morocco. You may easily imagine all we had to suffer on board the pirate vessel. My mother was still very handsome; our maids of honour, and even our waiting women, had more charms than are to be found in all Africa. As for myself, I was ravishing, was exquisite, grace itself, and I was a virgin! I did not remain so long; this flower, which had been reserved for the handsome Prince of Massa Carara, was plucked by the corsair captain. He was an abominable negro, and yet believed that he did me a great deal of honour. Certainly the Princess of Palestrina and myself must have been very strong to go through all that we experienced until our arrival at Morocco. But let us pass on; these are such common things as not to be worth mentioning.

"Morocco swam in blood when we arrived. Fifty sons of the Emperor Muley-Ismael had each their adherents; this produced fifty civil wars, of blacks against blacks, and blacks against tawnies, and tawnies against tawnies, and mulattoes against mulattoes. In short it was a continual carnage throughout the empire.

"No sooner were we landed, than the blacks of a contrary faction to that of my captain attempted to rob him of his booty. Next to jewels and gold we were the most valuable things he had. I was witness to such a battle as you have never seen in your European climates. The northern nations have not that heat in their blood, nor that raging lust for women, so common in Africa. It seems that you Europeans have only milk in your veins; but it is vitriol, it is fire which runs in those of the inhabitants of Mount Atlas and the neighbouring countries. They fought with the fury of the lions, tigers, and serpents of the country, to see who should have us. A Moor seized my mother by the right arm, while my captain's lieutenant held her by the left; a Moorish soldier had hold of her by one leg, and one of our corsairs held her by the other. Thus almost all our women were drawn in quarters by four men. My captain concealed me behind him; and with his drawn scimitar cut and slashed every one that opposed his fury. At length I saw all our Italian women, and my mother herself, torn, mangled, massacred, by the monsters who disputed over them. The slaves, my companions, those who had taken them, soldiers, sailors, blacks, whites, mulattoes, and at last my captain, all were killed, and I remained dying on a heap of dead. Such scenes as this were transacted through an extent of three hundred leagues—and yet they never missed the five prayers a day ordained by Mahomet.

"With difficulty I disengaged myself from such a heap of slaughtered bodies, and crawled to a large orange tree on the bank of a neighbouring rivulet, where I fell, oppressed with fright, fatigue, horror, despair, and hunger. Immediately after, my senses, overpowered, gave themselves up to sleep, which was yet more swooning than repose. I was in this state of weakness and insensibility, between life and death, when I felt myself pressed by something that moved upon my body. I opened my eyes, and saw a white man, of good countenance, who sighed, and who said between his teeth: '*O che sciagura d'essere senza coglioni!*'"

## XII. THE ADVENTURES OF THE OLD WOMAN CONTINUED.

"ASTONISHED and delighted to hear my native language, and no less surprised at what this man said, I made answer that there were much greater misfortunes than that of which he complained. I told him in a few words of the horrors which I had endured, and fainted a second time. He carried me to a neighbouring house, put me to bed, gave me food, waited upon me, consoled me, flattered me; he told me that he had never seen any one so beautiful as I, and that he never so much regretted the loss of what it was impossible to recover.

" 'I was born at Naples,' said he, 'there they geld two or three thousand children every year; some die of the operation, others acquire a voice more beautiful than that of women, and others are raised to offices of state. This operation was performed on me with great success and I was chapel musician to madam, the Princess of Palestrina.'

" 'To my mother!' cried I.

" 'Your mother!' cried he, weeping. 'What! can you be that young princess whom I brought up until the age of six years, and who promised so early to be as beautiful as you?'

" 'It is I, indeed; but my mother lies four hundred yards hence, torn in quarters, under a heap of dead bodies.'

"I told him all my adventures, and he made me acquainted with his; telling me that he had been sent to the Emperor of Morocco by a Christian power, to conclude a treaty with that prince, in consequence of which he was to be furnished with military stores and ships to help to demolish the commerce of other Christian Governments.

" 'My mission is done,' said this honest eunuch; 'I go to embark for Ceuta, and will take you to Italy. *Ma che sciagura d'essere senza coglioni!*' "

"I thanked him with tears of commiseration; and instead of taking me to Italy he conducted me to Algiers, where he sold me to the Dey. Scarcely was I sold, than the plague which had made the tour of Africa, Asia, and Europe, broke out with great malignancy in Algiers. You have seen earthquakes; but pray, miss, have you ever had the plague?"

"Never," answered Cunegonde.

"If you had," said the old woman, "you would acknowledge that it is far more terrible than an earthquake. It is common in Africa, and I caught it. Imagine to yourself the distressed situation of the daughter of a Pope, only fifteen years old, who, in less than three months, had felt the miseries of poverty and slavery, had been ravished almost every day, had beheld her mother drawn in quarters, had experienced famine and war, and was dying of the plague in Algiers. I did not die, however, but my eunuch, and the Dey, and almost the whole seraglio of Algiers perished.

"As soon as the first fury of this terrible pestilence was over, a sale was made of the Dey's slaves; I was purchased by a merchant, and carried to Tunis; this man sold me to another merchant, who sold me again to another at Tripoli; from Tripoli I was sold to Alexandria, from Alexandria to Smyrna, and from Smyrna to Constantinople. At length I became the property of an Aga of the Janissaries, who was soon ordered away to the defence of Azof, then besieged by the Russians.

"The Aga, who was a very gallant man, took his whole seraglio with him, and lodged us in a small fort on the Palus Méotides, guarded by two black eunuchs and twenty soldiers. The Turks killed prodigious numbers of the Russians, but the latter had their revenge. Azof was destroyed by fire, the inhabitants put to the sword, neither sex nor age was spared; until there remained only our little fort, and the enemy wanted to starve us out. The twenty Janissaries had sworn they would never surrender. The extremities of famine to which they were reduced, obliged them to eat our two eunuchs, for fear of violating their oath. And at the end of a few days they resolved also to devour the women.

"We had a very pious and humane Iman, who preached an excellent sermon, exhorting them not to kill us all at once.

" 'Only cut off a buttock of each of those ladies,' said he, 'and you'll fare extremely well; if you must go to it again, there will be the same entertainment a few days hence; heaven will accept of so charitable an action, and send you relief.'

"He had great eloquence; he persuaded them; we underwent this terrible operation. The Iman applied the same balsam to us, as he does to children after circumcision; and we all nearly died.

"Scarcely had the Janissaries finished the repast with which we had furnished them, than the Russians came in flat-bottomed boats; not a Janissary escaped. The Russians paid no attention to the condition we were in. There are French surgeons in all parts of the world; one of them who was very clever took us under his care—he cured us; and as long as I live I shall remember that as soon as my wounds were healed he made proposals to me. He bid us all be of good cheer, telling us that the like had happened in many sieges, and that it was according to the laws of war.

"As soon as my companions could walk, they were obliged to set out for Moscow. I fell to the share of a Boyard who made me his gardener, and gave me twenty lashes a day. But this nobleman having in two years' time been broke upon the wheel along with thirty more Boyards for some broils at court, I profited by that event; I fled. I traversed all Russia; I was a long time an inn-holder's servant at Riga, the same at Rostock, at Vismar, at Leipzig, at Cassel, at Utrecht, at Leyden, at the Hague, at Rotterdam. I waxed old in misery and disgrace, having only one-half of my posteriors, and always remembering I was a Pope's daughter. A hundred times I was upon the point of killing myself; but still I loved life. This ridiculous foible is perhaps one of our most fatal characteristics; for is there anything more absurd than to wish to carry continually a burden which one can always throw down? to detest existence and yet to cling to one's existence? in brief, to caress the serpent which devours us, till he has eaten our very heart?

"In the different countries which it has been my lot to traverse, and the numerous inns where I have been servant, I have taken notice of a vast number of people who held their own existence in abhorrence, and yet I never knew of more than eight who voluntarily put an end to their misery; three negroes, four Englishmen, and a German professor named Robek. I ended by being servant to the Jew, Don Issachar, who placed me near your presence, my fair lady. I am determined to share your fate, and have been much more affected with your misfortunes than with my own. I would never even have spoken to you of my misfortunes, had you not piqued me a little, and if it were not customary to tell stories on board a ship in order to pass away the time. In short, Miss Cunegonde, I have had experience, I know the world; therefore I advise you to divert yourself, and prevail upon each passenger to tell his story; and if there be one of them all, that has not cursed his life many a time, that has not frequently looked upon himself as the unhappiest of mortals, I give you leave to throw me headforemost into the sea."

## XIII. HOW CANDIDE WAS FORCED AWAY FROM HIS FAIR CUNEGONDE AND THE OLD WOMAN.

THE beautiful Cunegonde having heard the old woman's history, paid her all the civilities due to a person of her rank and merit. She likewise accepted her proposal, and engaged all the passengers, one after the other, to relate their adventures; and then both she and Candide allowed that the old woman was in the right.

"It is a great pity," said Candide, "that the sage Pangloss was hanged contrary to custom at an *auto-da-fé;* he would tell us most amazing things in regard to the physical and moral evils that overspread earth and sea, and I should be able, with due respect, to make a few objections."

While each passenger was recounting his story, the ship made her way. They landed at Buenos Ayres. Cunegonde, Captain Candide, and the old woman, waited on the Governor, Don Fernando d'Ibaraa, y Figueora, y Mascarenes, y Lampourdos, y Souza. This nobleman had a stateliness becoming a person who bore so many names. He spoke to men with so noble a disdain, carried his nose so loftily, raised his voice so unmercifully, assumed so imperious an air, and stalked with such intolerable pride, that those who saluted him were strongly inclined to give him a good drubbing. Cunegonde appeared to him the most beautiful he had ever met. The first thing he did was to ask whether she was not the captain's wife. The manner in which he asked the question alarmed Candide; he durst not say she was his wife, because indeed she was not; neither durst he say she was his sister, because it was not so; and although this obliging lie had been formerly much in favour among the ancients, and although it could be useful to the moderns, his soul was too pure to betray the truth.

"Miss Cunegonde," said he, "is to do me the honour to marry me, and we beseech your excellency to deign to sanction our marriage."

Don Fernando d'Ibaraa, y Figueora, y Mascarenes, y Lampourdos, y Souza, turning up his moustachios, smiled mockingly, and ordered Captain Candide to go and review his company. Candide obeyed, and the Governor remained alone with Miss Cunegonde. He declared his passion, protesting he would marry her the next day in the face of the church, or otherwise, just as should be agreeable to herself. Cunegonde asked a quarter of an hour to consider of it, to consult the old woman, and to take her resolution.

The old woman spoke thus to Cunegonde:

"Miss, you have seventy-two quarterings, and not a farthing; it is now in your power to be wife to the greatest lord in South America, who has very beautiful moustachios. Is it for you to pique yourself upon inviolable fidelity? You have been ravished by Bulgarians; a Jew and an Inquisitor have enjoyed your favours. Misfortune gives sufficient excuse. I own, that if I were in your place, I should have no scruple in marrying the Governor and in making the fortune of Captain Candide."

While the old woman spoke with all the prudence which age and experience gave, a small ship entered the port on board of which were an Alcalde and his alguazils, and this was what had happened.

As the old woman had shrewdly guessed, it was a Grey Friar who stole Cunegonde's money and jewels in the town of Badajos, when she and Candide were escaping. The Friar wanted to sell some of the diamonds to a jeweller; the jeweller knew them to be the Grand Inquisitor's. The Friar before he was hanged confessed he had stolen them. He described the persons, and the route they had taken. The flight of Cunegonde and Candide was already known. They were traced to Cadiz. A vessel was immediately sent in pursuit of them. The vessel was already in the port of Buenos Ayres. The report spread that the Alcalde was going to land, and that he was in pursuit of the murderers of my lord the Grand Inquisitor. The prudent old woman saw at once what was to be done.

"You cannot run away," said she to Cunegonde, "and you have nothing to fear, for it was not you that killed my lord; besides the Governor who loves you will not suffer you to be ill-treated; therefore stay."

She then ran immediately to Candide.

"Fly," said she, "or in an hour you will be burnt."

There was not a moment to lose; but how could he part from Cunegonde, and where could he flee for shelter?

## XIV. HOW CANDIDE AND CACAMBO WERE RECEIVED BY THE JESUITS OF PARAGUAY.

CANDIDE had brought such a valet with him from Cadiz, as one often meets with on the coasts of Spain and in the American colonies. He was a quarter Spaniard, born of a mongrel in Tucuman; he had been singing-boy, sacristan, sailor, monk, pedlar, soldier, and lackey. His name was Cacambo, and he loved his master, because his master was a very good man. He quickly saddled the two Andalusian horses.

"Come, master, let us follow the old woman's advice; let us start, and run without looking behind us."

Candide shed tears.

"Oh! my dear Cunegonde! must I leave you just at a time when the Governor was going to sanction our nuptials? Cunegonde, brought to such a distance what will become of you?"

"She will do as well as she can," said Cacambo; "the women are never at a loss, God provides for them, let us run."

"Whither art thou carrying me? Where shall we go? What shall we do without Cunegonde?" said Candide.

"By St. James of Compostella," said Cacambo, "you were going to fight against the Jesuits; let us go to fight for them; I know the road well, I'll conduct you to their kingdom, where they will be charmed to have a captain that understands the Bulgarian exercise. You'll make a prodigious fortune; if we cannot find our account in one world we shall in another. It is a great pleasure to see and do new things."

"You have before been in Paraguay, then?" said Candide.

"Ay, sure," answered Cacambo, "I was servant in the College of the Assumption, and am acquainted with the government of the good Fathers as well as I am with the streets of Cadiz. It is an admirable government. The kingdom is upwards of three hundred leagues in diameter, and divided into thirty provinces; there the Fathers possess all, and the people nothing; it is a masterpiece of reason and justice. For my part I see nothing so divine as the Fathers who here make war upon the kings of Spain and Portugal, and in Europe confess those kings; who here kill Spaniards, and in Madrid send them to heaven; this delights me, let us push forward. You are going to be the happiest of mortals. What pleasure will it be to those Fathers to hear that a captain who knows the Bulgarian exercise has come to them!"

As soon as they reached the first barrier, Cacambo told the advanced guard that a captain wanted to speak with my lord the Commandant. Notice was given to the main guard, and immediately a Paraguayan officer ran and laid himself at the feet of the Commandant, to impart this news to him. Candide and Cacambo were disarmed, and their two Andalusian horses seized. The strangers were introduced between two files of musketeers; the Commandant was at the further end, with the three-cornered cap on his head, his gown tucked up, a sword by his side, and a spontoon in his hand. He beckoned, and straightway the new-comers were encompassed by four-and-twenty soldiers. A sergeant told them they must wait, that the Commandant could not speak to them, and that the reverend Father Provincial does not suffer any Spaniard to open his mouth but in his presence, or to stay above three hours in the province.

"And where is the reverend Father Provincial?" said Cacambo.

"He is upon the parade just after celebrating mass," answered the sergeant, "and you cannot kiss his spurs till three hours hence."

"However," said Cacambo, "the captain is not a Spaniard, but a German, he is ready to perish with hunger as well as myself; cannot we have something for breakfast, while we wait for his reverence?"

The sergeant went immediately to acquaint the Commandant with what he had heard.

"God be praised!" said the reverend Commandant, "since he is a German, I may speak to him; take him to my arbour."

Candide was at once conducted to a beautiful summer-house, ornamented with a very pretty colonnade of green and gold marble, and with trellises, enclosing parraquets, humming-birds, fly-birds, guinea-hens, and all other rare birds. An excellent breakfast was provided in vessels of gold; and while the Paraguayans were eating maize out of wooden dishes, in the open fields and exposed to the heat of the sun, the reverend Father Commandant retired to his arbour.

He was a very handsome young man, with a full face, white skin but high in colour; he had an arched eyebrow, a lively eye, red ears, vermilion lips, a bold air, but such a boldness as neither belonged to a Spaniard nor a Jesuit. They returned their arms to Candide and Cacambo, and also the two Andalusian horses; to whom Cacambo gave some oats to eat just by the arbour, having an eye upon them all the while for fear of a surprise.

Candide first kissed the hem of the Commandant's robe, then they sat down to table.

"You are, then, a German?" said the Jesuit to him in that language.

"Yes, reverend Father," answered Candide.

As they pronounced these words they looked at each other with great amazement, and with such an emotion as they could not conceal.

"And from what part of Germany do you come?" said the Jesuit.

"I am from the dirty province of Westphalia," answered Candide; "I was born in the Castle of Thunder-ten-Tronckh."

"Oh! Heavens! is it possible?" cried the Commandant.

"What a miracle!" cried Candide.

"Is it really you?" said the Commandant.

"It is not possible!" said Candide.

They drew back; they embraced; they shed rivulets of tears.

"What, is it you, reverend Father? You, the brother of the fair Cunegonde! You, that was slain by the Bulgarians! You, the Baron's son! You, a Jesuit in Paraguay! I must confess this is a strange world that we live in. Oh, Pangloss! Pangloss! how glad you would be if you had not been hanged!"

The Commandant sent away the negro slaves and the Paraguayans, who served them with liquors in goblets of rock-crystal. He thanked God and St. Ignatius a thousand times; he clasped Candide in his arms; and their faces were all bathed with tears.

"You will be more surprised, more affected, and transported," said Candide, "when I tell you that Cunegonde, your sister, whom you believe to have been ripped open, is in perfect health."

"Where?"

"In your neighbourhood, with the Governor of Buenos Ayres; and I was going to fight against you."

Every word which they uttered in this long conversation but added wonder to wonder. Their souls fluttered on their tongues, listened in their ears, and sparkled in their eyes. As they were Germans, they sat a good while at table, waiting for the reverend Father Provincial, and the Commandant spoke to his dear Candide as follows.

## XV. HOW CANDIDE KILLED THE BROTHER OF HIS DEAR CUNEGONDE.

"I SHALL have ever present to my memory the dreadful day, on which I saw my father and mother killed, and my sister ravished. When the Bulgarians retired, my dear sister could not be found; but my mother, my father, and myself, with two maid-servants and three little boys all of whom had been slain, were put in a hearse, to be conveyed for interment to a chapel belonging to the Jesuits, within two leagues of our family seat. A Jesuit sprinkled us with some holy water; it was horribly salt; a few drops of it fell into my eyes; the father perceived that my eyelids stirred a little; he put his hand upon my heart and felt it beat. I received assistance, and at the end of three weeks I recovered. You know, my dear Candide, I was very pretty; but I grew much prettier, and the reverend Father Didrie, Superior of that House, conceived the tenderest friendship for me; he gave me the habit of the order, some years after I was sent to Rome. The Father-General needed new levies of young German-Jesuits. The sovereigns of Paraguay admit as few Spanish Jesuits as possible; they prefer those of other nations as being more subordinate to their commands. I was judged fit by the reverend Father-General to go and work in this vineyard. We set out—a Pole, a Tyrolese, and myself. Upon my arrival I was honoured with a sub-deaconship and a lieutenancy. I am to-day colonel and priest. We shall give a warm reception to the King of Spain's troops; I will answer for it that they shall be excommunicated and well beaten. Providence sends you here to assist us. But is it, indeed, true that my dear sister Cunegonde is in the neighbourhood, with the Governor of Buenos Ayres?"

Candide assured him on oath that nothing was more true, and their tears began afresh.

The Baron could not refrain from embracing Candide; he called him his brother, his saviour.

"Ah! perhaps," said he, "we shall together, my dear Candide, enter the town as conquerors, and recover my sister Cunegonde."

"That is all I want," said Candide, "for I intended to marry her, and I still hope to do so."

"You insolent!" replied the Baron, "would you have the impudence to marry my sister who has seventy-two quarterings! I find thou hast the most consummate effrontery to dare to mention so presumptuous a design!"

Candide, petrified at this speech, made answer:

"Reverend Father, all the quarterings in the world signify nothing; I rescued your sister from the arms of a Jew and of an Inquisitor; she has great obligations to me, she wishes to marry me; Master Pangloss always told me that all men are equal, and certainly I will marry her."

"We shall see that, thou scoundrel!" said the Jesuit Baron de Thunder-ten-Tronckh, and that instant struck him across the face with the flat of his sword. Candide in an instant drew his rapier, and plunged it up to the hilt in the Jesuit's belly; but in pulling it out reeking hot, he burst into tears.

"Good God!" said he, "I have killed my old master, my friend, my brother-in-law! I am the best-natured creature in the world, and yet I have already killed three men, and of these three two were priests."

Cacambo, who stood sentry by the door of the arbour, ran to him.

"We have nothing more for it than to sell our lives as dearly as we can," said his master to him, "without doubt some one will soon enter the arbour, and we must die sword in hand."

Cacambo, who had been in a great many scrapes in his lifetime, did not lose his head; he took the Baron's Jesuit habit, put it on Candide, gave him the square cap, and made him mount on horseback. All this was done in the twinkling of an eye.

"Let us gallop fast, master, everybody will take you for a Jesuit, going to give directions to your men, and we shall have passed the frontiers before they will be able to overtake us."

He flew as he spoke these words, crying out aloud in Spanish:

"Make way, make way, for the reverend Father Colonel."

## XVI. ADVENTURES OF THE TWO TRAVELLERS, WITH TWO GIRLS, TWO MONKEYS, AND THE SAVAGES CALLED OREILLONS.

CANDIDE and his valet had got beyond the barrier, before it was known in the camp that the German Jesuit was dead. The wary Cacambo had taken care to fill his wallet with bread, chocolate, bacon, fruit, and a few bottles of wine. With their Andalusian horses they penetrated into an unknown country, where they perceived no beaten track. At length they came to a beautiful meadow intersected with purling rills. Here our two adventurers fed their horses. Cacambo proposed to his master to take some food, and he set him an example.

"How can you ask me to eat ham," said Candide, "after killing the Baron's son, and being doomed never more to see the beautiful Cunegonde? What will it avail me to spin out my wretched days and drag them far from her in remorse and despair? And what will the *Journal of Trevoux* say?"

While he was thus lamenting his fate, he went on eating. The sun went down. The two wanderers heard some little cries which seemed to be uttered by women. They did not know whether they were cries of pain or joy; but they started up precipitately with that inquietude and alarm which every little thing inspires in an unknown country. The noise was made by two naked girls, who tripped along the mead, while two monkeys were pursuing them and biting their buttocks. Candide was moved with pity; he had learned to fire a gun in the Bulgarian service, and he was so clever at it, that he could hit a filbert in a hedge without touching a leaf of the tree. He took up his double-barrelled Spanish fusil, let it off, and killed the two monkeys.

"God be praised! My dear Cacambo, I have rescued those two poor creatures from a most perilous situation. If I have committed a sin in killing an Inquisitor and a Jesuit, I have made ample amends by saving the lives of these girls. Perhaps they are young ladies of family; and this adventure may procure us great advantages in this country."

He was continuing, but stopped short when he saw the two girls tenderly embracing the monkeys, bathing their bodies in tears, and rending the air with the most dismal lamentations.

"Little did I expect to see such good-nature," said he at length to Cacambo; who made answer:

"Master, you have done a fine thing now; you have slain the sweethearts of those two young ladies."

"The sweethearts! Is it possible? You are jesting, Cacambo, I can never believe it!"

"Dear master," replied Cacambo; "you are surprised at everything. Why should you think it so strange that in some countries there are monkeys which insinuate themselves into the good graces of the ladies; they are a fourth part human, as I am a fourth part Spaniard."

"Alas!" replied Candide, "I remember to have heard Master Pangloss say, that formerly such accidents used to happen; that these mixtures were productive of Centaurs, Fauns, and Satyrs; and that many of the ancients had seen such monsters, but I looked upon the whole as fabulous."

"You ought now to be convinced," said Cacambo, "that it is the truth, and you see what use is made of those creatures, by persons that have not had a proper education; all I fear is that those ladies will play us some ugly trick."

These sound reflections induced Candide to leave the meadow and to plunge into a wood. He supped there with Cacambo; and after cursing the Portuguese inquisitor, the Governor of Buenos Ayres, and the Baron, they fell asleep on moss. On awaking they felt that they could not move; for during the night the Oreillons, who inhabited that country, and to whom the ladies had denounced them, had bound them with cords made of the bark of trees. They were encompassed by fifty naked Oreillons, armed with bows and arrows, with clubs and flint hatchets. Some were making a large cauldron boil, others were preparing spits, and all cried:

"A Jesuit! a Jesuit! we shall be revenged, we shall have excellent cheer, let us eat the Jesuit, let us eat him up!"

"I told you, my dear master," cried Cacambo sadly, "that those two girls would play us some ugly trick."

Candide seeing the cauldron and the spits, cried:

"We are certainly going to be either roasted or boiled. Ah! what would Master Pangloss say, were he to see how pure nature is formed? Everything is right, may be, but I declare it is very hard to have lost Miss Cunegonde and to be put upon a spit by Oreillons."

Cacambo never lost his head.

"Do not despair," said he to the disconsolate Candide, "I understand a little of the jargon of these people, I will speak to them."

"Be sure," said Candide, "to represent to them how frightfully inhuman it is to cook men, and how very un-Christian."

"Gentlemen," said Cacambo, "you reckon you are to-day going to feast upon a Jesuit. It is all very well, nothing is more unjust than thus to treat your enemies. Indeed, the law of nature teaches us to kill our neighbour, and such is the practice all over the world. If we do not accustom ourselves to eating them, it is because we have better fare. But you have not the same resources as we; certainly it is much better to devour your enemies than to resign to the crows and rooks the fruits of your victory. But, gentlemen, surely you would not choose to eat your friends. You believe that you are going to spit a Jesuit, and he is your defender. It is the enemy of your enemies that you are going to roast. As for myself, I was born in your country; this gentleman is my master, and, far from being a Jesuit, he has just killed one, whose spoils he wears; and thence comes your mistake. To convince you of the truth of what I say, take his habit and carry it to the first barrier of the Jesuit kingdom, and inform yourselves whether my master did not kill a Jesuit officer. It will not take you long, and you can always eat us if you find that I have lied to you. But I have told you the truth. You are too well acquainted with the principles of public law, humanity, and justice not to pardon us."

The Oreillons found this speech very reasonable. They deputed two of their principal people with all expedition to inquire into the truth of the matter; these executed their commission like men of sense, and soon returned with good news. The Oreillons untied their prisoners, showed them all sorts of civilities, offered them girls, gave them refreshment, and reconducted them to the confines of their territories, proclaiming with great joy:

"He is no Jesuit! He is no Jesuit!"

Candide could not help being surprised at the cause of his deliverance.

"What people!" said he; "what men! what manners! If I had not been so lucky as to run Miss Cunegonde's brother through the body, I should have been devoured without redemption. But, after all, pure nature is good, since these people, instead of feasting upon my flesh, have shown me a thousand civilities, when then I was not a Jesuit."

## XVII. ARRIVAL OF CANDIDE AND HIS VALET AT EL DORADO, AND WHAT THEY SAW THERE.

"You see," said Cacambo to Candide, as soon as they had reached the frontiers of the Oreillons, "that this hemisphere is not better than the others, take my word for it; let us go back to Europe by the shortest way."

"How go back?" said Candide, "and where shall we go? to my own country? The Bulgarians and the Abares are slaying all; to Portugal? there I shall be burnt; and if we abide here we are every moment in danger of being spitted. But how can I resolve to quit a part of the world where my dear Cunegonde resides?"

"Let us turn towards Cayenne," said Cacambo, "there we shall find Frenchmen, who wander all over the world; they may assist us; God will perhaps have pity on us."

It was not easy to get to Cayenne; they knew vaguely in which direction to go, but rivers, precipices, robbers, savages, obstructed them all the way. Their horses died of fatigue. Their provisions were consumed; they fed a whole month upon wild fruits, and found themselves at last near a little river bordered with cocoa trees, which sustained their lives and their hopes.

Cacambo, who was as good a counsellor as the old woman, said to Candide:

"We are able to hold out no longer; we have walked enough. I see an empty canoe near the river-side; let us fill it with cocoanuts, throw ourselves into it, and go with the current; a river always leads to some inhabited spot. If we do not find pleasant things we shall at least find new things."

"With all my heart," said Candide, "let us recommend ourselves to Providence."

They rowed a few leagues, between banks, in some places flowery, in others barren; in some parts smooth, in others rugged. The stream ever widened, and at length lost itself under an arch of frightful rocks which reached to the sky. The two travellers had the courage to commit themselves to the current. The river, suddenly contracting at this place, whirled them along with a dreadful noise and rapidity. At the end of four-and-twenty hours they saw daylight again, but their canoe was dashed to pieces against the rocks. For a league they had to creep from rock to rock, until at length they discovered an extensive plain, bounded by inaccessible mountains. The country was cultivated as much for pleasure as for necessity. On all sides the useful was also the beautiful. The roads were covered, or rather adorned, with carriages of a glittering form and substance, in which were men and women of surprising beauty, drawn by large red sheep which surpassed in fleetness the finest coursers of Andalusia, Tetuan, and Mequinez.

"Here, however, is a country," said Candide, "which is better than Westphalia."

He stepped out with Cacambo towards the first village which he saw. Some children dressed in tattered brocades played at quoits on the outskirts. Our travellers from the other world amused themselves by looking on. The quoits were large round pieces, yellow, red, and green, which cast a singular lustre! The travellers picked a few of them off the ground; this was of gold, that of emeralds, the other of rubies—the least of them would have been the greatest ornament on the Mogul's throne.

"Without doubt," said Cacambo, "these children must be the king's sons that are playing at quoits!"

The village schoolmaster appeared at this moment and called them to school.

"There," said Candide, "is the preceptor of the royal family."

The little truants immediately quitted their game, leaving the quoits on the ground with all their other playthings. Candide gathered them up, ran to the master, and presented them to him in a most humble manner, giving him to understand by signs that their royal highnesses had forgotten their gold and jewels. The schoolmaster, smiling, flung them upon the ground; then, looking at Candide with a good deal of surprise, went about his business.

The travellers, however, took care to gather up the gold, the rubies, and the emeralds.

"Where are we?" cried Candide. "The king's children in this country must be well brought up, since they are taught to despise gold and precious stones."

Cacambo was as much surprised as Candide. At length they drew near the first house in the village. It was built like an European palace. A crowd of people pressed about the door, and there were still more in the house. They heard most agreeable music, and were aware of a delicious odour of cooking. Cacambo went up to the door and heard they were talking Peruvian; it was his mother tongue, for it is well known that Cacambo was born in Tucuman, in a village where no other language was spoken.

"I will be your interpreter here," said he to Candide; "let us go in, it is a public-house."

Immediately two waiters and two girls, dressed in cloth of gold, and their hair tied up with ribbons, invited them to sit down to table with the landlord. They served four dishes of soup, each garnished with two young parrots; a boiled condor which weighed two hundred pounds; two roasted monkeys, of excellent flavour; three hundred humming-birds in one dish, and six hundred fly-birds in another; exquisite ragouts; delicious pastries; the whole served up in dishes of a kind of rock-crystal. The waiters and girls poured out several liqueurs drawn from the sugar-cane.

Most of the company were chapmen and waggoners, all extremely polite; they asked Cacambo a few questions with the greatest circumspection, and answered his in the most obliging manner.

As soon as dinner was over, Cacambo believed as well as Candide that they might well pay their reckoning by laying down two of those large gold pieces which they had picked up. The landlord and landlady shouted with laughter and held their sides. When the fit was over:

"Gentlemen," said the landlord, "it is plain you are strangers, and such guests we are not accustomed to see; pardon us therefore for laughing when you offered us the pebbles from our highroads in payment of your reckoning. You doubtless have not the money of the country; but it is not necessary to have any money at all to dine in this house. All hostelries established for the convenience of commerce are paid by the government. You have fared but very indifferently because this is a poor village; but everywhere else, you will be received as you deserve."

Cacambo explained this whole discourse with great astonishment to Candide, who was as greatly astonished to hear it.

"What sort of a country then is this," said they to one another; "a country unknown to all the rest of the world, and where nature is of a kind so different from ours? It is probably the country where all is well; for there absolutely must be one such place. And, whatever Master Pangloss might say, I often found that things went very ill in Westphalia."

## XVIII. WHAT THEY SAW IN THE COUNTRY OF EL DORADO.

CACAMBO expressed his curiosity to the landlord, who made answer:

"I am very ignorant, but not the worse on that account. However, we have in this neighbourhood an old man retired from Court who is the most learned and most communicative person in the kingdom."

At once he took Cacambo to the old man. Candide acted now only a second character, and accompanied his valet. They entered a very plain house, for the door was only of silver, and the ceilings were only of gold, but wrought in so elegant a taste as to vie with the richest. The antechamber, indeed, was only encrusted with rubies and emeralds, but the order in which everything was arranged made amends for this great simplicity.

The old man received the strangers on his sofa, which was stuffed with humming-birds' feathers, and ordered his servants to present them with liqueurs in diamond goblets; after which he satisfied their curiosity in the following terms:

"I am now one hundred and seventy-two years old, and I learnt of my late father, Master of the Horse to the King, the amazing revolutions of Peru, of which he had been an eye-witness. The kingdom we now inhabit is the ancient country of the Incas, who quitted it very imprudently to conquer another part of the world, and were at length destroyed by the Spaniards.

"More wise by far were the princes of their family, who remained in their native country; and they ordained, with the consent of the whole nation, that none of the inhabitants should ever be permitted to quit this little kingdom; and this has preserved our innocence and happiness. The Spaniards have had a confused notion of this country, and have called it *El Dorado;* and an Englishman, whose name was Sir Walter Raleigh, came very near it about a hundred years ago; but being surrounded by inaccessible rocks and precipices, we have hitherto been sheltered from the rapaciousness of European nations, who have an inconceivable passion for the pebbles and dirt of our land, for the sake of which they would murder us to the last man."

The conversation was long: it turned chiefly on their form of government, their manners, their women, their public entertainments, and the arts. At length Candide, having always had a taste for metaphysics, made Cacambo ask whether there was any religion in that country.

The old man reddened a little.

"How then," said he, "can you doubt it? Do you take us for ungrateful wretches?"

Cacambo humbly asked, "What was the religion in El Dorado?"

The old man reddened again.

"Can there be two religions?" said he. "We have, I believe, the religion of all the world: we worship God night and morning."

"Do you worship but one God?" said Cacambo, who still acted as interpreter in representing Candide's doubts.

"Surely," said the old man, "there are not two, nor three, nor four.

I must confess the people from your side of the world ask very extraordinary questions."

Candide was not yet tired of interrogating the good old man; he wanted to know in what manner they prayed to God in El Dorado.

"We do not pray to Him," said the worthy sage; "we have nothing to ask of Him; He has given us all we need, and we return Him thanks without ceasing."

Candide having a curiosity to see the priests asked where they were. The good old man smiled.

"My friend," said he, "we are all priests. The King and all the heads of families sing solemn canticles of thanksgiving every morning, accompanied by five or six thousand musicians."

"What! have you no monks who teach, who dispute, who govern, who cabal, and who burn people that are not of their opinion?"

"We must be mad, indeed, if that were the case," said the old man; "here we are all of one opinion, and we know not what you mean by monks."

During this whole discourse Candide was in raptures, and he said to himself:

"This is vastly different from Westphalia and the Baron's castle. Had our friend Pangloss seen El Dorado he would no longer have said that the castle of Thunder-ten-Tronckh was the finest upon earth. It is evident that one must travel."

After this long conversation the old man ordered a coach and six sheep to be got ready, and twelve of his domestics to conduct the travellers to Court.

"Excuse me," said he, "if my age deprives me of the honour of accompanying you. The King will receive you in a manner that cannot displease you; and no doubt you will make an allowance for the customs of the country, if some things should not be to your liking."

Candide and Cacambo got into the coach, the six sheep flew, and in less than four hours they reached the King's palace situated at the extremity of the capital. The portal was two hundred and twenty feet high, and one hundred wide; but words are wanting to express the materials of which it was built. It is plain such materials must have prodigious superiority over those pebbles and sand which we call gold and precious stones.

Twenty beautiful damsels of the King's guard received Candide and Cacambo as they alighted from the coach, conducted them to the bath, and dressed them in robes woven of the down of humming-birds; after which the great crown officers, of both sexes, led them to the King's apartment, between two files of musicians, a thousand on each side. When they drew near to the audience chamber Cacambo asked one of the great officers in what way he should pay his obeisance to his Majesty; whether they should throw themselves upon their knees or on their stomachs; whether they should put their hands upon their heads or behind their backs; whether they should lick the dust off the floor; in a word, what was the ceremony?

"The custom," said the great officer, "is to embrace the King, and to kiss him on each cheek."

Candide and Cacambo threw themselves round his Majesty's neck. He received them with all the goodness imaginable, and politely invited them to supper.

While waiting they were shown the city, and saw the public edifices raised as high as the clouds, the market places ornamented with a thousand columns, the fountains of spring water, those of rose water, those of liqueurs drawn from sugar-cane, incessantly flowing into the great squares, which were paved with a kind of precious stone, which gave off a delicious fragrancy like that of cloves and cinnamon. Candide asked to see the court of justice, the parliament. They told him they had none, and that they were strangers to lawsuits. He asked if they had any prisons, and they answered no. But what surprised him most and gave him the greatest pleasure was the palace of sciences, where he saw a gallery two thousand feet long, and filled with instruments employed in mathematics and physics.

After rambling about the city the whole afternoon, and seeing but a thousandth part of it, they were reconducted to the royal palace, where Candide sat down to table with his Majesty, his valet Cacambo, and several ladies. Never was there a better entertainment, and never was more wit shown at a table than that which fell from his Majesty. Cacambo explained the King's *bon-mots* to Candide, and notwithstanding they were translated they still appeared to be *bon-mots*. Of all the things that surprised Candide this was not the least.

They spent a month in this hospitable place. Candide frequently said to Cacambo:

"I own, my friend, once more that the castle where I was born is nothing in comparison with this; but, after all, Miss Cunegonde is not here, and you have, without doubt, some mistress in Europe. If we abide here we shall only be upon a footing with the rest, whereas, if we return to our old world, only with twelve sheep laden with the pebbles of El Dorado, we shall be richer than all the kings in Europe. We shall have no more Inquisitors to fear, and we may easily recover Miss Cunegonde."

This speech was agreeable to Cacambo; mankind are so fond of roving, of making a figure in their own country, and of boasting of what they have seen in their travels, that the two happy ones resolved to be no longer so, but to ask his Majesty's leave to quit the country.

"You are foolish," said the King. "I am sensible that my kingdom is but a small place, but when a person is comfortably settled in any part he should abide there. I have not the right to detain strangers. It is a tyranny which neither our manners nor our laws permit. All men are free. Go when you wish, but the going will be very difficult. It is impossible to ascend that rapid river on which you came as by a miracle, and which runs under vaulted rocks. The mountains which surround my kingdom are ten thousand feet high, and as steep as walls; they are each over ten leagues in breadth, and there is no other way to descend them than by precipices. However, since you absolutely wish to depart, I shall give orders to my engineers to construct a machine that will convey you very safely. When we have conducted you over the mountains no one can accompany you further, for my subjects have made a vow never to quit the kingdom, and they are too wise to break it. Ask me besides anything that you please."

"We desire nothing of your Majesty," says Candide, "but a few sheep laden with provisions, pebbles, and the earth of this country."

The King laughed.

"I cannot conceive," said he, "what pleasure you Europeans find in our yellow clay, but take as much as you like, and great good may it do you."

At once he gave directions that his engineers should construct a machine to hoist up these two extraordinary men out of the kingdom. Three thousand good mathematicians went to work; it was ready in fifteen days, and did not cost more than twenty million sterling in the specie of that country. They placed Candide and Cacambo on the machine. There were two great red sheep saddled and bridled to ride upon as soon as they were beyond the mountains, twenty pack-sheep laden with provisions, thirty with presents of the curiosities of the country, and fifty with gold, diamonds, and precious stones. The King embraced the two wanderers very tenderly.

Their departure, with the ingenious manner in which they and their sheep were hoisted over the mountains, was a splendid spectacle. The mathematicians took their leave after conveying them to a place of safety, and Candide had no other desire, no other aim, than to present his sheep to Miss Cunegonde.

"Now," said he, "we are able to pay the Governor of Buenos Ayres if Miss Cunegonde can be ransomed. Let us journey towards Cayenne. Let us embark, and we will afterwards see what kingdom we shall be able to purchase."

## XIX. WHAT HAPPENED TO THEM AT SURINAM AND HOW CANDIDE GOT ACQUAINTED WITH MARTIN.

OUR travellers spent the first day very agreeably. They were delighted with possessing more treasure than all Asia, Europe, and Africa could scrape together. Candide, in his raptures, cut Cunegonde's name on the trees. The second day two of their sheep plunged into a morass, where they and their burdens were lost; two more died of fatigue a few days after; seven or eight perished with hunger in a desert; and others subsequently fell down precipices. At length, after travelling a hundred days, only two sheep remained. Said Candide to Cacambo:

"My friend, you see how perishable are the riches of this world; there is nothing solid but virtue, and the happiness of seeing Cunegonde once more."

"I grant all you say," said Cacambo, "but we have still two sheep remaining, with more treasure than the King of Spain will ever have; and I see a town which I take to be Surinam, belonging to the Dutch. We are at the end of all our troubles, and at the beginning of happiness."

As they drew near the town, they saw a negro stretched upon the ground, with only one moiety of his clothes, that is, of his blue linen drawers; the poor man had lost his left leg and his right hand.

"Good God!" said Candide in Dutch, "what art thou doing there, friend, in that shocking condition?"

"I am waiting for my master, Mynheer Vanderdendur, the famous merchant," answered the negro.

"Was it Mynheer Vanderdendur," said Candide, "that treated thee thus?"

"Yes, sir," said the negro, "it is the custom. They give us a pair of linen drawers for our whole garment twice a year. When we work at the sugar-canes, and the mill snatches hold of a finger, they cut off the hand; and when we attempt to run away, they cut off the leg; both cases have happened to me. This is the price at which you eat sugar in Europe. Yet when my mother sold me for ten patagons * on the coast of Guinea, she said to me: 'My dear child, bless our fetiches, adore them for ever; they will make thee live happily; thou hast the honour of being the slave of our lords, the whites, which is making the fortune of thy father and mother.' Alas! I know not whether I have made their fortunes; this I know, that they have not made mine. Dogs,

* Spanish half-crowns.

monkeys, and parrots are a thousand times less wretched than I. The Dutch fetiches, who have converted me, declare every Sunday that we are all of us children of Adam—blacks as well as whites. I am not a genealogist, but if these preachers tell truth, we are all second cousins. Now, you must agree, that it is impossible to treat one's relations in a more barbarous manner."

"Oh, Pangloss!" cried Candide, "thou hadst not guessed at this abomination; it is the end. I must at last renounce thy optimism."

"What is this optimism?" said Cacambo.

"Alas!" said Candide, "it is the madness of maintaining that everything is right when it is wrong."

Looking at the negro, he shed tears, and weeping, he entered Surinam.

The first thing they inquired after was whether there was a vessel in the harbour which could be sent to Buenos Ayres. The person to whom they applied was a Spanish sea-captain, who offered to agree with them upon reasonable terms. He appointed to meet them at a public-house, whither Candide and the faithful Cacambo went with their two sheep, and awaited his coming.

Candide, who had his heart upon his lips, told the Spaniard all his adventures, and avowed that he intended to elope with Miss Cunegonde.

"Then I will take good care not to carry you to Buenos Ayres," said the seaman. "I should be hanged, and so would you. The fair Cunegonde is my lord's favourite mistress."

This was a thunderclap for Candide: he wept for a long while. At last he drew Cacambo aside.

"Here, my dear friend," said he to him, "this thou must do. We have, each of us in his pocket, five or six millions in diamonds; you are more clever than I; you must go and bring Miss Cunegonde from Buenos Ayres. If the Governor makes any difficulty, give him a million; if he will not relinquish her, give him two; as you have not killed an Inquisitor, they will have no suspicion of you; I'll get another ship, and go and wait for you at Venice; that's a free country, where there is no danger either from Bulgarians, Abares, Jews, or Inquisitors."

Cacambo applauded this wise resolution. He despaired at parting from so good a master, who had become his intimate friend; but the pleasure of serving him prevailed over the pain of leaving him. They embraced with tears; Candide charged him not to forget the good old woman. Cacambo set out that very same day. This Cacambo was a very honest fellow.

Candide stayed some time longer in Surinam, waiting for another captain to carry him and the two remaining sheep to Italy. After he had hired domestics, and purchased everything necessary for a long voyage, Mynheer Vanderdendur, captain of a large vessel, came and offered his services.

"How much will you charge," said he to this man, "to carry me straight to Venice—me, my servants, my baggage, and these two sheep?"

The skipper asked ten thousand piastres. Candide did not hesitate.

"Oh! oh!" said the prudent Vanderdendur to himself, "this stranger gives ten thousand piastres unhesitatingly! He must be very rich."

Returning a little while after, he let him know that upon second consideration, he could not undertake the voyage for less than twenty thousand piastres.

"Well, you shall have them," said Candide.

"Ay!" said the skipper to himself, "this man agrees to pay twenty thousand piastres with as much ease as ten."

He went back to him again, and declared that he could not carry him to Venice for less than thirty thousand piastres.

"Then you shall have thirty thousand," replied Candide.

"Oh! oh!" said the Dutch skipper once more to himself, "thirty thousand piastres are a trifle to this man; surely these sheep must be laden with an immense treasure; let us say no more about it. First of all, let him pay down the thirty thousand piastres; then we shall see."

Candide sold two small diamonds, the least of which was worth more than what the skipper asked for his freight. He paid him in advance. The two sheep were put on board. Candide followed in a little boat to join the vessel in the roads. The skipper seized his opportunity, set sail, and put out to sea, the wind favouring him. Candide, dismayed and stupefied, soon lost sight of the vessel.

"Alas!" said he, "this is a trick worthy of the old world!"

He put back, overwhelmed with sorrow, for indeed he had lost sufficient to make the fortune of twenty monarchs. He waited upon the Dutch magistrate, and in his distress he knocked over loudly at the door. He entered and told his adventure, raising his voice with unnecessary vehemence. The magistrate began by fining him ten thousand piastres for making a noise; then he listened patiently, promised to examine into his affair at the skipper's return, and ordered him to pay ten thousand piastres for the expense of the hearing.

This drove Candide to despair; he had, indeed, endured misfortunes a thousand times worse; the coolness of the magistrate and of the skipper who had robbed him, roused his choler and flung him into a deep melancholy. The villainy of mankind presented itself before his imagination in all its deformity, and his mind was filled with gloomy ideas. At length hearing that a French vessel was ready to set sail for Bordeaux, as he had no sheep laden with diamonds to take along with him he hired a cabin at the usual price. He made it known in the town that he would pay the passage and board and give two thousand piastres to any honest man who would make the voyage with him, upon condition that this man was the most dissatisfied with his state, and the most unfortunate in the whole province.

Such a crowd of candidates presented themselves that a fleet of ships could hardly have held them. Candide being desirous of selecting from among the best, marked out about one-twentieth of them who seemed to be sociable men, and who all pretended to merit his preference. He assembled them at his inn, and gave them a supper on condition that each took an oath to relate his history faithfully, promising to choose him who appeared to be most justly discontented with his state, and to bestow some presents upon the rest.

They sat until four o'clock in the morning. Candide, in listening to all their adventures, was reminded of what the old woman had said to him in their voyage to Buenos Ayres, and of her wager that there was not a person on board the ship but had met with very great misfortunes. He dreamed of Pangloss at every adventure told to him.

"This Pangloss," said he, "would be puzzled to demonstrate his system. I wish that he were here. Certainly, if all things are good, it is in El Dorado and not in the rest of the world."

At length he made choice of a poor man of letters, who had worked ten years for the booksellers of Amsterdam. He judged that there was not in the whole world a trade which could disgust one more.

This philosopher was an honest man; but he had been robbed by his wife, beaten by his son, and abandoned by his daughter who got a Portuguese to run away with her. He had just been deprived of a small employment, on which he subsisted; and he was persecuted by the preachers of Surinam, who took him for a Socinian. We must allow that the others were at least as wretched as he; but Candide hoped that the philosopher would entertain him during the voyage. All the other candidates complained that Candide had done them great injustice; but he appeased them by giving one hundred piastres to each.

## XX. WHAT HAPPENED AT SEA TO CANDIDE AND MARTIN.

THE old philosopher, whose name was Martin, embarked then with Candide for Bordeaux. They had both seen and suffered a great deal;

and if the vessel had sailed from Surinam to Japan, by the Cape of Good Hope, the subject of moral and natural evil would have enabled them to entertain one another during the whole voyage.

Candide, however, had one great advantage over Martin, in that he always hoped to see Miss Cunegonde; whereas Martin had nothing at all to hope. Besides, Candide was possessed of money and jewels, and though he had lost one hundred large red sheep, laden with the greatest treasure upon earth; though the knavery of the Dutch skipper still sat heavy upon his mind; yet when he reflected upon what he had still left, and when he mentioned the name of Cunegonde, especially towards the latter end of a repast, he inclined to Pangloss's doctrine.

"But you, Mr. Martin," said he to the philosopher, "what do you think of all this? what are your ideas on moral and natural evil?"

"Sir," answered Martin, "our priests accused me of being a Socinian, but the real fact is I am a Manichean."

"You jest," said Candide; "there are no longer Manicheans in the world."

"I am one," said Martin. "I cannot help it; I know not how to think otherwise."

"Surely you must be possessed by the devil," said Candide.

"He is so deeply concerned in the affairs of this world," answered Martin, "that he may very well be in me, as well as in everybody else; but I own to you that when I cast an eye on this globe, or rather on this little ball, I cannot help thinking that God has abandoned it to some malignant being. I except, always, El Dorado. I scarcely ever knew a city that did not desire the destruction of a neighbouring city, nor a family that did not wish to exterminate some other family. Everywhere the weak execrate the powerful, before whom they cringe; and the powerful beat them like sheep whose wool and flesh they sell. A million regimented assassins, from one extremity of Europe to the other, get their bread by disciplined depredation and murder, for want of more honest employment. Even in those cities which seem to enjoy peace, and where the arts flourish, the inhabitants are devoured by more envy, care, and uneasiness than are experienced by a besieged town. Secret griefs are more cruel than public calamities. In a word I have seen so much, and experienced so much than I am a Manichean."

"There are, however, some things good," said Candide.

"That may be," said Martin; "but I know them not."

In the middle of this dispute they heard the report of cannon; it redoubled every instant. Each took out his glass. They saw two ships in close fight about three miles off. The wind brought both so near to the French vessel that our travellers had the pleasure of seeing the fight at their ease. At length one let off a broadside, so low and so truly aimed, that the other sank to the bottom. Candide and Martin could plainly perceive a hundred men on the deck of the sinking vessel; they raised their hands to heaven and uttered terrible outcries, and the next moment were swallowed up by the sea.

"Well," said Martin, "this is how men treat one another."

"It is true," said Candide; "there is something diabolical in this affair."

While speaking, he saw he knew not what, of a shining red, swimming close to the vessel. They put out the long-boat to see what it could be: it was one of his sheep! Candide was more rejoiced at the recovery of this one sheep than he had been grieved at the loss of the hundred laden with the large diamonds of El Dorado.

The French captain soon saw that the captain of the victorious vessel was a Spaniard, and that the other was a Dutch pirate, and the very same one who had robbed Candide. The immense plunder which this villain had amassed, was buried with him in the sea, and out of the whole only one sheep was saved.

"You see," said Candide to Martin, "that crime is sometimes punished. This rogue of a Dutch skipper has met with the fate he deserved."

"Yes," said Martin; "but why should the passengers be doomed also to destruction? God has punished the knave, and the devil has drowned the rest."

The French and Spanish ships continued their course, and Candide continued his conversation with Martin. They disputed fifteen successive days, and on the last of those fifteen days, they were as far advanced as on the first. But, however, they chatted, they communicated ideas, they consoled each other. Candide caressed his sheep.

"Since I have found thee again," said he, "I may likewise chance to find my Cunegonde."

## XXI. CANDIDE AND MARTIN, REASONING, DRAW NEAR THE COAST OF FRANCE.

At length they descried the coast of France.

"Were you ever in France, Mr. Martin?" said Candide.

"Yes," said Martin, "I have been in several provinces. In some one-half of the people are fools, in others they are too cunning; in some they are weak and simple, in others they affect to be witty; in all, the principal occupation is love, the next is slander, and the third is talking nonsense."

"But, Mr. Martin, have you seen Paris?"

"Yes, I have. All these kinds are found there. It is a chaos—a confused multitude, where everybody seeks pleasure and scarcely any one finds it, at least as it appeared to me. I made a short stay there. On my arrival I was robbed of all I had by pickpockets at the fair of St. Germain. I myself was taken for a robber and was imprisoned for eight days, after which I served as corrector of the press to gain the money necessary for my return to Holland on foot. I knew the whole scribbling rabble, the party rabble, the fanatic rabble. It is said that there are very polite people in that city, and I wish to believe it."

"For my part, I have no curiosity to see France," said Candide. "You may easily imagine that after spending a month at El Dorado I can desire to behold nothing upon earth but Miss Cunegonde. I go to await her at Venice. We shall pass through France on our way to Italy. Will you bear me company?"

"With all my heart," said Martin. "It is said that Venice is fit only for its own nobility, but that strangers meet with a very good reception if they have a good deal of money. I have none of it; you have, therefore I will follow you all over the world."

"But do you believe," said Candide, "that the earth was originally a sea, as we find it asserted in that large book belonging to the captain?"

"I do not believe a word of it," said Martin, "any more than I do of the many ravings which have been published lately."

"But for what end, then, has this world been formed?" said Candide.

"To plague us to death," answered Martin.

"Are you not greatly surprised," continued Candide, "at the love which these two girls of the Oreillons had for those monkeys, of which I have already told you?"

"Not at all," said Martin. "I do not see that that passion was strange. I have seen so many extraordinary things that I have ceased to be surprised."

"Do you believe," said Candide, "that men have always massacred each other as they do to-day, that they have always been liars, cheats, traitors, ingrates, brigands, idiots, thieves, scoundrels, gluttons, drunkards, misers, envious, ambitious, bloody-minded, calumniators, debauchees, fanatics, hypocrites, and fools?"

"Do you believe," said Martin, "that hawks have always eaten pigeons when they have found them?"

"Yes, without doubt," said Candide.

"Well, then," said Martin, "if hawks have always had the same character why should you imagine that men may have changed theirs?"

"Oh!" said Candide, "there is a vast deal of difference, for free will—"

And reasoning thus they arrived at Bordeaux.

## XXII. WHAT HAPPENED IN FRANCE TO CANDIDE AND MARTIN.

CANDIDE stayed in Bordeaux no longer than was necessary for the selling of a few of the pebbles of El Dorado, and for hiring a good chaise to hold two passengers; for he could not travel without his Philosopher Martin. He was only vexed at parting with his sheep, which he left to the Bordeaux Academy of Sciences, who set as a subject for that year's prize, "to find why this sheep's wool was red;" and the prize was awarded to a learned man of the North, who demonstrated by A plus B minus C divided by Z, that the sheep must be red, and die of the rot.

Meanwhile, all the travellers whom Candide met in the inns along his route, said to him, "We go to Paris." This general eagerness at length gave him, too, a desire to see this capital; and it was not so very great a *détour* from the road to Venice.

He entered Paris by the suburb of St. Marceau, and fancied that he was in the dirtiest village of Westphalia.

Scarcely was Candide arrived at his inn, than he found himself attacked by a slight illness, caused by fatigue. As he had a very large diamond on his finger, and the people of the inn had taken notice of a prodigiously heavy box among his baggage, there were two physicians to attend him, though he had never sent for them, and two devotees who warmed his broths.

"I remember," Martin said, "also to have been sick at Paris in my first voyage; I was very poor, thus I had neither friends, devotees, nor doctors, and I recovered."

However, what with physic and bleeding, Candide's illness became serious. A parson of the neighbourhood came with great meekness to ask for a bill for the other world payable to the bearer. Candide would do nothing for him; but the devotees assured him it was the new fashion. He answered that he was not a man of fashion. Martin wished to throw the priest out of the window. The priest swore that they would not bury Candide. Martin swore that he would bury the priest if he continued to be troublesome. The quarrel grew heated. Martin took him by the shoulders and roughly turned him out of doors; which occasioned great scandal and a law-suit.

Candide got well again, and during his convalescence he had very good company to sup with him. They played high. Candide wondered why it was that the ace never came to him; but Martin was not at all astonished.

Among those who did him the honours of the town was a little Abbé of Perigord, one of those busybodies who are ever alert, officious, forward, fawning, and complaisant; who watch for strangers in their passage through the capital, tell them the scandalous history of the town, and offer them pleasure at all prices. He first took Candide and Martin to La Comédie, where they played a new tragedy. Candide happened to be seated near some of the fashionable wits. This did not prevent his shedding tears at the well-acted scenes. One of these critics at his side said to him between the acts:

"Your tears are misplaced; that is a shocking actress; the actor who plays with her is yet worse; and the play is still worse than the actors. The author does not know a word of Arabic, yet the scene is in Arabia; moreover he is a man that does not believe in innate ideas; and I will bring you, to-morrow, twenty pamphlets written against him."

"How many dramas have you in France, sir?" said Candide to the Abbé.

"Five or six thousand."

"What a number!" said Candide. "How many good?"

"Fifteen or sixteen," replied the other.

"What a number!" said Martin.

Candide was very pleased with an actress who played Queen Elizabeth in a somewhat insipid tragedy sometimes acted.

"That actress," said he to Martin, "pleases me much; she has a likeness to Miss Cunegonde; I should be very glad to wait upon her."

The Perigordian Abbé offered to introduce him. Candide, brought up in Germany, asked what was the etiquette, and how they treated queens of England in France.

"It is necessary to make distinctions," said the Abbé. "In the provinces one takes them to the inn; in Paris, one respects them when they are beautiful, and throws them on the highway when they are dead."

"Queens on the highway!" said Candide.

"Yes, truly," said Martin, "the Abbé is right. I was in Paris when Miss Monime passed, as the saying is, from this life to the other. She was refused what people call the *honours of sepulture*—that is to say, of rotting with all the beggars of the neighbourhood in an ugly cemetery; she was interred all alone by her company at the corner of the Rue de Bourgogne, which ought to trouble her much, for she thought nobly."

"That was very uncivil," said Candide.

"What would you have?" said Martin; "these people are made thus. Imagine all contradictions, all possible incompatibilities—you will find them in the government, in the law-courts, in the churches, in the public shows of this droll nation."

"Is it true that they always laugh in Paris?" said Candide.

"Yes," said the Abbé, "but it means nothing, for they complain of everything with great fits of laughter; they even do the most detestable things while laughing."

"Who," said Candide, "is that great pig who spoke so ill of the piece at which I wept, and of the actors who gave me so much pleasure?"

"He is a bad character," answered the Abbé, "who gains his livelihood by saying evil of all plays and of all books. He hates whatever succeeds, as the eunuchs hate those who enjoy; he is one of the serpents of literature who nourish themselves on dirt and spite; he is a *folliculaire*."

"What is a *folliculaire?*" said Candide.

"It is," said the Abbé, "a pamphleteer—a Fréron."

Thus Candide, Martin, and the Perigordian conversed on the staircase, while watching every one go out after the performance.

"Although I am eager to see Cunegonde again," said Candide, "I should like to sup with Miss Clairon, for she appears to me admirable."

The Abbé was not the man to approach Miss Clairon, who saw only good company.

"She is engaged for this evening," he said, "but I shall have the honour to take you to the house of a lady of quality, and there you will know Paris as if you had lived in it for years."

Candide, who was naturally curious, let himself be taken to this lady's house, at the end of the Faubourg St. Honoré. The company was occupied in playing faro; a dozen melancholy punters held each in his hand a little pack of cards; a bad record of his misfortunes. Profound silence reigned; pallor was on the faces of the punters, anxiety on that of the banker, and the hostess, sitting near the unpitying banker, noticed with lynx-eyes all the doubled and other increased stakes, as each player dog's-eared his cards; she made them turn down the edges again with severe, but polite attention; she showed no vexation for fear of losing her customers. The lady insisted upon being called the Marchioness of Parolignac. Her daughter, aged fifteen, was among the punters, and notified with a covert glance the cheatings of the poor people who tried to repair the cruelties of fate. The Perigordian Abbé, Candide and Martin entered; no one rose, no one saluted them, no one looked at them; all were profoundly occupied with their cards.

"The Baroness of Thunder-ten-Tronckh was more polite," said Candide.

However, the Abbé whispered to the Marchioness, who half rose, honoured Candide with a gracious smile, and Martin with a condescending nod; she gave a seat and a pack of cards to Candide, who lost fifty thousand francs in two deals, after which they supped very gaily, and every one was astonished that Candide was not moved by his loss; the servants said among themselves, in the language of servants:—

"Some English lord is here this evening."

The supper passed at first like most Parisian suppers, in silence, followed by a noise of words which could not be distinguished, then with pleasantries of which most were insipid, with false news, with bad reasoning, a little politics, and much evil speaking; they also discussed new books.

"Have you seen," said the Perigordian Abbé, "the romance of Sieur Gauchat, doctor of divinity?"

"Yes," answered one of the guests, "but I have not been able to finish it. We have a crowd of silly writings, but all together do not approach the impertinence of 'Gauchat, Doctor of Divinity.' I am so satiated with the great number of detestable books with which we are inundated that I am reduced to punting at faro."

"And the *Mélanges* of Archdeacon Trublet, what do you say of that?" said the Abbé.

"Ah!" said the Marchioness of Parolignac, "the wearisome mortal! How curiously he repeats to you all that the world knows! How heavily he discusses that which is not worth the trouble of lightly remarking upon! How, without wit, he appropriates the wit of others! How he spoils what he steals! How he disgusts me! But he will disgust me no longer—it is enough to have read a few of the Archdeacon's pages."

There was at table a wise man of taste, who supported the Marchioness. They spoke afterwards of tragedies; the lady asked why there were tragedies which were sometimes played and which could not be read. The man of taste explained very well how a piece could have some interest, and have almost no merit; he proved in few words that it was not enough to introduce one or two of those situations which one finds in all romances, and which always seduce the spectator, but that it was necessary to be new without being odd, often sublime and always natural, to know the human heart and to make it speak; to be a great poet without allowing any person in the piece to appear to be a poet; to know language perfectly—to speak it with purity, with continuous harmony and without rhythm ever taking anything from sense."

"Whoever," added he, "does not observe all these rules can produce one or two tragedies, applauded at a theatre, but he will never be counted in the ranks of good writers. There are very few good tragedies; some are idylls in dialogue, well written and well rhymed, others political reasonings which lull to sleep, or amplifications which repel; others demoniac dreams in barbarous style, interrupted in sequence, with long apostrophes to the gods, because they do not know how to speak to men, with false maxims, with bombastic commonplaces!"

Candide listened with attention to this discourse, and conceived a great idea of the speaker, and as the Marchioness had taken care to place him beside her, he leaned towards her and took the liberty of asking who was the man who had spoken so well.

"He is a scholar," said the lady, "who does not play, whom the Abbé sometimes brings to supper; he is perfectly at home among tragedies and books, and he has written a tragedy which was hissed, and a book of which nothing has ever been seen outside his bookseller's shop excepting the copy which he dedicated to me."

"The great man!" said Candide. "He is another Pangloss!"

Then, turning towards him, he said:

"Sir, you think doubtless that all is for the best in the moral and physical world, and that nothing could be otherwise than it is?"

"I, sir!" answered the scholar, "I know nothing of all that; I find that all goes awry with me; that no one knows either what is his rank, nor what is his condition, what he does nor what he ought to do; and that except supper, which is always gay, and where there appears to be enough concord, all the rest of the time is passed in impertinent quarrels; Jansenist against Molinist, Parliament against the Church, men of letters against men of letters, courtesans against courtesans, financiers against the people, wives against husbands, relatives against relatives—it is eternal war."

"I have seen the worst," Candide replied. "But a wise man, who since has had the misfortune to be hanged, taught me that all is marvellously well; these are but the shadows on a beautiful picture."

"Your hanged man mocked the world," said Martin. "The shadows are horrible blots."

"They are men who make the blots," said Candide, "and they cannot be dispensed with."

"It is not their fault then," said Martin.

Most of the punters, who understood nothing of this language, drank, and Martin reasoned with the scholar, and Candide related some of his adventures to his hostess.

After supper the Marchioness took Candide into her boudoir, and made him sit upon a sofa.

"Ah, well!" said she to him, "you love desperately Miss Cunegonde of Thunder-ten-Tronckh?"

"Yes, madame," answered Candide.

The Marchioness replied to him with a tender smile:

"You answer me like a young man from Westphalia. A Frenchman would have said, 'It is true that I have loved Miss Cunegonde, but seeing you, madame, I think I no longer love her.' "

"Alas! madame," said Candide, "I will answer you as you wish."

"Your passion for her," said the Marchioness, "commenced by picking up her handkerchief. I wish that you would pick up my garter."

"With all my heart," said Candide. And he picked it up.

"But I wish that you would put it on," said the lady.

And Candide put it on.

"You see," said she, "you are a foreigner. I sometimes make my Parisian lovers languish for fifteen days, but I give myself to you the first night because one must do the honours of one's country to a young man from Westphalia."

The lady having perceived two enormous diamonds upon the hands of the young foreigner praised them with such good faith that from Candide's fingers they passed to her own.

Candide, returning with the Perigordian Abbé, felt some remorse in having been unfaithful to Miss Cunegonde. The Abbé sympathised in his trouble; he had had but a light part of the fifty thousand francs lost at play and of the value of the two brilliants, half given, half extorted. His design was to profit as much as he could by the advantages which the acquaintance of Candide could procure for him. He spoke much of Cunegonde, and Candide told him that he should ask forgiveness of that beautiful one for his infidelity when he should see her in Venice.

The Abbé redoubled his politeness and attentions, and took a tender interest in all that Candide said, in all that he did, in all that he wished to do.

"And so, sir, you have a rendezvous at Venice?"

"Yes, monsieur Abbé," answered Candide. "It is absolutely necessary that I go to meet Miss Cunegonde."

And then the pleasure of talking of that which he loved induced him to relate, according to his custom, part of his adventures with the fair Westphalian.

"I believe," said the Abbé, "that Miss Cunegonde has a great deal of wit, and that she writes charming letters?"

"I have never received any from her," said Candide, "for being expelled from the castle on her account I had not an opportunity for writing to her. Soon after that I heard she was dead; then I found her alive; then I lost her again; and last of all, I sent an express to her two thousand five hundred leagues from here, and I wait for an answer."

The Abbé listened attentively, and seemed to be in a brown study. He soon took his leave of the two foreigners after a most tender embrace. The following day Candide received, on awaking, a letter couched in these terms:

"My very dear love, for eight days I have been ill in this town. I learn that you are here. I would fly to your arms if I could but move. I was informed of your passage at Bordeaux, where I left faithful Cacambo and the old woman, who are to follow me very soon. The Governor of Buenos Ayres has taken all, but there remains to me your heart. Come! your presence will either give me life or kill me with pleasure."

This charming, this unhoped-for letter transported Candide with an inexpressible joy, and the illness of his dear Cunegonde overwhelmed him with grief. Divided between those two passions, he took his gold and his diamonds and hurried away, with Martin, to the hotel where Miss Cunegonde was lodged. He entered her room trembling, his heart palpitating, his voice sobbing; he wished to open the curtains of the bed, and asked for a light.

"Take care what you do," said the servant-maid; "the light hurts her," and immediately she drew the curtain again.

"My dear Cunegonde," said Candide, weeping, "how are you? If you cannot see me, at least speak to me."

"She cannot speak," said the maid.

The lady then put a plump hand out from the bed, and Candide bathed it with his tears and afterwards filled it with diamonds, leaving a bag of gold upon the easy chair.

In the midst of these transports in came an officer, followed by the Abbé and a file of soldiers.

"There," said he, "are the two suspected foreigners," and at the same time he ordered them to be seized and carried to prison.

"Travellers are not treated thus in El Dorado," said Candide.

"I am more a Manichean now than ever," said Martin.

"But pray, sir, where are you going to carry us?" said Candide.

"To a dungeon," answered the officer.

Martin, having recovered himself a little, judged that the lady who acted the part of Cunegonde was a cheat, that the Perigordian Abbé was a knave who had imposed upon the honest simplicity of Candide, and that the officer was another knave whom they might easily silence.

Candide, advised by Martin and impatient to see the real Cunegonde, rather than expose himself before a court of justice, proposed to the officer to give him three small diamonds, each worth about three thousand pistoles.

"Ah, sir," said the man with the ivory baton, "had you committed all the imaginable crimes you would be to me the most honest man in the world. Three diamonds! Each worth three thousand pistoles! Sir, instead of carrying you to jail I would lose my life to serve you. There are orders for arresting all foreigners, but leave it to me. I have a brother at Dieppe in Normandy! I'll conduct you thither, and if you have a diamond to give him he'll take as much care of you as I would."

"And why," said Candide, "should all foreigners be arrested?"

"It is," the Perigordian Abbé then made answer, "because a poor beggar of the country of Atrébatie heard some foolish things said.

This induced him to commit a parricide, not such as that of 1610 in the month of May, but such as that of 1594 in the month of December, and such as others which have been committed in other years and other months by other poor devils who had heard nonsense spoken."

The officer then explained what the Abbé meant.

"Ah, the monsters!" cried Candide. "What horrors among a people who dance and sing! Is there no way of getting quickly out of this country where monkeys provoke tigers? I have seen no bears in my country, but *men* I have beheld nowhere except in El Dorado. In the name of God, sir, conduct me to Venice, where I am to await Miss Cunegonde."

"I can conduct you no further than lower Normandy," said the officer.

Immediately he ordered his irons to be struck off, acknowledged himself mistaken, sent away his men, set out with Candide and Martin for Dieppe, and left them in the care of his brother.

There was then a small Dutch ship in the harbour. The Norman, who by the virtue of three more diamonds had become the most subservient of men, put Candide and his attendants on board a vessel that was just ready to set sail for Portsmouth in England.

This was not the way to Venice, but Candide thought he had made his way out of hell, and reckoned that he would soon have an opportunity for resuming his journey.

## XXIII. CANDIDE AND MARTIN TOUCHED UPON THE COAST OF ENGLAND, AND WHAT THEY SAW THERE.

"AH, Pangloss! Pangloss! Ah, Martin! Martin! Ah, my dear Cunegonde, what sort of a world is this?" said Candide on board the Dutch ship.

"Something very foolish and abominable," said Martin.

"You know England? Are they as foolish there as in France?"

"It is another kind of folly," said Martin. "You know that these two nations are at war for a few acres of snow in Canada, and that they spend over this beautiful war much more than Canada is worth. To tell you exactly, whether there are more people fit to send to a madhouse in one country than the other, is what my imperfect intelligence will not permit. I only know in general that the people we are going to see are very atrabilious."

Talking thus they arrived at Portsmouth. The coast was lined with crowds of people, whose eyes were fixed on a fine man kneeling, with his eyes bandaged, on board one of the men of war in the harbour. Four soldiers stood opposite to this man; each of them fired three balls at his head, with all the calmness in the world; and the whole assembly went away very well satisfied.

"What is all this?" said Candide; "and what demon is it that exercises his empire in this country?"

He then asked who was that fine man who had been killed with so much ceremony. They answered, he was an Admiral.

"And why kill this Admiral?"

"It is because he did not kill a sufficient number of men himself. He gave battle to a French Admiral; and it has been proved that he was not near enough to him."

"But," replied Candide, "the French Admiral was as far from the English Admiral."

"There is no doubt of it; but in this country it is found good, from time to time, to kill one Admiral to encourage the others."

Candide was so shocked and bewildered by what he saw and heard, that he would not set foot on shore, and he made a bargain with the Dutch skipper (were he even to rob him like the Surinam captain) to conduct him without delay to Venice.

The skipper was ready in two days. They coasted France; they passed in sight of Lisbon, and Candide trembled. They passed through the Straits, and entered the Mediterranean. At last they landed at Venice.

"God be praised!" said Candide, embracing Martin. "It is here that I shall see again my beautiful Cunegonde. I trust Cacambo as myself. All is well, all will be well, all goes as well as possible."

## XXIV. OF PAQUETTE AND FRIAR GIROFLÉE.

Upon their arrival at Venice, Candide went to search for Cacambo at every inn and coffee-house, and among all the ladies of pleasure, but to no purpose. He sent every day to inquire on all the ships that came in. But there was no news of Cacambo.

"What!" said he to Martin, "I have had time to voyage from Surinam to Bordeaux, to go from Bordeaux to Paris, from Paris to Dieppe, from Dieppe to Portsmouth, to coast along Portugal and Spain, to cross the whole Mediterranean, to spend some months, and yet the beautiful Cunegonde has not arrived! Instead of her I have only met a Parisian wench and a Perigordian Abbé. Cunegonde is dead without doubt, and there is nothing for me but to die. Alas! how much better it would have been for me to have remained in the paradise of El Dorado than to come back to this cursed Europe! You are in the right, my dear Martin: all is misery and illusion."

He fell into a deep melancholy, and neither went to see the opera, nor any of the other diversions of the Carnival; nay, he was proof against the temptations of all the ladies.

"You are in truth very simple," said Martin to him, "if you imagine that a mongrel valet, who has five or six millions in his pocket, will go to the other end of the world to seek your mistress and bring her to you to Venice. If he find her, he will keep her to himself; if he do not find her he will get another. I advise you to forget your valet Cacambo and your mistress Cunegonde."

Martin was not consoling. Candide's melancholy increased; and Martin continued to prove to him that there was very little virtue or happiness upon earth, except perhaps in El Dorado, where nobody could gain admittance.

While they were disputing on this important subject and waiting for Cunegonde, Candide saw a young Theatin friar in St. Mark's Piazza, holding a girl on his arm. The Theatin looked fresh coloured, plump, and vigorous; his eyes were sparkling, his air assured, his look lofty, and his step bold. The girl was very pretty, and sang; she looked amorously at her Theatin, and from time to time pinched his fat cheeks.

"At least you will allow me," said Candide to Martin, "that these two are happy. Hitherto I have met with none but unfortunate people in the whole habitable globe, except in El Dorado; but as to this pair, I would venture to lay a wager that they are very happy."

"I lay you they are not," said Martin.

"We need only ask them to dine with us," said Candide, "and you will see whether I am mistaken."

Immediately he accosted them, presented his compliments, and invited them to his inn to eat some macaroni, with Lombard partridges, and caviare, and to drink some Montepulciano, Lachrymæ Christi, Cyprus and Samos wine. The girl blushed, the Theatin accepted the invitation and she followed him, casting her eyes on Candide with confusion and surprise, and dropping a few tears. No sooner had she set foot in Candide's apartment than she cried out:

"Ah! Mr. Candide does not know Paquette again."

Candide had not viewed her as yet with attention, his thoughts being entirely taken up with Cunegonde; but recollecting her as she spoke.

"Alas!" said he, "my poor child, it is you who reduced Doctor Pangloss to the beautiful condition in which I saw him?"

"Alas! it was I, sir, indeed," answered Paquette. "I see that you have heard all. I have been informed of the frightful disasters that befell the family of my lady Baroness, and the fair Cunegonde. I swear to you that my fate has been scarcely less sad. I was very innocent when you knew me. A Grey Friar, who was my confessor, easily seduced me. The consequences were terrible. I was obliged to quit the castle some time after the Baron had sent you away with kicks on the backside. If a famous surgeon had not taken compassion on me, I should have died. For some time I was this surgeon's mistress, merely out of gratitude. His wife, who was mad with jealousy, beat me every day unmercifully; she was a fury. The surgeon was one of the ugliest of men, and I the most wretched of women, to be continually beaten for a man I did not love. You know, sir, what a dangerous thing it is for an ill-natured woman to be married to a doctor. Incensed at the behaviour of his wife, he one day gave her so effectual a remedy to cure her of a slight cold, that she died two hours after, in most horrid convulsions. The wife's relations prosecuted the husband; he took flight, and I was thrown into jail. My innocence would not have saved me if I had not been good-looking. The judge set me free, on condition that he succeeded the surgeon. I was soon supplanted by a rival, turned out of doors quite destitute, and obliged to continue this abominable trade, which appears so pleasant to you men, while to us women it is the utmost abyss of misery. I have come to exercise the profession at Venice. Ah! sir, if you could only imagine what it is to be obliged to caress indifferently an old merchant, a lawyer, a monk, a gondolier, an abbé, to be exposed to abuse and insults; to be often reduced to borrowing a petticoat, only to go and have it raised by a disagreeable man; to be robbed by one of what one has earned from another; to be subject to the extortions of the officers of justice; and to have in prospect only a frightful old age, a hospital, and a dung-hill; you would conclude that I am one of the most unhappy creatures in the world."

Paquette thus opened her heart to honest Candide, in the presence of Martin, who said to his friend:

"You see that already I have won half the wager."

Friar Giroflée stayed in the dining-room, and drank a glass or two of wine while he was waiting for dinner.

"But," said Candide to Paquette, "you looked so gay and content when I met you; you sang and you behaved so lovingly to the Theatin, that you seemed to me as happy as you pretend to be now the reverse."

"Ah! sir," answered Paquette, "this is one of the miseries of the trade. Yesterday I was robbed and beaten by an officer; yet to-day I must put on good humour to please a friar."

Candide wanted no more convincing; he owned that Martin was in the right. They sat down to table with Paquette and the Theatin; the repast was entertaining; and towards the end they conversed with all confidence.

"Father," said Candide to the Friar, "you appear to me to enjoy a state that all the world might envy; the flower of health shines in your face, your expression makes plain your happiness; you have a very pretty girl for your recreation, and you seem well satisfied with your state as a Theatin."

"My faith, sir," said Friar Giroflée, "I wish that all the Theatins were at the bottom of the sea. I have been tempted a hundred times to set fire to the convent, and go and become a Turk. My parents forced me at the age of fifteen to put on this detestable habit, to increase the fortune of a cursed elder brother, whom God confound. Jealousy, discord, and fury, dwell in the convent. It is true I have preached a few bad sermons that have brought me in a little money, of which the prior stole half, while the rest serves to maintain my girls; but when I return at night to the monastery, I am ready to dash my head against the walls of the dormitory; and all my fellows are in the same case."

Martin turned towards Candide with his usual coolness.

"Well," said he, "have I not won the whole wager?"

Candide gave two thousand piastres to Paquette, and one thousand to Friar Giroflée.

"I'll answer for it," said he, "that with this they will be happy."

"I do not believe it at all," said Martin; "you will, perhaps, with these piastres only render them the more unhappy."

"Let that be as it may," said Candide, "but one thing consoles me. I see that we often meet with those whom we expected never to see more; so that, perhaps, as I have found my red sheep and Paquette, it may well be that I shall also find Cunegonde."

"I wish," said Martin, "she may one day make you very happy; but I doubt it very much."

"You are very hard of belief," said Candide.

"I have lived," said Martin.

"You see those gondoliers," said Candide, "are they not perpetually singing?"

"You do not see them," said Martin, "at home with their wives and brats. The Doge has his troubles, the gondoliers have theirs. It is true that, all things considered, the life of a gondolier is preferable to that of a Doge; but I believe the difference to be so trifling that it is not worth the trouble of examining."

"People talk," said Candide, "of the Senator Pococurante, who lives in that fine palace on the Brenta, where he entertains foreigners in the politest manner. They pretend that this man has never felt any uneasiness."

"I should be glad to see such a rarity," said Martin.

Candide immediately sent to ask the Lord Pococurante permission to wait upon him the next day.

## XXV. THE VISIT TO LORD POCOCURANTE, A NOBLE VENETIAN.

CANDIDE and Martin went in a gondola on the Brenta, and arrived at the palace of the noble Signor Pococurante. The gardens, laid out with taste, were adorned with fine marble statues. The palace was beautifully built. The master of the house was a man of sixty, and very rich. He received the two travellers with polite indifference, which put Candide a little out of countenance, but was not at all disagreeable to Martin.

First, two pretty girls, very neatly dressed, served them with chocolate, which was frothed exceedingly well. Candide could not refrain from commending their beauty, grace, and address.

"They are good enough creatures," said the Senator. "I make them lie with me sometimes, for I am very tired of the ladies of the town, of their coquetries, of their jealousies, of their quarrels, of their humours, of their pettinesses, of their prides, of their follies, and of the sonnets which one must make, or have made, for them. But after all, these two girls begin to weary me."

After breakfast, Candide walking into a long gallery was surprised by the beautiful pictures. He asked, by what master were the two first.

"They are by Raphael," said the Senator. "I bought them at a great price, out of vanity, some years ago. They are said to be the finest things in Italy, but they do not please me at all. The colours are too dark, the figures are not sufficiently rounded, nor in good relief; the draperies in no way resemble stuffs. In a word, whatever may be said, I do not find there a true imitation of nature. I only care for a picture when I think I see nature itself; and there are none of this sort. I have a great many pictures, but I prize them very little."

While they were waiting for dinner Pococurante ordered a concert. Candide found the music delicious.

"This noise," said the Senator, "may amuse one for half an hour; but if it were to last longer it would grow tiresome to everybody, though they durst not own it. Music, to-day, is only the art of executing difficult things, and that which is only difficult cannot please long. Perhaps I should be fonder of the opera if they had not found the secret of making of it a monster which shocks me. Let who will go to see bad tragedies set to music, where the scenes are contrived for no other end than to introduce two or three songs ridiculously out of place, to show off an actress's voice. Let who will, or who can, die away with pleasure at the sight of an eunuch quavering the *rôle* of Cæsar, or of Cato, and strutting awkwardly upon the stage. For my part I have long since renounced those paltry entertainments which constitute the glory of modern Italy, and are purchased so dearly by sovereigns."

Candide disputed the point a little, but with discretion. Martin was entirely of the Senator's opinion.

They sat down to table, and after an excellent dinner they went into the library. Candide, seeing a Homer magnificently bound, commended the virtuoso on his good taste.

"There," said he, "is a book that was once the delight of the great Pangloss, the best philosopher in Germany."

"It is not mine," answered Pococurante coolly. "They used at one time to make me believe that I took a pleasure in reading him. But that continual repetition of battles, so extremely like one another; those gods that are always active without doing anything decisive; that Helen who is the cause of the war, and who yet scarcely appears in the piece; that Troy, so long besieged without being taken; all these together caused me great weariness. I have sometimes asked learned men whether they were not as weary as I of that work. Those who were sincere have owned to me that the poem made them fall asleep; yet it was necessary to have it in their library as a monument of antiquity, or like those rusty medals which are no longer of use in commerce."

"But your Excellency does not think thus of Virgil?" said Candide.

"I grant," said the Senator, "that the second, fourth, and sixth books of his *Æneid* are excellent, but as for his pious Æneas, his strong Cloanthus, his friend Achates, his little Ascanius, his silly King Latinus, his bourgeois Amata, his insipid Lavinia, I think there can be nothing more flat and disagreeable. I prefer Tasso a good deal, or even the soporific tales of Ariosto."

"May I presume to ask you, sir," said Candide, "whether you do not receive a great deal of pleasure from reading Horace?"

"There are maxims in this writer," answered Pococurante, "from which a man of the world may reap great benefit, and being written in energetic verse they are more easily impressed upon the memory. But I care little for his journey to Brundusium, and his account of a bad dinner, or of his low quarrel between one Rupilius whose words he says were full of poisonous filth, and another whose language was imbued with vinegar. I have read with much distaste his indelicate verses against old women and witches; nor do I see any merit in telling his friend Mæcenas that if he will but rank him in the choir of lyric poets, his lofty head shall touch the stars. Fools admire everything in an author of reputation. For my part, I read only to please myself. I like only that which serves my purpose."

Candide, having been educated never to judge for himself, was much surprised at what he heard. Martin found there was a good deal of reason in Pococurante's remarks.

"Oh! here is Cicero," said Candide. "Here is the great man whom I fancy you are never tired of reading."

"I never read him," replied the Venetian. "What is it to me whether he pleads for Rabirius or Cluentius? I try causes enough myself; his philosophical works seem to me better, but when I found that he doubted of everything, I concluded that I knew as much as he, and that I had no need of a guide to learn ignorance."

"Ha! here are four-score volumes of the Academy of Sciences," cried Martin. "Perhaps there is something valuable in this collection."

"There might be," said Pococurante, "if only one of those rakers of rubbish had shown how to make pins; but in all these volumes there is nothing but chimerical systems, and not a single useful thing."

"And what dramatic works I see here," said Candide, "in Italian, Spanish, and French."

"Yes," replied the Senator, "there are three thousand, and not three dozen of them good for anything. As to those collections of sermons, which altogether are not worth a single page of Seneca, and those huge volumes of theology, you may well imagine that neither I nor any one else ever opens them."

Martin saw some shelves filled with English books.

"I have a notion," said he, "that a Republican must be greatly pleased with most of these books, which are written with a spirit of freedom."

"Yes," answered Pococurante, "it is noble to write as one thinks; this is the privilege of humanity. In all our Italy we write only what we do not think; those who inhabit the country of the Cæsars and the Antoninuses dare not acquire a single idea without the permission of a Dominican friar. I should be pleased with the liberty which inspires the English genius if passion and party spirit did not corrupt all that is estimable in this precious liberty."

Candide, observing a Milton, asked whether he did not look upon this author as a great man.

"Who?" said Pococurante, "that barbarian, who writes a long commentary in ten books of harsh verse on the first chapter of Genesis; that coarse imitator of the Greeks, who disfigures the Creation, and who, while Moses represents the Eternal producing the world by a word, makes the Messiah take a great pair of compasses from the armoury of heaven to circumscribe His work? How can I have any esteem for a writer who has spoiled Tasso's hell and the devil, who transforms Lucifer sometimes into a toad and other times into a pigmy, who makes him repeat the same things a hundred times, who makes him dispute on theology, who, by a serious imitation of Ariosto's comic invention of firearms, represents the devils cannonading in heaven? Neither I nor any man in Italy could take pleasure in those melancholy extravagances; and the marriage of Sin and Death, and the snakes brought forth by Sin, are enough to turn the stomach of any one with the least taste, [and his long description of a pest-house is good only for a grave-digger]. This obscure, whimsical, and disagreeable poem was despised upon its first publication, and I only treat it now as it was treated in its own country by contemporaries. For the matter of that I say what I think, and I care very little whether others think as I do."

Candide was grieved at this speech, for he had a respect for Homer and was fond of Milton.

"Alas!" said he softly to Martin, "I am afraid that this man holds our German poets in very great contempt."

"There would not be much harm in that," said Martin.

"Oh! what a superior man," said Candide below his breath. "What a great genius is this Pococurante! Nothing can please him."

After their survey of the library they went down into the garden, where Candide praised its several beauties.

"I know of nothing in so bad a taste," said the master. "All you see here is merely trifling. After to-morrow I will have it planted with a nobler design."

"Well," said Candide to Martin when they had taken their leave, "you will agree that this is the happiest of mortals, for he is above everything he possesses."

"But do you not see," answered Martin, "that he is disgusted with all he possesses? Plato observed a long while ago that those stomachs are not the best that reject all sorts of food."

"But is there not a pleasure," said Candide, "in criticising everything, in pointing out faults where others see nothing but beauties?"

"That is to say," replied Martin, "that there is some pleasure in having no pleasure."

"Well, well," said Candide, "I find that I shall be the only happy man when I am blessed with the sight of my dear Cunegonde."

"It is always well to hope," said Martin.

However, the days and the weeks passed. Cacambo did not come, and Candide was so overwhelmed with grief that he did not even reflect that Paquette and Friar Giroflée did not return to thank him.

## XXVI. OF A SUPPER WHICH CANDIDE AND MARTIN TOOK WITH SIX STRANGERS, AND WHO THEY WERE.

ONE evening that Candide and Martin were going to sit down to supper with some foreigners who lodged in the same inn, a man whose complexion was as black as soot, came behind Candide, and taking him by the arm, said:

"Get yourself ready to go along with us; do not fail."

Upon this he turned round and saw—Cacambo! Nothing but the sight of Cunegonde could have astonished and delighted him more. He was on the point of going mad with joy. He embraced his dear friend.

"Cunegonde is here, without doubt; where is she? Take me to her that I may die of joy in her company."

"Cunegonde is not here," said Cacambo, "she is at Constantinople."

"Oh, heavens! at Constantinople! But were she in China I would fly thither; let us be off."

"We shall set out after supper," replied Cacambo. "I can tell you nothing more; I am a slave, my master awaits me, I must serve him at table; speak not a word, eat, and then get ready."

Candide, distracted between joy and grief, delighted at seeing his faithful agent again, astonished at finding him a slave, filled with the fresh hope of recovering his mistress, his heart palpitating, his understanding confused, sat down to table with Martin, who saw all these scenes quite unconcerned, and with six strangers who had come to spend the Carnival at Venice.

Cacambo waited at table upon one of the strangers; towards the end of the entertainment he drew near his master, and whispered in his ear:

"Sire, your Majesty may start when you please, the vessel is ready."

On saying these words he went out. The company in great surprise looked at one another without speaking a word, when another domestic approached his master and said to him:

"Sire, your Majesty's chaise is at Padua, and the boat is ready."

The master gave a nod and the servant went away. The company all stared at one another again, and their surprise redoubled. A third valet came up to a third stranger, saying:

"Sire, believe me, your Majesty ought not to stay here any longer. I am going to get everything ready."

And immediately he disappeared. Candide and Martin did not doubt that this was a masquerade of the Carnival. Then a fourth domestic said to a fourth master:

"Your Majesty may depart when you please."

Saying this he went away like the rest. The fifth valet said the same thing to the fifth master. But the sixth valet spoke differently to the sixth stranger, who sat near Candide. He said to him:

"Faith, Sire, they will no longer give credit to your Majesty nor to me, and we may perhaps both of us be put in jail this very night. Therefore I will take care of myself. Adieu."

The servants being all gone, the six strangers, with Candide and Martin, remained in a profound silence. At length Candide broke it.

"Gentlemen," said he, "this is a very good joke indeed, but why should you all be kings? For me I own that neither Martin nor I is a king."

Cacambo's master then gravely answered in Italian:

"I am not at all joking. My name is Achmet III. I was Grand Sultan many years. I dethroned my brother; my nephew dethroned me, my viziers were beheaded, and I am condemned to end my days in the old Seraglio. My nephew, the great Sultan Mahmoud, permits me to travel sometimes for my health, and I am come to spend the Carnival at Venice."

A young man who sat next to Achmet, spoke then as follows:

"My name is Ivan. I was once Emperor of all the Russias, but was dethroned in my cradle. My parents were confined in prison and I was educated there; yet I am sometimes allowed to travel in company with persons who act as guards; and I am come to spend the Carnival at Venice."

The third said:

"I am Charles Edward, King of England; my father has resigned all his legal rights to me. I have fought in defence of them; and above eight hundred of my adherents have been hanged, drawn, and quartered. I have been confined in prison; I am going to Rome, to pay a visit to the King, my father, who was dethroned as well as myself and my grandfather, and I am come to spend the Carnival at Venice."

The fourth spoke thus in his turn:

"I am the King of Poland; the fortune of war has stripped me of my hereditary dominions; my father underwent the same vicissitudes; I resign myself to Providence in the same manner as Sultan Achmet, the Emperor Ivan, and King Charles Edward, whom God long preserve; and I am come to the Carnival at Venice."

The fifth said:

"I am King of Poland also; I have been twice dethroned; but Providence has given me another country, where I have done more good than all the Sarmatian kings were ever capable of doing on the banks of the Vistula; I resign myself likewise to Providence, and am come to pass the Carnival at Venice."

It was now the sixth monarch's turn to speak:

"Gentlemen," said he, "I am not so great a prince as any of you; however, I am a king. I am Theodore, elected King of Corsica; I had the title of Majesty, and now I am scarcely treated as a gentleman. I have coined money, and now am not worth a farthing; I have had two secretaries of state, and now I have scarce a valet; I have seen myself on a throne, and I have seen myself upon straw in a common jail in London. I am afraid that I shall meet with the same treatment here though, like your majesties, I am come to see the Carnival at Venice."

The other five kings listened to this speech with generous compassion. Each of them gave twenty sequins to King Theodore to buy him clothes and linen; and Candide made him a present of a diamond worth two thousand sequins.

"Who can this private person be," said the five kings to one another, "who is able to give, and really has given, a hundred times as much as any of us?"

Just as they rose from table, in came four Serene Highnesses, who had also been stripped of their territories by the fortune of war, and were come to spend the Carnival at Venice. But Candide paid no regard to these newcomers, his thoughts were entirely employed on his voyage to Constantinople, in search of his beloved Cunegonde.

## XXVII. CANDIDE'S VOYAGE TO CONSTANTINOPLE.

THE faithful Cacambo had already prevailed upon the Turkish skipper, who was to conduct the Sultan Achmet to Constantinople, to receive Candide and Martin on his ship. They both embarked after having made their obeisance to his miserable Highness.

"You see," said Candide to Martin on the way, "we supped with six dethroned kings, and of those six there was one to whom I gave charity. Perhaps there are many other princes yet more unfortunate. For my part, I have only lost a hundred sheep; and now I am flying into Cunegonde's arms. My dear Martin, yet once more Pangloss was right: all is for the best."

"I wish it," answered Martin.

"But," said Candide, "it was a very strange adventure we met with at Venice. It has never before been seen or heard that six dethroned kings have supped together at a public inn."

"It is not more extraordinary," said Martin, "than most of the things that have happened to us. It is a very common thing for kings to be dethroned; and as for the honour we have had of supping in their company, it is a trifle not worth our attention."

No sooner had Candide got on board the vessel than he flew to his old valet and friend Cacambo, and tenderly embraced him.

"Well," said he, "what news of Cunegonde? Is she still a prodigy of beauty? Does she love me still? How is she? Thou hast doubtless bought her a palace at Constantinople?"

"My dear master," answered Cacambo, "Cunegonde washes dishes on the banks of the Propontis, in the service of a prince, who has very few dishes to wash; she is a slave in the family of an ancient sovereign named Ragotsky, to whom the Grand Turk allows three crowns a day in his exile. But what is worse still is, that she has lost her beauty and has become horribly ugly."

"Well, handsome or ugly," replied Candide, "I am a man of honour, and it is my duty to love her still. But how came she to be reduced to so abject a state with the five or six millions that you took to her?"

"Ah!" said Cacambo, "was I not to give two millions to Senor Don Fernando d'Ibaraa, y Figueora, y Mascarenes, y Lampourdos, y Souza, Governor of Buenos Ayres, for permitting Miss Cunegonde to come away? And did not a corsair bravely rob us of all the rest? Did not this corsair carry us to Cape Matapan, to Milo, to Nicaria, to Samos, to Petra, to the Dardanelles, to Marmora, to Scutari? Cunegonde and the old woman serve the prince I now mentioned to you, and I am slave to the dethroned Sultan."

"What a series of shocking calamities!" cried Candide. "But after all, I have some diamonds left; and I may easily pay Cunegonde's ransom. Yet it is a pity that she is grown so ugly."

Then, turning towards Martin: "Who do you think," said he, "is most to be pitied—the Sultan Achmet, the Emperor Ivan, King Charles Edward, or I?"

"How should I know!" answered Martin. "I must see into your hearts to be able to tell."

"Ah!" said Candide, "if Pangloss were here, he could tell."

"I know not," said Martin, "in what sort of scales your Pangloss would weigh the misfortunes of mankind and set a just estimate on their sorrows. All that I can presume to say is, that there are millions of people upon earth who have a hundred times more to complain of than King Charles Edward, the Emperor Ivan, or the Sultan Achmet."

"That may well be," said Candide.

In a few days they reached the Bosphorus, and Candide began by paying a very high ransom for Cacambo. Then without losing time, he and his companions went on board a galley, in order to search on the banks of the Propontis for his Cunegonde, however ugly she might have become.

Among the crew there were two slaves who rowed very badly, and to whose bare shoulders the Levantine captain would now and then apply blows from a bull's pizzle. Candide, from a natural impulse, looked at these two slaves more attentively than at the other oarsmen, and approached them with pity. Their features though greatly disfigured, had a slight resemblance to those of Pangloss and the unhappy Jesuit and Westphalian Baron, brother to Miss Cunegonde. This moved and saddened him. He looked at them still more attentively.

"Indeed," said he to Cacambo, "if I had not seen Master Pangloss hanged, and if I had not had the misfortune to kill the Baron, I should think it was they that were rowing."

At the names of the Baron and of Pangloss, the two galley-slaves uttered a loud cry, held fast by the seat, and let drop their oars. The captain ran up to them and redoubled his blows with the bull's pizzle.

"Stop! stop! sir," cried Candide. "I will give you what money you please."

"What! it is Candide!" said one of the slaves.

"What! it is Candide!" said the other.

"Do I dream?" cried Candide; "am I awake? or am I on board a galley? Is this the Baron whom I killed? Is this Master Pangloss whom I saw hanged?"

"It is we! it is we!" answered they.

"Well! is this the great philosopher?" said Martin.

"Ah! captain," said Candide, "what ransom will you take for Monsieur de Thunder-ten-Tronckh, one of the first barons of the empire, and for Monsieur Pangloss, the profoundest metaphysician in Germany?"

"Dog of a Christian," answered the Levantine captain, "since these two dogs of Christian slaves are barons and metaphysicians, which I doubt not are high dignities in their country, you shall give me fifty thousand sequins."

"You shall have them, sir. Carry me back at once to Constantinople, and you shall receive the money directly. But no; carry me first to Miss Cunegonde."

Upon the first proposal made by Candide, however, the Levantine captain had already tacked about, and made the crew ply their oars quicker than a bird cleaves the air.

Candide embraced the Baron and Pangloss a hundred times.

"And how happened it, my dear Baron, that I did not kill you? And, my dear Pangloss, how came you to life again after being hanged? And why are you both in a Turkish galley?"

"And it is true that my dear sister is in this country?" said the Baron.

"Yes," answered Cacambo.

"Then I behold, once more, my dear Candide," cried Pangloss.

Candide presented Martin and Cacambo to them; they embraced each other, and all spoke at once. The galley flew; they were already in the port. Instantly Candide sent for a Jew, to whom he sold for fifty thousand sequins a diamond worth a hundred thousand, though the fellow swore to him by Abraham that he could give him no more. He immediately paid the ransom for the Baron and Pangloss. The latter threw himself at the feet of his deliverer, and bathed them with his tears; the former thanked him with a nod, and promised to return him the money on the first opportunity.

"But is it indeed possible that my sister can be in Turkey?" said he.

"Nothing is more possible," said Cacambo, "since she scours the dishes in the service of a Transylvanian prince."

Candide sent directly for two Jews and sold them some more diamonds, and then they all set out together in another galley to deliver Cunegonde from slavery.

## XXVIII. WHAT HAPPENED TO CANDIDE, CUNEGONDE, PANGLOSS, MARTIN, ETC.

"I ASK your pardon once more," said Candide to the Baron, "your pardon, reverend father, for having run you through the body."

"Say no more about it," answered the Baron. "I was a little too hasty, I own, but since you wish to know by what fatality I came to be a galley-slave I will inform you. After I had been cured by the surgeon of the college of the wound you gave me, I was attacked and carried off by a party of Spanish troops, who confined me in prison at Buenos Ayres at the very time my sister was setting out thence. I asked leave to return to Rome to the General of my Order. I was appointed chaplain to the French Ambassador at Constantinople. I had not been eight days in this employment when one evening I met with a young Ichoglan, who was a very handsome fellow. The weather was warm. The young man wanted to bathe, and I took this opportunity of bathing also. I did not know that it was a capital crime for a Christian to be found naked with a young Mussulman. A cadi ordered me a hundred blows on the soles of the feet, and condemned me to the galleys. I do not think there ever was a greater act of injustice. But I should be glad to know how my sister came to be scullion to a Transylvanian prince who has taken shelter among the Turks."

"But you, my dear Pangloss," said Candide, "how can it be that I behold you again?"

"It is true," said Pangloss, "that you saw me hanged. I should have been burnt, but you may remember it rained exceedingly hard when they were going to roast me; the storm was so violent that they despaired of lighting the fire, so I was hanged because they could do no better. A surgeon purchased my body, carried me home, and dissected me. He began with making a crucial incision on me from the navel to the clavicula. One could not have been worse hanged than I was. The executioner of the Holy Inquisition was a sub-deacon, and knew how to burn people marvellously well, but he was not accustomed to hanging. The cord was wet and did not slip properly, and besides it was badly tied; in short, I still drew my breath, when the crucial incision made me give such a frightful scream that my surgeon fell flat upon his back, and imagining that he had been dissecting the devil he ran away, dying with fear, and fell down the staircase in his flight. His wife, hearing the noise, flew from the next room. She saw me stretched out upon the table with my crucial incision. She was seized with yet greater fear than her husband, fled, and tumbled over him. When they came to themselves a little, I heard the wife say to her husband: 'My dear, how could you take it into your head to dissect a heretic? Do you not know that these people always have the devil in their bodies? I will go and fetch a priest this minute to exorcise him.' At this proposal I shuddered, and mustering up what little courage I had still remaining I cried out aloud, 'Have mercy on me!' At length the Portuguese barber plucked up his spirits. He sewed up my wounds; his wife even nursed me. I was upon my legs at the end of fifteen days. The barber found me a place as lackey to a knight of Malta who was going to Venice, but finding that my master had no money to pay me my wages I entered the service of a Venetian merchant, and went with him to Constantinople. One day I took it into my head to step into a mosque, where I saw an old Iman and a very pretty young devotee who was saying her paternosters. Her bosom was uncovered, and between her breasts she had a beautiful bouquet of tulips, roses, anemones, ranunculus, hyacinths, and auriculas. She dropped her bouquet; I picked it up, and presented it to her with a profound reverence. I was so long in delivering it that the Iman began to get angry, and seeing that I was a Christian he called out for help. They carried me before the cadi, who ordered me a hundred lashes on the soles of the feet and sent me to the galleys. I was chained to the very same galley and the same bench as the young Baron. On board this galley there were four young men from Marseilles, five Neapolitan priests, and two monks from Corfu, who told us similar adventures happened daily. The Baron maintained that he had suffered greater injustice than I, and I insisted that it was far more innocent to take up a bouquet and place it again on a woman's bosom than to be found stark naked with an Ichoglan. We were continually disputing, and received twenty lashes with a bull's pizzle when the concatenation of universal events brought you to our galley, and you were good enough to ransom us."

"Well, my dear Pangloss," said Candide to him, "when you had been hanged, dissected, whipped, and were tugging at the oar, did you always think that everything happens for the best?"

"I am still of my first opinion," answered Pangloss, "for I am a philosopher and I cannot retract, especially as Liebnitz could never be wrong; and besides, the pre-established harmony is the finest thing in the world, and so is his *plenum* and *materia subtilis.*

## XXIX. HOW CANDIDE FOUND CUNEGONDE AND THE OLD WOMAN AGAIN.

WHILE Candide, the Baron, Pangloss, Martin, and Cacambo were relating their several adventures, were reasoning on the contingent or non-contingent events of the universe, disputing on effects and causes, on moral and physical evil, on liberty and necessity, and on the consolations a slave may feel even on a Turkish galley, they arrived at the house of the Transylvanian prince on the banks of the Propontis. The first objects which met their sight were Cunegonde and the old woman hanging towels out to dry.

The Baron paled at this sight. The tender, loving Candide, seeing his beautiful Cunegonde embrowned, with blood-shot eyes, withered neck, wrinkled cheeks, and rough, red arms, recoiled three paces, seized with horror, and then advanced out of good manners. She embraced Candide and her brother; they embraced the old woman, and Candide ransomed them both.

There was a small farm in the neighbourhood which the old woman proposed to Candide to make a shift with till the company could be provided for in a better manner. Cunegonde did not know she had grown ugly, for nobody had told her of it; and she reminded Candide of his promise in so positive a tone that the good man durst not refuse her. He therefore intimated to the Baron that he intended marrying his sister.

"I will not suffer," said the Baron, "such meanness on her part, and such insolence on yours; I will never be reproached with this scandalous thing; my sister's children would never be able to enter the church in Germany. No; my sister shall only marry a baron of the empire."

Cunegonde flung herself at his feet, and bathed them with her tears; still he was inflexible.

"Thou foolish fellow," said Candide; "I have delivered thee out of the galleys, I have paid thy ransom, and thy sister's also; she was a scullion, and is very ugly, yet I am so condescending as to marry her; and dost thou pretend to oppose the match? I should kill thee again, were I only to consult my anger."

"Thou mayest kill me again," said the Baron, "but thou shalt not marry my sister, at least whilst I am living."

## XXX. THE CONCLUSION.

AT the bottom of his heart Candide had no wish to marry Cunegonde. But the extreme impertinence of the Baron determined him to conclude the match, and Cunegonde pressed him so strongly that he could not go from his word. He consulted Pangloss, Martin, and the faithful Cacambo. Pangloss drew up an excellent memorial, wherein he proved that the Baron had no right over his sister, and that according to all the laws of the empire, she might marry Candide with her left hand. Martin was for throwing the Baron into the sea; Cacambo decided that it would be better to deliver him up again to the captain of the galley, after which they thought to send him back to the General Father of the Order at Rome by the first ship. This advice was well received, the old woman approved it; they said not a word to his sister; the thing was executed for a little money, and they had the double pleasure of entrapping a Jesuit, and punishing the pride of a German baron.

It is natural to imagine that after so many disasters Candide married, and living with the philosopher Pangloss, the philosopher Martin, the prudent Cacambo, and the old woman, having besides brought so many diamonds from the country of the ancient Incas, must have led a very happy life. But he was so much imposed upon by the Jews that he had nothing left except his small farm; his wife became uglier every day, more peevish and unsupportable; the old woman was infirm and even more fretful than Cunegonde. Cacambo, who worked in the garden, and took vegetables for sale to Constantinople, was fatigued with hard work, and cursed his destiny. Pangloss was in despair at not shining in some German university. For Martin, he was firmly persuaded that he would be as badly off elsewhere, and therefore bore things patiently. Candide, Martin, and Pangloss sometimes disputed about morals and metaphysics. They often saw passing under the windows of their farm boats full of Effendis, Pashas, and Cadis, who were going into banishment to Lemnos, Mitylene, or Erzeroum. And they saw other Cadis, Pashas, and Effendis coming to supply the place of the exiles, and afterwards exiled in their turn. They saw heads decently impaled for presentation to the Sublime Porte. Such spectacles as these increased the number of their dissertations; and when they did not dispute time hung so heavily upon their hands, that one day the old woman ventured to say to them:

"I want to know which is worse, to be ravished a hundred times by negro pirates, to have a buttock cut off, to run the gauntlet among the Bulgarians, to be whipped and hanged at an *auto-da-fé*, to be dissected, to row in the galleys—in short, to go through all the miseries we have undergone, or to stay here and have nothing to do?"

"It is a great question," said Candide.

This discourse gave rise to new reflections, and Martin especially concluded that man was born to live either in a state of distracting inquietude or of lethargic disgust. Candide did not quite agree to that, but he affirmed nothing. Pangloss owned that he had always suffered horribly, but as he had once asserted that everything went wonderfully well, he asserted it still though he no longer believed it.

What helped to confirm Martin in his detestable principles, to stagger Candide more than ever, and to puzzle Pangloss, was that one day they saw Paquette and Friar Giroflée land at the farm in extreme misery. They had soon squandered their three thousand piastres, parted, were reconciled, quarrelled again, were thrown into gaol, had escaped, and Friar Giroflée had at length become Turk. Paquette continued her trade wherever she went, but made nothing of it.

"I foresaw," said Martin to Candide, "that your presents would soon be dissipated, and only make them the more miserable. You have rolled in millions of money, you and Cacambo; and yet you are not happier than Friar Giroflée and Paquette."

"Ha!" said Pangloss to Paquette, "Providence has then brought you amongst us again, my poor child! Do you know that you cost me the tip of my nose, an eye, and an ear, as you may see? What a world this is!"

And now this new adventure set them philosophising more than ever.

In the neighbourhood there lived a very famous Dervish who was esteemed the best philosopher in all Turkey, and they went to consult him. Pangloss was the speaker.

"Master," said he, "we come to beg you to tell why so strange an animal as man was made."

"With what meddlest thou?" said the Dervish; "is it thy business?"

"But, reverend father," said Candide, "there is horrible evil in this world."

"What signifies it," said the Dervish, "whether there be evil or good? When his highness sends a ship to Egypt, does he trouble his head whether the mice on board are at their ease or not?"

"What, then, must we do?" said Pangloss.

"Hold your tongue," answered the Dervish.

"I was in hopes," said Pangloss, "that I should reason with you a little about causes and effects, about the best possible worlds, the origin of evil, the nature of the soul, and the pre-established harmony."

At these words, the Dervish shut the door in their faces.

During this conversation, the news was spread that two Viziers and the Mufti had been strangled at Constantinople, and that several of their friends had been impaled. This catastrophe made a great noise for some hours. Pangloss, Candide, and Martin, returning to the little farm, saw a good old man taking the fresh air at his door under an orange bower. Pangloss, who was as inquisitive as he was argumentative, asked the old man what was the name of the strangled Mufti.

"I do not know," answered the worthy man, "and I have not known the name of any Mufti, nor of any Vizier. I am entirely ignorant of the event you mention; I presume in general that they who meddle with the administration of public affairs die sometimes miserably, and that they deserve it; but I never trouble my head about what is transacting at Constantinople; I content myself with sending there for sale the fruits of the garden which I cultivate."

Having said these words, he invited the strangers into his house; his two sons and two daughters presented them with several sorts of sherbet, which they made themselves, with Kaimak enriched with the candied-peel of citrons, with oranges, lemons, pine-apples, pistachio-nuts, and Mocha coffee unadulterated with the bad coffee of Batavia or the American islands. After which the two daughters of the honest Mussulman perfumed the strangers' beards.

"You must have a vast and magnificent estate," said Candide to the Turk.

"I have only twenty acres," replied the old man; "I and my children cultivate them; our labour preserves us from three great evils—weariness, vice, and want."

Candide, on his way home, made profound reflections on the old man's conversation.

"This honest Turk," said he to Pangloss and Martin, "seems to be in a situation far preferable to that of the six kings with whom we had the honour of supping."

"Grandeur," said Pangloss, "is extremely dangerous according to the testimony of philosophers. For, in short, Eglon, King of Moab, was assassinated by Ehud; Absalom was hung by his hair, and pierced with three darts; King Nadab, the son of Jeroboam, was killed by Baasa; King Ela by Zimri; Ahaziah by Jehu; Athaliah by Jehoiada; the Kings Jehoiakim, Jeconiah, and Zedekiah, were led into captivity. You know how perished Crœsus, Astyages, Darius, Dionysius of Syracuse, Pyrrhus, Perseus, Hannibal, Jugurtha, Ariovistus, Cæsar, Pompey, Nero, Otho, Vitellius, Domitian, Richard II. of England, Edward II., Henry VI., Richard III., Mary Stuart, Charles I., the three Henrys of France, the Emperor Henry IV.! You know—"

"I know also," said Candide, "that we must cultivate our garden."

"You are right," said Pangloss, "for when man was first placed in the Garden of Eden, he was put there *ut operaretur eum*, that he might cultivate it; which shows that man was not born to be idle.

"Let us work," said Martin, "without disputing; it is the only way to render life tolerable."

The whole little society entered into this laudable design, according to their different abilities. Their little plot of land produced plentiful crops. Cunegonde was, indeed, very ugly, but she became an excellent pastry cook; Paquette worked at embroidery; the old woman looked after the linen. They were all, not excepting Friar Giroflée, of some service or other; for he made a good joiner, and became a very honest man.

Pangloss sometimes said to Candide:

"There is a concatenation of events in this best of all possible worlds: for if you had not been kicked out of a magnificent castle for love of Miss Cunegonde: if you had not been put into the Inquisition: if you had not walked over America: if you had not stabbed the Baron: if you had not lost all your sheep from the fine country of El Dorado: you would not be here eating perserved citrons and pistachio-nuts."

"All that is very well," answered Candide, "but let us cultivate our garden."

# POPE

## *The Rape of the Lock*

### Canto I

What dire offence from am'rous causes springs,
What mighty contests rise from trivial things,
I sing—This verse to Caryl, Muse! is due:
This, ev'n Belinda may vouchsafe to view:
Slight is the subject, but not so the praise,
If she inspire, and he approve my lays.
  Say what strange motive, Goddess! could compel
A well-bred lord t' assault a gentle belle?
O say what stranger cause, yet unexplor'd,
Could make a gentle belle reject a lord?
In tasks so bold, can little men engage,
And in soft bosoms dwells such mighty rage?
  Sol through white curtains shot a tim'rous ray,
And oped those eyes that must eclipse the day:
Now lap-dogs give themselves the rousing shake,
And sleepless lovers, just at twelve, awake:
Thrice rung the bell, the slipper knock'd the ground,
And the press'd watch returned a silver sound.
Belinda still her downy pillow prest,
Her guardian Sylph prolonged the balmy rest:
'Twas he had summon'd to her silent bed
The morning-dream that hover'd o'er her head,
A Youth more glitt'ring than a birth-night beau,
(That ev'n in slumber caus'd her cheek to glow)
Seem'd to her ear his winning lips to lay,
And thus in whispers said, or seem'd to say.
  "Fairest of mortals, thou distinguished care
Of thousand bright inhabitants of air!
If e'er one vision touch'd thy infant thought,
Of all the nurse and all the priest have taught;
Of airy elves by moonlight shadows seen,
The silver token, and the circled green,
Or virgins visited by angel-pow'rs,
With golden crowns and wreaths of heav'nly flow'rs;

Hear and believe! thy own importance know,
Nor bound thy narrow views to things below.
Some secret truths, from learned pride conceal'd,
To maids alone and children are reveal'd:
What though no credit doubting wits may give?
The fair and innocent shall still believe.
Know then, unnumber'd spirits round thee fly,
The light militia of the lower sky:
These, though unseen, are ever on the wing,
Hang o'er the Box, and hover round the Ring.
Think what an equipage thou hast in air,
And view with scorn two pages and a chair.
As now your own, our beings were of old,
And once inclos'd in woman's beauteous mould;
Thence, by a soft transition, we repair
From earthly vehicles to these of air.
Think not, when woman's transient breath is fled,
That all her vanities at once are dead;
Succeeding vanities she still regards,
And though she plays no more, o'erlooks the cards.
Her joy in gilded chariots, when alive,
And love of ombre, after death survive.
For when the fair in all their pride expire,
To their first elements their souls retire:
The sprites of fiery termagants in flame
Mount up, and take a salamander's name.
Soft yielding minds to water glide away,
And sip, with nymphs, their elemental tea.
The graver prude sinks downward to a gnome,
In search of mischief still on earth to roam.
The light coquettes in sylphs aloft repair,
And sport and flutter in the fields of air.
"Know farther yet; whoever fair and chaste
Rejects mankind, is by some sylph embrac'd:
For spirits, freed from mortal laws, with ease
Assume what sexes and what shapes they please.
What guards the purity of melting maids,
In courtly balls, and midnight masquerades,
Safe from the treach'rous friend, the daring spark,
The glance by day, the whisper in the dark,
When kind occasion prompts their warm desires,
When music softens, and when dancing fires?
'Tis but their sylph, the wise celestials know,

Though honour is the word with men below.
"Some nymphs there are, too conscious of their face,
For life predestin'd to the gnomes' embrace.
These swell their prospects and exalt their pride,
When offers are disdain'd, and love deny'd:
Then gay ideas crowd the vacant brain,
While peers, and dukes, and all their sweeping train,
And garters, stars, and coronets appear,
And in soft sounds, Your Grace salutes their ear.
'Tis these that early taint the female soul,
Instruct the eyes of young coquettes to roll,
Teach infant-cheeks a bidden blush to know,
And little hearts to flutter at a beau.
"Oft, when the world imagine women stray,
The sylphs through mystic mazes guide their way,
Through all the giddy circle they pursue,
And old impertinence expel by new.
What tender maid but must a victim fall
To one man's treat, but for another's ball?
When Florio speaks what virgin could withstand,
If gentle Damon did not squeeze her hand?
With varying vanities, from ev'ry part,
They shift the moving toyshop of their heart;
Where wigs with wigs, with sword-knots sword-knots strive,
Beaux banish beaux, and coaches coaches drive.
This erring mortals levity may call;
Oh blind to truth! the sylphs contrive it all.
"Of these am I, who thy protection claim,
A watchful sprite, and Ariel is my name.
Late, as I rang'd the crystal wilds of air,
In the clear mirror of thy ruling star
I saw, alas! some dread event impend,
Ere to the main this morning sun descend;
But heav'n reveals not what, or how, or where:
Warn'd by the sylph, oh pious maid, beware!
This to disclose is all thy guardian can:
Beware of all, but most beware of man!"
He said; when Shock, who thought she slept too long,
Leap'd up, and wak'd his mistress with his tongue.
'Twas then, Belinda, if report say true,
Thy eyes first open'd on a billet-doux;
Wounds, charms, and ardours were no sooner read,
But all the vision vanish'd from thy head.

And now, unveil'd, the toilet stands display'd,
Each silver vase in mystic order laid.
First, rob'd in white, the nymph intent adores,
With head uncover'd, the cosmetic pow'rs.
A heav'nly image in the glass appears,
To that she bends, to that her eyes she rears;
Th' inferior priestess, at her altar's side,
Trembling begins the sacred rites of Pride.
Unnumber'd treasures ope at once, and here
The various off'rings of the world appear;
From each she nicely culls with curious toil,
And decks the goddess with the glitt'ring spoil.
This casket India's glowing gems unlocks,
And all Arabia breathes from yonder box.
The tortoise here and elephant unite,
Transform'd to combs, the speckled, and the white.
Here files of pins extend their shining rows.
Puffs, powders, patches, bibles, billet-doux.
Now awful beauty puts on all its arms;
The fair each moment rises in her charms,
Repairs her smiles, awakens ev'ry grace,
And calls forth all the wonders of her face;
Sees by degrees a purer blush arise,
And keener lightnings quicken in her eyes.
The busy sylphs surround their darling care,
These set the head, and those divide the hair,
Some fold the sleeve, whilst others plait the gown;
And Betty's prais'd for labours not her own.

## CANTO II

NOT with more glories, in th' ethereal plain,
The Sun first rises o'er the purpled main,
Than, issuing forth, the rival of his beams
Launch'd on the bosom of the silver Thames.
Fair nymphs, and well-drest youths around her shone,
But ev'ry eye was fix'd on her alone.
On her white breast a sparkling cross she wore,
Which Jews might kiss, and infidels adore.
Her lively looks a sprightly mind disclose,
Quick as her eyes, and as unfix'd as those:
Favours to none, to all she smiles extends;

Oft she rejects, but never once offends.
Bright as the sun, her eyes the gazers strike,
And, like the sun, they shine on all alike.
Yet graceful ease, and sweetness void of pride,
Might hide her faults, if belles had faults to hide:
If to her share some female errors fall,
Look on her face, and you'll forget 'em all.
  This nymph, to the destruction of mankind,
Nourish'd two locks, which graceful hung behind
In equal curls, and well conspir'd to deck
With shining ringlets the smooth iv'ry neck.
Love in these labyrinths his slaves detains,
And mighty hearts are held in slender chains.
With hairy springes we the birds betray,
Slight lines of hair surprise the finny prey,
Fair tresses man's imperial race insnare,
And beauty draws us with a single hair.
  Th' advent'rous baron the bright locks admir'd;
He saw, he wish'd, and to the prize aspir'd.
Resolv'd to win, he meditates the way,
By force to ravish, or by fraud betray;
For when success a lover's toil attends,
Few ask, if fraud or force attain'd his ends.
  For this, ere Phœbus rose, he had implor'd
Propitious heav'n, and ev'ry pow'r ador'd,
But chiefly Love—to Love an altar built,
Of twelve vast French romances, neatly gilt.
There lay three garters, half a pair of gloves;
And all the trophies of his former loves;
With tender billet-doux he lights the pyre,
And breathes three am'rous sighs to raise the fire.
Then prostrate falls, and begs with ardent eyes
Soon to obtain, and long possess the prize:
The pow'rs gave ear, and granted half his pray'r,
The rest, the winds dispers'd in empty air.
  But now secure the painted vessel glides,
The sun-beams trembling on the floating tides:
While melting music steals upon the sky,
And soften'd sounds along the waters die;
Smooth flow the waves, the zephyrs gently play,
Belinda smil'd, and all the world was gay.
All but the sylph—with careful thoughts opprest,
Th' impending woe sat heavy on his breast.

He summons strait his denizens of air;
The lucid squadrons round the sails repair:
Soft o'er the shrouds aërial whispers breathe,
That seem'd but zephyrs to the train beneath.
Some to the sun their insect-wings unfold,
Waft on the breeze, or sink in clouds of gold;
Transparent forms, too fine for mortal sight,
Their fluid bodies half dissolv'd in light.
Loose to the wind their airy garments flew,
Thin glitt'ring textures of the filmy dew,
Dipt in the richest tincture of the skies,
Where light disports in ever-mingling dyes,
While ev'ry beam new transient colours flings,
Colours that change whene'er they wave their wings.
Amid the circle, on the gilded mast,
Superior by the head, was Ariel plac'd;
His purple pinions op'ning to the sun,
He rais'd his azure wand, and thus begun.
"Ye sylphs and sylphids, to your chief give ear!
Fays, fairies, genii, elves, and dæmons, hear!
Ye know the spheres, and various tasks assign'd
By laws eternal to th' aërial kind.
Some in the fields of purest æther play,
And bask and whiten in the blaze of day.
Some guide the course of wand'ring orbs on high,
Or roll the planets through the boundless sky.
Some less refin'd, beneath the moon's pale light
Pursue the stars that shoot athwart the night,
Or suck the mists in grosser air below,
Or dip their pinions in the painted bow,
Or brew fierce tempests on the wintry main,
Or o'er the glebe distil the kindly rain.
Others on earth o'er human race preside,
Watch all their ways, and all their actions guide:
Of these the chief the care of nations own,
And guard with arms divine the British throne.
"Our humbler province is to tend the fair,
Not a less pleasing, though less glorious care;
To save the powder from too rude a gale,
Nor let th' imprison'd essences exhale;
To draw fresh colours from the vernal flow'rs;
To steal from rainbows ere they drop in show'rs
A brighter wash; to curl their waving hairs,

Assist their blushes, and inspire their airs;
Nay oft, in dreams, invention we bestow,
To change a flounce, or add a furbelow.
"This day, black omens threat the brightest fair,
That e'er deserv'd a watchful spirit's care;
Some dire disaster, or by force, or slight;
But what, or where, the fates have wrapt in night.
Whether the nymph shall break Diana's law,
Or some frail china jar receive a flaw;
Or stain her honour, or her new brocade;
Forget her pray'rs, or miss a masquerade;
Or lose her heart, or necklace, at a ball;
Or whether Heav'n has doom'd that Shock must fall.
Haste then, ye spirits! to your charge repair:
The flutt'ring fan be Zephyretta's care;
The drops to thee, Brillante, we consign;
And, Momentilla, let the watch be thine;
Do thou, Crispissa, tend her fav'rite lock;
Ariel himself shall be the guard of Shock.
"To fifty chosen sylphs, of special note,
We trust th' important charge, the petticoat:
Oft have we known that seven-fold fence to fail,
Though stiff with hoops, and arm'd with ribs of whale;
Form a strong line about the silver bound,
And guard the wide circumference around.
"Whatever spirit, careless of his charge,
His post neglects, or leaves the fair at large,
Shall feel sharp vengeance soon o'ertake his sins,
Be stop'd in vials, or transfix'd with pins;
Or plung'd in lakes of bitter washes lie,
Or wedg'd whole ages in a bodkin's eye:
Gums and pomatums shall his flight restrain,
While clog'd he beats his silken wings in vain;
Or alum styptics with contracting pow'r
Shrink his thin essence like a rivel'd flow'r:
Or, as Ixion fix'd, the wretch shall feel
The giddy motion of the whirling mill,
In fumes of burning chocolate shall glow,
And tremble at the sea that froths below!"
He spoke; the spirits from the sails descend;
Some, orb in orb, around the nymph extend;
Some thrid the mazy ringlets of her hair;
Some hang upon the pendants of her ear;

With beating hearts the dire event they wait,
Anxious, and trembling for the birth of Fate.

## CANTO III

CLOSE by those meads, for ever crown'd with flow'rs,
Where Thames with pride surveys his rising tow'rs,
There stands a structure of majestic frame,
Which from the neighb'ring Hampton takes its name.
Here Britain's statesmen oft the fall foredoom
Of foreign tyrants and of nymphs at home;
Here thou, great Anna! whom three realms obey,
Dost sometimes counsel take—and sometimes tea.
  Hither the heroes and the nymphs resort,
To taste awhile the pleasures of a court;
In various talk th' instructive hours they past,
Who gave the ball, or paid the visit last;
One speaks the glory of the British Queen,
And one describes a charming Indian screen;
A third interprets motions, looks, and eyes;
At ev'ry word a reputation dies.
Snuff, or the fan, supply each pause of chat,
With singing, laughing, ogling, *and all that.*
  Meanwhile, declining from the noon of day,
The sun obliquely shoots his burning ray;
The hungry judges soon the sentence sign,
And wretches hang that jury-men may dine;
The merchant from th' Exchange returns in peace,
And the long labours of the toilet cease.
Belinda now, whom thirst of fame invites,
Burns to encounter two advent'rous knights,
At ombre singly to decide their doom;
And swells her breast with conquests yet to come.
Straight the three bands prepare in arms to join,
Each band the number of the sacred nine.
Soon as she spreads her hand, th' aërial guard
Descend, and sit on each important card:
First Ariel perch'd upon a Matadore,
Then each, according to the rank they bore;
For sylphs, yet mindful of their ancient race,
Are, as when women, wondrous fond of place.
  Behold, four kings in majesty rever'd,

With hoary whiskers and a forky beard;
And four fair queens, whose hands sustain a flow'r,
Th' expressive emblem of their softer pow'r;
Four knaves in garbs succinct, a trusty band,
Caps on their heads, and halberts in their hand;
And parti-colour'd troops, a shining train,
Draw forth to combat on the velvet plain.
  The skillful nymph reviews her force with care:
Let spades be trumps! she said, and trumps they were.
  Now move to war her sable Matadores,
In show like leaders of the swarthy Moors.
Spadillio first, unconquerable lord!
Led off two captive trumps, and swept the board.
As many more Manillio forc'd to yield,
And march'd a victor from the verdant field.
Him Basto follow'd, but his fate more hard
Gain'd but one trump and one plebian card.
With his broad sabre next, a chief in years,
The hoary Majesty of Spades appears,
Puts forth one manly leg, to sight reveal'd,
The rest, his many-colour'd robe conceal'd.
The rebel Knave, who dares his prince engage,
Proves the just victim of his royal rage.
Ev'n mighty Pam, that kings and queens o'erthrew
And mow'd down armies in the fights of Lu,
Sad chance of war! now destitute of aid,
Falls undistinguish'd by the victor spade!
  Thus far both armies to Belinda yield;
Now to the baron fate inclines the field.
His warlike Amazon her host invades,
Th' imperial consort of the crown of spades.
The club's black tyrant first her victim dy'd,
Spite of his haughty mien, and barb'rous pride:
What boots the regal circle on his head,
His giant limbs, in state unwieldy spread;
That long behind he trails his pompous robe,
And, of all monarchs, only grasps the globe?
  The baron now his diamonds pours apace;
Th' embroider'd King who shows but half his face,
And his refulgent Queen, with pow'rs combin'd
Of broken troops an easy conquest find.
Clubs, diamonds, hearts, in wild disorder seen,
With throngs promiscuous strow the level green.

Thus when dispers'd a routed army runs,
Of Asia's troops, and Afric's sable sons,
With like confusion different nations fly,
Of various habit, and of various dye,
The pierc'd battalions disunited fall,
In heaps on heaps; one fate o'erwhelms them all.
 The Knave of diamonds tries his wily arts,
And wins (oh shameful chance!) the Queen of hearts.
At this, the blood the virgin's cheek forsook,
A livid paleness spreads o'er all her look;
She sees, and trembles at th' approaching ill,
Just in the jaws of ruin, and codille.
And now, (as oft in some distemper'd state)
On one nice trick depends the gen'ral fate.
An Ace of hearts steps forth: the King unseen
Lurk'd in her hand, and mourn'd his captive Queen:
He springs to vengeance with an eager pace,
And falls like thunder on the prostrate Ace.
The nymph exulting fills with shouts the sky;
The walls, the woods, and long canals reply.
 Oh thoughtless mortals! ever blind to fate,
Too soon dejected, and too soon elate.
Sudden, these honours shall be snatch'd away,
And curs'd for ever this victorious day.
 For lo! the board with cups and spoons is crown'd,
The berries crackle, and the mill turns round;
On shining altars of Japan they raise
The silver lamp; the fiery spirits blaze:
From silver spouts the grateful liquors glide,
While China's earth receives the smoking tide:
At once they gratify their scent and taste,
And frequent cups prolong the rich repast.
Straight hover round the fair her airy band;
Some, as she sipp'd, the fuming liquor fann'd,
Some o'er her lap their careful plumes display'd,
Trembling, and conscious of the rich brocade.
Coffee, (which makes the politician wise,
And see through all things with his half-shut eyes)
Sent up in vapours to the baron's brain
New stratagems, the radiant lock to gain.
Ah cease, rash youth! desist ere 'tis too late,
Fear the just gods, and think of Scylla's fate!
Chang'd to a bird, and sent to flit in air,

She dearly pays for Nisus' injur'd hair!
   But when to mischief mortals bend their will,
How soon they find fit instruments of ill!
Just then, Clarissa drew with tempting grace
A two-edg'd weapon from her shining case:
So ladies in romance assist their knight,
Present the spear, and arm him for the fight.
He takes the gift with rev'rence, and extends
The little engine on his fingers' ends;
This just behind Belinda's neck he spread,
As o'er the fragrant steams she bends her head.
Swift to the lock a thousand sprites repair,
A thousand wings, by turns, blow back the hair;
And thrice they twitch'd the diamond in her ear;
Thrice she look'd back, and thrice the foe drew near.
Just in that instant, anxious Ariel sought
The close recesses of the virgin's thought;
As on the nosegay in her breast reclin'd,
He watch'd th' ideas rising in her mind,
Sudden he view'd, in spite of all her art,
An earthly lover lurking at her heart.
Amaz'd, confus'd, he found his pow'r expir'd,
Resign'd to fate, and with a sigh retir'd.
   The peer now spreads the glitt'ring forfex wide,
T' inclose the Lock; now joins it, to divide.
Ev'n then, before the fatal engine clos'd,
A wretched sylph too fondly interpos'd;
Fate urg'd the shears, and cut the sylph in twain,
(But airy substance soon unites again)
The meeting points the sacred hair dissever
From the fair head, for ever, and for ever!
   Then flash'd the living lightning from her eyes,
And screams of horror rend th' affrighted skies.
Not louder shrieks to pitying heav'n are cast,
When husbands, or when lap-dogs breathe their last;
Or when rich china vessels fall'n from high,
In glitt'ring dust and painted fragments lie!
   "Let wreaths of triumph now my temples twine,"
(The victor cry'd) "the glorious prize is mine!
While fish in streams, or birds delight in air,
Or in a coach and six the British fair,
As long as Atalantis shall be read,
Or the small pillow grace a lady's bed,

While visits shall be paid on solemn days,
When num'rous wax-lights in bright order blaze,
While nymphs take treats, or assignations give,
So long my honour, name, and praise shall live!
What time would spare, from steel receives its date,
And monuments, like men, submit to fate!
Steel could the labour of the gods destroy,
And strike to dust th' imperial tow'rs of Troy;
Steel could the works of mortal pride confound,
And hew triumphal arches to the ground.
What wonder then, fair nymph! thy hairs should feel,
The conq'ring force of unresisted steel?"

## CANTO IV

BUT anxious cares the pensive nymph oppress'd,
And secret passions labour'd in her breast.
Not youthful kings in battle seiz'd alive,
Not scornful virgins who their charms survive,
Not ardent lovers robb'd of all their bliss,
Not ancient ladies when refus'd a kiss,
Not tyrants fierce that unrepenting die,
Not Cynthia when her manteau's pinned awry,
E'er felt such rage, resentment, and despair,
As thou, sad virgin! for thy ravish'd hair.
  For, that sad moment, when the sylphs withdrew,
And Ariel weeping from Belinda flew,
Umbriel, a dusky, melancholy sprite,
As ever sully'd the fair face of light,
Down to the central earth, his proper scene,
Repair'd to search the gloomy cave of Spleen.
  Swift on his sooty pinions flits the gnome,
And in a vapour reach'd the dismal dome.
No cheerful breeze this sullen region knows,
The dreaded East is all the wind that blows.
Here in a grotto, shelter'd close from air,
And screen'd in shades from day's detested glare,
She sighs for ever on her pensive bed,
Pain at her side, and Megrim at her head.
  Two handmaids wait the throne: alike in place,
But diff'ring far in figure and in face.
Here stood Ill-nature like an ancient maid,

Her wrinkled form in black and white array'd;
With store of pray'rs, for mornings, nights, and noons.
Her hand is fill'd; her bosom with lampoons.
  There Affectation, with a sickly mien,
Shows in her cheek the roses of eighteen,
Practis'd to lisp, and hang the head aside,
Faints into airs, and languishes with pride,
On the rich quilt sinks with becoming woe,
Wrapt in a gown, for sickness, and for show.
The fair-ones feel such maladies as these,
When each new night-dress gives a new disease.
  A constant vapour o'er the palace flies;
Strange phantoms rising as the mists arise;
Dreadful, as hermits' dreams in haunted shades,
Or bright, as visions of expiring maids.
Now glaring fields, and snakes on rolling spires,
Pale spectres, gaping tombs, and purple fires:
Now lakes of liquid gold, Elysian scenes,
And crystal domes, and angels in machines.
  Unnumber'd throngs on ev'ry side are seen,
Of bodies chang'd to various forms by Spleen.
Here living tea-pots stand, one arm held out,
One bent; the handle this, and that the spout:
A pipkin there, like Homer's tripod walks;
Here sighs a jar, and there a goose-pie talks;
Men prove with child, as pow'rful fancy works,
And maids turn'd bottles, call aloud for corks.
  Safe past the gnome through this fantastic band,
A branch of healing spleenwort in his hand.
Then thus address'd the pow'r—"Hail, wayward queen!
Who rule the sex to fifty from fifteen:
Parent of vapours and of female wit,
Who give th' hysteric, or poetic fit,
On various tempers act by various ways,
Make some take physic, others scribble plays;
Who cause the proud their visits to delay,
And send the godly in a pet to pray.
A nymph there is, that all thy pow'r disdains,
And thousands more in equal mirth maintains.
But oh! if e'er thy gnome could spoil a grace,
Or raise a pimple on a beauteous face,
Like citron-waters matrons' cheeks inflame,
Or change complexions at a losing game;

If e'er with airy horns I planted heads,
Or rumpled petticoats, or tumbled beds,
Or caus'd suspicion when no soul was rude,
Or discompos'd the head-dress of a prude,
Or e'er to costive lap-dog gave disease,
Which not the tears of brightest eyes could ease:
Hear me, and touch Belinda with chagrin,
That single act gives half the world the spleen."
  The goddess with a discontented air
Seems to reject him, though she grants his pray'r.
A wondrous bag with both her hands she binds,
Like that where once Ulysses held the winds;
There she collects the force of female lungs,
Sighs, sobs, and passions, and the war of tongues.
A vial next she fills with fainting fears,
Soft sorrows, melting griefs, and flowing tears.
The gnome rejoicing bears her gifts away,
Spreads his black wings, and slowly mounts to day.
  Sunk in Thalestris' arms the nymph he found,
Her eyes dejected, and her hair unbound.
Full o'er their heads the swelling bag he rent,
And all the furies issu'd at the vent.
Belinda burns with more than mortal ire,
And fierce Thalestris fans the rising fire.
"Oh wretched maid!" she spread her hands, and cry'd
(While Hampton's echoes, "Wretched maid!" reply'd)
"Was it for this you took such constant care
The bodkin, comb, and essence to prepare?
For this your locks in paper durance bound,
For this with tort'ring irons wreath'd around?
For this with fillets strain'd your tender head,
And bravely bore the double loads of lead?
Gods! shall the ravisher display your hair,
While the fops envy, and the ladies stare!
Honour forbid! at whose unrival'd shrine
Ease, pleasure, virtue, all our sex resign.
Methinks already I your tears survey,
Already hear the horrid things they say,
Already see you a degraded toast,
And all your honour in a whisper lost!
How shall I, then, your helpless fame defend?
'Twill then be infamy to seem your friend!
And shall this prize, th' inestimable prize,

Expos'd through crystal to the gazing eyes,
And heighten'd by the diamond's circling rays,
On that rapacious hand for ever blaze?
Sooner shall grass in Hyde-park Circus grow,
And wits take lodgings in the sound of Bow;
Sooner let earth, air, sea, to chaos fall,
Men, monkeys, lap-dogs, parrots, perish all!"
She said; then raging to Sir Plume repairs,
And bids her beau demand the precious hairs:
(Sir Plume of amber snuff-box justly vain,
And the nice conduct of a clouded cane)
With earnest eyes, and round unthinking face,
He first the snuff-box open'd, then the case,
And thus broke out—"My Lord, why, what the devil?
Z—ds! damn the lock! 'fore Gad, you must be civil!
Plague on't! 'tis past a jest—nay prithee, pox!
Give her the hair"—he spoke, and rapp'd his box.
"It grieves me much" (reply'd the peer again)
"Who speaks so well should ever speak in vain.
But by this lock, this sacred lock I swear,
(Which never more shall join its parted hair;
Which never more its honours shall renew,
Clipp'd from the lovely head where late it grew)
That while my nostrils draw the vital air,
This hand, which won it, shall for ever wear."
He spoke, and speaking, in proud triumph spread
The long-contended honours of her head.
But Umbriel, hateful gnome! forbears not so;
He breaks the vial whence the sorrows flow.
Then see! the nymph in beauteous grief appears,
Her eyes half-languishing, half-drown'd in tears;
On her heav'd bosom hung her drooping head,
Which, with a sigh, she rais'd; and thus she said.
"For ever curs'd be this detested day,
Which snatch'd my best, my fav'rite curl away!
Happy! ah ten times happy had I been,
If Hampton-Court these eyes had never seen!
Yet am not I the first mistaken maid,
By love of courts to num'rous ills betray'd.
Oh had I rather un-admir'd remain'd
In some lone isle, or distant northern land;
Where the gilt chariot never marks the way,
Where none learn ombre, none e'er taste bohea!

There kept my charms conceal'd from mortal eye,
Like roses, that in deserts bloom and die.
What mov'd my mind with youthful lords to roam?
Oh had I stay'd, and said my prayers at home!
'Twas this, the morning omens seem'd to tell,
Thrice from my trembling hand the patch-box fell;
The tott'ring china shook without a wind,
Nay, Poll sat mute, and Shock was most unkind!
A sylph too warn'd me of the threats of fate,
In mystic visions, now believ'd too late!
See the poor remnants of these slighted hairs!
My hands shall rend what ev'n thy rapine spares:
These in two sable ringlets taught to break,
Once gave new beauties to the snowy neck;
The sister-lock now sits uncouth, alone,
And in its fellow's fate foresees its own;
Uncurl'd it hangs, the fatal shears demands,
And tempts, once more, thy sacrilegious hands.
Oh hadst thou, cruel! been content to seize
Hairs less in sight, or any hairs but these!"

## Canto V

She said: the pitying audience melt in tears;
But Fate and Jove had stopp'd the Baron's ears.
In vain Thalestris with reproach assails,
For who can move when fair Belinda fails?
Not half so fix'd the Trojan could remain,
While Anna begg'd and Dido rag'd in vain.
Then grave Clarissa graceful wav'd her fan;
Silence ensu'd, and thus the nymph began.
"Say why are beauties prais'd and honour'd most,
The wise man's passion, and the vain man's toast?
Why deck'd with all that land and sea afford,
Why angels call'd, and angel-like ador'd?
Why round our coaches crowd the white-glov'd beaux,
Why bows the side-box from its inmost rows;
How vain are all these glories, all our pains,
Unless good sense preserve what beauty gains:
That men may say, when we the front-box grace,
'Behold the first in virtue as in face!'
Oh! if to dance all night, and dress all day,

Charm'd the small-pox, or chas'd old-age away;
Who would not scorn what housewife's cares produce,
Or who would learn one earthly thing of use?
To patch, nay ogle, might become a saint,
Nor could it sure be such a sin to paint.
But since, alas! frail beauty must decay,
Curl'd or uncurl'd, since locks will turn to grey;
Since painted, or not painted, all shall fade,
And she who scorns a man, must die a maid;
What then remains, but well our pow'r to use,
And keep good-humour still whate'er we lose?
And trust me, dear! good-humour can prevail,
When airs, and flights, and screams, and scolding fail.
Beauties in vain their pretty eyes may roll;
Charms strike the sight, but merit wins the soul."
   So spoke the dame, but no applause ensu'd;
Belinda frown'd, Thalestris call'd her prude.
"To arms, to arms!" the fierce virago cries,
And swift as lightning to the combat flies.
All side in parties, and begin th' attack;
Fans clap, silks rustle, and tough whalebones crack;
Heroes' and heroines' shouts confus'dly rise,
And bass and treble voices strike the skies.
No common weapons in their hands are found,
Like gods they fight, nor dread a mortal wound.
   So when bold Homer makes the gods engage,
And heav'nly breasts with human passions rage;
'Gainst Pallas, Mars; Latona, Hermes arms;
And all Olympus rings with loud alarms:
Jove's thunder roars, heav'n trembles all around,
Blue Neptune storms, the bellowing deeps resound:
Earth shakes her nodding tow'rs, the ground gives way,
And the pale ghosts start at the flash of day!
   Triumphant Umbriel on a sconce's height
Clapp'd his glad wings, and sate to view the fight:
Prop'd on their bodkin spears, the sprites survey
The growing combat, or assist the fray.
   While through the press enrag'd Thalestris flies,
And scatters death around from both her eyes,
A beau and witling perish'd in the throng,
One dy'd in metaphor, and one in song.
"O cruel nymph! a living death I bear,"

Cried Dapperwit, and sunk beside his chair.
A mournful glance Sir Fopling upwards cast,
"Those eyes are made so killing"—was his last.
Thus on Mæander's flow'ry margin lies
Th' expiring swan, and as he sings he dies.
When bold Sir Plume had drawn Clarissa down,
Chloe stepp'd in, and kill'd him with a frown;
She smil'd to see the doughty hero slain,
But, at her smile, the beau reviv'd again.
Now Jove suspends his golden scales in air,
Weighs the men's wits against the lady's hair;
The doubtful beam long nods from side to side;
At length the wits mount up, the hairs subside.
See fierce Belinda on the baron flies,
With more than usual lightning in her eyes:
Nor fear'd the chief th' unequal fight to try,
Who sought no more than on his foe to die.
But this bold lord with manly strength endu'd,
She with one finger and a thumb subdu'd:
Just where the breath of life his nostrils drew,
A charge of snuff the wily virgin threw;
The gnomes direct, to ev'ry atom just,
The pungent grains of titillating dust.
Sudden, with starting tears each eye o'erflows,
And the high dome re-echoes to his nose.
Now meet thy fate, incens'd Belinda cry'd,
And drew a deadly bodkin from her side.
(The same, his ancient personage to deck,
Her great-great-grandsire wore about his neck,
In three seal-rings; which after, melted down,
Form'd a vast buckle for his widow's gown:
Her infant grandame's whistle next it grew,
The bells she jingled, and the whistle blew;
Then in a bodkin grac'd her mother's hairs,
Which long she wore, and now Belinda wears.)
"Boast not my fall" (he cry'd) "insulting foe!
Thou by some other shalt be laid as low,
Nor think, to die dejects my lofty mind:
All that I dread is leaving you behind!
Rather than so, ah let me still survive,
And burn in Cupid's flames—but burn alive."
"Restore the lock!" she cries; and all around

"Restore the lock!" the vaulted roofs rebound.
Not fierce Othello in so loud a strain
Roar'd for the handkerchief that caus'd his pain.
But see how oft ambitious aims are cross'd,
And chiefs contend 'till all the prize is lost!
The lock, obtain'd with guilt, and kept with pain,
In ev'ry place is sought, but sought in vain:
With such a prize no mortal must be blest,
So heav'n decrees! with heav'n who can contest?
Some thought it mounted to the lunar sphere,
Since all things lost on earth are treasur'd there.
There hero's wits are kept in pond'rous vases,
And beau's in snuff-boxes and tweezer-cases.
There broken vows, and death-bed alms are found,
And lovers' hearts with ends of riband bound,
The courtier's promises, and sick man's pray'rs,
The smiles of harlots, and the tears of heirs,
Cages for gnats, and chains to yoke a flea,
Dry'd butterflies, and tomes of casuistry.
But trust the Muse—she saw it upward rise,
Though mark'd by none but quick, poetic eyes:
(So Rome's great founder to the heav'ns withdrew,
To Proculus alone confess'd in view)
A sudden star, it shot through liquid air,
And drew behind a radiant trail of hair.
Not Berenice's locks first rose so bright,
The heav'ns bespangling with dishevel'd light.
The sylphs behold it kindling as it flies,
And pleas'd pursue its progress through the skies.
This the beau monde shall from the Mall survey,
And hail with music its propitious ray.
This the blest lover shall for Venus take,
And send up vows from Rosamonda's lake.
This Partridge soon shall view in cloudless skies,
When next he looks through Galileo's eyes;
And hence th' egregious wizard shall foredoom
The fate of Louis, and the fall of Rome.
Then cease, bright Nymph! to mourn thy ravish'd hair,
Which adds new glory to the shining sphere!
Not all the tresses that fair head can boast,
Shall draw such envy as the lock you lost.
For, after all the murders of your eye,

When, after millions slain, yourself shall die:
When those fair suns shall set, as set they must,
And all those tresses shall be laid in dust,
This lock, the Muse shall consecrate to fame,
And 'midst the stars inscribe Belinda's name.

## SAINT-SIMON

# *The Prince de Condé*

M. LE PRINCE, who for more than two years had not appeared at the Court, died at Paris a little after midnight on the night between Easter Sunday and Monday, the last of March and the first of April, and in his seventy-sixth year. No man had ever more ability of all kinds,—extending even to the arts and mechanics,—more valor, and, when it pleased him, more discernment, grace, politeness, and nobility. But then no man had ever before so many useless talents, so much genius of no avail, or an imagination so calculated to be a bugbear to itself and a plague to others. Abjectly and vilely servile even to lackeys, he scrupled not to use the lowest and paltriest means to gain his ends. Unnatural son, cruel father, terrible husband, detestable master, pernicious neighbor; without friendship, without friends—incapable of having any—jealous, suspicious, even restless, full of slyness and artifices to discover and to scrutinize all (in which he was unceasingly occupied, aided by an extreme vivacity and a surprising penetration), choleric and headstrong to excess even for trifles, difficult of access, never in accord with himself, and keeping all around him in a tremble; to conclude, impetuosity and avarice were his masters, which monopolized him always. With all this he was a man difficult to be proof against when he put in play the pleasing qualities he possessed.

Madame la Princesse, his wife, was his continual victim. She was disgustingly ugly, virtuous, and foolish, a little humpbacked, and stunk like a skunk, even from a distance. All these things did not hinder M. le Prince from being jealous of her even to fury up to the very last. The piety, the indefatigable attention of Madame la Princesse, her sweetness, her novice-like submission, could not guarantee her from frequent injuries, or from kicks, and blows with the fist, which were not rare. She was not mistress even of the most trifling things; she did not dare to propose or ask anything. He made her set out from one place to another the moment the fancy took him. Often when seated in their coach he made her descend, or return from the end of the street, then recommence the journey after dinner, or the next day. This seesawing lasted once fifteen days running, before a trip to Fontainebleau. At other times he sent for her from church, made her quit high mass, and sometimes sent for her the moment she was going to receive the Sacrament; she was obliged to return at once and put off her communion to another occasion. It was not that he wanted her, but it was merely to gratify his whim that he thus troubled her.

He was always of uncertain habits, and had four dinners ready for him every day; one at Paris, one at Ecouen, one at Chantilly, and one where the Court was. But the expense of this arrangement was not great; he dined on soup, and the half of a fowl roasted upon a crust of bread; the other half serving for the next day. He rarely invited anybody to dinner, but when he did, no man could be more polite or attentive to his guests.

Formerly he had been in love with several ladies of the Court; then, nothing cost too much. He was grace, magnificence, gallantry in person—a Jupiter transformed into a shower of gold. Now he disguised himself as a lackey, another time as a female broker in articles for the toilet; and now in another fashion. He was the most ingenious man in the world. He once gave a grand *fête* solely for the purpose of retarding the journey into Italy of a lady with whom he was enamored, with whom he was on good terms, and whose husband he amused by making verses. He hired all the houses on one side of a street near St. Sulpice, furnished them, and pierced the connecting walls, in order to be able thus to reach the place of rendezvous without being suspected.

Jealous and cruel to his mistresses, he had, among others, the Marquise de Richelieu; whom I name, because she is not worth the trouble of being silent upon. He was hopelessly smitten and spent millions upon her and to learn her movements. He knew that the Comte de Roucy shared her favors (it was for her that sagacious Comte proposed to put straw before the house in order to guarantee her against the sound of the church bells, of which she complained). M. le Prince reproached her for favoring the Count. She defended herself; but he watched her so closely, that he brought home the offense to her without her being able to deny it. The fear of losing a lover so rich as was M. le Prince furnished her on the spot with an excellent suggestion for putting him at ease. She proposed to make an appointment at her own house with the Comte de Roucy, M. le Prince's people to lie in wait, and when the Comte appeared, to make away with him. Instead of the success she expected from a proposition so humane and ingenious, M. le Prince was so horror struck, that he warned the Comte de Roucy, and never saw the Marquise de Richelieu again all his life.

The most surprising thing was, that with so much ability, penetration, activity, and valor, as had M. le Prince, with the desire to be as great a warrior as the Great Condé, his father, he could never succeed in understanding even the first elements of the military art. Instructed as he was by his father, he never acquired the least aptitude in war. It was a profession he was not born for, and for which he could not qualify himself by study.

During the last fifteen or twenty years of his life, he was accused of something more than fierceness and ferocity. Wanderings were noticed in his conduct, which were not exhibited in his own house alone. Entering one morning into the apartment of the Maréchale de Noailles (she herself has related this to me) as her bed was being made, and there being only the counterpane to put on, he stopped short at the door, crying with transport, "Oh, the nice bed, the nice bed!" took a spring, leaped upon the bed, rolled himself upon it seven or eight times, then descended and made his excuses to the Maréchale, saying that her bed was so clean and so well made, that he could not hinder himself from jumping upon it; and this, although there had never been anything between them; and when the Maréchale, who all her life had been above suspicion, was at an age at which she could not give birth to any. Her servants remained stupefied, and she as much as they. She got out of the difficulty by laughing and treating it as a joke. It was whispered that there were times when M. le Prince believed himself a dog, or some other beast, whose manners he imitated; and I have known people very worthy of faith who have assured me they have seen him at the going to bed of the King suddenly throw his head into the air several times running, and open his mouth quite wide, like a dog when barking, yet without making a noise. It is certain, that for a long time nobody saw him except a single valet, who had control over him, and who did not annoy him.

In the latter part of his life he attended in a ridiculously minute manner to his diet and its results, and entered into discussions which drove his doctors to despair. Fever and gout at last attacked him, and he augmented them by the course he pursued. Finot, our physician and his, at times knew not what to do with him. What embarrassed Finot most, as he related to us more than once, was that M. le Prince would eat nothing, for the simple reason, as he alleged, that he was dead, and that dead men did not eat! It was necessary, however, that he should take something, or he would have really died. Finot and another doctor who attended him, determined to agree with him that he was dead, but to maintain that dead men sometimes eat. They offered to produce dead men of this kind; and in point of fact, led to M. le Prince some persons unknown to him, who pretended to be dead, but who ate nevertheless. This trick succeeded, but he would never eat except with these men and Finot. On that condition he ate well, and this jealousy lasted a long time, and drove Finot to despair by its duration; who, nevertheless, sometimes nearly died of laughter in relating to us what passed at these repasts, and the conversation from the other world heard there.

M. le Prince's malady augmenting, Madame la Princesse grew bold enough to ask him if he did not wish to think of his conscience, and to see a confessor? He amused himself tolerably long in refusing to do so. Some months before he had seen in secret Père de la Tour. He had sent to the reverend father asking him to come by night and disguised. Père de la Tour, surprised to the last degree at so wild a proposition, replied that the respect he owed to the cloth would prevent him visiting M. le Prince in disguise; but that he would come in his ordinary attire. M. le Prince agreed to this last imposed condition. He made the Père de la Tour enter at night by a little back door, at which an attendant was waiting to receive him. He was led by this attendant, who had a lantern in one hand and a key in the other, through many long and obscure passages, and through many doors, which were opened and closed upon him as he passed. Having arrived at last at the sick chamber, he confessed M. le Prince, and was conducted out of the house in the same manner and by the same way as before. These visits were repeated during several months.

The Prince's malady rapidly increased, and became extreme. The doctors found him so ill on the night of Easter Sunday that they proposed to him the Sacrament for the next day. He disputed with them, and said that if he was so very bad it would be better to take the Sacraments at once, and have done with them. They in their turn opposed this, saying there was no need of so much hurry. At last, for fear of incensing him, they consented, and he received all-hurriedly the last Sacraments. A little while after he called M. le Duc to him, and spoke of the honors he wished at his funeral, mentioning those which had been omitted at the funeral of his father, but which he did not wish to be omitted from his. He talked of nothing but this and of the sums he had spent at Chantilly, until his reason began to wander.

Not a soul regretted him; neither servants nor friends, neither child nor wife. Indeed the Princess was so ashamed of her tears that she made excuses for them.

# SAINT-SIMON

## *The Death of Monseigneur**

On Saturday, the 11th of the month, and the day before Quasimodo, I had been walking all the morning, and I had entered all alone into my cabinet a little before dinner, when a courier sent by Madame de Saint-Simon, gave me a letter from her, in which I was informed that Monseigneur was ill.

I learned afterward that this Prince, while on his way to Meudon for the Easter *fêtes*, met at Chaville a priest, who was carrying Our Lord to a sick person. Monseigneur, and Madame de Bourgogne, who was with him, knelt down to adore the host, and then Monseigneur inquired what was the malady of the patient. "The smallpox," he was told. That disease was very prevalent just then. Monseigneur had had it, but very lightly, and when young. He feared it very much, and was struck with the answer he now received. In the evening he said to Boudin, his chief doctor, "I should not be surprised if I were to have the smallpox." The day, however, passed over as usual.

On the morrow, Thursday, the 9th, Monseigneur rose, and meant to go out wolf hunting; but as he was dressing, such a fit of weakness seized him, that he fell into his chair. Boudin made him get into bed again; but all the day his pulse was in an alarming state. The King, only half informed by Fagon of what had taken place, believed there was nothing the matter, and went out walking at Marly after dinner, receiving news from time to time. Monseigneur le Duc de Bourgogne and Madame de Bourgogne dined at Meudon, and they would not quit Monseigneur for one moment. The Princess added to the strict duties of a daughter-in-law all that her gracefulness could suggest, and gave everything to Monseigneur with her own hand. Her heart could not have been troubled by what her reason foresaw; but, nevertheless, her care and attention were extreme, without any airs of affectation or acting. The Duc de Bourgogne, simple and holy as he was, and full of the idea of his duty, exaggerated his attention; and although there was a strong suspicion of the smallpox, neither quitted Monseigneur, except for the King's supper.

* Monseigneur, with whom Saint-Simon was not on good terms, was the Dauphin, the son of Louis XIV. At his death his older son, the Duc de Bourgogne, became heir to the throne.

The next day, Friday, the 10th, in reply to his express demands, the King was informed of the extremely dangerous state of Monseigneur. He had said on the previous evening that he would go on the following morning to Meudon, and remain there during all the illness of Monseigneur whatever its nature might be. He was now as good as his word. Immediately after mass he set out for Meudon. Before doing so, he forbade his children, and all who had not had the smallpox, to go there, which was suggested by a motive of kindness. With Madame de Maintenon and a small suite, he had just taken up his abode in Meudon, when Madame de Saint-Simon sent me the letter of which I have just made mention.

I will continue to speak of myself with the same truthfulness I speak of others, and with as much exactness as possible. According to the terms on which I was with Monseigneur and his intimates, may be imagined the impression made upon me by this news. I felt that one way or other, well or ill, the malady of Monseigneur would soon terminate. I was quite at my ease at La Ferté. I resolved therefore to wait there until I received fresh particulars. I dispatched a courier to Madame de Saint-Simon, requesting her to send me another the next day, and I passed the rest of this day, in an ebb and flow of feelings; the man and the Christian struggling against the man and the courtier, and in the midst of a crowd of vague fancies catching glimpses of the future, painted in the most agreeable colors.

The courier I expected so impatiently arrived the next day, Sunday, after dinner. The smallpox had declared itself, I learned, and was going on as well as could be wished. I believed Monseigneur saved, and wished to remain at my own house; nevertheless I took advice, as I have done all my life, and with great regret set out the next morning. At La Queue, about six leagues from Versailles, I met a financier of the name of La Fontaine, whom I knew well. He was coming from Paris and Versailles, and came up to me as I changed horses. Monseigneur, he said, was going on admirably; and he added details which convinced me he was out of all danger. I arrived at Versailles, full of this opinion, which was confirmed by Madame de Saint-Simon and everybody I met, so that nobody any longer feared, except on account of the treacherous nature of this disease in a very fat man of fifty.

The King held his Council, and worked in the evening with his ministers as usual. He saw Monseigneur morning and evening, oftentimes in the afternoon, and always remained long by the bedside. On the Monday I arrived he had dined early, and had driven to Marly, where the Duchesse de Bourgogne joined him. He saw in passing on the outskirts of the garden of Versailles his grandchildren, who had come out to meet him, but he would not let them come near, and said "good day" from a distance. The Duchesse de Bourgogne had had the smallpox, but no trace was left.

The King only liked his own houses, and could not bear to be anywhere else. This was why his visits to Meudon were few and short, and only made from complaisance. Madame de Maintenon was still more out of her element there. Although her chamber was everywhere a sanctuary, where only ladies entitled to the most extreme familiarity entered, she always wanted another retreat near at hand entirely inaccessible except to the Duchesse de Bourgogne alone, and that only for a few instants at a time. Thus she had Saint Cyr for Versailles and for Marly; and at Marly also a particular retiring place; at Fontainebleau she had her town house. Seeing therefore that Monseigneur was getting on well, and that a long sojourn at Meudon would be necessary, the upholsterers of the King were ordered to furnish a house in the park which once belonged to the Chancellor le Tellier, but which Monseigneur had bought.

When I arrived at Versailles, I wrote to M. de Beauvilliers at Meudon praying him to apprise the King that I had returned on account of the illness of Monseigneur, and that I would have gone to see him, but that, never having had the smallpox, I was included in the prohibition. M. de Beauvilliers did as I asked, and sent word back to me that my return had been very well timed, and that the King still forbade me as well as Madame de Saint-Simon to go to Meudon. This fresh prohibition did not distress me in the least. I was informed of all that was passing there, and that satisfied me.

There were yet contrasts at Meudon worth noticing. Mademoiselle Choin never appeared while the King was with Monseigneur, but kept close in her loft. When the coast was clear she came out, and took up her position at the sick man's bedside. All sorts of compliments passed between her and Madame de Maintenon, yet the two ladies never met. The King asked Madame de Maintenon if she had seen Mademoiselle Choin, and upon learning that she had not, was but ill pleased. Therefore Madame de Maintenon sent excuses and apologies to Mademoiselle Choin, and hoped, she said, to see her soon,—strange compliments from one chamber to another under the same roof. They never saw each other afterward.

It should be observed, that Père Tellier was also incognito at Meudon, and dwelt in a retired room from which he issued to see the King, but never approached the apartments of Monseigneur.

Versailles presented another scene. Monseigneur le Duc and Madame la Duchesse de Bourgogne held their Court openly there; and this Court resembled the first gleamings of the dawn. All the Court assembled there; all Paris also; and as discretion and precaution were never French virtues, all Meudon came as well. People were believed when they declared that they had not entered the apartments of Monseigneur that day, and consequently could not bring the infection. When the Prince and Princess rose, when they went to bed, when they dined and supped with the ladies,—all public conversations—all meals—all assemblies—were opportunities of paying court to them. The apartments could not contain the crowd. The characteristic features of the room were many. Couriers arrived every quarter of an hour, and reminded people of the illness of Monseigneur—he was going on as well as could be expected; confidence and hope were easily felt; but there was an extreme desire to please at the new Court. The young Prince and Princess exhibited majesty and gravity, mixed with gayety; obligingly received all, continually spoke to every one; the crowd wore an air of complaisance; reciprocal satisfaction showed in every face, the Duc and Duchesse de Berry were treated almost as nobody. Thus five days fled away in increasing thought of future events—in preparation to be ready for whatever might happen.

On Tuesday, the 14th of April I went to see the Chancellor, and asked for information upon the state of Monseigneur. He assured me it was good, and repeated to me the words Fagon had spoken to him, "that things were going on according to their wishes, and beyond their hopes." The Chancellor appeared to me very confident, and I had faith in him, so much the more, because he was on an extremely good footing with Monseigneur. The Prince, indeed, had so much recovered, that the fish women came in a body the self-same day to congratulate him, as they did after his attack of indigestion. They threw themselves at the foot of his bed, which they kissed several times, and in their joy said they would go back to Paris and have a *Te Deum* sung. But Monseigneur, who was not insensible to these marks of popular affection, told them it was not yet time, thanked them, and gave them a dinner, and some money.

As I was going home, I saw the Duchesse d'Orléans walking on a terrace. She called to me; but I pretended not to notice her, because La Montauban was with her, and hastened home, my mind filled with this news, and withdrew to my cabinet. Almost immediately afterward Madame la Duchesse d'Orléans joined me there. We were bursting to speak to each other alone, upon a point on which our thoughts were alike. She had left Meudon not an hour before, and she had the same tale to tell as the Chancellor. Everybody was at ease there, she said; and then she extolled the care and capacities of the doctors, exaggerating their success; and, to speak frankly and to our shame, she and I lamented together to see Monseigneur, in spite of his age and his fat, escape from so dangerous an illness. She reflected seriously but wittily, that after an illness of this sort, apoplexy was not to be looked for; that an attack of indigestion was equally unlikely to arise, considering the care Monseigneur had taken not to over-gorge himself since his recent danger; and we concluded more than dolefully, that henceforth we must make up our minds that the Prince would live and reign for a long time. In a word, we let ourselves loose in this rare conversation, although not without an occasional scruple of conscience which disturbed it. Madame de Saint-Simon all-devoutly tried what she could to put a drag upon our tongues, but the drag broke, so to speak, and we continued our free discourse, humanly speaking very reasonable on our parts, but which we felt, nevertheless, was not according to religion. Thus two hours passed, seemingly very short. Madame d'Orléans went away, and I repaired with Madame de Saint-Simon to receive a numerous company.

While thus all was tranquillity at Versailles, and even at Meudon, everything had changed its aspect at the *château.* The King had seen Monseigneur several times during the day; but in his after-dinner visit he was so much struck with the extraordinary swelling of the face and of the head, that he shortened his stay, and on leaving the *château* shed tears. He was reassured as much as possible, and after the council he took a walk in the garden.

Nevertheless Monseigneur had already mistaken Madame la Princesse de Conti for some one else; and Boudin, the doctor, was alarmed. Monseigneur himself had been so from the first, and he admitted that, for a long time before being attacked, he had been very unwell, and so much on Good Friday, that he had been unable to read his prayer book at chapel.

Toward four o'clock he grew worse, so much so that Boudin proposed to Fagon to call in other doctors, more familiar with the disease than they were. But Fagon flew into a rage at this, and would call in nobody. He declared that it would be better to act for themselves, and to keep Monseigneur's state secret, although it was hourly growing worse, and toward seven o'clock was perceived by several valets and courtiers. But nobody dared to open his mouth before Fagon, and the King was actually allowed to go to supper and to finish it without interruption, believing on the faith of Fagon that Monseigneur was going on well.

While the King supped thus tranquilly, all those who were in the sick chamber began to lose their wits. Fagon and the others poured down physic on physic, without leaving time for any to work. The *curé,* who was accustomed to go and learn the news every evening, found, against all custom, the doors thrown wide open, and the valets in confusion. He entered the chamber, and perceiving what was the matter, ran to the bedside, took the hand of Monseigneur, spoke to him of God, and seeing him full of consciousness, but scarcely able to speak, drew from him a sort of confession, of which nobody had hitherto thought, and suggested some acts of contrition. The poor Prince repeated distinctly several words suggested to him, and confusedly answered others, struck his breast, squeezed the *curé's* hand, appeared penetrated with the best sentiments, and received with a contrite and willing air the absolution of the *curé*.

As the King rose from the supper table, he well nigh fell backward when Fagon, coming forward, cried in great trouble that all was lost. It may be imagined what terror seized all the company at this abrupt passage from perfect security to hopeless despair. The King, scarcely master of himself, at once began to go toward the apartment of Monseigneur, and repelled very stiffly the indiscreet eagerness of some courtiers who wished to prevent him, saying that he would see his son again, and be quite certain that nothing could be done. As he was about to enter the chamber, Madame la Princesse de Conti presented herself before him, and prevented him from going in. She pushed him back with her hands, and said that henceforth he had only to think of himself. Then the King, nearly fainting from a shock so complete and so sudden, fell upon a sofa that stood near. He asked unceasingly for news of all who passed, but scarce anybody dared to reply to him. He had sent for Père Tellier who went into Monseigneur's room; but it was no longer time. It is true the Jesuit, perhaps to console the King, said that he gave him a well-founded absolution. Madame de Maintenon hastened after the King, and sitting down beside him on the same sofa, tried to cry. She endeavored to lead away the King into the carriage already waiting for him in the courtyard, but he would not go, and sat thus outside the door until Monseigneur had expired.

The agony, without consciousness, of Monseigneur lasted more than an hour after the King had come into the cabinet. Madame la Duchesse and Madame la Princesse de Conti divided their cares between the dying man and the King, to whom they constantly came back; while the faculty confounded, the valets bewildered, the courtiers hurrying and murmuring, hustled against each other, and moved unceasingly to and fro, backward and forward, in the same narrow space. At last the fatal moment arrived. Fagon came out, and allowed so much to be understood.

The King, much afflicted, and very grieved that Monseigneur's confession had been so tardily made, abused Fagon a little; and went away led by Madame de Maintenon and the two Princesses. He was somewhat struck by finding the vehicle of Monseigneur outside; and made a sign that he would have another coach, for that one made him suffer, and left the *château.* He was not, however, so much occupied with his grief that he could not call Pontchartrain to arrange the hour of the council of the next day. I will not comment on this coolness, and shall merely say it surprised extremely all present; and that if Pontchartrain had not said the council could be put off, no interruption to business would have taken place. The King got into his coach with difficulty, supported on both sides. Madame de Maintenon seated herself beside him. A crowd of officers of Monseigneur lined both sides of the court on their knees, as he passed out, crying to him with strange howlings to have compassion on them, for they had lost all, and must die of hunger.

While Meudon was filled with horror, all was tranquil at Versailles, without the least suspicion. We had supped. The company some time after had retired, and I was talking with Madame de Saint-Simon, who had nearly finished undressing herself to go to bed, when a servant of Madame la Duchesse de Berry, who had formerly belonged to us, entered, all terrified. He said that there must be some bad news from Meudon, since Monseigneur le Duc de Bourgogne had just whispered in the ear of M. le Duc de Berry, whose eyes had at once become red, that he left the table, and that all the company shortly after him rose with precipitation. So sudden a change rendered my surprise extreme. I ran in hot haste to Madame la Duchesse de Berry's. Nobody was there. Everybody had gone to Madame la Duchesse de Bourgogne. I followed on with all speed.

I found all Versailles assembled on arriving, all the ladies hastily dressed—the majority having been on the point of going to bed—all the doors open, and all in trouble. I learned that Monseigneur had received extreme unction, that he was without consciousness and beyond hope, and that the King had sent word to Madame de Bourgogne that he was going to Marly, and that she was to meet him as he passed through the avenue between the two stables.

The spectacle before me attracted all the attention I could bestow. The two Princes and the two Princesses were in the little cabinet behind the bed. The bed toilet was as usual in the chamber of the Duchesse de Bourgogne, which was filled with all the Court in confusion. She came and went from the cabinet to the chamber, waiting for the moment when she was to meet the King; and her demeanor, always distinguished by the same graces, was one of trouble and compassion, which the trouble and compassion of others induced them to take for grief. Now and then, in passing, she said a few rare words. All present were in truth expressive personages. Whoever had eyes, without any knowledge of the Court, could see the interests of all who were interested painted on their faces, and the indifference of the indifferent; these tranquil, the former penetrated with grief, or gravely attentive to themselves to hide their emancipation and their joy.

For my part, my first care was to inform myself thoroughly of the state of affairs, fearing lest there might be too much alarm for too trifling a cause; then, recovering myself, I reflected upon the misery common to all men, and that I myself should find myself some day at the gates of death. Joy nevertheless found its way through the momentary reflections of religion and of humanity, by which I tried to master myself. My own private deliverance seemed so great and so unhoped for, that it appeared to me that the State must gain everything by such a loss. And with these thoughts I felt, in spite, of myself, a lingering fear lest the sick man should recover, and was extremely ashamed of it.

Wrapped up thus in myself, I did not fail, nevertheless, to cast clandestine looks upon each face, to see what was passing there. I saw Madame la Duchesse d'Orléans arrive, but her countenance, majestic and constrained, said nothing. She went into the little cabinet, whence she presently issued with the Duc d'Orléans, whose activity and turbulent air marked his emotion at the spectacle more than any other sentiment. They went away, and I noticed this expressly, on account of what happened afterward in my presence.

Soon afterward I caught a distinct glimpse of the Duc de Bourgogne, who seemed much moved and troubled; but the glance with which I probed him rapidly, revealed nothing tender, and told merely of a mind profoundly occupied with the bearings of what had taken place.

Valets and chamber-women were already indiscreetly crying out; and THEIR grief showed well that they were about to lose something.

Toward half past twelve we had news of the King, and immediately after Madame de Bourgogne came out of the little cabinet with the Duke, who seemed more touched than when I first saw him. The Princess took her scarf and her coifs from the toilet, standing with a deliberate air, her eyes scarcely wet—a fact betrayed by inquisitive glances cast rapidly to the right and left—and, followed only by her ladies, went to her coach by the great staircase.

I took the opportunity to go to the Duchesse d'Orléans, where I found many people. Their presence made me very impatient; the Duchess, who was equally impatient, took a light and went in. I whispered in the ear of the Duchesse de Villeroy, who thought as I thought of this event. She nudged me, and said in a very low voice that I must contain myself. I was smothered with silence, amid the complaints and the narrative surprises of these ladies; but at last M. le Duc d'Orléans appeared at the door of his cabinet, and beckoned me to come to him.

I followed him into the cabinet where we were alone. What was my surprise, remembering the terms on which he was with Monseigneur, to see the tears streaming from his eyes.

"Sir!" exclaimed I, rising. He understood me at once; and answered in a broken voice, really crying: "You are right to be surprised—I am surprised myself; but such a spectacle touches. He was a man with whom I passed much of my life, and who treated me well when he was uninfluenced. I feel very well that my grief won't last long; in a few days I shall discover motives of joy; at present, blood, relationship, humanity, —all work; and my entrails are moved." I praised his sentiments, but repeated my surprise. He rose, thrust his head into a corner, and with his nose there, wept bitterly and sobbed, which if I had not seen I could not have believed.

After a little silence, however, I exhorted him to calm himself. I represented to him that, everybody knowing on what terms he had been with Monseigneur, he would be laughed at, as playing a part, if his eyes showed that he had been weeping. He did what he could to remove the marks of his tears, and we then went back into the other room.

The interview of the Duchesse de Bourgogne with the King had not been long. She met him in the avenue between the two stables, got down, and went to the door of the carriage. Madame de Maintenon cried out, "Where are you going? We bear the plague about with us." I do not know what the King said or did. The Princess returned to her carriage, and came back to Versailles, bringing in reality the first news of the actual death of Monseigneur.

Acting upon the advice of M. de Beauvilliers, all the company had gone into the *salon*. The two Princes, Monseigneur de Bourgogne and M. de Berry, were there, seated on one sofa, their Princesses at their side; all the rest of the company were scattered about in confusion, seated or standing, some of the ladies being on the floor, near the sofa. There could be no doubt of what had happened. It was plainly written on every face in the chamber and throughout the apartment. Monseigneur was no more: it was known: it was spoken of: constraint with respect to him no longer existed. Amid the surprise, the confusion, and the movements that prevailed, the sentiments of all were painted to the life in looks and gestures.

In the outside rooms were heard the constrained groans and sighs of the valets—grieving for the master they had lost as well as for the master that had succeeded. Farther on began the crowd of courtiers of all kinds. The greater number—that is to say the fools—pumped up sighs as well as they could, and with wandering but dry eyes, sung the praises of Monseigneur—insisting especially on his goodness. They pitied the King for the loss of so good a son. The keener began already to be uneasy about the health of the King; and admired themselves for preserving so much judgment amid so much trouble, which could be perceived by the frequency of their repetitions. Others, really afflicted —the discomfited Cabal—wept bitterly, and kept themselves under with an effort as easy to notice as sobs. The most strong-minded or the wisest, with eyes fixed on the ground, in corners, meditated on the consequences of such an event—and especially on their own interests. Few words passed in conversation—here and there an exclamation wrung from grief was answered by some neighboring grief—a word every quarter of an hour—somber and haggard eyes—movements quite involuntary of the hands—immobility of all other parts of the body. Those who already looked upon the event as favorable in vain exaggerated their gravity so as to make it resemble chagrin and severity; the veil over their faces was transparent and hid not a single feature. They remained as motionless as those who grieved most, fearing opinion, curiosity, their own satisfaction, their every movement; but their eyes made up for their immobility. Indeed they could not refrain from repeatedly changing their attitude like people ill at ease, sitting or standing, from avoiding each other too carefully, even from allowing their eyes to meet—nor repress a manifest air of liberty—nor conceal their increased liveliness—nor put out a sort of brilliancy which distinguished them in spite of themselves.

The two princes, and the two princesses who sat by their sides, were more exposed to view than any other. The Duc de Bourgogne wept with tenderness, sincerity, and gentleness, the tears of nature, of religion, and of patience. M. le Duc de Berry also sincerely shed abundance of tears, but bloody tears, so to speak, so great appeared their bitterness; and he uttered not only sobs, but cries, nay, even yells. He was silent sometimes, but from suffocation, and then would burst out again with such a noise, such a trumpet sound of despair, that the majority present burst out also at these dolorous repetitions, either impelled by affliction or decorum. He became so bad, in fact, that his people were forced to undress him then and there, put him to bed, and call in the doctor. Madame la Duchesse de Berry was beside herself, and we shall soon see why. The most bitter despair was painted with horror on her face. There was seen written, as it were, a sort of furious grief, based on interest, not affection; now and then came dry lulls deep and sullen, then a torrent of tears and involuntary gestures, yet restrained, which showed extreme bitterness of mind, fruit of the profound meditation that had preceded. Often aroused by the cries of her husband, prompt to assist him, to support him, to embrace him, to give her smelling bottle, her care for him was evident; but soon came another profound reverie—then a gush of tears assisted to suppress her cries. As for Madame la Duchesse de Bourgogne, she consoled her husband with less trouble than she had to appear herself in want of consolation. Without attempting to play a part, it was evident that she did her best to acquit herself of a pressing duty of decorum. But she found extreme difficulty in keeping up appearances. When the Prince her brother-in-law howled, she blew her nose. She had brought some tears along with her and kept them up with care; and these combined with the art of the handkerchief, enabled her to redden her eyes, and make them swell, and smudge her face; but her glances often wandered on the sly to the countenances of all present.

Madame arrived, in full dress she knew not why, and howling she knew not why, inundated everybody with her tears in embracing them, making the *château* echo with renewed cries, and furnished the odd spectacle of a princess putting on her robes of ceremony in the dead of night to come and cry among a crowd of women with but little on except their nightdresses,—almost as masqueraders.

In the gallery several ladies, Madame la Duchesse d'Orléans, Madame de Castries, and Madame de Saint-Simon among the rest, finding no one close by, drew near each other by the side of a tent bedstead, and began to open their hearts to each other, which they did with the more freedom, inasmuch as they had but one sentiment in common upon what had occurred. In this gallery, and in the *salon*, there were always during the night several beds in which, for security's sake, certain Swiss guards and servants slept. These beds had been put in their usual place this evening before the bad news came from Meudon. In the midst of the conversation of the ladies, Madame de Castries touched the bed, felt something move, and was much terrified. A moment after they saw a sturdy arm, nearly naked, raise on a sudden the curtains, and thus show them a great brawny Swiss under the sheets, half awake, and wholly amazed. The fellow was a long time in making out his position, fixing his eyes upon every face one after the other; but at last, not judging it advisable to get up in the midst of such a grand company, he reburied himself in his bed, and closed the curtains. Apparently the good man had gone to bed before anything had been known, and had slept so soundly ever since that he had not been aroused until then. The saddest sights have often the most ridiculous contrasts. This caused some of the ladies to laugh, and made Madame d'Orléans fear lest the conversation should have been overheard. But after reflection, the sleep and the stupidity of the sleeper reassured her.

I had some doubts yet as to the event that had taken place; for I did not like to abandon myself to belief, until the word was pronounced by some one in whom I could have faith. By chance I met D'O, and I asked him. He answered me clearly that Monseigneur was no more. Thus answered, I tried not to be glad. I know not if I succeeded well, but at least it is certain, that neither joy nor sorrow blunted my cruriosity, and that while taking due care to preserve all decorum, I did not consider myself in any way forced to play the doleful. I no longer feared any fresh attack from the citadel of Meudon, nor any cruel charges from its implacable garrison. I felt, therefore, under no constraint, and followed every face with my glances, and tried to scrutinize them unobserved. It must be admitted, that for him who is well acquainted with the privacies of a Court, the first sight of rare events of this nature, so interesting in so many different respects, is extremely satisfactory. Every countenance recalls the cares, the intrigues, the labors employed in the advancement of fortunes—in the overthrow of rivals; the relations, the coldness, the hatreds, the evil offices done, the baseness of all; hope, despair, rage, satisfaction, express themselves in the features. See how all eyes wander to and fro examining what passes around—how some are astonished to find others more mean, or less mean than was expected! Thus this spectacle produced a pleasure, which, hollow as it may be, is one of the greatest a Court can bestow.

The turmoil in this vast apartment lasted about an hour; at the end of which M. de Beauvilliers thought it was high time to deliver the Princes of their company. The rooms were cleared. M. le Duc de Berry went away to his rooms, partly supported by his wife. All through the night he asked, amid tears and cries, for news from Meudon; he would not understand the cause of the King's departure to Marly. When at length the mournful curtain was drawn from before his eyes, the state he fell into cannot be described. The night of Monseigneur and Madame de Bourgogne was more tranquil. Some one having said to the Princess, that having no real cause to be affected, it would be terrible to play a part, she replied, quite naturally, that without feigning, pity touched her and decorum controlled her; and indeed she kept herself within these bounds with truth and decency. Their chamber, in which they invited several ladies to pass the night in armchairs, became immediately a palace of Morpheus. All quietly fell asleep. The curtains were left open, so that the Prince and Princess could be seen sleeping profoundly. They woke up once or twice for a moment. In the morning the Duke and Duchess rose early, their tears quite dried up. They shed no more for this cause, except on special and rare occasions. The ladies who had watched and slept in their chamber, told their friends how tranquil the night had been. But nobody was surprised, and as there was no longer a Monseigneur, nobody was scandalized. Madame de Saint-Simon and I remained up two hours before going to bed, and then went there without feeling any want of rest. In fact, I slept so little that at seven in the morning I was up; but it must be admitted that such restlessness is sweet, and such reawakenings are savory.

Horror reigned at Meudon. As soon as the King left, all the courtiers left also, crowding into the first carriages that came. In an instant Meudon was empty. Mademoiselle Choin remained alone in her garret, and unaware of what had taken place. She learned it only by the cry raised. Nobody thought of telling her. At last some friends went up to her, hurried her into a hired coach, and took her to Paris. The dispersion was general. One or two valets, at the most, remained near the body. La Vrillière, to his praise be it said, was the only courtier who, not having abandoned Monseigneur during life, did not abandon him after his death. He had some difficulty to find somebody to go in search of Capuchins to pray over the corpse. The decomposition became so rapid and so great, that the opening of windows was not enough; the Capuchins, La Vrillière, and the valets, were compelled to pass the night outside.

## EDMOND AND JULES DE GONCOURT

# From the *Journals*

### 1855

*January.*—I ran onto a mistress I had had during my last year in school. I remember having desired her very much and loved her a little, and I can still see her in that tiny flat in the rue d'Isly at noon, with the sun streaming in and settling itself down like a bird. I would open the door, mornings, when the water carrier arrived. She would go down the street in a little bonnet to buy two cutlets for us and would put on her petticoat before she cooked them; and we would lunch off one end of the table out of the electro-plate utensil and drink out of the same glass. There were still girls like her in those days, girls with a little of the *grisette* left under their cashmere shawls.

I met her again. She was still the same girl, with the eyes I had loved, her little nose, her lips flat as if crushed by kisses, her supple figure. And yet she was not the same. The pretty girl was not on the town any more; she was living respectably, conjugally, with a photographer. Housewifery had left its mark on her. The shadow of the savings bank lay on her forehead. She mends linen now, looks after her kitchen, scolds her servant like a legitimate spouse, and is studying English and the piano. She frequents only married women and is ambitious to be married herself. She has buried her Bohemian existence in the cooking pot. Her lover, an American named Peterson, whose blood was bothering him and who took a mistress only because it was doctor's orders, drags her to a café every evening and there, by way of amusement, he plays dominoes with her, surrounded night after night by the same faces of his compatriots.

This man, who is stolidity and ponderation incarnate, emerges from his imperturbability only over dominoes, and then not in a café but in bed. They go to bed. Just as she is dozing off she feels her American stirring and rumbling indistinctly; soon he flies into a passion over the mistakes she made, her lack of concentration, her flighty French brain. She succeeds in dropping off to sleep, nevertheless, but after a half-hour or an hour of furious silence during which he is eating himself up, the American shakes her awake in order to say to her, "If you had put down the five-three instead of the two-three we would have won." And with that he goes back over the whole game.

## 1857

*August 23.*—Murger told us the funeral oration pronounced over Planche by Buloz, editor of the *Revue des Deux Mondes*: "I had as lief have lost 20,000 francs."

## 1859

*January 27.*—This morning Scholl said to me something amusing about Barrière: "Yes, yes, he has talent; but he doesn't know how to make people forgive him for having it."

*Undated.*—Nothing is more charming, more exquisite, than the French wit of certain foreigners—the wit of Galiani, of the Prince de Ligne, of Heine.

## 1861

*Sunday, April 18.*—Flaubert told us today that before taking *Madame Bovary* to Lévy, he had offered it to Jacottet, of the Librairie Nouvelle. "Your book is very good," Jacottet said; "it is *chiselled;* but of course you cannot aspire to the success of Amédée Achard, who has two books with me now; and I cannot contract to publish you this year." Flaubert was raging: "It's *chiselled!* What a piece of insolence on the part of a publisher! I don't mind a publisher exploiting an author; but he has no right to express a literary judgment. I have always been grateful to Lévy for the fact that he has never said a word to me about my book."

## 1862

*Friday, February 21.*—We dined with Flaubert at the Charles Edmonds'. Conversation turned upon his love affair with Mme Colet, and her novel about Flaubert and herself, *Elle et lui.* There was no bitterness, no remains of resentment in him, as he spoke of her. Apparently she had intoxicated him with her insane and furious love. There is a truculence of nature in Flaubert that takes pleasure in passionate, high-strung women and probably wears love out by its gross emotions, its harsh transports, and its violent frenzies.

One day she pursued him to his mother's house and demanded an explanation in the presence of his mother. It appears that his mother had always felt that her son's harshness towards his mistress was in some way an injury done to all womankind. "It was the only cloud between my mother and me," Flaubert said. He confessed, nevertheless, that he had loved Mme Colet madly, to the point, one day, of wanting to kill her; and as he rushed upon her there came into his mind an hallucinating vision of himself prosecuted. "I could hear the creaking of the chair in the dock in which I sat." •

*Undated.* —C— found himself at supper with R— at the Maison d'Or. The whim took them suddenly not to sup by themselves. One of them, after having run in vain, went out and leant over the staircase to send the doorman to look for some of their friends. He found the man deep in a book and was sufficiently curious to ask what he was reading. "I am reading what His Grace told me to read," the big blond fellow said with a simple air.

"Whose Grace?"

"His Grace the Bishop of Nancy, from where I come. He said to me: 'You are going to Paris. It is a place of perdition. Read Tertullian.' And I am reading Tertullian."

It was true: the man was reading a Father of the Church in the staircase of the Maison d'Or, between errands to the house of that beautiful lady, La Farcy. The imagination of man can never match the incredible and antithetical strangeness of life.

*Monday, March 3.*—A very light snowfall. We took a cab to Théophile Gautier's. . . . We asked if we were disturbing him, to which he answered, "Not at all. I never work at home. I can only work at *Le Moniteur*, in the printing shop. They print as I write. The only thing that sets me going is the smell of printer's ink. And then, there is the law of pressure. That is inescapable. I am bound to deliver my copy. Yes, that's the only place where I can work. If I were to write a novel now, I could only write it there, where they would set it up ten lines at a go while I wrote. Looking at a proof sheet, one can judge one's work. What one has written becomes impersonal. A manuscript, now, is yourself, it's your hand, it clings to you by certain filaments, it is not detached from you. All my life I have had places arranged for me to work in, and I have never been able to work in them. I need action round me. I work well when there is an orgy going on about me; whereas if I shut myself up to write, the solitude depresses me. One might be able to work pretty well in a servant's garret, at a deal table, with cheap white paper and a pot so that one wouldn't have to go down into the courtyard from time to time."

Then he began to criticize Gounod's *Reine de Saba*, and as we confessed ourselves completely deaf to music, unless it be perhaps a military band, he exclaimed: "I am glad to hear you say that. I am the same way. I prefer silence to music. Having lived part of my life with a singer, I finally learnt to tell good music from bad; but I don't really care which is which. It's interesting, you know, that all the writers of my time are like that. Balzac execrated music, and Hugo cannot bear it. Lamartine himself, who is a human piano for sale or for hire, had a horror of it. Nobody cares for it but a few painters. Composers nowadays have reached a deadly stage of Gluckism, writing things that are broad, slow, slow. . . . They're going back to plain chant. That Gounod is a complete ass.* In the second act there are two choruses of Israelites and Sabaeans chattering beside a pool before washing their bottoms. A very nice chorus, I grant you; but that's all. And the whole house sighs, and there is a general *ah-h-h!* of relief, so dull is the rest of the opera. Verdi: ask me what Verdi is. Verdi is a Dennery, a Guilbert de Pixerécourt. Do you want to know what his musical ideas are? When the words are sad, he goes *troo, troo, troo;* when they are gay he sings *tra, tra, tra.* He would never have a piccolo in a funeral march. Now, Rossini would. He's the fellow who, in *Semiramide*, brings on the shade of Ninus to the air of a ravishing waltz. And there you have the whole of Verdi's musical genius."

With which Gautier began to complain of our times. "It may be because I am beginning to be an old man; but there's no air in our times. It isn't enough to have wings: you have to have air. I do not feel contemporary. In 1830, yes, it was superb; but I was two or three years too young. I was not borne along in midstream. I wasn't ripe. I should have written other things."

Finally we talked about Flaubert, about his methods, his patience, his seven years spent on a single book of four hundred pages. "Imagine!" exclaimed Gautier. "The other day Flaubert said to me: 'It's finished. I have only ten more pages to write. But I have already got the ends of the sentences.' You see? He already had the music of the ends of the sentences which he hadn't yet begun. He had his ends. Isn't that funny? Eh! What? Now, for my part, I believe that what you need most of all in a sentence is *ocular rhythm.* For example, a sentence that is very long in getting started should not end thinly, abruptly—except for deliberate effect. And then, often Flaubert's rhythms are audible to him alone; they escape the rest of us. A book is not written to be read

* My brother and I sought to depict our contemporaries essentially as human beings and tried to report their conversation in the picturesqueness of its verity. The characteristic quality, I may say the beauty, of Gautier's conversation resided in his fantastic paradoxes. To take this absolute negation of music, this grossly abusive banter, for the true feeling of the illustrious writer about M. Gounod would be to prove oneself either unintelligent or very hostile to the stenographer of this antimusical outburst.—E. de G.

aloud, but he bawls his aloud to himself. There are bawlings in his sentences which seem to him harmonious, but that you have to be able to read the way he does if you are to get that bawling effect. We both have pages, you in your *Venice* and I in a lot of things everybody knows, that are as rhythmical as anything he has written, and they have cost us much less effort.

"You know, the poor fellow has one remorse that is poisoning his life. It is going to put him in the grave. You don't know what that remorse is. It's that, in *Madame Bovary*, he stuck two genitives one right on top of the other: *Une couronne de fleurs d'oranger*. It made him miserable; but there was not a thing he could do about it, try as he did. Do you want to see the house?"

## 1863

*Undated.*—A very fine remark of old Rothschild's pronounced the other day at Walewski's. Calvet-Rogniat having asked him why Consols had gone down the day before, he answered: "Do I know why stocks go up or down? If I knew that I should be a rich man."

*September 14.*—Magny dinner. . . . Sainte-Beuve left early, the rest of us sitting and drinking the mixture of rum and curaçao he always brews for these dinners.

"By the way, Gautier; you are just back from Madame Sand's, at Nohant. Did you find it amusing?"

"As funny as a monastery of Moravian brethren. I arrived late in the day. The house is far from the railway station. They left my box in a bush. I reached the house by way of the farms, followed by dogs that frightened me. They gave me dinner. The food was good, but there was too much game and chicken. I don't like it. Marchal, the painter, was there, and Madame Calamatta, and Alexandre Dumas the younger."

"What kind of life do they lead at Nohan?"

"You breakfast at ten o'clock. On the last stroke, when the hand is exactly on the hour, everybody sits down. Madame Sand arrives with the air of a somnambulist and remains asleep throughout the meal. After breakfast, you go out into the garden. There you play at bowls, for it wakes her up. She sits down and begins to chat. There is general conversation, at that hour, about pronunciation: for example, comparison of *d'ailleurs* and *meilleur*. The talk is wildly gay, I must tell you, and the jokes are stercoraceous."

"How awful!"

"However, not one word about the relations between the sexes. I believe you would be thrown out of the house if you made the slightest allusion to sex. At three o'clock Madame Sand goes upstairs to grind out copy until six. Then you dine; but you dine a little hurriedly so that there may be time for Marie Caillot to dine. She is the servant in the house, a little Fadette that Madame Sand found thereabouts to act in the theatre she has on the place. Marie Caillot joins you afterwards in the drawing room.

"After dinner Madame Sand plays patience without uttering a word, until midnight. On the second day, I want to tell you, I said that if there was no talk about literature I was going to leave. Ah, literature! . . . It seemed to bring them back from another world. I forgot to tell you that the great preoccupation of the moment is mineralogy. Each person has his hammer and never goes out of doors without it. So, I declared that Jean Jacques Rousseau was incomparably the worst writer in all French literature, and that set off an argument with Madame Sand which lasted until one in the morning.

"There is no gainsaying that Manceau did a good job at Nohant, so far as copy goes. Madame Sand cannot sit down in a room without pens springing up, and blue ink, and cigarette papers, and Turkish tobacco, and striped note paper. She certainly uses it. You've heard that she goes back to work at midnight and works until four in the morning. Let me tell you what happened to her. Something fantastic. One day she finished a novel at one o'clock in the morning . . . and immediately started another. Turning out copy is a natural function with Madame Sand.

"On the whole, she does you very well. The service, for instance, is absolutely soundless. In the vestibule there is a box with two compartments: one for letters intended for the post, the other for letters intended for the household. If you want anything, you write for it and sign your name, indicating where your room is. I needed a comb. I wrote: 'Monsieur Gautier, such-and-such a room' and what I wanted. The next morning at six o'clock there were thirty combs for me to choose from."

## 1864

*March 14.*—Magny dinner. . . . [Gautier] spoke of the profund tedium in which he lived; of the perpetual plaguing of the two selves within him, one of them saying, when his evening clothes are laid out: "Go to bed. What do you want to go there for?" and the other, once he has got to bed, saying: "You ought to have gone. You would have had such a good time."

## 1865

*Undated.*—I was wondering how justice came to be in the world when, walking by the river, I saw a group of children at play. The biggest boy was saying:

"Let's organize a law court. I'll be the court."

## 1866

*Undated.*—That which, perhaps, hears more silly remarks than anything else in the world, is a picture in a museum.

## 1867

*January 2.*—Dined at the princess's with Gautier, Octave Feuillet and Amédée Achard, a wilted man of fashion, a mind without emphasis, an expressionless voice—the archetype of nonentity.

Ponsard pulled to pieces by Gautier and ourselves, the princess arguing against us. When we had finished, someone asked Gautier why he did not write the things he had just said. "Let me tell you a little story," Gautier replied with perfect self-possession. "One day, Monsieur Walewski told me that I was to stop being indulgent to writers, I had his authority to write exactly what I thought of all the plays produced. 'But,' said I, 'it is So-and-so's play that is opening this week.' 'Indeed?' said he. 'In that case, suppose you begin the week following.' Well, I am still waiting for the week following."

*February 3.*—They say that during one of Ollivier's interviews with the emperor, the emperor asked him to tell him very frankly what people were saying about him; to speak as if he were not addressing his sovereign. Ollivier having said finally that people thought his faculties were declining, the emperor remarked impassively, "That is consistent with the reports that have reached me."

The story is like him, and in his impersonality he attains a certain grandeur.

*Undated.*—There are two great currents in the history of humanity: baseness, which makes conservatives; and envy, which makes revolutionaries.

## 1868

*January 3.*—La Païva dislikes a grate fire. She came into her drawing room dripping with emeralds all over the flesh of her shoulders and arms. "I am still a little blue with cold. My maid has just done my hair with the windows wide open," she said. Out of doors it was snowing, and the night was so cold that, coming here, we shivered for the ill-clad poor of Paris. This woman is not built like the rest of humanity. She lives in icy air and water like a kind of boreal dragon in a Scandinavian myth.

At table she developed a theory of will power that was frightening, saying that everything was the result of the exercise of the will, that there were no circumstances, that one created one's own circumstances, that people who were unfortunate were so because they wanted to be so. And when Taine—dining with her for the first time—corroborated her thesis by a little speech on the power of concentration, citing Newton as usual and saying that the great physicist used to concentrate so fixedly that in his periods of meditation he seemed like an idiot, La Païva spoke of a woman who, to accomplish a certain unrevealed purpose, cut herself off from the world and lived three years alone, scarcely eating a morsel and having to be reminded of food, walled up within herself and given over wholly to the plan she was developing. And, after a moment of silence, La Païva added, "I was that woman."

*April 5.*—"A woman who has never been pretty has never been young." I read this in a book picked up by chance in a lending library; and read, written in the margin in a woman's hand, "How sadly true!"

*October 29.*—The English are sharpers as a nation and honest as individuals; the French are honest as a nation and sharpers as individuals.

# WILLIAM CONGREVE

# *The Way of the World*

TO THE RIGHT HONOURABLE

## RALPH, EARL OF MOUNTAGUE, &c.

My Lord,—Whether the world will arraign me of vanity, or not, that I have presumed to dedicate this comedy to your lordship, I am yet in doubt: though it may be it is some degree of vanity even to doubt of it. One who has at any time had the honour of your lordship's conversation, cannot be supposed to think very meanly of that which he would prefer to your perusal: yet it were to incur the imputation of too much sufficiency, to pretend to such a merit as might abide the test of your lordship's censure.

Whatever value may be wanting to this play while yet it is mine, will be sufficiently made up to it, when it is once become your lordship's; and it is my security, that I cannot have overrated it more by my dedication, than your lordship will dignifie it by your patronage.

That it succeeded on the stage, was almost beyond my expectation; for but little of it was prepared for that general taste which seems now to be predominant in the pallats of our audience.

Those characters which are meant to be ridiculed in most of our comedies, are of fools so gross, that in my humble opinion, they should rather disturb than divert the well-natured and reflecting part of an audience; they are rather objects of charity than contempt; and instead of moving our mirth, they ought very often to excite our compassion.

This reflection moved me to design some characters, which should appear ridiculous not so much through a natural folly (which is incorrigible, and therefore not proper for the stage) as through an affected wit; a wit, which at the same time that it is affected, is also false. As there is some difficulty in the formation of a character of this nature, so there is some hazard which attends the progress of its success, upon the stage: for many come to a play, so over-charged with criticism, that they very often let fly their censure, when through their rashness they have mistaken their aim. This I had occasion lately to observe: for this play had been acted two or three days, before some of these hasty judges could find the leisure to distinguish betwixt the character of a Witwoud and a Truewit.

I must beg your lordship's pardon for this digression from the true course of this epistle; but that it may not seem altogether impertinent, I beg, that I may plead the occasion of it, in part of that excuse of which I stand in need, for recommending this comedy to your protection. It is only by the countenance of your lordship, and the *few* so qualified, that such who write with care and pains can hope to be distinguished: for the prostituted name of *poet* promiscuously levels all that bear it.

Terence, the most correct writer in the world, had a Scipio and a Lelius, if not to assist him, at least to support him in his reputation: and notwithstanding his extraordinary merit, it may be, their countenance was not more than necessary.

The purity of his stile, the delicacy of his turns, and the justness of his characters, were all of them beauties, which the greater part of his audience were incapable of tasting: some of the coursest strokes of Plautus, so severely censured by Horace, were more likely to affect the multitude; such, who come with expectation to laugh at the last act of a play, and are better entertained with two or three unseasonable jests, than with the artful solution of the fable.

As Terence excelled in his performances, so had he great advantages to encourage his undertakings; for he built most on the foundations of Menander: his plots were generally modelled, and his characters ready drawn to his hand. He copied Menander; and Menander had no less light in the formation of his characters, from the observations of Theophrastus, of whom he was a disciple; and Theophrastus it is known was not only the disciple, but the immediate successor of Aristotle, the first and greatest judge of poetry. These were great models to design by; and the further advantage which Terence possessed, towards giving his plays the due ornaments of purity of style and justness of manners, was not less considerable, from the freedom of conversation, which was permitted him with Lelius and Scipio, two of the greatest and most polite men of his age. And indeed, the privilege of such a conversation is the only certain means of attaining to the perfection of dialogue.

If it has happened in any part of this comedy, that I have gained a turn of style, or expression more correct, or at least more corrigible than in those which I have formerly written, I must, with equal pride and gratitude, ascribe it to the honour of your lordship's admitting me into your conversation, and that of a society where everybody else was so well worthy of you, in your retirement last summer from the town: for it was immediately after, that this comedy was written. If I have failed in my performance, it is only to be regretted, where there were so many, not inferior either to a Scipio or a Lelius, that there should be one wanting, equal in capacity to a Terence.

If I am not mistaken, poetry is almost the only art which has not yet laid claim to your lordship's patronage. Architecture and painting, to the great honour of our country, have flourished under your influence and protection. In the meantime, poetry, the eldest sister of all arts, and parent of most, seems to have resigned her birthright, by having neglected to pay her duty to your lordship; and by permitting others of a later extraction to prepossess that place in your esteem, to which none can pretend a better title. Poetry, in its nature, is sacred to the good and great; the relation between them is reciprocal, and they are ever propitious to it. It is the privilege of poetry to address to them, and it is their prerogative alone to give it protection.

This received maxim is a general apology for all writers who consecrate their labours to great men: but I could wish, at this time, that this address were exempted from the common pretence of all dedications; and that as I can distinguish your lordship even among the most deserving, so this offering might become remarkable by some particular instance of respect, which should assure your lordship that I am, with all due sense of your extream worthiness and humanity, my lord, your lordship's most obedient and most obliged humble servant,

WILL. CONGREVE

## DRAMATIS PERSONÆ

| | |
|---|---|
| FAINALL, in love with Mrs. Marwood | Mr. BETTERTON. |
| MIRABELL, in love with Mrs. Millamant | Mr. VERBRUGGEN. |
| WITWOUD } Followers of Mrs. Millamant | Mr. BOWEN. |
| PETULANT } Followers of Mrs. Millamant | Mr. BOWMAN. |
| Sir WILFULL WITWOUD, Half-brother to Witwoud, and Nephew to Lady Wishfort | Mr. UNDERHILL. |
| WAITWELL, Servant to Mirabell | Mr. BRIGHT. |
| Lady WISHFORT, Enemy to Mirabell, for having falsely pretended love to her | Mrs. LEIGH. |
| Mrs. MILLAMANT, a fine lady, Niece to Lady Wishfort, and loves Mirabell | Mrs. BRACEGIRDLE. |
| Mrs. MARWOOD, Friend to Mr. Fainall, and likes Mirabell | Mrs. BARRY. |
| Mrs. FAINALL, Daughter to Lady Wishfort, and wife to Fainall, formerly friend to Mirabell | Mrs. BOWMAN. |
| FOIBLE, Woman to Lady Wishfort | Mrs. WILLIS. |
| MINCING, Woman to Mrs. Millamant | Mrs. PRINCE. |

Dancers, Footmen, and Attendants.

SCENE—LONDON.

*The time equal to that of the presentation.*

## PROLOGUE

SPOKEN BY MR. BETTERTON

OF those few fools, who with ill stars are curst,
Sure scribling fools, called poets, fare the worst:
For they're a sort of fools which Fortune makes,
And after she has made 'em fools, forsakes.
With Nature's oafs 'tis quite a diff'rent case,
For Fortune favours all her Idiot-race:
In her own nest the Cuckow-eggs we find,
O'er which she broods to hatch the Changling-kind.
No portion for her own she has to spare,

So much she doats on her adopted care.
  Poets are bubbles, by the town drawn in,
Suffered at first some trifling stakes to win:
But what unequal hazards do they run!
Each time they write they venture all they've won:
The squire that's buttered still, is sure to be undone.
This author, heretofore, has found your favour,
But pleads no merit from his past behaviour.
To build on that might prove a vain presumption,
Should grants to poets made, admit resumption:
And in Parnassus he must lose his seat,
If that be found a forfeited estate.
  He owns, with toil, he wrought the following scenes,
But if they're naught ne'er spare him for his pains:
Damn him the more; have no commiseration
For dulness on mature deliberation.
He swears he'll not resent one hissed-off scene,
Nor, like those peevish wits, his play maintain,
Who, to assert their sense, your taste arraign.
Some plot we think he has, and some new thought;
Some humour too, no farce; but that's a fault.
Satire, he thinks, you ought not to expect;
For so reformed a town, who dares correct?
To please, this time, has been his sole pretence,
He'll not instruct, lest it should give offence.
Should he by chance a knave or fool expose,
That hurts none here, sure here are none of those.
In short, our play shall (with your leave to shew it)
Give you one instance of a passive poet.
Who to your judgments yields all resignation;
So save or damn, after your own discretion.

## ACT I

SCENE I—*A Chocolate-house.* MIRABELL *and* FAINALL [*rising from Cards*], BETTY *waiting*

*Mira.* You are a fortunate man, Mr. Fainall.

*Fain.* Have we done?

*Mira.* What you please. I'll play on to entertain you.

*Fain.* No, I'll give you your revenge another time, when you are not so indifferent; you are thinking of something else now, and play too negligently; the coldness of a losing gamester lessens the pleasure of the winner. I'd no more play with a man that slighted his ill fortune, than I'd make love to a woman who undervalued the loss of her reputation.

*Mira.* You have a taste extreamly delicate, and are for refining on your pleasures.

*Fain.* Prithee, why so reserved? Something has put you out of humour.

*Mira.* Not at all: I happen to be grave to-day; and you are gay; that's all.

*Fain.* Confess, Millamant and you quarrelled last night, after I left you; my fair cousin has some humours that would tempt the patience of a Stoick. What, some coxcomb came in, and was well received by her, while you were by.

*Mira.* Witwoud and Petulant; and what was worse, her aunt, your wife's mother, my evil genius; or to sum up all in her own name, my old Lady Wishfort came in—

*Fain.* O there it is then—she has a lasting passion for you, and with reason.—What, then my wife was there?

*Mira.* Yes, and Mrs. Marwood and three or four more, whom I never saw before; seeing me, they all put on their grave faces, whispered one another, then complained aloud of the vapours, and after fell into a profound silence.

*Fain.* They had a mind to be rid of you.

*Mira.* For which reason I resolved not to stir. At last the good old lady broke through her painful taciturnity, with an invective against long visits. I would not have understood her, but Millamant joining in the argument, I rose and with a constrained smile told her I thought nothing was so easie as to know when a visit began to be troublesome; she redened and I withdrew, without expecting her reply.

*Fain.* You were to blame to resent what she spoke only in compliance with her aunt.

*Mira.* She is more mistress of herself, than to be under the necessity of such a resignation.

*Fain.* What? though half her fortune depends upon her marrying with my lady's approbation?

*Mira.* I was then in such a humour, that I should have been better pleased if she had been less discreet.

*Fain.* Now I remember, I wonder not they were weary of you; last night was one of their cabal-nights; they have 'em three times a week, and meet by turns, at one another's apartments, where they come together like the coroner's inquest, to sit upon the murdered reputations of the week. You and I are excluded; and it was once proposed that all the male sex should be excepted; but somebody moved that to avoid scandal there might be one man of the community; upon which motion Witwoud and Petulant were enrolled members.

*Mira.* And who may have been the foundress of this sect? My Lady Wishfort, I warrant, who publishes her detestation of mankind; and full of the vigour of fifty-five, declares for a friend and ratafia; and let posterity shift for itself, she'll breed no more.

*Fain.* The discovery of your sham addresses to her, to conceal your love to her neice, has provoked this separation: had you dissembled better, things might have continued in the state of nature.

*Mira.* I did as much as man could, with any reasonable conscience; I proceeded to the very last act of flattery with her, and was guilty of a song in her commendation. Nay, I got a friend to put her into a lampoon, and complement her with the imputation of an affair with a young fellow, which I carried so far, that I told her the malicious town took notice that she was grown fat of a sudden; and when she lay in of a dropsie, persuaded her she was reported to be in labour. The devil's in't, if an old woman is to be flattered further, unless a man should endeavour downright personally to debauch her; and that my vertue forbad me. But for the discovery of this amour, I am indebted to your friend, or your wife's friend, Mrs. Marwood.

*Fain.* What should provoke her to be your enemy, unless she has made you advances, which you have slighted? Women do not easily forgive omissions of that nature.

*Mira.* She was always civil to me, 'till of late; I confess I am not one of those coxcombs who are apt to interpret a woman's good manners to her prejudice; and think that she who does not refuse 'em everything, can refuse 'em nothing.

*Fain.* You are a gallant man, Mirabell; and though you may have cruelty enough, not to satisfie a lady's longing; you have too much generosity, not to be tender of her honour. Yet you speak with an indifference which seems to be affected; and confesses you are conscious of a negligence.

*Mira.* You pursue the argument with a distrust that seems to be unaffected, and confesses you are conscious of a concern for which the lady is more indebted to you, than is your wife.

*Fain.* Fie, fie, friend, if you grow censorious I must leave you;—I'll look upon the gamesters in the next room.

*Mira.* Who are they?

*Fain.* Petulant and Witwoud.—Bring me some chocolate.

*Mira.* Betty, what says your clock?

*Bet.* Turned of the last canonical hour, sir.

*Mira.* How pertinently the jade answers me! Ha! almost one a clock! [*Looking on his watch.*] O, y'are come—

## Scene II. mirabell *and* footman

*Mira.* Well, is the grand affair over? You have been something tedious.

*Serv.* Sir, there's such coupling at Pancras, that they stand behind one another, as 'twere in a country dance. Ours was the last couple to lead up; and no hopes appearing of dispatch, besides, the parson growing hoarse, we were afraid his lungs would have failed before it came to our turn; so we drove round to Duke's Place; and there they were riveted in a trice.

*Mira.* So, so, you are sure they are married.

*Serv.* Married and bedded, sir: I am witness.

*Mira.* Have you the certificate?

*Serv.* Here it is, sir.

*Mira.* Has the tailor brought Waitwell's cloaths home, and the new liveries?

*Serv.* Yes, sir.

*Mira.* That's well. Do you go home again, d'ye hear, and adjourn the consummation 'till farther order; bid Waitwell shake his ears, and Dame Partlet rustle up her feathers, and meet me at one a clock by Rosamond's Pond; that I may see her before she returns to her lady: and as you tender your ears be secret.

## Scene III. mirabell, fainall, betty

*Fain.* Joy of your success, Mirabell; you look pleased.

*Mira.* Ay; I have been engaged in a matter of some sort of mirth, which is not yet ripe for discovery. I am glad this is not a cabal-night. I wonder, Fainall, that you who are married, and of consequence should be discreet, will suffer your wife to be of such a party.

*Fain.* Faith, I am not jealous. Besides, most who are engaged are women and relations; and for the men, they are of a kind too contemptible to give scandal.

*Mira.* I am of another opinion. The greater the coxcomb, always the more the scandal: for a woman who is not a fool, can have but one reason for associating with a man who is one.

*Fain.* Are you jealous as often as you see Witwoud entertained by Millamant?

*Mira.* Of her understanding I am, if not of her person.

*Fain.* You do her wrong; for to give her her due, she has wit.

*Mira.* She has beauty enough to make any man think so; and complaisance enough not to contradict him who shall tell her so.

*Fain.* For a passionate lover, methinks you are a man somewhat too discerning in the failings of your mistress.

*Mira.* And for a discerning man, somewhat too passionate a lover; for I like her with all her faults; nay, like her for her faults. Her follies are so natural, or so artful, that they become her; and those affectations which in another woman would be odious, serve but to make her more agreeable. I'll tell thee, Fainall, she once used me with that insolence, that in revenge I took her to pieces; sifted her, and separated her failings; I studied 'em, and got 'em by rote. The catalogue was so large, that I was not without hopes, one day or other, to hate her heartily: to which end I so used myself to think of 'em, that at length, contrary to my design and expectation, they gave me every hour less and less disturbance; 'till in a few days it became habitual to me, to remember 'em without being displeased. They are now grown as familiar to me as my own frailties; and in all probability in a little time longer I shall like 'em as well.

*Fain.* Marry her, marry her; be half as well acquainted with her charms, as you are with her defects, and my life on't, you are your own man again.

*Mira.* Say you so?

*Fain.* I, I, I have experience: I have a wife, and so forth.

## SCENE IV. [*To them*] MESSENGER

*Mess.* Is one Squire Witwoud here?

*Bet.* Yes; what's your business?

*Mess.* I have a letter for him, from his brother, Sir Wilfull, which I am charged to deliver into his own hands.

*Bet.* He's in the next room, friend—that way.

## Scene V. mirabell, fainall, betty

*Mira.* What, is the chief of that noble family in town, Sir Wilfull Witwoud?

*Fain.* He is expected to-day. Do you know him?

*Mira.* I have seen him, he promises to be an extraordinary person; I think you have the honour to be related to him.

*Fain.* Yes; he is half-brother to this Witwoud by a former wife, who was sister to my Lady Wishfort, my wife's mother. If you marry Millamant, you must call cousins too.

*Mira.* I had rather be his relation than his acquaintance.

*Fain.* He comes to town in order to equip himself for travel.

*Mira.* For travel! Why the man that I mean is above forty.

*Fain.* No matter for that; 'tis for the honour of England, that all Europe should know we have blockheads of all ages.

*Mira.* I wonder there is not an act of parliament to save the credit of the nation, and prohibit the exportation of fools.

*Fain.* By no means, 'tis better as 'tis; 'tis better to trade with a little loss, than to be quite eaten up, with being overstocked.

*Mira.* Pray, are the follies of this knight-errant, and those of the squire his brother, anything related?

*Fain.* Not at all; Witwoud grows by the knight, like a medlar grafted on a crab. One will melt in your mouth, and t'other set your teeth on edge; one is all pulp, and the other all core.

*Mira.* So one will be rotten before he be ripe, and the other will be rotten without ever being ripe at all.

*Fain.* Sir Wilfull is an odd mixture of bashfulness and obstinacy.—But when he's drunk, he's as loving as the monster in the "Tempest;" and much after the same manner. To give t'other his due, he has something of good nature, and does not always want wit.

*Mira.* Not always; but as often as his memory fails him, and his commonplace of comparisons. He is a fool with a good memory, and some few scraps of other folks' wit. He is one whose conversation can never be approved, yet it is now and then to be endured. He has indeed one good quality, he is not exceptious; for he so passionately affects the reputation of understanding raillery, that he will construe an affront into a jest; and call downright rudeness and ill language, satire and fire.

*Fain.* If you have a mind to finish his picture, you have an opportunity to do it at full length. Behold the original.

## SCENE VI. [*To them*] WITWOUD

*Wit.* Afford me your compassion, my dears; pity me, Fainall, Mirabell, pity me.

*Mira.* I do from my soul.

*Fain.* Why, what's the matter?

*Wit.* No letters for me, Betty?

*Bet.* Did not a messenger bring you one but now, sir?

*Wit.* Ay, but no other?

*Bet.* No, sir.

*Wit.* That's hard, that's very hard;—a messenger, a mule, a beast of burden, he has brought me a letter from the fool my brother, as heavy as a panegyrick in a funeral sermon, or a copy of commendatory verses from one poet to another. And what's worse, 'tis as sure a forerunner of the author, as an epistle dedicatory.

*Mira.* A fool, and your brother, Witwoud!

*Wit.* Ay, ay, my half-brother. My half-brother he is, no nearer upon honour.

*Mira.* Then 'tis possible he may be but half a fool.

*Wit.* Good, good, Mirabell, *le drole!* Good, good, hang him, don't let's talk of him;—Fainall, how does your lady? Gad! I say anything in the world to get this fellow out of my head. I beg pardon that I should ask a man of pleasure, and the town, a question at once so foreign and domestick. But I talk like an old maid at a marriage, I don't know what I say: but she's the best woman in the world.

*Fain.* 'Tis well you don't know what you say, or else your commendation would go near to make me either vain or jealous.

*Wit.* No man in town lives well with a wife but Fainall. Your judgment, Mirabell?

*Mira.* You had better step and ask his wife, if you would be credibly informed.

*Wit.* Mirabell.

*Mira.* Ay.

*Wit.* My dear, I ask ten thousand pardons;—Gad I have forgot what I was going to say to you.

*Mira.* I thank you heartily, heartily.

*Wit.* No, but prithee excuse me,—my memory is such a memory.

*Mira.* Have a care of such apologies, Witwoud;—for I never knew a fool but he affected to complain, either of the spleen or his memory.

*Fain.* What have you done with Petulant?

*Wit.* He's reckoning his mony,—my mony it was—I have no luck to-day.

*Fain.* You may allow him to win of you at play;—for you are sure to be too hard for him at repartee: since you monopolise the wit that is between you, the fortune must be his of course.

*Mira.* I don't find that Petulant confesses the superiority of wit to be your talent, Witwoud.

*Wit.* Come, come, you are malicious now, and would breed debates —Petulant's my friend, and a very honest fellow, and a very pretty fellow, and has a smattering—faith and troth a pretty deal of an odd sort of a small wit: Nay, I'll do him justice. I'm his friend, I won't wrong him.—And if he had any judgment in the world,—he would not be altogether contemptible. Come, come, don't detract from the merits of my friend.

*Fain.* You don't take your friend to be over-nicely bred.

*Wit.* No, no, hang him, the rogue has no manners at all, that I must own—no more breeding than a bum-baily, that I grant you.—'Tis pity; the fellow has fire and life.

*Mira.* What, courage?

*Wit.* Hum, faith I don't know as to that,—I can't say as to that.—Yes, faith, in a controversie he'll contradict anybody.

*Mira.* Though 'twere a man whom he feared, or a woman whom he loved.

*Wit.* Well, well, he does not always think before he speaks;—We have all our failings; you are too hard upon him, you are, faith. Let me excuse him,—I can defend most of his faults, except one or two; one he has, that's the truth on't, if he were my brother, I could not acquit him —that indeed I could wish were otherwise.

*Mira.* Ay marry, what's that, Witwoud?

*Wit.* O pardon me—expose the infirmities of my friend.—No, my dear, excuse me there.

*Fain.* What I warrant he's unsincere, or 'tis some such trifle.

*Wit.* No, no, what if he be? 'Tis no matter for that, his wit will excuse that: a wit should no more be sincere, than a woman constant; one argues a decay of parts, as t'other of beauty.

*Mira.* Maybe you think him too positive?

*Wit.* No, no, his being positive is an incentive to argument, and keeps up conversation.

*Fain.* Too illiterate.

*Wit.* That! that's his happiness—his want of learning gives him the more opportunities to shew his natural parts.

*Mira.* He wants the words.

*Wit.* Ay; but I like him for that now; for his want of words gives me the pleasure very often to explain his meaning.

*Fain.* He's impudent.

*Wit.* No, that's not it.

*Mira.* Vain.

*Wit.* No.

*Mira.* What, he speaks unseasonable truths sometimes, because he has not wit enough to invent an evasion.

*Wit.* Truths! Ha, ha, ha! No, no, since you will have it,—I mean, he never speaks truth at all,—that's all. He will lie like a chambermaid, or a woman of quality's porter. Now that is a fault.

## SCENE VII. [*To them*] COACHMAN

*Coach.* Is Master Petulant here, mistress?

*Bet.* Yes.

*Coach.* Three gentlewomen in a coach would speak with him.

*Fain.* O brave Petulant, three!

*Bet.* I'll tell him.

*Coach.* You must bring two dishes of chocolate and a glass of cinnamon-water.

## SCENE VIII. MIRABELL, FAINALL, WITWOUD

*Wit.* That should be for two fasting strumpets, and a bawd troubled with wind. Now you may know what the three are.

*Mira.* You are very free with your friend's acquaintance.

*Wit.* Ay, ay, friendship without freedom is as dull as love without enjoyment, or wine without toasting; but to tell you a secret, these are trulls whom he allows coach-hire, and something more by the week, to call on him once a day at publick places.

*Mira.* How!

*Wit.* You shall see he won't go to 'em because there's no more company here to take notice of him—Why this is nothing to what he used to do;—before he found out this way, I have known him call for himself—

*Fain.* Call for himself? What dost thou mean?

*Wit.* Mean, why he would slip you out of this chocolate-house, just when you had been talking to him—as soon as your back was turned—whip he was gone;—then trip to his lodging, clap on a hood and scarf, and a mask, slap into a hackney-coach, and drive hither to the door again in a trice; where he would send in for himself, that I mean, call for himself, wait for himself, nay and what's more, not finding himself, sometimes leave a letter for himself.

*Mira.* I confess this is something extraordinary—I believe he waits for himself now, he is so long a coming; O I ask his pardon.

### Scene IX. PETULANT, MIRABELL, FAINALL, WITWOUD, BETTY

*Bet.* Sir, the coach stays.

*Pet.* Well, well; I come.—'Sbud a man had as good be a professed midwife, as a professed whoremaster, at this rate; to be knocked up and raised at all hours, and in all places. Pox on 'em, I won't come—D'ye hear, tell 'em I won't come.—Let 'em snivel and cry their hearts out.

*Fain.* You are very cruel, Petulant.

*Pet.* All's one, let it pass—I have a humour to be cruel.

*Mira.* I hope they are not persons of condition that you use at this rate.

*Pet.* Condition, condition's a dried fig, if I am not in humour.—By this hand, if they were your—a—a—your what-dee-call-'ems themselves, they must wait or rub off, if I want appetite.

*Mira.* What-dee-call-'ems! What are they, Witwoud?

*Wit.* Empresses, my dear—by your what-dee-call-'ems he means sultana queens.

*Pet.* Ay, Roxolana's.

*Mira.* Cry you mercy.

*Fain.* Witwoud says they are—

*Pet.* What does he say th'are?

*Wit.* I; fine ladies I say.

*Pet.* Pass on, Witwoud—Harkee, by this light his relations—two coheiresses his cousins, and an old aunt, who loves catter-wauling better than a conventicle.

*Wit.* Ha, ha, ha; I had a mind to see how the rogue would come off. —Ha, ha, ha; Gad I can't be angry with him, if he had said they were my mother and my sisters.

*Mira.* No!

*Wit.* No; the rogue's wit and readiness of invention charm me, dear Petulant.

*Bet.* They are gone, sir, in great anger.

*Pet.* Enough, let 'em trundel. Anger helps complexion, saves paint.

*Fain.* This continence is all dissembled; this is in order to have something to brag of the next time he makes court to Millamant, and swear he has abandoned the whole sex for her sake.

*Mira.* Have you not left off your impudent pretensions there yet? I shall cut your throat, sometime or other, Petulant, about that business.

*Pet.* Ay, ay, let that pass—there are other throats to be cut.—

*Mira.* Meaning mine, sir?

*Pet.* Not I—I mean nobody—I know nothing.—But there are uncles and nephews in the world—and they may be rivals—What then? All's one for that—

*Mira.* How! Harkee, Petulant, come hither—Explain, or I shall call your interpreter.

*Pet.* Explain; I know nothing.—Why you have an uncle, have you not, lately come to town, and lodges by my Lady Wishfort's?

*Mira.* True.

*Pet.* Why that's enough—you and he are not friends; and if he should marry and have a child, you may be disinherited, ha?

*Mira.* Where hast thou stumbled upon all this truth?

*Pet.* All's one for that; why then say I know something.

*Mira.* Come, thou art an honest fellow, Petulant, and shalt make love to my mistress, thou shalt, faith. What hast thou heard of my uncle?

*Pet.* I, nothing I. If throats are to be cut, let swords clash; snug's the word, I shrug and am silent.

*Mira.* O raillery, raillery. Come, I know thou art in the women's secrets.—What you're a cabalist, I know you staid at Millamant's last night, after I went. Was there any mention made of my uncle or me? Tell me; if thou hadst but good nature equal to thy wit, Petulant, Tony Witwoud, who is now thy competitor in fame, would shew as dim by thee as a dead whiting's eye by a pearl of Orient; he would no more be seen by thee, than Mercury is by the sun: Come, I'm sure thou wo't tell me.

*Pet.* If I do, will you grant me common sense then, for the future?

*Mira.* Faith I'll do what I can for thee, and I'll pray that Heaven may grant it thee in the meantime.

*Pet.* Well, harkee.

*Fain.* Petulant and you both will find Mirabell as warm a rival as a lover.

*Wit.* Pshaw, pshaw, that she laughs at Petulant is plain. And for my part—but that it is almost a fashion to admire her, I should—harkee—to tell you a secret, but let it go no further—between friends, I shall never break my heart for her.

*Fain.* How!

*Wit.* She's handsome; but she's a sort of an uncertain woman.

*Fain.* I thought you had died for her.

*Wit.* Umh—no—

*Fain.* She has wit.

*Wit.* 'Tis what she will hardly allow anybody else—Now, demme, I should hate that, if she were as handsome as Cleopatra. Mirabell is not so sure of her as he thinks for.

*Fain.* Why do you think so?

*Wit.* We staid pretty late there last night; and heard something of an uncle to Mirabell, who is lately come to town,—and is between him and the best part of his estate; Mirabell and he are at some distance, as my Lady Wishfort has been told; and you know she hates Mirabell, worse than a Quaker hates a parrot, or than a fishmonger hates a hard frost. Whether this uncle has seen Mrs. Millamant or not, I cannot say; but there were items of such a treaty being in embrio; and if it should come to life, poor Mirabell would be in some sort unfortunately fobbed i'faith.

*Fain.* 'Tis impossible Millamant should harken to it.

*Wit.* Faith, my dear, I can't tell; she's a woman and a kind of a humorist.

*Mira.* And this is the sum of what you could collect last night.

*Pet.* The quintessence. Maybe Witwoud knows more, he stayed longer.—Besides they never mind him; they say anything before him.

*Mira.* I thought you had been the greatest favourite.

*Pet.* Ay, *tête à tête;* but not in publick, because I make remarks.

*Mira.* You do?

*Pet.* Ay, ay, pox I'm malicious, man. Now he's soft, you know, they are not in awe of him—the fellow's well bred, he's what you call a—what-d'ye-call-'em. A fine gentleman, but he's silly withal.

*Mira.* I thank you, I know as much as my curiosity requires. Fainall, are you for the Mall?

*Fain.* Ay, I'll take a turn before dinner.

*Wit.* Ay, we'll all walk in the Park, the ladies talked of being there.

*Mira.* I thought you were obliged to watch for your brother Sir Wilfull's arrival.

*Wit.* No, no, he comes to his aunt's, my Lady Wishfort; pox on him, I shall be troubled with him too; what shall I do with the fool?

*Pet.* Beg him for his estate; that I may beg you afterwards; and so have but one trouble with you both.

*Wit.* O rare Petulant; thou art as quick as fire in a frosty morning; thou shalt to the Mall with us; and we'll be very severe.

*Pet.* Enough, I'm in a humour to be severe.

*Mira.* Are you? Pray then walk by yourselves,—let not us be accessary to your putting the ladies out of countenance, with your senseless ribaldry; which you roar out aloud as often as they pass by you; and when you have made a handsome woman blush, then you think you have been severe.

*Pet.* What, what? Then let 'em either shew their innocence by not understanding what they hear, or else shew their discretion by not hearing what they would not be thought to understand.

*Mira.* But hast not thou then sense enough to know that thou ought'st to be most ashamed of thyself, when thou hast put another out of countenance?

*Pet.* Not I, by this hand—I always take blushing either for a sign of guilt, or ill breeding.

*Mira.* I confess you ought to think so. You are in the right, that you may plead the error of your judgment in defence of your practice.

Where modesty's ill manners, 'tis but fit
That impudence and malice pass for wit.

## ACT II

### SCENE I. *St. James's Park.* MRS. FAINALL *and* MRS. MARWOOD

*Mrs. Fain.* Ay, ay, dear Marwood, if we will be happy, we must find the means in ourselves, and among ourselves. Men are ever in extreams; either doating, or averse. While they are lovers, if they have fire and sense, their jealousies are insupportable: and when they cease to love (we ought to think at least) they loath; they look upon us with horror and distaste; they meet us like the ghosts of what we were, and as from such, fly from us.

*Mrs. Mar.* True, 'tis an unhappy circumstance of life, that love should ever die before us; and that the man so often should outlive the lover. But say what you will, 'tis better to be left, then never to have been loved. To pass our youth in dull indifference, to refuse the sweets of life because they once must leave us, is as preposterous as to wish to have been born old, because we one day must be old. For my part, my youth may wear and waste, but it shall never rust in my possession.

*Mrs. Fain.* Then it seems you dissemble an aversion to mankind, only in compliance to my mother's humour.

*Mrs. Mar.* Certainly. To be free; I have no taste of those insipid dry discourses, with which our sex of force must entertain themselves, apart from men. We may affect endearments to each other, profess eternal friendships, and seem to dote like lovers; but 'tis not in our natures long to persevere. Love will resume his empire in our breasts, and every heart, or soon or late, receive and readmit him as its lawful tyrant.

*Mrs. Fain.* Bless me, how have I been deceived! Why you profess a libertine.

*Mrs. Mar.* You see my friendship by my freedom. Come, be as sincere, acknowledge that your sentiments agree with mine.

*Mrs. Fain.* Never.

*Mrs. Mar.* You hate mankind?

*Mrs. Fain.* Heartily, inveterately.

*Mrs. Mar.* Your husband?

*Mrs. Fain.* Most transcendently; ay, though I say it, meritoriously.

*Mrs. Mar.* Give me your hand upon it.

*Mrs. Fain.* There.

*Mrs. Mar.* I join with you; what I have said has been to try you.

*Mrs. Fain.* Is it possible? Dost thou hate those vipers men?

*Mrs. Mar.* I have done hating 'em, and am now come to despise 'em; the next thing I have to do, is eternally to forget 'em.

*Mrs. Fain.* There spoke the spirit of an Amazon, a Penthesilea.

*Mrs. Mar.* And yet I am thinking sometimes to carry my aversion further.

*Mrs. Fain.* How?

*Mrs. Mar.* Faith by marrying; if I could but find one that loved me very well, and would be thoroughly sensible of ill usage, I think I should do myself the violence of undergoing the ceremony.

*Mrs. Fain.* You would not make him a cuckold?

*Mrs. Mar.* No; but I'd make him believe I did, and that's as bad.

*Mrs. Fain.* Why had not you as good do it?

*Mrs. Mar.* O if he should ever discover it, he would then know the worst, and be out of his pain; but I would have him ever to continue upon the rack of fear and jealousie.

*Mrs. Fain.* Ingenious mischief! Would thou wert married to Mirabell.

*Mrs. Mar.* Would I were.

*Mrs. Fain.* You change colour.

*Mrs. Mar.* Because I hate him.

*Mrs. Fain.* So do I; but I can hear him named. But what reason have you to hate him in particular?

*Mrs. Mar.* I never loved him; he is, and always was, insufferably proud.

*Mrs. Fain.* By the reason you give for your aversion, one would think it dissembled; for you have laid a fault to his charge of which his enemies must acquit him.

*Mrs. Mar.* O then it seems you are one of his favourable enemies. Methinks you look a little pale, and now you flush again.

*Mrs. Fain.* Do I? I think I am a little sick o' the sudden.

*Mrs. Mar.* What ails you?

*Mrs. Fain.* My husband. Don't you see him? He turned short upon me unawares, and has almost overcome me.

## SCENE II. [*To them*] FAINALL *and* MIRABELL

*Mrs. Mar.* Ha, ha, ha; he comes opportunely for you.

*Mrs. Fain.* For you, for he has brought Mirabell with him.

*Fain.* My dear.

*Mrs. Fain.* My soul.

*Fain.* You don't look well to-day, child.

*Mrs. Fain.* D'ye think so?

*Mira.* He is the only man that does, madam.

*Mrs. Fain.* The only man that would tell me so at least; and the only man from whom I could hear it without mortification.

*Fain.* O my dear, I am satisfied of your tenderness; I know you cannot resent anything from me; especially what is an effect of my concern.

*Mrs. Fain.* Mr. Mirabell, my mother interrupted you in a pleasant relation last night: I would fain hear it out.

*Mira.* The persons concerned in that affair have yet a tolerable reputation.—I am afraid Mr. Fainall will be censorious.

*Mrs. Fain.* He has a humour more prevailing than his curiosity, and will willingly dispence with the hearing of one scandalous story, to avoid giving an occasion to make another by being seen to walk with his wife. This way, Mr. Mirabell, and I dare promise you will oblige us both.

## SCENE III. FAINALL, MRS. MARWOOD

*Fain.* Excellent creature! Well, sure if I should live to be rid of my wife, I should be a miserable man.

*Mrs. Mar.* Ay!

*Fain.* For having only that one hope, the accomplishment of it, of consequence must put an end to all my hopes; and what a wretch is he who must survive his hopes! Nothing remains when that day comes, but to sit down and weep like Alexander, when he wanted other worlds to conquer.

*Mrs. Mar.* Will you not follow 'em?

*Fain.* Faith, I think not.

*Mrs. Mar.* Pray let us; I have a reason.

*Fain.* You are not jealous?

*Mrs. Mar.* Of whom?

*Fain.* Of Mirabell.

*Mrs. Mar.* If I am, is it inconsistent with my love to you that I am tender of your honour?

*Fain.* You would intimate then, as if there were a fellow-feeling between my wife and him.

*Mrs. Mar.* I think she does not hate him to that degree she would be thought.

*Fain.* But he, I fear, is too insensible.

*Mrs. Mar.* It may be you are deceived.

*Fain.* It may be so. I do not now begin to apprehend it.

*Mrs. Mar.* What?

*Fain.* That I have been deceived, madam, and you are false.

*Mrs. Mar.* That I am false! What mean you?

*Fain.* To let you know I see through all your little arts—Come, you both love him; and both have equally dissembled your aversion. Your mutual jealousies of one another, have made you clash 'till you have both struck fire. I have seen the warm confession redening on your cheeks, and sparkling from your eyes.

*Mrs. Mar.* You do me wrong.

*Fain.* I do not—'twas for my ease to oversee and wilfully neglect the gross advances made him by my wife; that by permitting her to be engaged, I might continue unsuspected in my pleasures; and take you oftener to my arms in full security. But could you think, because the nodding husband would not wake, that e'er the watchful lover slept?

*Mrs. Mar.* And wherewithal can you reproach me?

*Fain.* With infidelity, with loving another, with love of Mirabell.

*Mrs. Mar.* 'Tis false. I challenge you to shew an instance that can confirm your groundless accusation. I hate him.

*Fain.* And wherefore do you hate him? He is insensible, and your resentment follows his neglect. An instance! The injuries you have done him are a proof: your interposing in his love. What cause had you to make discoveries of his pretended passion? To undeceive the credulous aunt, and be the officious obstacle of his match with Millamant?

*Mrs. Mar.* My obligations to my lady urged me: I had professed a friendship to her; and could not see her easie nature so abused by that dissembler.

*Fain.* What, was it conscience then? Professed a friendship! O the pious friendships of the female sex!

*Mrs. Mar.* More tender, more sincere, and more enduring, than all the vain and empty vows of men, whether professing love to us, or mutual faith to one another.

*Fain.* Ha, ha, ha; you are my wife's friend too.

*Mrs. Mar.* Shame and ingratitude! Do you reproach me? You, you upbraid me! Have I been false to her, through strict fidelity to you, and sacrified my friendship to keep my love inviolate? And have you the baseness to charge me with the guilt, unmindful of the merit! To you it should be meritorious, that I have been vicious: And do you reflect that guilt upon me, which should lie buried in your bosom?

*Fain.* You misinterpret my reproof. I meant but to remind you of the slight account you once could make of strictest ties, when set in competition with your love to me.

*Mrs. Mar.* 'Tis false, you urged it with deliberate malice—'twas spoke in scorn, and I never will forgive it.

*Fain.* Your guilt, not your resentment, begets your rage. If yet you loved, you could forgive a jealousie: but you are stung to find you are discovered.

*Mrs. Mar.* It shall be all discovered. You too shall be discovered; be sure you shall. I can but be exposed—if I do it myself I shall prevent your baseness.

*Fain.* Why, what will you do?

*Mrs. Mar.* Disclose it to your wife; own what has past between us.

*Fain.* Frenzy!

*Mrs. Mar.* By all my wrongs I'll do't—I'll publish to the world the injuries you have done me, both in my fame and fortune: With both I trusted you, you bankrupt in honour, as indigent of wealth.

*Fain.* Your fame I have preserved. Your fortune has been bestowed as the prodigality of your love would have it, in pleasures which we both have shared. Yet, had not you been false, I had e'er this repaid it —'Tis true—had you permitted Mirabell with Millamant to have stollen their marriage, my lady had been incensed beyond all means of reconcilement: Millamant had forfeited the moiety of her fortune; which then would have descended to my wife;—And wherefore did I marry, but to make lawful prize of a rich widow's wealth, and squander it on love and you?

*Mrs. Mar.* Deceit and frivolous pretence.

*Fain.* Death, am I not married? What's pretence? Am I not imprisoned, fettered? Have I not a wife? Nay, a wife that was a widow, a young widow, a handsome widow; and would be again a widow, but that I have a heart of proof, and something of a constitution to bustle through the ways of wedlock and this world. Will you yet be reconciled to truth and me?

*Mrs. Mar.* Impossible. Truth and you are inconsistent—I hate you, and shall for ever.

*Fain.* For loving you?

*Mrs. Mar.* I loath the name of love after such usage; and next to the guilt with which you would asperse me, I scorn you most. Farewell.

*Fain.* Nay, we must not part thus.

*Mrs. Mar.* Let me go.

*Fain.* Come, I'm sorry.

*Mrs. Mar.* I care not—let me go—break my hands, do—I'd leave 'em to get loose.

*Fain.* I would not hurt you for the world. Have I no other hold to keep you here?

*Mrs. Mar.* Well, I have deserved it all.

*Fain.* You know I love you.

*Mrs. Mar.* Poor dissembling!—O that—Well, it is not yet—

*Fain.* What? What is it not? What is it not yet? It is not yet too late—

*Mrs. Mar.* No, it is not yet too late—I have that comfort.

*Fain.* It is, to love another.

*Mrs. Mar.* But not to loath, detest, abhor mankind, myself and the whole treacherous world.

*Fain.* Nay, this is extravagance.—Come, I ask your pardon—no tears—I was to blame, I could not love you and be easie in my doubts—pray forbear—I believe you; I'm convinced I've done you wrong; and any way, every way will make amends;—I'll hate my wife yet more, damn her, I'll part with her, rob her of all she's worth, and we'll retire somewhere, anywhere, to another world, I'll marry thee—be pacified.—'Sdeath they come, hide your face, your tears—you have a mask, wear it a moment. This way, this way, be persuaded.

## Scene IV. MIRABELL *and* MRS. FAINALL

*Mrs. Fain.* They are here yet.

*Mira.* They are turning into the other walk.

*Mrs. Fain.* While I only hated my husband, I could bear to see him; but since I have despised him, he's too offensive.

*Mira.* O you should hate with prudence.

*Mrs. Fain.* Yes, for I have loved with indiscretion.

*Mira.* You should have just so much disgust for your husband as may be sufficient to make you relish your lover.

*Mrs. Fain.* You have been the cause that I have loved without bounds, and would you set limits to that aversion, of which you have been the occasion? Why did you make me marry this man?

*Mira.* Why do we daily commit disagreeable and dangerous actions? To save that idol reputation. If the familiarities of our loves had produced that consequence, of which you were apprehensive, where could you have fixed a father's name with credit, but on a husband? I knew Fainall to be a man lavish of his morals, an interested and professing friend, a false and a designing lover; yet one whose wit and outword fair behaviour have gained a reputation with the town, enough to make that woman stand excused, who has suffered herself to be won by his addresses. A better man ought not to have been sacrificed to the occasion; a worse had not answered to the purpose. When you are weary of him, you know your remedy.

*Mrs. Fain.* I ought to stand in some degree of credit with you, Mirabell.

*Mira.* In justice to you, I have made you privy to my whole design, and put it in your power to ruin or advance my fortune.

*Mrs. Fain.* Whom have you instructed to represent your pretended uncle?

*Mira.* Waitwell, my servant.

*Mrs. Fain.* He is an humble servant to foible my mother's woman, and may win her to your interest.

*Mira.* Care is taken for that—she is won and worn by this time. They were married this morning.

*Mrs. Fain.* Who?

*Mira.* Waitwell and Foible. I would not tempt my servant to betray me by trusting him too far. If your mother, in hopes to ruin me, should consent to marry my pretended uncle, he might, like Mosca in the "Fox," stand upon terms; so I made him sure before-hand.

*Mrs. Fain.* So, if my poor mother is caught in a contract, you will discover the imposture betimes; and release her by producing a certificate of her gallant's former marriage.

*Mira.* Yes, upon condition that she consent to my marriage with her niece, and surrender the moiety of her fortune in her possession.

*Mrs. Fain.* She talked last night of endeavoring at a match between Millamant and your uncle.

*Mira.* That was by Foible's direction, and my instruction, that she might seem to carry it more privately.

*Mrs. Fain.* Well, I have an opinion of your success; for I believe my lady will do anything to get an husband; and when she has this, which you have provided for her, I suppose she will submit to anything to get rid of him.

*Mira.* Yes, I think the good lady would marry anything that resembled a man, though 'twere no more than what a butler could pinch out of a napkin.

*Mrs. Fain.* Female frailty! We must all come to it, if live to be old, and feel the craving of a false appetite when the true is decayed.

*Mira.* An old woman's appetite is depraved like that of a girl—'tis the green-sickness of a second childhood; and like the faint offer of a latter spring, serves but to usher in the fall; and withers in an affected bloom.

*Mrs. Fain.* Here's your mistress.

## Scene V. [*To them*] MRS. MILLAMANT, WITWOUD, MINCING

*Mira.* Here she comes i'faith full sail, with her fan spread and streamers out, and a shoal of fools for tenders—Ha, no, I cry her mercy.

*Mrs. Fain.* I see but one poor empty sculler; and he tows her woman after him.

*Mira.* You seem to be unattended, madam,—you used to have the *beau-mond* throng after you; and a flock of gay fine perukes hovering round you.

*Wit.* Like moths about a candle—I had like to have lost my comparison for want of breath.

*Milla.* O I have denied myself airs to-day. I have walked as fast through the croud—

*Wit.* As a favorite just disgraced; and with as few followers.

*Milla.* Dear Mr. Witwoud, truce with your similitudes: for I am as sick of 'em—

*Wit.* As a physician of a good air—I cannot help it, madam, though 'tis against myself.

*Milla.* Yet again! Mincing, stand between me and his wit.

*Wit.* Do, Mrs. Mincing, like a skreen before a great fire. I confess I do blaze to-day, I am too bright.

*Mrs. Fain.* But, dear Millamant, why were you so long?

*Milla.* Long! Lord, have I not made violent haste? I have asked every living thing I met for you; I have inquired after you, as after a new fashion.

*Wit.* Madam, truce with your similitudes—No, you met her husband, and did not ask him for her.

*Mira.* By your leave, Witwoud, that were like enquiring after an old fashion, to ask a husband for his wife.

*Wit.* Hum, a hit, a hit, a palpable hit, I confess it.

*Mrs. Fain.* You were dressed before I came abroad.

*Milla.* Ay, that's true—O but then I had—Mincing, what had I? Why was I so long?

*Minc.* O mem, your laship staid to peruse a pacquet of letters.

*Milla.* O ay, letters—I had letters—I am persecuted with letters—I hate letters—nobody knows how to write letters; and yet one has 'em, one does not know why—they serve one to pin up one's hair.

*Wit.* Is that the way? Pray, madam, do you pin up your hair with all your letters? I find I must keep copies.

*Milla.* Only with those in verse, Mr. Witwoud. I never pin up my hair with prose. I think I tried once, Mincing.

*Minc.* O mem, I shall never forget it.

*Milla.* Ay, poor Mincing tift and tift all the morning.

*Minc.* 'Till I had the cramp in my fingers, I'll vow, mem. And all to no purpose. But when your laship pins it up with poetry, it sits so pleasant the next day as anything, and is so pure and so crips.

*Wit.* Indeed, so crips?

*Minc.* You're such a critick, Mr. Witwoud.

*Milla.* Mirabell, did you take exceptions last night? O ay, and went away—Now I think on't I'm angry—no, now I think on't I'm pleased —for I believe I gave you some pain.

*Mira.* Does that please you?

*Milla.* Infinitely; I love to give pain.

*Mira.* You would affect a cruelty which is not in your nature; your true vanity is in the power of pleasing.

*Milla.* O I ask your pardon for that—one's cruelty is one's power, and when one parts with one's cruelty, one parts with one's power; and when one has parted with that, I fancy one's old and ugly.

*Mira.* Ay, ay, suffer your cruelty to ruin the object of your power, to destroy your lover—and then how vain, how lost a thing you'll be? Nay, 'tis true: you are no longer handsome when you've lost your lover; your beauty dies upon the instant: For beauty is the lover's gift; 'tis he bestows your charms—your glass is all a cheat. The ugly and the old, whom the looking-glass mortifies, yet after commendation can be flattered by it, and discover beauties in it: for that reflects our praises, rather than your face.

*Milla.* O the vanity of these men! Fainall, d'ye hear him? If they did not commend us, we were not handsome! Now you must know they could not commend one, if one was not handsome. Beauty the lover's gift—Lord, what is a lover, that it can give? Why one makes lovers as fast as one pleases, and they live as long as one pleases, and they die as soon as one pleases: and then if one pleases one makes more.

*Wit.* Very pretty. Why you make no more of making of lovers, madam, than of making so many card-matches.

*Milla.* One no more owes one's beauty to a lover, than one's wit to an eccho: they can but reflect what we look and say; vain empty things if we are silent or unseen, and want a being.

*Mira.* Yet, to those two vain empty things, you owe two the greatest pleasures of your life.

*Milla.* How so?

*Mira.* To your lover you owe the pleasure of hearing yourselves praised; and to an eccho the pleasure of hearing yourselves talk.

*Wit.* But I know a lady that loves talking so incessantly, she won't give an eccho fair play; she has that everlasting rotation of tongue, that an eccho must wait 'till she dies, before it can catch her last words.

*Milla.* O fiction; Fainall, let us leave these men.

*Mira.* Draw off Witwoud. [*Aside to* Mrs. Fainall.

*Mrs. Fain.* Immediately; I have a word or two for Mr. Witwoud.

## Scene VI. Millamant, Mirabell, Mincing

*Mira.* I would beg a little private audience too—you had the tyranny to deny me last night; though you knew I came to impart a secret to you that concerned my love.

*Milla.* You saw I was engaged.

*Mira.* Unkind. You had the leisure to entertain a herd of fools; things who visit you from their excessive idleness; bestowing on your easiness that time, which is the incumbrance of their lives. How can you find delight in such society? It is impossible they should admire you, they are not capable: or if they were, it should be to you as a mortification; for sure to please a fool is some degree of folly.

*Milla.* I please myself—besides, sometimes to converse with fools is for my health.

*Mira.* Your health! Is there a worse disease than the conversation of fools?

*Milla.* Yes, the vapours; fools are physick for it, next to *assa-fœtida.*

*Mira.* You are not in a course of fools?

*Milla.* Mirabell, if you persist in this offensive freedom, you'll displease me—I think I must resolve after all, not to have you—we shan't agree.

*Mira.* Not in our physick it may be.

*Milla.* And yet our distemper in all likelihood will be the same; for we shall be sick of one another. I shan't endure to be reprimanded, nor instructed; 'tis so dull to act always by advice, and so tedious to be told of one's faults—I can't bear it. Well, I won't have you, Mirabell—I'm resolved—I think—You may go—ha, ha, ha. What would you give, that you could help loving me?

*Mira.* I would give something that you did not know, I could not help it.

*Milla.* Come, don't look grave then. Well, what do you say to me?

*Mira.* I say that a man may as soon make a friend by his wit, or a fortune by his honesty, as win a woman with plain-dealing and sincerity.

*Milla.* Sententious Mirabell! Prithee don't look with that violent and inflexible wise face, like Solomon at the dividing of the child in an old tapestry hanging.

*Mira.* You are merry, madam, but I would persuade you for a moment to be serious.

*Milla.* What, with that face? No, if you keep your countenance, 'tis impossible I should hold mine. Well, after all, there is something very moving in a lovesick face. Ha, ha, ha—Well I won't laugh, don't be peevish—Heigho! Now I'll be melancholy, as melancholy as a watch-light. Well, Mirabell, if ever you will win me woo me now—Nay, if you are so tedious, fare you well;—I see they are walking away.

*Mira.* Can you not find in the variety of your disposition one moment—

*Milla.* To hear you tell me Foible's married, and your plot like to speed.—No.

*Mira.* But how you came to know it—

*Milla.* Without the help of the devil, you can't imagine; unless she should tell me herself. Which of the two it may have been, I will leave you to consider; and when you have done thinking of that, think of me.

## SCENE VII. MIRABELL *alone*

*Mira.* I have something more—Gone—think of you! To think of a whirlwind, though 'twere in a whirlwind, were a case of more steady contemplation; a very tranquility of mind and mansion. A fellow that lives in a windmill, has not a more whimsical dwelling than the heart of a man that is lodged in a woman. There is no point of the compass to which they cannot turn, and by which they are not turned; and by one as well as another; for motion not method is their occupation. To know this, and yet continue to be in love, is to be made wise from the dictates of reason, and yet persevere to play the fool by the force of instinct.—O here come my pair of turtles,—what, billing so sweetly! Is not Valentine's Day over with you yet?

## Scene VIII. [*To him*] WAITWELL, FOIBLE

*Mira.* Sirrah, Waitwell, why sure you think you were married for your own recreation, and not for my conveniency.

*Wait.* Your pardon, sir. With submission, we have indeed been solacing in lawful delights; but still with an eye to business, sir. I have instructed her as well as I could. If she can take your directions as readily as my instructions, sir, your affairs are in a prosperous way.

*Mira.* Give you joy, Mrs. Foible.

*Foib.* O-las, sir, I'm so ashamed—I'm afraid my lady has been in a thousand inquietudes for me. But I protest, sir, I made as much haste as I could.

*Wait.* That she did indeed, sir. It was my fault that she did not make more.

*Mira.* That I believe.

*Foib.* But I told my lady as you instructed me, sir. That I had a prospect of seeing Sir Rowland your uncle; and that I would put her ladiship's picture in my pocket to shew him; which I'll be sure to say has made him so enamoured of her beauty, that he burns with impatience to lye at her ladiship's feet and worship the original.

*Mira.* Excellent Foible! Matrimony has made you eloquent in love.

*Wait.* I think she has profited, sir. I think so.

*Foib.* You have seen Madam Millamant, sir?

*Mira.* Yes.

*Foib.* I told her, sir, because I did not know that you might find an opportunity; she had so much company last night.

*Mira.* Your diligence will merit more—In the meantime—

[*Gives mony.*

*Foib.* O dear sir, your humble servant.

*Wait.* Spouse.

*Mira.* Stand off, sir, not a penny.—Go on and prosper, Foible—the lease shall be made good and the farm stocked, if we succeed.

*Foib.* I don't question your generosity, sir: and you need not doubt of success. If you have no more commands, sir, I'll be gone; I'm sure my lady is at her toilet, and can't dress 'till I come.—O dear, I'm sure that [*looking out*] was Mrs. Marwood that went by in a mask; if she has seen me with you I'm sure she'll tell my lady. I'll make haste home and prevent her. Your servant, sir. B'w'y, Waitwell.

SCENE IX. MIRABELL, WAITWELL

*Wait.* Sir Rowland if you please. The jade's so pert upon her preferment she forgets herself.

*Mira.* Come, sir, will you endeavour to forget yourself—and transform into Sir Rowland.

*Wait.* Why, sir; it will be impossible I should remember myself—married,, knighted and attended all in one day! 'Tis enough to make any man forget himself. The difficulty will be how to recover my acquaintance and familiarity with my former self; and fall from my transformation to a reformation into Waitwell. Nay, I shan't be quite the same Waitwell neither—for now I remember me, I'm married, and can't be my own man again.

Ay there's my grief; that's the sad change of life;
To lose my title, and yet keep my wife.

## ACT III

SCENE I.—*A Room in* LADY WISHFORT'S *House.* LADY WISHFORT *at her toilet,* PEG *waiting*

*Lady.* Merciful, no news of Foible yet?

*Peg.* No, madam.

*Lady.* I have no more patience—if I have not fretted myself 'till I am pale again, there's no veracity in me. Fetch me the red—the red, do you hear, sweetheart? An errant ash colour, as I'm a person. Look you how this wench stirs! Why dost thou not fetch me a little red? Didst thou not hear me, mopus?

*Peg.* The red ratafia does your ladiship mean, or the cherry-brandy?

*Lady.* Ratafia, fool. No, fool. Not the ratafia, fool—grant me patience! I mean the Spanish paper, idiot, complexion darling. Paint, paint, paint, dost thou understand that, changeling, dangling thy hands like bobbins before thee? Why dost thou not stir, puppet? thou wooden thing upon wires.

*Peg.* Lord, madam, your ladiship is so impatient—I cannot come at the paint, madam, Mrs. Foible has locked it up, and carried the key with her.

*Lady*. A pox take you both—fetch me the cherry-brandy then.

## Scene II. lady wishfort

I'm as pale and as faint, I look like Mrs. Qualmsick the curate's wife, that's always breeding—Wench, come, come, wench, what art thou doing, sipping? tasting? Save thee, dost thou not know the bottle?

## Scene III. lady wishfort, peg *with a bottle and china cup*

*Peg*. Madam, I was looking for a cup.

*Lady*. A cup, save thee, and what a cup hast thou brought! Dost thou take me for a fairy, to drink out of an acorn? Why didst thou not bring thy thimble? Hast thou ne'er a brass thimble clinking in thy pocket with a bit of nutmeg? I warrant thee. Come, fill, fill.—So—again. See who that is.—[*One knocks.*] Set down the bottle first. Here, here, under the table—What, wouldst thou go with the bottle in thy hand like a tapster. As I'm a person, this wench has lived in an inn upon the road, before she came to me, like Maritornes the Asturian in *Don Quixote*. No Foible yet?

*Peg*. No, Madam, Mrs. Marwood.

*Lady*. O Marwood, let her come in. Come in, good Marwood.

## Scene IV. [*To them*] mrs. marwood

*Mrs. Mar*. I'm surprised to find your ladiship in dishabillé at this time of day.

*Lady*. Foible's a lost thing; has been abroad since morning, and never heard of since.

*Mrs. Mar*. I saw her but now, as I came masked through the Park, in conference with Mirabell.

*Lady*. With Mirabell! You call my blood into my face, with mentioning that traitor. She durst not have the confidence. I sent her to negotiate an affair, in which if I'm detected I'm undone. If that wheadling villain has wrought upon Foible to detect me, I'm ruined. Oh my dear friend, I'm a wretch of wretches if I'm detected.

*Mrs. Mar*. O madam, you cannot suspect Mrs. Foible's integrity.

*Lady*. O, he carries poison in his tongue that would corrupt integrity itself. If she has given him an opportunity, she has as good as put her integrity into his hands. Ah, dear Marwood, what's integrity to an opportunity?—Hark! I hear her.—Dear friend, retire into my closet, that I may examine her with more freedom—You'll pardon me, dear friend, I can make bold with you—There are books over the chimney —Quarles and Pryn, and the *Short View of the Stage*, with Bunyan's works to entertain you.—Go, you thing, and send her in. [*To* PEG.

SCENE V. LADY WISHFORT, FOIBLE

*Lady*. O Foible, where hast thou been? what hast thou been doing?

*Foib*. Madam, I have seen the party.

*Lady*. But what hast thou done?

*Foib*. Nay, 'tis your ladiship has done, and are to do; I have only promised. But a man so enamoured—so transported. Well, if worshipping of pictures be a sin—poor Sir Rowland, I say.

*Lady*. The miniature has been counted like—But hast thou not betrayed me, Foible? Hast thou not detected me to that faithless Mirabell?—What hadst thou to do with them in the Park? Answer me, has he got nothing out of thee?

*Foib*. So, the devil has been beforehand with me, what shall I say?—Alas, madam, could I help it, if I met that confident thing? Was I in fault? If you had heard how he used me, and all upon your ladiship's account, I'm sure you would not suspect my fidelity. Nay, if that had been the worst I could have born: but he had a fling at your ladiship too; and then I could not hold: but i'faith I gave him his own.

*Lady*. Me? What did the filthy fellow say?

*Foib*. O madam; 'tis a shame to say what he said—with his taunts and his fleers, tossing up his nose. Humh (says he), what you are a hatching some plot (says he), you are so early abroad, or catering (says he), ferreting for some disbanded officer, I warrant—half pay is but thin subsistance (says he)—Well, what pension does your lady propose? Let me see (says he), what she must come down pretty deep now, she's superannuated (says he) and—

*Lady*. Ods my life, I'll have him, I'll have him murdered. I'll have him poisoned. Where does he eat? I'll marry a drawer to have him poisoned in his wine. I'll send for Robin from Lockets—immediately.

*Foib*. Poison him? Poisoning's too good for him. Starve him, madam, starve him; marry Sir Rowland, and get him disinherited. O you would bless yourself, to hear what he said.

*Lady*. A villain, superannuated!

*Foib*. Humh (says he), I hear you are laying designs against me too (says he), and Mrs. Millamant is to marry my uncle (he does not suspect a word of your ladiship); but (says he) I'll fit you for that, I warrant you (says he), I'll hamper you for that (says he), you and your old frippery too (says he), I'll handle you—

*Lady.* Audacious villain! handle me, would he durst—Frippery? old frippery! Was there ever such a foul-mouthed fellow? I'll be married to-morrow, I'll be contracted to-night.

*Foib.* The sooner the better, madam.

*Lady.* Will Sir Rowland be here, say'st thou? when, Foible?

*Foib.* Incontinently, madam. No new sheriff's wife expects the return of her husband after knighthood, with that impatience in which Sir Rowland burns for the dear hour of kissing your ladiship's hand after dinner.

*Lady.* Frippery! superannuated frippery! I'll frippery the villain; I'll reduce him to frippery and rags: a tatterdemallion—I hope to see him hung with tatters, like a Long-Lane penthouse, or a gibbet-thief. A slander-mouthed railer: I warrant the spendthrift prodigal's in debt as much as the million lottery, or the whole court upon a birthday. I'll spoil his credit with his tailor. Yes, he shall have my niece with her fortune, he shall.

*Foib.* He! I hope to see him lodge in Ludgate first, and angle into Black-Fryars for brass farthings, with an old mitten.

*Lady.* Ay, dear Foible; thank thee for that, dear Foible. He has put me out of all patience. I shall never recompose my features to receive Sir Rowland with any oeconomy of face. This wretch has fretted me that I am absolutely decayed. Look, Foible.

*Foib.* Your ladiship has frowned a little too rashly, indeed, madam. There are some cracks discernible in the white vernish.

*Lady.* Let me see the glass—Cracks, say'st thou? Why, I am arrantly fleaed—I look like an old peeled wall. Thou must repair me, Foible, before Sir Rowland comes; or I shall never keep up to my picture.

*Foib.* I warrant you, madam; a little art once made your picture like you; and now a little of the same art must make you like your picture. Your picture must sit for you, madam.

*Lady.* But art thou sure Sir Rowland will not fail to come? Or will a not fail when he does come? Will he be importunate, Foible, and push? For if he should not be importunate—I shall never break decorums—I shall die with confusion, if I am forced to advance—Oh no, I can never advance—I shall swoon if he should expect advances. No, I hope Sir Rowland is better bred, than to put a lady to the necessity of breaking her forms. I won't be too coy neither.—I won't give him despair—but a little disdain is not amiss; a little scorn is alluring.

*Foib.* A little scorn becomes your ladiship.

*Lady*. Yes, but tenderness becomes me best—a sort of a dyingness—You see that picture has a sort of a—Ha, Foible? A swimmingness in the eyes—Yes, I'll look so—my niece affects it; but she wants features. Is Sir Rowland handsome? Let my toilet be removed—I'll dress above. I'll receive Sir Rowland here. Is he handsome? Don't answer me. I won't know: I'll be surprized. I'll be taken by surprize.

*Foib*. By storm, madam. Sir Rowland's a brisk man.

*Lady*. Is he! O then he'll importune, if he's a brisk man. I shall save decorums if Sir Rowland importunes. I have a mortal terror at the apprehension of offending against decorums. O I'm glad he's a brisk man. Let my things be removed, good Foible.

## SCENE VI. MRS. FAINALL, FOIBLE

*Mrs. Fain.* O Foible, I have been in a fright, lest I should come too late. That devil, Marwood, saw you in the Park with Mirabell, and I'm afraid will discover it to my lady.

*Foib.* Discover what, madam?

*Mrs. Fain.* Nay, nay, put not on that strange face. I am privy to the whole design, and know that Waitwell, to whom thou wert this morning married, is to personate Mirabell's uncle, and as such, winning my lady, to involve her in those difficulties from which Mirabell only must release her, by his making his conditions to have my cousin and her fortune left to her own disposal.

*Foib.* O dear madam, I beg your pardon. It was not my confidence in your ladiship that was deficient; but I thought the former good correspondence between your ladiship and Mr. Mirabell, might have hindered his communicating this secret.

*Mrs. Fain.* Dear Foible, forget that.

*Foib.* O dear madam, Mr. Mirabell is such a sweet winning gentleman—But your ladiship is the pattern of generosity.—Sweet lady, to be so good! Mr. Mirabell cannot chuse but be grateful. I find your ladiship has his heart still. Now, madam, I can safely tell your ladiship our success, Mrs. Marwood had told my lady; but I warrant I managed myself. I turned it all for the better. I told my lady that Mr. Mirabell railed at her. I laid horrid things to his charge, I'll vow; and my lady is so incensed, that she'll be contracted to Sir Rowland to-night, she says;—I warrant I worked her up, that he may have her for asking for, as they say of a Welsh maiden-head.

*Mrs. Fain.* O rare Foible!

*Foib.* Madam, I beg your ladiship to acquaint Mr. Mirabell of his success. I would be seen as little as possible to speak to him—besides, I believe Madam Marwood watches me.—She has a month's mind; but I know Mr. Mirabell can't abide her.—[*Calls.*] John—remove my lady's toilet. Madam, your servant. My lady is so impatient, I fear she'll come for me, if I stay.

*Mrs. Fain.* I'll go with you up the back stairs, lest I should meet her.

## Scene VII. mrs. marwood *alone*

*Mrs. Mar.* Indeed, Mrs. Engine, is it thus with you? Are you become a go-between of this importance? Yes, I shall watch you. Why this wench is the *pass-par-toute*, a very master-key to everybody's strong box. My friend Fainall, have you carried it so swimmingly? I thought there was something in it; but it seems it's over with you. Your loathing is not from a want of appetite then, but from a surfeit. Else you could never be so cool to fall from a principal to be an assistant; to procure for him! A pattern of generosity, that I confess. Well, Mr. Fainall, you have met with your match.—O man, man! Woman, woman! The devil's an ass: if I were a painter, I would draw him like an idiot, a driveler with a bib and bells. Man should have his head and horns, and woman the rest of him. Poor simple fiend! Madam Marwood has a month's mind, but he can't abide her—'Twere better for him you had not been his confessor in that affair; without you could have kept his counsel closer. I shall not prove another pattern of generosity—he has not obliged me to that with those excesses of himself; and now I'll have none of him. Here comes the good lady, panting ripe; with a heart full of hope, and a head full of care, like any chymist upon the day of projection.

## Scene VIII. [*To her*] lady wishfort

*Lady.* O dear Marwood, what shall I say for this rude forgetfulness—but my dear friend is all goodness.

*Mrs. Mar.* No apologies, dear madam. I have been very well entertained.

*Lady.* As I'm a person I am in a very chaos to think I should so forget myself—but I have such an olio of affairs really I know not what to do.—[*Calls*]—Foible—I expect my nephew Sir Wilfull every moment too:—Why, Foible—He means to travel for improvement.

*Mrs. Mar.* Methinks Sir Wilfull should rather think of marrying than travelling at his years. I hear he is turned of forty.

*Lady.* O he's in less danger of being spoiled by his travels—I am against my nephew's marrying too young. It will be time enough when he comes back, and has acquired discretion to chuse for himself.

*Mrs. Mar.* Methinks Mrs. Millamant and he would make a very fit match. He may travel afterwards. 'Tis a thing very usual with young gentlemen.

*Lady.* I promise you I have thought on't—and since 'tis your judgment, I'll think on't again. I assure you I will; I value your judgment extreamly. On my word I'll propose it.

### SCENE IX. [*To them*] FOIBLE

*Lady.* Come, come, Foible—I had forgot my nephew will be here before dinner—I must make haste.

*Foib.* Mr. Witwoud and Mr. Petulant are come to dine with your ladiship.

*Lady.* O dear, I can't appear 'till I am dressed. Dear Marwood, shall I be free with you again, and beg you to entertain 'em. I'll make all imaginable haste. Dear friend, excuse me.

### SCENE X. MRS. MARWOOD, MRS. MILLAMANT, MINCING

*Milla.* Sure never anything was so unbred as that odious man.—Marwood, your servant.

*Mrs. Mar.* You have a colour, what's the matter?

*Milla.* That horrid fellow Petulant has provoked me into a flame—I have broke my fan—Mincing, lend me yours;—Is not all the powder out of my hair?

*Mrs. Mar.* No. What has he done?

*Milla.* Nay, he has done nothing; he has only talked—Nay, he has said nothing neither; but he has contradicted everything that has been said. For my part, I thought Witwoud and he would have quarrelled.

*Minc.* I vow, mem, I thought once they would have fitt.

*Milla.* Well, 'tis a lamentable thing I swear, that one has not the liberty of chusing one's acquaintance as one does one's cloaths.

*Mrs. Mar.* If we had that liberty, we should be as weary of one set of acquaintance, though never so good, as we are of one suit, though never so fine. A fool and a doily stuff would now and then find days of grace, and be worn for variety.

*Milla.* I could consent to wear 'em, if they would wear alike; but fools never wear out—they are such *drap-de-berry* things! Without one could give 'em to one's chambermaid after a day or two.

*Mrs. Mar.* 'Twere better so indeed. Or what think you of the playhouse? A fine gay glosly fool should be given there, like a new masking habit, after the masquerade is over, and we have done with the disguise.

For a fool's visit is always a disguise; and never admitted by a woman of wit, but to blind her affair with a lover of sense. If you would but appear barefaced now, and own Mirabell; you might as easily put off Petulant and Witwould, as your hood and scarf. And indeed 'tis time, for the town has found it: the secret is grown too big for the pretence: 'tis like Mrs. Primly's great belly; she may lace it down before, but it burnishes on her hips. Indeed, Millamant, you can no more conceal it, than my Lady Strammel can her face, that goodly face, which in defiance of her Rhenishwine tea, will not be comprehended in a mask.

*Milla.* I'll take my death, Marwood, you are more censorious than a decayed beauty, or a discarded toast; Mincing, tell the men they may come up. My aunt is not dressing here; their folly is less provoking than your malice.

## Scene XI. millamant, marwood

*Milla.* The town has found it. What has it found? That Mirabell loves me is no more a secret, than it is a secret that you discovered it to my aunt, or than the reason why you discovered it is a secret.

*Mrs. Mar.* You are nettled.

*Milla.* You're mistaken. Ridiculous!

*Mrs. Mar.* Indeed, my dear, you'll tear another fan, if you don't mitigate those violent airs.

*Milla.* O silly! Ha, ha, ha. I could laugh immoderately. Poor Mirabell! His constancy to me has quite destroyed his complaisance for all the world beside. I swear, I never enjoined it him, to be so coy—If I had the vanity to think he would obey me, I would command him to shew more gallantry—'tis hardly well bred to be so particular on one hand, and so insensible on the other. But I despair to prevail, and so let him follow his own way. Ha, ha, ha. Pardon me, dear creature, I must laugh, ha, ha, ha; though I grant you 'tis a little barbarous, ha, ha, ha.

*Mrs. Mar.* What pity 'tis, so much fine railery, and delivered with so significant gesture, should be so unhappily directed to miscarry.

*Milla.* Hæ! Dear creature, I ask your pardon—I swear I did not mind you.

*Mrs. Mar.* Mr. Mirabell and you both may think it a thing impossible, when I shall tell him by telling you—

*Milla.* O dear, what? for it is the same thing, if I hear it—ha, ha, ha.

*Mrs. Mar.* That I detest him, hate him, madam.

*Milla.* O madam, why so do I—and yet the creature loves me, ha, ha, ha. How can one forbear laughing to think of it—I am a Sybil if I am not amazed to think what he can see in me. I'll take my death, I think you are handsomer—and within a year or two as young.—If you could but stay for me, I should overtake you—but that cannot be—Well, that thought makes me melancholick—now I'll be sad.

*Mrs. Mar.* Your merry note may be changed sooner than you think.

*Milla.* D'ye say so? Then I'm resolved I'll have a song to keep up my spirits.

SCENE XII. [*To them*] MINCING

*Minc.* The gentlemen stay but to comb, madam; and will wait on you.

*Milla.* Desire Mrs.— that is in the next room to sing the song I would have learnt yesterday. You shall hear it, madam—Not that there's any great matter in it—but 'tis agreeable to my humour.

SONG

*Set by Mr. John Eccles*

I

Love's but the frailty of the mind,
When 'tis not with ambition joined;
A sickly flame, which if not fed expires;
And feeding, wastes in self-consuming fires.

II

'Tis not to wound a wanton boy
Or am'rous youth, that gives the joy;
But 'tis the glory to have pierced a swain,
For whom inferior beauties sighed in vain.

III

Then I alone the conquest prize,
When I insult a rival's eyes:
If there's delight in love, 'tis when I see
That heart which others bleed for, bleed for me.

SCENE XIII. [*To them*] PETULANT, WITWOUD

*Milla.* Is your animosity composed, gentlemen?

*Wit.* Raillery, raillery, madam, we have no animosity—we hit off a little wit now and then, but no animosity—The falling out of wits is like the falling out of lovers—We agree in the main, like treble and base. Ha, Petulant!

*Pet.* Ay, in the main—but when I have a humour to contradict—

*Wit.* Ay, when he has a humour to contradict, then I contradict too. What, I know my cue. Then we contradict one another like two battledores; for contradictions beget one another like Jews.

*Pet.* If he says black's black—if I have a humour to say 'tis blue—let that pass—all's one for that. If I have a humour to prove it, it must be granted.

*Wit.* Not positively must—but it may—it may.

*Pet.* Yes, it positively must, upon proof positive.

*Wit.* Ay, upon proof positive it must; but upon proof presumptive it only may. That's a logical distinction now, madam.

*Mrs. Mar.* I perceive your debates are of importance, and very learnedly handled.

*Pet.* Importance is one thing, and learning's another; but a debate's a debate, that I assert.

*Wit.* Petulant's an enemy to learning; he relies altogether on his parts.

*Pet.* No, I'm no enemy to learning; it hurts not me.

*Mrs. Mar.* That's a sign indeed it's no enemy to you.

*Pet.* No, no, it's no enemy to anybody, but them that have it.

*Milla.* Well, an illiterate man's my aversion, I wonder at the impudence of any illiterate man, to offer to make love.

*Wit.* That I confess I wonder at too.

*Milla.* Ah! to marry an ignorant! that can hardly read or write.

*Pet.* Why should a man be any further from being married though he can't read, than he is from being hanged? The ordinary's paid for setting the psalm, and the parish-priest for reading the ceremony. And for the rest which is to follow in both cases, a man may do it without book—so all's one for that.

*Milla.* D'ye hear the creature? Lord, here's company, I'll be gone.

SCENE XIV. SIR WILFULL WITWOUD *in a riding dress*, MRS. MARWOOD, PETULANT, WITWOUD, FOOTMAN

*Wit.* In the name of Bartlemew and his fair, what have we here?

*Mrs. Mar.* 'Tis your brother, I fancy. Don't you know him?

*Wit.* Not I—Yes, I think it is he—I've almost forgot him; I have not seen him since the Revolution.

*Foot.* Sir, my lady's dressing. Here's company; if you please to walk in, in the meantime.

*Sir Wil.* Dressing! What, it's but morning here I warrant with you in London; we should count it towards afternoon in our parts, down in Shropshire.—Why then belike my aunt han't dined yet—ha, friend?

*Foot.* Your aunt, sir?

*Sir Wil.* My aunt, sir, yes, my aunt, sir, and your lady, sir; your lady is my aunt, sir—Why, what do'st thou not know me, friend? Why then send somebody hither that does. How long hast thou lived with thy lady, fellow, ha?

*Foot.* A week, sir; longer than anybody in the house, except my lady's woman.

*Sir Wil.* Why then belike thou dost not know thy lady, if thou see'st her, ha, friend?

*Foot.* Why truly, sir, I cannot safely swear to her face in a morning, before she is dressed. 'Tis like I may give a shrewd guess at her by this time.

*Sir Wil.* Well, prithee try what thou canst do; if thou canst not guess, enquire her out, do'st hear, fellow? And tell her, her nephew, Sir Wilfull Witwould, is in the house.

*Foot.* I shall, sir.

*Sir Wil.* Hold ye, hear me, friend; a word with you in your ear, prithee who are these gallants?

*Foot.* Really, sir, I can't tell; here come so many here, 'tis hard to know 'em all.

## SCENE XV. SIR WILFULL WITWOUD, PETULANT, WITWOUD, MRS. MARWOOD

*Sir Wil.* Oons this fellow knows less than a starling; I don't think a' knows his own name.

*Mrs. Mar.* Mr. Witwoud, your brother is not behind-hand in forgetfulness—I fancy he has forgot you too.

*Wit.* I hope so—the devil take him that remembers first, I say.

*Sir Wil.* Save you, gentlemen and lady.

*Mrs. Mar.* For shame, Mr. Witwoud; why won't you speak to him? And you, sir.

*Wit.* Petulant, speak.

*Pet.* And you, sir.

*Sir Wil.* No offence, I hope. [*Salutes* MARWOOD.

*Mrs. Mar.* No, sure, sir.

*Wit.* This is a vile dog, I see that already. No offence! Ha, ha, ha, to him; to him, Petulant, smoke him.

*Pet.* It seems as if you had come a journey, sir; hem, hem.
[*Surveying him round.*

*Sir Wil.* Very likely, sir, that it may seem so.

*Pet.* No offence, I hope, sir.

*Wit.* Smoke the boots, the boots; Petulant, the boots; ha, ha, ha.

*Sir Wil.* Maybe not, sir; thereafter as 'tis meant, sir.

*Pet.* Sir, I presume upon the information of your boots.

*Sir Wil.* Why, 'tis like you may, sir: if you are not satisfied with the information of my boots, sir, if you will step to the stable, you may enquire further of my horse, sir.

*Pet.* Your horse, sir! Your horse is an ass, sir!

*Sir Wil.* Do you speak by way of offence, sir?

*Mrs. Mar.* The gentleman's merry, that's all, sir.—S'life, we shall have a quarrel betwixt an horse and an ass, before they find one another out. You must not take anything amiss from your friends, sir. You are among your friends here, though it may be you don't know it.—If I am not mistaken, you are Sir Wilfull Witwoud.

*Sir Wil.* Right, lady; I am Sir Wilfull Witwoud, so I write myself; no offence to anybody, I hope; and nephew to the Lady Wishfort of this mansion.

*Mrs. Mar.* Don't you know this gentleman, sir?

*Sir Wil.* Hum! What, sure 'tis not—Yea, by'r lady, but 'tis—'Sheart, I know not whether 'tis or no—Yea, but 'tis, by the Rekin. Brother Antony! What, Tony, i'faith! What do'st thou not know me? By'r Lady, nor I thee, thou art so becravated, and so beperriwiged—'Sheart, why do'st not speak? Art thou o'erjoyed?

*Wit.* Odso, brother, is it you? Your servant, brother.

*Sir Wil.* Your servant! Why yours, sir. Your servant again—'Sheart, and your friend and servant to that—And a—(*puff*) and a flap dragon for your service, sir: and a hare's foot, and a hare's scut for your service, sir; an you be so cold and so courtly!

*Wit.* No offence, I hope, brother.

*Sir Wil.* 'Sheart, sir, but there is, and much offence.—A pox, is this your Inns o' Court breeding, not to know your friends and your relations, your elders, and your betters?

*Wit.* Why, brother Wilfull of Salop, you may be as short as a Shrewsbury cake, if you please. But I tell you 'tis not modish to know relations in town. You think you're in the country, where great lubberly brothers slabber and kiss one another when they meet, like a call of serjeants—'Tis not the fashion here; 'tis not indeed, dear brother.

*Sir Wil.* The fashion's a fool; and you're a fop, dear brother. 'Sheart, I've suspected this—By'r Lady I conjectured you were a fop, since you began to change the stile of your letters, and write in a scrap of paper gilt round the edges, no bigger than a subpæna. I might expect this when you left off Honoured Brother; and hoping you are in good health, and so forth—to begin with a Rat me, knight, I'm so sick of a last night's debauch—O'ds heart, and then tell a familiar tale of a cock and a bull, and a whore and a bottle, and so conclude—You could write news before you were out of your time, when you lived with honest Pumple-Nose, the attorney of Furnival's Inn—You could intreat to be remembered then to your friends round the Rekin. We could have Gazettes then, and Dawks's Letter, and the Weekly Bill, 'till of late days.

*Pet.* 'Slife, Witwoud, were you ever an attorney's clerk? Of the family of the Furnivals. Ha, ha, ha!

*Wit.* Ay, ay, but that was but for a while. Not long, not long; pshaw, I was not in my own power then. An orphan, and this fellow was my guardian; ay, ay, I was glad to consent to that man to come to London. He had the disposal of me then. If I had not agreed to that, I might have been bound prentice to a felt-maker in Shrewsbury; this fellow would have bound me to a maker of felts.

*Sir Wil.* 'Sheart, and better than to be bound to a maker of fops; where, I suppose, you have served your time; and now you may set up for yourself.

*Mrs. Mar.* You intend to travel, sir, as I'm informed.

*Sir Wil.* Belike I may, madam. I may chance to sail upon the salt seas, if my mind hold.

*Pet.* And the wind serve.

*Sir Wil.* Serve or not serve, I shan't ask license of you, sir; nor the weather-cock your companion. I direct my discourse to the lady, sir. 'Tis like my aunt may have told you, madam—Yes, I have settled my concerns, I may say now, and am minded to see foreign parts. If an how that the peace holds, whereby that is taxes abate.

*Mrs. Mar.* I thought you had designed for France at all adventures.

*Sir Wil.* I can't tell that; 'tis like I may, and 'tis like I may not. I am somewhat dainty in making a resolution,—because when I make it I keep it. I don't stand shill I, shall I, then; if I say't, I'll do't: But I have thoughts to tarry a small matter in town, to learn somewhat of your lingo first, before I cross the seas. I'd gladly have a spice of your French as they say, whereby to hold discourse in foreign countries.

*Mrs. Mar.* Here's an academy in town for that use.

*Sir Wil.* There is? 'Tis like there may.

*Mrs. Mar.* No doubt you will return very much improved.

*Wit.* Yes, refined like a Dutch skipper from a whale-fishing.

## Scene XVI. [*To them*] lady wishford *and* fainall

*Lady*. Nephew, you are welcome.

*Sir Wil.* Aunt, your servant.

*Fain.* Sir Wilfull, your most faithful servant.

*Sir Wil.* Cousin Fainall, give me your hand.

*Lady*. Cousin Witwoud, your servant; Mr. Petulant, your servant—nephew, you are welcome again. Will you drink anything after your journey, nephew, before you eat? Dinner's almost ready.

*Sir Wil.* I'm very well thank you, aunt— however, I thank you for your courteous offer. 'Sheart, I was afraid you would have been in the fashion too, and have remembered to have forgot your relations. Here's your Cousin Tony, belike, I mayn't call him brother for fear of offence.

*Lady*. O he's a rallier, nephew—my cousin's a wit; and your great wits always rally their best friends to chuse. When you have been abroad, nephew, you'll understand raillery better.

[Fain. *and* Mrs. Marwood *talk apart.*

*Sir Wil.* Why then let him hold his tongue in the meantime; and rail when that day comes.

## Scene XVII. [*To them*] mincing

*Minc.* Mem, I come to acquaint your laship that dinner is impatient.

*Sir Wil.* Impatient? Why then belike it won't stay 'till I pull off my boots. Sweetheart, can you help me to a pair of slippers?—My man's with his horses, I warrant.

*Lady*. Fie, fie, nephew, you would not pull off your boots here—go down into the hall—dinner shall stay for you.—My nephew's a little unbred, you'll pardon him, madam—Gentlemen, will you walk? Marwood?

*Mrs. Mar.* I'll follow you, madam,—before Sir Wilfull is ready.

## Scene XVIII. marwood, fainall

*Fain.* Why then Foible's a bawd, an errant, rank, match-making bawd. And I, it seems, am a husband, a rank-husband; and my wife a very errant, rank-wife,—all in the way of the world. 'Sdeath, to be a cuckold by anticipation, a cuckold in embrio? Sure I was born with budding antlers like a young satyr, or a citizen's child. 'Sdeath, to be outwitted, to be outjilted—out-matrimonied—If I had kept my speed like a stag, 'twere somewhat—but to crawl after, with my horns like a snail, and be outstripped by my wife—'tis scurvy wedlock.

*Mrs. Mar.* Then shake it off, you have often wished for an opportunity to part;—and now you have it. But first prevent their plot,—the half of Millamant's fortune is too considerable to be parted with, to a foe, to Mirabell.

*Fain.* Dam him, that had been mine, had you not made that fond discovery—that had been forfeited, had they been married. My wife had added lustre to my horns, by that encrease of fortune, I could have worn 'em tipt with gold, though my forehead had been furnished like a deputy-lieutenant's hall.

*Mrs. Mar.* They may prove a cap of maintenance to you still, if you can away with your wife. And she's no worse than when you had her—I dare swear she had given up her game, before she was married.

*Fain.* Hum! That may be—

*Mrs. Mar.* You married her to keep you; and if you can contrive to have her keep you better than you expected, why should you not keep her longer than you intended?

*Fain.* The means, the means.

*Mrs. Mar.* Discover to my lady your wife's conduct; threaten to part with her—my lady loves her, and will come to any composition to save her reputation. Take the opportunity of breaking it, just upon the discovery of this imposture. My lady will be enraged beyond bounds, and sacrifice niece, and fortune, and all at that conjuncture. And let me alone to keep her warm; if she should flag in her part, I will not fail to prompt her.

*Fain.* Faith, this has an appearance.

*Mrs. Mar.* I'm sorry I hinted to my lady to endeavour a match between Millamant and Sir Wilfull, that may be an obstacle.

*Fain.* O for that matter leave me to manage him; I'll disable him for that, he will drink like a Dane: after dinner, I'll set his hand in.

*Mrs. Mar.* Well, how do you stand affected towards your lady?

*Fain.* Why faith I'm thinking of it.—Let me see—I am married already; so that's over—My wife has plaid the jade with me—well, that's over too—I never loved her, or if I had, why that would have been over too by this time—Jealous of her I cannot be, for I am certain; so there's an end of jealousie. Weary of her, I am and shall be—No, there's no end of that; no, no, that were too much to hope. Thus far concerning my repose. Now for my reputation—As to my own, I married not for it; so that's out of the question.—And as to my part in my wife's—why she had parted with hers before; so bringing none to me, she can take none from me; 'tis against all rule of play, that I should lose to one who has not wherewithal to stake.

*Mrs. Mar.* Besides, you forget, marriage is honourable.

*Fain.* Hum! Faith and that's well thought on; marriage is honourable, as you say; and if so, wherefore should cuckoldom be a discredit, being derived from so honourable a root?

*Mrs. Mar.* Nay, I know not; if the root be honourable, why not the branches?

*Fain.* So, so, why this point's clear.—Well, how do we proceed?

*Mrs. Mar.* I will contrive a letter which shall be delivered to my lady at the time when that rascal who is to act Sir Rowland is with her. It shall come as from an unknown hand—for the less I appear to know of the truth, the better I can play the incendiary. Besides, I would not have Foible provoked if I could help it,—because you know she knows some passages—nay, I expect all will come out—but let the mine be sprung first, and then I care not if I am discovered.

*Fain.* If the worst come to the worst, I'll turn my wife out to grass—I have already a deed of settlement of the best part of her estate; which I wheadled out of her; and that you shall partake at least.

*Mrs. Mar.* I hope you are convinced that I hate Mirabell now: you'll be no more jealous?

*Fain.* Jealous, no,—by this kiss—let husbands be jealous; but let the lover still believe: or if he doubt, let it be only to endear his pleasure, and prepare the joy that follows, when he proves his mistress true. But let husbands' doubts convert to endless jealousie; or if they have belief, let it corrupt to superstition, and blind credulity. I am single, and will herd no more with 'em. True, I wear the badge, but I'll disown the order. And since I take my leave of 'em, I care not if I leave 'em a common motto to their common crest.

All husbands must, or pain, or shame, endure;
The wife too jealous are, fools to secure.

## ACT IV

### Scene I. [*Scene continues*] LADY WISHFORT *and* FOIBLE

*Lady.* Is Sir Rowland coming say'st thou, Foible? and are things in order?

*Foib.* Yes, madam. I have put wax-lights in the sconces; and placed the footmen in a row in the hall, in their best liveries, with the coachman and postilion to fill up the equipage.

*Lady.* Have you pullvilled the coachman and postilion, that they may not stink of the stable, when Sir Rowland comes by?

*Foib.* Yes, madam.

*Lady.* And are the dancers and the music ready, that he may be entertained in all points with correspondence to his passion?

*Foib.* All is ready, madam.

*Lady.* And—well—and how do I look, Foible?

*Foib.* Most killing well, madam.

*Lady.* Well, and how shall I receive him? In what figure shall I give his heart the first impression? There is a great deal in the first impression. Shall I sit?—No, I won't sit—I'll walk—ay, I'll walk from the door upon his entrance; and then turn full upon him—No, that will be too sudden. I'll lye—ay, I'll lye down—I'll receive him in my little dressing-room, there's a couch—yes, yes, I'll give the first impression on a couch—I won't lye neither, but loll and lean upon one elbow; with one foot a little dangling off, jogging in a thoughtful way—yes—and then as soon as he appears, start, ay, start and be surprized, and rise to meet him in a pretty disorder—yes—O, nothing is more alluring than a levee from a couch in some confusion—it shews the foot to advantage, and furnishes with blushes, and re-composing airs beyond comparison. Hark! There's a coach.

*Foib.* 'Tis he, madam.

*Lady.* O dear, has my nephew made his addresses to Millamant? I ordered him.

*Foib.* Sir Wilfull is set in to drinking, madam, in the parlour.

*Lady.* Ods my life, I'll send him to her. Call her down, Foible; bring her hither. I'll send him as I go—When they are together, then come to me, Foible, that I may not be too long alone with Sir Rowland.

## SCENE II. MRS. MILLAMANT, MRS. FAINALL, FOIBLE

*Foib.* Madam, I stayed here, to tell your ladiship that Mr. Mirabell has waited this half-hour for an opportunity to talk with you. Though my lady's orders were to leave you and Sir Wilfull together. Shall I tell Mr. Mirabell that you are at leisure?

*Milla.* No—What would the dear man have? I am thoughtful, and would amuse myself,—bid him come another time.

There never yet was woman made,
Nor shall, but to be cursed.

[*Repeating and walking about.*

That's hard!

*Mrs. Fain.* You are very fond of Sir John Suckling to-day, Millamant, and the poets.

*Milla.* He? Ay, and filthy verses—so I am.

*Foib.* Sir Wilfull is coming, madam. Shall I send Mr. Mirabell away?

*Milla.* Ay, if you please, Foible, send him away,—or send him hither,—just as you will, dear Foible.—I think I'll see him—Shall I? Ay, let the wretch come.

Thyrsis, a youth of the inspired train. [*Repeating.*

Dear Fainall, entertain Sir Wilfull—thou hast philosophy to undergo a fool, thou art married and hast patience—I would confer with my own thoughts.

*Mrs. Fain.* I am obliged to you, that you would make me your proxy in this affair; but I have business of my own.

SCENE III. [*To them*] SIR WILFULL

*Mrs. Fain.* O Sir Wilfull; you are come at the critical instant. There's your mistress up to the ears in love and contemplation, pursue your point, now or never.

*Sir Wil.* Yes; my aunt will have it so,—I would gladly have been encouraged with a bottle or two, because I'm somewhat wary at first, before I am acquainted—[*This while* MILLA. *walks about repeating to herself.*] But I hope, after a time, I shall break my mind—that is upon further acquaintance.—So for the present, cousin, I'll take my leave—if so be you'll be so kind to make my excuse, I'll return to my company—

*Mrs. Fain.* O fie, Sir Wilfull! What, you must not be daunted.

*Sir Wil.* Daunted, no, that's not it, it is not so much for that—for if so be that I set on't, I'll do't. But only for the present, 'tis sufficient 'till further acquaintance, that's all—your servant.

*Mrs. Fain.* Nay, I'll swear you shall never lose so favourable an opportunity, if I can help it. I'll leave you together, and lock the door.

SCENE IV. SIR WILFULL, MILLAMANT

*Sir Wil.* Nay, nay, cousin,—I have forgot my gloves.—What d'ye do? 'Sheart, a' has locked the door indeed, I think—Nay, Cousin Fainall, open the door—Pshaw, what a vixon trick is this?—Nay, now a' has seen me too—cousin, I made bold to pass through as it were—I think this door's inchanted—

*Milla.* [*repeating*].

I prithee spare me, gentle boy,
Press me no more for that slight toy.

*Sir Wil.* Anan? Cousin, your servant.

*Milla.* That foolish trifle of a heart–
Sir Wilfull!

*Sir Wil.* Yes–your servant. No offence, I hope, cousin.

*Milla.* [*repeating.*]

I swear it will not do its part,
Though thou dost thine, employ'st thy power and art.

Natural, easie Suckling!

*Sir Wil.* Anan? Suckling? No such suckling neither, cousin, nor stripling: I thank Heaven, I'm no minor.

*Milla.* Ah, rustick, ruder than Gothick.

*Sir Wil.* Well, well, I shall understand your lingo one of these days, cousin, in the meanwhile I must answer in plain English.

*Milla.* Have you any business with me, Sir Wilfull?

*Sir Wil.* Not at present, cousin.–Yes, I made bold to see, to come and know if that how you were disposed to fetch a walk this evening, if so be that I might not be troublesome, I would have sought a walk with you.

*Milla.* A walk? What then?

*Sir Wil.* Nay, nothing–only for the walk's sake, that's all–

*Milla.* I nauseate walking; 'tis a country diversion, I loath the country and everything that relates to it.

*Sir Wil.* Indeed! Hah! Look ye, look ye, you do? Nay, 'tis like you may–Here are choice of pastimes here in town, as plays and the like, that must be confessed indeed–

*Milla. Ah l'etourdie!* I hate the town too.

*Sir Wil.* Dear heart, that's much–Hah! that you should hate 'em both! Hah! 'tis like you may; there are some can't relish the town, and others can't away with the country,–'tis like you may be one of those, cousin.

*Milla.* Ha, ha, ha. Yes, 'tis like I may.–You have nothing further to say to me?

*Sir Wil.* Not at present, cousin.–'Tis like when I have an opportunity to be more private, I may break my mind in some measure–I conjecture you partly guess–However, that's as time shall try,–but spare to speak and spare to speed, as they say.

*Milla.* If it is of no great importance, Sir Wilfull, you will oblige me to leave me: I have just now a little business–

*Sir Wil.* Enough, enough, cousin: yes, yes, all a case—when you're disposed, when you're disposed. Now's as well as another time; and another time as well as now. All's one for that.—Yes, yes, if your concerns call you, there's no haste; it will keep cold as they say—Cousin, your servant.—I think this door's locked.

*Milla.* You may go this way, sir.

*Sir Wil.* Your servant, then with your leave I'll return to my company.

*Milla.* Ay, ay; ha, ha, ha.

Like Phœbus sung the no less am'rous boy.

## Scene V. MILLAMANT, MIRABELL

*Mira.* Like Daphne she, as lovely and as coy.
Do you lock yourself up from me, to make my search more curious? Or is this pretty artifice contrived, to signifie that here the chance must end, and my pursuit be crowned, for you can fly no further?

*Milla.* Vanity! No—I'll fly and be followed to the last moment, though I am upon the very verge of matrimony, I expect you should sollicit me as much as if I were wavering at the grate of a monastery, with one foot over the threshold. I'll be sollicited to the very last, nay and afterwards.

*Mira.* What, after the last?

*Milla.* O, I should think I was poor and had nothing to bestow, if I were reduced to an inglorious ease, and freed from the agreeable fatigues of sollicitation.

*Mira.* But do not you know, that when favours are conferred upon instant and tedious sollicitation, that they deminish in their value, and that both the giver loses the grace, and the receiver lessens his pleasure?

*Milla.* It may be in things of common application; but never sure in love. O, I hate a lover that can dare to think he draws a moment's air, independent on the bounty of his mistress. There is not so impudent a thing in nature, as the sawcy look of an assured man, confident of success. The pedantick arrogance of a very husband has not so pragmatical an air. Ah! I'll never marry, unless I am first made sure of my will and pleasure.

*Mira.* Would you have 'em both before marriage? Or will you be contented with the first now, and stay for the other 'till after grace?

*Milla.* Ah, don't be so impertinent—My dear liberty, shall I leave thee? My faithful solitude, my darling contemplation, must I bid you then adieu? Ay-h, adieu—my morning thoughts, agreeable wakings, indolent slumbers, all ye *douceurs*, ye *someils du matin*, adieu—I can't do't, 'tis more than impossible—Positively, Mirabell, I'll lye abed in a morning as long as I please.

*Mira.* Then I'll get up in a morning as early as I please.

*Milla.* Ah! Idle creature, get up when you will—And d'ye hear, I won't be called names after I'm married; positively I won't be called names.

*Mira.* Names!

*Milla.* Ay, as wife, spouse, my dear, joy, jewel, love, sweetheart, and the rest of that nauseous cant, in which men and their wives are so fulsomly familiar—I shall never bear that—Good Mirabell, don't let us be familiar or fond, nor kiss before folks, like my Lady Fadler and Sir Francis: nor go to Hide Park together the first Sunday in a new chariot, to provoke eyes and whispers; and then never be seen there together again; as if we were proud of one another the first week, and ashamed of one another ever after. Let us never visit together, nor go to a play together, but let us be very strange and well bred: let us be as strange as if we had been married a great while; and as well bred as if we were not married at all.

*Mira.* Have you any more conditions to offer? Hitherto your demands are pretty reasonable.

*Milla.* Trifles,—as liberty to pay and receive visits to and from whom I please; to write and receive letters, without interrogatories or wry faces on your part; to wear what I please; and chuse conversation with regard only to my own taste; to have no obligation upon me to converse with wits that I don't like, because they are your acquaintance; or to be intimate with fools because they may be your relations. Come to dinner when I please, dine in my dressing-room when I'm out of humour, without giving a reason. To have my closet inviolate; to be sole empress of my tea-table, which you must never presume to approach without first asking leave. And lastly, wherever I am, you shall always knock at the door before you come in. These articles subscribed, if I continue to endure you a little longer, I may by degrees dwindle into a wife.

*Mira.* Your bill of fare is something advanced in this latter account. Well, have I liberty to offer conditions—that when you are dwindled into a wife, I may not be beyond measure enlarged into a husband?

*Milla.* You have free leave, propose your utmost, speak and spare not.

*Mira.* I thank you. *Inprimis* then, I covenant that your acquaintance be general; that you admit no sworn confident, or intimate of your own sex; no she friend to skreen her affairs under your countenance, and tempt you to make trial of a mutual secresie. No decoy-duck to wheadle you a *fop—scrambling* to the play in a mask—then bring you home in a pretended fright, when you think you shall be found out—and rail at me for missing the play, and disappointing the frolick which you had to pick me up and prove my constancy.

*Milla.* Detestable *inprimis!* I go to the play in a mask!

*Mira. Item,* I article, that you continue to like your own face as long as I shall: and while it passes currant with me, that you endeavour not to new coin it. To which end, together with all vizards for the day, I prohibit all masks for the night, made of oiled-skins and I know not what—hog's bones, hare's gall, pig water, and the marrow of a roasted cat. In short, I forbid all commerce with the gentlewoman in *what-d'ye-call-it* Court. *Item,* I shut my doors against all bauds with baskets, and pennyworths of *muslin, china, fans, atlasses,* etc.—*Item,* when you shall be breeding—

*Milla.* Ah! name it not.

*Mira.* Which may be presumed, with a blessing on our endeavours—

*Milla.* Odious endeavours!

*Mira.* I denounce against all strait lacing, squeezing for a shape, 'till you mould my boy's head like a sugar-loaf; and instead of a man-child, make me father to a crooked-billet. Lastly, to the dominion of the *tea-table* I submit.—But with *proviso,* that you exceed not in your province; but restrain yourself to native and simple *tea-table* drinks, as *tea, chocolate,* and *coffee.* As likewise to genuine and authorised *tea-table* talk—such as mending of fashions, spoiling reputations, railing at absent friends, and so forth—but that on no account you encroach upon the men's prerogative, and presume to drink healths, or toast fellows; for prevention of which, I banish all *foreign forces,* all auxiliaries to the *tea-table,* as *orange-brandy,* all *anniseed, cinamon, citron* and *Barbado's-waters,* together with *ratafia* and the most noble spirit of *clary.*—But for *couslip-wine, poppy-water,* and all *dormitives,* those I allow.—These *provisos* admitted, in other things I may prove a tractable and complying husband.

*Milla.* O horrid *provisos!* filthy strong waters! I toast fellows, odious men! I hate your odious *provisos.*

*Mira.* Then we're agreed. Shall I kiss your hand upon the contract? and here comes one to be a witness to the sealing of the deed.

## Scene VI. [*To them*] MRS. FAINALL

*Milla.* Fainall, what shall I do? Shall I have him? I think I must have him.

*Mrs. Fain.* Ay, ay, take him, take him, what should you do?

*Milla.* Well then—I'll take my death I'm in a horrid fright—Fainall, I shall never say it—Well—I think—I'll endure you.

*Mrs. Fain.* Fy, fy, have him, have him, and tell him so in plain terms: for I am sure you have a mind to him.

*Milla.* Are you? I think I have—and the horrid man looks as if he thought so too—Well, you ridiculous thing you, I'll have you—I won't be kissed, nor I won't be thanked—Here, kiss my hand though—so, hold your tongue now, don't say a word.

*Mrs. Fain.* Mirabell, there's a necessity for your obedience;—you have neither time to talk nor stay. My mother is coming; and in my conscience, if she should see you, would fall into fits, and maybe not recover time enough to return to Sir Rowland; who, as Foible tells me, is in a fair way to succeed. Therefore spare your extacies for another occasion, and slip down the back stairs, where Foible waits to consult you.

*Milla.* Ay, go, go. In the meantime I suppose you have said something to please me.

*Mira.* I am all obedience.

## SCENE VII. MILLAMANT, MRS. FAINALL

*Mrs. Fain.* Yonder Sir Wilfull's drunk; and so noisie that my mother has been forced to leave Sir Rowland to appease him; but he answers her only with singing and drinking—What they may have done by this time I know not; but Petulant and he were upon quarrelling as I came by.

*Milla.* Well, if Mirabell should not make a good husband, I am a lost thing; for I find I love him violently.

*Mrs. Fain.* So it seems; for you mind not what's said to you.—If you doubt him, you had best take up with Sir Wilfull.

*Milla.* How can you name that superannuated lubber? foh!

## SCENE VIII. [*To them*] WITWOUD *from drinking*

*Mrs. Fain.* So, is the fray made up, that you have left 'em?

*Wit.* Left 'em? I could stay no longer—I have laughed like ten christnings—I am tipsie with laughing—if I had staid any longer I should have burst,—I must have been let out and pieced in the sides like an unsized camlet—Yes, yes, the fray is composed; my lady came in like a *noli prosequi*, and stopt the proceedings.

*Milla.* What was the dispute?

*Wit.* That's the jest; there was no dispute. They could neither of 'em speak for rage; and so fell a sputtering at one another like two roasting apples.

SCENE IX. [*To them*] PETULANT *drunk*

*Wit.* Now, Petulant? all's over, all's well? Gad, my head begins to whim it about—Why dost thou not speak? thou art both as drunk and as mute as a fish.

*Pet.* Look you, Mrs. Millamant—if you can love me, dear nymph—say it—and that's the conclusion—pass on, or pass off,—that's all.

*Wit.* Thou hast uttered volumes, folios, in less than *decimo sexto*, my dear Lacedemonian. Sirrah, Petulant, thou art an epitomiser of words.

*Pet.* Witwoud—you are an annihilator of sense.

*Wit.* Thou art a retailer of phrases; and dost deal in remnants of remnants, like a maker of pincushions—thou art in truth (metaphorically speaking) a speaker of shorthand.

*Pet.* Thou art (without a figure) just one half of an ass, and Baldwin yonder, thy half-brother, is the rest—a gemini of asses split, would make just four of you.

*Wit.* Thou dost bite, my dear mustard-seed; kiss me for that.

*Pet.* Stand off—I'll kiss no more males,—I have kissed your *twin* yonder in a humour of reconciliation, 'till he (*hiccup*) rises upon my stomach like a radish.

*Milla.* Eh! filthy creature—what was the quarrel?

*Pet.* There was no quarrel—there might have been a quarrel.

*Wit.* If there had been words enow between 'em to have expressed provocation, they had gone together by the ears like a pair of castanets.

*Pet.* You were the quarrel.

*Milla.* Me!

*Pet.* If I have a humour to quarrel, I can make less matters conclude premises.—If you are not handsom, what then; if I have a humour to prove it?—If I shall have my reward, say so; if not, fight for your face the next time yourself—I'll go sleep.

*Wit.* Do, wrap thyself up like a woodlouse, and dream revenge—and hear me, if thou canst learn to write by to-morrow morning, pen me a challenge—I'll carry it for thee.

*Pet.* Carry your mistress's monkey a spider,—go flea dogs, and read romances—I'll go to bed to my maid.

*Mrs. Fain.* He's horribly drunk—how came you all in this pickle?

*Wit.* A plot, a plot, to get rid of the knight,—your husband's advice; but he sneaked off.

SCENE X. SIR WILFULL *drunk*, LADY WISHFORT, WITWOUD, MILLAMANT, MRS. FAINALL

*Lady.* Out upon't, out upon't, at years of discretion, and comport yourself at this rantipole rate.

*Sir Wil.* No offence, aunt.

*Lady.* Offence? As I'm a person, I'm ashamed of you—Fogh! how you stink of wine! D'ye think my niece will ever endure such a *borachio!* you're an absolute *borachio.*

*Sir Wil. Borachio!*

*Lady.* At a time when you should commence an amour, and put your best foot foremost—

*Sir Wil.* 'Sheart, an you grutch me your liquor, make a bill—give me more drink, and take my purse. [*Sings.*

Prithee fill me the glass
'Till it laugh in my face,
With ale that is potent and mellow;
He that whines for a lass
Is an ignorant ass,
For a *bumper* has not its fellow.

But if you would have me marry my cousin, say the word, and I'll do't—Wilfull will do't, that's the word—Wilfull will do't, that's my crest—my motto I have forgot.

*Lady.* My nephew's a little overtaken, cousin—but 'tis with drinking your health—O' my word you are obliged to him—

*Sir Wil. In vino veritas,* aunt:—If I drunk your health to-day, cousin, I am a *borachio.* But if you have a mind to be married say the word, and send for the piper, Wilfull will do't. If not, dust it away, and let's have t'other round—Tony, 'odsheart, where's Tony—Tony's an honest fellow, but he spits after a bumper, and that's a fault. [*Sings.*

We'll drink and we'll never ha' done, boys,
Put the glass then around with the sun, boys,
Let Apollo's example invite us;
For he's drunk every night,
And that makes him so bright,
That he's able next morning to light us.

The sun's a good pimple, an honest soaker, he has a cellar at your Antipodes. If I travel, aunt, I touch at your Antipodes—your Antipodes are a good rascally sort of topsie-turvy fellows—if I had a bumper I'd stand upon my head and drink a health to 'em—A match or no match, cousin, with the hard name—aunt, Wilfull will do't. If she has her maidenhead let her look to't; if she has not, let her keep her own counsel in the meantime, and cry out at the nine months' end.

*Milla.* Your pardon, madam, I can stay no longer—Sir Wilfull grows very powerful. Egh! how he smells! I shall be overcome if I stay. Come, cousin.

## SCENE XI. LADY WISHFORT, SIR WILFULL WITWOUD, MR. WITWOUD, FOIBLE

*Lady.* Smells! he would poison a tallow-chandler and his family. Beastly creature, I know not what to do with him.—Travel, quoth a; ay travel, travel, get thee gone, get thee but far enough, to the Saracens, or the Tartars, or the Turks—for thou art not fit to live in a Christian commonwealth, thou beastly pagan.

*Sir Wil.* Turks, no; no Turks, aunt: your Turks are infidels, and believe not in the grape. Your Mahometan, your Mussulman is a dry stinkard—no offence, aunt. My map says that your Turk is not so honest a man as your Christian—I cannot find by the map that your mufti is orthodox—whereby it is a plain case, that orthodox is a hard word, aunt, and (*hiccup*) Greek for claret. [*Sings.*

To drink is a Christian diversion
Unknown to the Turk or the Persian:
  Let Mahometan fools
  Live by heathenish rules,
And be damned over tea-cups and coffee.
  But let British lads sing,
  Crown a health to the king,
And a fig for your sultan and Sophy.

Ah, Tony! [FOIBLE *whispers* LADY WISHFORT.

*Lady.* Sir Rowland impatient? Good lack! what shall I do with this beastly tumbril?—Go lie down and sleep, you sot—or as I'm a person, I'll have you bastinadoed with broom-sticks. Call up the wenches with broom-sticks.

*Sir Wil.* Ahey? Wenches, where are the wenches?

*Lady.* Dear Cousin Witwoud, get him away, and you will bind me to you inviolably. I have an affair of moment that invades me with some precipitation.—You will oblige me to all futurity.

*Wit.* Come, knight—pox on him, I don't know what to say to him—will you go to a cock-match?

*Sir Wil.* With a wench, Tony? Is she a shake-bag, sirrah? Let me bite your cheek for that.

*Wit.* Horrible! He has a breath like a bagpipe—Ay, ay, come, will you march, my Salopian?

*Sir Wil.* Lead on, little Tony—I'll follow thee, my Anthony, my Tantony. Sirrah, thou shalt be my Tantony, and I'll be thy pig.

—And a fig for your sultan and Sophy.

*Lady.* This will never do. It will never make a match—at least before he has been abroad.

SCENE XII. LADY WISHFORT, WAITWELL *disguised as for* SIR ROWLAND

*Lady.* Dear Sir Rowland, I am confounded with confusion at the retrospection of my own rudeness,—I have more pardons to ask than the pope distributes in the year of jubile. But I hope where there is likely to be so near an alliance, we may unbend the severity of decorum, and dispense with a little ceremony.

*Wait.* My impatience, madam, is the effect of my transport;—and 'till I have the possession of your adorable person, I am tantalised on the rack; and do but hang, madam, on the tenter of expectation.

*Lady.* You have excess of gallantry, Sir Rowland; and press things to a conclusion, with a most prevailing vehemence.—But a day or two for decency of marriage—

*Wait.* For decency of funeral, madam. The delay will break my heart—or if that should fail, I shall be poisoned. My nephew will get an inkling of my designs, and poison me,—and I would willingly starve him before I die—I would gladly go out of the world with that satisfaction.—That would be some comfort to me, if I could but live so long as to be revenged on that unnatural viper.

*Lady.* Is he so unnatural, say you? Truly I would contribute much both to the saving of your life, and the accomplishment of your revenge—not that I respect myself; though he has been a perfidious wretch to me.

*Wait.* Profidious to you!

*Lady.* O Sir Rowland, the hours that he has died away at my feet, the tears that he has shed, the oaths that he has sworn, the palpitations that he has felt, the trances and the tremblings, the ardors and the ecstacies, the kneelings, and the risings, the heart-heavings and the hand-gripings, the pangs and the pathetick regards of his protesting eyes! Oh, no memory can register.

*Wait.* What, my rival! Is the rebel my rival? a' dies.

*Lady.* No, don't kill him at once, Sir Rowland, starve him gradually inch by inch.

*Wait.* I'll do't. In three weeks he shall be bare-foot; in a month out at knees with begging an alms,—he shall starve upward and upward, 'till he has nothing living but his head, and then go out in a stink like a candle's end upon a save-all.

*Lady.* Well, Sir Rowland, you have the way,—you are no novice in the labyrinth of love—you have the clue—But as I am a person, Sir Rowland, you must not attribute my yielding to any sinister appetite, or indigestion of widow-hood; nor impute my complacency to any lethargy of continence—I hope you do not think me prone to any iteration of nuptials—

*Wait.* Far be it from me—

*Lady.* If you do, I protest I must recede—or think that I have made a prostitution of decorums, but in the vehemence of compassion, and to save the life of a person of so much importance—

*Wait.* I esteem it so—

*Lady.* Or else you wrong my condescension—

*Wait.* I do not, I do not—

*Lady.* Indeed you do.

*Wait.* I do not, fair shrine of virtue.

*Lady.* If you think the least scruple of carnality was an ingredient—

*Wait.* Dear madam, no. You are all camphire and frankincense, all chastity and odour.

*Lady.* Or that—

## Scene XIII. [*To them*] FOIBLE

*Foib.* Madam, the dancers are ready, and there's one with a letter, who must deliver it into your own hands.

*Lady.* Sir Rowland, will you give me leave? Think favourably, judge candidly, and conclude you have found a person who would suffer racks in honour's cause, dear Sir Rowland, and will wait on you incessantly.

## Scene XIV. WAITWELL, FOIBLE

*Wait.* Fie, fie!—What a slavery have I undergone; spouse, hast thou any cordial, I want spirits.

*Foib.* What a washy rogue art thou, to pant thus for a quarter of an hour's lying and swearing to a fine lady?

*Wait.* O, she is the antidote to desire. Spouse, thou wilt fare the worse for't—I shall have no appetite to iteration of nuptials this eight and forty hours—By this hand I'd rather be a chairman in the dog-days, than act Sir Rowland 'till this time to-morrow.

## Scene XV. [*To them*] Lady *with a letter*

*Lady.* Call in the dancers;—Sir Rowland, we'll sit, if you please, and see the entertainment. [*Dance.*

Now with your permission, Sir Rowland, I will peruse my letter—I would open it in your presence, because I would not make you uneasie. If it should make you uneasie I would burn it—speak if it does—but you may see, the superscription is like a woman's hand.

*Foib.* By heaven! Mrs. Marwood's, I know it,—my heart akes—get it from her— [*To him.*

*Wait.* A woman's hand? No, madam, that's no woman's hand, I see that already. That's somebody whose throat must be cut.

*Lady.* Nay, Sir Rowland, since you give me a proof of your passion by your jealousie, I promise you I'll make a return, by a frank communication—You shall see it—we'll open it together—look you here.

[*Reads.*] "Madam, though unknown to you,"—Look you there, 'tis from nobody that I know—"I have that honour for your character, that I think myself obliged to let you know you are abused. He who pretends to be Sir Rowland is a cheat and a rascal—" Oh heavens! what's this?

*Foib.* Unfortunate, all's ruined.

*Wait.* How, how, let me see, let me see [*reading*], "A rascal and disguised, and suborned for that imposture,"—O villany! O villany!—"by the contrivance of—"

*Lady.* I shall faint, I shall die, oh!

*Foib.* Say 'tis your nephew's hand.—Quickly, his plot, swear, swear it. [*To him.*

*Wait.* Here's a villain! Madam, don't you perceive it, don't you see it?

*Lady.* Too well, too well. I have seen too much.

*Wait.* I told you at first I knew the hand—A woman's hand? The rascal writes a sort of a large hand; your Roman hand—I saw there was a throat to be cut presently. If he were my son, as he is my nephew, I'd pistol him–

*Foib.* O treachery! But are you sure, Sir Rowland, it is his writing?

*Wait.* Sure? Am I here? do I live? do I love this pearl of India? I have twenty letters in my pocket from him, in the same character.

*Lady.* How!

*Foib.* O what luck it is, Sir Rowland, that you were present at this juncture! This was the business that brought Mr. Mirabell disguised to Madam Millamant this afternoon. I thought something was contriving, when he stole by me and would have hid his face.

*Lady.* How, how!–I heard the villain was in the house indeed; and now I remember, my niece went away abruptly, when Sir Wilfull was to have made his addresses.

*Foib.* Then, then, madam, Mr. Mirabell waited for her in her chamber; but I would not tell your ladiship to discompose you when you were to receive Sir Rowland.

*Wait.* Enough, his date is short.

*Foib.* No, good Sir Rowland, don't incur the law.

*Wait.* Law! I care not for law. I can but die, and 'tis in a good cause–my lady shall be satisfied of my truth and innocence, though it cost me my life.

*Lady.* No, dear Sir Rowland, don't fight, if you should be killed I must never shew my face; or hanged–O consider my reputation, Sir Rowland–No, you shan't fight.–I'll go in and examine my niece; I'll make her confess. I conjure you, Sir Rowland, by all your love, not to fight.

*Wait.* I am charmed, madam, I obey. But some proof you must let me give you;–I'll go for a black box, which contains the writings of my whole estate, and deliver that into your hands.

*Lady.* Ay, dear Sir Rowland, that will be some comfort, bring the black box.

*Wait.* And may I presume to bring a contract to be signed this night? May I hope so far?

*Lady.* Bring what you will; but come alive, pray come alive. O this is a happy discovery.

*Wait.* Dead or alive I'll come–and married we will be in spight of treachery; ay, and get an heir that shall defeat the last remaining glimpse of hope in my abandoned nephew. Come, my buxom widow:

E'er long you shall substantial proof receive
That I'm an arrant knight–

*Foib.* Or arrant knave.

# ACT V

## SCENE I. [*Scene continues*] LADY WISHFORT *and* FOIBLE

*Lady.* Out of my house, out of my house, thou viper, thou serpent, that I have fostered; thou bosom traitress, that I raised from nothing—begone, begone, begone, go, go,—that I took from washing of old gause and weaving of dead hair, with a bleak blue nose, over a chafing-dish of starved embers, and dining behind a traver's rag, in a shop no bigger than a birdcage,—go, go, starve again, do, do.

*Foib.* Dear madam, I'll beg pardon on my knees.

*Lady.* Away, out, out, go set up for yourself again—do, drive a trade, do, with your threepenny-worth of small ware, flaunting upon a packthread, under a brandy-feller's bulk, or against a dead wall by a ballad-monger. Go, hang out an old frisoneer-gorget with a yard of yellow colberteen again; do; an old gnawed mask, two rows of pins and a child's fiddle; a glass necklace with the beads broken, and a quilted nightcap with one ear. Go, go, drive a trade.—These were your commodities, you treacherous trull, this was the merchandize you dealt in, when I took you into my house, placed you next myself, and made you governante of my whole family. You have forgot this, have you, now you have feathered your nest?

*Foib.* No, no, dear madam. Do but hear me, have but a moment's patience—I'll confess all. Mr. Mirabell seduced me; I am not the first that he has wheadled with his dissembling tongue; your ladiship's own wisdom has been deluded by him, then how should I, a poor ignorant, defend myself? O madam, if you knew but what he promised me, and how he assured me your ladiship should come to no damage—or else the wealth of the Indies should not have bribed me to conspire against so good, so sweet, so kind a lady as you have been to me.

*Lady.* No damage? What, to betray me, to marry me to a cast-serving-man; to make me a receptacle, an hospital for a decayed pimp? No damage? O thou frontless impudence, more than a big-bellied actress.

*Foib.* Pray do but hear me, madam, he could not marry your ladiship, madam—no indeed, his marriage was to have been void in law; for he was married to me first, to secure your ladiship. He could not have bedded your ladiship; for if he had consummated with your ladiship, he must have run the risque of the law, and been put upon his clergy—Yes indeed, I enquired of the law in that case before I would meddle or make.

*Lady.* What, then I have been your property, have I? I have been convenient to you, it seems,—while you were catering for Mirabell; I have been broaker for you? What, have you made a passive bawd of me?—This exceeds all precedent; I am brought to fine uses, to become a botcher of second-hand marriages between Abigails and Andrews! I'll couple you. Yes, I'll baste you together, you and your Philander. I'll Duke's Place you, as I'm a person. Your turtle is in custody already: you shall coo in the same cage, if there be constable or warrant in the parish.

*Foib.* O that ever I was born, O that I was ever married,—a bride, ay, I shall be a Bridewell-bride. Oh!

## SCENE II. MRS. FAINALL, FOIBLE

*Mrs. Fain.* Poor Foible, what's the matter?

*Foib.* O madam, my lady's gone for a constable; I shall be had to a justice, and put to Bridewell to beat hemp; poor Waitwell's gone to prison already.

*Mrs. Fain.* Have a good heart, Foible, Mirabell's gone to give security for him. This is all Marwood's and my husband's doing.

*Foib.* Yes, yes; I know it, madam; she was in my lady's closet, and overheard all that you said to me before dinner. She sent the letter to my lady; and that missing effect, Mr. Fainall laid this plot to arrest Waitwell, when he pretended to go for the papers; and in the meantime Mrs. Marwood declared all to my lady.

*Mrs. Fain.* Was there no mention made of me in the letter?—My mother does not suspect my being in the confederacy? I fancy Marwood has not told her, though she has told my husband.

*Foib.* Yes, madam; but my lady did not see that part: we stifled the letter before she read so far. Has that mischievous devil told Mr. Fainall of your ladiship then?

*Mrs. Fain.* Ay, all's out, my affair with Mirabell, everything discovered. This is the last day of our living together, that's my comfort.

*Foib.* Indeed, madam, and so 'tis a comfort if you knew all,—he has been even with your ladiship; which I could have told you long enough since, but I love to keep peace and quietness by my good will: I had rather bring friends together than set 'em at distance. But Mrs. Marwood and he are nearer related than ever their parents thought for.

*Mrs. Fain.* Say'st thou so, Foible? Canst thou prove this?

*Foib.* I can take my oath of it, madam, so can Mrs. Mincing; we have had many a fair word from Madam Marwood, to conceal something that passed in our chamber one evening when you were at Hide Park; —and we were thought to have gone a walking: but we went up unawares,—though we were sworn to secresie too; Madam Marwood took a book and swore us upon it: but it was but a book of poems,—so long as it was not a Bible-oath, we may break it with a safe conscience.

*Mrs. Fain.* This discovery is the most opportune thing I could wish. Now Mincing?

## SCENE III. [*To them*] MINCING

*Minc.* My lady would speak with Mrs. Foible, mem. Mr. Mirabell is with her; he has set your spouse at liberty, Mrs. Foible, and would have you hide yourself in my lady's closet, 'till my old lady's anger is abated. O, my old lady is in a perilous passion at something Mr. Fainall has said; he swears, and my old lady cries. There's a fearful hurricane I vow. He says, mem, how that he'll have my lady's fortune made over to him, or he'll be divorced.

*Mrs. Fain.* Does your lady or Mirabell know that?

*Minc.* Yes, mem, they have sent me to see if Sir Wilfull be sober, and to bring him to them. My lady is resolved to have him I think, rather than lose such a vast sum as six thousand pound. O, come, Mrs. Foible, I hear my old lady.

*Mrs. Fain.* Foible, you must tell Mincing that she must prepare to vouch when I call her.

*Foib.* Yes, yes, madam.

*Minc.* O yes, mem, I'll vouch anything for your ladiship's service, be what it will.

## SCENE IV. MRS. FAINALL, LADY WISHFORT, MARWOOD

*Lady.* O my dear friend, how can I enumerate the benefits that I have received from your goodness? To you I owe the timely discovery of the false vows of Mirabell; to you I owe the detection of the impostor Sir Rowland. And now you are become an intercessor with my son-in-law, to save the honour of my house, and compound for the frailties of my daughter. Well, friend, you are enough to reconcile me to the bad world, or else I would retire to desarts and solitudes; and feed harmless sheep by groves and purling streams. Dear Marwood, let us leave the world, and retire by ourselves and be shepherdesses.

*Mrs. Mar.* Let us first dispatch the affair in hand, madam. We shall have leisure to think of retirement afterwards. Here is one who is concerned in the treaty.

*Lady.* O daughter, daughter, is it possible thou should'st be my child, bone of my bone, and flesh of my flesh, and as I may say, another me, and yet transgress the most minute particle of severe virtue? Is it possible you should lean aside to iniquity, who have been cast in the direct mold of virtue? I have not only been a mold but a pattern for you, and a model for you, after you were brought into the world.

*Mrs. Fain.* I don't understand your ladiship.

*Lady.* Not understand? Why, have you not been naught? Have you not been sophisticated? Not understand? Here I am ruined to compound for your caprices and your cuckoldoms. I must pawn my plate and my jewels, and ruin my niece, and all little enough–

*Mrs. Fain.* I am wronged and abused, and so are you. 'Tis a false accusation, as false as hell, as false as your friend there, ay, or your friend's friend, my false husband.

*Mrs. Mar.* My friend, Mrs. Fainall? Your husband my friend, what do you mean?

*Mrs. Fain.* I know what I mean, madam, and so do you; and so shall the world at a time convenient.

*Mrs. Mar.* I am sorry to see you so passionate, madam. More temper would look more like innocence. But I have done. I am sorry my zeal to serve your ladiship and family should admit of misconstruction, or make me liable to affronts. You will pardon me, madam, if I meddle no more with an affair in which I am not personally concerned.

*Lady.* O dear friend, I am so ashamed that you should meet with such returns–You ought to ask pardon on your knees, ungrateful creature; she deserves more from you, than all your life can accomplish– O don't leave me destitute in this perplexity;–no, stick to me, my good genius.

*Mrs. Fain.* I tell you, madam, you're abused–Stick to you? ay, like a leach, to suck your best blood–she'll drop off when she's full. Madam, you shan't pawn a bodkin, nor part with a brass counter, in composition for me. I defie 'em all. Let 'em prove their aspersions: I know my own innocence, and dare stand a trial.

## SCENE V. LADY WISHFORT, MARWOOD

*Lady.* Why, if she should be innocent, if she should be wronged after all, ha? I don't know what to think,–and I promise you, her education has been unexceptionable–I may say it; for I chiefly made it my own care to initiate her very infancy in the rudiments of virtue, and to impress upon her tender years a young odium and aversion to the very sight of men,—ay, friend, she would ha' shrieked if she had but seen a man, 'till she was in her teens. As I'm a person 'tis true.—She was never suffered to play with a male-child, though but in coats; nay, her very babies were of the feminine gender,—O, she never looked a man in the face but her own father, or the chaplain, and him we made a shift to put upon her for a woman, by the help of his long garments, and his sleek face; 'till she was going in her fifteen.

*Mrs. Mar.* 'Twas much she should be deceived so long.

*Lady.* I warrant you, or she would never have born to have been catechised by him; and have heard his long lectures against singing and dancing, and such debaucheries; and going to filthy plays; and prophane musick-meetings, where the lewd trebles squeek nothing but bawdy, and the bases roar blasphemy. O, she would have swooned at the sight or name of an obscene play-book—and can I think after all this, that my daughter can be naught? What, a whore? And thought it excommunication to set her foot within the door of a play-house. O dear friend, I can't believe it, no, no; as she says, let him prove it, let him prove it.

*Mrs. Mar.* Prove it, madam? What, and have your name prostituted in a publick court; yours and your daughter's reputation worried at the bar by a pack of bawling lawyers? To be ushered in with an *O yes* of scandal; and have your case opened by an old fumbling leacher in a quoif like a man midwife, to bring your daughter's infamy to light; to be a theme for legal punsters, and quiblers by the statute; and become a jest, against a rule of court, where there is no precedent for a jest in any record; not even in Doomsday Book: to discompose the gravity of the bench, and provoke naughty interrogatories in more naughty law Latin; while the good judge, tickled with the proceeding, simpers under a grey beard, and figes off and on his cushion as if he had swallowed cantharides, or sate upon cow-itch.

*Lady.* O, 'tis very hard!

*Mrs. Mar.* And then to have my young revellers of the Temple take notes, like prentices at a conventicle; and after talk it over again in Commons, or before drawers in an eating-house.

*Lady.* Worse and worse.

*Mrs. Mar.* Nay, this is nothing; if it would end here 'twere well. But it must after this be consigned by the shorthand writers to the publick press; and from thence be transferred to the hands, nay, into the throats and lungs of hawkers, with voices more licentious than the loud flounder-man's: and this you must hear 'till you are stunned; nay, you must hear nothing else for some days.

*Lady*. O, 'tis insupportable. No, no, dear friend, make it up, make it up; ay, ay, I'll compound. I'll give up all, myself and my all, my niece and her all—anything, everything for composition.

*Mrs. Mar.* Nay, madam, I advise nothing, I only lay before you, as a friend, the inconveniencies which perhaps you have overseen. Here comes Mr. Fainall, if he will be satisfied to huddle up all in silence, I shall be glad. You must think I would rather congratulate than condole with you.

## SCENE VI. FAINALL, LADY WISHFORT, MRS. MARWOOD

*Lady*. Ay, ay, I do not doubt it, dear Marwood: no, no, I do not doubt it.

*Fain.* Well, madam; I have suffered myself to be overcome by the importunity of this lady your friend; and am content you shall enjoy your own proper estate during life; on condition you oblige yourself never to marry, under such penalty as I think convenient.

*Lady*. Never to marry?

*Fain.* No more Sir Rowlands,—the next imposture may not be so timely detected.

*Mrs. Mar.* That condition, I dare answer, my lady will consent to, without difficulty; she has already but too much experienced the perfidiousness of men. Besides, madam, when we retire to our pastoral solitude we shall bid adieu to all other thoughts.

*Lady*. Ay, that's true; but in case of necessity; as of health, or some such emergency—

*Fain.* O, if you are prescribed marriage, you shall be considered; I will only reserve to myself the power to chuse for you. If your physick be wholsome, it matters not who is your apothecary. Next, my wife shall settle on me the remainder of her fortune, not made over already; and for her maintenance depend entirely on my discretion.

*Lady*. This is most inhumanly savage; exceeding the barbarity of a Muscovite husband.

*Fain.* I learned it from his czarish majesty's retinue, in a winter evening's conference over brandy and pepper, amongst other secrets of matrimony and policy, as they are at present practised in the northern hemisphere. But this must be agreed unto, and that positively. Lastly, I will be endowed, in right of my wife, with that six thousand pound, which is the moiety of Mrs. Millamant's fortune in your possession; and which she has forfeited (as will appear by the last will and testament of your deceased husband, Sir Jonathan Wishfort) by her disobedience in contracting herself against your consent or knowledge; and by refusing the offered match with Sir Wilfull Witwoud, which you, like a careful aunt, had provided for her.

*Lady.* My nephew was *non compos;* and could not make his addresses.

*Fain.* I come to make demands—I'll hear no objections.

*Lady.* You will grant me time to consider?

*Fain.* Yes, while the instrument is drawing, to which you must set your hand 'till more sufficient deeds can be perfected: which I will take care shall be done with all possible speed. In the meanwhile I will go for the said instrument, and 'till my return you may ballance this matter in your own discretion.

## SCENE VII. LADY WISHFORT, MRS. MARWOOD

*Lady.* This insolence is beyond all precedent, all parallel; must I be subject to this merciless villain?

*Mrs. Mar.* 'Tis severe indeed, madam, that you should smart for your daughter's wantonness.

*Lady.* 'Twas against my consent that she married this barbarian, but she would have him, though her year was not out.—Ah! her first husband, my son Languish, would not have carried it thus. Well, that was my choice, this is hers; she is matched now with a witness—I shall be mad, dear friend, is there no comfort for me? Must I live to be confiscated at this rebel-rate?—Here come two more of my Egyptian plagues too.

## SCENE VIII. [*To them*] MILLAMANT, SIR WILFULL

*Sir. Wil.* Aunt, your servant.

*Lady.* Out, caterpillar, call not me aunt; I know thee not.

*Sir Wil.* I confess I have been a little in disguise, as they say—'Sheart! and I'm sorry for't. What would you have? I hope I committed no offence, aunt—and if I did I am willing to make satisfaction; and what can a man say fairer? If I have broke anything I'll pay for't, an it cost a pound. And so let that content for what's past, and make no more words. For what's to come, to pleasure you I'm willing to marry my cousin. So pray let's all be friends, she and I are agreed upon the matter before a witness.

*Lady.* How's this, dear niece? Have I any comfort? Can this bė true?

*Milla.* I am content to be a sacrifice to your repose, madam; and to convince you that I had no hand in the plot, as you were misinformed, I have laid my commands on Mirabell to come in person, and be a witness that I give my hand to this flower of knighthood; and for the contract that passed between Mirabell and me, I have obliged him to make a resignation of it in your ladiship's presence;—he is without, and waits your leave for admittance.

*Lady.* Well, I'll swear I am something revived at this testimony of your obedience; but I cannot admit that traitor,—I fear I cannot fortifie myself to support his appearance. He is as terrible to me as a Gorgon; if I see him I fear I shall turn to stone, petrifie incessantly.

*Milla.* If you disoblige him he may resent your refusal, and insist upon the contract still. Then 'tis the last time he will be offensive to you.

*Lady.* Are you sure it will be the last time?—If I were sure of that—shall I never see him again?

*Milla.* Sir Wilfull, you and he are to travel together, are you not?

*Sir Wil.* 'Sheart, the gentleman's a civil gentleman, aunt, let him come in; why, we are sworn brothers and fellow-travellers.—We are to be Pylades and Orestes, he and I—he is to be my interpreter in foreign parts. He has been over-seas once already; and with proviso that I marry my cousin, will cross 'em once again, only to bear me company.—'Sheart, I'll call him in,—an I set on't once, he shall come in; and see who'll hinder him. [*Goes to the door and hems.*

*Mrs. Mar.* This is precious fooling, if it would pass; but I'll know the bottom of it.

*Lady.* O dear Marwood, you are not going?

*Mar.* Not far, madam; I'll return immediately.

## Scene IX. LADY WISHFORT, MILLAMANT, SIR WILFULL, MIRABELL

*Sir Wil.* Look up, man, I'll stand by you, 'sbud, an she do frown, she can't kill you;—besides—harkee, she dare not frown desperately, because her face is none of her own; 'sheart, and she should her forehead would wrinkle like the coat of a cream-cheese; but mum for that, fellow-traveller.

*Mira.* If a deep sense of the many injuries I have offered to so good a lady, with a sincere remorse, and a hearty contrition, can but obtain the least glance of compassion, I am too happy—Ah, madam, there was a time—but let it be forgotten—I confess I have deservedly forfeited the high place I once held, of sighing at your feet; nay, kill me not, by turning from me in disdain—I come not to plead for favour;—nay, not for pardon; I am a suppliant only for pity—I am going where I never shall behold you more—

*Sir Wil.* How, fellow-traveller!—You shall go by yourself then.

*Mira.* Let me be pitied first; and afterwards forgotten—I ask no more.

*Sir Wil.* By'r Lady, a very reasonable request, and will cost you nothing, aunt.—Come, come, forgive and forget, aunt, why you must an you are a Christian.

*Mira.* Consider, madam, in reality, you could not receive much prejudice; it was an innocent device; though I confess it had a face of guiltiness, it was at most an artifice which love contrived—and errors which love produces have ever been accounted venial. At least think it is punishment enough, that I have lost what in my heart I hold most dear, that to your cruel indignation I have offered up this beauty, and with her my peace and quiet; nay, all my hopes of future comfort.

*Sir Wil.* An he does not move me, would I may never be o' the quorum,—an it were not as good a deed as to drink, to give her to him again, I would I might never take shipping—Aunt, if you don't forgive quickly, I shall melt, I can tell you that. My contract went no farther than a little mouth-glew, and that's hardly dry;—one doleful sigh more from my fellow-traveller and 'tis dissolved.

*Lady.* Well, nephew, upon your account—Ah, he has a false insinuating tongue—Well, sir, I will stifle my just resentment at my nephew's request.—I will endeavour what I can to forget,—but on proviso that you resign the contract with my niece immediately.

*Mira.* It is in writing and with papers of concern; but I have sent my servant for it, and will deliver it to you, with all acknowledgments for your transcendent goodness.

*Lady.* Oh, he has witchcraft in his eyes and tongue;—when I did not see him I could have bribed a villain to his assassination; but his appearance rakes the embers which have so long lain smothered in my breast.— [*Aside.*

SCENE X. [*To them*] FAINALL, MRS. MARWOOD

*Fain.* Your date of deliberation, madam, is expired. Here is the instrument, are you prepared to sign?

*Lady.* If I were prepared, I am not impowered. My niece exerts a lawful claim, having matched herself by my direction to Sir Wilfull.

*Fain.* That sham is too gross to pass on me—though 'tis imposed on you, madam.

*Milla.* Sir, I have given my consent.

*Mira.* And, sir, I have resigned my pretensions.

*Sir Wil.* And, sir, I assert my right; and will maintain it in defiance of you, sir, and of your instrument. 'Sheart, an you talk of an instrument, sir, I have an old fox by my thigh shall hack your instrument of ram vellam to shreds, sir. It shall not be sufficient for a mittimus or a tailor's measure; therefore withdraw your instrument, sir, or by'r Lady I shall draw mine.

*Lady.* Hold, nephew, hold.

*Milla.* Good Sir Wilfull, respite your valour.

*Fain.* Indeed? Are you provided of your guard, with your single beef-eater there? But I'm prepared for you; and insist upon my first proposal. You shall submit your own estate to my management, and absolutely make over my wife's to my sole use; as pursuant to the purport and tenor of this other covenant.—I suppose, madam, your consent is not requisite in this case; nor, Mr. Mirabell, your resignation; nor, Sir Wilfull, your right—you may draw your fox if you please sir, and make a bear-garden flourish somewhere else: for here it will not avail. This, my Lady Wishfort, must be subscribed, or your darling daughter's turned adrift, like a leaky hulk to sink or swim, as she and the current of this lewd town can agree.

*Lady.* Is there no means, no remedy, to stop my ruin? Ungrateful wretch! dost thou not owe thy being, thy subsistance, to my daughter's fortune?

*Fain.* I'll answer you when I have the rest of it in my possession.

*Mira.* But that you would not accept of a remedy from my hands—I own I have not deserved you should owe any obligation to me; or else perhaps I could davise—

*Lady.* O what? what? to save me and my child from ruin, from want, I'll forgive all that's past; nay, I'll consent to anything to come, to be delivered from this tyranny.

*Mira.* Ay, madam; but that is too late, my reward is intercepted. You have disposed of her, who only could have made me a compensation for all my services;—but be it as it may, I am resolved I'll serve you, you shall not be wronged in this savage manner.

*Lady.* How! Dear Mr. Mirabell, can you be so generous at last! But it is not possible. Harkee, I'll break my nephew's match, you shall have my niece yet, and all her fortune, if you can but save me from this imminent danger.

*Mira.* Will you? I take you at your word. I ask no more. I must have leave for two criminals to appear.

*Lady.* Ay, ay, anybody, anybody.

*Mira.* Foible is one, and a penitent.

SCENE XI. [*To them*] MRS. FAINALL, FOIBLE, MINCING. MIRA. *and* LADY *go to* MRS. FAIN. *and* FOIBLE

*Mrs. Mar.* O my shame! these corrupt things are brought hither to expose me. [*To* FAIN.

*Fain.* If it must all come out, why let 'em know it, 'tis but *the way of the world.* That shall not urge me to relinquish or abate one title of my terms, no, I will insist the more.

*Foib.* Yes indeed, madam, I'll take my Bible-oath of it.

*Minc.* And so will I, mem.

*Lady.* O Marwood, Marwood, art thou false? my friend deceive me? Hast thou been a wicked accomplice with that profligate man?

*Mrs. Mar.* Have you so much ingratitude and injustice, to give credit against your friend, to the aspersions of two such mercenary truls?

*Minc.* Mercenary, mem? I scorn your words. 'Tis true we found you and Mr. Fainall in the blue garret; by the same token, you swore us to secresie upon Messalinas's poems. Mercenary? No, if we would have been mercenary, we should have held our tongues; you would have bribed us sufficiently.

*Fain.* Go, you are an insignificant thing.—Well, what are you the better for this! Is this Mr. Mirabell's expedient? I'll be put off no longer —You, thing, that was a wife, shall smart for this. I will not leave thee wherewithal to hide thy shame: your body shall be naked as your reputation.

*Mrs. Fain.* I despise you, and defie your malice—you have aspersed me wrongfully—I have proved your falsehood—go you and your treacherous—I will not name it, but starve together—perish.

*Fain.* Not while you are worth a groat, indeed, my dear. Madam, I'll be fooled no longer.

*Lady.* Ah, Mr. Mirabell, this is small comfort, the detection of this affair.

*Mira.* O in good time—Your leave for the other offender and penitent to appear, madam.

SCENE XII. [*To them*] WAITWELL *with a box of writings*

*Lady.* O Sir Rowland—Well, rascal.

*Wait.* What your ladiship pleases.—I have brought the black box at last, madam.

*Mira.* Give it me. Madam, you remember your promise.

*Lady.* Ay, dear sir.

*Mira.* Where are the gentlemen?

*Wait.* At hand, sir, rubbing their eyes,—just risen from sleep.

*Fain.* S'death, what's this to me? I'll not wait your private concerns.

SCENE XIII. [*To them*] PETULANT, WITWOUD

*Pet.* How now? what's the matter? who's hand's out?

*Wit.* Hey day! what, are you all got together, like players at the end of the last act?

*Mira.* You may remember, gentlemen, I once requested your hands as witnesses to a certain parchment.

*Wit.* Ay, I do, my hand I remember—Petulant set his mark.

*Mira.* You wrong him, his name is fairly written, as shall appear—You do not remember, gentlemen, anything of what that parchment contained? [*Undoing the box.*

*Wit.* No.

*Pet.* Not I. I writ, I read nothing.

*Mira.* Very well, now you shall know—Madam, your promise.

*Lady.* Ay, ay, sir, upon my honour.

*Mira.* Mr. Fainall, it is now time that you should know that your lady, while she was at her own disposal, and before you had by your insinuations wheadled her out of a pretended settlement of the greatest part of her fortune—

*Fain.* Sir! pretended!

*Mira.* Yes, sir. I say that this lady while a widow, having it seems received some cautions respecting your inconstancy and tyranny of temper, which from her own partial opinion and fondness of you she could never have suspected—she did, I say, by the wholesome advice of friends and of sages learned more in the laws of this land, deliver this same as her act and deed to me in trust, and to the uses within mentioned. You may read if you please—[*holding out the parchment*] though perhaps what is written on the back may serve your occasions.

*Fain.* Very likely, sir. What's here? Damnation!

[*Reads.*] "A deed of conveyance of the whole estate real of Arabella Languish, widow, in trust to Edward Mirabell."—Confusion!

*Mira.* Even so, sir, 'tis *the way of the world*, sir; of the widows of the world. I suppose this deed may bear an elder date than what you have obtained from your lady.

*Fain.* Perfidious fiend! then thus I'll be revenged.—

[*Offers to run at* MRS. FAIN.

*Sir Wil.* Hold, sir, now you may make your bear-garden flourish somewhere else, sir.

*Fain.* Mirabell, you shall hear of this, sir, be sure you shall.—Let me pass, oaf.

*Mrs. Fain.* Madam, you seem to stifle your resentment: you had better give it vent.

*Mrs. Mar.* Yes, it shall have vent—and to your confusion, or I'll perish in the attempt.

SCENE XIV (THE LAST). LADY WISHFORT, MILLAMANT, MIRABELL, MRS. FAINALL, SIR WILFULL, PETULANT, WITWOUD, FOIBLE, MINCING, WAITWELL

*Lady.* O daughter, daughter, 'tis plain thou hast inherited thy mother's prudence.

*Mrs. Fain.* Thank Mr. Mirabell, a cautious friend, to whose advice all is owing.

*Lady.* Well, Mr. Mirabell, you have kept your promise—and I must perform mine.—First I pardon for your sake Sir Rowland there and Foible—the next thing is to break the matter to my nephew—and how to do that—

*Mira.* For that, madam, give yourself no trouble,—let me have your consent—Sir Wilfull is my friend; he has had compassion upon lovers, and generously engaged a volunteer in this action, for our service; and now designs to prosecute his travels.

*Sir Wil.* 'Sheart, aunt, I have no mind to marry. My cousin's a fine lady, and the gentleman loves her, and she loves him, and they deserve one another; my resolution is to see foreign parts—I have set on't—and when I'm set on't, I must do't. And if these two gentlemen would travel too, I think they may be spared.

*Pet.* For my part, I say little—I think things are best off or on.

*Wit.* I gad, I understand nothing of the matter,—I'm in a maze yet, like a dog in a dancing-school.

*Lady.* Well, sir, take her, and with her all the joy I can give you.

*Milla.* Why does not the man take me? Would you have me give myself to you over again?

*Mira.* Ay, and over and over again.—[*Kisses her hand.*] I would have you as often as possibly I can. Well, Heaven grant I love you not too well, that's all my fear.

*Sir Wil.* 'Sheart, you'll have time enough to toy after you're married; or if you will toy now, let us have a dance in the meantime; that we who are not lovers may have some other employment, besides looking on.

*Mira.* With all my heart, dear Sir Wilfull. What shall we do for musick?

*Foib.* O sir, some that were provided for Sir Rowland's entertainment are yet within call. [*A dance.*

*Lady.* As I am a person I can hold out no longer;—I have wasted my spirits so to-day already, that I am ready to sink under the fatigue; and I cannot but have some fears upon me yet, that my son Fainall will pursue some desperate course.

*Mira.* Madam, disquiet not yourself on that account; to my knowledge his circumstances are such, he must of force comply. For my part, I will contribute all that in me lyes to a reunion; in the meantime, madam [*to* Mrs. Fain.], let me before these witnesses restore to you this deed of trust; it may be a means, well managed, to make you live easily together.

From hence let those be warned, who mean to wed;
Lest mutual falshood stain the bridal-bed:
For each deceiver to his cost may find,
That marriage frauds too oft are paid in kind.

[*Exeunt omnes.*

# EPILOGUE

SPOKEN BY MRS. BRACEGIRDLE

AFTER our epilogue this crowd dismisses,
I'm thinking how this play'll be pulled to pieces.
But pray consider, e'er you doom its fall,
How hard a thing 'twould be, to please you all.
There are some criticks so with spleen diseased,
They scarcely come inclining to be pleased:
And sure he must have more than mortal skill,
Who pleases any one against his will.
Then, all bad poets we are sure are foes,
And how their number's swelled the town well knows:
In shoals, I've marked 'em judging in the pit;
Though they're on no pretence for judgment fit,
But that they have been damned for want of wit.
Since when, they by their own offences taught,
Set up for spies on plays, and finding fault.
Others there are whose malice we'de prevent;
Such, who watch plays, with scurrilous intent
To mark out who by Characters are meant.
And though no perfect likeness they can trace;
Yet each pretends to know the Copied Face.
These, with false glosses feed their own ill-nature,
And turn to Libel, what was meant a Satire.
May such malicious Fops this fortune find,
To think themselves alone the Fools designed:
If any are so arrogantly vain,
To think they singly can support a Scene,
And furnish Fool enough to entertain.
For well the learned and the judicious know,
That Satire scorns to stoop so meanly low,
As any one abstracted Fop to show.
For, as when painters form a matchless face,
They from each Fair one catch some different grace;
And shining features in one portrait blend,
To which no single beauty must pretend:
So poets oft, do in one piece expose
Whole *belles assemblées* of *cocquets* and *beaux*.

# APHORISMS

## II

GOETHE:

THERE is nothing so horrible as imagination devoid of taste.

WE do not learn to know men through their coming to us. To find out what sort of persons they are, we must go to them.

THE intelligent man finds almost everything ridiculous, the sensible man hardly anything.

LORD HALIFAX:

MEN are not hanged for stealing horses, but that horses may not be stolen.

BY that time men are fit for company, they see the objections to it.

A WIFE is to thank God her husband hath faults . . . a husband without faults is a dangerous observer.

THOSE friends who are above interest are seldom above jealousy.

THE excessive desire of pleasing goes along almost always with the apprehension of not being liked.

FULLER

BETTER to sit up all night, than to go to bed with a dragon.

JEREMY TAYLOR

THERE is no refuge from confession but suicide and suicide is confession.

DANIEL WEBSTER

VIRTUE knows to a farthing what it has lost through not being vice.

HORACE WALPOLE

CLEVER liars give details, but the cleverest don't.

ANONYMOUS

INJUSTICE is relatively easy to bear; what stings is justice.

H. L. MENCKEN

BEWARE of all enterprises that require new clothes.

THOREAU

EVERY one thinks himself well-bred.

SHAFTESBURY

THEY say Princes learn no art truly, but the art of horsemanship. The reason is, the brave beast is no flatterer. He will throw a prince as soon as his groom.

BEN JONSON

# LUCIAN OF SAMOSATA

## *Zeus Cross-Examined*

CYNISCUS. ZEUS

*Cyn.* Zeus: I am not going to trouble you with requests for a fortune or a throne; you get prayers enough of that sort from other people, and from your habit of convenient deafness I gather that you experience a difficulty in answering them. But there is one thing I should like, which would cost you no trouble to grant.

*Zeus.* Well, Cyniscus? You shall not be disappointed, if your expectations are as reasonable as you say.

*Cyn.* I want to ask you a plain question.

*Zeus.* Such a modest petition is soon granted; ask what you will.

*Cyn.* Well then: you know your Homer and Hesiod, of course? Is it all true that they sing of Destiny and the Fates—that whatever they spin for a man at his birth must inevitably come about?

*Zeus.* Unquestionably. Nothing is independent of their control. From their spindle hangs the life of all created things; whose end is predetermined even from the moment of their birth; and that law knows no change.

*Cyn.* Then when Homer says, for instance, in another place,

> Lest unto Hell thou go, *outstripping Fate*,

he is talking nonsense, of course?

*Zeus.* Absolute nonsense. Such a thing is impossible: the law of the Fates, the thread of Destiny, is over all. No; so long as the poets are under the inspiration of the Muses, they speak truth: but once let those Goddesses leave them to their own devices, and they make blunders and contradict themselves. Nor can we blame them: they are but men; how should they know truth, when the divinity whose mouthpieces they were is departed from them?

*Cyn.* That point is settled, then. But there is another thing I want to know. There are three Fates, are there not,—Clotho, Lachesis, and Atropus?

*Zeus.* Quite so.

*Cyn.* But one also hears a great deal about Destiny and Fortune. Who are they, and what is the extent of their power? Is it equal to that of the Fates? or greater perhaps? People are always talking about the insuperable might of Fortune and Destiny.

*Zeus.* It is not proper, Cyniscus, that you should know all. But what made you ask me about the Fates?

*Cyn.* Ah, you must tell me one thing more first. Do the Fates also control you Gods? Do *you* depend from their thread?

*Zeus.* We do. Why do you smile?

*Cyn.* I was thinking of that bit in Homer, where he makes you address the Gods in council, and threaten to suspend all the world from a golden cord. You said, you know, that you would let the cord down from Heaven, and all the Gods together, if they liked, might take hold of it and try to pull you down, and they would never do it: whereas you, if you had a mind to it, could easily pull them up,

And Earth and Sea withal.

I listened to that passage with shuddering reverence; I was much impressed with the idea of your strength. Yet now I understand that you and your cord and your threats all depend from a mere cobweb. It seems to me Clotho should be the one to boast: she has you dangling from her distaff, like a sprat at the end of a fishing-line.

*Zeus.* I do not catch the drift of your questions.

*Cyn.* Come, I will speak my mind; and in the name of Destiny and the Fates take not my candour amiss. If the case stands thus, if the Fates are mistresses of all, and their decisions unalterable, then why do men sacrifice to *you*, and bring hecatombs, and pray for good at *your* hands? If our prayers can neither save us from evil nor procure us any boon from Heaven, I fail to see what we get for our trouble.

*Zeus.* These are nice questions! I see how it is,—you have been with the sophists; accursed race! who would deny us all concern in human affairs. Yes, these are just the points they raise, impiously seeking to pervert mankind from the way of sacrifice and prayer: it is all thrown away, forsooth! the Gods take no thought for mankind; they have no power on the earth.—Ah well; they will be sorry for it some day.

*Cyn.* Now, by Clotho's own spindle, my questions are free from all sophistic taint. How it has come about, I know not; but one word has brought up another, and the end of it is—there is no use in sacrifice. Let us begin again. I will put you a few more questions; answer me frankly, but think before you speak, this time.

*Zeus.* Well; if you have the time to waste on such tomfoolery.

*Cyn.* Everything proceeds from the Fates, you say?

*Zeus.* Yes.

*Cyn.* And is it in your power to unspin what they have spun?

*Zeus.* It is not.

*Cyn.* Shall I proceed, or is the inference clear?

*Zeus.* Oh, clear enough. But you seem to think that people sacrifice to us from ulterior motives; that they are driving a bargain with us, *buying* blessings, as it were: not at all; it is a disinterested testimony to our superior merit.

*Cyn.* There you are, then. As you say, sacrifice answers no useful purpose; it is just our good-natured way of acknowledging your superiority. And mind you, if we had a sophist here, he would want to know all about that superiority. You are our fellow slaves, he would say; if the Fates are our mistresses, they are also yours. Your immortality will not serve you; that only makes things worse. We mortals, after all, are liberated by death: but for you there is no end to the evil; that long thread of yours means eternal servitude.

*Zeus.* But this eternity is an eternity of happiness; the life of Gods is one round of blessings.

*Cyn.* Not all Gods' lives. Even in Heaven there are distinctions, not to say mismanagement. *You* are happy, of course: you are king, and you can haul up earth and sea as it were a bucket from the well. But look at Hephaestus: a cripple; a common blacksmith. Look at Prometheus: *he* gets nailed up on Caucasus. And I need not remind you that your own father lies fettered in Tartarus at this hour. It seems, too, that Gods are liable to fall in love; and to receive wounds; nay, they may even have to take service with mortal men; witness your brother Posidon, and Apollo, servants to Laomedon and to Admetus. I see no great happiness in all this; some of you I dare say have a very pleasant time of it, but not so others. I might have added, that you are subject to robbery like the rest of us; your temples get plundered, and the richest of you becomes a pauper in the twinkling of an eye. To more than one of you it has even happened to be melted down, if he was a gold or a silver God. All destiny, of course.

*Zeus.* Take care, Cyniscus: you are going too far. You will repent of this one day.

*Cyn.* Spare your threats: you know that nothing can happen to me, except what Fate has settled first. I notice, for instance, that even temple-robbers do not always get punished; most of them, indeed, slip through your hands. Not destined to be caught, I suppose.

*Zeus.* I knew it! you are one of those who would abolish Providence.

*Cyn.* You seem to be very much afraid of these gentlemen, for some reason. Not one word can I say, but you must think I picked it up from them. Oblige me by answering another question; I could desire no better authority than yours. What *is* this Providence? Is she a Fate too? or some greater, a mistress of the Fates?

*Zeus.* I have already told you that there are things which it is not proper for you to know. You said you were only going to ask me one question, instead of which you go on quibbling without end. I see what it is you are at: you want to make out that we Gods take no thought for human affairs.

*Cyn.* It is nothing to do with me: it was you who said just now that the Fates ordained everything. Have you thought better of it? Are you going to retract what you said? Are the Gods going to push Destiny aside and make a bid for government?

*Zeus.* Not at all; but the Fates work *through us.*

*Cyn.* I see: you are their servants, their underlings. But that comes to the same thing: it is still they who design; you are only their tools, their instruments.

*Zeus.* How do you make that out?

*Cyn.* I suppose it is pretty much the same as with a carpenter's adze and drill: they do assist him in his work, but no one would describe them as the workmen; we do not say that a ship has been turned out by such and such an adze, or by such and such a drill; we name the shipwright. In the same way, Destiny and the Fates are the universal shipwrights, and you are their drills and adzes; and it seems to me that instead of paying their respects and their sacrifices to you, men ought to sacrifice to Destiny, and implore *her* favours; though even that would not meet the case, because I take it that things are settled once and for all, and that the Fates themselves are not at liberty to chop and change. If some one gave the spindle a turn in the wrong direction, and undid all Clotho's work, Atropus would have something to say on the subject.

*Zeus.* So! You would deprive even the Fates of honour? You seem determined to reduce all to one level. Well, we Gods have at least one claim on you: we do prophesy and foretell what the Fates have disposed.

*Cyn.* Now even granting that you do, what is the use of knowing what one has to expect, when one can by no possibility take any precautions? Are you going to tell me that a man who finds out that he is to die by a steel point can escape the doom by shutting himself up? Not he. Fate will take him out hunting, and there will be his steel: Adrastus will hurl his spear at the boar, miss the brute, and get Croesus's son; Fate's inflexible law directs his aim. The full absurdity of the thing is seen in the case of Laïus:

> Seek not for offspring in the Gods' despite;
> Beget a child, and thou begett'st thy slayer.

Was not this advice superfluous, seeing that the end must come? Accordingly we find that the oracle does not deter Laïus from begetting a son, nor that son from being his slayer. On the whole, I cannot see that your prophecies entitle you to reward, even setting aside the obscurity of the oracles, which are generally contrived to cut both ways. You omitted to mention, for instance, whether Croesus—'the Halys crossed' —should destroy his own or Cyrus's 'mighty realm.' It might be either, so far as the oracle goes.

*Zeus.* Apollo was angry with Croesus. When Croesus boiled that lamb and tortoise together in the cauldron, he was making trial of Apollo.

*Cyn.* Gods ought not to be angry. After all, I suppose it was fated that the Lydian should misinterpret that oracle; his case only serves to illustrate that general ignorance of the future, which Destiny has appointed for mankind. At that rate, your prophetic power too seems to be in her hands.

*Zeus.* You leave us nothing, then? We exercise no control, we are not entitled to sacrifice, we are very drills and adzes. But you may well despise me: why do I sit here listening to all this, with my thunder-bolt beneath my arm?

*Cyn.* Nay, smite, if the thunder-bolt is my destiny. I shall think none the worse of you; I shall know it is all Clotho's doing; I will not even blame the bolt that wounds me. And by the way—talking of thunderbolts—there is one thing I will ask you and Destiny to explain; you can answer for her. Why is it that you leave all the pirates and temple-robbers and ruffians and perjurers to themselves, and direct your shafts (as you are always doing) against an oak-tree or a stone or a harmless mast, or even an honest, God-fearing traveller? . . . No answer? Is this one of the things it is not proper for me to know?

*Zeus.* It is, Cyniscus. You are a meddlesome fellow; I don't know where you picked up all these ideas.

*Cyn.* Well, I suppose I must not ask you all (Providence and Destiny and you) why honest Phocion died in utter poverty and destitution, like Aristides before him, while those two unwhipped puppies, Callias and Alcibiades, and the ruffian Midias, and that Aeginetan libertine Charops, who starved his own mother to death, were all rolling in money? nor again why Socrates was handed over to the Eleven instead of Meletus? nor yet why the effeminate Sardanapalus was a king, and one high-minded Persian after another went to the cross for refusing to countenance his doings? I say nothing of our own days, in which villains and money-grubbers prosper, and honest men are oppressed with want and sickness and a thousand distresses, and can hardly call their souls their own.

*Zeus.* Surely you know, Cyniscus, what punishments await the evildoers after death, and how happy will be the lot of the righteous?

*Cyn.* Ah, to be sure: Hades—Tityus—Tantalus. Whether there is such a place as Hades, I shall be able to satisfy myself when I die. In the meantime, I had rather live a pleasant life here, and have a score or so of vultures at my liver when I am dead, than thirst like Tantalus in this world, on the chance of drinking with the heroes in the Isles of the Blest, and reclining in the fields of Elysium.

*Zeus.* What! you doubt that there are punishments and rewards to come? You doubt of that judgement-seat before which every soul is arraigned?

*Cyn.* I *have* heard mention of a judge in that connexion; one Minos, a Cretan. Ah, yes, tell me about him: they say he is your son?

*Zeus.* And what of him?

*Cyn.* Whom does he punish in particular?

*Zeus.* Whom but the wicked? Murderers, for instance, and temple-robbers.

*Cyn.* And whom does he send to dwell with the heroes?

*Zeus.* Good men and God-fearing, who have led virtuous lives.

*Cyn.* Why?

*Zeus.* Because they deserve punishment and reward respectively.

*Cyn.* Suppose a man commits a crime accidentally: does he punish him just the same?

*Zeus.* Certainly not.

*Cyn.* Similarly, if a man involuntarily performed a good action, he would not reward him?

*Zeus.* No.

*Cyn.* Then there is no one for him to reward or punish.

*Zeus.* How so?

*Cyn.* Why, we men do nothing of our own free will: we are obeying an irresistible impulse,—that is, if there is any truth in what we settled just now, about Fate's being the cause of everything. Does a man commit a murder? Fate is the murderess. Does he rob a temple? He has her instructions for it. So if there is going to be any justice in Minos's sentences, he will punish Destiny, not Sisyphus; Fate, not Tantalus. What harm did these men do? They only obeyed orders.

*Zeus.* I am not going to speak to you any more. You are an unscrupulous man; a sophist. I shall go away and leave you to yourself.

*Cyn.* I wanted to ask you where the Fates lived; and how they managed to attend to all the details of such a vast mass of business, just those three. I do not envy them their lot; they must have a busy time of it, with so much on their hands. Their destiny, apparently, is no better than other people's. I would not exchange with them, if I had the choice; I had rather be poorer than I am, than sit before such a spindleful, watching every thread.—But never mind, if you would rather not answer. Your previous replies have quite cleared up my doubts about Destiny and Providence; and for the rest, I expect I was not destined to hear it.

# MAUPASSANT

## *The Jewels*

A CERTAIN Monsieur Lantin met a young girl from the country at the house of his chief assistant, and he was caught in the net of love at once. She was the daughter of a tax-collector who had died a few months before and her mother brought her to Paris and took her about to the houses of her friends hoping to find a husband for her. They were poor and honest, and they lived quietly and unpretentiously. The girl's beauty had the charm of angelic modesty, the faint smile on her lips seemed to come from a tender heart, and no one doubted that she was one of those innocent girls to whom every young man dreams of trusting his whole life.

Every one who knew her sang her praises, and every one who knew her said over and over, "The man who wins her will be lucky—he could not do better."

Monsieur Lantin was chief clerk in the Ministry of the Interior at that time, and his salary was thirty-five hundred francs a year. He proposed for her and married her, and he was unbelievably happy. She managed his house so cleverly and so economically that they lived in luxury. She paid her husband all the delightful little attentions, and she was so affectionate and so charming that when he had been married to her for six years he loved her more than he had ever loved her before.

She had only two tastes that he did not like—she was too fond of the theatre and too fond of imitation jewels. Her friends were the wives of unimportant officials and they often gave her boxes for popular plays—sometimes even for first nights. She was always dragging her husband with her and he found them unbearably tiresome after his day at the Ministry. He began begging her to ask some older woman who could bring her home after the play, and he was properly grateful when he managed to persuade her that the arrangement was perfectly respectable.

When she went to the theatre she naturally wanted to look her best, and her gowns always suited her though they were still simple. Her quiet charms and her irresistibly gentle smile seemed to acquire a fresh distinction from her simple gowns, but she began to put two enormous rhinestones in her ears and she wore strings of imitation pearls and bracelets and combs that played at being set with precious stones.

Her husband was distressed by this passion for false glitter, and he was always saying, "My dear, women who can not buy real jewels should adorn themselves only with their own beauty and charm, the rarest jewels after all."

But she always smiled sweetly and she always said, "What can I do about it? I love these things. I know you are right—they are my vice. I should have loved jewels."

Then she would slip the pearls round her fingers or hold the paste diamonds in the lamplight, and she always said, "See how beautifully they are made. One would swear they were real."

And he always smiled and said, "You have the tastes of a gypsy."

Sometimes, when they were alone by their fireside, she brought out the leather box that held what Monsieur Lantin called her trash. She put the box on the tea-table and then she examined her false jewels with such passionate interest that she seemed to be tasting a secret joy. Sometimes she insisted on fastening one of the necklaces around her husband's throat, and then she laughed and told him how absurd he looked and kissed him passionately.

One night she came home from the opera shivering with cold. The next morning she had a little cough and the next week she died of pneumonia.

Lantin almost followed her to the grave. His despair was so terrible that his hair was white in a month. He wept all day and his soul was torn by memories of the smile and the voice and all the charms of his dead wife. Time did not lessen his grief. When the other clerks in his office were talking over the news of the day they often saw his face twitch, and then his eyes filled with tears and he broke into sobs. He kept his wife's bedroom just as she had left it and he constantly shut himself up to think of her in that room where even her gowns were hanging just where she had kept them.

His existence soon became a struggle. His wife had found his salary quite enough for the household, but now it was hardly enough for him alone and he wondered how she had managed to give him the good wine and the good food that he could no longer buy with his small salary. He ran into debt and one morning when he found himself penniless a week before the end of the month he thought of selling some of his wife's imitation jewels—he still had a grudge against them in the bottom of his heart and the mere sight of them left a little stain on the memory of his beloved.

He looked through the heap of tinsel that she had left. She had gone on buying it until the end of her life and nearly every day she had brought home a new treasure. He finally settled on a long string of diamonds that she had seemed to prefer and that he thought might be worth six or eight francs since it was of unusually fine workmanship for an imitation.

He put it in his pocket and walked along the boulevards towards the Ministry, looking for a responsible jeweller. He was ashamed to show his poverty by trying to sell something that would bring him only a few francs, but he went into a shop at last.

"I would like to ask what value you would put on this," he said to the shopkeeper.

The man looked at the string, turned it over and over, weighed it, looked at it again through a magnifying-glass, whispered something to his clerk, and then laid it on the counter and walked away to judge its effect from a distance. Monsieur Lantin was annoyed by so much ceremony and he was about to say that he knew it was worth very little when the jeweller said, "It is worth twelve or fifteen thousand francs, sir, but you will have to tell me exactly how you came by it."

The bereaved husband stared at the shopkeeper with his eyes and his mouth wide open. He was quite unable to understand but finally he stammered, "You say . . . you are sure?"

The jeweller misunderstood his surprise and he said dryly, "You can ask if any one will give you more, but it is not worth more than fifteen thousand francs to me. Come back here if you cannot do better."

Monsieur Lantin was sure that he was going mad and that he must take his necklace and be alone to think. But when he was back in the street he told himself that he had been an imbecile not to take the jeweller at his word since he evidently did not know glass from diamonds.

He went into another shop not far down the Rue de la Paix, and as soon as the jeweller saw the string he exclaimed, "I know that necklace well. It was bought here."

Monsieur Lantin was even more disturbed.

"How much is it worth?" he asked.

"I sold it for twenty-five thousand francs, sir, and I will give you eighteen thousand for it if you will tell me how it came into your possession."

This time Monsieur Lantin was overcome by his astonishment.

"Examine it carefully, sir. I have always thought it an imitation."

"Will you give me your name?" the jeweller asked him.

"Certainly. My name is Lantin. I am in the Ministry of the Interior and I live at number 16, Rue des Martyrs."

The man opened his books, looked through them, and said, "This necklace was sent to Madame Lantin at that address on the twentieth of July, eighteen seventy-six."

The two men looked at each. The government clerk was senseless with surprise and the jeweller suspected a thief. The jeweller spoke first.

"Will you leave the necklace here for twenty-four hours? I will give you a receipt."

"Certainly," Monsieur Lantin stammered again. And he walked out of the shop folding the paper.

He crossed the street and walked up it again before he noticed that he was going the wrong way. He crossed the Seine and when he realized his mistake he came back to the Champs Elysées—all without one clear idea in his head. He tried to understand what had happened. His wife could not have bought the necklace herself. . . . Certainly not. . . . Then it must have been a gift. Whose gift . . . And why did he give it to her?

He stood quite still in the middle of the Champs Elysées. A horrible suspicion slipped into his mind. . . . Then all of the other jewels had been presents too! The earth shook under his feet. . . . The tree across the street was falling. He threw out his arms and fell unconscious. He came to himself in the pharmacy where some passers-by had carried him, and he asked to be taken home and shut himself up alone there.

He wept all day and bit a handkerchief to keep himself from screaming. Then he went to bed and slept heavily from sorrow and exhaustion.

A ray of sunlight woke him, and he rose wearily to dress for the Ministry. But he knew he could not work, and he sent a note to his chief. Then he remembered that he must go back to the jeweller's and his face turned purple from shame; but he could not leave the string of diamonds with the man, and he finally dressed and went out.

The day was fine and the sky was blue above the radiant city. Men were strolling about with their hands in their pockets. Lantin looked at them.

"People who have money enough must always be happy. They can even forget their sorrows by travelling about and amusing themselves. I could do that if I were rich."

He began to realize that he was hungry and that he had eaten nothing for twenty-four hours, but his pockets were empty and he thought of the necklace again. Eighteen thousand francs was a great deal of money.

He turned into the Rue de la Paix, and walked up and down across from the jeweller's shop. Eighteen thousand francs was a great deal of money. Twenty times he almost went in, and mortification stopped him every time. But he was hungry and he had nothing in his pockets. He ran across the street and rushed into the shop without giving himself time to change his mind.

The jeweller smiled politely and offered him a chair. The clerks looked at him with knowing smiles in their eyes and on their lips.

"I have looked into the matter, sir," the man told him, "and I am willing to pay you the price I offered."

"I will take it," the poor government clerk stammered.

The jeweller took eighteen thousand-franc bills from a drawer, counted them, and offered them to Lantin, who signed a receipt and put them in his pocket with trembling hands. As he was going out he turned to the smiling shopkeeper and lowered his eyes.

"I have . . . I have some other jewels . . . that I inherited from the same person. Will you consider buying them?"

"Certainly, sir," the merchant said, bowing. One of the clerks went outside where he could laugh comfortably and another blew his nose violently.

"I will bring them," Lantin said, calmly and seriously, but with a very red face. He took a cab so that he could go for them quickly.

He was back in less than an hour without even stopping for breakfast. The proprietor and his clerks examined the pieces one by one and carefully considered their value although nearly all of them had been bought in the shop. Lantin argued about their valuations, lost his temper, insisted on seeing the records of the sales, and talked louder and louder as the figures grew larger.

The earrings were worth twenty thousand francs, the bracelets thirty-five thousand, the pins and rings and pendants sixteen thousand. A set of emeralds and sapphires was worth fourteen thousand and a gold chain with one beautiful diamond pendant was worth forty thousand—altogether, a hundred and ninety-six thousand francs.

"You see the advantage of putting all one's savings in precious stones," the jeweller said, laughing good-naturedly.

"They are as good an investment as any other," Lantin answered gravely. And he went away after he had arranged to have another jeweller's valuation the next day.

He looked up at the column in the Place Vendôme as if it were merely a greased pole that he wanted to climb—he could have played leap frog over the emperor's statue perched up there in the sky. He lunched at Voisin's and drank a twenty franc bottle of wine. Then he took a carriage and drove through the Bois. He looked contemptuously at the private carriages and longed to call out to their owners, "I am rich too! I have two hundred thousand francs!"

He suddenly thought of the Ministry. He drove to it and walked boldly into his chief's office.

"I have come, sir, to offer you my resignation," he said. "I have inherited three hundred thousand francs."

Then he went out and shook hands with his old colleagues and told them what wonderful things he was going to do. But he dined alone at the Café Anglais. He happened to sit near a gentleman who seemed to him a person of distinction and he could not resist telling him that he had just inherited four hundred thousand francs.

For the first time in his life he was not bored at the theatre and after the play he went off with some girls.

He was married again six months later. His second wife was virtuous, but she was not charming. He was very unhappy with her.

# HENRY JAMES

# *Washington Square*

## I

DURING a portion of the first half of the present century, and more particularly during the latter part of it, there flourished and practised in the city of New York a physician who enjoyed perhaps an exceptional share of the consideration which, in the United States, has always been bestowed upon distinguished members of the medical profession. This profession in America has constantly been held in honour, and more successfully than elsewhere has put forward a claim to the epithet of "liberal." In a country in which, to play a social part, you must either earn your income or make believe that you earn it, the healing art has appeared in a high degree to combine two recognised sources of credit. It belongs to the realm of the practical, which in the United States is a great recommendation; and it is touched by the light of science—a merit appreciated in a community in which the love of knowledge has not always been accompanied by leisure and opportunity. It was an element in Dr. Sloper's reputation that his learning and his skill were very evenly balanced; he was what you might call a scholarly doctor, and yet there was nothing abstract in his remedies—he always ordered you to take something. Though he was felt to be extremely thorough, he was not uncomfortably theoretic, and if he sometimes explained matters rather more minutely than might seem of use to the patient, he never went so far (like some practitioners one has heard of) as to trust to the explanation alone, but always left behind him an inscrutable prescription. There were some doctors that left the prescription without offering any explanation at all; and he did not belong to that class either, which was, after all, the most vulgar. It will be seen that I am describing a clever man; and this is really the reason why Dr. Sloper had become a local celebrity. At the time at which we are chiefly concerned with him, he was some fifty years of age, and his popularity was at its height. He was very witty, and he passed in the best society of New York for a man of the world—which, indeed, he was, in a very sufficient degree. I hasten to add, to anticipate possible misconception, that he was not the least of a charlatan. He was a thoroughly honest man—honest in a degree of which he had perhaps lacked the opportunity to give the complete measure; and, putting aside the great good-nature of the circle in which he practised, which was rather fond of boasting that it possessed the "brightest" doctor in the country, he daily justified his claim to the talents attributed to him by the popular voice. He was an observer, even a philosopher, and to be bright was so natural to him, and (as the popular voice said) came so easily, that he never aimed at mere effect, and had none of the little tricks and pretensions of second-rate reputations. It must be confessed that fortune had favoured him, and that he had found the path to prosperity very soft to his tread. He had married at the age of twenty-seven, for love, a very charming girl, Miss Catherine Harrington, of New York, who, in addition to her charms, had brought him a solid dowry. Mrs. Sloper was amiable, graceful, accomplished, elegant, and in 1820 she had been one of the pretty girls of the small but promising capital which clustered about the Battery and overlooked the Bay, and of which the uppermost boundary was indicated by the grassy waysides of Canal Street. Even at the age of twenty-seven Austin Sloper had made his mark sufficiently to mitigate the anomaly of his having been chosen among a dozen suitors by a young woman of high fashion, who had ten thousand dollars of income and the most charming eyes in the island of Manhattan. These eyes, and some of their accompaniments, were for about five years a source of extreme satisfaction to the young physician, who was both a devoted and a very happy husband. The fact of his having married a rich woman made no difference in the line he had traced for himself, and he cultivated his profession with as definite a purpose as if he still had no other resources than his fraction of the modest patrimony which on his father's death he had shared with his brothers and sisters. This purpose had not been preponderantly to make money—it had been rather to learn something and to do something. To learn something interesting, and to do something useful—this was, roughly speaking, the programme he had sketched, and of which the accident of his wife having an income appeared to him in no degree to modify the validity. He was fond of his practice, and of exercising a skill of which he was agreeably conscious, and it was so patent a truth that if he were not a doctor there was nothing else he could be, that a doctor he persisted in being, in the best possible conditions. Of course his easy domestic situation saved him a good deal of drudgery, and his wife's affiliation to the "best people" brought him a good many of those patients whose symptoms are, if not more interesting in themselves than those of the lower orders, at least more consistently displayed. He desired experience, and in the course of twenty years he got a great deal. It must be added that it came to him in some forms which, whatever might have been their intrinsic value, made it the reverse of welcome. His first child, a little boy of extraordinary promise, as the Doctor, who was not addicted to easy enthusiasms, firmly believed, died at three years of age, in spite of everything that the mother's tenderness and the father's science could invent to save him. Two years later Mrs. Sloper gave birth to a second infant—an infant of a sex which rendered the poor child, to the Doctor's sense, an inadequate substitute for his lamented first-born, of whom he had promised himself to make an admirable man. The little girl was a disappointment; but this was not the worst. A week after her birth the young mother, who, as the phrase is, had been doing well, suddenly betrayed alarming symptoms, and before another week had elapsed Austin Sloper was a widower.

For a man whose trade was to keep people alive, he had certainly done poorly in his own family; and a bright doctor who within three years loses his wife and his little boy should perhaps be prepared to see either his skill or his affection impugned. Our friend, however, escaped criticism: that is, he escaped all criticism but his own, which was much the most competent and most formidable. He walked under the weight of this very private censure for the rest of his days, and bore for ever the scars of a castigation to which the strongest hand he knew had treated him on the night that followed his wife's death. The world, which, as I have said, appreciated him, pitied him too much to be ironical; his misfortune made him more interesting, and even helped him to be the fashion. It was observed that even medical families cannot escape the more insidious forms of disease, and that, after all, Dr. Sloper had lost other patients beside the two I have mentioned; which constituted an honourable precedent. His little girl remained to him, and though she was not what he had desired, he proposed to himself to make the best of her. He had on hand a stock of unexpended authority, by which the child, in its early years, profited largely. She had been named, as a matter of course, after her poor mother, and even in her most diminutive babyhood the Doctor never called her anything but Catherine. She grew up a very robust and healthy child, and her father, as he looked at her, often said to himself that, such as she was, he at least need have no fear of losing her. I say "such as she was," because, to tell the truth —But this is a truth of which I will defer the telling.

## II

WHEN the child was about ten years old, he invited his sister, Mrs. Penniman, to come and stay with him. The Miss Slopers had been but two in number, and both of them had married early in life. The younger, Mrs. Almond by name, was the wife of a prosperous merchant, and the mother of a blooming family. She bloomed herself, indeed, and was a comely, comfortable, reasonable woman, and a favourite with her clever brother, who, in the matter of women, even when they were nearly related to him, was a man of distinct preferences. He preferred Mrs. Almond to his sister Lavinia, who had married a poor clergyman, of a sickly constitution and a flowery style of eloquence, and then, at the age of thirty-three, had been left a widow, without children, without fortune—with nothing but the memory of Mr. Penniman's flowers of speech, a certain vague aroma of which hovered about her own conversation. Nevertheless he had offered her a home under his own roof, which Lavinia accepted with the alacrity of a woman who had spent the ten years of her married life in the town of Poughkeepsie. The Doctor had not proposed to Mrs. Penniman to come and live with him indefinitely; he had suggested that she should make an asylum of his house while she looked about for unfurnished lodgings. It is uncertain whether Mrs. Penniman ever instituted a search for unfurnished lodgings, but it is beyond dispute that she never found them. She settled herself with her brother and never went away, and when Catherine was twenty years old her Aunt Lavinia was still one of the most striking features of her immediate *entourage*. Mrs. Penniman's own account of the matter was that she had remained to take charge of her niece's education. She had given this account, at least, to every one but the Doctor, who never asked for explanations which he could entertain himself any day with inventing. Mrs. Penniman, moreover, though she had a good deal of a certain sort of artificial assurance, shrank, for indefinable reasons, from presenting herself to her brother as a fountain of instruction. She had not a high sense of humour, but she had enough to prevent her from making this mistake; and her brother, on his side, had enough to excuse her, in her situation, for laying him under contribution during a considerable part of a lifetime. He therefore assented tacitly to the proposition which Mrs. Penniman had tacitly laid down, that it was of importance that the poor motherless girl should have a brilliant woman near her. His assent could only be tacit, for he had never been dazzled by his sister's intellectual lustre. Save when he fell in love with Catherine Harrington, he had never been dazzled, indeed, by any feminine characteristics whatever; and though he was to a certain extent what is called a ladies' doctor, his private opinion of the more complicated sex was not exalted. He regarded its complications as more curious than edifying, and he had an idea of the beauty of *reason,* which was, on the whole, meagrely gratified by what he observed in his female patients. His wife had been a reasonable woman, but she was a bright exception; among several things that he was sure of, this was perhaps the principal. Such a conviction, of course, did little either to mitigate or to abbreviate his widowhood; and it set a limit to his recognition, at the best, of Catherine's possibilities and of Mrs. Penniman's ministrations. He, nevertheless, at the end of six months, accepted his sister's permanent presence as an accomplished fact, and as Catherine grew older perceived that there were in effect good reasons why she should have a companion of her own imperfect sex. He was extremely polite to Lavinia, scrupulously, formally polite; and she had never seen him in anger but once in her life, when he lost his temper in a theological discussion with her late husband. With her he never discussed theology, nor, indeed, discussed anything; he contented himself with making known, very distinctly, in the form of a lucid ultimatum, his wishes with regard to Catherine.

Once, when the girl was about twelve years old, he had said to her: "Try and make a clever woman of her, Lavinia; I should like her to be a clever woman."

Mrs. Penniman, at this, looked thoughtful a moment. "My dear Austin," she then inquired, "do you think it is better to be clever than to be good?"

"Good for what?" asked the Doctor. "You are good for nothing unless you are clever."

From this assertion Mrs. Penniman saw no reason to dissent; she possibly reflected that her own great use in the world was owing to her aptitude for many things.

"Of course I wish Catherine to be good," the Doctor said next day; "but she won't be any the less virtuous for not being a fool. I am not afraid of her being wicked; she will never have the salt of malice in her character. She is as good as good bread, as the French say; but six years hence I don't want to have to compare her to good bread and butter."

"Are you afraid she will turn insipid? My dear brother, it is I who supply the butter; so you needn't fear!" said Mrs. Penniman, who had taken in hand the child's accomplishments, overlooking her at the piano, where Catherine displayed a certain talent, and going with her to the dancing-class, where it must be confessed that she made but a modest figure.

Mrs. Penniman was a tall, thin, fair, rather faded woman, with a perfectly amiable disposition, a high standard of gentility, a taste for light literature, and a certain foolish indirectness and obliquity of character. She was romantic, she was sentimental, she had a passion for little secrets and mysteries—a very innocent passion, for her secrets had hitherto always been as unpractical as addled eggs. She was not absolutely veracious; but this defect was of no great consequence, for she had never had anything to conceal. She would have liked to have a lover, and to correspond with him under an assumed name in letters left at a shop; I am bound to say that her imagination never carried the intimacy farther than this. Mrs. Penniman had never had a lover, but her brother, who was very shrewd, understood her turn of mind. "When Catherine is about seventeen," he said to himself, "Lavinia will try and persuade her that some young man with a moustache is in love with her. It will be quite untrue; no young man, with a moustache or without, will ever be in love with Catherine. But Lavinia will take it up, and talk to her about it; perhaps, even, if her taste for clandestine operations doesn't prevail with her, she will talk to me about it. Catherine won't see it, and won't believe it, fortunately for her peace of mind; poor Catherine isn't romatic."

She was a healthy well-grown child, without a trace of her mother's beauty. She was not ugly; she had simply a plain, dull, gentle countenance. The most that had ever been said for her was that she had a "nice" face, and, though she was an heiress, no one had ever thought of regarding her as a belle. Her father's opinion of her moral purity was abundantly justified; she was excellently, imperturbably good; affectionate, docile, obedient, and much addicted to speaking the truth. In her younger years she was a good deal of a romp, and, though it is an awkward confession to make about one's heroine, I must add that she was something of a glutton. She never, that I know of, stole raisins out of the pantry; but she devoted her pocket-money to the purchase of cream-cakes. As regards this, however, a critical attitude would be inconsistent with a candid reference to the early annals of any biographer. Catherine was decidedly not clever; she was not quick with her book, nor, indeed, with anything else. She was not abnormally deficient, and she mustered learning enough to acquit herself respectably in conversation with her contemporaries, among whom it must be avowed, however, that she occupied a secondary place. It is well known that in New York it is possible for a young girl to occupy a primary one. Catherine, who was extremely modest, had no desire to shine, and on most social occasions, as they are called, you would have found her lurking in the background. She was extremely fond of her father, and very much afraid of him; she thought him the cleverest and handsomest and most celebrated of men. The poor girl found her account so completely in the exercise of her affections that the little tremor of fear that mixed itself with her filial passion gave the thing an extra relish rather than blunted its edge. Her deepest desire was to please him, and her conception of happiness was to know that she had succeeded in pleasing him. She had never succeeded beyond a certain point. Though, on the whole, he was very kind to her, she was perfectly aware of this, and to go beyond the point in question seemed to her really something to live for. What she could not know, of course, was that she disappointed him, though on three or four occasions the Doctor had been almost frank about it. She grew up peacefully and prosperously, but at the age of eighteen Mrs. Penniman had not made a clever woman of her. Dr. Sloper would have liked to be proud of his daughter; but there was nothing to be proud of in poor Catherine. There was nothing, of course, to be ashamed of; but this was not enough for the Doctor, who was a proud man and would have enjoyed being able to think of his daughter as an unusual girl. There would have been a fitness in her being pretty and graceful, intelligent and distinguished; for her mother had been the most charming woman of her little day, and as regards her father, of course he knew his own value. He had moments of irritations at having produced a commonplace child, and he even went so far at times as to take a certain satisfaction in the thought that his wife had not lived to find her out. He was naturally slow in making this discovery himself, and it was not till Catherine had become a young lady grown that he regarded the matter as settled. He gave her the benefit of a great many doubts; he was in no haste to conclude. Mrs. Penniman frequently assured him that his daughter had a delightful nature; but he knew how to interpret this assurance. It meant, to his sense, that Catherine was not wise enough to discover that her aunt was a goose—a limitation of mind that could not fail to be agreeable to Mrs. Penniman. Both she and her brother, however, exaggerated the young girl's limitations; for Catherine, though she was very fond of her aunt, and conscious of the gratitude she owed her, regarded her without a particle of that gentle dread which gave its stamp to her admiration of her father. To her mind there was nothing of the infinite about Mrs. Penniman; Catherine saw her all at once, as it were, and was not dazzled by the apparition; whereas her father's great faculties seemed, as they stretched away, to lose themselves in a sort of luminous vagueness, which indicated, not that they stopped, but that Catherine's own mind ceased to follow them.

It must not be supposed that Dr. Sloper visited his disappointment upon the poor girl, or ever let her suspect that she had played him a trick. On the contrary, for fear of being unjust to her, he did his duty with exemplary zeal, and recognised that she was a faithful and affectionate child. Besides, he was a philosopher; he smoked a good many cigars over his disappointment, and in the fulness of time he got used to it. He satisfied himself that he had expected nothing, though, indeed, with a certain oddity of reasoning. "I expect nothing," he said to himself, "so that if she gives me a surprise, it will be all clear gain. If she doesn't, it will be no loss." This was about the time Catherine had reached her eighteenth year, so that it will be seen her father had not been precipitate. At this time she seemed not only incapable of giving surprises; it was almost a question whether she could have received one —she was so quiet and irresponsive. People who expressed themselves roughly called her stolid. But she was irresponsive because she was shy, uncomfortably, painfully shy. This was not always understood, and she sometimes produced an impression of insensibility. In reality she was the softest creature in the world.

## III

As a child she had promised to be tall, but when she was sixteen she ceased to grow, and her stature, like most other points in her composition, was not unusual. She was strong, however, and properly made, and, fortunately, her health was excellent. It has been noted that the Doctor was a philosopher, but I would not have answered for his philosophy if the poor girl had proved a sickly and suffering person. Her appearance of health constituted her principal claim to beauty, and her clear, fresh complexion, in which white and red were very equally distributed, was, indeed, an excellent thing to see. Her eye was small and quiet, her features were rather thick, her tresses brown and smooth. A dull, plain girl she was called by rigorous critics—a quiet, ladylike girl by those of the more imaginative sort; but by neither class was she very elaborately discussed. When it had been duly impressed upon her that she was a young lady—it was a good while before she could believe it —she suddenly developed a lively taste for dress: a lively taste is quite the expression to use. I feel as if I ought to write it very small, her judgment in this matter was by no means infallible; it was liable to confusions and embarrassments. Her great indulgence of it was really the desire of a rather inarticulate nature to manifest itself; she sought to be eloquent in her garments, and to make up for her diffidence of speech by a fine frankness of costume. But if she expresed herself in her clothes it is certain that people were not to blame for not thinking her a witty person. It must be added that though she had the expectation of a fortune—Dr. Sloper for a long time had been making twenty thousand dollars a year by his profession, and laying aside the half of it—the amount of money at her disposal was not greater than the allowance made to many poorer girls. In those days in New York there were still a few altar-fires flickering in the temple of Republican simplicity, and Dr. Sloper would have been glad to see his daughter present herself, with a classic grace, as a priestess of this mild faith. It made him fairly grimace, in private, to think that a child of his should be both ugly and overdressed. For himself, he was fond of the good things of life, and he made a considerable use of them; but he had a dread of vulgarity, and even a theory that it was increasing in the society that surrounded him. Moreover, the standard of luxury in the United States thirty years ago was carried by no means so high as at present, and Catherine's clever father took the old-fashioned view of the education of young persons. He had no particular theory on the subject; it had scarcely as yet become a necessity of self-defence to have a collection of theories. It simply appeared to him proper and reasonable that a well-bred young woman should not carry half her fortune on her back. Catherine's back was a broad one, and would have carried a good deal; but to the weight of the paternal displeasure she never ventured to expose it, and our heroine was twenty years old before she treated herself, for evening wear, to a red satin gown trimmed with gold fringe; though this was an article which, for many years, she had coveted in secret. It made her look, when she sported it, like a woman of thirty; but oddly enough, in spite of her taste for fine clothes, she had not a grain of coquetry, and her anxiety when she put them on was as to whether they, and not she, would look well. It is a point on which history has not been explicit, but the assumption is warrantable; it was in the royal raiment just mentioned that she presented herself at a little entertainment given by her aunt, Mrs. Almond. The girl was at this time in her twenty-first year, and Mrs. Almond's party was the beginning of something very important.

Some three or four years before this Dr. Sloper had moved his household gods up town, as they say in New York. He had been living ever since his marriage in an edifice of red brick, with granite copings and an enormous fanlight over the door, standing in a street within five minutes' walk of the City Hall, which saw its best days (from the social point of view) about 1820. After this, the tide of fashion began to set steadily northward, as, indeed, in New York, thanks to the narrow channel in which it flows, it is obliged to do, and the great hum of traffic rolled farther to the right and left of Broadway. By the time the Doctor changed his residence the murmur of trade had become a mighty uproar, which was music in the ears of all good citizens interested in the commercial development, as they delighted to call it, of their fortunate isle. Dr. Sloper's interest in this phenomenon was only indirect—though, seeing that, as the years went on, half his patients came to be overworked men of business, it might have been more immediate—and when most of his neighbours' dwellings (also ornamented with granite copings and large fanlights) had been converted into offices, warehouses, and shipping agencies, and otherwise applied to the base uses of commerce, he determined to look out for a quieter home. The ideal of quiet and of genteel retirement, in 1835, was found in Washington Square, where the Doctor built himself a handsome, modern, wide-fronted house, with a big balcony before the drawing-room windows, and a flight of marble steps ascending to a portal which was also faced with white marble. This structure, and many of its neighbours, which it exactly resembled, were supposed, forty years ago, to embody the last results of architectural science, and they remain to this day very solid and honourable dwellings. In front of them was the Square, containing a considerable quantity of inexpensive vegetation, enclosed by a wooden paling, which increased its rural and accessible appearance; and round the corner was the more august precinct of the Fifth Avenue, taking its origin at this point with a spacious and confident air which already marked it for high destinies. I know not whether it is owing to the tenderness of early associations, but this portion of New York appears to many persons the most delectable. It has a kind of established repose which is not of frequent occurrence in other quarters of the long, shrill city; it has a riper, richer, more honourable look than any of the upper ramifications of the great longitudinal thoroughfare—the look of having had something of a social history. It was here, as you might have been informed on good authority, that you had come into a world which appeared to offer a variety of sources of interest; it was here that your grandmother lived, in venerable solitude, and dispensed a hospitality which commended itself alike to the infant imagination and the infant palate; it was here that you took your first walks abroad, following the nursery-maid with unequal step and sniffing up the strange odour of the ailantus-trees which at that time formed the principal umbrage of the Square, and diffused an aroma that you were not yet critical enough to dislike as it deserved; it was here, finally, that your first school, kept by a broad-bosomed, broad-based old lady with a ferule, who was always having tea in a blue cup, with a saucer that didn't match, enlarged the circle both of your observations and your sensations. It was here, at any rate, that my heroine spent many years of her life; which is my excuse for this topographical parenthesis.

Mrs. Almond lived much farther up town, in an embryonic street with a high number—a region where the extension of the city began to assume a theoretic air, where poplars grew beside the pavement (when there was one), and mingled their shade with the steep roofs of desultory Dutch houses, and where pigs and chickens disported themselves in the gutter. These elements of rural picturesqueness have now wholly departed from New York street scenery; but they were to be found within the memory of middle-aged persons, in quarters which now would blush to be reminded of them. Catherine had a great many cousins, and with her Aunt Almond's children, who ended by being nine in number, she lived on terms of considerable intimacy. When she was younger they had been rather afraid of her; she was believed, as the phrase is, to be highly educated, and a person who lived in the intimacy of their Aunt Penniman had something of reflected grandeur. Mrs. Penniman, among the little Almonds, was an object of more admiration than sympathy. Her manners were strange and formidable, and her mourning robes—she dressed in black for twenty years after her husband's death, and then suddenly appeared one morning with pink roses in her cap—were complicated in odd, unexpected places with buckles, bugles, and pins, which discouraged familiarity. She took children too hard, both for good and for evil, and had an oppressive air of expecting subtle things of them, so that going to see her was a good deal like being taken to church and made to sit in a front pew. It was discovered after a while, however, that Aunt Penniman was but an accident in Catherine's existence, and not a part of its essence, and that when the girl came to spend a Saturday with her cousins, she was available for "follow-my-master," and even for leap-frog. On this basis an understanding was easily arrived at, and for several years Catherine fraternised with her young kinsmen. I say young kinsmen, because seven of the little Almonds were boys, and Catherine had a preference for those games which are most conveniently played in trousers. By degrees, however, the little Almonds' trousers began to lengthen, and the wearers to disperse and settle themselves in life. The elder children were older than Catherine, and the boys were sent to college or placed in counting-rooms. Of the girls, one married very punctually, and the other as punctually became engaged. It was to celebrate this latter event that Mrs. Almond gave the little party I have mentioned. Her daughter was to marry a stout young stockbroker, a boy of twenty; it was thought a very good thing.

## IV

MRS. PENNIMAN, with more buckles and bangles than ever, came, of course, to the entertainment, accompanied by her niece; the Doctor, too, had promised to look in later in the evening. There was to be a good deal of dancing, and before it had gone very far, Marian Almond came up to Catherine, in company with a tall young man. She introduced the young man as a person who had a great desire to make our heroine's acquaintance, and as a cousin of Arthur Townsend, her own intended.

Marian Almond was a pretty little person of seventeen, with a very small figure and a very big sash, to the elegance of whose manners matrimony had nothing to add. She already had all the airs of a hostess, receiving the company, shaking her fan, saying that with so many people to attend to she should have no time to dance. She made a long speech about Mr. Townsend's cousin, to whom she administered a tap with her fan before turning away to other cares. Catherine had not understood all that she said; her attention was given to enjoying Marian's ease of manner and flow of ideas, and to looking at the young man, who was remarkably handsome. She had succeeded, however, as she often failed to do when people were presented to her, in catching his name, which appeared to be the same as that of Marian's little stock-broker. Catherine was always agitated by an introduction; it seemed a difficult moment, and she wondered that some people—her new acquaintance at this moment, for instance—should mind it so little. She wondered what she ought to say, and what would be the consequences of her saying nothing. The consequences at present were very agreeable. Mr. Townsend, leaving her no time for embarrassment, began to talk with an easy smile, as if he had known her for a year.

"What a delightful party! What a charming house! What an interesting family! What a pretty girl your cousin is!"

These observations, in themselves of no great profundity, Mr. Townsend seemed to offer for what they were worth, and as a contribution to an acquaintance. He looked straight into Catherine's eyes. She answered nothing; she only listened, and looked at him; and he, as if he expected no particular reply, went on to say many other things in the same comfortable and natural manner. Catherine, though she felt tongue-tied, was conscious of no embarrassment; it seemed proper that he should talk, and that she should simply look at him. What made it natural was that he was so handsome, or rather, as she phrased it to herself, so beautiful. The music had been silent for a while, but it suddenly began again; and then he asked her, with a deeper, intenser smile, if she would do him the honour of dancing with him. Even to this inquiry she gave no audible assent; she simply let him put his arm round her waist—as she did so it occurred to her more vividly than it had ever done before, that this was a singular place for a gentleman's arm to be—and in a moment he was guiding her round the room in the harmonious rotation of the polka. When they paused she felt that she was red; and then, for some moments, she stopped looking at him. She fanned herself, and looked at the flowers that were painted on her fan. He asked her if she would begin again, and she hesitated to answer, still looking at the flowers.

"Does it make you dizzy?" he asked, in a tone of great kindness.

Then Catherine looked up at him; he was certainly beautiful, and not at all red. "Yes," she said; she hardly knew why, for dancing had never made her dizzy.

"Ah, well, in that case," said Mr. Townsend, "we we will sit still and talk. I will find a good place to sit."

He found a good place—a charming place; a little sofa that seemed meant only for two persons. The rooms by this time were very full; the dancers increased in number, and people stood close in front of them, turning their backs, so that Catherine and her companion seemed secluded and unobserved. "*We* will talk," the young man had said; but he still did all the talking. Catherine leaned back in her place, with her eyes fixed upon him, smiling and thinking him very clever. He had features like young men in pictures; Catherine had never seen such features—so delicate, so chiselled and finished—among the young New Yorkers whom she passed in the streets and met at parties. He was tall and slim, but he looked extremely strong. Catherine thought he looked like a statue. But a statue would not talk like that, and, above all, would not have eyes of so rare a colour. He had never been at Mrs. Almond's before; he felt very much like a stranger; and it was very kind of Catherine to take pity on him. He was Arthur Townsend's cousin—not very near; several times removed—and Arthur had brought him to present him to the family. In fact, he was a great stranger in New York. It was his native place; but he had not been there for many years. He had been knocking about the world, and living in far-away lands; he had only come back a month or two before. New York was very pleasant, only he felt lonely.

"You see, people forget you," he said, smiling at Catherine with his delightful gaze, while he leaned forward obliquely, turning towards her, with his elbows on his knees.

It seemed to Catherine that no one who had once seen him would ever forget him; but though she made this reflection she kept it to herself, almost as you would keep something precious.

They sat there for some time. He was very amusing. He asked her about the people that were near them; he tried to guess who some of them were, and he made the most laughable mistakes. He criticised them very freely, in a positive, off-hand way. Catherine had never heard any one—especially any young man—talk just like that. It was the way a young man might talk in a novel; or better still, in a play, on the stage, close before the footlights, looking at the audience, and with every one looking at him, so that you wondered at his presence of mind. And yet Mr. Townsend was not like an actor; he seemed so sincere, so natural. This was very interesting; but in the midst of it Marian Almond came pushing through the crowd, with a little ironical cry, when she found these young people still together, which made every one turn round, and cost Catherine a conscious blush. Marian broke up their talk, and told Mr. Townsend—whom she treated as if she were already married, and he had become her cousin—to run away to her mother, who had been wishing for the last half-hour to introduce him to Mr. Almond.

"We shall meet again!" he said to Catherine as he left her, and Catherine thought it a very original speech.

Her cousin took her by the arm, and made her walk about. "I needn't ask you what you think of Morris!" the young girl exclaimed.

"Is that his name?"

"I don't ask you what you think of his name, but what you think of himself," said Marian.

"Oh, nothing particular!" Catherine answered, dissembling for the first time in her life.

"I have half a mind to tell him that!" cried Marian. "It will do him good. He's so terribly conceited."

"Conceited?" said Catherine, staring.

"So Arthur says, and Arthur knows about him."

"Oh, don't tell him!" Catherine murmured imploringly.

"Don't tell him he's conceited? I have told him so a dozen times."

At this profession of audacity Catherine looked down at her little companion in amazement. She supposed it was because Marian was going to be married that she took so much on herself; but she wondered too, whether, when she herself should become engaged, such exploits would be expected of her,

Half an hour later she saw her Aunt Penniman sitting in the embrasure of a window, with her head a little on one side, and her gold eyeglass raised to her eyes, which were wandering about the room. In front of her was a gentleman, bending forward a little, with his back turned to Catherine. She knew his back immediately, though she had never seen it; for when he had left her, at Marian's instigation, he had retreated in the best order, without turning round. Morris Townsend—the name had already become very familiar to her, as if some one had been repeating it in her ear for the last half-hour—Morris Townsend was giving his impressions of the company to her aunt, as he had done to herself; he was saying clever things, and Mrs. Penniman was smiling, as if she approved of them. As soon as Catherine had perceived this she moved away; she would not have liked him to turn round and see her. But it gave her pleasure—the whole thing. That he should talk with Mrs. Penniman, with whom she lived and whom she saw and talked with every day—that seemed to keep him near her, and to make him even easier to contemplate than if she herself had been the object of his civilities; and that Aunt Lavinia should like him, should not be shocked or startled by what he said, this also appeared to the girl a personal gain; for Aunt Lavinia's standard was extremely high, planted as it was over the grave of her late husband, in which, as she had convinced every one, the very genius of conversation was buried. One of the Almond boys, as Catherine called him, invited our heroine to dance a quadrille, and for a quarter of an hour her feet at least were occupied. This time she was not dizzy; her head was very clear. Just when the dance was over, she found herself in the crowd face to face with her father. Dr. Sloper had usually a little smile, never a very big one, and with his little smile playing in his clear eyes and on his neatly-shaved lips, he looked at his daughter's crimson gown.

"Is it possible that this magnificent person is my child?" he said.

You would have surprised him if you had told him so; but it is a literal fact that he almost never addressed his daughter save in the ironical form. Whenever he addressed her he gave her pleasure; but she had to cut her pleasure out of the piece, as it were. There were portions left over, light remnants and snippets of irony, which she never knew what to do with, which seemed too delicate for her own use; and yet Catherine, lamenting the limitations of her understanding, felt that they were too valuable to waste and had a belief that if they passed over her head they yet contributed to the general sum of human wisdom.

"I am not magnificent," she said mildly, wishing that she had put on another dress.

"You are sumptuous, opulent, expensive," her father rejoined. "You look as if you had eighty thousand a year."

"Well, so long as I haven't—" said Catherine illogically. Her conception of her prospective wealth was as yet very indefinite.

"So long as you haven't you shouldn't look as if you had. Have you enjoyed your party?"

Catherine hesitated a moment; and then, looking away, "I am rather tired," she murmured. I have said that this entertainment was the beginning of something important for Catherine. For the second time in her life she made an indirect answer; and the beginning of a period of dissimulation is certainly a significant date. Catherine was not so easily tired as that.

Nevertheless, in the carriage, as they drove home, she was as quiet as if fatigue had been her portion. Dr. Sloper's manner of addressing his sister Lavinia had a good deal of resemblance to the tone he had adopted towards Catherine.

"Who was the young man that was making love to you?" he presently asked.

"Oh, my good brother!" murmured Mrs. Penniman, in deprecation.

"He seemed uncommonly tender. Whenever I looked at you, for half an hour, he had the most devoted air."

"The devotion was not to me," said Mrs. Penniman. "It was to Catherine; he talked to me of her."

Catherine had been listening with all her ears. "Oh, Aunt Penniman!" she exclaimed faintly.

"He is very handsome; he is very clever; he expressed himself with a great deal—a great deal of felicity," her aunt went on.

"He is in love with this regal creature, then?" the Doctor inquired humorously.

"Oh, father," cried the girl, still more faintly, devoutly thankful the carriage was dark.

"I don't know that; but he admired her dress."

Catherine did not say to herself in the dark, "My dress only?" Mrs. Penniman's announcement struck her by its richness, not by its meagreness.

"You see," said her father, "he thinks you have eighty thousand a year."

"I don't believe he thinks of that," said Mrs. Penniman; "he is too refined."

"He must be tremendously refined not to think of that!"

"Well, he is!" Catherine exclaimed, before she knew it.

"I thought you had gone to sleep," her father answered. "The hour has come!" he added to himself. "Lavinia is going to get up a romance for Catherine. It's a shame to play such tricks on the girl. What is the gentleman's name?" he went on, aloud.

"I didn't catch it, and I didn't like to ask him. He asked to be introduced to me," said Mrs. Penniman, with a certain grandeur; "but you know how indistinctly Jefferson speaks." Jefferson was Mr. Almond. "Catherine, dear, what was the gentleman's name?"

For a minute, if it had not been for the rumbling of the carriage, you might have heard a pin drop.

"I don't know, Aunt Lavinia," said Catherine, very softly. And, with all his irony, her father believed her.

## V

He learned what he had asked some three or four days later, after Morris Townsend, with his cousin, had called in Washington Square. Mrs. Penniman did not tell her brother, on the drive home, that she had intimated to this agreeable young man, whose name she did not know, that, with her niece, she should be very glad to see him; but she was greatly pleased, and even a little flattered, when, late on a Sunday afternoon, the two gentlemen made their appearance. His coming with Arthur Townsend made it more natural and easy; the latter young man was on the point of becoming connected with the family, and Mrs. Penniman had remarked to Catherine that, as he was going to marry Marian, it would be polite in him to call. These events came to pass late in the autumn, and Catherine and her aunt had been sitting together in the closing dusk, by the firelight, in the high back parlour.

Arthur Townsend fell to Catherine's portion, while his companion placed himself on the sofa, beside Mrs. Penniman. Catherine had hitherto not been a harsh critic; she was easy to please—she liked to talk with young men. But Marian's betrothed, this evening, made her feel vaguely fastidious; he sat looking at the fire and rubbing his knees with his hands. As for Catherine, she scarcely even pretended to keep up the conversation; her attention had fixed itself on the other side of the room; she was listening to what went on between the other Mr. Townsend and her aunt. Every now and then he looked over at Catherine herself and smiled, as if to show that what he said was for her benefit too. Catherine would have liked to change her place, to go and sit near them, where she might see and hear him better. But she was afraid of seeming bold—of looking eager; and, besides, it would not have been polite to Marian's little suitor. She wondered why the other gentleman had picked out her aunt—how he came to have so much to say to Mrs. Penniman, to whom, usually, young men were not especially devoted. She was not at all jealous of Aunt Lavinia, but she was a little envious, and above all she wondered; for Morris Townsend was an object on which she found that her imagination could exercise itself indefinitely. His cousin had been describing a house that he had taken in view of his union with Marian, and the domestic conveniences he meant to introduce into it; how Marian wanted a larger one, and Mrs. Almond recommended a smaller one, and how he himself was convinced that he had got the neatest house in New York.

"It doesn't matter," he said; "it's only for three or four years. At the end of three or four years we'll move. That's the way to live in New York—to move every three or four years. Then you always get the last thing. It's because the city's growing so quick—you've got to keep up with it. It's going straight up town—that's where New York's going. If I wasn't afraid Marian would be lonely, I'd go up there—right up to the top—and wait for it. Only have to wait ten years—they'd all come up after you. But Marian says she wants some neighbours—she doesn't want to be a pioneer. She says that if she's got to be the first settler she had better go out to Minnesota. I guess we'll move up little by little; when we get tired of one street we'll go higher. So you see we'll always have a new house; it's a great advantage to have a new house; you get all the latest improvements. They invent everything all over again about every five years, and it's a great thing to keep up with the new things. I always try and keep up with the new things of every kind. Don't you think that's a good motto for a young couple—to keep 'going higher'? That's the name of that piece of poetry—what do they call it?—*Excelsior!*"

Catherine bestowed on her junior visitor only just enough attention to feel that this was not the way Mr. Morris Townsend had talked the other night, or that he was talking now to her fortunate aunt. But suddenly his aspiring kinsman became more interesting. He seemed to have become conscious that she was affected by his companion's presence, and he thought it proper to explain it.

"My cousin asked me to bring him, or I shouldn't have taken the liberty. He seemed to want very much to come; you know he's awfully sociable. I told him I wanted to ask you first, but he said Mrs. Penniman had invited him. He isn't particular what he says when he wants to come somewhere! But Mrs. Penniman seems to think it's all right."

"We are very glad to see him," said Catherine. And she wished to talk more about him; but she hardly knew what to say. "I never saw him before," she went on presently.

Arthur Townsend stared.

"Why, he told me he talked with you for over half an hour the other night."

"I mean before the other night. That was the first time."

"Oh, he has been away from New York—he has been all round the world. He doesn't know many people here, but he's very sociable, and he wants to know every one."

"Every one?" said Catherine.

"Well, I mean all the good ones. All the pretty young ladies—like Mrs. Penniman!" and Arthur Townsend gave a private laugh.

"My aunt likes him very much," said Catherine.

"Most people like him—he's so brilliant."

"He's more like a foreigner," Catherine suggested.

"Well, I never knew a foreigner!" said young Townsend, in a tone which seemed to indicate that his ignorance had been optional.

"Neither have I," Catherine confessed, with more humility. "They say they are generally brilliant," she added vaguely.

"Well, the people of this city are clever enough for me. I know some of them that think they are too clever for me; but they ain't!"

"I suppose you can't be too clever," said Catherine, still with humility.

"I don't know. I know some people that call my cousin too clever."

Catherine listened to this statement with extreme interest, and a feeling that if Morris Townsend had a fault it would naturally be that one. But she did not commit herself, and in a moment she asked: "Now that he has come back, will he stay here always?"

"Ah," said Arthur, "if he can get something to do."

"Something to do?"

"Some place or other; some business."

"Hasn't he got any?" said Catherine, who had never heard of a young man—of the upper class—in this situation.

"No; he's looking round. But he can't find anything."

"I am very sorry," Catherine permitted herself to observe.

"Oh, he doesn't mind," said young Townsend. "He takes it easy—he isn't in a hurry. He is very particular."

Catherine thought he naturally would be, and gave herself up for some moments to the contemplation of this idea, in several of its bearings.

"Won't his father take him into his business—his office?" she at last inquired.

"He hasn't got any father—he has only got a sister. Your sister can't help you much."

It seemed to Catherine that if she were his sister she would disprove this axiom. "Is she—is she pleasant?" she asked in a moment.

"I don't know—I believe she's very respectable," said young Townsend. And then he looked across to his cousin and began to laugh. "Look here, we are talking about you," he added.

Morris Townsend paused in his conversation with Mrs. Penniman, and stared, with a little smile. Then he got up, as if he were going.

"As far as you are concerned, I can't return the compliment," he said to Catherine's companion. "But as regards Miss Sloper, it's another affair."

Catherine thought this little speech wonderfully well turned; but she was embarrassed by it, and she also got up. Morris Townsend stood looking at her and smiling; he put out his hand for farewell. He was going, without having said anything to her; but even on these terms she was glad to have seen him.

"I will tell her what you have said—when you go!" said Mrs. Penniman, with an insinuating laugh.

Catherine blushed, for she felt almost as if they were making sport of her. What in the world could this beautiful young man have said? He looked at her still, in spite of her blush; but very kindly and respectfully.

"I have had no talk with you," he said, "and that was what I came for. But it will be a good reason for coming another time; a little pretext—if I am obliged to give one. I am not afraid of what your aunt will say when I go."

With this the two young men took their departure; after which Catherine, with her blush still lingering, directed a serious and interrogative eye to Mrs. Penniman. She was incapable of elaborate artifice, and she resorted to no jocular device—to no affectation of the belief that she had been maligned—to learn what she desired.

"What did you say you would tell me?" she asked.

Mrs. Penniman came up to her, smiling and nodding a little, looked at her all over, and gave a twist to the knot of ribbon in her neck. "It's a great secret, my dear child; but he is coming a-courting!"

Catherine was serious still. "Is that what he told you!"

"He didn't say so exactly. But he left me to guess it. I'm a good guesser."

"Do you mean a-courting me?"

"Not me, certainly, miss; though I must say he is a hundred times more polite to a person who has no longer extreme youth to recommend her than most of the young men. He is thinking of some one else." And Mrs. Penniman gave her niece a delicate little kiss. "You must be very gracious to him."

Catherine stared—she was bewildered. "I don't understand you," she said; "he doesn't know me."

"Oh yes, he does; more than you think. I have told him all about you."

"Oh, Aunt Penniman!" murmured Catherine, as if this had been a breach of trust. "He is a perfect stranger—we don't know him." There was infinite modesty in the poor girl's "we."

Aunt Penniman, however, took no account of it; she spoke even with a touch of acrimony. "My dear Catherine, you know very well that you admire him!"

"Oh, Aunt Penniman!" Catherine could only murmur again. It might very well be that she admired him—though this did not seem to her a thing to talk about. But that this brilliant stranger—this sudden apparition, who had barely heard the sound of her voice—took that sort of interest in her that was expressed by the romantic phrase of which Mrs. Penniman had just made use: this could only be a figment of the restless brain of Aunt Lavinia, whom every one knew to be a woman of powerful imagination.

## VI

MRS. PENNIMAN even took for granted at times that other people had as much imagination as herself; so that when, half an hour later, her brother came in, she addressed him quite on this principle.

"He has just been here, Austin; it's such a pity you missed him."

"Whom in the world have I missed?" asked the Doctor.

"Mr. Morris Townsend; he has made us such a delightful visit."

"And who in the world is Mr. Morris Townsend?"

"Aunt Penniman means the gentleman—the gentleman whose name I couldn't remember," said Catherine.

"The gentleman at Elizabeth's party who was so struck with Catherine," Mrs. Penniman added.

"Oh, his name is Morris Townsend, is it? And did he come here to propose to you?"

"Oh, father," murmured the girl for all answer, turning away to the window, where the dusk had deepened to darkness.

"I hope he won't do that without your permission," said Mrs. Penniman, very graciously.

"After all, my dear, he seems to have yours," her brother answered.

Lavinia simpered, as if this might not be quite enough, and Catherine, with her forehead touching the window-panes, listened to this exchange of epigrams as reservedly as if they had not each been a pin-prick in her own destiny.

"The next time he comes," the Doctor added, "you had better call me. He might like to see me."

Morris Townsend came again, some five days afterwards; but Dr. Sloper was not called, as he was absent from home at the time. Catherine was with her aunt when the young man's name was brought in, and Mrs. Penniman, effacing herself and protesting, made a great point of her niece's going into the drawing-room alone.

"This time it's for you—for you only," she said. "Before, when he talked to me, it was only preliminary—it was to gain my confidence. Literally, my dear, I should not have the *courage* to show myself to-day."

And this was perfectly true. Mrs. Penniman was not a brave woman, and Morris Townsend had struck her as a young man of great force of character, and of remarkable powers of satire; a keen, resolute, brilliant nature, with which one must exercise a great deal of tact. She said to herself that he was "imperious," and she liked the word and the idea. She was not the least jealous of her niece, and she had been perfectly happy with Mr. Penniman, but in the bottom of her heart she permitted herself the observation: "That's the sort of husband I should have had!" He was certainly much more imperious—she ended by calling it imperial—than Mr. Penniman.

So Catherine saw Mr. Townsend alone, and her aunt did not come in even at the end of the visit. The visit was a long one; he sat there—in the front parlour, in the biggest armchair—for more than an hour. He seemed more at home this time—more familiar; lounging a little in the chair, slapping a cushion that was near him with his stick, and looking round the room a good deal, and at the objects it contained, as well as at Catherine; whom, however, he also contemplated freely. There was a smile of respectful devotion in his handsome eyes which seemed to Catherine almost solemnly beautiful; it made her think of a young knight in a poem. His talk, however, was not particularly knightly; it was light and easy and friendly; it took a practical turn, and he asked a number of questions about herself—what were her tastes—if she liked this and that—what were her habits. He said to her, with his charming smile, "Tell me about yourself; give me a little sketch." Catherine had very little to tell, and she had no talent for sketching; but before he went she had confided to him that she had a secret passion for the theatre, which had been but scantily gratified, and a taste for operatic music—that of Bellini and Donizetti, in especial (it must be remembered in extenuation of this primitive young woman that she held these opinions in an age of general darkness)—which she rarely had an occasion to hear, except on the hand-organ. She confessed that she was not particularly fond of literature. Morris Townsend agreed with her that books were tiresome things; only, as he said, you had to read a good many before you found it out. He had been to places that people had written books about, and they were not a bit like the descriptions. To see for yourself—that was the great thing; he always tried to see for himself. He had seen all the principal actors—he had been to all the best theatres in London and Paris. But the actors were always like the authors—they always exaggerated. He liked everything to be natural. Suddenly he stopped, looking at Catherine with his smile.

"That's what I like you for; you are so natural! Excuse me," he added; "you see I am natural myself!"

And before she had time to think whether she excused him or not—which afterwards, at leisure, she became conscious that she did—he began to talk about music, and to say that it was his greatest pleasure in life. He had heard all the great singers in Paris and London—Pasta and Rubini and Lablache—and when you had done that, you could say that you knew what singing was.

"I sing a little myself," he said; "some day I will show you. Not to-day, but some other time."

And then he got up to go; he had omitted, by accident, to say that he would sing to her if she would play to him. He thought of this after he got into the street; but he might have spared his compunction, for Catherine had not noticed the lapse. She was thinking only that "some other time" had a delightful sound; it seemed to spread itself over the future.

This was all the more reason, however, though she was ashamed and uncomfortable, why she should tell her father that Mr. Morris Townsend had called again. She announced the fact abruptly, almost violently, as soon as the Doctor came into the house; and having done so—it was her duty—she took measures to leave the room. But she could not leave it fast enough; her father stopped her just as she reached the door.

"Well, my dear, did he propose to you to-day?" the Doctor asked.

This was just what she had been afraid he would say; and yet she had no answer ready. Of course she would have liked to take it as a joke—as her father must have meant it; and yet she would have liked, also, in denying it, to be a little positive, a little sharp; so that he would perhaps not ask the question again. She didn't like it—it made her unhappy. But Catherine could never be sharp; and for a moment she only stood, with her hand on the door-knob, looking at her satiric parent, and giving a little laugh.

"Decidedly," said the Doctor to himself, "my daughter is not brilliant!"

But he had no sooner made this reflexion than Catherine found something; she had decided, on the whole, to take the thing as a joke.

"Perhaps he will do it the next time!" she exclaimed, with a repetition of her laugh. And she quickly got out of the room.

The Doctor stood staring; he wondered whether his daughter were serious. Catherine went straight to her own room, and by the time she reached it she bethought herself that there was something else—something better—she might have said. She almost wished, now, that her father would ask his question again, so that she might reply: "Oh yes, Mr. Morris Townsend proposed to me, and I refused him!"

The Doctor, however, began to put his questions elsewhere; it naturally having occurred to him that he ought to inform himself properly about this handsome young man who had formed the habit of running in and out of his house. He addressed himself to the younger of his sisters, Mrs. Almond—not going to her for the purpose; there was no such hurry as that—but having made a note of the matter for the first opportunity. The Doctor was never eager, never impatient nor nervous; but he made notes of everything, and he regularly consulted his notes. Among them the information he obtained from Mrs. Almond about Morris Townsend took its place.

"Lavinia has already been to ask me," she said. "Lavinia is most excited; I don't understand it. It's not, after all, Lavinia that the young man is supposed to have designs upon. She is very peculiar."

"Ah, my dear," the Doctor replied, "she has not lived with me these twelve years without my finding it out!"

"She has got such an artificial mind," said Mrs. Almond, who always enjoyed an opportunity to discuss Lavinia's peculiarities with her brother. "She didn't want me to tell you that she had asked me about Mr. Townsend; but I told her I would. She always wants to conceal everything."

"And yet at moments no one blurts things out with such crudity. She is like a revolving lighthouse; pitch darkness alternating with a dazzling brilliancy! But what did you tell her?" the Doctor asked.

"What I tell you; that I know very little of him."

"Lavinia must have been disappointed at that," said the Doctor; "she would prefer him to have been guilty of some romantic crime. However, we must make the best of people. They tell me our gentleman is the cousin of the little boy to whom you are about to entrust the future of your little girl."

"Arthur is not a little boy; he is a very old man; you and I will never be so old. He is a distant relation of Lavinia's *protégé*. The name is the same, but I am given to understand that there are Townsends and Townsends. So Arthur's mother tells me; she talked about 'branches'—younger branches, elder branches, inferior branches—as if it were a royal house. Arthur, it appears, is of the reigning line, but poor Lavinia's young man is not. Beyond this, Arthur's mother knows very little about him; she has only a vague story that he has been 'wild.' But I know his sister a little, and she is a very nice woman. Her name is Mrs. Montgomery; she is a widow, with a little property and five children. She lives in the Second Avenue."

"What does Mrs. Montgomery say about him?"

"That he has talents by which he might distinguish himself."

"Only he is lazy, eh?"

"She doesn't say so."

"That's family pride," said the Doctor. "What is his profession?"

"He hasn't got any; he is looking for something. I believe he was once in the Navy."

"Once? What is his age?"

"I suppose he is upwards of thirty. He must have gone into the Navy very young. I think Arthur told me that he inherited a small property—which was perhaps the cause of his leaving the Navy—and that he spent it all in a few years. He travelled all over the world, lived abroad, amused himself. I believe it was a kind of system, a theory he had. He has lately come back to America, with the intention, as he tells Arthur, of beginning life in earnest."

"Is he in earnest about Catherine, then?"

"I don't see why you should be incredulous," said Mrs. Almond. "It seems to me that you have never done Catherine justice. You must remember that she has the prospect of thirty thousand a year."

The Doctor looked at his sister a moment, and then, with the slightest touch of bitterness: "You at least appreciate her," he said.

Mrs. Almond blushed.

"I don't mean that is her only merit; I simply mean that it is a great one. A great many young men think so; and you appear to me never to have been properly aware of that. You have always had a little way of alluding to her as an unmarriageable girl."

"My allusions are as kind as yours, Elizabeth," said the Doctor frankly. "How many suitors has Catherine had, with all her expectations—how much attention has she ever received? Catherine is not unmarriageable, but she is absolutely unattractive. What other reason is there for Lavinia being so charmed with the idea that there is a lover in the house? There has never been one before, and Lavinia, with her sensitive, sympathetic nature, is not used to the idea. It affects her imagination. I must do the young men of New York the justice to say that they strike me as very disinterested. They prefer pretty girls—lively girls—girls like your own. Catherine is neither pretty nor lively."

"Catherine does very well; she has a style of her own—which is more than my poor Marian has, who has no style at all," said Mrs. Almond. "The reason Catherine has received so little attention is that she seems to all the young men to be older than themselves. She is so large, and she dresses—so richly. They are rather afraid of her, I think; she looks as if she had been married already, and you know they don't like married women. And if our young men appear disinterested," the Doctor's wiser sister went on, "it is because they marry, as a general thing, so young, before twenty-five, at the age of innocence and sincerity, before the age of calculation. If they only waited a little, Catherine would fare better."

"As a calculation? Thank you very much," said the Doctor.

"Wait till some intelligent man of forty comes along, and he will be delighted with Catherine," Mrs. Almond continued.

"Mr. Townsend is not old enough, then; his motives may be pure."

"It is very possible that his motives are pure; I should be very sorry to take the contrary for granted. Lavinia is sure of it, and, as he is a very prepossessing youth, you might give him the benefit of the doubt."

Dr. Sloper reflected a moment.

"What are his present means of subsistence?"

"I have no idea. He lives, as I say, with his sister."

"A widow, with five children? Do you mean he lives *upon* her?"

Mrs. Almond got up, and with a certain impatience: "Had you not better ask Mrs. Montgomery herself?" she inquired.

"Perhaps I may come to that," said the Doctor. "Did you say the Second Avenue?" He made a note of the Second Avenue.

## VII

He was, however, by no means so much in earnest as this might seem to indicate; and, indeed, he was more than anything else amused with the whole situation. He was not in the least in a state of tension or of vigilance with regard to Catherine's prospects; he was even on his guard against the ridicule that might attach itself to the spectacle of a house thrown into agitation by its daughter and heiress receiving attentions unprecedented in its annals. More than this, he went so far as to promise himself some entertainment from the little drama—if drama it was—of which Mrs. Penniman desired to represent the ingenious Mr. Townsend as the hero. He had no intention, as yet, of regulating the *dénouement*. He was perfectly willing, as Elizabeth had suggested, to give the young man the benefit of every doubt. There was no great danger in it; for Catherine, at the age of twenty-two, was, after all, a rather mature blossom, such as could be plucked from the stem only by a vigorous jerk. The fact that Morris Townsend was poor—was not of necessity against him; the Doctor had never made up his mind that his daughter should marry a rich man. The fortune she would inherit struck him as a very sufficient provision for two reasonable persons, and if a penniless swain who could give a good account of himself should enter the lists, he should be judged quite upon his personal merits. There were other things besides. The Doctor thought it very vulgar to be precipitate in accusing people of mercenary motives, inasmuch as his door had as yet not been in the least besieged by fortune-hunters; and, lastly, he was very curious to see whether Catherine might really be loved for her moral worth. He smiled as he reflected that poor Mr. Townsend had been only twice to the house, and he said to Mrs. Penniman that the next time he should come she must ask him to dinner.

He came very soon again, and Mrs. Penniman had of course great pleasure in executing this mission. Morris Townsend accepted her invitation with equal good grace, and the dinner took place a few days later. The Doctor had said to himself, justly enough, that they must not have the young man alone; this would partake too much of the nature of encouragement. So two or three other persons were invited; but Morris Townsend, though he was by no means the ostensible, was the real, occasion of the feast. There is every reason to suppose that he desired to make a good impression; and if he fell short of this result, it was not for want of a good deal of intelligent effort. The Doctor talked to him very little during dinner; but he observed him attentively, and after the ladies had gone out he pushed him the wine and asked him several questions. Morris was not a young man who needed to be pressed, and he found quite enough encouragement in the superior quality of the claret. The Doctor's wine was admirable, and it may be communicated to the reader that while he sipped it Morris reflected that a cellar-full of good liquor—there was evidently a cellar-full here—would be a most attractive idiosyncrasy in a father-in-law. The Doctor was struck with his appreciative guest; he saw that he was not a commonplace young man. "He has ability," said Catherine's father, "decided ability; he has a very good head if he chooses to use it. And he is uncommonly well turned out; quite the sort of figure that pleases the ladies. But I don't think I like him." The Doctor, however, kept his reflexions to himself, and talked to his visitors about foreign lands, concerning which Morris offered him more information than he was ready, as he mentally phrased it, to swallow. Dr. Sloper had travelled but little, and he took the liberty of not believing everything this anecdotical idler narrated. He prided himself on being something of a physiognomist, and while the young man, chatting with easy assurance, puffed his cigar and filled his glass again, the Doctor sat with his eyes quietly fixed on his bright, expressive face. "He has the assurance of the devil himself," said Morris's host; "I don't think I ever saw such assurance. And his powers of invention are most remarkable. He is very knowing; they were not so knowing as that in my time. And a good head, did I say? I should think so—after a bottle of Madeira and a bottle and a half of claret!"

After dinner Morris Townsend went and stood before Catherine, who was standing before the fire in her red satin gown.

"He doesn't like me—he doesn't like me at all!" said the young man.

"Who doesn't like you?" asked Catherine.

"Your father; extraordinary man!"

"I don't see how you know," said Catherine, blushing.

"I feel; I am very quick to feel."

"Perhaps you are mistaken."

"Ah, well; you ask him and you will see."

"I would rather not ask him, if there is any danger of his saying what you think."

Morris looked at her with an air of mock melancholy.

"It wouldn't give you any pleasure to contradict him?"

"I never contradict him," said Catherine.

"Will you hear me abused without opening your lips in my defence?"

"My father won't abuse you. He doesn't know you enough."

Morris Townsend gave a loud laugh, and Catherine began to blush again.

"I shall never mention you," she said, to take refuge from her confusion.

"That is very well; but it is not quite what I should have liked you to say. I should have liked you to say: 'If my father doesn't think well of you, what does it matter?'"

"Ah, but it would matter; I couldn't say that!" the girl exclaimed.

He looked at her for a moment, smiling a little; and the Doctor, if he had been watching him just then, would have seen a gleam of fine impatience in the sociable softness of his eye. But there was no impatience in his rejoinder—none, at least, save what was expressed in a little appealing sigh. "Ah, well, then, I must not give up the hope of bringing him round!"

He expressed it more frankly to Mrs. Penniman later in the evening. But before that he sang two or three songs at Catherine's timid request; not that he flattered himself that this would help to bring her father round. He had a sweet, light tenor voice, and when he had finished every one made some exclamation—every one, that is, save Catherine, who remained intensely silent. Mrs. Penniman declared that his manner of singing was "most artistic," and Dr. Sloper said it was "very taking—very taking indeed"; speaking loudly and distinctly, but with a certain dryness.

"He doesn't like me—he doesn't like me at all," said Morris Townsend, addressing the aunt in the same manner as he had done the niece. "He thinks I'm all wrong."

Unlike her niece, Mrs. Penniman asked for no explanation. She only smiled very sweetly, as if she understood everything; and, unlike Catherine too, she made no attempt to contradict him. "Pray, what does it matter?" she murmured softly.

"Ah, you say the right thing!" said Morris, greatly to the gratification of Mrs. Penniman, who prided herself on always saying the right thing.

The Doctor, the next time he saw his sister Elizabeth, let her know that he had made the acquaintance of Lavinia's *protégé.*

"Physically," he said, "he's uncommonly well set up. As an anatomist, it is really a pleasure to me to see such a beautiful structure; although, if people were all like him, I suppose there would be very little need for doctors."

"Don't you see anything in people but their bones?" Mrs. Almond rejoined. "What do you think of him as a father?"

"As a father? Thank Heaven I am not his father!"

"No; but you are Catherine's. Lavinia tells me she is in love."

"She must get over it. He is not a gentleman."

"Ah, take care! Remember that he is a branch of the Townsends."

"He is not what I call a gentleman. He has not the soul of one. He is extremely insinuating; but it's a vulgar nature. I saw through it in a minute. He is altogether too familiar—I hate familiarity. He is a plausible coxcomb."

"Ah, well," said Mrs. Almond; "if you make up your mind so easily, it's a great advantage."

"I don't make up my mind easily. What I tell you is the result of thirty years of observation; and in order to be able to form that judgment in a single evening, I have had to spend a lifetime in study."

"Very possibly you are right. But the thing is for Catherine to see it."

"I will present her with a pair of spectacles!" said the Doctor.

## VIII

IF it were true that she was in love, she was certainly very quiet about it; but the Doctor was of course prepared to admit that her quietness might mean volumes. She had told Morris Townsend that she would not mention him to her father, and she saw no reason to retract this vow of discretion. It was no more than decently civil, of course, that after having dined in Washington Square, Morris should call there again; and it was no more than natural that, having been kindly received on this occasion, he should continue to present himself. He had had plenty of leisure on his hands; and thirty years ago, in New York, a young man of leisure had reason to be thankful for aids to self-oblivion. Catherine said nothing to her father about these visits, though they had rapidly become the most important, the most absorbing thing in her life. The girl was very happy. She knew not as yet what would come of it; but the present had suddenly grown rich and solemn. If she had been told she was in love, she would have been a good deal surprised; for she had an idea that love was an eager and exacting passion, and her own heart was filled in these days with the impulse of self-effacement and sacrifice. Whenever Morris Townsend had left the house, her imagination projected itself, with all its strength, into the idea of his soon coming back; but if she had been told at such a moment that he would not return for a year, or even that he would never return, she would not have complained nor rebelled, but would have humbly accepted the decree, and sought for consolation in thinking over the times she had already seen him, the words he had spoken, the sound of his voice, of his tread, the expression of his face. Love demands certain things as a right; but Catherine had no sense of her rights; she had only a consciousness of immense and unexpected favours. Her very gratitude for these things had hushed itself; for it seemed to her that there would be something of impudence in making a festival of her secret. Her father suspected Morris Townsend's visits, and noted her reserve. She seemed to beg pardon for it; she looked at him constantly in silence, as if she meant to say that she said nothing because he was afraid of irritating him. But the poor girl's dumb eloquence irritated him more than anything else would have done, and he caught himself murmuring more than once that it was a grievous pity his only child was a simpleton. His murmurs, however, were inaudible; and for a while he said nothing to any one. He would have liked to know exactly how often young Townsend came; but he had determined to ask no questions of the girl herself—to say nothing more to her that would show that he watched her. The Doctor had a great idea of being largely just: he wished to leave his daughter her liberty, and interfere only when the danger should be proved. It was not in his manner to obtain information by indirect methods, and it never even occurred to him to question the servants. As for Lavinia, he hated to talk to her about the matter; she annoyed him with her mock romanticism. But he had to come to this. Mrs. Penniman's convictions as regards the relations of her niece and the clever young visitor who saved appearances by coming ostensibly for both the ladies—Mrs. Penniman's convictions had passed into a riper and richer phase. There was to be no crudity in Mrs. Penniman's treatment of the situation; she had become as uncommunicative as Catherine herself. She was tasting of the sweets of concealment; she had taken up the line of mystery. "She would be enchanted to be able to prove to herself that she is persecuted," said the Doctor; and when at last he questioned her, he was sure she would contrive to extract from his words a pretext for this belief.

"Be so good as to let me know what is going on in the house," he said to her, in a tone which, under the circumstances, he himself deemed genial.

"Going on, Austin?" Mrs. Penniman exclaimed. "Why, I am sure I don't know! I believe that last night the old grey cat had kittens!"

"At her age?" said the Doctor. "The idea is startling—almost shocking. Be so good as to see that they are all drowned. But what else has happened?"

"Ah, the dear little kittens!" cried Mrs. Penniman. "I wouldn't have them drowned for the world!"

Her brother puffed his cigar a few moments in silence. "Your sympathy with kittens, Lavinia," he presently resumed, "arises from a feline element in your own character."

"Cats are very graceful and very clean," said Mrs. Penniman, smiling.

"And very stealthy. You are the embodiment both of grace and of neatness; but you are wanting in frankness."

"You certainly are not, dear brother."

"I don't pretend to be graceful, though I try to be neat. Why haven't you let me know that Mr. Morris Townsend is coming to the house four times a week?"

Mrs. Penniman lifted her eyebrows. "Four times a week?"

"Five times, if you prefer it. I am away all day, and I see nothing. But when such things happen, you should let me know."

Mrs. Penniman, with her eyebrows still raised, reflected intently. "Dear Austin," she said at last, "I am incapable of betraying a confidence. I would rather suffer anything."

"Never fear; you shall not suffer. To whose confidence is it you allude? Has Catherine made you take a vow of eternal secrecy?"

"By no means. Catherine has not told me as much as she might. She has not been very trustful."

"It is the young man, then, who has made you his confidante? Allow me to say that it is extremely indiscreet of you to form secret alliances with young men. You don't know where they may lead you."

"I don't know what you mean by an alliance," said Mrs. Penniman. "I take a great interest in Mr. Townsend; I won't conceal that. But that's all."

"Under the circumstances, that is quite enough. What is the source of your interest in Mr. Townsend?"

"Why," said Mrs. Penniman, musing, and then breaking into her smile, "that he is so interesting!"

The Doctor felt that he had need of his patience. "And what makes him interesting?—his good looks?"

"His misfortunes, Austin."

"Ah, he has had misfortunes? That, of course, is always interesting. Are you at liberty to mention a few of Mr. Townsend's?"

"I don't know that he would like it," said Mrs. Penniman. "He has told me a great deal about himself—he has told me, in fact, his whole history. But I don't think I ought to repeat those things. He would tell them to you, I am sure, if he thought you would listen to him kindly. With kindness you may do anything with him."

The Doctor gave a laugh. "I shall request him very kindly, then, to leave Catherine alone."

"Ah!" said Mrs. Penniman, shaking her forefinger at her brother, with her little finger turned out, "Catherine had probably said something to him kinder than that."

"Said that she loved him? Do you mean that?"

Mrs. Penniman fixed her eyes on the floor. "As I tell you, Austin, she doesn't confide in me."

"You have an opinion, I suppose, all the same. It is that I ask you for; though I don't conceal from you that I shall not regard it as conclusive."

Mrs. Penniman's gaze continued to rest on the carpet; but at last she lifted it, and then her brother thought it very expressive. "I think Catherine is very happy; that is all I can say."

"Townsend is trying to marry her—is that what you mean?"

"He is greatly interested in her."

"He finds her such an attractive girl?"

"Catherine has a lovely nature, Austin," said Mrs. Penniman, "and Mr. Townsend has had the intelligence to discover that."

"With a little help from you, I suppose. My dear Lavinia," cried the Doctor, "you are an admirable aunt!"

"So Mr. Townsend says," observed Lavinia, smiling.

"Do you think he is sincere?" asked her brother.

"In saying that?"

"No; that's of course. But in his admiration for Catherine?"

"Deeply sincere. He has said to me the most appreciative, the most charming things about her. He would say them to you, if he were sure you would listen to him—gently."

"I doubt whether I can undertake it. He appears to require a great deal of gentleness."

"He is a sympathetic, sensitive nature," said Mrs. Penniman.

Her brother puffed his cigar again in silence. "These delicate qualities have survived his vicissitudes, eh? All this while you haven't told me about his misfortunes."

"It is a long story," said Mrs. Penniman, "and I regard it as a sacred trust. But I suppose there is no objection to my saying that he has been wild—he frankly confesses that. But he has paid for it."

"That's what has impoverished him, eh?"

"I don't mean simply in money. He is very much alone in the world."

"Do you mean that he has behaved so badly that his friends have given him up?"

"He has had false friends, who have deceived and betrayed him."

"He seems to have some good ones too. He has a devoted sister, and half-a-dozen nephews and nieces."

Mrs. Penniman was silent a minute. "The nephews and nieces are children, and the sister is not a very attractive person."

"I hope he doesn't abuse her to you," said the Doctor; "for I am told he lives upon her."

"Lives upon her?"

"Lives with her, and does nothing for himself; it is about the same thing."

"He is looking for a position—most earnestly," said Mrs. Penniman. "He hopes every day to find one."

"Precisely. He is looking for it here—over there in the front parlour. The position of husband of a weak-minded woman with a large fortune would suit him to perfection!"

Mrs. Penniman was truly amiable, but she now gave signs of temper. She rose with much animation, and stood for a moment looking at her brother. "My dear Austin," she remarked, "if you regard Catherine as a weak-minded woman, you are particularly mistaken!" And with this she moved majestically away.

## IX

IT was a regular custom with the family in Washington Square to go and spend Sunday evening at Mrs. Almond's. On the Sunday after the conversation I have just narrated, this custom was not intermitted; and on this occasion, towards the middle of the evening, Dr. Sloper found reason to withdraw to the library, with his brother-in-law, to talk over a matter of business. He was absent some twenty minutes, and when he came back into the circle, which was enlivened by the presence of several friends of the family, he saw that Morris Townsend had come in and had lost as little time as possible in seating himself on a small sofa, beside Catherine. In the large room, where several different groups had been formed, and the hum of voices and of laughter was loud, these two young persons might confabulate, as the Doctor phrased it to himself, without attracting attention. He saw in a moment, however, that his daughter was painfully conscious of his own observation. She sat motionless, with her eyes bent down, staring at her open fan, deeply flushed, shrinking together as if to minimise the indiscretion of which she confessed herself guilty.

The Doctor almost pitied her. Poor Catherine was not defiant; she had no genius for bravado; and as she felt that her father viewed her companion's attentions with an unsympathising eye, there was nothing but discomfort for her in the accident of seeming to challenge him. The Doctor felt, indeed, so sorry for her that he turned away, to spare her the sense of being watched; and he was so intelligent a man that, in his thoughts, he rendered a sort of poetic justice to her situation.

"It must be deucedly pleasant for a plain inanimate girl like that to have a beautiful young fellow come and sit down beside her and whisper to her that he is her slave—if that is what this one whispers. No wonder she likes it, and that she thinks me a cruel tyrant; which of course she does, though she is afraid—she hasn't the animation necessary—to admit it to herself. Poor old Catherine!" mused the Doctor; "I verily believe she is capable of defending me when Townsend abuses me!"

And the force of this reflexion, for the moment, was such in making him feel the natural opposition between his point of view and that of an infatuated child, that he said to himself that he was perhaps, after all, taking things too hard and crying out before he was hurt. He must not condemn Morris Townsend unheard. He had a great aversion to taking things too hard; he thought that half the discomfort and many of the disappointments of life came from it; and for an instant he asked himself whether, possibly, he did not appear ridiculous to this intelligent young man, whose private perception of incongruities he suspected of being keen. At the end of a quarter of an hour Catherine had got rid of him, and Townsend was now standing before the fireplace in conversation with Mrs. Almond.

"We will try him again," said the Doctor. And he crossed the room and joined his sister and her companion, making her a sign that she should leave the young man to him. She presently did so, while Morris looked at him, smiling, without a sign of evasiveness in his affable eye.

"He's amazingly conceited!" thought the Doctor; and then he said aloud: "I am told you are looking out for a position."

"Oh, a position is more than I should presume to call it," Morris Townsend answered. "That sounds so fine. I should like some quiet work—something to turn an honest penny."

"What sort of thing should you prefer?"

"Do you mean what am I fit for? Very little, I am afraid. I have nothing but my good right arm, as they say in the melodramas."

"You are too modest," said the Doctor. "In addition to your good right arm, you have your subtle brain. I know nothing of you but what I see; but I see by your physiognomy that you are extremely intelligent."

"Ah," Townsend murmured, "I don't know what to answer when you say that! You advise me, then, not to despair?"

And he looked at his interlocutor as if the question might have a double meaning. The Doctor caught the look and weighed it a moment before he replied. "I should be very sorry to admit that a robust and well-disposed young man need ever despair. If he doesn't succeed in one thing, he can try another. Only, I should add, he should choose his line with discretion."

"Ah, yes, with discretion," Morris Townsend repeated sympathetically. "Well, I have been indiscreet, formerly; but I think I have got over it. I am very steady now." And he stood a moment, looking down at his remarkably neat shoes. Then at last, "Were you kindly intending to propose something for my advantage?" he inquired, looking up and smiling.

"Damn his impudence!" the Doctor exclaimed privately. But in a moment he reflected that he himself had, after all, touched first upon this delicate point, and that his words might have been construed as an offer of assistance. "I have no particular proposal to make," he presently said; "but it occurred to me to let you know that I have you in my mind. Sometimes one hears of opportunities. For instance—should you object to leaving New York—to going to a distance?"

"I am afraid I shouldn't be able to manage that. I must seek my fortune here or nowhere. You see," added Morris Townsend, "I have ties—I have responsibilities here. I have a sister, a widow, from whom I have been separated for a long time, and to whom I am almost everything. I shouldn't like to say to her that I must leave her. She rather depends upon me, you see."

"Ah, that's very proper; family feeling is very proper," said Dr. Sloper. "I often think there is not enough of it in our city. I think I have heard of your sister."

"It is possible, but I rather doubt it; she lives so very quietly."

"As quietly, you mean," the Doctor went on, with a short laugh, "as a lady may do who has several young children."

"Ah, my little nephews and nieces—that's the very point! I am helping to bring them up," said Morris Townsend. "I am a kind of amateur tutor; I give them lessons."

"That's very proper, as I say; but it is hardly a career."

"It won't make my fortune!" the young man confessed.

"You must not be too much bent on a fortune," said the Doctor. "But I assure you I will keep you in mind; I won't lose sight of you!"

"If my situation becomes desperate I shall perhaps take the liberty of reminding you!" Morris rejoined, raising his voice a little, with a brighter smile, as his interlocutor turned away.

Before he left the house the Doctor had a few words with Mrs. Almond.

"I should like to see his sister," he said. "What do you call her? Mrs. Montgomery. I should like to have a little talk with her."

"I will try and manage it," Mrs. Almond responded. "I will take the first opportunity of inviting her, and you shall come and meet her. Unless, indeed," Mrs. Almond added, "she first takes it into her head to be sick and to send for you."

"Ah no, not that; she must have trouble enough without that. But it would have its advantages, for then I should see the children. I should like very much to see the children."

"You are very thorough. Do you want to catechise them about their uncle!"

"Precisely. Their uncle tells me he has charge of their education, that he saves their mother the expense of school-bills. I should like to ask them a few questions in the commoner branches."

"He certainly has not the cut of a schoolmaster!" Mrs. Almond said to herself a short time afterwards, as she saw Morris Townsend in a corner bending over her niece, who was seated.

And there was, indeed, nothing in the young man's discourse at this moment that savoured of the pedagogue.

"Will you meet me somewhere to-morrow or next day?" he said, in a low tone, to Catherine.

"Meet you?" she asked, lifting her frightened eyes.

"I have something particular to say to you—very particular."

"Can't you come to the house? Can't you say it there?"

Townsend shook his head gloomily. "I can't enter your doors again!"

"Oh, Mr. Townsend!" murmured Catherine. She trembled as she wondered what had happened, whether her father had forbidden it.

"I can't in self-respect," said the young man. "Your father has insulted me."

"Insulted you!"

"He has taunted me with my poverty."

"Oh, you are mistaken—you misunderstood him!" Catherine spoke with energy, getting up from her chair.

"Perhaps I am too proud—too sensitive. But would you have me otherwise?" he asked tenderly.

"Where my father is concerned, you must not be sure. He is full of goodness," said Catherine.

"He laughed at me for having no position! I took it quietly; but only because he belongs to you."

"I don't know," said Catherine; "I don't know what he thinks. I am sure he means to be kind. You must not be too proud."

"I will be proud only of you," Morris answered. "Will you meet me in the Square in the afternoon?"

A great blush on Catherine's part had been the answer to the declaration I have just quoted. She turned away, heedless of his question.

"Will you meet me?" he repeated. "It is very quiet there; no one need see us—toward dusk?"

"It is you who are unkind, it is you who laugh, when you say such things as that."

"My dear girl!" the young man murmured.

"You know how little there is in me to be proud of. I am ugly and stupid."

Morris greeted this remark with an ardent murmur, in which she recognised nothing articulate but an assurance that she was his own dearest.

But she went on. "I am not even—I am not even—" And she paused a moment.

"You are not what?"

"I am not even brave."

"Ah, then, if you are afraid, what shall we do?"

She hesitated a while; then at last—"You must come to the house," she said; "I am not afraid of that."

"I would rather it were in the Square," the young man urged. "You know how empty it is, often. No one will see us."

"I don't care who sees us! But leave me now."

He left her resignedly; he had got what he wanted. Fortunately he was ignorant that half an hour later, going home with her father and feeling him near, the poor girl, in spite of her sudden declaration of courage, began to tremble again. Her father said nothing; but she had an idea his eyes were fixed upon her in the darkness. Mrs. Penniman also was silent; Morris Townsend had told her that her niece preferred, unromantically, an interview in a chintz-covered parlour to a sentimental tryst beside a fountain sheeted with dead leaves, and she was lost in wonderment at the oddity—almost the perversity—of the choice.

## X

CATHERINE received the young man the next day on the ground she had chosen—amid the chaste upholstery of a New York drawing-room furnished in the fashion of fifty years ago. Morris had swallowed his pride and made the effort necessary to cross the threshold of her too derisive parent—an act of magnanimity which could not fail to render him doubly interesting.

"We must settle something—we must take a line," he declared, passing his hand through his hair and giving a glance at the long narrow mirror which adorned the space between the two windows, and which had at its base a little gilded bracket covered by a thin slab of white marble, supporting in its turn a backgammon board folded together in the shape of two volumes, two shining folios inscribed in letters of greenish gilt, *History of England*. If Morris had been pleased to describe the master of the house as a heartless scoffer, it is because he thought him too much on his guard, and this was the easiest way to express his own dissatisfaction—a dissatisfaction which he had made a point of concealing from the Doctor. It will probably seem to the reader, however, that the Doctor's vigilance was by no means excessive, and that these two young people had an open field. Their intimacy was now considerable, and it may appear that for a shrinking and retiring person our heroine has been liberal of her favours. The young man, within a few days, has made her listen to things for which she had not supposed that she was prepared; having a lively foreboding of difficulties, he proceeded to gain as much ground as possible in the present. He remembered that fortune favours the brave, and even if he had forgotten it, Mrs. Penniman would have remembered it for him. Mrs. Penniman delighted of all things in a drama, and she flattered herself that a drama would now be enacted. Combining as she did the zeal of the prompter with the impatience of the spectator, she had long since done her utmost to pull up the curtain. She too expected to figure in the performance—to be the confidante, the Chorus, to speak the epilogue. It may even be said that there were times when she lost sight altogether of the modest heroine of the play, in the contemplation of certain great passages which would naturally occur between the hero and herself.

What Morris had told Catherine at last was simply that he loved her, or rather adored her. Virtually, he had made known as much already—his visits had been a series of eloquent intimations of it. But now he had affirmed it in lover's vows, and, as a memorable sign of it, he had passed his arm round the girl's waist and taken a kiss. This happy certitude had come sooner than Catherine expected, and she had regarded it, very naturally, as a priceless treasure. It may even be doubted whether she had ever definitely expected to possess it; she had not been waiting for it, and she had never said to herself that at a given moment it must come. As I have tried to explain, she was not eager and exacting; she took what was given her from day to day; and if the delightful custom of her lover's visits, which yielded her a happiness in which confidence and timidity were strangely blended, had suddenly come to an end, she would not only not have spoken of herself as one of the forsaken, but she would not have thought of herself as one of the disappointed. After

Morris had kissed her, the last time he was with her, as a ripe assurance of his devotion, she begged him to go away, to leave her alone, to let her think. Morris went away, taking another kiss first. But Catherine's meditations had lacked a certain coherence. She felt his kisses on her lips and on her cheeks for a long time afterwards; the sensation was rather an obstacle than an aid to reflexion. She would have liked to see her situation all clearly before her, to make up her mind what she should do if, as she feared, her father should tell her that he disapproved of Morris Townsend. But all that she could see with any vividness was that it was terribly strange that any one should disapprove of him; that there must in that case be some mistake, some mystery, which in a little while would be set at rest. She put off deciding and choosing; before the vision of a conflict with her father she dropped her eyes and sat motionless, holding her breath and waiting. It made her heart beat, it was intensely painful. When Morris kissed her and said these things—that also made her heart beat; but this was worse, and it frightened her. Nevertheless, to-day, when the young man spoke of settling something, taking a line, she felt that it was the truth, and she answered very simply and without hesitating.

"We must do our duty," she said; "we must speak to my father. I will do it to-night; you must do it to-morrow."

"It is very good of you to do it first," Morris answered. "The young man—the happy lover—generally does that. But just as you please!"

It pleased Catherine to think that she should be brave for his sake, and in her satisfaction she even gave a little smile. "Women have more tact," she said; "they ought to do it first. They are more conciliating; they can persuade better."

"You will need all your powers of persuasion. But, after all," Morris added, "you are irresistible."

"Please don't speak that way—and promise me this. To-morrow, when you talk with father, you will be very gentle and respectful."

"As much so as possible," Morris promised. "It won't be much use, but I shall try. I certainly would rather have you easily than have to fight for you."

"Don't talk about fighting; we shall not fight."

"Ah, we must be prepared," Morris rejoined; "you especially, because for you it must come hardest. Do you know the first thing your father will say to you?"

"No, Morris; please tell me."

"He will tell you I am mercenary."

"Mercenary?"

"It's a big word; but it means a low thing. It means that I am after your money."

"Oh!" murmured Catherine softly.

The exclamation was so deprecating and touching that Morris indulged in another little demonstration of affection. "But he will be sure to say it," he added.

"It will be easy to be prepared for that," Catherine said. "I shall simply say that he is mistaken—that other men may be that way, but that you are not."

"You must make a great point of that, for it will be his own great point."

Catherine looked at her lover a minute, and then she said, "I shall persuade him. But I am glad we shall be rich," she added.

Morris turned away, looking into the crown of his hat. "No, it's a misfortune," he said at last. "It is from that our difficulty will come."

"Well, if it is the worst misfortune, we are not so unhappy. Many people would not think it so bad. I will persuade him, and after that we shall be very glad we have money."

Morris Townsend listened to this robust logic in silence. "I will leave my defence to you; it's a charge that a man has to stoop to defend himself from."

Catherine on her side was silent for a while; she was looking at him while he looked, with a good deal of fixedness, out of the window. "Morris," she said abruptly, "are you very sure you love me?"

He turned round, and in a moment he was bending over her. "My own dearest, can you doubt it?"

"I have only known it five days," she said; "but now it seems to me as if I could never do without it."

"You will never be called upon to try!" And he gave a little tender, reassuring laugh. Then, in a moment, he added, "There is something you must tell me, too." She had closed her eyes after the last word she uttered, and kept them closed; and at this she nodded her head, without opening them. "You must tell me," he went on, "that if your father is dead against me, if he absolutely forbids our marriage, you will still be faithful."

Catherine opened her eyes, gazing at him, and she could give no better promise than what he read there.

"You will cleave to me?" said Morris. "You know you are your own mistress—you are of age."

"Ah, Morris!" she murmured, for all answer. Or rather not for all; for she put her hand into his own. He kept it a while, and presently he kissed her again. This is all that need be recorded of their conversation; but Mrs. Penniman, if she had been present, would probably have admitted that it was as well it had not taken place beside the fountain in Washington Square.

## XI

CATHERINE listened for her father when he came in that evening, and she heard him go to his study. She sat quiet, though her heart was beating fast, for nearly half an hour; then she went and knocked at his door—a ceremony without which she never crossed the threshold of this apartment. On entering it now she found him in his chair beside the fire, entertaining himself with a cigar and the evening paper.

"I have something to say to you," she began very gently; and she sat down in the first place that offered.

"I shall be very happy to hear it, my dear," said her father. He waited—waited, looking at her, while she stared, in a long silence, at the fire. He was curious and impatient, for he was sure she was going to speak of Morris Townsend; but he let her take her own time, for he was determined to be very mild.

"I am engaged to be married!" Catherine announced at last, still staring at the fire.

The Doctor was startled; the accomplished fact was more than he had expected. But he betrayed no surprise. "You do right to tell me," he simply said. "And who is the happy mortal whom you have honoured with your choice?"

"Mr. Morris Townsend." And as she pronounced her lover's name, Catherine looked at him. What she saw was her father's still grey eye and his clear-cut, definite smile. She contemplated these objects for a moment, and then she looked back at the fire; it was much warmer.

"When was this arrangement made?" the Doctor asked.

"This afternoon—two hours ago."

"Was Mr. Townsend here?"

"Yes, father; in the front parlour." She was very glad that she was not obliged to tell him that the ceremony of their betrothal had taken place out there under the bare ailantus-trees.

"Is it serious?" said the Doctor.

"Very serious, father."

Her father was silent a moment. "Mr. Townsend ought to have told me."

"He means to tell you to-morrow."

"After I know all about it from you? He ought to have told me before. Does he think I didn't care—because I left you so much liberty?"

"Oh no," said Catherine; "he knew you would care. And we have been so much obliged to you for—for the liberty."

The Doctor gave a short laugh. "You might have made a better use of it, Catherine."

"Please don't say that, father," the girl urged softly, fixing her dull and gentle eyes upon him.

He puffed his cigar awhile, meditatively. "You have gone very fast," he said at last.

"Yes," Catherine answered simply; "I think we have."

Her father glanced at her an instant, removing his eyes from the fire. "I don't wonder Mr. Townsend likes you. You are so simple and so good."

"I don't know why it is—but he *does* like me. I am sure of that."

"And are you very fond of Mr. Townsend?"

"I like him very much, of course—or I shouldn't consent to marry him."

"But you have known him a very short time, my dear."

"Oh," said Catherine, with some eagerness, "it doesn't take long to like a person—when once you begin."

"You must have begun very quickly. Was it the first time you saw him—that night at your aunt's party?"

"I don't know, father," the girl answered. "I can't tell you about that."

"Of course; that's your own affair. You will have observed that I have acted on that principle. I have not interfered, I have left you your liberty, I have remembered that you are no longer a little girl—that you have arrived at years of discretion."

"I feel very old—and very wise," said Catherine, smiling faintly.

"I am afraid that before long you will feel older and wiser yet. I don't like your engagement."

"Ah!" Catherine exclaimed softly, getting up from her chair.

"No, my dear. I am sorry to give you pain; but I don't like it. You should have consulted me before you settled it. I have been too easy with you, and I feel as if you had taken advantage of my indulgence. Most decidedly, you should have spoken to me first."

Catherine hesitated a moment, and then—"It was because I was afraid you wouldn't like it!" she confessed.

"Ah, there it is! You had a bad conscience."

"No, I have not a bad conscience, father!" the girl cried out, with considerable energy. "Please don't accuse me of anything so dreadful." These words, in fact, represented to her imagination something very terrible indeed, something base and cruel, which she associated with malefactors and prisoners.

"It was because I was afraid—afraid—" she went on.

"If you were afraid, it was because you had been foolish!"

"I was afraid you didn't like Mr. Townsend."

"You were quite right. I don't like him."

"Dear father, you don't know him," said Catherine, in a voice so timidly argumentative that it might have touched him.

"Very true; I don't know him intimately. But I know him enough. I have my impression of him. You don't know him either."

She stood before the fire, with her hands lightly clasped in front of her; and her father, leaning back in his chair and looking up at her, made this remark with a placidity that might have been irritating.

I doubt, however, whether Catherine was irritated, though she broke into a vehement protest. "I don't know him?" she cried. "Why, I know him—better than I have ever known any one!"

"You know a part of him—what he has chosen to show you. But you don't know the rest."

"The rest? What is the rest?"

"Whatever it may be. There is sure to be plenty of it."

"I know what you mean," said Catherine, remembering how Morris had forewarned her. "You mean that he is mercenary."

Her father looked up at her still, with his cold, quiet reasonable eye. "If I meant it, my dear, I should say it! But there is an error I wish particularly to avoid—that of rendering Mr. Townsend more interesting to you by saying hard things about him."

"I won't think them hard if they are true," said Catherine.

"If you don't, you will be a remarkably sensible young woman!"

"They will be your reasons, at any rate, and you will want me to hear your reasons."

The Doctor smiled a little. "Very true. You have a perfect right to ask for them." And he puffed his cigar a few moments. "Very well, then, without accusing Mr. Townsend of being in love only with your fortune—and with the fortune that you justly expect—I will say that there is every reason to suppose that these good things have entered into his calculation more largely than a tender solicitude for your happiness strictly requires. There is, of course, nothing impossible in an intelligent young man entertaining a disinterested affection for you. You are an honest, amiable girl, and an intelligent young man might easily find it out. But the principal thing that we know about this young man—who is, indeed, very intelligent—leads us to suppose that, however much he may value your personal merits, he values your money more. The principal thing we know about him is that he has led a life of dissipation, and has spent a fortune of his own in doing so. That is enough for me, my dear. I wish you to marry a young man with other antecedents—a young man who could give positive guarantees. If Morris Townsend has spent his own fortune in amusing himself, there is every reason to believe that he would spend yours."

The Doctor delivered himself of these remarks slowly, deliberately, with occasional pauses and prolongations of accent, which made no great allowance for poor Catherine's suspense as to his conclusion. She sat down at last, with her head bent and her eyes still fixed upon him; and strangely enough—I hardly know how to tell it—even while she felt that what he said went so terribly against her, she admired his neatness and nobleness of expression. There was something hopeless and oppressive in having to argue with her father; but she too, on her side, must try to be clear. He was so quiet; he was not at all angry; and she too must be quiet. But her very effort to be quiet made her tremble.

"That is not the principal thing we know about him," she said; and there was a touch of her tremor in her voice. "There are other things—many other things. He has very high abilities—he wants so much to do something. He is kind, and generous, and true," said poor Catherine, who had not suspected hitherto the resources of her eloquence. "And his fortune—his fortune that he spent—was very small!"

"All the more reason he shouldn't have spent it," cried the Doctor, getting up, with a laugh. Then as Catherine, who had also risen to her feet again, stood there in her rather angular earnestness, wishing so much and expressing so little, he drew her towards him and kissed her. "You won't think me cruel?" he said, holding her a moment.

This question was not reassuring; it seemed to Catherine, on the contrary, to suggest possibilities which made her feel sick. But she answered coherently enough—"No, dear father; because if you knew how I feel—and you must know, you know everything—you would be so kind, so gentle."

"Yes, I think I know how you feel," the Doctor said. "I will be very kind—be sure of that. And I will see Mr. Townsend to-morrow. Meanwhile, and for the present, be so good as to mention to no one that you are engaged."

## XII

On the morrow, in the afternoon, he stayed at home, awaiting Mr. Townsend's call—a proceeding by which it appeared to him (justly perhaps, for he was a very busy man) that he paid Catherine's suitor great honour, and gave both these young people so much the less to complain of. Morris presented himself with a countenance sufficiently serene—he appeared to have forgotten the "insult" for which he had solicited Catherine's sympathy two evenings before, and Dr. Sloper lost no time in letting him know that he had been prepared for his visit.

"Catherine told me yesterday what has been going on between you," he said. "You must allow me to say that it would have been becoming of you to give me notice of your intentions before they had gone so far."

"I should have done so," Morris answered, "if you had not had so much the appearance of leaving your daughter at liberty. She seems to me quite her own mistress."

"Literally, she is. But she has not emancipated herself morally quite so far, I trust, as to choose a husband without consulting me. I have left her at liberty, but I have not been in the least indifferent. The truth is that your little affair has come to a head with a rapidity that surprises me. It was only the other day that Catherine made your acquaintance."

"It was not long ago, certainly," said Morris, with great gravity. "I admit that we have not been slow to—to arrive at an understanding. But that was very natural, from the moment we were sure of ourselves—and of each other. My interest in Miss Sloper began the first time I saw her."

"Did it not by chance precede your first meeting?" the Doctor asked.

Morris looked at him an instant. "I certainly had already heard that she was a charming girl."

"A charming girl—that's what you think her?"

"Assuredly. Otherwise I should not be sitting here."

The Doctor meditated a moment. "My dear young man," he said at last, "you must be very susceptible. As Catherine's father, I have, I trust, a just and tender appreciation of her many good qualities; but I don't mind telling you that I have never thought of her as a charming girl, and never expected any one else to do so."

Morris Townsend received this statement with a smile that was not wholly devoid of deference. "I don't know what I might think of her if I were her father. I can't put myself in that place. I speak from my own point of view."

"You speak very well," said the Doctor; "but that is not all that is necessary. I told Catherine yesterday that I disapproved of her engagement."

"She let me know as much, and I was very sorry to hear it. I am greatly disappointed." And Morris sat in silence awhile, looking at the floor.

"Did you really expect I would say I was delighted, and throw my daughter into your arms?"

"Oh no; I had an idea you didn't like me."

"What gave you the idea?"

"The fact that I am poor."

"That has a harsh sound," said the Doctor, "but it is about the truth—speaking of you strictly as a son-in-law. Your absence of means, of a profession, of visible resources or prospects, places you in a category from which it would be imprudent for me to select a husband for my daughter, who is a weak young woman with a large fortune. In any other capacity I am perfectly prepared to like you. As a son-in-law, I abominate you!"

Morris Townsend listened respectfully. "I don't think Miss Sloper is a weak woman," he presently said.

"Of course you must defend her—it's the least you can do. But I have known my child twenty years, and you have known her six weeks. Even if she were not weak, however, you would still be a penniless man."

"Ah, yes; that is *my* weakness! And therefore, you mean, I am mercenary—I only want your daughter's money."

"I don't say that. I am not obliged to say it; and to say it, save under stress of compulsion, would be very bad taste. I say simply that you belong to the wrong category."

"But your daughter doesn't marry a category," Townsend urged, with his handsome smile. "She marries an individual—an individual whom she is so good as to say she loves."

"An individual who offers so little in return!"

"Is it possible to offer more than the most tender affection and a lifelong devotion?" the young man demanded.

"It depends how we take it. It is possible to offer a few other things besides; and not only is it possible, but it's usual. A lifelong devotion is measured after the fact; and meanwhile it is customary in these cases to give a few material securities. What are yours? A very handsome face and figure, and a very good manner. They are excellent as far as they go, but they don't go far enough."

"There is one thing you should add to them," said Morris; "the word of a gentleman!"

"The word of a gentleman that you will always love Catherine? You must be a very fine gentleman to be sure of that."

"The word of a gentleman that I am not mercenary; that my affection for Miss Sloper is as pure and disinterested a sentiment as was ever lodged in a human breast! I care no more for her fortune than for the ashes in that grate."

"I take note—I take note," said the Doctor. "But having done so, I turn to our category again. Even with that solemn vow on your lips, you take your place in it. There is nothing against you but an accident, if you will; but with my thirty years' medical practice, I have seen that accidents may have far-reaching consequences."

Morris smoothed his hat—it was already remarkably glossy—and continued to display a self-control which, as the Doctor was obliged to admit, was extremely creditable to him. But his disappointment was evidently keen.

"Is there nothing I can do to make you believe in me?"

"If there were I should be sorry to suggest it, for—don't you see?—I don't want to believe in you!" said the Doctor, smiling.

"I would go and dig in the fields."

"That would be foolish."

"I will take the first work that offers, to-morrow."

"Do so by all means—but for your own sake, not for mine."

"I see; you think I am an idler!" Morris exclaimed, a little too much in the tone of a man who has made a discovery. But he saw his error immediately, and blushed.

"It doesn't matter what I think, when once I have told you I don't think of you as a son-in-law."

But Morris persisted. "You think I would squander her money."

The Doctor smiled. "It doesn't matter, as I say; but I plead guilty to that."

"That's because I spent my own, I suppose," said Morris. "I frankly confess that. I have been wild. I have been foolish. I will tell you every crazy thing I ever did, if you like. There were some great follies among the number—I have never concealed that. But I have sown my wild oats. Isn't there some proverb about a reformed rake? I was not a rake, but I assure you I have reformed. It is better to have amused oneself for a while and have done with it. Your daughter would never care for a milksop; and I will take the liberty of saying that you would like one quite as little. Besides, between my money and hers there is a great difference. I spent my own; it was because it was my own that I spent it. And I made no debts; when it was gone I stopped. I don't owe a penny in the world."

"Allow me to inquire what you are living on now—though I admit," the Doctor added, "that the question, on my part, is inconsistent."

"I am living on the remnants of my property," said Morris Townsend.

"Thank you!" the Doctor gravely replied.

Yes, certainly, Morris's self-control was laudable. "Even admitting I attach an undue importance to Miss Sloper's fortune," he went on, "would not that be in itself an assurance that I should take much care of it?"

"That you should take too much care would be quite as bad as that you should take too little. Catherine might suffer as much by your economy as by your extravagance."

"I think you are very unjust!" The young man made this declaration decently, civilly, without violence.

"It is your privilege to think so, and I surrender my reputation to you! I certainly don't flatter myself I gratify you."

"Don't you care a little to gratify your daughter? Do you enjoy the idea of making her miserable?"

"I am perfectly resigned to her thinking me a tyrant for a twelvemonth."

"For a twelvemonth!" exclaimed Morris, with a laugh.

"For a lifetime, then! She may as well be miserable in that way as in the other."

Here at last Morris lost his temper. "Ah, you are not polite, sir!" he cried.

"You push me to it—you argue too much."

"I have a great deal at stake."

"Well, whatever it is," said the Doctor, "you have lost it!"

"Are you sure of that?" asked Morris; "are you sure your daughter will give me up?"

"I mean, of course, you have lost it as far as I am concerned. As for Catherine's giving you up—no, I am not sure of it. But as I shall strongly recommend it, as I have a great fund of respect and affection in my daughter's mind to draw upon, and as she has the sentiment of duty developed in a very high degree, I think it extremely possible."

Morris Townsend began to smooth his hat again. "I too have a fund of affection to draw upon!" he observed at last.

The Doctor at this point showed his own first symptoms of irritation. "Do you mean to defy me?"

"Call it what you please, sir! I mean not to give your daughter up."

The Doctor shook his head. "I haven't the least fear of your pining away your life. You are made to enjoy it."

Morris gave a laugh. "Your opposition to my marriage is all the more cruel, then! Do you intend to forbid your daughter to see me again?"

"She is past the age at which people are forbidden, and I am not a father in an old-fashioned novel. But I shall strongly urge her to break with you."

"I don't think she will," said Morris Townsend.

"Perhaps not. But I shall have done what I could."

"She has gone too far," Morris went on.

"To retreat? Then let her stop where she is."

"Too far to stop, I mean."

The Doctor looked at him a moment; Morris had his hand on the door. "There is a great deal of impertinence in your saying it."

"I will say no more, sir!" Morris answered; and, making his bow, he left the room.

## XIII

It may be thought the Doctor was too positive, and Mrs. Almond intimated as much. But, as he said, he had his impression; it seemed to him sufficient, and he had no wish to modify it. He had passed his life in estimating people (it was part of the medical trade), and in nineteen cases out of twenty he was right.

"Perhaps Mr. Townsend is the twentieth case," Mrs. Almond suggested.

"Perhaps he is, though he doesn't look to me at all like a twentieth case. But I will give him the benefit of the doubt, and, to make sure, I will go and talk with Mrs. Montgomery. She will almost certainly tell me I have done right; but it is just possible that she will prove to me that I have made the greatest mistake of my life. If she does, I will beg Mr. Townsend's pardon. You needn't invite her to meet me, as you kindly proposed; I will write her a frank letter, telling her how matters stand, and asking leave to come and see her."

"I am afraid the frankness will be chiefly on your side. The poor little woman will stand up for her brother, whatever he may be."

"Whatever he may be? I doubt that. People are not always so fond of their brothers."

"Ah," said Mrs. Almond, "when it's a question of thirty thousand a year coming into a family—"

"If she stands up for him on account of the money, she will be a humbug. If she is a humbug I shall see it. If I see it, I won't waste time with her."

"She is not a humbug—she is an exemplary woman. She will not wish to play her brother a trick simply because he is selfish."

"If she is worth talking to, she will sooner play him a trick than that he should play Catherine one. Has she seen Catherine, by the way—does she know her?"

"Not to my knowledge. Mr. Townsend can have had no particular interest in bringing them together."

"If she is an exemplary woman, no. But we shall see to what extent she answers your description."

"I shall be curious to hear her description of you!" said Mrs. Almond, with a laugh. "And, meanwhile, how is Catherine taking it?"

"As she takes everything—as a matter of course."

"Doesn't she make a noise? Hasn't she made a scene?"

"She is not scenic."

"I thought a love-lorn maiden was always scenic."

"A fantastic widow is more so. Lavinia has made me a speech; she thinks me very arbitrary."

"She has a talent for being in the wrong," said Mrs. Almond. "But I am very sorry for Catherine, all the same."

"So am I. But she will get over it."

"You believe she will give him up?"

"I count upon it. She has such an admiration for her father."

"Oh, we know all about that! But it only makes me pity her the more. It makes her dilemma the more painful, and the effort of choosing between you and her lover almost impossible."

"If she can't choose, all the better."

"Yes, but he will stand there entreating her to choose, and Lavinia will pull on that side."

"I am glad she is not on my side; she is capable of ruining an excellent cause. The day Lavinia gets into your boat it capsizes. But she had better be careful," said the Doctor. "I will have no treason in my house!"

"I suspect she will be careful; for she is at bottom very much afraid of you."

"They are both afraid of me—harmless as I am!" the Doctor answered. "And it is on that that I build—on the salutary terror I inspire!"

## XIV

He wrote his frank letter to Mrs. Montgomery, who punctually answered it, mentioning an hour at which he might present himself in the Second Avenue. She lived in a neat little house of red brick, which had been freshly painted, with the edges of the bricks very sharply marked out in white. It has now disappeared, with its companions, to make room for a row of structures more majestic. There were green shutters upon the windows, without slats, but pierced with little holes, arranged in groups; and before the house was a diminutive yard, ornamented with a bush of mysterious character, and surrounded by a low wooden paling, painted in the same green as the shutters. The place looked like a magnified baby-house, and might have been taken down from a shelf in a toy-shop. Dr. Sloper, when he went to call, said to himself, as he glanced at the objects I have enumerated, that Mrs. Montgomery was evidently a thrifty and self-respecting little person—the modest proportions of her dwelling seemed to indicate that she was of small stature—who took a virtuous satisfaction in keeping herself tidy, and had resolved that, since she might not be splendid, she would at least be immaculate. She received him in a little parlour, which was precisely the parlour he had expected: a small unspeckled bower, ornamented with a desultory foliage of tissue-paper, and with clusters of glass drops, amid which—to carry out the analogy—the temperature of the leafy season was maintained by means of a cast-iron stove, emitting a dry blue flame, and smelling strongly of varnish. The walls were embellished with engravings swathed in pink gauze, and the tables ornamented with volumes of extracts from the poets, usually bound in black cloth stamped with florid designs in jaundiced gilt. The Doctor had time to take cognisance of these details, for Mrs. Montgomery, whose conduct he pronounced under the circumstances inexcusable, kept him waiting some ten minutes before she appeared. At last, however, she rustled in, smoothing down a stiff poplin dress, with a little frightened flush in a gracefully-rounded cheek.

She was a small, plump, fair woman, with a bright, clear eye, and an extraordinary air of neatness and briskness. But these qualities were evidently combined with an unaffected humility, and the Doctor gave her his esteem as soon as he had looked at her. A brave little person, with lively perceptions, and yet a disbelief in her own talent for social, as distinguished from practical, affairs—this was his rapid mental *résumé* of Mrs. Montgomery, who, as he saw, was flattered by what she regarded as the honour of his visit. Mrs. Montgomery, in her little red house in the Second Avenue, was a person for whom Dr. Sloper was one of the great men, one of the fine gentlemen of New York; and while she fixed her agitated eyes upon him, while she clasped her mittened hands together in her glossy poplin lap, she had the appearance of saying to herself that he quite answered her idea of what a distinguished guest would naturally be. She apologised for being late; but he interrupted her.

"It doesn't matter," he said; "for while I sat here I had time to think over what I wish to say to you, and to make up my mind how to begin."

"Oh, do begin!" murmured Mrs. Montgomery.

"It is not so easy," said the Doctor, smiling. "You will have gathered from my letter that I wish to ask you a few questions, and you may not find it very comfortable to answer them."

"Yes; I have thought what I should say. It is not very easy."

"But you must understand my situation—my state of mind. Your brother wishes to marry my daughter, and I wish to find out what sort of a young man he is. A good way to do so seemed to be to come and ask you; which I have proceeded to do."

Mrs. Montgomery evidently took the situation very seriously; she was in a state of extreme moral concentration. She kept her pretty eyes, which were illumined by a sort of brilliant modesty, attached to his own countenance, and evidently paid the most earnest attention to each of his words. Her expression indicated that she thought his idea of coming to see her a very superior conception, but that she was really afraid to have opinions on strange subjects.

"I am extremely glad to see you," she said, in a tone which seemed to admit, at the same time, that this had nothing to do with the question.

The Doctor took advantage of this admission. "I didn't come to see you for your pleasure; I came to make you say disagreeable things—and you can't like that. What sort of a gentleman is your brother?"

Mrs. Montgomery's illuminated gaze grew vague, and began to wander. She smiled a little, and for some time made no answer, so that the Doctor at last became impatient. And her answer, when it came, was not satisfactory. "It is difficult to talk about one's brother."

"Not when one is fond of him, and when one has plenty of good to say."

"Yes, even then, when a good deal depends on it," said Mrs. Montgomery.

"Nothing depends on it, for you."

"I mean for—for—" and she hesitated.

"For your brother himself. I see!"

"I mean for Miss Sloper," said Mrs. Montgomery.

The Doctor liked this; it had the accent of sincerity. "Exactly; that's the point. If my poor girl should marry your brother, everything—as regards her happiness—would depend on his being a good fellow. She is the best creature in the world, and she could never do him a grain of injury. He, on the other hand, if he should not be all that we desire, might make her very miserable. That is why I want you to throw some light upon his character, you know. Of course you are not bound to do it. My daughter, whom you have never seen, is nothing to you; and I, possibly, am only an indiscreet and impertinent old man. It is perfectly open to you to tell me that my visit is in very bad taste and that I had better go about my business. But I don't think you will do this; because I think we shall interest you, my poor girl and I. I am sure that if you were to see Catherine, she would interest you very much. I don't mean because she is interesting in the usual sense of the word, but because you would feel sorry for her. She is so soft, so simple-minded, she would be such an easy victim! A bad husband would have remarkable facilities for making her miserable; for she would have neither the intelligence nor the resolution to get the better of him, and yet she would have an exaggerated power of suffering. I see," added the Doctor, with his most insinuating, his most professional laugh, "you are already interested!"

"I have been interested from the moment he told me he was engaged," said Mrs. Montgomery.

"Ah! he says that—he calls it an engagement?"

"Oh, he has told me you didn't like it."

"Did he tell you that I don't like *him?*"

"Yes, he told me that too. I said I couldn't help it!" added Mrs. Montgomery.

"Of course you can't. But what you can do is to tell me I am right—to give me an attestation, as it were." And the Doctor accompanied this remark with another professional smile.

Mrs. Montgomery, however, smiled not at all; it was obvious that she could not take the humorous view of his appeal. "That is a good deal to ask," she said at last.

"There can be no doubt of that; and I must, in conscience, remind you of the advantages a young man marrying my daughter would enjoy. She has an income of ten thousand dollars in her own right, left her by her mother; if she marries a husband I approve, she will come into almost twice as much more at my death."

Mrs. Montgomery listened in great earnestness to this splendid financial statement; she had never heard thousands of dollars so familiarly talked about. She flushed a little with excitement. "Your daughter will be immensely rich," she said softly.

"Precisely—that's the bother of it."

"And if Morris should marry her, he—he—" And she hesitated timidly.

"He would be master of all that money? By no means. He would be master of the ten thousand a year that she has from her mother; but I should leave every penny of my own fortune, earned in the laborious exercise of my profession, to public institutions."

Mrs. Montgomery dropped her eyes at this, and sat for some time gazing at the straw matting which covered her floor.

"I suppose it seems to you," said the Doctor, laughing, "that in so doing I should play your brother a very shabby trick."

"Not at all. That is too much money to get possession of so easily, by marrying. I don't think it would be right."

"It's right to get all one can. But in this case your brother wouldn't be able. If Catherine marries without my consent, she doesn't get a penny from my own pocket."

"Is that certain?" asked Mrs. Montgomery, looking up.

"As certain as that I sit here!"

"Even if she should pine away?"

"Even if she should pine to a shadow, which isn't probable."

"Does Morris know this?"

"I shall be most happy to inform him!" the Doctor exclaimed.

Mrs. Montgomery resumed her meditations, and her visitor, who was prepared to give time to the affair, asked himself whether, in spite of her little conscientious air, she was not playing into her brother's hands. At the same time he was half ashamed of the ordeal to which he had subjected her, and was touched by the gentleness with which she bore it. "If she were a humbug," he said, "she would get angry; unless she be very deep indeed. It is not probable that she is as deep as that."

"What makes you dislike Morris so much?" she presently asked, emerging from her reflexions.

"I don't dislike him in the least as a friend, as a companion. He seems to me a charming fellow, and I should think he would be excellent company. I dislike him, exclusively, as a son-in-law. If the only office of a son-in-law were to dine at the paternal table, I should set a high value upon your brother. He dines capitally. But that is a small part of his function, which, in general, is to be a protector and caretaker of my child, who is singularly ill-adapted to take care of herself. It is there that he doesn't satisfy me. I confess I have nothing but my impression to go by; but I am in the habit of trusting my impression. Of course you are at liberty to contradict it flat. He strikes me as selfish and shallow."

Mrs. Montgomery's eyes expanded a little, and the Doctor fancied he saw the light of admiration in them. "I wonder you have discovered he is selfish!" she exclaimed.

"Do you think he hides it so well?"

"Very well indeed," said Mrs. Montgomery. "And I think we are all rather selfish," she added quickly.

"I think so too; but I have seen people hide it better than he. You see I am helped by a habit I have of dividing people into classes, into types. I may easily be mistaken about your brother as an individual, but his type is written on his whole person."

"He is very good-looking," said Mrs. Montgomery.

The Doctor eyed her a moment. "You women are all the same! But the type to which your brother belongs was made to be the ruin of you, and you were made to be its handmaids and victims. The sign of the type in question is the determination—sometimes terrible in its quiet intensity—to accept nothing of life but its pleasures, and to secure these pleasures chiefly by the aid of your complaisant sex. Young men of this class never do anything for themselves that they can get other people to do for them, and it is the infatuation, the devotion, the superstition of others that keeps them going. These others in ninety-nine cases out of a hundred are women. What our young friends chiefly insist upon is that some one else shall suffer for them; and women do that sort of thing, as you must know, wonderfully well." The Doctor paused a moment, and then he added abruptly, "You have suffered immensely for your brother!"

This exclamation was abrupt, as I say, but it was also perfectly calculated. The Doctor had been rather disappointed at not finding his compact and comfortable little hostess surrounded in a more visible degree by the ravages of Morris Townsend's immorality; but he had said to himself that this was not because the young man had spared her, but because she had contrived to plaster up her wounds. They were aching there, behind the varnished stove, the festooned engravings, beneath her own neat little poplin bosom; and if he could only touch the tender spot, she would make a movement that would betray her. The words I have just quoted were an attempt to put his finger suddenly upon the place; and they had some of the success that he looked for. The tears sprang for a moment to Mrs. Montgomery's eyes, and she indulged in a proud little jerk of the head.

"I don't know how you have found that out!" she exclaimed.

"By a philosophic trick—by what they call induction. You know you have always your option of contradicting me. But kindly answer me a question. Don't you give your brother money! I think you ought to answer that."

"Yes, I have given him money," said Mrs. Montgomery.

"And you have not had much to give him?"

She was silent a moment. "If you ask me for a confession of poverty, that is easily made. I am very poor."

"One would never suppose it from your—your charming house," said the Doctor. "I learned from my sister that your income was moderate, and your family numerous."

"I have five children," Mrs. Montgomery observed; "but I am happy to say I can bring them up decently."

"Of course you can—accomplished and devoted as you are! But your brother has counted them over, I suppose?"

"Counted them over?"

"He knows there are five, I mean. He tells me it is he that brings them up."

Mrs. Montgomery stared a moment, and then quickly—"Oh yes; he teaches them—Spanish."

The Doctor laughed out. "That must take a great deal off your hands! Your brother also knows, of course, that you have very little money."

"I have often told him so!" Mrs. Montgomery exclaimed, more unreservedly than she had yet spoken. She was apparently taking some comfort in the Doctor's clairvoyancy.

"Which means that you have often occasion to, and that he often sponges on you. Excuse the crudity of my language; I simply express a fact. I don't ask you how much of your money he has had, it is none of my business. I have ascertained what I suspected—what I wished." And the Doctor got up, gently smoothing his hat. "Your brother lives on you," he said as he stood there.

Mrs. Montgomery quickly rose from her chair, following her visitor's movements with a look of fascination. But then, with a certain inconsequence—"I have never complained of him!" she said.

"You needn't protest—you have not betrayed him. But I advise you not to give him any more money."

"Don't you see it is in my interest that he should marry a rich person?" she asked. "If, as you say, he lives on me, I can only wish to get rid of him, and to put obstacles in the way of his marrying is to increase my own difficulties."

"I wish very much you would come to me with your difficulties," said the Doctor. "Certainly, if I throw him back on your hands, the least I can do is to help you to bear the burden. If you will allow me to say so, then, I shall take the liberty of placing in your hands, for the present, a certain fund for your brother's support."

Mrs. Montgomery stared; she evidently thought he was jesting; but she presently saw that he was not, and the complication of her feelings became painful. "It seems to me that I ought to be very much offended with you," she murmured.

"Because I have offered you money? That's a superstition," said the Doctor. "You must let me come and see you again, and we will talk about these things. I suppose that some of your children are girls."

"I have two little girls," said Mrs. Montgomery.

"Well, when they grow up, and begin to think of taking husbands, you will see how anxious you will be about the moral character of these gentlemen. Then you will understand this visit of mine!"

"Ah, you are not to believe that Morris's moral character is bad!"

The Doctor looked at her a little, with folded arms. "There is something I should greatly like—as a moral satisfaction. I should like to hear you say—'He is abominably selfish!'"

The words came out with the grave distinctness of his voice, and they seemed for an instant to create, to poor Mrs. Montgomery's troubled vision, a material image. She gazed at it an instant, and then she turned away. "You distress me, sir!" she exclaimed. "He is, after all, my brother, and his talents, his talents—" On these last words her voice quavered, and before he knew it she had burst into tears.

"His talents are first-rate!" said the Doctor. "We must find a proper field for them!" And he assured her most respectfully of his regret at having so greatly discomposed her. "It's all for my poor Catherine," he went on. "You must know her, and you will see."

Mrs. Montgomery brushed away her tears, and blushed at having shed them. "I should like to know your daughter," she answered; and then, in an instant—"Don't let her marry him!"

Dr. Sloper went away with the words gently humming in his ears—"Don't let her marry him!" They gave him the moral satisfaction of which he had just spoken, and their value was the greater that they had evidently cost a pang to poor little Mrs. Montgomery's family pride.

## XV

HE had been puzzled by the way that Catherine carried herself; her attitude at this sentimental crisis seemed to him unnaturally passive. She had not spoken to him again after that scene in the library, the day before his interview with Morris; and a week had elapsed without making any change in her manner. There was nothing in it that appealed for pity, and he was even a little disappointed at her not giving him an opportunity to make up for his harshness by some manifestation of liberality which should operate as a compensation. He thought a little of offering to take her for a tour in Europe; but he was determined to do this only in case she should seem mutely to reproach him. He had an idea that she would display a talent for mute reproaches, and he was surprised at not finding himself exposed to these silent batteries. She said nothing, either tacitly or explicitly, and as she was never very talkative, there was now no especial eloquence in her reserve. And poor Catherine was not sulky—a style of behaviour for which she had too little histrionic talent; she was simply very patient. Of course she was thinking over her situation, and she was apparently doing so in a deliberate and unimpassioned manner, with a view of making the best of it.

"She will do as I have bidden her," said the Doctor, and he made the further reflexion that his daughter was not a woman of a great spirit. I know not whether he had hoped for a little more resistance for the sake of a little more entertainment; but he said to himself, as he had said before, that though it might have its momentary alarms, paternity was, after all, not an exciting vocation.

Catherine, meanwhile, had made a discovery of a very different sort; it had become vivid to her that there was a great excitement in trying to be a good daughter. She had an entirely new feeling, which may be described as a state of expectant suspense about her own actions. She watched herself as she would have watched another person, and wondered what she would do. It was as if this other person, who was both herself and not herself, had suddenly sprung into being, inspiring her with a natural curiosity as to the performance of untested functions.

"I am glad I have such a good daughter," said her father, kissing her, after the lapse of several days.

"I am trying to be good," she answered, turning away, with a conscience not altogether clear.

"If there is anything you would like to say to me, you know you must not hesitate. You needn't feel obliged to be so quiet. I shouldn't care that Mr. Townsend should be a frequent topic of conversation, but whenever you have anything particular to say about him I shall be very glad to hear it."

"Thank you," said Catherine; "I have nothing particular at present."

He never asked her whether she had seen Morris again, because he was sure that if this had been the case she would tell him. She had, in fact, not seen him, she had only written him a long letter. The letter at least was long for her; and, it may be added, that it was long for Morris; it consisted of five pages, in a remarkably neat and handsome hand. Catherine's handwriting was beautiful, and she was even a little proud of it; she was extremely fond of copying, and possessed volumes of extracts which testified to this accomplishment; volumes which she had exhibited one day to her lover, when the bliss of feeling that she was important in his eyes was exceptionally keen. She told Morris in writing that her father had expressed the wish that she should not see him again, and that she begged he would not come to the house until she should have "made up her mind." Morris replied with a passionate epistle, in which he asked to what, in Heaven's name, she wished to make up her mind. Had not her mind been made up two weeks before, and could it be possible that she entertained the idea of throwing him off? Did she mean to break down at the very beginning of their ordeal, after all the promises of fidelity she had both given and extracted? And he gave an account of his own interview with her father—an account not identical at all points with that offered in these pages. "He was terribly violent," Morris wrote; "but you know my self-control. I have need of it all when I remember that I have it in my power to break in upon your cruel captivity." Catherine sent him, in answer to this, a note of three lines. "I am in great trouble; do not doubt of my affection, but let me wait a little and think." The idea of a struggle with her father, of setting up her will against his own, was heavy on her soul, and it kept her formally submissive, as a great physical weight keeps us motionless. It never entered into her mind to throw her lover off; but from the first she tried to assure herself that there would be a peaceful way out of their difficulty. The assurance was vague, for it contained no element of positive conviction that her father would change his mind. She only had an idea that if she should be very good, the situation would in some mysterious manner improve. To be good, she must be patient, respectful, abstain from judging her father too harshly, and from committing any act of open defiance. He was perhaps right, after all, to think as he did; by which Catherine meant not in the least that his judgement of Morris's motives in seeking to marry her was perhaps a just one, but that it was probably natural and proper that conscientious parents should be suspicious and even unjust. There were probably people in the world as bad as her father supposed Morris to be, and if there were the slightest chance of Morris being one of these sinister persons, the Doctor was right in taking it into account. Of course he could not know what she knew, how the purest love and truth were seated in the young man's eyes; but Heaven, in its time, might appoint a way of bringing him to such knowledge. Catherine expected a good deal of Heaven, and referred to the skies the initiative, as the French say, in dealing with her dilemma. She could not imagine herself imparting any kind of knowledge to her father, there was something superior even in his injustice and absolute in his mistakes. But she could at least be good, and if she were only good enough, Heaven would invent some way of reconciling all things—the dignity of her father's errors and the sweetness of her own confidence, the strict performance of her filial duties and the enjoyment of Morris Townsend's affection. Poor Catherine would have been glad to regard Mrs. Penniman as an illuminating agent, a part which this lady herself indeed was but imperfectly prepared to play. Mrs. Penniman took too much satisfaction in the sentimental shadows of this little drama to have, for the moment, any great interest in dissipating them. She wished the plot to thicken, and the advice that she gave her niece tended, in her own imagination, to produce this result. It was rather incoherent counsel, and from one day to another it contradicted itself; but it was pervaded by an earnest desire that Catherine should do something striking. "You must *act*, my dear; in your situation the great thing is to act," said Mrs. Penniman, who found her niece altogether beneath her opportunities. Mrs. Penniman's real hope was that the girl would make a secret marriage, at which she should officiate as brideswoman or duenna. She had a vision of this ceremony being performed in some subterranean chapel—subterranean chapels in New York were not frequent, but Mrs. Penniman's imagination was not chilled by trifles—and of the guilty couple—she liked to think of poor Catherine and her suitor as the guilty couple—being shuffled away in a fast-whirling vehicle to some obscure lodging in the suburbs, where she would pay them (in a thick veil) clandestine visits, where they would endure a period of romantic privation, and where ultimately, after she should have been their earthly providence, their intercessor, their advocate, and their medium of communication with the world, they should be reconciled to her brother in an artistic tableau, in which she herself should be somehow the central figure. She hesitated as yet to recommend this course to Catherine, but she attempted to draw an attractive picture of it to Morris Townsend. She was in daily communication with the young man, whom she kept informed by letters of the state of affairs in Washington Square. As he had been banished, as she said, from the house, she no longer saw him; but she ended by writing to him that she longed for an interview. This interview could take place only on neutral ground, and she bethought herself greatly before selecting a place of meeting. She had an inclination for Greenwood Cemetery, but she gave it up as too distant; she could not absent herself for so long, as she said, without exciting suspicion. Then she thought of the Battery, but that was rather cold and windy, besides one's being exposed to intrusion from the Irish emigrants who at this point alight, with large appetites, in the New World; and at last she fixed upon an oyster saloon in the Seventh Avenue, kept by a negro—an establishment of which she knew nothing save that she had noticed it in passing. She made an appointment with Morris Townsend to meet him there, and she went to the tryst at dusk, enveloped in an impenetrable veil. He kept her waiting for half an hour—he had almost the whole width of the city to traverse—but she liked to wait, it seemed to intensify the situation. She ordered a cup of tea, which proved excessively bad, and this gave her a sense that she was suffering in a romantic cause. When Morris at last arrived, they sat together for half an hour in the duskiest corner of a back shop; and it is hardly too much to say that this was the happiest half-hour that Mrs. Penniman had known for years. The situation was really thrilling, and it scarcely seemed to her a false note when her companion asked for an oyster stew, and proceeded to consume it before her eyes. Morris, indeed, needed all the satisfaction that stewed oysters could give him, for it may be intimated to the reader that he regarded Mrs. Penniman in the light of a fifth wheel to his coach. He was in a state of irritation natural to a gentleman of fine parts who had been snubbed in a benevolent attempt to confer a distinction upon a young woman of inferior characteristics, and the insinuating sympathy of this somewhat desiccated matron appeared to offer him no practical relief. He thought her a humbug, and he judged of humbugs with a good deal of confidence. He had listened and made himself agreeable to her at first, in order to get a footing in Washington Square; and at present he needed all his self-command to be decently civil. It would have gratified him to tell her that she was a fantastic old woman, and that he should like to put her into an omnibus and send her home. We know, however, that Morris possessed the virtue of self-control, and he had, moreover, the constant habit of seeking to be agreeable; so that, although Mrs. Penniman's demeanour only exasperated his already unquiet nerves, he listened to her with a sombre deference in which she found much to admire.

## XVI

THEY had of course immediately spoken of Catherine. "Did she send me a message, or—or anything?" Morris asked. He appeared to think that she might have sent him a trinket or a lock of her hair.

Mrs. Penniman was slightly embarrassed, for she had not told her niece of her intended expedition. "Not exactly a message," she said; "I didn't ask her for one, because I was afraid to—to excite her."

"I am afraid she is not very excitable!" And Morris gave a smile of some bitterness.

"She is better than that. She is steadfast—she is true!"

"Do you think she will hold fast, then?"

"To the death!"

"Oh, I hope it won't come to that," said Morris.

"We must be prepared for the worst, and that is what I wish to speak to you about."

"What do you call the worst?"

"Well," said Mrs. Penniman, "my brother's hard, intellectual nature."

"Oh, the devil!"

"He is impervious to pity," Mrs. Penniman added, by way of explanation.

"Do you mean that he won't come round?"

"He will never be vanquished by argument. I have studied him. He will be vanquished only by the accomplished fact."

"The accomplished fact?"

"He will come round afterwards," said Mrs. Penniman, with extreme significance. "He cares for nothing but facts; he must be met by facts!"

"Well," rejoined Morris, "it is a fact that I wish to marry his daughter. I met him with that the other day, but he was not all vanquished."

Mrs. Penniman was silent a little, and her smile beneath the shadow of her capacious bonnet, on the edge of which her black veil was arranged curtain-wise, fixed itself upon Morris's face with a still more tender brilliancy. "Marry Catherine first and meet him afterwards!" she exclaimed.

"Do you recommend that?" asked the young man, frowning heavily.

She was a little frightened, but she went on with considerable boldness. "That is the way I see it: a private marriage—a private marriage." She repeated the phrase because she liked it.

"Do you mean that I should carry Catherine off? What do they call it—elope with her?"

"It is not a crime when you are driven to it," said Mrs. Penniman. "My husband, as I have told you, was a distinguished clergyman; one of the most eloquent men of his day. He once married a young couple that had fled from the house of the young lady's father. He was so interested in their story. He had no hesitation, and everything came out beautifully. The father was afterwards reconciled, and thought everything of the young man. Mr. Penniman married them in the evening, about seven o'clock. The church was so dark, you could scarcely see; and Mr. Penniman was intensely agitated; he was so sympathetic. I don't believe he could have done it again."

"Unfortunately Catherine and I have not Mr. Penniman to marry us," said Morris.

"No, but you have me!" rejoined Mrs. Penniman expressively. "I can't perform the ceremony, but I can help you. I can watch."

"The woman's an idiot," thought Morris; but he was obliged to say something different. It was not, however, materially more civil. "Was it in order to tell me this that you requested I would meet you here?"

Mrs. Penniman had been conscious of a certain vagueness in her errand, and of not being able to offer him any very tangible reward for his long walk. "I thought perhaps you would like to see one who is so near to Catherine," she observed, with considerable majesty. "And also," she added, "that you would value an opportunity of sending her something."

Morris extended his empty hands with a melancholy smile. "I am greatly obliged to you, but I have nothing to send."

"Haven't you a *word?*" asked his companion, with her suggestive smile coming back.

Morris frowned again. "Tell her to hold fast," he said rather curtly.

"That is a good word—a noble word. It will make her happy for many days. She is very touching, very brave," Mrs. Penniman went on, arranging her mantle and preparing to depart. While she was so engaged she had an inspiration. She found the phrase that she could boldly offer as a vindication of the step she had taken. "If you marry Catherine at all risks," she said, "you will give my brother a proof of your being what he pretends to doubt."

"What he pretends to doubt?"

"Don't you know what that is?" Mrs. Penniman asked almost playfully.

"It does not concern me to know," said Morris grandly.

"Of course it makes you angry."

"I despise it," Morris declared.

"Ah, you know what it is, then?" said Mrs. Penniman, shaking her finger at him. "He pretends that you like—you like the money."

Morris hesitated a moment; and then, as if he spoke advisedly—"I *do* like the money!"

"Ah, but not—but not as he means it. You don't like it more than Catherine?"

He leaned his elbows on the table and buried his head in his hands. "You torture me!" he murmured. And, indeed, this was almost the effect of the poor lady's too importunate interest in his situation.

But she insisted on making her point. "If you marry her in spite of him, he will take for granted that you expect nothing of him, and are prepared to do without it. And so he will see that you are disinterested."

Morris raised his head a little, following this argument, "And what shall I gain by that?"

"Why, that he will see that he has been wrong in thinking that you wished to get his money."

"And seeing that I wish he would go to the deuce with it, he will leave it to a hospital. Is that what you mean?" asked Morris.

"No, I don't mean that; though that would be very grand!" Mrs. Penniman quickly added. "I mean that having done you such an injustice, he will think it his duty, at the end, to make some amends."

Morris shook his head, though it must be confessed he was a little struck with this idea. "Do you think he is so sentimental?"

"He is not sentimental," said Mrs. Penniman; "but, to be perfectly fair to him, I think he has, in his own narrow way, a certain sense of duty."

There passed through Morris Townsend's mind a rapid wonder as to what he might, even under a remote contingency, be indebted to from the action of this principle in Dr. Sloper's breast, and the inquiry exhausted itself in his sense of the ludicrous. "Your brother has no duties to me," he said presently, "and I none to him."

"Ah, but he has duties to Catherine."

"Yes, but you see that on that principle Catherine has duties to him as well."

Mrs. Penniman got up, with a melancholy sigh, as if she thought him very unimaginative. "She has always performed them faithfully; and now, do you think she has no duties to *you?*" Mrs. Penniman always, even in conversation, italicised her personal pronouns.

"It would sound harsh to say so! I am so grateful for her love," Morris added.

"I will tell her you said that! And now, remember that if you need me, I am there." And Mrs. Penniman, who could think of nothing more to say, nodded vaguely in the direction of Washington Square.

Morris looked some moments at the sanded floor of the shop; he seemed to be disposed to linger a moment. At last, looking up with a certain abruptness, "It is your belief that if she marries me he will cut her off?" he asked.

Mrs. Penniman stared a little, and smiled. "Why, I have explained to you what I think would happen—that in the end it would be the best thing to do."

"You mean that, whatever she does, in the long run she will get the money?"

"It doesn't depend upon her, but upon you. Venture to appear as disinterested as you are!" said Mrs. Penniman ingeniously. Morris dropped his eyes on the sanded floor again, pondering this; and she pursued. "Mr. Penniman and I had nothing, and we were very happy. Catherine, moreover, has her mother's fortune, which, at the time my sister-in-law married, was considered a very handsome one."

"Oh, don't speak of that!" said Morris; and, indeed, it was quite superfluous, for he had contemplated the fact in all its lights.

"Austin married a wife with money—why shouldn't you?"

"Ah! but your brother was a doctor," Morris objected.

"Well, all young men can't be doctors!"

"I should think it an extremely loathsome profession," said Morris, with an air of intellectual independence. Then in a moment, he went on rather inconsequently, "Do you suppose there is a will already made in Catherine's favour?"

"I suppose so—even doctors must die; and perhaps a little in mine," Mrs. Penniman frankly added.

"And you believe he would certainly change it—as regards Catherine?"

"Yes; and then change it back again."

"Ah, but one can't depend on that!" said Morris.

"Do you want to *depend* on it?" Mrs. Penniman asked.

Morris blushed a little. "Well, I am certainly afraid of being the cause of an injury to Catherine."

"Ah! you must not be afraid. Be afraid of nothing, and everything will go well!"

And then Mrs. Penniman paid for her cup of tea, and Morris paid for his oyster stew, and they went out together into the dimly-lighted wilderness of the Seventh Avenue. The dusk had closed in completely and the street lamps were separated by wide intervals of a pavement in which cavities and fissures played a disproportionate part. An omnibus, emblazoned with strange pictures, went tumbling over the dislocated cobble-stones.

"How will you go home?" Morris asked, following this vehicle with an interested eye. Mrs. Penniman had taken his arm.

She hesitated a moment. "I think this manner would be pleasant," she said; and she continued to let him feel the value of his support.

So he walked with her through the devious ways of the west side of the town, and through the bustle of gathering nightfall in populous streets, to the quiet precinct of Washington Square. They lingered a moment at the foot of Dr. Sloper's white marble steps, above which a spotless white door, adorned with a glittering silver plate, seemed to figure, for Morris, the closed portal of happiness; and then Mrs. Penniman's companion rested a melancholy eye upon a lighted window in the upper part of the house.

"That is my room—my dear little room!" Mrs. Penniman remarked.

Morris started. "Then I needn't come walking round the Square to gaze at it."

"That's as you please. But Catherine's is behind; two noble windows on the second floor. I think you can see them from the other street."

"I don't want to see them, ma'am!" And Morris turned his back to the house.

"I will tell her you have been *here*, at any rate," said Mrs. Penniman, pointing to the spot where they stood; "and I will give her your message—that she is to hold fast!"

"Oh, yes! of course. You know I write her all that."

"It seems to say more when it is spoken! And remember, if you need me, that I am *there*"; and Mrs. Penniman glanced at the third floor.

On this they separated, and Morris, left to himself, stood looking at the house a moment; after which he turned away, and took a gloomy walk round the Square, on the opposite side, close to the wooden fence. Then he came back, and paused for a minute in front of Dr. Sloper's dwelling. His eyes travelled over it; they even rested on the ruddy windows of Mrs. Penniman's apartment. He thought it a devilish comfortable house.

## XVII

MRS. PENNIMAN told Catherine that evening—the two ladies were sitting in the back parlour—that she had had an interview with Morris Townsend; and on receiving this news the girl started with a sense of pain. She felt angry for the moment; it was almost the first time she had ever felt angry. It seemed to her that her aunt was meddlesome; and from this came a vague apprehension that she would spoil something.

"I don't see why you should have seen him. I don't think it was right," Catherine said.

"I was so sorry for him—it seemed to me some one ought to see him."

"No one but I," said Catherine, who felt as if she were making the most presumptuous speech of her life, and yet at the same time had an instinct that she was right in doing so.

"But you wouldn't, my dear," Aunt Lavinia rejoined; "and I didn't know what might have become of him."

"I have not seen him, because my father has forbidden it," Catherine said very simply.

There was a simplicity in this, indeed, which fairly vexed Mrs. Penniman. "If your father forbade you to go to sleep, I suppose you would keep awake!" she commented.

Catherine looked at her. "I don't understand you. You seem to be very strange."

"Well, my dear, you will understand me some day!" And Mrs. Penniman, who was reading the evening paper, which she perused daily from the first line to the last, resumed her occupation. She wrapped herself in silence; she was determined Catherine should ask her for an account of her interview with Morris. But Catherine was silent for so long, that she almost lost patience; and she was on the point of remarking to her that she was very heartless, when the girl at last spoke.

"What did he say?" she asked.

"He said he is ready to marry you any day, in spite of everything."

Catherine made no answer to this, and Mrs. Penniman almost lost patience again; owing to which she at last volunteered the information that Morris looked very handsome, but terribly haggard.

"Did he seem sad?" asked her niece.

"He was dark under the eyes," said Mrs. Penniman. "So different from when I first saw him; though I am not sure that if I had seen him in this condition the first time, I should not have been even more struck with him. There is something brilliant in his very misery."

This was, to Catherine's sense, a vivid picture, and though she disapproved, she felt herself gazing at it. "Where did you see him?" she asked presently.

"In—in the Bowery; at a confectioner's," said Mrs. Penniman, who had a general idea that she ought to dissemble a little.

"Whereabouts is the place?" Catherine inquired, after another pause.

"Do you wish to go there, my dear?" said her aunt.

"Oh no!" And Catherine got up from her seat and went to the fire, where she stood looking a while at the glowing coals.

"Why are you so dry, Catherine?" Mrs. Penniman said at last.

"So dry?"

"So cold—so irresponsive."

The girl turned very quickly. "Did *he* say that?"

Mrs. Penniman hesitated a moment. "I will tell you what he said. He said he feared only one thing—that you would be afraid."

"Afraid of what?"

"Afraid of your father."

Catherine turned back to the fire again, and then, after a pause, she said—"I *am* afraid of my father."

Mrs. Penniman got quickly up from her chair and approached her niece. "Do you mean to give him up, then?"

Catherine for some time never moved; she kept her eyes on the coals. At last she raised her head and looked at her aunt. "Why do you push me so?" she asked.

"I don't push you. When have I spoken to you before?"

"It seems to me that you have spoken to me several times."

"I am afraid it is necessary, then, Catherine," said Mrs. Penniman, with a good deal of solemnity. "I am afraid you don't feel the importance—" She paused a little; Catherine was looking at her. "The importance of not disappointing that gallant young heart!" And Mrs. Penniman went back to her chair, by the lamp, and, with a little jerk, picked up the evening paper again.

Catherine stood there before the fire, with her hands behind her, looking at her aunt, to whom it seemed that the girl had never had just this dark fixedness in her gaze. "I don't think you understand—or that you know me," she said.

"If I don't, it is not wonderful; you trust me so little."

Catherine made no attempt to deny this charge, and for some time more nothing was said. But Mrs. Penniman's imagination was restless, and the evening paper failed on this occasion to enchain it.

"If you succumb to the dread of your father's wrath," she said, "I don't know what will become of us."

"Did *he* tell you to say these things to me?"

"He told me to use my influence."

"You must be mistaken," said Catherine. "He trusts me."

"I hope he may never repent of it!" And Mrs. Penniman gave a little sharp slap to her newspaper. She knew not what to make of her niece, who had suddenly become stern and contradictious.

This tendency on Catherine's part was presently even more apparent. "You had much better not make any more appointments with Mr. Townsend," she said. "I don't think it is right."

Mrs. Penniman rose with considerable majesty. "My poor child, are you jealous of me?" she inquired.

"Oh, Aunt Lavinia!" murmured Catherine, blushing.

"I don't think it is your place to teach me what is right."

On this point Catherine made no concession. "It can't right to deceive."

"I certainly have not deceived *you!*"

"Yes; but I promised my father—"

"I have no doubt you promised your father. But I have promised him nothing!"

Catherine had to admit this, and she did so in silence. "I don't believe Mr. Townsend himself likes it," she said at last.

"Doesn't like meeting me?"

"Not in secret."

"It was not in secret; the place was full of people."

"But it was a secret place—away off in the Bowery."

Mrs. Penniman flinched a little. "Gentlemen enjoy such things," she remarked presently. "I know what gentlemen like."

"My father wouldn't like it, if he knew."

"Pray, do you propose to inform him?" Mrs. Penniman inquired.

"No, Aunt Lavinia. But please don't do it again."

"If I do it again, you will inform him: is that what you mean? I do not share your dread of my brother; I have always known how to defend my own position. But I shall certainly never again take any step on your behalf; you are much too thankless. I knew you were not a spontaneous nature, but I believed you were firm, and I told your father that he would find you so. I am disappointed—but your father will not be!" And with this, Mrs. Penniman offered her niece a brief good-night, and withdrew to her own apartment.

## XVIII

CATHERINE sat alone by the parlour fire—sat there for more than an hour, lost in her meditations. Her aunt seemed to her aggressive and foolish, and to see it so clearly—to judge Mrs. Penniman so positively—made her feel old and grave. She did not resent the imputation of weakness; it made no impression on her, for she had not the sense of weakness, and she was not hurt at not being appreciated. She had an immense respect for her father, and she felt that to displease him would be a misdemeanour analogous to an act of profanity in a great temple;

but her purpose had slowly ripened, and she believed that her prayers had purified it of its violence. The evening advanced, and the lamp burned dim without her noticing it; her eyes were fixed upon her terrible plan. She knew her father was in his study—that he had been there all the evening; from time to time she expected to hear him move. She thought he would perhaps come, as he sometimes came, into the parlour. At last the clock struck eleven, and the house was wrapped in silence; the servants had gone to bed. Catherine got up and went slowly to the door of the library, where she waited a moment, motionless. Then she knocked, and then she waited again. Her father had answered her, but she had not the courage to turn the latch. What she had said to her aunt was true enough—she was afraid of him; and in saying that she had no sense of weakness she meant that she was not afraid of herself. She heard him move within, and he came and opened the door for her.

"What is the matter?" asked the Doctor. "You are standing there like a ghost."

She went into the room, but it was some time before she contrived to say what she had come to say. Her father, who was in his dressing-gown and slippers, had been busy at his writing-table, and after looking at her for some moments, and waiting for her to speak, he went and seated himself at his papers again. His back was turned to her—she began to hear the scratching of his pen. She remained near the door, with her heart thumping beneath her bodice; and she was very glad that his back was turned, for it seemed to her that she could more easily address herself to this portion of his person than to his face. At last she began, watching it while she spoke.

"You told me that if I should have anything more to say about Mr. Townsend you would be glad to listen to it."

"Exactly, my dear," said the Doctor, not turning round, but stopping his pen.

Catherine wished it would go on, but she herself continued. "I thought I would tell you that I have not seen him again, but that I should like to do so."

"To bid him good-bye?" asked the Doctor.

The girl hesitated a moment. "He is not going away."

The Doctor wheeled slowly round in his chair, with a smile that seemed to accuse her of an epigram; but extremes meet, and Catherine had not intended one. "It is not to bid him good-bye, then?" her father said.

"No, father, not that; at least, not for ever. I have not seen him again, but I should like to see him," Catherine repeated.

The Doctor slowly rubbed his under lip with the feather of his quill.

"Have you written to him?"

"Yes, four times."

"You have not dismissed him, then. Once would have done that."

"No," said Catherine; "I have asked him—asked him to wait."

Her father sat looking at her, and she was afraid he was going to break out into wrath; his eyes were so fine and cold.

"You are a dear, faithful child," he said at last. "Come here to your father." And he got up, holding out his hands toward her.

The words were a surprise, and they gave her an exquisite joy. She went to him, and he put his arm round her tenderly, soothingly; and then he kissed her. After this he said:

"Do you wish to make me very happy?"

"I should like to—but I am afraid I can't," Catherine answered.

"You can if you will. It all depends on your will."

"Is it to give him up?" said Catherine.

"Yes, it is to give him up."

And he held her still, with the same tenderness, looking into her face and resting his eyes on her averted eyes. There was a long silence; she wished he would release her.

"You are happier than I, father," she said, at last.

"I have no doubt you are unhappy just now. But it is better to be unhappy for three months and get over it, than for many years and never get over it."

"Yes, if that were so," said Catherine.

"It would be so; I am sure of that." She answered nothing, and he went on. "Have you no faith in my wisdom, in my tenderness, in my solicitude for your future?"

"Oh, father!" murmured the girl.

"Don't you suppose that I know something of men: their vices, their follies, their falsities?"

She detached herself, and turned upon him. "He is not vicious—he is not false!"

Her father kept looking at her with his sharp, pure eye. "You make nothing of my judgment, then?"

"I can't believe that!"

"I don't ask you to believe it, but to take it on trust."

Catherine was far from saying to herself that this was an ingenious sophism; but she met the appeal none the less squarely. "What has he done—what do you know?"

"He has never done anything—he is a selfish idler."

"Oh, father, don't abuse him!" she exclaimed pleadingly.

"I don't mean to abuse him; it would be a great mistake. You may do as you choose," he added, turning away.

"I may see him again?"

"Just as you choose."

"Will you forgive me?"

"By no means."

"It will only be for once."

"I don't know what you mean by once. You must either give him up or continue the acquaintance."

"I wish to explain—to tell him to wait."

"To wait for what?"

"Till you know him better—till you consent."

"Don't tell him any such nonsense as that. I know him well enough, and I shall never consent."

"But we can wait a long time," said poor Catherine, in a tone which was meant to express the humblest conciliation, but which had upon her father's nerves the effect of an iteration not characterised by tact.

The Doctor answered, however, quietly enough: "Of course you can wait till I die, if you like."

Catherine gave a cry of natural horror.

"Your engagement will have one delightful effect upon you; it will make you extremely impatient for that event."

Catherine stood staring, and the Doctor enjoyed the point he had made. It came to Catherine with the force—or rather with the vague impressiveness—of a logical axiom which it was not in her province to controvert; and yet, though it was a scientific truth, she felt wholly unable to accept it.

"I would rather not marry, if that were true," she said.

"Give me a proof of it, then; for it is beyond a question that by engaging yourself to Morris Townsend you simply wait for my death."

She turned away, feeling sick and faint; and the Doctor went on. "And if you wait for it with impatience, judge, if you please, what *his* eagerness will be!"

Catherine turned it over—her father's words had such an authority for her that her very thoughts were capable of obeying him. There was a dreadful ugliness in it, which seemed to glare at her through the interposing medium of her own feebler reason. Suddenly, however, she had an inspiration—she almost knew it to be an inspiration.

"If I don't marry before your death, I will not after," she said.

To her father, it must be admitted, this seemed only another epigram; and as obstinacy, in unaccomplished minds, does not usually select such a mode of expression, he was the more surprised at this wanton play of a fixed idea.

"Do you mean that for an impertinence?" he inquired; an inquiry of which, as he made it, he quite perceived the grossness.

"An impertinence? Oh, father, what terrible things you say!"

"If you don't wait for my death, you might as well marry immediately; there is nothing else to wait for."

For some time Catherine made no answer; but finally she said:

"I think Morris—little by little—might persuade you."

"I shall never let him speak to me again. I dislike him too much."

Catherine gave a long, low sigh; she tried to stifle it, for she had made up her mind that it was wrong to make a parade of her trouble, and to endeavour to act upon her father by the meretricious aid of emotion. Indeed, she even thought it wrong—in the sense of being inconsiderate—to attempt to act upon his feelings at all; her part was to effect some gentle, gradual change in his intellectual perception of poor Morris's character. But the means of effecting such a change were at present shrouded in mystery, and she felt miserably helpless and hopeless. She had exhausted all arguments, all replies. Her father might have pitied her, and in fact he did so; but he was sure he was right.

"There is one thing you can tell Mr. Townsend when you see him again," he said: "that if you marry without my consent, I don't leave you a farthing of money. That will interest him more than anything else you can tell him.

"That would be very right," Catherine answered. "I ought not in that case to have a farthing of your money."

"My dear child," the Doctor observed, laughing, "your simplicity is touching. Make that remark, in that tone, and with that expression of countenance, to Mr. Townsend, and take a note of his answer. It won't be polite—it will express irritation; and I shall be glad of that, as it will put me in the right; unless, indeed—which is perfectly possible—you should like him the better for being rude to you."

"He will never be rude to me," said Catherine gently.

"Tell him what I say, all the same."

She looked at her father, and her quiet eyes filled with tears.

"I think I will see him, then," she murmured, in her timid voice.

"Exactly as you choose!" And he went to the door and opened it for her to go out. The movement gave her a terrible sense of his turning her off.

"It will be only once, for the present," she added, lingering a moment.

"Exactly as you choose," he repeated, standing there with his hand on the door. "I have told you what I think. If you see him, you will be an ungrateful, cruel child; you will have given your old father the greatest pain of his life."

This was more than the poor girl could bear; her tears overflowed, and she moved towards her grimly consistent parent with a pitiful cry. Her hands were raised in supplication, but he sternly evaded this appeal. Instead of letting her sob out her misery on his shoulder, he simply took her by the arm and directed her course across the threshold, closing the door gently but firmly behind her. After he had done so, he remained listening. For a long time there was no sound; he knew that she was standing outside. He was sorry for her, as I have said; but he was so sure he was right. At last he heard her move away, and then her footstep creaked faintly upon the stairs.

The Doctor took several turns round his study, with his hands in his pockets, and a thin sparkle, possibly of irritation, but partly also of something like humour, in his eye. "By Jove," he said to himself, "I believe she will stick—I believe she will stick!" And this idea of Catherine "sticking" appeared to have a comical side, and to offer a prospect of entertainment. He determined, as he said to himself, to see it out.

## XIX

IT was for reasons connected with this determination that on the morrow he sought a few words of private conversation with Mrs. Penniman. He sent for her to the library, and he there informed her that he hoped very much that, as regarded this affair of Catherine's, she would mind her *p's* and *q's*.

"I don't know what you mean by such an expression," said his sister. "You speak as if I were learning the alphabet."

"The alphabet of common sense is something you will never learn," the Doctor permitted himself to respond.

"Have you called me here to insult me?" Mrs. Penniman inquired.

"Not at all. Simply to advise you. You have taken up young Townsend; that's your own affair. I have nothing to do with your sentiments, your fancies, your affections, your delusions; but what I request of you is that you will keep these things to yourself. I have explained my views to Catherine; she understands them perfectly, and anything that she does further in the way of encouraging Mr. Townsend's attentions will be in deliberate opposition to my wishes. Anything that you should do in the way of giving her aid and comfort will be—permit me the expression—distinctly treasonable. You know high treason is a capital offence; take care how you incur the penalty."

Mrs. Penniman threw back her head, with a certain expansion of the eye which she occasionally practised. "It seems to me that you talk like a great autocrat."

"I talk like my daughter's father."

"Not like your sister's brother!" cried Lavinia.

"My dear Lavinia," said the Doctor, "I sometimes wonder whether

I am your brother. We are so extremely different. In spite of differences, however, we can, at a pinch, understand each other; and that is the essential thing just now. Walk straight with regard to Mr. Townsend; that's all I ask. It is highly probable you have been corresponding with him for the last three weeks—perhaps even seeing him. I don't ask you—you needn't tell me." He had a moral conviction that she would contrive to tell a fib about the matter, which it would disgust him to listen to. "Whatever you have done, stop doing it. That's all I wish."

"Don't you wish also by chance to murder your child?" Mrs. Penniman inquired.

"On the contrary, I wish to make her live and be happy."

"You will kill her; she passed a dreadful night."

"She won't die of one dreadful night, nor of a dozen. Remember that I am a distinguished physician."

Mrs. Penniman hesitated a moment. Then she risked her retort. "Your being a distinguished physician has not prevented you from already losing *two members* of your family!"

She had risked it, but her brother gave her such a terribly incisive look—a look so like a surgeon's lancet—that she was frightened at her courage. And he answered her in words that corresponded to the look: "It may not prevent me, either, from losing the society of still another."

Mrs. Penniman took herself off, with whatever air of depreciated merit was at her command, and repaired to Catherine's room, where the poor girl was closeted. She knew all about her dreadful night, for the two had met again, the evening before, after Catherine left her father. Mrs. Penniman was on the landing of the second floor when her niece came upstairs. It was not remarkable that a person of so much subtlety should have discovered that Catherine had been shut up with the Doctor. It was still less remarkable that she should have felt an extreme curiosity to learn the result of this interview, and that this sentiment, combined with her great amiability and generosity, should have prompted her to regret the sharp words lately exchanged between her niece and herself. As the unhappy girl came into sight, in the dusky corridor, she made a lively demonstration of sympathy. Catherine's bursting heart was equally oblivious. She only knew that her aunt was taking her into her arms. Mrs. Penniman drew her into Catherine's own room, and the two women sat there together, far into the small hours; the younger one with her head on the other's lap, sobbing and sobbing at first in a soundless, stifled manner, and then at last perfectly still. It gratified Mrs. Penniman to be able to feel conscientiously that this scene virtually removed the interdict which Catherine had placed upon her further communion with Morris Townsend. She was not gratified, however, when, in coming back to her niece's room before breakfast, she found that Catherine had risen and was preparing herself for this meal.

"You should not go to breakfast," she said; "you are not well enough, after your fearful night."

"Yes, I am very well, and I am only afraid of being late."

"I can't understand you!" Mrs. Penniman cried. "You should stay in bed for three days."

"Oh, I could never do that!" said Catherine, to whom this idea presented no attractions.

Mrs. Penniman was in despair, and she noted, with extreme annoyance, that the trace of the night's tears had completely vanished from Catherine's eyes. She had a most impracticable *physique*. "What effect do you expect to have upon your father," her aunt demanded, "if you come plumping down, without a vestige of any sort of feeling, as if nothing in the world had happened?"

"He would not like me to lie in bed," said Catherine simply.

"All the more reason for your doing it. How else do you expect to move him?"

Catherine thought a little. "I don't know how; but not in that way. I wish to be just as usual." And she finished dressing, and, according to her aunt's expression, went plumping down into the paternal presence. She was really too modest for consistent pathos.

And yet it was perfectly true that she had had a dreadful night. Even after Mrs. Penniman left her she had had no sleep. She lay staring at the uncomforting gloom, with her eyes and ears filled with the movement with which her father had turned her out of his room, and of the words in which he had told her that she was a heartless daughter. Her heart was breaking. She had heart enough for that. At moments it seemed to her that she believed him, and that to do what she was doing, a girl must indeed be bad. She *was* bad; but she couldn't help it. She would try to appear good, even if her heart were perverted; and from time to time she had a fancy that she might accomplish something by ingenious concessions to form, though she should persist in caring for Morris. Catherine's ingenuities were indefinite, and we are not called upon to expose their hollowness. The best of them perhaps showed itself in that freshness of aspect which was so discouraging to Mrs. Penniman, who was amazed at the absence of haggardness in a young woman who for a whole night had lain quivering beneath a father's curse. Poor Catherine was conscious of her freshness; it gave her a feeling about the future which rather added to the weight upon her mind. It seemed a proof that she was strong and solid and dense, and would live to a great age—longer than might be generally convenient; and this idea was depressing, for it appeared to saddle her with a pretension the more, just when the cultivation of any pretension was inconsistent with her doing right. She wrote that day to Morris Townsend, requesting him to come and see her on the morrow; using very few words, and explaining nothing. She would explain everything face to face.

## XX

On the morrow, in the afternoon, she heard his voice at the door, and his step in the hall. She received him in the big, bright front parlour, and she instructed the servant that if any one should call she was particularly engaged. She was not afraid of her father's coming in, for at that hour he was always driving about town. When Morris stood there before her, the first thing that she was conscious of was that he was even more beautiful to look at than fond recollection had painted him; the next was that he had pressed her in his arms. When she was free again it appeared to her that she had now indeed thrown herself into the gulf of defiance, and even, for an instant, that she had been married to him.

He told her that she had been very cruel, and had made him very unhappy; and Catherine felt acutely the difficulty of her destiny, which forced her to give pain in such opposite quarters. But she wished that, instead of reproaches, however tender, he would give her help; he was certainly wise enough, and clever enough, to invent some issue from their troubles. She expressed this belief, and Morris received the assurance as if he thought it natural; but he interrogated, at first—as was natural too—rather than committed himself to marking out a course.

"You should not have made me wait so long," he said. "I don't know how I have been living; every hour seemed like years. You should have decided sooner."

"Decided?" Catherine asked.

"Decided whether you would keep me or give me up."

"Oh, Morris," she cried, with a long tender murmur, "I never thought of giving you up!"

"What, then, were you waiting for?" The young man was ardently logical.

"I thought my father might—might—" and she hesitated.

"Might see how unhappy you were?"

"Oh no! But that he might look at it differently."

"And now you have sent for me to tell me that at last he does so. Is that it?"

This hypothetical optimism gave the poor girl a pang. "No, Morris," she said solemnly, "he looks at it still in the same way."

"Then why have you sent for me?"

"Because I wanted to see you!" cried Catherine piteously.

"That's an excellent reason, surely. But did you want to look at me only? Have you nothing to tell me?"

His beautiful persuasive eyes were fixed upon her face, and she wondered what answer would be noble enough to make to such a gaze as that. For a moment her own eyes took it in, and then—"I *did* want to look at you!" she said gently. But after this speech, most inconsistently, she hid her face.

Morris watched her for a moment, attentively. "Will you marry me to-morrow?" he asked suddenly.

"To-morrow?"

"Next week, then. Any time within a month."

"Isn't it better to wait?" said Catherine.

"To wait for what?"

She hardly knew for what; but this tremendous leap alarmed her. "Till we have thought about it a little more."

He shook his head, sadly and reproachfully. "I thought you had been thinking about it these three weeks. Do you want to turn it over in your mind for five years? You have given me more than time enough. My poor girl," he added in a moment, "you are not sincere!"

Catherine coloured from brow to chin, and her eyes filled with tears. "Oh, how can you say that?" she murmured.

"Why, you must take me or leave me," said Morris, very reasonably. "You can't please your father and me both; you must choose between us."

"I have chosen you!" she said passionately.

"Then marry me next week."

She stood gazing at him. "Isn't there any other way?"

"None that I know of for arriving at the same result. If there is, I should be happy to hear of it."

Catherine could think of nothing of the kind, and Morris's luminosity seemed almost pitiless. The only thing she could think of was that her father might, after all, come round, and she articulated, with an awkward sense of her helplessness in doing so, a wish that this miracle might happen.

"Do you think it is in the least degree likely?" Morris asked.

"It would be, if he could only know you!"

"He can know me if he will. What is to prevent it?"

"His ideas, his reasons," said Catherine. "They are so—so terribly strong." She trembled with the recollection of them yet.

"Strong?" cried Morris. "I would rather you should think them weak."

"Oh, nothing about my father is weak!" said the girl.

Morris turned away, walking to the window, where he stood looking out. "You are terribly afraid of him!" he remarked at last.

She felt no impulse to deny it, because she had no shame in it; for if it was no honour to herself, at least it was an honour to him. "I suppose I must be," she said simply.

"Then you don't love me—not as I love you. If you fear your father more than you love me, then your love is not what I hoped it was."

"Ah, my friend!" she said, going to him.

"Do *I* fear anything?" he demanded, turning round on her. "For your sake what am I not ready to face?"

"You are noble—you are brave!" she answered, stopping short at a distance that was almost respectful.

"Small good it does me, if you are so timid."

"I don't think that I am—*really*," said Catherine.

"I don't know what you mean by 'really.' It is really enough to make us miserable."

"I should be strong enough to wait—to wait a long time."

"And suppose after a long time your father should hate me worse than ever?"

"He wouldn't—he couldn't!"

"He would be touched by my fidelity? Is that what you mean? If he is so easily touched, then why should you be afraid of him?"

This was much to the point, and Catherine was struck by it. "I will try not to be," she said. And she stood there submissively, the image, in advance, of a dutiful and responsible wife. This image could not fail to recommend itself to Morris Townsend, and he continued to give proof of the high estimation in which he held her. It could only have been at the prompting of such a sentiment that he presently mentioned to her that the course recommended by Mrs. Penniman was an immediate union, regardless of consequences.

"Yes, Aunt Penniman would like that," Catherine said simply—and yet with a certain shrewdness. It must, however, have been in pure simplicity, and from motives quite untouched by sarcasm, that, a few moments after, she went on to say to Morris that her father had given her a message for him. It was quite on her conscience to deliver this message, and had the mission been ten times more painful she would have as scrupulously performed it. "He told me to tell you—to tell you very distinctly, and directly from himself, that if I marry without his consent, I shall not inherit a penny of his fortune. He made a great point of this. He seemed to think—he seemed to think—"

Morris flushed, as any young man of spirit might have flushed at an imputation of baseness.

"What did he seem to think?"

"That it would make a difference."

"It *will* make a difference—in many things. We shall be by many thousands of dollars the poorer; and that is a great difference. But it will make none in my affection."

"We shall not want the money," said Catherine; "for you know I have a good deal myself."

"Yes, my deal girl, I know you have something. And he can't touch that!"

"He would never," said Catherine. "My mother left it to me."

Morris was silent a while. "He was very positive about this, was he?" he asked at last. "He thought such a message would annoy me terribly, and make me throw off the mask, eh?"

"I don't know what he thought," said Catherine wearily.

"Please tell him that I care for his message as much as for that!" And Morris snapped his fingers sonorously.

"I don't think I could tell him that."

"Do you know you sometimes disappoint me?" said Morris.

"I should think I might. I disappoint every one—father and Aunt Penniman."

"Well, it doesn't matter with me, because I am fonder of you than they are."

"Yes, Morris," said the girl, with her imagination—what there was of it—swimming in this happy truth, which seemed, after all, invidious to no one.

"Is it your belief that he will stick to it—stick to it forever, to this idea of disinheriting you?—that your goodness and patience will never wear out his cruelty?"

"The trouble is that if I marry you, he will think I am not good. He will think that a proof."

"Ah, then, he will never forgive you!"

This idea, sharply expressed by Morris's handsome lips, renewed for a moment, to the poor girl's temporarily pacified conscience, all its dreadful vividness. "Oh, you must love me very much!" she cried.

"There is no doubt of that, my dear!" her lover rejoined. "You don't like that word 'disinherited,'" he added in a moment.

"It isn't the money; it is that he should—that he should feel so."

"I suppose it seems to you a kind of curse," said Morris. "It must be very dismal. But don't you think," he went on presently, "that if you were to try to be very clever, and to set rightly about it, you might in the end conjure it away? Don't you think," he continued further, in a tone of sympathetic speculation, "that a really clever woman, in your place, might bring him round at last? Don't you think—"

Here, suddenly, Morris was interrupted; these ingenious inquiries had not reached Catherine's ears. The terrible word "disinheritance," with all its impressive moral reprobation, was still ringing there; seemed indeed to gather force as it lingered. The mortal chill of her situation struck more deeply into her child-like heart, and she was overwhelmed by a feeling of loneliness and danger. But her refuge was there, close to her, and she put out her hands to grasp it. "Ah, Morris," she said, with a shudder, "I will marry you as soon as you please." And she surrendered herself, leaning her head on his shoulder.

"My dear good girl!" he exclaimed, looking down at his prize. And then he looked up again, rather vaguely, with parted lips and lifted eyebrows.

## XXI

Dr. Sloper very soon imparted his conviction to Mrs. Almond, in the same terms in which he had announced it to himself. "She's going to stick, by Jove! she's going to stick."

"Do you mean that she is going to marry him?" Mrs. Almond inquired.

"I don't know that; but she is not going to break down. She is going to drag out the engagement, in the hope of making me relent."

"And shall you not relent?"

"Shall a geometrical proposition relent? I am not so superficial."

"Doesn't geometry treat of surfaces?" asked Mrs. Almond, who, as we know, was clever, smiling.

"Yes; but it treats of them profoundly. Catherine and her young man are my surfaces; I have taken their measure."

"You speak as if it surprised you."

"It is immense; there will be a great deal to observe."

"You are shockingly cold-blooded!" said Mrs Almond.

"I need to be with all this hot blood about me. Young Townsend indeed is cool; I must allow him that merit."

"I can't judge him," Mrs. Almond answered; "but I am not at all surprised at Catherine."

"I confess I am a little; she must have been so deucedly divided and bothered."

"Say it amuses you outright! I don't see why it should be such a joke that your daughter adores you."

"It is the point where the adoration stops that I find it interesting to fix."

"It stops where the other sentiment begins."

"Not at all—that would be simple enough. The two things are extremely mixed up, and the mixture is extremely odd. It will produce some third element, and that's what I am waiting to see. I wait with suspense—with positive excitement; and that is a sort of emotion that I didn't suppose Catherine would ever provide for me. I am really very much obliged to her."

"She will cling," said Mrs. Almond; "she will certainly cling."

"Yes; as I say, she will stick."

"Cling is prettier. That's what those very simple natures always do, and nothing could be simpler than Catherine. She doesn't take many impressions; but when she takes one she keeps it. She is like a copper kettle that receives a dent; you may polish up the kettle, but you can't efface the mark."

"We must try and polish up Catherine," said the Doctor. "I will take her to Europe."

"She won't forget him in Europe."

"He will forget her, then."

Mrs. Almond looked grave. "Should you really like that?"

"Extremely!" said the Doctor.

Mrs. Penniman, meanwhile, lost little time in putting herself again in communication with Morris Townsend. She requested him to favour her with another interview, but she did not on this occasion select an oyster saloon as the scene of their meeting. She proposed that he should join her at the door of a certain church, after service on Sunday afternoon, and she was careful not to appoint the place of worship which she usually visited, and where, as she said, the congregation would have spied upon her. She picked out a less elegant resort, and on issuing from its portal at the hour she had fixed she saw the young man standing apart. She offered him no recognition till she had crossed the street and he had followed her to some distance. Here, with a smile—"Excuse my apparent want of cordiality," she said. "You know what to believe about that. Prudence before everything." And on his asking her in what direction they should walk, "Where we shall be least observed," she murmured.

Morris was not in high good-humour, and his response to this speech was not particularly gallant. "I don't flatter myself we shall be much observed anywhere." Then he turned recklessly toward the centre of the town. "I hope you have come to tell me that he has knocked under," he went on.

"I am afraid I am not altogether a harbinger of good; and yet, too, I am to a certain extent a messenger of peace. I have been thinking a great deal, Mr. Townsend," said Mrs. Penniman.

"You think too much."

"I suppose I do; but I can't help it, my mind is so terribly active.

When I give myself, I give myself. I pay the penalty in my headaches, my famous headaches—a perfect circlet of pain! But I carry it as a queen carries her crown. Would you believe that I have one now? I wouldn't however, have missed our rendezvous for anything. I have something very important to tell you."

"Well, let's have it," said Morris.

"I was perhaps a little headlong the other day in advising you to marry immediately. I have been thinking it over, and now I see it just a little differently."

"You seem to have a great many different ways of seeing the same object."

"Their number is infinite!" said Mrs. Penniman, in a tone which seemed to suggest that this convenient faculty was one of her brightest attributes.

"I recommend you to take one way and stick to it," Morris replied.

"Ah! but it isn't easy to choose. My imagination is never quiet, never satisfied. It makes me a bad adviser, perhaps; but it makes me a capital friend!"

"A capital friend who gives bad advice!" said Morris.

"Not intentionally—and who hurries off, at every risk, to make the most humble excuses!"

"Well, what do you advise me now?"

"To be very patient; to watch and wait."

"And is that bad advice or good?"

"That is not for me to say," Mrs. Penniman rejoined, with some dignity. "I only pretend it's sincere."

"And will you come to me next week and recommend something different and equally sincere?"

"I may come to you next week and tell you that I am in the streets!"

"In the streets?"

"I have had a terrible scene with my brother, and he threatens, if anything happens, to turn me out of the house. You know I am a poor woman."

Morris had a speculative idea that she had a little property; but he naturally did not press this.

"I should be very sorry to see you suffer martyrdom for me," he said. "But you make your brother out a regular Turk."

Mrs. Penniman hesitated a little.

"I certainly do not regard Austin as a satisfactory Christian."

"And am I to wait till he is converted?"

"Wait, at any rate, till he is less violent. Bide your time, Mr. Townsend; remember the prize is great!"

Morris walked along some time in silence, tapping the railings and gate posts very sharply with his stick.

"You certainly are devilish inconsistent!" he broke out at last. "I have already got Catherine to consent to a private marriage."

Mrs. Penniman was indeed inconsistent, for at this news she gave a little jump of gratification.

"Oh! when and where?" she cried. And then she stopped short.

Morris was a little vague about this.

"That isn't fixed; but she consents. It's deuced awkward, now, to back out."

Mrs. Penniman, as I say, had stopped short; and she stood there with her eyes fixed brilliantly on her companion.

"Mr. Townsend," she proceeded, "shall I tell you something? Catherine loves you so much that you may do anything."

This declaration was slightly ambiguous, and Morris opened his eyes.

"I am happy to hear it! But what do you mean by 'anything'?"

"You may postpone—you may change about; she won't think the worse of you."

Morris stood there still, with his raised eyebrows; then he said simply and rather dryly—"Ah!" After this he remarked to Mrs. Penniman that if she walked so slowly she would attract notice, and he succeeded, after a fashion, in hurrying her back to the domicile of which her tenure had become so insecure.

## XXII

HE had slightly misrepresented the matter in saying that Catherine had consented to take the great step. We left her just now declaring that she would burn her ships behind her; but Morris, after having elicited this declaration, had become conscious of good reasons for not taking it up. He avoided, gracefully enough, fixing a day, though he left her under the impression that he had his eye on one. Catherine may have had her difficulties; but those of her circumspect suitor are also worthy of consideration. The prize was certainly great; but it was only to be won by striking the happy mean between precipitancy and caution. It would be all very well to take one's jump and trust to Providence; Providence was more especially on the side of clever people, and clever people were known by an indisposition to risk their bones. The ultimate reward of a union with a young woman who was both unattractive and impoverished ought to be connected with immediate disadvantages by some very palpable chain. Between the fear of losing Catherine and her possible fortune altogether, and the fear of taking her too soon and finding this possible fortune as void of actuality as a collection of emptied bottles, it was not comfortable for Morris Townsend to choose; a fact that should be remembered by readers disposed to judge harshly of a young man who may have struck them as making but an indifferently successful use of fine natural parts. He had not forgotten that in any event Catherine had her own ten thousand a year; he had devoted an abundance of meditation to this circumstance. But with his fine parts he rated himself high, and he had a perfectly definite appreciation of his value, which seemed to him inadequately represented by the sum I have mentioned. At the same time he reminded himself that this sum was considerable, that everything is relative, and that if a modest income is less desirable than a large one, the complete absence of revenue is nowhere accounted an advantage. These reflexions gave him plenty of occupation, and made it necessary that he should trim his sail. Dr. Sloper's opposition was the unknown quantity in the problem he had to work out. The natural way to work it out was by marrying Catherine; but in mathematics there are many short cuts, and Morris was not without a hope that he should yet discover one. When Catherine took him at his word and consented to renounce the attempt to mollify her father, he drew back skilfully enough, as I have said, and kept the wedding-day still an open question. Her faith in his sincerity was so complete that she was incapable of suspecting that he was playing with her; her trouble just now was of another kind. The poor girl had an admirable sense of honour; and from the moment she had brought herself to the point of violating her father's wish, it seemed to her that she had no right to enjoy his protection. It was on her conscience that she ought to live under his roof only so long as she conformed to his wisdom. There was a great deal of glory in such a position, but poor Catherine felt that she had forfeited her claim to it. She had cast her lot with a young man against whom he had solemnly warned her, and broken the contract under which he provided her with a happy home. She could not give up the young man, so she must leave the home; and the sooner the object of her preference offered her another the sooner her situation would lose its awkward twist. This was close reasoning; but it was commingled with an infinite amount of merely instinctive penitence. Catherine's days at this time were dismal, and the weight of some of her hours was almost more than she could bear. Her father never looked at her, never spoke of her. He knew perfectly what he was about, and this was part of a plan. She looked at him as much as she dared (for she was afraid of seeming to offer herself to his observation), and she pitied him for the sorrow she had brought upon him. She held up her head and busied her hands, and went about her daily occupations; and when the state of things in

Washington Square seemed intolerable, she closed her eyes and indulged herself with an intellectual vision of the man for whose sake she had broken a sacred law. Mrs. Penniman, of the three persons in Washington Square, had much the most of the manner that belongs to a great crisis. If Catherine was quiet, she was quietly quiet, as I may say, and her pathetic effects, which there was no one to notice, were entirely unstudied and unintended. If the Doctor was stiff and dry and absolutely indifferent to the presence of his companions, it was so lightly, neatly, easily done, that you would have had to know him well to discover that, on the whole, he rather enjoyed having to be so disagreeable. But Mrs. Penniman was elaborately reserved and significantly silent; there was a richer rustle in the very deliberate movements to which she confined herself, and when she occasionally spoke, in connexion with some very trivial event, she had the air of meaning something deeper than what she said. Between Catherine and her father nothing had passed since the evening she went to speak to him in his study. She had something to say to him—it seemed to her she ought to say it; but she kept it back, for fear of irritating him. He also had something to say to her; but he was determined not to speak first. He was interested, as we know, in seeing how, if she were left to herself, she would "stick." At last she told him she had seen Morris Townsend again, and that their relations remained quite the same.

"I think we shall marry—before very long. And probably, meanwhile, I shall see him rather often; about once a week, not more."

The Doctor looked at her coldly from head to foot, as if she had been a stranger. It was the first time his eyes had rested on her for a week, which was fortunate, if that was to be their expression. "Why not three times a day?" he asked. "What prevents your meeting as often as you choose?"

She turned away a moment; there were tears in her eyes. Then she said, "It is better once a week."

"I don't see how it is better. It is as bad as it can be. If you flatter yourself that I care for little modifications of that sort, you are very much mistaken. It is as wrong of you to see him once a week as it would be to see him all day long. Not that it matters to me, however."

Catherine tried to follow these words, but they seemed to lead towards a vague horror from which she recoiled. "I think we shall marry pretty soon," she repeated at last.

Her father gave her his dreadful look again, as if she were some one else. "Why do you tell me that? It's no concern of mine."

"Oh, father!" she broke out, "don't you care, even if you do feel so?"

"Not a button. Once you marry, it's quite the same to me when or where or why you do it; and if you think to compound for your folly by hoisting your flag in this way, you may spare yourself the trouble."

With this he turned away. But the next day he spoke to her of his own accord, and his manner was somewhat changed. "Shall you be married within the next four or five months?" he asked.

"I don't know, father," said Catherine. "It is not very easy for us to make up our minds."

"Put it off, then, for six months, and in the meantime I will take you to Europe. I should like you very much to go."

It gave her such delight, after his words of the day before, to hear that he should "like" her to do something, and that he still had in his heart any of the tenderness of preference, that she gave a little exclamation of joy. But then she became conscious that Morris was not included in this proposal, and that—as regards really going—she would greatly prefer to remain at home with him. But she blushed, none the less, more comfortably than she had done of late. "It would be delightful to go to Europe," she remarked, with a sense that the idea was not original, and that her tone was not all it might be.

"Very well, then, we will go. Pack up your clothes."

"I had better tell Mr. Townsend," said Catherine.

Her father fixed his cold eyes upon her. "If you mean that you had better ask his leave, all that remains to me is to hope he will give it."

The girl was sharply touched by the pathetic ring of the words; it was the most calculated, the most dramatic little speech the Doctor had ever uttered. She felt that it was a great thing for her, under the circumstances, to have this fine opportunity of showing him her respect; and yet there was something else that she felt as well, and that she presently expressed. "I sometimes think that if I do what you dislike so much, I ought not to stay with you."

"To stay with me?"

"If I live with you, I ought to obey you."

"If that's your theory, it's certainly mine," said the Doctor, with a dry laugh.

"But if I don't obey you, I ought not to live with you—to enjoy your kindness and protection."

This striking argument gave the Doctor a sudden sense of having underestimated his daughter; it seemed even more than worthy of a young woman who had revealed the quality of unaggressive obstinacy. But it displeased him—displeased him deeply, and he signified as much. "That idea is in very bad taste," he said. "Did you get it from Mr. Townsend?"

"Oh no; it's my own!" said Catherine eagerly.

"Keep it to yourself, then," her father answered, more than ever determined she should go to Europe.

## XXIII

IF Morris Townsend was not to be included in this journey, no more was Mrs. Penniman, who would have been thankful for an invitation, but who (to do her justice) bore her disappointment in a perfectly lady-like manner. "I should enjoy seeing the works of Raphael and the ruins—the ruins of the Pantheon," she said to Mrs. Almond; "but, on the other hand, I shall not be sorry to be alone and at peace for the next few months in Washington Square. I want rest; I have been through so much in the last four months." Mrs. Almond thought it rather cruel that her brother should not take poor Lavinia abroad; but she easily understood that, if the purpose of his expedition was to make Catherine forget her lover, it was not in his interest to give his daughter this young man's best friend as a companion. "If Lavinia had not been so foolish, she might visit the ruins of the Pantheon," she said to herself; and she continued to regret her sister's folly, even though the latter assured her that she had often heard the relics in question most satisfactorily described by Mr. Penniman. Mrs. Penniman was perfectly aware that her brother's motive in undertaking a foreign tour was to lay a trap for Catherine's constancy; and she imparted this conviction very frankly to her niece.

"He thinks it will make you forget Morris," she said (she always called the young man "Morris" now); "out of sight, out of mind, you know. He thinks that all the things you will see over there will drive him out of your thoughts."

Catherine looked greatly alarmed. "If he thinks that, I ought to tell him beforehand."

Mrs. Penniman shook her head. "Tell him afterwards, my dear! After he has had all the trouble and the expense! That's the way to serve him." And she added, in a softer key, that it must be delightful to think of those who love us among the ruins of the Pantheon.

Her father's displeasure had cost the girl, as we know, a great deal of deep-welling sorrow—sorrow of the purest and most generous kind, without a touch of resentment or rancour; but for the first time, after he had dismissed with such contemptuous brevity her apology for being a charge upon him, there was a spark of anger in her grief. She had felt his contempt; it had scorched her; that speech about her bad taste made her ears burn for three days. During this period she was less considerate; she had an idea—a rather vague one, but it was agreeable to her sense of injury—that now she was absolved from penance, and might do what she chose. She chose to write to Morris Townsend to meet her in the Square and take her to walk about the town. If she were going to Europe out of respect to her father, she might at least give herself this satisfaction. She felt in every way at present more free and more resolute; there was a force that urged her. Now at last, completely and unreservedly, her passion possessed her.

Morris met her at last, and they took a long walk. She told him immediately what had happened—that her father wished to take her away. It would be for six months, to Europe; she would do absolutely what Morris should think best. She hoped inexpressibly that he would think it best she should stay at home. It was some time before he said what he thought: he asked, as they walked along, a great many questions. There was one that especially struck her; it seemed so incongruous.

"Should you like to see all those celebrated things over there?"

"Oh no, Morris!" said Catherine, quite deprecatingly.

"Gracious Heaven, what a dull woman!" Morris exclaimed to himself.

"He thinks I will forget you," said Catherine: "that all these things will drive you out of my mind."

"Well, my dear, perhaps they will!"

"Please don't say that," Catherine answered gently, as they walked along. "Poor father will be disappointed."

Morris gave a little laugh. "Yes, I verily believe that your poor father will be disappointed! But you will have seen Europe," he added humorously. "What a take-in!"

"I don't care for seeing Europe," Catherine said.

"You ought to care, my dear. And it may mollify your father."

Catherine, conscious of her obstinacy, expected little of this, and could not rid herself of the idea that in going abroad and yet remaining firm, she should play her father a trick. "Don't you think it would be a kind of deception?" she asked.

"Doesn't he want to deceive you?" cried Morris. "It will serve him right! I really think you had better go."

"And not be married for so long?"

"Be married when you come back. You can buy your wedding clothes in Paris." And then Morris, with great kindness of tone, explained his view of the matter. It would be a good thing that she should go; it would put them completely in the right. It would show they were reasonable and willing to wait. Once they were so sure of each other, they could afford to wait—what had they to fear? If there was a particle of chance that her father would be favourably affected by her going, that ought to settle it; for, after all, Morris was very unwilling to be the cause of her being disinherited. It was not for himself, it was for her and for her children. He was willing to wait for her; it would be hard, but he could do it. And over there, among beautiful scenes and noble monuments, perhaps the old gentleman would be softened; such things were supposed to exert a humanising influence. He might be touched by her gentleness, her patience, her willingness to make any sacrifice but *that* one; and if she should appeal to him some day, in some celebrated spot—in Italy, say, in the evening; in Venice, in a gondola, by moonlight—if she should be a little clever about it and touch the right chord, perhaps he would fold her in his arms and tell her that he forgave her. Catherine was immensely struck with this conception of the affair, which seemed eminently worthy of her lover's brilliant intellect; though she viewed it askance in so far as it depended upon her own powers of execution. The idea of being "clever" in a gondola by moonlight appeared to her to involve elements of which her grasp was not active. But it was settled between them that she should tell her father that she was ready to follow him obediently anywhere, making the mental reservation that she loved Morris Townsend more than ever.

She informed the Doctor she was ready to embark, and he made rapid arrangements for this event. Catherine had many farewells to make, but with only two of them are we actively concerned. Mrs. Penniman took a discriminating view of her niece's journey; it seemed to her very proper that Mr. Townsend's destined bride should wish to embellish her mind by a foreign tour.

"You leave him in good hands," she said, pressing her lips to Catherine's forehead. (She was very fond of kissing people's foreheads; it was an involuntary expression of sympathy with the intellectual part.) "I shall see him often; I shall feel like one of the vestals of old, tending the sacred flame."

"You behave beautifully about not going with us," Catherine answered, not presuming to examine this analogy.

"It is my pride that keeps me up," said Mrs. Penniman, tapping the body of her dress, which always gave forth a sort of metallic ring.

Catherine's parting with her lover was short, and few words were exchanged.

"Shall I find you just the same when I come back?" she asked; though the question was not the fruit of scepticism.

"The same—only more so!" said Morris, smiling.

It does not enter into our scheme to narrate in detail Dr. Sloper's proceedings in the eastern hemisphere. He made the grand tour of Europe, travelled in considerable splendour, and (as was to have been expected in a man of his high cultivation) found so much in art and antiquity to interest him, that he remained abroad, not for six months, but for twelve. Mrs. Penniman, in Washington Square, accommodated herself to his absence. She enjoyed her uncontested dominion in the empty house, and flattered herself that she made it more attractive to their friends than when her brother was at home. To Morris Townsend, at least, it would have appeared that she made it singularly attractive. He was altogether her most frequent visitor, and Mrs. Penniman was very fond of asking him to tea. He had his chair—a very easy one at the fireside in the back parlour (when the great mahogany sliding-doors, with silver knobs and hinges, which divided this apartment from its more formal neighbour, were closed), and he used to smoke cigars in the Doctor's study, where he often spent an hour in turning over the curious collections of its absent proprietor. He thought Mrs. Penniman a goose, as we know; but he was no goose himself, and, as a young man of luxurious tastes and scanty resources, he found the house a perfect castle of indolence. It became for him a club with a single member. Mrs. Penniman saw much less of her sister than while the Doctor was at home; for Mrs. Almond had felt moved to tell her that she disapproved of her relations with Mr. Townsend. She had no business to be so friendly to a young man of whom their brother thought so meanly, and Mrs. Almond was surprised at her levity in foisting a most deplorable engagement upon Catherine.

"Deplorable?" cried Lavinia. "He will make her a lovely husband!"

"I don't believe in lovely husbands," said Mrs. Almond; "I only believe in good ones. If he marries her, and she comes into Austin's money, they may get on. He will be an idle, amiable, selfish, and doubtless tolerably good-natured fellow. But if she doesn't get the money and he finds himself tied to her, Heaven have mercy on her! He will have none. He will hate her for his disappointment, and take his revenge; he will be pitiless and cruel. Woe betide poor Catherine! I recommend you to talk a little with his sister; it's a pity Catherine can't marry *her!*"

Mrs. Penniman had no appetite whatever for conversation with Mrs. Montgomery, whose acquaintance she made no trouble to cultivate; and the effect of this alarming forecast of her niece's destiny was to make her think it indeed a thousand pities that Mr. Townsend's generous nature should be embittered. Bright enjoyment was his natural element, and how could he be comfortable if there should prove to be nothing to enjoy? It became a fixed idea with Mrs. Penniman that he should yet enjoy her brother's fortune, on which she had acuteness enough to perceive that her own claim was small.

"If he doesn't leave it to Catherine, it certainly won't be to leave it to me," she said.

## XXIV

THE Doctor, during the first six months he was abroad, never spoke to his daughter of their little difference; partly on system, and partly because he had a great many other things to think about. It was idle to attempt to ascertain the state of her affections without direct inquiry, because, if she had not had an expressive manner among the familiar influences of home, she failed to gather animation from the mountains of Switzerland or the monuments of Italy. She was always her father's docile and reasonable associate—going through their sight-seeing in deferential silence, never complaining of fatigue, always ready to start at the hour he had appointed over-night, making no foolish criticisms and indulging in no refinements of appreciation. "She is about as intelligent as the bundle of shawls," the Doctor said; her main superiority being that while the bundle of shawls sometimes got lost, or tumbled out of the carriage, Catherine was always at her post, and had a firm and ample seat. But her father had expected this, and he was not constrained to set down her intellectual limitations as a tourist to sentimental depression; she had completely divested herself of the characteristics of a victim, and during the whole time that they were abroad she never uttered an audible sigh. He supposed she was in correspondence with Morris Townsend; but he held his peace about it, for he never saw the young man's letters, and Catherine's own missives were always given to the courier to post. She heard from her lover with considerable regularity, but his letters came enclosed in Mrs. Penniman's; so that whenever the Doctor handed her a packet addressed in his sister's hand, he was an involuntary instrument of the passion he condemned. Catherine made this reflexion, and six months earlier she would have felt bound to give him warning; but now she deemed herself absolved. There was a sore spot in her heart that his own words had made when once she spoke to him as she thought honour prompted; she would try and please him as far as she could, but she would never speak that way again. She read her lover's letters in secret.

One day at the end of the summer, the two travellers found themselves in a lonely valley of the Alps. They were crossing one of the passes, and on the long ascent they had got out of the carriage and had wandered much in advance. After a while the Doctor descried a footpath which, leading through a transverse valley, would bring them out, as he justly supposed, at a much higher point of the ascent. They followed this devious way, and finally lost the path; the valley proved very wild and rough, and their walk became rather a scramble. They were good walkers, however, and they took their adventure easily; from time to time they stopped, that Catherine might rest; and then she sat upon a stone and looked about her at the hard-featured rocks and the glowing sky. It was late in the afternoon, in the last of August; night was coming on, and, as they had reached a great elevation, the air was cold and sharp. In the west there was a great suffusion of cold, red light, which made the sides of the little valley look only the more rugged and dusky. During one of their pauses, her father left her and wandered away to some high place, at a distance, to get a view. He was out of sight; she sat there alone, in the stillness, which was just touched by the vague murmur, somewhere, of a mountain brook. She thought of Morris Townsend, and the place was so desolate and lonely that he seemed very far away. Her father remained absent a long time; she began to wonder what had become of him. But at last he reappeared, coming towards her in the clear twilight, and she got up, to go on. He made no motion to proceed, however, but came close to her, as if he had something to say. He stopped in front of her and stood looking at her, with eyes that had kept the light of the flushing snow-summits on which they had just been fixed. Then, abruptly, in a low tone, he asked her an unexpected question:

"Have you given him up?"

The question was unexpected, but Catherine was only superficially unprepared.

"No, father!" she answered.

He looked at her again for some moments, without speaking.

"Does he write to you?" he asked.

"Yes—about twice a month."

The Doctor looked up and down the valley, swinging his stick; then he said to her, in the same low tone:

"I am very angry."

She wondered what he meant—whether he wished to frighten her. If he did, the place was well chosen; this hard, melancholy dell, abandoned by the summer light, made her feel her loneliness. She looked around her, and her heart grew cold; for a moment her fear was great. But she could think of nothing to say, save to murmur gently, "I am sorry."

"You try my patience," her father went on, "and you ought to know what I am, I am not a very good man. Though I am very smooth externally, at bottom I am very passionate; and I assure you I can be very hard."

She could not think why he told her these things. Had he brought her there on purpose, and was it part of a plan? What was the plan? Catherine asked herself. Was it to startle her suddenly into a retractation—to take an advantage of her by dread? Dread of what? The place was ugly and lonely, but the place could do her no harm. There was a kind of still intensity about her father, which made him dangerous, but Catherine hardly went so far as to say to herself that it might be part of his plan to fasten his hand—the neat, fine, supple hand of a distinguished physician—in her throat. Nevertheless, she receded a step.

"I am sure you can be anything you please," she said. And it was her simple belief.

"I am very angry," he replied, more sharply.

"Why has it taken you so suddenly?"

"It has not taken me suddenly. I have been raging inwardly for the last six months. But just now this seemed a good place to flare out. It's so quiet, and we are alone."

"Yes, it's very quiet," said Catherine vaguely, looking about her. "Won't you come back to the carriage?"

"In a moment. Do you mean that in all this time you have not yielded an inch?"

"I would if I could, father; but I can't."

The Doctor looked round him too. "Should you like to be left in such a place as this, to starve?"

"What do you mean?" cried the girl.

"That will be your fate—that's how he will leave you."

He would not touch her, but he had touched Morris. The warmth came back to her heart. "That is not true, father," she broke out, "and you ought not to say it! It is not right, and it's not true!"

He shook his head slowly. "No, it's not right, because you won't believe it. But it *is* true. Come back to the carriage."

He turned away, and she followed him; he went faster, and was presently much in advance. But from time to time he stopped, without turning round, to let her keep up with him, and she made her way forward with difficulty, her heart beating with the excitement of having for the first time spoken to him in violence. By this time it had grown almost dark, and she ended by losing sight of him. But she kept her course, and after a little, the valley making a sudden turn, she gained the road, where the carriage stood waiting. In it sat her father, rigid and silent; in silence, too, she took her place beside him.

It seemed to her, later, in looking back upon all this, that for days afterwards not a word had been exchanged between them. The scene had been a strange one, but it had not permanently affected her feeling towards her father, for it was natural, after all, that he should occasionally make a scene of some kind, and he had let her alone for six months. The strangest part of it was that he had said he was not a good man; Catherine wondered a great deal what he had meant by that. The statement failed to appeal to her credence, and it was not grateful to any resentment that she entertained. Even in the utmost bitterness that she might feel, it would give her no satisfaction to think him less complete. Such a saying as that was a part of his great subtlety—men so clever as he might say anything and mean anything. And as to his being hard, that surely, in a man, was a virtue.

He let her alone for six months more—six months during which she accommodated herself without a protest to the extension of their tour. But he spoke again at the end of this time; it was at the very last, the night before they embarked for New York, in the hotel at Liverpool. They had been dining together in a great dim, musty sitting-room; and then the cloth had been removed, and the Doctor walked slowly up and down. Catherine at last took her candle to go to bed, but her father motioned her to stay.

"What do you mean to do when you get home?" he asked, while she stood there with her candle in her hand.

"Do you mean about Mr. Townsend?"

"About Mr. Townsend."

"We shall probably marry."

The Doctor took several turns again while she waited. "Do you hear from him as much as ever?"

"Yes; twice a month," said Catherine promptly.

"And does he always talk about marriage?"

"Oh yes! That is, he talks about other things to, but he always says something about that."

"I am glad to hear he varies his subjects; his letters might otherwise be monotonous."

"He writes beautifully," said Catherine, who was very glad of a chance to say it.

"They always write beautifully. However, in a given case that doesn't diminish the merit. So, as soon as you arrive, you are going off with him?"

This seemed a rather gross way of putting it, and something that there was of dignity in Catherine resented it. "I cannot tell you till we arrive," she said.

"That's reasonable enough," her father answered. "That's all I ask of you—that you *do* tell me, that you give me definite notice. When a poor man is to lose his only child, he likes to have an inkling of it beforehand."

"Oh, father, you will not lose me!" Catherine said, spilling her candle-wax.

"Three days before will do," he went on, "if you are in a position to be positive then. He ought to be very thankful to me, do you know. I have done a mighty good thing for him in taking you abroad; your value is twice as great, with all the knowledge and taste that you have acquired. A year ago, you were perhaps a little limited—a little rustic; but now you have seen everything, and appreciated everything, and you will be a most entertaining companion. We have fattened the sheep for him before he kills it!" Catherine turned away, and stood staring at the blank door. "Go to bed," said her father; "and, as we don't go aboard till noon, you may sleep late. We shall probably have a most uncomfortable voyage."

## XXV

THE voyage was indeed uncomfortable, and Catherine, on arriving in New York, had not the compensation of "going off," in her father's phrase, with Morris Townsend. She saw him, however, the day after she landed; and, in the meantime, he formed a natural subject of conversation between our heroine and her Aunt Lavinia, with whom, the night she disembarked, the girl was closeted for a long time before either lady retired to rest.

"I have seen a great deal of him," said Mrs. Penniman. "He is not very easy to know. I suppose you think you know him; but you don't, my dear. You will some day; but it will only be after you have lived with him. I may almost say *I* have lived with him," Mrs. Penniman proceeded, while Catherine stared. "I think I know him now; I have had such remarkable opportunities. You will have the same—or rather, you will have better!" and Aunt Lavinia smiled. "Then you will see what I mean. It's a wonderful character, full of passion and energy, and just as true!"

Catherine listened with a mixture of interest and apprehension. Aunt Lavinia was intensely sympathetic, and Catherine, for the past year, while she wandered through foreign galleries and churches, and rolled over the smoothness of posting roads, nursing the thoughts that never passed her lips, had often longed for the company of some intelligent person of her own sex. To tell her story to some kind woman—at moments it seemed to her that this would give her comfort, and she had more than once been on the point of taking the landlady, or the nice young person from the dressmaker's, into her confidence. If a woman had been near her she would on certain occasions have treated such a companion to a fit of weeping; and she had an apprehension that, on her return, this would form her response to Aunt Lavinia's first embrace. In fact, however, the two ladies had met, in Washington Square, without tears, and when they found themselves alone together a certain dryness fell upon the girl's emotion. It came over her with a greater force that Mrs. Penniman had enjoyed a whole year of her lover's society, and it was not a pleasure to her to hear her aunt explain and interpret the young man, speaking of him as if her own knowledge of him were supreme. It was not that Catherine was jealous; but her sense of Mrs. Penniman's innocent falsity, which had lain dormant, began to haunt her again, and she was glad that she was safely at home.

With this, however, it was a blessing to be able to talk of Morris, to sound his name, to be with a person who was not unjust to him.

"You have been very kind to him," said Catherine. "He has written me that, often. I shall never forget that, Aunt Lavinia."

"I have done what I could; it has been very little. To let him come and talk to me, and give him his cup of tea—that was all. Your Aunt Almond thought it was too much, and used to scold me terribly; but she promised me, at least, not to betray me."

"To betray you?"

"Not to tell your father. He used to sit in your father's study!" said Mrs. Penniman, with a little laugh.

Catherine was silent a moment. This idea was disagreeable to her, and she was reminded again, with pain, of her aunt's secretive habits. Morris, the reader may be informed, had had the tact not to tell her that he sat in her father's study. He had known her but for a few months, and her aunt had known her for fifteen years; and yet he would not have made the mistake of thinking that Catherine would see the joke of the thing. "I am sorry you made him go into father's room," she said, after a while.

"I didn't make him go; he went himself. He liked to look at the books, and all those things in the glass cases. He knows all about them; he knows all about everything."

Catherine was silent again; then, "I wish he had found some employment," she said.

"He has found some employment! It's beautiful news, and he told me to tell you as soon as you arrived. He has gone into partnership with a commission merchant. It was all settled, quite suddenly, a week ago."

This seemed to Catherine indeed beautiful news; it had a fine prosperous air. "Oh, I'm so glad!" she said; and now, for a moment, she was disposed to throw herself on Aunt Lavinia's neck.

"It's much better than being under some one; and he has never been used to that," Mrs. Penniman went on. "He is just as good as his partner—they are perfectly equal! You see how right he was to wait. I should like to know what your father can say now! They have got an office in Duane Street, and little printed cards; he brought me one to show me. I have got it in my room, and you shall see it to-morrow. That's what he said to me the last time he was here—'You see how right I was to wait!' He has got other people under him, instead of being a subordinate. He could never be a subordinate; I have often told him I could never think of him in that way."

Catherine assented to this proposition, and was very happy to know that Morris was his own master; but she was deprived of the satisfaction of thinking that she might communicate this news in triumph to her father. Her father would care equally little whether Morris were established in business or transported for life. Her trunks had been brought into her room, and further reference to her lover was for a short time suspended, while she opened them and displayed to her aunt some of the spoils of foreign travel. These were rich and abundant; and Catherine had brought home a present to every one—to every one save Morris, to whom she had brought simply her undiverted heart. To Mrs. Penniman she had been lavishly generous, and Aunt Lavinia spent half an hour in unfolding and folding again, with little ejaculations of gratitude and taste. She marched about for some time in a splendid cashmere shawl, which Catherine had begged her to accept, settling it on her shoulders, and twisting down her head to see how low the point descended behind.

"I shall regard it only as a loan," she said. "I will leave it to you again when I die; or rather," she added, kissing her niece again, "I will leave it to your first-born little girl!" And draped in her shawl, she stood there smiling.

"You had better wait till she comes," said Catherine.

"I don't like the way you say that," Mrs. Penniman rejoined, in a moment. "Catherine, are you changed?"

"No; I am the same."

"You have not swerved a line?"

"I am exactly the same," Catherine repeated, wishing her aunt were a little less sympathetic.

"Well, I am glad!" and Mrs. Penniman surveyed her cashmere in the glass. Then, "How is your father?" she asked in a moment, with her eyes on her niece. "Your letters were so meagre—I could never tell!"

"Father is very well."

"Ah, you know what I mean," said Mrs. Penniman, with a dignity to which the cashmere gave a richer effect. "Is he still implacable!"

"Oh yes!"

"Quite unchanged?"

"He is, if possible, more firm."

Mrs. Penniman took off her great shawl, and slowly folded it up. "That is very bad. You had no success with your little project?"

"What little project?"

"Morris told me all about it. The idea of turning the tables on him, in Europe; of watching him, when he was agreeably impressed by some celebrated sight—he pretends to be so artistic, you know—and then just pleading with him and bringing him round."

"I never tried it. It was Morris's idea; but if he had been with us, in Europe, he would have seen that father was never impressed in that way. He *is* artistic—tremendously artistic; but the more celebrated places we visited, and the more he admired them, the less use it would have been to plead with him. They seemed only to make him more determined—more terrible," said poor Catherine. "I shall never bring him round, and I expect nothing now."

"Well, I must say," Mrs. Penniman answered, "I never supposed you were going to give it up."

"I have given it up. I don't care now."

"You have grown very brave," said Mrs. Penniman, with a short laugh. "I didn't advise you to sacrifice your property."

"Yes, I am braver than I was. You asked me if I had changed; I have changed in that way. Oh," the girl went on, "I have changed very much. And it isn't my property. If *he* doesn't care for it, why should I?"

Mrs. Penniman hesitated. "Perhaps he does care for it."

"He cares for it for my sake, because he doesn't want to injure me. But he will know—he knows already—how little he need be afraid about that. Besides," said Catherine, "I have got plenty of money of my own. We shall be very well off; and now hasn't he got his business? I am delighted about that business." She went on talking, showing a good deal of excitement as she proceeded. Her aunt had never seen her with just this manner, and Mrs. Penniman, observing her, set it down to foreign travel, which had made her more positive, more mature. She thought also that Catherine had improved in appearance; she looked rather handsome. Mrs. Penniman wondered whether Morris Townsend would be struck with that. While she was engaged in this speculation, Catherine broke out, with a certain sharpness, "Why are you so contradictory, Aunt Penniman? You seem to think one thing at one time, and another at another. A year ago, before I went away, you wished me not to mind about displeasing father; and now you seem to recommend me to take another line. You change about so."

This attack was unexpected, for Mrs. Penniman was not used, in any discussion, to seeing the war carried into her own country—possibly because the enemy generally had doubts of finding subsistence there. To her own consciousness, the flowery fields of her reason had rarely been ravaged by a hostile force. It was perhaps on this account that in defending them she was majestic rather than agile.

"I don't know what you accuse me of, save of being too deeply interested in your happiness. It is the first time I have been told I am capricious. That fault is not what I am usually reproached with."

"You were angry last year that I wouldn't marry immediately, and now you talk about my winning my father over. You told me it would serve him right if he should take me to Europe for nothing. Well, he has taken me for nothing, and you ought to be satisfied. Nothing is changed—nothing but my feeling about father. I don't mind nearly so much now. I have been as good as I could, but he doesn't care. Now I don't care either. I don't know whether I have grown bad; perhaps I have. But I don't care for that. I have come home to be married—that's all I know. That ought to please you, unless you have taken up some new idea; you are so strange. You may do as you please; but you must never speak to me again about pleading with father. I shall never plead with him for anything; that is all over. He has put me off. I am come home to be married."

This was a more authoritative speech than she had ever heard on her niece's lips, and Mrs. Penniman was proportionately startled. She was indeed a little awestruck, and the force of the girl's emotion and resolution left her nothing to reply. She was easily frightened, and she always carried off her discomfiture by a concession; a concession which was often accompanied, as in the present case, by a little nervous laugh.

## XXVI

IF she had disturbed her niece's temper—she began from this moment forward to talk a good deal about Catherine's temper, an article which up to that time had never been mentioned in connexion with our heroine—Catherine had opportunity, on the morrow, to recover her serenity. Mrs. Penniman had given her a message from Morris Townsend, to the effect that he would come and welcome her home on the day after her arrival. He came in the afternoon; but, as may be imagined, he was not on this occasion made free of Dr. Sloper's study. He had been coming and going, for the past year, so comfortably and irresponsibly, that he had a certain sense of being wronged by finding himself reminded that he must now limit has horizon to the front parlour, which was Catherine's particular province.

"I am very glad you have come back," he said; "it makes me very happy to see you again." And he looked at her, smiling, from head to foot; though it did not appear, afterwards, that he agreed with Mrs. Penniman (who, womanlike, went more into details) in thinking her embellished.

To Catherine he appeared resplendent; it was some time before she could believe again that this bautiful young man was her own exclusive property. They had a great deal of characteristic lovers' talk—a soft exchange of inquiries and assurances. In these matters Morris had an excellent grace, which flung a picturesque interest even over the account of his début in the commission business—a subject as to which his companion earnestly questioned him. From time to time he got up from the sofa where they sat together, and walked about the room;

after which he came back, smiling and passing his hand through his hair. He was unquiet, as was natural in a young man who has just been reunited to a long-absent mistress, and Catherine made the reflexion that she had never seen him so excited. It gave her pleasure, somehow, to note this fact. He asked her questions about her travels, to some of which she was unable to reply, for she had forgotten the names of places, and the order of her father's journey. But for the moment she was so happy, so lifted up by the belief that her troubles at last were over, that she forgot to be ashamed of her meagre answers. It seemed to her now that she could marry him without the remnant of a scruple or a single tremor save those that belonged to joy. Without waiting for him to ask, she told him that her father had come back in exactly the same state of mind—that he had not yielded an inch.

"We must not expect it now," she said, "and we must do without it."

Morris sat looking and smiling. "My poor dear girl!" he exclaimed.

"You mustn't pity me," said Catherine; "I don't mind it now—I am used to it."

Morris continued to smile, and then he got up and walked about again. "You had better let me try him!"

"Try to bring him over? You would only make him worse," Catherine answered resolutely.

"You say that because I managed it so badly before. But I should manage it differently now. I am much wiser; I have had a year to think of it. I have more tact."

"Is that what you have been thinking of for a year?"

"Much of the time. You see, the idea sticks in my crop. I don't like to be beaten."

"How are you beaten if we marry?"

"Of course, I am not beaten on the main issue; but I am, don't you see, on all the rest of it—on the question of my reputation, of my relations with your father, of my relations with my own children, if we should have any."

"We shall have enough for our children—we shall have enough for everything. Don't you expect to succeed in business?"

"Brilliantly, and we shall certainly be very comfortable. But it isn't of the mere material comfort I speak; it is of the moral comfort," said Morris—"of the intellectual satisfaction!"

"I have great moral comfort now," Catherine declared, very simply.

"Of course you have. But with me it is different. I have staked my pride on proving to your father that he is wrong; and now that I am at the head of a flourishing business, I can deal with him as an equal. I have a capital plan—do let me go at him!"

He stood before her with his bright face, his jaunty air, his hands in his pockets; and she got up, with her eyes resting on his own. "Please don't, Morris; please don't," she said; and there was a certain mild, sad firmness in her tone which he heard for the first time. "We must ask no favours of him—we must ask nothing more. He won't relent, and nothing good will come of it. I know it now—I have a very good reason."

"And pray, what is your reason?"

She hesitated to bring it out, but at last it came. "He is not very fond of me!"

"Oh, bother!" cried Morris angrily.

"I wouldn't say such a thing without being sure. I saw it, I felt it, in England, just before he came away. He talked to me one night—the last night; and then it came over me. You can tell when a person feels that way. I wouldn't accuse him if he hadn't made me feel that way. I don't accuse him; I just tell you that that's how it is. He can't help it; we can't govern our affections. Do I govern mine? mightn't he say that to me? It's because he is so fond of my mother, whom we lost so long ago. She was beautiful, and very, very brilliant; he is always thinking of her. I am not at all like her; Aunt Penniman has told me that. Of course, it isn't my fault; but neither is it his fault. All I mean is, it's true; and it's a stronger reason for his never being reconciled than simply his dislike for you."

" 'Simply?' " cried Morris, with a laugh, "I am much obliged for that!"

"I don't mind about his disliking you now; I mind everything less. I feel differently; I feel separated from my father."

"Upon my word," said Morris, "you are a queer family!"

"Don't say that—don't say anything unkind," the girl entreated. "You must be very kind to me now, because, Morris—because," and she hesitated a moment—"because I have done a great deal for you."

"Oh, I know that, my dear!"

She had spoken up to this moment without vehemence or outward sign of emotion, gently, reasoningly, only trying to explain. But her emotion had been ineffectually smothered, and it betrayed itself at last in the trembling of her voice. "It is a great thing to be separated like that from your father, when you have worshipped him before. It has made me very unhappy; or it would have made me so if I didn't love you. You can tell when a person speaks to you as if—as if—"

"As if what?"

"As if they despised you!" said Catherine passionately. "He spoke that way the night before we sailed. It wasn't much, but it was enough, and I thought of it on the voyage, all the time. Then I made up my mind. I will never ask him for anything again, or expect anything from him. It would not be natural now. We must be very happy together, and we must not seem to depend upon his forgiveness. And Morris, Morris, you must never despise me!"

This was an easy promise to make, and Morris made it with fine effect. But for the moment he undertook nothing more onerous.

## XXVII

THE Doctor, of course, on his return, had a good deal of talk with his sisters. He was at no great pains to narrate his travels or to communicate his impressions of distant lands to Mrs. Penniman, upon whom he contented himself with bestowing a momento of his enviable experience, in the shape of a velvet gown. But he conversed with her at some length about matters nearer home, and lost no time in assuring her that he was still an inflexible father.

"I have no doubt you have seen a great deal of Mr. Townsend, and done your best to console him for Catherine's absence," he said. "I don't ask you, and you needn't deny it. I wouldn't put the question to you for the world, and expose you to the inconvenience of having to—a—excogitate an answer. No one has betrayed you, and there has been no spy upon your proceedings. Elizabeth has told no tales, and has never mentioned you except to praise your good looks and good spirits. The thing is simply an inference of my own—an induction, as the philosophers say. It seems to me likely that you would have offered an asylum to an interesting sufferer. Mr. Townsend has been a good deal in the house; there is something in the house that tells me so. We doctors, you know, end by acquiring fine perceptions, and it is impressed upon my sensorium that he has sat in these chairs, in a very easy attitude, and warmed himself at that fire. I don't grudge him the comfort of it; it is the only one he will ever enjoy at my expense. It seems likely, indeed, that I shall be able to economise at his own. I don't know what you may have said to him, or what you may say hereafter; but I should like you to know that if you have encouraged him to believe that he will gain anything by hanging on, or that I have budged a hair's-breadth from the position I took up a year ago, you have played him a trick for which he may exact reparation. I'm not sure that he may not bring a suit against you. Of course you have done it conscientiously; you have made yourself believe that I can be tired out. This is the most baseless hallucination that ever visited the brain of a genial optimist. I am not in the least tired; I am as fresh as when I started; I am good for fifty years yet. Catherine appears not to have budged an inch either; she is equally fresh; so we are about where we were before. This, however, you know as well as I. What I wish is simply to give you notice of my own state of mind! Take it to heart, dear Lavinia. Beware of the just resentment of a deluded fortune-hunter!"

"I can't say I expected it," said Mrs. Penniman. "And I had a sort of foolish hope that you would come home without that odious ironical tone with which you treat the most sacred subjects."

"Don't undervalue irony, it is often of great use. It is not, however, always necessary, and I will show you how gracefully I can lay it aside. I should like to know whether you think Morris Townsend will hang on."

"I will answer you with your own weapons," said Mrs. Penniman. "You had better wait and see!"

"Do you call such a speech as that one of my own weapons? I never said anything so rough."

"He will hang on long enough to make you very uncomfortable, then."

"My dear Lavinia," exclaimed the Doctor, "do you call that irony? I call it pugilism."

Mrs. Penniman, however, in spite of her pugilism, was a good deal frightened, and she took counsel of her fears. Her brother meanwhile took counsel, with many reservations, of Mrs. Almond, to whom he was no less generous than to Lavinia, and a good deal more communicative.

"I suppose she has had him there all the while," he said. "I must look into the state of my wine! You needn't mind telling me now; I have already said all I mean to say to her on the subject."

"I believe he was in the house a good deal," Mrs. Almond answered. "But you must admit that your leaving Lavinia quite alone was a great change for her, and that it was natural she should want some society."

"I do admit that, and that is why I shall make no row about the wine; I shall set it down as compensation to Lavinia. She is capable of telling me that she drank it all herself. Think of the inconceivable bad taste, in the circumstances, of that fellow making free with the house—or coming there at all! If that doesn't describe him, he is indescribable."

"His plan is to get what he can. Lavinia will have supported him for a year," said Mrs. Almond. "It's so much gained."

"She will have to support him for the rest of his life, then!" cried the Doctor. "But without wine, as they say at the *tables d'hôte*."

"Catherine tells me he has set up a business, and is making a great deal of money."

The Doctor stared. "She has not told me that—and Lavinia didn't deign. Ah!" he cried, "Catherine has given me up. Not that it matters, for all that the business amounts to."

"She has not given up Mr. Townsend," said Mrs. Almond. "I saw that in the first half minute. She has come home exactly the same."

"Exactly the same; not a grain more intelligent. She didn't notice a stick or a stone all the while we were away—not a picture nor a view, not a statue nor a cathedral."

"How could she notice? She had other things to think of; they are never for an instant out of her mind. She touches me very much."

"She would touch me if she didn't irritate me. That's the effect she has upon me now. I have tried everything upon her; I really have been quite merciless. But it is of no use whatever; she is absolutely *glued*. I have passed, in consequence, into the exasperated stage. At first I had a good deal of a certain genial curiosity about it; I wanted to see if she really would stick. But, good Lord, one's curiosity is satisfied! I see she is capable of it, and now she can let go."

"She will never let go," said Mrs. Almond.

"Take care, or you will exasperate me too. If she doesn't let go, she will be shaken off—sent tumbling into the dust! That's a nice position for my daughter. She can't see that if you are going to be pushed you had better jump. And then she will complain of her bruises."

"She will never complain," said Mrs. Almond.

"That I shall object to even more. But the deuce will be that I can't prevent anything."

"If she is to have a fall," said Mrs. Almond, with a gentle laugh, "we must spread as many carpets as we can." And she carried out this idea by showing a great deal of motherly kindness to the girl.

Mrs. Penniman immediately wrote to Morris Townsend. The intimacy between these two was by this time consummate, but I must content myself with noting but a few of its features. Mrs. Penniman's own share in it was a singular sentiment, which might have been misinterpreted, but which in itself was not discreditable to the poor lady. It was a romantic interest in this attractive and unfortunate young man, and yet it was not such an interest as Catherine might have been jealous of. Mrs. Penniman had not a particle of jealousy of her niece. For herself, she felt as if she were Morris's mother or sister—a mother or sister of an emotional temperament—and she had an absorbing desire to make him comfortable and happy. She had striven to do so during the year that her brother left her an open field, and her efforts had been attended with the success that has been pointed out. She had never had a child of her own, and Catherine, whom she had done her best to invest with the importance that would naturally belong to a youthful Penniman, had only partly rewarded her zeal. Catherine, as an object of affection and solicitude, had never had that picturesque charm which (as it seemed to her) would have been a natural attribute of her own progeny. Even the maternal passion in Mrs. Penniman would have been romantic and factitious, and Catherine was not constituted to inspire a romantic passion. Mrs. Penniman was as fond of her as ever, but she had grown to feel that with Catherine she lacked opportunity. Sentimentally speaking, therefore, she had (though she had not disinherited her niece) adopted Morris Townsend, who gave her opportunity in abundance. She would have been very happy to have a handsome and tyrannical son, and would have taken an extreme interest in his love affairs. This was the light in which she had come to regard Morris, who had conciliated her at first, and made his impression by his delicate and calculated deference—a sort of exhibition to which Mrs. Penniman was particularly sensitive. He had largely abated his deference afterwards, for he economised his resources, but the impression was made, and the young man's very brutality came to have a sort of filial value. If Mrs. Penniman had had a son, she would probably have been afraid of him, and at this stage of our narrative she was certainly afraid of Morris Townsend. This was one of the results of his domestication in Washington Square. He took his ease with her—as, for that matter, he would certainly have done with his own mother.

## XXVIII

THE letter was a word of warning; it informed him that the Doctor had come home more impracticable than ever. She might have reflected that Catherine would supply him with all the information he needed on this point; but we know that Mrs. Penniman's reflexions were rarely just; and, moreover, she felt that it was not for her to depend on what Catherine might do. She was to do her duty, quite irrespective of Catherine. I have said that her young friend took his ease with her, and it is an illustration of the fact that he made no answer to her letter. He took note of it, amply; but he lighted his cigar with it, and he waited, in tranquil confidence that he should receive another. "His state of mind really freezes my blood," Mrs. Penniman had written, alluding to her brother; and it would have seemed that upon this statement she could hardly improve. Nevertheless, she wrote again, expressing herself with the aid of a different figure. "His hatred of you burns with a lurid flame—the flame that never dies," she wrote. "But it doesn't light up the darkness of your future. If my affection could do so, all the years of your life would be an eternal sunshine. I can extract nothing from C.; she is so terribly secretive, like her father. She seems to expect to be married very soon, and has evidently made preparations in Europe—quantities of clothing, ten pairs of shoes, etc. My dear friend, you cannot set up in married life simply with a few pairs of shoes, can you? Tell me what you think of this. I am intensely anxious to see you; I have so much to say. I miss you dreadfully; the house seems so empty without you. What is the news down town? Is the business extending? That dear little business—I think it's so brave of you! Couldn't I come to your office?—just for three minutes? I might pass for a customer—is that what you call them? I might come in to buy something—some shares or some railroad things. *Tell me what you think of this plan.* I would carry a little reticule, like a woman of the people."

In spite of the suggestion about the reticule, Morris appeared to think poorly of the plan, for he gave Mrs. Penniman no encouragement whatever to visit his office, which he had already represented to her as a place peculiarly and unnaturally difficult to find. But as she persisted in desiring an interview—up to the last, after months of intimate colloquy, she called these meetings "interviews"—he agreed that they should take a walk together, and was even kind enough to leave his office for this purpose, during the hours at which business might have been supposed to be liveliest. It was no surprise to him, when they met at a street corner, in a region of empty lots and undeveloped pavements (Mrs. Penniman being attired as much as possible like a "woman of the people"), to find that, in spite of her urgency, what she chiefly had to convey to him was the assurance of her sympathy. Of such assurances, however, he had already a voluminous collection, and it would not have been worth his while to forsake a fruitful avocation merely to hear Mrs. Penniman say, for the thousandth time, that she had made his cause her own. Morris had something of his own to say. It was not an easy thing to bring out, and while he turned it over the difficulty made him acrimonious.

"Oh yes, I know perfectly that he combines the properties of a lump of ice and a red-hot coal," he observed. "Catherine has made it thoroughly clear, and you have told me so till I am sick of it. You needn't tell me again; I am perfectly satisfied. He will never give us a penny; I regard that as mathematically proved."

Mrs. Penniman at this point had an inspiration.

"Couldn't you bring a lawsuit against him?" She wondered that this simple expedient had never occurred to her before.

"I will bring a lawsuit against *you,*" said Morris, "if you ask me any more such aggravating questions. A man should know when he is beaten," he added, in a moment. "I must give her up!"

Mrs. Penniman received this declaration in silence, though it made her heart beat a little. It found her by no means unprepared, for she had accustomed herself to the thought that, if Morris should decidedly not be able to get her brother's money, it would not do for him to marry

Catherine without it. "It would not do" was a vague way of putting the thing; but Mrs. Penniman's natural affection completed the idea, which, though it had not as yet been so crudely expressed between them as in the form that Morris had just given it, had nevertheless been implied so often, in certain easy intervals of talk, as he sat stretching his legs in the Doctor's well-stuffed armchairs, that she had grown first to regard it with an emotion which she flattered herself was philosophic, and then to have a secret tenderness for it. The fact that she kept her tenderness secret proves, of course, that she was ashamed of it; but she managed to blink her shame by reminding herself that she was, after all, the official protector of her niece's marriage. Her logic would scarcely have passed muster with the Doctor. In the first place, Morris *must* get the money, and she would help him to it. In the second, it was plain it would never come to him, and it would be a grievous pity he should marry without it—a young man who might so easily find something better. After her brother had delivered himself, on his return from Europe, of that incisive little address that has been quoted, Morris's cause seemed so hopeless that Mrs. Penniman fixed her attention exclusively upon the latter branch of her argument. If Morris had been her son, she would certainly have sacrificed Catherine to a superior conception of his future; and to be ready to do so as the case stood was therefore even a finer degree of devotion. Nevertheless, it checked her breath a little to have the sacrificial knife, as it were, suddenly thrust into her hand.

Morris walked along a moment, and then he repeated harshly:

"I must give her up!"

"I think I understand you," said Mrs. Penniman gently.

"I certainly say it distinctly enough—brutally and vulgarly enough."

He was ashamed of himself, and his shame was uncomfortable; and as he was extremely intolerant of discomfort, he felt vicious and cruel. He wanted to abuse somebody, and he began, cautiously—for he was always cautious—with himself.

"Couldn't you take her down a little?" he asked.

"Take her down?"

"Prepare her—try and ease me off."

Mrs. Penniman stopped, looking at him very solemnly.

"My poor Morris, do you know how much she loves you?"

"No, I don't. I don't want to know. I have always tried to keep from knowing. It would be too painful."

"She will suffer much," said Mrs. Penniman.

"You must console her. If you are as good a friend to me as you pretend to be, you will manage it."

Mrs. Penniman shook her head sadly.

"You talk of my 'pretending' to like you; but I can't pretend to hate you. I can only tell her I think very highly of you; and how will that console her for losing you?"

"The Doctor will help you. He will be delighted at the thing being broken off, and, as he is a knowing fellow, he will invent something to comfort her."

"He will invent a new torture!" cried Mrs. Penniman. "Heaven deliver her from her father's comfort. It will consist of his crowing over her and saying, 'I always told you so!' "

Morris coloured a most uncomfortable red.

"If you don't console her any better than you console me, you certainly won't be of much use! It's a damned disagreeable necessity; I feel it extremely, and you ought to make it easy for me."

"I will be your friend for life!" Mrs. Penniman declared.

"Be my friend *now!*" And Morris walked on.

She went with him; she was almost trembling.

"Should you like me to tell her?" she asked.

"You mustn't tell her, but you can—you can—" And he hesitated, trying to think what Mrs. Penniman could do. "You can explain to her why it is. It's because I can't bring myself to step in between her and her father—to give him the pretext he grasps at so eagerly (it's a hideous sight) for depriving her of her rights."

Mrs. Penniman felt with remarkable promptitude the charm of this formula.

"That's so like you," she said; "it's so finely felt."

Morris gave his stick an angry swing.

"Oh, botheration!" he exclaimed perversely.

Mrs. Penniman, however, was not discouraged.

"It may turn out better than you think. Catherine is, after all, so very peculiar." And she thought she might take it upon herself to assure him that, whatever happened, the girl would be very quiet—she wouldn't make a noise. They extended their walk, and, while they proceeded, Mrs. Penniman took upon herself other things besides, and ended by having assumed a considerable burden; Morris being ready enough, as may be imagined, to put everything off upon her. But he was not for a single instant the dupe of her blundering alacrity; he knew that of what she promised she was competent to perform but an insignificant fraction, and the more she professed her willingness to serve him, the greater fool he thought her.

"What will you do if you don't marry her?" she ventured to inquire in the course of this conversation.

"Something brilliant," said Morris. "Shouldn't you like me to do something brilliant?"

The idea gave Mrs. Penniman exceeding pleasure.

"I shall feel sadly taken in if you don't."

"I shall have to, to make up for this. This isn't at all brilliant, you know."

Mrs. Penniman mused a little, as if there might be some way of making out that it was; but she had to give up the attempt, and, to carry off the awkwardness of failure, she risked a new inquiry.

"Do you mean—do you mean another marriage?"

Morris greeted this question with a reflexion which was hardly the less impudent from being inaudible. "Surely, women are more crude than men!" And then he answered audibly:

"Never in the world!"

Mrs. Penniman felt disappointed and snubbed, and she relieved herself in a little vaguely-sarcastic cry. He was certainly perverse.

"I give her up, not for another woman, but for a wider career!" Morris announced.

This was very grand; but still Mrs. Penniman, who felt that she had exposed herself, was faintly rancorous.

"Do you mean never to come to see her again?" she asked, with some sharpness.

"Oh no, I shall come again; but what is the use of dragging it out? I have been four times since she came back, and it's terribly awkward work. I can't keep it up indefinitely; she oughtn't to expect that, you know. A woman should never keep a man dangling!" he added finely.

"Ah, but you must have your last parting!" urged his companion, in whose imagination the idea of last partings occupied a place inferior in dignity only to that of first meetings.

## XXIX

HE came again, without managing the last parting; and again and again, without finding that Mrs. Penniman had as yet done much to pave the path of retreat with flowers. It was devilish awkward, as he said, and he felt a lively animosity for Catherine's aunt, who, as he had now quite formed the habit of saying to himself, had dragged him into the mess and was bound in common charity to get him out of it. Mrs. Penniman, to tell the truth, had, in the seclusion of her own apartment— and, I may add, amid the suggestiveness of Catherine's, which wore in those days the appearance of that of a young lady laying out her *trousseau*—Mrs. Penniman had measured her responsibilities, and taken fright at their magnitude. The task of preparing Catherine and easing off Morris presented difficulties which increased in the execution, and even led the impulsive Lavinia to ask herself whether the modification of the young man's original project had been conceived in a happy spirit. A brilliant future, a wider career, a conscience exempt from the reproach of interference between a young lady and her natural rights—these excellent things might be too troublesomely purchased. From Catherine herself Mrs. Penniman received no assistance whatever; the poor girl was apparently without suspicion of her danger. She looked at her lover with eyes of undiminished trust, and though she had less confidence in her aunt than in a young man with whom she had exchanged so many tender vows, she gave her no handle for explaining or confessing. Mrs. Penniman, faltering and wavering, declared Catherine was very stupid, put off the great scene, as she would have called it, from day to day, and wandered about very uncomfortably, primed, to repletion, with her apology, but unable to bring it to the light. Morris's own scenes were very small ones just now; but even these were beyond his strength. He made his visit as brief as possible, and while he sat with his mistress, found terribly little to talk about. She was waiting for him, in vulgar parlance, to name the day; and so long as he was unprepared to be explicit on this point it seemed a mockery to pretend to talk about matters more abstract. She had no airs and no arts; she never attempted to disguise her expectancy. She was waiting on his good pleasure, and would wait modestly and patiently; his hanging back at this supreme time might appear strange, but of course he must have a good reason for it. Catherine would have made a wife of the gentle old-fashioned pattern—regarding reasons as favours and windfalls, but no more expecting one every day than she would have expected a bouquet of camellias. During the period of her engagement, however, a young lady even of the most slender pretensions counts upon more bouquets than at other times; and there was a want of perfume in the air at this moment which at last excited the girl's alarm.

"Are you sick?" she asked of Morris. "You seem so restless, and you look pale."

"I am not at all well," said Morris; and it occurred to him that, if he could only make her pity him enough, he might get off.

"I am afraid you are overworked; you oughtn't to work so much."

"I must do that." And then he added, with a sort of calculated brutality, "I don't want to owe you everything!"

"Ah, how can you say that?"

"I am too proud," said Morris.

"Yes—you are too proud!"

"Well, you must take me as I am," he went on, "you can never change me."

"I don't want to change you," she said gently. "I will take you as you are!" And she stood looking at him.

"You know people talk tremendously about a man's marrying a rich girl," Morris remarked. "It's excessively disagreeable."

"But I am not rich!" said Catherine.

"You are rich enough to make me talked about!"

"Of course you are talked about. It's an honour!"

"It's an honour I could easily dispense with."

She was on the point of asking him whether it were not a compensation for this annoyance that the poor girl who had the misfortune to bring it upon him, loved him so dearly and believed in him so truly; but she hesitated, thinking that this would perhaps seem an exacting speech, and while she hesitated, he suddenly left her.

The next time he came, however, she brought it out, and she told him again that he was too proud. He repeated that he couldn't change, and this time she felt the impulse to say that with a little effort he might change.

Sometimes he thought that if he could only make a quarrel with her it might help him; but the question was how to quarrel with a young woman who had such treasures of concession. "I suppose you think the effort is all on your side!" he was reduced to exclaiming. "Don't you believe that I have my own effort to make?"

"It's all yours now," she said. "My effort is finished and done with!"

"Well, mine is not."

"We must bear things together," said Catherine. "That's what we ought to do."

Morris attempted a natural smile. "There are some things which we can't very well bear together—for instance, separation."

"Why do you speak of separation?"

"Ah! you don't like it; I knew you wouldn't!"

"Where are you going, Morris?" she suddenly asked.

He fixed his eye on her for a moment, and for a part of that moment she was afraid of it. "Will you promise not to make a scene?"

"A scene!—do I make scenes?"

"All women do!" said Morris, with the tone of large experience.

"I don't. Where are you going?"

"If I should say I was going away on business, should you think it very strange?"

She wondered a moment, gazing at him. "Yes—no. Not if you will take me with you."

"Take you with me—on business?"

"What is your business? Your business is to be with me."

"I don't earn my living with you," said Morris. "Or rather," he cried with a sudden inspiration, "that's just what I do—or what the world says I do!"

This ought perhaps to have been a great stroke, but it miscarried. "Where are you going?" Catherine simply repeated.

"To New Orleans. About buying some cotton."

"I am perfectly willing to go to New Orleans," Catherine said.

"Do you suppose I would take you to a nest of yellow fever?" cried Morris. "Do you suppose I would expose you at such a time as this?"

"If there is yellow fever, why should you go? Morris, you must not go!"

"It is to make six thousand dollars," said Morris. "Do you grudge me that satisfaction?"

"We have no need of six thousand dollars. You think too much about money!"

"You can afford to say that? This is a great chance; we heard of it last night." And he explained to her in what the chance consisted; and told her a long story, going over more than once several of the details, about the remarkable stroke of business which he and his partner had planned between them.

But Catherine's imagination, for reasons best known to herself, absolutely refused to be fired. "If you can go to New Orleans, I can go," she said. "Why shouldn't you catch yellow fever quite as easily as I? I am every bit as strong as you, and not in the least afraid of any fever. When we were in Europe, we were in very unhealthy places; my father used to make me take some pills. I never caught anything, and I never was nervous. What will be the use of six thousand dollars if you die of a fever? When persons are going to be married they oughtn't to think so much about business. You shouldn't think about cotton, you should think about me. You can go to New Orleans some other time—there will always be plenty of cotton. It isn't the moment to choose—we have waited too long already." She spoke more forcibly and volubly than he had ever heard her, and she held his arm in her two hands.

"You said you wouldn't make a scene!" cried Morris. "I call this a scene."

"It's you that are making it! I have never asked you anything before. We have waited too long already." And it was a comfort to her to think that she had hitherto asked so little; it seemed to make her right to insist the greater now.

Morris bethought himself a little. "Very well, then; we won't talk about it any more. I will transact my business by letter." And he began to smooth his hat, as if to take leave.

"You won't go?" And she stood looking up at him.

He could not give up his idea of provoking a quarrel; it was so much the simplest way! He bent his eyes on her upturned face, with the darkest frown he could achieve. "You are not discreet. You mustn't bully me!"

But, as usual, she conceded everything. "No, I am not discreet; I know I am too pressing. But isn't it natural? It is only for a moment."

"In a moment you may do a great deal of harm. Try and be calmer the next time I come."

"When will you come?"

"Do you want to make conditions?" Morris asked. "I will come next Saturday."

"Come to-morrow," Catherine begged; "I want you to come to-morrow. I will be very quiet," she added; and her agitation had by this time become so great that the assurance was not becoming. A sudden fear had come over her; it was like the solid conjunction of a dozen disembodied doubts, and her imagination, at a single bound, had traversed an enormous distance. All her being, for the moment, centred in the wish to keep him in the room.

Morris bent his head and kissed her forehead. "When you are quiet, you are perfection," he said; "but when you are violent, you are not in character."

It was Catherine's wish that there should be no violence about her save the beating of her heart, which she could not help; and she went on, as gently as possible, "Will you promise to come to-morrow?"

"I said Saturday!" Morris answered, smiling. He tried a frown at one moment, a smile at another; he was at his wit's end.

"Yes, Saturday too," she answered, trying to smile. "But to-morrow first." He was going to the door, and she went with him quickly. She leaned her shoulder against it; it seemed to her that she would do anything to keep him.

"If I am prevented from coming to-morrow, you will say I have deceived you!" he said.

"How can you be prevented? You can come if you will."

"I am a busy man—I am not a dangler!" cried Morris sternly.

His voice was so hard and unnatural that, with a helpless look at him, she turned away; and then he quickly laid his hand on the door-knob. He felt as if he were absolutely running away from her. But in an instant she was close to him again, and murmuring in a tone none the less penetrating for being low, "Morris, you are going to leave me."

"Yes, for a little while."

"For how long?"

"Till you are reasonable again."

"I shall never be reasonable in that way!" And she tried to keep him longer; it was almost a struggle. "Think of what I have done!" she broke out. "Morris, I have given up everything!"

"You shall have everything back!"

"You wouldn't say that if you didn't mean something. What is it?—what has happened?—what have I done?—what has changed you?"

"I will write to you—that is better," Morris stammered.

"Ah, you won't come back!" she cried, bursting into tears.

"Dear Catherine," he said, "don't believe that! I promise you that you shall see me again!" And he managed to get away and to close the door behind him.

## XXX

It was almost her last outbreak of passive grief; at least, she never indulged in another that the world knew anything about. But this one was long and terrible; she flung herself on the sofa and gave herself up to her misery. She hardly knew what had happened; ostensibly she had only had a difference with her lover, as other girls had had before, and the thing was not only not a rupture, but she was under no obligation to regard it even as a menace. Nevertheless, she felt a wound, even if he had not dealt it; it seemed to her that a mask had suddenly fallen from his face. He had wished to get away from her; he had been angry and cruel, and said strange things, with strange looks. She was smothered and stunned; she buried her head in the cushions, sobbing and talking to herself. But at last she raised herself, with the fear that either her father or Mrs. Penniman would come in; and then she sat there, staring before her, while the room grew darker. She said to herself that perhaps he would come back to tell her he had not meant what he said; and she listened for his ring at the door, trying to believe that this was probable. A long time passed, but Morris remained absent; the shadows gathered; the evening settled down on the meagre elegance of the light, clear-coloured room; the fire went out. When it had grown dark, Catherine went to the window and looked out; she stood there for half an hour, on the mere chance that he would come up the steps. At last she turned away, for she saw her father come in. He had seen her at the window looking out, and he stopped a moment at the bottom of the white steps, and gravely, with an air of exaggerated courtesy, lifted his hat to her. The gesture was so incongruous to the condition she was in, this stately tribute of respect to a poor girl despised and forsaken was so out of place, that the thing gave her a kind of horror, and she hurried away to her room. It seemed to her that she had given Morris up.

She had to show herself half an hour later, and she was sustained at table by the immensity of her desire that her father should not perceive that anything had happened. This was a great help to her afterwards, and it served her (though never as much as she supposed) from the first. On this occasion Dr. Sloper was rather talkative. He told a great many stories about a wonderful poodle that he had seen at the house of an old lady whom he had visited professionally. Catherine not only tried to appear to listen to the anecdotes of the poodle, but she endeavoured to interest herself in them, so as not to think of her scene with Morris. That perhaps was an hallucination; he was mistaken, she was jealous; people didn't change like that from one day to another. Then she knew that she had had doubts before—strange suspicions, that were at once vague and acute—and that he had been different ever since her return from Europe: whereupon she tried again to listen to her father, who told a story so remarkably well. Afterwards she went straight to her own room; it was beyond her strength to undertake to spend the evening with her aunt. All the evening, alone, she questioned herself. Her trouble was terrible; but was it a thing of her imagination, engendered by an extravagant sensibility, or did it represent a clear-cut reality, and had the worst that was possible actually come to pass? Mrs. Penniman, with a degree of tact that was as unusual as it was commendable, took the line of leaving her alone. The truth is, that her suspicions having been aroused, she indulged a desire, natural to a timid person, that the explosion should be localised. So long as the air still vibrated she kept out of the way.

She passed and repassed Catherine's door several times in the course of the evening, as if she expected to hear a plaintive moan behind it. But the room remained perfectly still; and accordingly, the last thing before retiring to her own couch, she applied for admittance. Catherine was sitting up, and had a book that she pretended to be reading. She had no wish to go to bed, for she had no expectation of sleeping. After Mrs. Penniman had left her she sat up half the night, and she offered her visitor no inducement to remain. Her aunt came stealing in very gently, and approached her with great solemnity.

"I am afraid you are in trouble, my dear. Can I do anything to help you?"

"I am not in any trouble whatever, and do not need any help," said Catherine, fibbing roundly, and proving thereby that not only our faults, but our most involuntary misfortunes, tend to corrupt our morals.

"Has nothing happened to you?"

"Nothing whatever."

"Are you very sure, dear?"

"Perfectly sure."

"And can I really do nothing for you?"

"Nothing, aunt, but kindly leave me alone," said Catherine.

Mrs. Penniman, though she had been afraid of too warm a welcome before, was now disappointed at so cold a one; and in relating afterwards, as she did to many persons, and with considerable variations of detail, the history of the termination of her niece's engagement, she was usually careful to mention that the young lady, on a certain occasion, had "hustled" her out of the room. It was characteristic of Mrs. Penniman that she related this fact, not in the least out of malignity to Catherine, whom she very sufficiently pitied, but simply from a natural disposition to embellish any subject that she touched.

Catherine, as I have said, sat up half the night, as if she still expected to hear Morris Townsend ring at the door. On the morrow this expectation was less unreasonable; but it was not gratified by the reappearance of the young man. Neither had he written; there was not a word of explanation or reassurance. Fortunately for Catherine she could take refuge from her excitement, which had now become intense, in her determination that her father should see nothing of it. How well she deceived her father we shall have occasion to learn; but her innocent arts were of little avail before a person of the rare perspicacity of Mrs. Penniman. This lady easily saw that she was agitated, and if there was any agitation going forward, Mrs. Penniman was not a person to forfeit her natural share in it. She returned to the charge the next evening, and requested her niece to lean upon her—to unburden her heart. Perhaps she should be able to explain certain things that now seemed dark, and that she knew more about than Catherine supposed. If Catherine had been frigid the night before, to-day she was haughty.

"You are completely mistaken, and I have not the least idea what you mean. I don't know what you are trying to fasten on me, and I have never had less need of any one's explanations in my life."

In this way the girl delivered herself, and from hour to hour kept her aunt at bay. From hour to hour Mrs. Penniman's curiosity grew. She would have given her little finger to know what Morris had said and done, what tone he had taken, what pretext he had found. She wrote to him, naturally, to request an interview; but she received, as naturally, no answer to her petition. Morris was not in a writing mood; for Catherine had addressed him two short notes which met with no acknowledgment. These notes were so brief that I may give them entire. "Won't you give me some sign that you didn't mean to be so cruel as you seemed on Tuesday?"—that was the first; the other was a little longer. "If I was unreasonable or suspicious on Tuesday—if I annoyed you or troubled you in any way—I beg your forgiveness, and I promise never again to be so foolish. I am punished enough, and I don't understand.

Dear Morris, you are killing me!" These notes were despatched on the Friday and Saturday; but Saturday and Sunday passed without bringing the poor girl the satisfaction she desired. Her punishment accumulated; she continued to bear it, however, with a good deal of superficial fortitude. On Saturday morning the Doctor, who had been watching in silence, spoke to his sister Lavinia.

"The thing has happened—the scoundrel has backed out!"

"Never!" cried Mrs. Penniman, who had bethought herself what she should say to Catherine, but was not provided with a line of defence against her brother, so that indignant negation was the only weapon in her hands.

"He has begged for a reprieve, then, if you like that better!"

"It seems to make you very happy that your daughter's affections have been trifled with."

"It does," said the Doctor; "for I had foretold it! It's a great pleasure to be in the right."

"Your pleasures make one shudder!" his sister exclaimed.

Catherine went rigidly through her usual occupations; that is, up to the point of going with her aunt to church on Sunday morning. She generally went to afternoon service as well; but on this occasion her courage faltered, and she begged of Mrs. Penniman to go without her.

"I am sure you have a secret," said Mrs. Penniman, with great significance, looking at her rather grimly.

"If I have, I shall keep it!" Catherine answered, turning away.

Mrs. Penniman started for church; but before she had arrived, she stopped and turned back, and before twenty minutes had elapsed she re-entered the house, looked into the empty parlours, and then went upstairs and knocked at Catherine's door. She got no answer; Catherine was not in her room, and Mrs. Penniman presently ascertained that she was not in the house. "She has gone to him, she has fled!" Lavinia cried, clasping her hands with admiration and envy. But she soon perceived that Catherine had taken nothing with her—all her personal property in her room was intact—and then she jumped at the hypothesis that the girl had gone forth, not in tenderness, but in resentment. "She has followed him to his own door—she has burst upon him in his own apartment!" It was in these terms that Mrs. Penniman depicted to herself her niece's errand, which, viewed in this light, gratified her sense of the picturesque only a shade less strongly than the idea of a clandestine marriage. To visit one's lover, with tears and reproaches, at his own residence, was an image so agreeable to Mrs. Penniman's mind that she felt a sort of æsthetic disappointment at its lacking, in this case, the harmonious accompaniments of darkness and storm. A quiet Sunday afternoon appeared an inadequate setting for it; and, indeed, Mrs. Penniman was quite out of humour with the conditions of the time, which passed very slowly as she sat in the front parlour in her bonnet and her cashmere shawl, awaiting Catherine's return.

This event at last took place. She saw her—at the window—mount the steps, and she went to await her in the hall, where she pounced upon her as soon as she had entered the house, and drew her into the parlour, closing the door with solemnity. Catherine was flushed, and her eye was bright. Mrs. Penniman hardly knew what to think.

"May I venture to ask where you have been?" she demanded.

"I have been to take a walk," said Catherine. "I thought you had gone to church."

"I did go to church; but the service was shorter than usual. And pray, where did you walk?"

"I don't know!" said Catherine.

"Your ignorance is most extraordinary! Dear Catherine, you can trust me."

"What am I to trust you with?"

"With your secret—your sorrow."

"I have no sorrow!" said Catherine fiercely.

"My poor child," Mrs. Penniman insisted, "you can't deceive me. I know everything. I have been requested to—a—to converse with you."

"I don't want to converse!"

"It will relieve you. Don't you know Shakespeare's lines?—'the grief that does not speak!' My dear girl, it is better as it is."

"What is better?" Catherine asked.

She was really too perverse. A certain amount of perversity was to be allowed for in a young lady whose lover had thrown her over; but not such an amount as would prove inconvenient to his apologists. "That you should be reasonable," said Mrs. Penniman, with some sternness. "That you should take counsel of worldly prudence, and submit to practical considerations. That you should agree to—a—separate."

Catherine had been ice up to this moment, but at this word she flamed up. "Separate? What do you know about our separating?"

Mrs. Penniman shook her head with a sadness in which there was almost a sense of injury. "Your pride is my pride, and your susceptibilities are mine. I see your side perfectly, but I also"—and she smiled with melancholy suggestiveness—"I also see the situation as a whole!"

This suggestiveness was lost upon Catherine, who repeated her violent inquiry. "Why do you talk about separation; what do you know about it?"

"We must study resignation," said Mrs. Penniman, hesitating, but sententious at a venture.

"Resignation to what?"

"To a change of—of our plans."

"My plans have not changed!" said Catherine, with a little laugh.

"Ah, but Mr. Townsend's have," her aunt answered very gently.

"What do you mean?"

There was an imperious brevity in the tone of this inquiry, against which Mrs. Penniman felt bound to protest; the information with which she had undertaken to supply her niece was, after all, a favour. She had tried sharpness, and she had tried sternness: but neither would do; she was shocked at the girl's obstinacy. "Ah, well," she said, "if he hasn't told you! . . ." and she turned away.

Catherine watched her a moment in silence; then she hurried after her, stopping her before she reached the door. "Told me what? What do you mean? What are you hinting at and threatening me with?"

"Isn't it broken off?" asked Mrs. Penniman.

"My engagement? Not in the least!"

"I beg your pardon in that case. I have spoken too soon!"

"Too soon! Soon or late," Catherine broke out, "you speak foolishly and cruelly!"

"What has happened between you, then?" asked her aunt, struck by the sincerity of this cry. "For something certainly has happened."

"Nothing has happened but that I love him more and more!"

Mrs. Penniman was silent an instant. "I suppose that's the reason you went to see him this afternoon."

Catherine flushed as if she had been struck. "Yes, I did go to see him! But that's my own business."

"Very well, then; we won't talk about it." And Mrs. Penniman moved towards the door again. But she was stopped by a sudden imploring cry from the girl.

"Aunt Lavinia, *where* has he gone?"

"Ah, you admit, then, that he has gone away? Didn't they know at his house?"

"They said he had left town. I asked no more questions; I was ashamed," said Catherine, simply enough.

"You needn't have taken so compromising a step if you had had a little more confidence in me," Mrs. Penniman observed, with a good deal of grandeur.

"Is it to New Orleans?" Catherine went on irrelevantly.

It was the first time Mrs. Penniman had heard of New Orleans in this connexion; but she was averse to letting Catherine know that she was in the dark. She attempted to strike an illumination from the instructions she had received from Morris. "My dear Catherine," she said, "when a separation has been agreed upon, the farther he goes away the better."

"Agreed upon? Has he agreed upon it with you?" A consummate sense of her aunt's meddlesome folly had come over her during the last five minutes, and she was sickened at the thought that Mrs. Penniman had been let loose, as it were, upon her happiness.

"He certainly has sometimes advised with me," said Mrs. Penniman.

"Is it you, then, that have changed him and made him so unnatural?" Catherine cried. "Is it you that have worked on him and taken him from me? He doesn't belong to you, and I don't see how you have anything to do with what is between us! Is it you that have made this plot and told him to leave me? How could you be so wicked, so cruel? What have I ever done to you; why can't you leave me alone? I was afraid you would spoil everything; for you *do* spoil everything you touch; I was afraid of you all the time we were abroad; I had no rest when I thought that you were always talking to him." Catherine went on with growing vehemence, pouring out in her bitterness and in the clairvoyance of her passion (which suddenly, jumping all processes, made her judge her aunt finally and without appeal) the uneasiness which had lain for so many months upon her heart.

Mrs. Penniman was scared and bewildered; she saw no prospect of introducing her little account of the purity of Morris's motives. "You are a most ungrateful girl!" she cried. "Do you scold me for talking with him? I am sure we never talked of anything but you!"

"Yes; and that was the way you worried him; you made him tired of my very name! I wish you had never spoken of me to him; I never asked your help!"

"I am sure if it hadn't been for me he would never have come to the house, and you would never have known what he thought of you," Mrs. Penniman rejoined, with a good deal of justice.

"I wish he never had come to the house, and that I never had known it! That's better than this," said poor Catherine.

"You are a very ungrateful girl," Aunt Lavinia repeated.

Catherine's outbreak of anger and the sense of wrong gave her, while they lasted, the satisfaction that comes from all assertion of force; they hurried her along, and there is always a sort of pleasure in cleaving the air. But at the bottom she hated to be violent, and she was conscious of no aptitude for organised resentment. She calmed herself with a great effort, but with great rapidity, and walked about the room a few moments, trying to say to herself that her aunt had meant everything for the best. She did not succeed in saying it with much conviction, but after a little she was able to speak quietly enough.

"I am not ungrateful, but I am very unhappy. It's hard to be grateful for that," she said. "Will you please tell me where he is?"

"I haven't the least idea; I am not in secret correspondence with him!"

And Mrs. Penniman wished indeed that she were, so that she might let him know how Catherine abused her, after all she had done.

"Was it a plan of his, then, to break off—?" By this time Catherine had become completely quiet.

Mrs. Penniman began again to have a glimpse of her chance for explaining. "He shrank—he shrank," she said. "He lacked courage, but it was the courage to injure you! He couldn't bear to bring down on you your father's curse."

Catherine listened to this with her eyes fixed upon her aunt, and continued to gaze at her for some time afterwards. "Did he tell you to say that?"

"He told me to say many things—all so delicate, so discriminating. And he told me to tell you he hoped you wouldn't despise him."

"I don't," said Catherine. And then she added: "And will he stay away for ever?"

"Oh, for ever is a long time. Your father, perhaps, won't live for ever."

"Perhaps not."

"I am sure you appreciate—you understand—even though your heart bleeds," said Mrs. Penniman. "You doubtless think him too scrupulous. So do I, but I respect his scruples. What he asks of you is that you should do the same."

Catherine was still gazing at her aunt, but she spoke at last, as if she had not heard or not understood her. "It has been a regular plan, then. He has broken it off deliberately; he has given me up."

"For the present, dear Catherine. He has put it off only."

"He has left me alone," Catherine went on.

"Haven't you *me?*" asked Mrs. Penniman, with much expression.

Catherine shook her head slowly. "I don't believe it!" and she left the room.

## XXXI

THOUGH she had forced herself to be calm, she preferred practising this virtue in private, and she forbore to show herself at tea—a repast which, on Sundays, at six o'clock, took the place of dinner. Dr. Sloper and his sister sat face to face, but Mrs. Penniman never met her brother's eye. Late in the evening she went with him, but without Catherine, to their sister Almond's, where, between the two ladies, Catherine's unhappy situation was discussed with a frankness that was conditioned by a good deal of mysterious reticence on Mrs. Penniman's part.

"I am delighted he is not to marry her," said Mrs. Almond, "but he ought to be horsewhipped all the same."

Mrs. Penniman, who was shocked at her sister's coarseness, replied that he had been actuated by the noblest of motives—the desire not to impoverish Catherine.

"I am very happy that Catherine is not to be impoverished—but I hope he may never have a penny too much! And what does the poor girl say to *you?*" Mrs. Almond asked.

"She says I have a genius for consolation," said Mrs. Penniman.

This was the account of the matter that she gave to her sister, and it was perhaps with the consciousness of genius that, on her return that evening to Washington Square, she again presented herself for admittance at Catherine's door. Catherine came and opened it; she was apparently very quiet.

"I only want to give you a little word of advice," she said. "If your father asks you, say that everything is going on."

Catherine stood there, with her hand on the knob, looking at her aunt, but not asking her to come in. "Do you think he will ask me?"

"I am sure he will. He asked me just now, on our way home from your Aunt Elizabeth's. I explained the whole thing to your Aunt Elizabeth. I said to your father I know nothing about it."

"Do you think he will ask me when he sees—when he sees—?" But here Catherine stopped.

"The more he sees the more disagreeable he will be," said her aunt.

"He shall see as little as possible!" Catherine declared.

"Tell him you are to be married."

"So I am," said Catherine softly; and she closed the door upon her aunt.

She could not have said this two days later—for instance, on Tuesday, when she at last received a letter from Morris Townsend. It was an epistle of considerable length, measuring five large square pages, and written at Philadelphia. It was an explanatory document, and it explained a great many things, chief among which were the considerations that had led the writer to take advantage of an urgent "professional" absence to try and banish from his mind the image of one whose path he had crossed only to scatter it with ruins. He ventured to expect but partial success in this attempt, but he could promise her that, whatever his failure, he would never again interpose between her generous heart and her brilliant prospects and filial duties. He closed with an intimation that his professional pursuits might compel him to travel for some months, and with the hope that when they should each have accommodated themselves to what was sternly involved in their respective positions—even should this result not be reached for years—they should meet as friends, as fellow-sufferers, as innocent but philosophic victims of a great social law. That her life should be peaceful and happy was the dearest wish of him who ventured still to subscribe himself her most obedient servant. The letter was beautifully written, and Catherine, who kept it for many years after this, was able, when her sense of the bitterness of its meaning and the hollowness of its tone had grown less acute, to admire its grace of expression. At present, for a long time after she received it, all she had to help her was the determination, daily more rigid, to make no appeal to the compassion of her father.

He suffered a week to elapse, and then one day, in the morning, at an hour at which she rarely saw him, he strolled into the back parlour. He had watched his time, and he found her alone. She was sitting with some work, and he came and stood in front of her. He was going out, he had on his hat and was drawing on his gloves.

"It doesn't seem to me that you are treating me just now with all the consideration I deserve," he said in a moment.

"I don't know what I have done," Catherine answered, with her eyes on her work.

"You have apparently quite banished from your mind the request I made you at Liverpool, before we sailed; the request that you would notify me in advance before leaving my house."

"I have not left your house!" said Catherine.

"But you intend to leave it, and by what you gave me to understand, your departure must be impending. In fact, though you are still here in body, you are already absent in spirit. Your mind has taken up its residence with your prospective husband, and you might quite as well be lodged under the conjugal roof, for all the benefit we get from your society."

"I will try and be more cheerful!" said Catherine.

"You certainly ought to be cheerful, you ask a great deal if you are not. To the pleasure of marrying a brilliant young man, you add that of having your own way; you strike me as a very lucky young lady!"

Catherine got up; she was suffocating. But she folded her work, deliberately and correctly, bending her burning face upon it. Her father stood where he had planted himself; she hoped he would go, but he smoothed and buttoned his gloves, and then he rested his hands upon his hips.

"It would be a convenience to me to know when I may expect to have an empty house," he went on. "When you go, your aunt marches."

She looked at him at last, with a long silent gaze, which, in spite of her pride and her resolution, uttered part of the appeal she had tried not to make. Her father's cold grey eye sounded her own, and he insisted on his point.

"Is it to-morrow? Is it next week, or the week after?"

"I shall not go away!" said Catherine.

The Doctor raised his eyebrows. "Has he backed out?"

"I have broken off my engagement."

"Broken it off?"

"I have asked him to leave New York, and he has gone away for a long time."

The Doctor was both puzzled and disappointed, but he solved his perplexity by saying to himself that his daughter simply misrepresented—justifiably, if one would, but nevertheless misrepresented—the facts; and he eased off his disappointment, which was that of a man losing a chance for a little triumph that he had rather counted on, by a few words that he uttered aloud.

"How does he take his dismissal?"

"I don't know!" said Catherine, less ingeniously than she had hitherto spoken.

"You mean you don't care? You are rather cruel, after encouraging him and playing with him for so long!"

The Doctor had his revenge, after all.

## XXXII

Our story has hitherto moved with very short steps, but as it approaches its termination it must take a long stride. As time went on, it might have appeared to the Doctor that his daughter's account of her rupture with Morris Townsend, mere bravado as he had deemed it, was in some degree justified by the sequel. Morris remained as rigidly and unremittingly absent as if he had died of a broken heart, and Catherine had apparently buried the memory of this fruitless episode as deep as if it had terminated by her own choice. We know that she had been deeply and incurably wounded, but the Doctor had no means of knowing it. He was certainly curious about it, and would have given a good deal to discover the exact truth; but it was his punishment that he never knew—his punishment, I mean, for the abuse of sarcasm in his relations with his daughter. There was a good deal of effective sarcasm in her keeping him in the dark, and the rest of the world conspired with her, in this sense, to be sarcastic. Mrs. Penniman told him nothing, partly because he never questioned her—he made too light of Mrs. Penniman for that—and partly because she flattered herself that a tormenting reserve, and a serene profession of ignorance, would avenge her for his theory that she had meddled in the matter. He went two or three times to see Mrs. Montgomery, but Mrs. Montgomery had nothing to impart. She simply knew that her brother's engagement was broken off, and now that Miss Sloper was out of danger she preferred not to bear witness in any way against Morris. She had done so before—however unwillingly—because she was sorry for Miss Sloper; but she was not sorry for Miss Sloper now—not at all sorry. Morris had told her nothing about his relations with Miss Sloper at the time, and he had told her nothing since. He was always away, and he very seldom wrote to her; she believed he had gone to California. Mrs. Almond had, in her sister's phrase, "taken up" Catherine violently since the recent catastrophe; but though the girl was very grateful to her for her kindness, she revealed no secrets, and the good lady could give the Doctor no satisfaction. Even, however, had she been able to narrate to him the private history of his daughter's unhappy love affair, it would have given her a certain comfort to leave him in ignorance; for Mrs. Almond was at this time not altogether in sympathy with her brother. She had guessed for herself that Catherine had been cruelly jilted—she knew nothing from Mrs. Penniman, for Mrs. Penniman had not ventured to lay the famous explanation of Morris's motives before Mrs. Almond, though she had thought it good enough for Catherine—and she pronounced her brother too consistently indifferent to what the poor creature must have suffered and must still be suffering. Dr. Sloper had his theory, and he rarely altered his theories. The marriage would have been an abominable one, and the girl had had a blessed escape. She was not to be pitied for that, and to pretend to condole with her would have been to make concessions to the idea that she had ever had a right to think of Morris.

"I put my foot on this idea from the first, and I keep it there now," said the Doctor. "I don't see anything cruel in that; one can't keep it there too long." To this Mrs. Almond more than once replied that if Catherine had got rid of her incongruous lover, she deserved the credit of it, and that to bring herself to her father's enlightened view of the matter must have cost her an effort that he was bound to appreciate.

"I am by no means sure she has got rid of him," the Doctor said. "There is not the smallest probability that, after having been as obstinate as a mule for two years, she suddenly became amenable to reason. It is infinitely more probable that he got rid of her."

"All the more reason you should be gentle with her."

"I *am* gentle with her. But I can't do the pathetic; I can't pump up tears, to look graceful, over the most fortunate thing that ever happened to her."

"You have no sympathy," said Mrs. Almond; "that was never your strong point. You have only to look at her to see that, right or wrong, and whether the rupture came from herself or from him, her poor little heart is grievously bruised."

"Handling bruises—and even dropping tears on them—doesn't make them any better! My business is to see she gets no more knocks, and that I shall carefully attend to. But I don't at all recognise your description of Catherine. She doesn't strike me in the least as a young woman going about in search of a moral poultice. In fact, she seems to me much better than while the fellow was hanging about. She is perfectly comfortable and blooming; she eats and sleeps, takes her usual exercise, and overloads herself, as usual, with finery. She is always knitting some purse or embroidering some handkerchief, and it seems to me she turns these articles out about as fast as ever. She hasn't much to say; but when had she anything to say? She had her little dance, and now she is sitting down to rest. I suspect that, on the whole, she enjoys it."

"She enjoys it as people enjoy getting rid of a leg that has been crushed. The state of mind after amputation is doubtless one of comparative repose."

"If your leg is a metaphor for young Townsend, I can assure you he has never been crushed. Crushed? Not he! He is alive and perfectly intact, and that's why I am not satisfied."

"Should you have liked to kill him?" asked Mrs. Almond.

"Yes, very much. I think it is quite possible that it is all a blind."

"A blind?"

"An arrangement between them. *Il fait le mort*, as they say in France; but he is looking out of the corner of his eye. You can depend upon it he has not burned his ships; he has kept one to come back in. When I am dead, he will set sail again, and then she will marry him."

"It is interesting to know that you accuse your only daughter of being the vilest of hypocrites," said Mrs. Almond.

"I don't see what difference her being my only daughter makes. It is better to accuse one than a dozen. But I don't accuse any one. There is not the smallest hypocrisy about Catherine, and I deny that she even pretends to be miserable."

The Doctor's idea that the thing was a "blind" had its intermissions and revivals; but it may be said on the whole to have increased as he grew older; together with his impression of Catherine's blooming and comfortable condition. Naturally, if he had not found grounds for viewing her as a lovelorn maiden during the year or two that followed her great trouble, he found none at a time when she had completely recovered her self-possession. He was obliged to recognise the fact that if the two young people were waiting for him to get out of the way, they were at least waiting very patiently. He had heard from time to time that Morris was in New York; but he never remained there long, and, to the best of the Doctor's belief, had no communication with Catherine. He was sure they never met, and he had reason to suspect that Morris never wrote to her. After the letter that has been mentioned, she heard from him twice again, at considerable intervals; but on none of these occasions did she write herself. On the other hand, as the Doctor observed, she averted herself rigidly from the idea of marrying other people. Her opportunities for doing so were not numerous, but they occurred often enough to test her disposition. She refused a widower, a man with a genial temperament, a handsome fortune, and three little girls (he had heard that she was very fond of children, and he pointed to his own with some confidence); and she turned a deaf ear to the solicitations of a clever young lawyer, who, with the prospect of a great practice, and the reputation of a most agreeable man, had had the shrewdness, when he came to look about him for a wife, to believe that she would suit him better than several younger and prettier girls. Mr. Macalister, the widower, had desired to make a marriage of reason, and had chosen Catherine for what he supposed to be her latent matronly qualities; but John Ludlow, who was a year the girl's junior, and spoken of always as a young man who might have his "pick," was seriously in love with her. Catherine, however, would never look at him; she made it plain to him that she thought he came to see her too often. He afterwards consoled himself, and married a very different person, little Miss Sturtevant, whose attractions were obvious to the dullest comprehension. Catherine, at the time of these events, had left her thirtieth year well behind her, and had quite taken her place as an old maid. Her father would have preferred she should marry, and he once told her that he hoped she would not be too fastidious. "I should like to see you an honest man's wife before I die," he said. This was after John Ludlow had been compelled to give it up, though the Doctor had advised him to persevere. The Doctor exercised no further pressure, and had the credit of not "worrying" at all over his daughter's singleness. In fact he worried rather more than appeared, and there were considerable periods during which he felt sure that Morris Townsend was hidden behind some door. "If he is not, why doesn't she marry?" he asked himself. "Limited as her intelligence may be, she must understand perfectly well that she is made to do the usual thing." Catherine, however, became an admirable old maid. She formed habits, regulated her days upon a system of her own, interested herself in charitable institutions, asylums, hospitals, and aid societies; and went generally, with an even and noiseless step, about the rigid business of her life. This life had, however, a secret history as well as a public one—if I may talk of the public history of a mature and diffident spinster for whom publicity had always a combination of terrors. From her own point of view the great facts of her career were that Morris Townsend had trifled with her affection, and that her father had broken its spring. Nothing could ever alter these facts; they were always there, like her name, her age, her plain face. Nothing could ever undo the wrong or cure the pain that Morris had inflicted on her, and nothing could ever make her feel towards her father as she felt in her younger years. There was something dead in her life, and her duty was to try and fill the void. Catherine recognised this duty to the utmost; she had a great disapproval of brooding and moping. She had, of course, no faculty for quenching memory in dissipation; but she mingled freely in the usual gaieties of the town, and she became at last an inevitable figure at all respectable entertainments. She was greatly liked, and as time went on she grew to be a sort of kindly maiden aunt to the younger portion of society. Young girls were apt to confide to her their love affairs (which they never did to Mrs. Penniman), and young men to be fond of her without knowing why. She developed a few harmless eccentricities; her habits, once formed, were rather stiffly maintained; her opinions, on all moral and social matters, were extremely conservative; and before she was forty she was regarded as an old-fashioned person, and an authority on customs that had passed away. Mrs. Penniman, in comparison, was quite a girlish figure; she grew younger as she advanced in life. She lost none of her relish for beauty and mystery, but she had little opportunity to exercise it. With Catherine's later wooers she failed to establish relations as intimate as those which had given her so many interesting hours in the society of Morris Townsend. These gentlemen had an indefinable mistrust of her good offices, and they never talked to her about Catherine's charms. Her ringlets, her buckles and bangles, glistened more brightly with each succeeding year, and she remained quite the same officious and imaginative Mrs. Penniman, and the odd mixture of impetuosity and circumspection, that we have hitherto known. As regards one point, however, her circumspection prevailed, and she must be given due credit for it. For upwards of seventeen years she never mentioned Morris Townsend's name to her niece. Catherine was grateful to her, but this consistent silence, so little in accord with her aunt's character, gave her a certain alarm, and she could never wholly rid herself of a suspicion that Mrs. Penniman sometimes had news of him.

## XXXIII

Little by little Dr. Sloper had retired from his profession; he visited only those patients in whose symptoms he recognised a certain originality. He went again to Europe, and remained two years; Catherine went with him, and on this occasion Mrs. Penniman was of the party. Europe apparently had few surprises for Mrs. Penniman, who frequently remarked, in the most romantic sites—"You know I am very familiar with all this." It should be added that such remarks were usually not addressed to her brother, or yet to her niece, but to fellow-tourists who happened to be at hand, or even to the cicerone or the goat-herd in the foreground.

One day, after his return from Europe, the Doctor said something to his daughter that made her start—it seemed to come from so far out of the past.

"I should like you to promise me something before I die."

"Why do you talk about your dying?" she asked.

"Because I am sixty-eight years old."

"I hope you will live a long time," said Catherine.

"I hope I shall! But some day I shall take a bad cold, and then it will not matter much what any one hopes. That will be the manner of my exit, and when it takes place, remember I told you so. Promise me not to marry Morris Townsend after I am gone."

This was what made Catherine start, as I have said; but her start was a silent one, and for some moments she said nothing. "Why do you speak of him?" she asked at last.

"You challenge everything I say. I speak of him because he's a topic, like any other. He's to be seen, like any one else, and he is still looking for a wife—having had one and got rid of her, I don't know by what means. He has lately been in New York, and at your cousin Marian's house; your Aunt Elizabeth saw him there."

"They neither of them told me," said Catherine.

"That's their merit; it's not yours. He has grown fat and bald, and he has not made his fortune. But I can't trust those facts alone to steel your heart against him, and that's why I ask you to promise."

"Fat and bald": these words presented a strange image to Catherine's mind, out of which the memory of the most beautiful young man in the world had never faded. "I don't think you understand," she said. "I very seldom think of Mr. Townsend."

"It will be very easy for you to go on, then. Promise me, after my death, to do the same."

Again, for some moments, Catherine was silent; her father's request deeply amazed her; it opened an old wound and made it ache afresh. "I don't think I can promise that," she answered.

"It would be a great satisfaction," said her father.

"You don't understand. I can't promise that."

The Doctor was silent a minute. "I ask you for a particular reason. I am altering my will."

This reason failed to strike Catherine; and indeed she scarcely understood it. All her feelings were merged in the sense that he was trying to treat her as he had treated her years before. She had suffered from it then; and now all her experience, all her acquired tranquillity and rigidity, protested. She had been so humble in her youth that she could now afford to have a little pride, and there was something in this request, and in her father's thinking himself so free to make it, that seemed an injury to her dignity. Poor Catherine's dignity was not aggressive; it never sat in state; but if you pushed far enough you could find it. Her father had pushed very far.

"I can't promise," she simply repeated.

"You are very obstinate," said the Doctor.

"I don't think you understand."

"Please explain, then."

"I can't explain," said Catherine. "And I can't promise."

"Upon my word," her father exclaimed, "I had no idea how obstinate you are!"

She knew herself that she was obstinate, and it gave her a certain joy. She was now a middle-aged woman.

About a year after this, the accident that the Doctor had spoken of occurred; he took a violent cold. Driving out to Bloomingdale one April day to see a patient of unsound mind, who was confined in a private asylum for the insane, and whose family greatly desired a medical opinion from an eminent source, he was caught in a spring shower, and being in a buggy, without a hood, he found himself soaked to the skin. He came home with an ominous chill, and on the morrow he was seriously ill. "It is congestion of the lungs," he said to Catherine; "I shall need very good nursing. It will make no difference, for I shall not recover; but I wish everything to be done, to the smallest detail, as if I should. I hate an ill-conducted sick-room; and you will be so good as to nurse me on the hypothesis that I shall get well." He told her which of his fellow-physicians to send for, and gave her a multitude of minute directions; it was quite on the optimistic hypothesis that she nursed him. But he had never been wrong in his life, and he was not wrong now. He was touching his seventieth year, and though he had a very well-tempered constitution, his hold upon life had lost its firmness. He died after three weeks' illness, during which Mrs. Penniman, as well as his daughter, had been assiduous at his bedside.

On his will being opened after a decent interval, it was found to consist of two portions. The first of these dated from ten years back, and consisted of a series of dispositions by which he left the great mass of property to his daughter, with becoming legacies to his two sisters. The second was a codicil, of recent origin, maintaining the annuities to Mrs. Penniman and Mrs. Almond, but reducing Catherine's share to a fifth of what he had first bequeathed her. "She is amply provided for from her mother's side," the document ran, "never having spent more than a fraction of her income from this source; so that her fortune is already more than sufficient to attract those unscrupulous adventurers whom she has given me reason to believe that she persists in regarding as an interesting class." The large remainder of his property, therefore, Dr. Sloper had divided into seven unequal parts, which he left, as endowments, to as many different hospitals and schools of medicine, in various cities of the Union.

To Mrs. Penniman it seemed monstrous that a man should play such tricks with other people's money; for after his death, of course, as she said, it was other people's. "Of course, you will dispute the will," she remarked, fatuously, to Catherine.

"Oh no," Catherine answered, "I like it very much. Only I wish it had been expressed a little differently!"

## XXXIV

IT was her habit to remain in town very late in the summer; she preferred the house in Washington Square to any other habitation whatever, and it was under protest that she used to go to the seaside for the month of August. At the sea she spent her month at an hotel. The year that her father died she intermitted this custom altogether, not thinking it consistent with deep mourning; and the year after that she put off her departure till so late that the middle of August found her still in the heated solitude of Washington Square. Mrs. Penniman, who was fond of a change, was usually eager for a visit to the country; but this year she appeared quite content with such rural impressions as she could gather, at the parlour window, from the ailantus-trees behind the wooden paling. The peculiar fragrance of this vegetation used to diffuse itself in the evening air, and Mrs. Penniman, on the warm nights of July, often sat at the open window and inhaled it. This was a happy moment for Mrs. Penniman; after the death of her brother she felt more free to obey her impulses. A vague oppression had disappeared from her life, and she enjoyed a sense of freedom of which she had not been conscious since the memorable time, so long ago, when the Doctor went abroad with Catherine and left her at home to entertain Morris Townsend. The year that had elapsed since her brother's death reminded her of that happy time, because, although Catherine, in growing older, had become a person to be reckoned with, yet her society was a very different thing, as Mrs. Penniman said, from that of a tank of cold water. The elder lady hardly knew what use to make of this larger margin of her life; she sat and looked at it very much as she had often sat, with her poised needle in her hand, before her tapestry frame. She had a confident hope, however, that her rich impulses, her talent for embroidery, would still find their application, and this confidence was justified before many months had elapsed.

Catherine continued to live in her father's house in spite of its being represented to her that a maiden lady of quiet habits might find a more convenient abode in one of the smaller dwellings, with brown stone fronts, which had at this time begun to adorn the transverse thoroughfares in the upper part of the town. She liked the earlier structure—it had begun by this time to be called an "old" house—and proposed to herself to end her days in it. If it was too large for a pair of unpretending gentlewomen, this was better than the opposite fault; for Catherine had no desire to find herself in closer quarters with her aunt. She expected to spend the rest of her life in Washington Square, and to enjoy Mrs. Penniman's society for the whole of this period; as she had a conviction that, long as she might live, her aunt would live at least as long, and always retain her brilliancy and activity. Mrs. Penniman suggested to her the idea of a rich vitality.

On one of those warm evenings in July of which mention has been made, the two ladies sat together at an open window, looking out on the quiet Square. It was too hot for lighted lamps, for reading, or for work; it might have appeared too hot even for conversation, Mrs. Penniman having long been speechless. She sat forward in the window, half on the balcony, humming a little song. Catherine was within the room, in a low rocking-chair, dressed in white, and slowly using a large palmetto fan. It was in this way, at this season, that the aunt and niece, after they had had tea, habitually spent their evenings.

"Catherine," said Mrs. Penniman at last, "I am going to say something that will surprise you."

"Pray do," Catherine answered; "I like surprises. And it is so quiet now."

"Well, then, I have seen Morris Townsend."

If Catherine was surprised, she checked the expression of it; she gave neither a start nor an exclamation. She remained, indeed, for some moments intensely still, and this may very well have been a symptom of emotion. "I hope he was well," she said at last.

"I don't know; he is a great deal changed. He would like very much to see you."

"I would rather not see him," said Catherine quickly.

"I was afraid you would say that. But you don't seem surprised!"

"I am—very much."

"I met him at Marian's," said Mrs. Penniman. "He goes to Marian's, and they are so afraid you will meet him there. It's my belief that that's why he goes. He wants so much to see you." Catherine made no response to this, and Mrs. Penniman went on. "I didn't know him at first; he is so remarkably changed. But he knew me in a minute. He says I am not in the least changed. You know how polite he always was. He was coming away when I came, and we walked a little distance together. He is still very handsome, only, of course, he looks older, and he is not so—so animated as he used to be. There was a touch of sadness about him; but there was a touch of sadness about him before—especially when he went away. I am afraid he has not been very successful—that he has never got thoroughly established. I don't suppose he is sufficiently plodding, and that, after all, is what succeeds in this world." Mrs. Penniman had not mentioned Morris Townsend's name to her niece for upwards of the fifth of a century; but now that she had broken the spell, she seemed to wish to make up for lost time, as if there had been a sort of exhilaration in hearing herself talk of him. She proceeded, however, with considerable caution, pausing occasionally to let Catherine give some sign. Catherine gave no other sign than to stop the rocking of her chair and the swaying of her fan; she sat motionless and silent. "It was on Tuesday last," said Mrs. Penniman, "and I have been hesitating ever since about telling you. I didn't know how you might like it. At last I thought that it was so long ago that you would probably not have any particular feeling. I saw him again, after meeting him at Marian's. I met him in the street, and he went a few steps with me. The first thing he said was about you; he asked ever so many questions. Marian didn't want me to speak to you; she didn't want you to know that they receive him. I told him I was sure that after all these years you couldn't have any feeling about that; you couldn't grudge him the hospitality of his own cousin's house. I said you would be bitter indeed if you did that. Marian has the most extraordinary ideas about what happened between you; she seems to think he behaved in some very unusual manner. I took the liberty of reminding her of the real facts, and placing the story in its true light. *He* has no bitterness, Catherine, I can assure you; and he might be excused for it, for things have not gone well with him. He has been all over the world, and tried to establish himself everywhere; but his evil star was against him. It is most interesting to hear him talk of his evil star. Everything failed; everything but his—you know, you remember—his proud, high spirit. I believe he married some lady somewhere in Europe. You know they marry in such a peculiar matter-of-course way in Europe; a marriage of reason they call it. She died soon afterwards; as he said to me, she only flitted across his life. He has not been in New York for ten years; he came back a few days ago. The first thing he did was to ask me about you. He had heard you had never married; he seemed very much interested about that. He said you had been the real romance of his life."

Catherine had suffered her companion to proceed from point to point, and pause to pause, without interrupting her; she fixed her eyes on the ground and listened. But the last phrase I have quoted was followed by a pause of peculiar significance, and then, at last, Catherine spoke. It will be observed that before doing so she had received a good deal of information about Morris Townsend. "Please say no more; please don't follow up that subject."

"Doesn't it interest you?" asked Mrs. Penniman, with a certain timorous archness.

"It pains me," said Catherine.

"I was afraid you would say that. But don't you think you could get used to it? He wants so much to see you."

"Please don't, Aunt Lavinia," said Catherine, getting up from her seat. She moved quickly away, and went to the other window, which stood open to the balcony; and here, in the embrasure, concealed from her aunt by the white curtains, she remained a long time, looking out into the warm darkness. She had had a great shock; it was as if the gulf of the past had suddenly opened, and a spectral figure had risen out of it. There were some things she believed she had got over, some feelings that she had thought of as dead; but apparently there was a certain vitality in them still. Mrs. Penniman had made them stir themselves. It was but a momentary agitation, Catherine said to herself; it would presently pass away. She was trembling, and her heart was beating so that she could feel it; but this also would subside. Then, suddenly, while she waited for a return of her calmness, she burst into tears. But her tears flowed very silently, so that Mrs. Penniman had no observation of them. It was perhaps, however, because Mrs. Penniman suspected them that she said no more that evening about Morris Townsend.

## XXXV

HER refreshed attention to this gentleman had not those limits of which Catherine desired, for herself, to be conscious; it lasted long enough to enable her to wait another week before speaking of him again. It was under the same circumstances that she once more attacked the subject. She had been sitting with her niece in the evening; only on this occasion, as the night was not so warm, the lamp had been lighted, and Catherine had placed herself near it with a morsel of fancy-work. Mrs. Penniman went and sat alone for half an hour on the balcony; then she came in, moving vaguely about the room. At last she sank into a seat near Catherine, with clasped hands, and a little look of excitement.

"Shall you be angry if I speak to you again about *him?*" she asked.

Catherine looked up at her quietly. "Who is *he?*"

"He whom you once loved."

"I shall not be angry, but I shall not like it."

"He sent you a message," said Mrs. Penniman. "I promised him to deliver it, and I must keep my promise."

In all these years Catherine had had time to forget how little she had to thank her aunt for in the season of her misery; she had long ago forgiven Mrs. Penniman for taking too much upon herself. But for a moment this attitude of interposition and disinterestedness, this carrying of messages and redeeming of promises, brought back the sense that her companion was a dangerous woman. She had said she would not be angry; but for an instant she felt sore. "I don't care what you do with your promise!" she answered.

Mrs. Penniman, however, with her high conception of the sanctity of pledges, carried her point. "I have gone too far to retreat," she said, though precisely what this meant she was not at pains to explain. "Mr. Townsend wishes most particularly to see you, Catherine; he believes that if you knew how much, and why, he wishes it, you would consent to do so."

"There can be no reason," said Catherine; "no good reason."

"His happiness depends upon it. Is not that a good reason?" asked Mrs. Penniman impressively.

"Not for me. My happiness does not."

"I think you will be happier after you have seen him. He is going away again—going to resume his wanderings. It is a very lonely, restless, joyless life. Before he goes he wishes to speak to you; it is a fixed idea with him—he is always thinking of it. He has something very important to say to you. He believes that you never understood him—that you never judged him rightly, and the belief has always weighed upon him terribly. He wishes to justify himself; he believes that in a very few words he could do so. He wishes to meet you as a friend."

Catherine listened to this wonderful speech without pausing in her work; she had now had several days to accustom herself to think of Morris Townsend again as an actuality. When it was over she said simply, "Please say to Mr. Townsend that I wish he would leave me alone."

She had hardly spoken when a sharp, firm ring at the door vibrated through the summer night. Catherine looked up at the clock; it marked a quarter-past nine—a very late hour for visitors, especially in the empty condition of the town. Mrs. Penniman at the same moment gave a little start, and then Catherine's eyes turned quickly to her aunt. They met Mrs. Penniman's and sounded them for a moment, sharply. Mrs. Penniman was blushing; her look was a conscious one; it seemed to confess something. Catherine guessed its meaning, and rose quickly from her chair.

"Aunt Penniman," she said, in a tone that scared her companion, "have you taken the *liberty* . . . ?"

"My dearest Catherine," stammered Mrs. Penniman, "just wait till you see him!"

Catherine had frightened her aunt, but she was also frightened herself; she was on the point of rushing to give orders to the servant, who was passing to the door, to admit no one; but the fear of meeting her visitor checked her.

"Mr. Morris Townsend."

This was what she heard, vaguely but recognisably articulated by the domestic, while she hesitated. She had her back turned to the door of the parlour, and for some moments she kept it turned, feeling that he had come in. He had not spoken, however, and at last she faced about. Then she saw a gentleman standing in the middle of the room, from which her aunt had discreetly retired.

She would never have known him. He was forty-five years old, and his figure was not that of the straight, slim young man she remembered. But it was a very fine person, and a fair and lustrous beard, spreading itself upon a well-presented chest, contributed to its effect. After a moment Catherine recognised the upper half of the face, which, though her visitor's clustering locks had grown thin, was still remarkably handsome. He stood in a deeply deferential attitude, with his eyes on her face. "I have ventured—I have ventured," he said; and then he paused, looking about him, as if he expected her to ask him to sit down. It was the old voice, but it had not the old charm. Catherine, for a minute, was conscious of a distinct determination not to invite him to take a seat. Why had he come? It was wrong of him to come. Morris was embarrassed, but Catherine gave him no help. It was not that she was glad of his embarrassment; on the contrary, it excited all her own liabilities of this kind, and gave her great pain. But how could she welcome him when she felt so vividly that he ought not to have come? "I wanted so much—I was determined," Morris went on. But he stopped again; it was not easy. Catherine still said nothing, and he may well have recalled with apprehension her ancient faculty of silence. She continued to look at him, however, and as she did so she made the strangest observation. It seemed to be he, and yet not he; it was the man who had been everything, and yet this person was nothing. How long ago it was—how old she had grown—how much she had lived! She had lived on something that was connected with *him,* and she had consumed it in doing so. This person did not look unhappy. He was fair and well-preserved, perfectly dressed, mature and complete. As Catherine looked at him, the story of his life defined itself in his eyes; he had made himself comfortable, and he had never been caught. But even while her perception opened itself to this, she had no desire to catch him; his presence was painful to her, and she only wished he would go.

"Will you not sit down?" he asked.

"I think we had better not," said Catherine.

"I offend you by coming?" He was very grave; he spoke in a tone of the richest respect.

"I don't think you ought to have come."

"Did not Mrs. Penniman tell you—did she not give you my message?"

"She told me something, but I did not understand."

"I wish you would let *me* tell you—let me speak for myself."

"I don't think it is necessary," said Catherine.

"Not for you, perhaps, but for me. It would be a great satisfaction—and I have not many." He seemed to be coming nearer; Catherine turned away. "Can we not be friends again?" he said.

"We are not enemies," said Catherine. "I have none but friendly feelings to you."

"Ah, I wonder whether you know the happiness it gives me to hear you say that!" Catherine uttered no intimation that she measured the influence of her words; and he presently went on, "You have not changed—the years have passed happily for you."

"They have passed very quietly," said Catherine.

"They have left no marks; you are admirably young." This time he succeeded in coming nearer—he was close to her; she saw his glossy perfumed beard, and his eyes above it looking strange and hard. It was very different from his old—from his young—face. If she had first seen him this way she would not have liked him. It seemed to her that he was smiling, or trying to smile. "Catherine," he said, lowering his voice, "I have never ceased to think of you."

"Please don't say those things," she answered.

"Do you hate me?"

"Oh no," said Catherine.

Something in her tone discouraged him, but in a moment he recovered himself. "Have you still some kindness for me, then?"

"I don't know why you have come here to ask me such things!" Catherine exclaimed.

"Because for many years it has been the desire of my life that we should be friends again."

"That is impossible."

"Why so? Not if you will allow it."

"I will not allow it!" said Catherine.

He looked at her again in silence. "I see; my presence troubles you and pains you. I will go away; but you must give me leave to come again."

"Please don't come again," she said.

"Never?—never?"

She made a great effort; she wished to say something that would make it impossible he should ever again cross her threshold. "It is wrong of you. There is no propriety in it—no reason for it."

"Ah, dearest lady, you do me injustice!" cried Morris Townsend. "We have only waited, and now we are free."

"You treated me badly," said Catherine.

"Not if you think of it rightly. You had your quiet life with your father—which was just what I could not make up my mind to rob you of."

"Yes; I had that."

Morris felt it to be a considerable damage to his cause that he could not add that she had had something more besides; for it is needless to say that he had learnt the contents of Dr. Sloper's will. He was nevertheless not at a loss. "There are worse fates than that!" he exclaimed, with expression; and he might have been supposed to refer to his own unprotected situation. Then he added, with a deeper tenderness, "Catherine, have you never forgiven me?"

"I forgave you years ago, but it is useless for us to attempt to be friends."

"Not if we forget the past. We have still a future, thank God!"

"I can't forget—I don't forget," said Catherine. "You treated me too badly. I felt it very much; I felt it for years." And then she went on, with her wish to show him that he must not come to her this way, "I can't begin again—I can't take it up. Everything is dead and buried. It was too serious; it made a great change in my life. I never expected to see you here."

"Ah, you are angry!" cried Morris, who wished immensely that he could extort some flash of passion from her mildness. In that case he might hope.

"No, I am not angry. Anger does not last, that way, for years. But there are other things. Impressions last, when they have been strong. But I can't talk."

Morris stood stroking his beard, with a clouded eye. "Why have you never married?" he asked abruptly. "You have had opportunities."

"I didn't wish to marry."

"Yes, you are rich, you are free; you had nothing to gain."

"I had nothing to gain," said Catherine.

Morris looked vaguely round him, and gave a deep sigh. "Well, I was in hopes that we might still have been friends."

"I meant to tell you, by my aunt, in answer to your message–if you had waited for an answer–that it was unnecessary for you to come in that hope."

"Good-bye, then," said Morris. "Excuse my indiscretion."

He bowed, and she turned away–standing there, averted, with her eyes on the ground, for some moments after she had heard him close the door of the room.

In the hall he found Mrs. Penniman, fluttered and eager; she appeared to have been hovering there under the irreconcilable promptings of her curiosity and her dignity.

"That was a precious plan of yours!" said Morris, clapping on his hat.

"Is she so hard?" asked Mrs. Penniman.

"She doesn't care a button for me–with her confounded little dry manner."

"Was it very dry?" pursued Mrs. Penniman, with solicitude.

Morris took no notice of her question; he stood musing an instant, with his hat on. "But why the deuce, then, would she never marry?"

"Yes–why indeed?" sighed Mrs. Penniman. And then, as if from a sense of the inadequacy of this explanation, "But you will not despair –you will come back?"

"Come back? Damnation!" And Morris Townsend strode out of the house, leaving Mrs. Penniman staring.

Catherine, meanwhile, in the parlour, picking up her morsel of fancy work, had seated herself with it again–for life, as it were.

# APHORISMS

## III

DR. JOHNSON:

No man is a hypocrite in his pleasures.

SOLITUDE is dangerous to reason without being favorable to virtue.

SIR, all the arguments which are brought to represent poverty as no evil show it to be evidently a great evil. You never find people labouring to convince you that you may live very happily upon a plentiful fortune.

NOTHING is more hopeless than a scheme of merriment.

SIR, claret is the liquor for boys; port for men; but he who aspires to be a hero must drink brandy.

MRS. MONTAGU has dropt me. Now, Sir, there are people whom one should like very well to drop, but would not wish to be dropt by.

HAZLITT:

MAN is a *make-believe* animal—he is never so truly himself as when he is acting a part.

FASHION is gentility running away from vulgarity and afraid of being overtaken.

HE who is not in some measure a pedant, though he may be a wise, cannot be a very happy man.

BARBARISM and rusticity may perhaps be instructed, but false refinement is incorrigible.

WE grow tired of everything but turning others into ridicule, and congratulating ourselves on their defects.

NEVER trust a man who speaks well of everybody.

CHURTON COLLINS

NOWHERE probably is there more true feeling, and nowhere worse taste, than in a churchyard.

BENJAMIN JOWETT

THE nearest than any honest man can come to the thing called impartiality is to confess that he is partial.

CHESTERTON

IN 1799 General Tamax received a proposal from Napoleon, who wished to enter the Russian service, but they were unable to agree, as Napoleon demanded the rank of Major.

TOLSTOY

## SAINTE-BEUVE

# *Madame Récamier*

In the month of May last there vanished a figure unique among the women who have reigned by their beauty and by their grace; a salon was closed which for a long time had united, under a charming influence, the most illustrious and the most diverse personages, and in which even the most obscure had had at one time or another their chance of appearing. The first in renown in this group of memorable names were stricken by death almost at the same time with her who had been their principal attraction and bond. A few only survive, dispersed to-day and unconsoled; and those who have done no more than pass through this elect society have the right, and almost the duty, to talk about it, as of a thing which is henceforth of interest to all and which has become a portion of history.

The salon of Madame Récamier was much else besides, but it was also, especially in the last years, a center and home of letters. This type of social organ, which has been so active in France and which has exercised so real a dominion (this very salon of Madame Récamier is proof of it), does not go back farther than the seventeenth century. It is in the celebrated Hôtel de Rambouillet that we are agreed to place the establishment of polite society, of the society where people gathered together for the purpose of talking among themselves of beautiful things and particularly of the things of the mind. But the solemnity of this Rambouillet circle accords little with the idea which I should now like to evoke, and I shall do better to seek in places more modest and more reserved the true antecedents of the type of salon whose last representative we have just seen disappear. Toward the middle of the seventeenth century, at the end of the Faubourg St.-Jacques, just outside the Port Royal monastery, a lady went into retirement who had been famous for her intellectual talents and for the long splendor of her triumphs—the Marquise de Sablé. In this semi-retreat, with its window opening on the convent and its door still ajar toward the world, this old friend of M. de La Rochefoucauld, still active in mind, still taking an interest in everything, continued to gather about her, until the year 1678, when she died, the most distinguished and the most varied persons,—old friends who had remained faithful and who came a long way to see her, from the city or the court; recluses, in a not too strict sense of the word, who, like herself, had been of the great world, and whose mind retirement had served only to sharpen and adorn; recluses by profession, whom, now and again, by her gracious importunity, she wrested from their vow of silence. These recluses, when they happened to be Arnauld or Nicole, could hardly, indeed, have been without worldly charm, and Pascal, once or twice, must have been of their number. This little salon of Madame de Sablé, so hidden, so much visited, and which, under the shadow the cloister yet not too much feeling its influence, combined something of the advantages of both worlds, appears to me to be the earliest model of the salon which we have seen in our own day at the Abbaye-aux-Bois. It is only of this last that I have here to speak.

M. de Châteaubriand reigned there, and when he was present everything began or ended in him; but he was not always there, and even when he was, there were places and appropriate attentions and *asides* for each. Everything was talked of, but in confidence, as it were, and in tones a little more subdued than elsewhere. Everybody, or at least a great many, frequented this salon, and yet there was about it nothing of the commonplace; you breathed there, from the moment you entered, an air of discretion and of mystery. Graciousness, but a graciousness at once sincere and discriminating, something personal—I know not what—put you immediately at your ease, and tempered the first effect of initiation into what had ever so little the character of a sanctuary. Distinction was there, and familiarity, or at least naturalness, a great ease in the choice of subjects (of much importance to the play of conversation), a prompt way of entering into what you were saying, which was not merely politeness and good-will, but which testified to a more genuine interest. From the first the eye was met with a smile which said clearly, "I understand," and which irradiated everything with a gentle light. You did not go away, even for the first time, without having been touched in some private region of mind and heart, and you felt flattered and above all grateful. There were many distinguished salons in the eighteenth century, those of Madame Geoffrin, of Madame d'Houdetot, of Madame Suard. Madame Récamier knew them all and could describe them very well; anyone who wished to write of them with taste would have done well first to talk them over with her. But none of them could have resembled her own.

That was because she herself resembled no one. M. de Châteaubriand was the pride of her salon, but she was its soul, and it is she whom we must try to show to those who never knew her; for to recall her to those who have known her is superfluous, to paint her for them impossible. I shall take care here not to attempt her biography; biography women should never have—wretched word fit only for men and unpleasantly reminiscent of study and research. Even when they have nothing of moment to conceal, women cannot but lose charm in the text of an extended narration. Can, indeed, the life of a woman be told? It is felt—it passes—it appears. I should wish even to set down no date whatever, for dates in such a subject are scarcely in taste. However, since there is no help, let us note merely that Jeanne-Françoise-Julie-Adélaïde Bernard was born at Lyons, the birthplace of Louise Labé, December 3, 1777. Of all the baptismal names that I have just enumerated, the only one by which she was ordinarily known was Julie, altered to Juliette—although there was never to be a Romeo. She was married at Paris in her sixteenth year (April 24, 1793) to Jacques-Rose Récamier, a banker, already rich or soon to become so. At the beginning of the Consulate, we find her shining in society, fêted, applauded, the youngest queen of the world of elegance, giving the tone to fashion, with art creating simple things fit only for beings of the highest beauty. We who were not there can speak only with an extreme reserve of this epoch, mythological, as it were, of Madame Récamier, in which, from afar, she seems a goddess upon the clouds; we cannot speak of it as would be fitting—not indeed that there is anything to conceal, but because such beauty, youthful and tender, was possessed of subtle graces that cannot be described, at least not by one who has not seen them for himself. Who that had seen only the sunset would think to paint the dawn? Nevertheless, since one cannot well understand the character and the gracious genius of Madame Récamier, that ambition of the heart which in her showed so much strength and persistence underneath the delicacy; since one cannot well grasp her spirit and her total personality in the absence of a very definite notion as to what inspired her during this period—not so different, in fact, from what inspired her to the end—I shall touch rapidly some of the authentic elements in the legend which for her, as for all beings that wield enchantment, already hides the truth. When we wish to judge Madame de Sévigné or Madame de Maintenon, and interpret to ourselves their natures, we must of necessity have a general idea and a *theory* regarding them. To understand well, for example, what Madame de Maintenon was in relation to Louis XIV, or Madame de Sévigné in relation to her daughter, and what kind of sentiment or passion they brought to their object, one must first have asked oneself several questions concerning the youth of these two women, or more simply one must have asked oneself one question, always the first and almost the only one that needs to be asked in speaking of a woman: Was she ever in love? and in what manner did she love?

I shall then ask the question, or rather, in the case of Madame Récamier, the question arises of itself; and for her as for Madame de Maintenon, and for Madame de Sévigné (Madame de Sévigné not yet a mother), I answer boldly, *No.* No, she never loved, never loved with passion and with fire; but the immense need of loving which is felt by every tender soul was changed with her into an infinite need of pleasing, or, better, of being loved, and into an active determination and a fervent desire to pay in kindness for all that she received. We who have seen her in her last years, and upon whom as we passed have fallen the rays of this divine goodness, well do we know whether she was able to pay that debt, and whether indeed friendship did not find out in her that flame which love had never found.

Two epochs, very distinct, are to be noted in the life of Madame Récamier: her time of youth, of triumph and of beauty, the long bright morning that lasted till the sunset; and afterward the evening when the sun had gone—her old age I can never name it. In these two epochs, so diversely colored, she was at bottom the same, but she no doubt appeared to be very different. She was the same in two essential particulars, which alone explain her nature: the one that in her youth, when her life was gayest, she remained ever pure; the other that, withdrawn to a quiet privacy and collected within herself, she still kept her desire of conquest and her gentle skill in winning hearts—yes, let us not shun the word, her coquetry. But (may the orthodox doctors forgive me the expression) it was a coquetry of the angels.

There are natures which are born pure and which have received, whether they willed it or no, the gift of innocence. Like Arethusa, they traverse the bitter sea; they resist the flames like those children of Scripture whom their good angel saved, and whom in the very midst of the furnace he refreshed with fragrant dew. Madame Récamier, in her youth, had need of this angel beside her and within her, for the world that she passed through and in which she dwelt was a motley world, and ardent, and she was at no pains not to tempt it. If I am to be truthful, I must a little lower the tone, descend a moment from the ideal plane of Laura and of Beatrice where it has been our wont to place her, and speak of her, in fine, more familiarly and in prose. I trust that when all is said she will have lost nothing.

When, radiant, she first appears under the Consulate, we see her forthwith surrounded, admired, and passionately loved. Lucien, the brother of the Consul, is the first historical personage who loves her (for I do not take account of Barère, who had known her formerly as a child). Lucien loves, he is not repelled, he will never be accepted. Just there is the nice distinction. It will be the same with all those who now press about her, as with all who shall succeed them. I saw not long since in the palace of the late king of Holland, at The Hague, a very beautiful statute of Eve. Eve, in her first flower of youth, stands opposite the serpent, who points out to her the apple; she gazes at it, she turns half round toward Adam, she makes as if to consult him. Eve is at that extreme moment of innocence when one plays with danger, when in secret one talks about it with oneself or with another. Now this indefinable moment, which in the case of Eve did not last, and which ended so badly, began often anew and was prolonged in a thousand recurrences during the brilliant and sometimes thoughtless youth of which we speak; but always it was restrained in time and overcome by a more powerful sentiment, by I know not what secret virtue. This young woman, confronted with the passions which she excited and of whose existence she was unaware, exhibited the imprudences, confidences, curiosities, almost of a child or of a schoolgirl. She went into danger with a smile on her face, in careless security, with love and charity, somewhat at those very Christian kings of old were wont on a day in holy week to go to certain of the sick that they might make them whole. She had no doubt of her high prerogative, of her gentle magic, of her power. She first insisted, almost, on wounding your heart, in order that the pleasure and the miracle of healing it might later be hers. If you fell to murmuring or grew impatient, she would say to you, with hopeless clemency, "Come and I will cure you." And with some, with most, she succeeded. All of her friends—with but very few exceptions—had commenced by loving her. She had had many, and almost all of them she had kept. M. de Montlosier observed to her one day that she might save like the Cid, *Five hundred of my friends*. She was a true magician in the way she had of converting love insensibly into friendship, while leaving to friendship all the bloom of love and all its perfume. She would have liked to stop everything at *April*. It was there her heart had stayed, in this time of earliest spring, when the orchard trees are covered with white blossoms and the leaves have not yet come.

I might here recount from memory many things, if my pen were but light enough to pass over these flowers without causing them to fade. To her new friends (as she was sometimes pleased to call them) Madame Récamier used often and gladly to speak of the old days and of the people she had known. "It is a way," she said, "of sharing the past with my friends."

Her intimacy with Madame de Staël, with Madame Moreau, with the wounded and the conquered, very early threw her into the ranks of those opposed to the Empire, but there was a moment when she had not yet chosen her color. Fouché, noting the power exercised by this young woman, conceived the idea of making her his tool. He wished, in the beginning, to introduce Madame Récamier into the imperial household as lady of honor; he did not like the nobility, and he would have been glad to have there a person at once influential and devoted. She declined to lend herself to such a rôle. Shortly afterwards she was in the opposition, by virtue especially of her friends and of the notions that were held regarding her.

She was not yet there when one day she dined with one of the sisters of Bonaparte. It was desired that she should meet the First Consul, who was, in fact, present. The intention was that she should be beside him at table; but by a mistake which occurred at the moment of sitting down she found herself instead at the side of Cambacérès, whereupon Bonaparte jestingly remarked: "*Eh bien!* Consul Cambacérès, always next to the prettiest!"

Madame Récamier's father, Monsieur Bernard, held a post in the mail service and was a royalist; under the Consulate he was compromised, arrested, and placed in confinement. Madame Récamier learned of this suddenly, while Madame Bacciochi, Bonaparte's sister, was dining with her at her house. Madame Bacciochi promised to do everything possible to interest the Consul. After the dinner Madame Récamier went out and tried to see Fouché, who, however, refused to see her, "for fear of having his feelings touched," he said, "and that in an affair of state." She then hurried to rejoin, at the Théâtre-Français, Madam Bacciochi, who was in the company of her sister Pauline, now all taken up with the casque of Lafon: "Just look," she was saying, "how ill that casque is put on, how far off it is on one side!" Madame Récamier was in agony; Madame Bacciochi wished to remain till the end of the tragedy, because, perhaps, of her sister Pauline. Bernadotte was in the box; he saw the altered air of Madame Récamier; he gave her his arm to escort her, and offered to go himself, on the instant, and see the Consul. It was at this moment that Bernadotte's warm feeling for her had its beginning; before this time he did not know her. He obtained pardon for her father. What is said on this point in the *Mémorial de Sainte-Hélène* [1] is inexact. Madame Récamier did not see Bonaparte on this occasion; Bernadotte took in hand the entire affair.

Bernadotte, then, loved her, and was one of her knights. The Montmorencys, at that time returned from the Emigration, were her knights no less. Mathieu de Montmorency, later the most saintly of men, Adrien (later Duke de Laval), and long afterwards the son of Adrien, who thus became the rival of his own father—all loved her passionately. Henri de Laval often encountered at her house the Duke de Laval, his father; he always held fast, however, and made no move to depart, a procedure which greatly vexed the good duke, and as he was a man

[1] A book of memoirs compiled by Las Cases from conversations with Napoleon at St. Helena.

of wit, he wrote to Madame Récamier in the most agreeable manner in the world: "My son is enamored of you, you know whether I am myself; well, after all, it is the fate of the Montmorencys:

*"Ils ne mouraient pas tous, mais tous étaient frappés."* [2]

Madame Récamier was the first to tell of these things, and she would smile at them gayly. She kept almost till the end her girlish laughter, her youthful way of putting her handkerchief to her mouth as if to restrain a gush of merriment. But, in her youth, this childlike spontaneity, with its accompaniment of graceful coquetry, led more than once (can one wonder?) to serious complications. Not all the men who were drawn to her and fascinated by her were so easy to guide and to elude as was the peaceful dynasty of the Montmorencys. She must have had to do at times with fits of violence and revolt hard even for her gentle hand to soothe. As she played thus with human passions, seeking only to charm them, but inflaming them more than she knew, it was as if the youngest of the graces were to harness up lions and tease them for her sport. Imprudent as innocence itself, as I have said, she loved peril, the peril of others if not her own; and—why should I not say it?—in this hazardous and too easily cruel game she brought sorrow, kind and tender though she was, to many hearts; some, without wishing it, she greatly embittered, not only hearts of desperate and rebellious men, but also those of hapless rivals, abandoned for her without her knowing it, and wounded. There is here a serious side which at the last her charity in some degree comprehended; it is a lesson which the high solemnity that attaches to her noble memory does not forbid us to recall. With her instinctive purity and heavenly goodness, she herself was aware of it: for this reason she did not regret her youth—she the admired and the adored—nor its bright morning hours, nor its times of storm, even the most resplendent. She had no idea of a perfect happiness divorced from duty; she placed the ideal of romance where she herself had so little met with it—in marriage; and she told how more than once in her happiest days, in the midst of gayeties where she was queen, she had stolen away for a moment and gone apart to weep.

It is thus that I conceive her when she was in the whirl of society, before her retreat. A series of chapters might be written regarding her, which here I cannot even sketch. One of these chapters would be that of her relations and of her intimacy with Madame de Staël. The two were alike brilliant influences, very distinct from each other, very often intersecting, almost never rivals, and mutually, in a high degree, complementary. It was in 1807, at the Château de Coppet, in the home

[2] They did not all die, but all were smitten.

of Madame de Staël, that Madame Récamier saw Prince August of Prussia, one of those vanquished at Jena; she, in her turn, soon vanquished and conquered him—a royal prisoner, brusque in demeanor, and sometimes embarrassing. This brusqueness sometimes gave him away. Once when he was riding horseback with Madame Récamier and wanted to say a word to her privately, he turned to Benjamin Constant, who was of the party, and said, "Monsieur de Constant, suppose you galloped on a bit." And Monsieur de Constant had his laugh at German finesse.

Another chapter would treat of the easy conquest which Madame Récamier made at Lyons of the mild Ballanche, who gave himself to her from the first day, without ever even telling her of it. Another chapter would describe her less simple relations, relations less easy at first but finally so well defined, with M. de Châteaubriand. Madame Récamier had seen him for the first time at the home of Madame de Staël, in 1801; she saw him for the second time in 1816 or 1817, not long before the death of Madame de Staël, and this time also at her house. But these were only chance meetings, and the real intimacy was not effected till late, at the time when M. de Châteaubriand left the ministry, and at the Abbaye-aux-Bois.

There would also be a chapter to write on her intimacy with Benjamin Constant, which does not date earlier than 1814–15. The letters of Benjamin Constant addressed to Madame Récamier would here be of great assistance; but they would be very inadequate, from the point of view of the truth, unless they were supplemented by their counterpart, that is to say, by what he wrote for himself at the conclusion of their relations (many persons have read it), and, finally, unless everything was lighted up by the kind of moral commentary not ordinarily to be found in lawyers' pleas. But that reminds me that an unpleasant dispute has been begun on this subject, and I hasten to leave it.

Before that on Benjamin Constant there would still be a chapter to write on the journey to Italy in 1813, the sojourn at Rome, the intimacy with Canova, the marble bust which Canova executed, and which this time, to be ideal, had only to copy its model; and then the sojourn at Naples with Queen. Caroline and Murat. The heart of Murat, if I mistake not, remained a little touched. But enough of rapid perspectives.

When Madame Récamier saw the hour approaching when beauty droops and wanes, she did what very few women are wise enough to do: she did not struggle; she accepted, with taste, the first marks of time. She understood that after such successes as she had enjoyed, the last means of appearing still beautiful was to pretend to beauty no more. To a woman who saw her again after a number of years and was complimenting her upon her appearance, she replied: "Ah, my dear friend, I can henceforth have no illusions. From the day when I noticed that the little chimney-sweeps in the street no longer turned round to look at me, I understood that all was over." She was right. She was sensitive to all attention and to all praise, not less to the exclamation of a child or of the humblest woman than to the declaration of a prince. From the side of her elegant barouche, as it made its way very slowly through the crowds, she thanked every one for his admiration with a bow and a smile.

At two periods Monsieur Récamier had suffered serious financial reverses: the first time at the beginning of the Empire, the second time in the first years of the Restoration. It was on the latter occasion, in 1819, that Madame Récamier retired to an apartment of the Abbaye-aux-Bois. She never had a more distinguished position in society than when she lived in this humble asylum in a remote corner of Paris. It was from this place that her gracious genius, freed from too lively complications, made its goodness more and more felt. It may be said that she perfected the art of friendship and made it take a step forward: it was like one fine art the more which she had introduced into life, and which adorned, ennobled, and ordered whatever was about her. The spirit of party was then at its height. She disarmed angry passions, she softened asperities; she charmed away rudeness and sowed seeds of indulgence. She could not rest until she had brought together at her house her friends of opposite camps, and by her gentle mediation had reconciled them to each other. It is by such influences that society becomes society so far as is possible, by such influences that it acquires all its pliancy and all its grace. Thus it is that a woman, without forsaking her sphere, performs in the highest degree the work of civilization, thus it is that Eurydice fulfills in her own manner the rôle of Orpheus. It was by Orpheus that wild life was tamed; it is by Eurydice that civilized life is brought to its true goal and crowned.

One day, in 1802, during the brief peace of Amiens, not in the fine mansion on the Rue du Mont-Blanc, which Madame Récamier then occupied, but in the drawing-room of the Château de Clichy, where she was spending the summer, there were assembled a group of men representing many diverse opinions—Adrien and Mathieu de Montmorency; General Moreau; some Englishmen of distinction, Mr. Fox, Mr. Erskine; and many others: they stood there confronting one another, they remained on their guard; no one was willing to commit himself. M. de Narbonne, who was of the company, endeavored to start the conversation going, but for all his talents he had been unable to succeed. Madame Récamier entered: she spoke first to Mr. Fox, she said a word to each, she presented them one to another with appropriate words of praise—and on the instant the conversation became general, the natural bond was discovered.

What she did on this day, she did every day. In her little salon at the Abbaye-aux-Bois, she thought of everything, she flung wide her net of sympathy. Not a talent, not a quality, not a distinction, but she loved to become acquainted with it, to welcome it to her house, to serve it, to bring it to the light, above all to put it in harmony with everything about her, to mark it at its heart with a little sign all her own. Ambition had its part in all this, beyond doubt; but what adorable ambition, especially when, addressing herself as she did to the most famous, she did not neglect even the most obscure, and when she made it her special task to seek out the most miserable. It was characteristic of this manifold nature of Madame Récamier to be at once universal and very particular, to exclude nothing—or, I shall better say, to attract to herself all things and yet choose what she would.

The choice she made might even appear unique. M. de Châteaubriand, during the last twenty years, was the grand center of her world, the grand interest of her life, the one to whom I will not say she sacrificed all the rest (she sacrificed no one but herself), but to whom she subordinated everything. He had his antipathies, his aversions, and even his bitternesses, all of which are apparent enough to-day in his *Mémoires d'Outre-Tombe*. All these things she tempered and corrected. How ingenious she was in making him speak when silent, in putting into his mouth amiable words, words friendly to others, which no doubt he had just spoken to her in intimacy, but which he was not always disposed to repeat before witnesses! How she played the coquette for his glory! How well she sometimes succeeded in making him really gay, lovable, altogether happy, eloquent, all those things he could so easily be the moment he wished it! By her gentle influence over him she very well justified the remark of Bernardin de Saint-Pierre, who said: "There is in woman a light joyousness that drives away the sadness of man." And in this instance with what a sadness she had to do!—a sadness which René had brought with him from the womb of his mother, and which grew greater with the years! Never was Madame de Maintenon at such pains to relieve the tedium of Louis XIV as was Madame Récamier to amuse M. de Châteaubriand. "I have always observed," Boileau used to say on coming back from Versailles, "that when the conversation did not turn upon his own praise, the King at once grew restless, and was ready either to yawn or to depart." Every great poet, as he grows old, is in this respect a little like Louis the Fourteenth. Madame Récamier had every day a thousand gracious inventions wherewith to renew for Châteaubriand the word of praise, and to give it freshness. From every side she rallied round him new friends and admirers. She made us all fast to the feet of her statue with a chain of gold.

An observer of mind no less delicate than just, who knew her well, said of Madame Récamier: "She has in her character what Shakespeare calls *the milk of human kindness*—a tender and compassionate sweetness. She sees the defects of her friends, but she is as tender with these as she would be with their bodily ills." She was a sister of charity to their sorrows, to their weaknesses, and, a little, to their faults.

That there were not in the long run certain disadvantages in this habitual procedure, mingled with a great charm; that in this atmosphere, so mild and so calming, while she polished and refined the mind, she did not a little relax it and render it complaisant, I dare not deny—and I dare it the less because I think that I myself, perhaps, experienced this effect. Certainly it was a salon where not politeness alone, but also charity, did injury in some degree to truth. Decidedly there were some things which she did not wish to see, and which for her did not exist. She did not believe in evil. In her inveterate innocence—I insist upon it—she remained very much a child. Shall we then complain? After all, is there another place on earth where we shall meet with a friendliness so real in the midst of an illusion so adorned? A bitter moralist, La Rochefoucauld, has said: "If we never flattered ourselves, we should have but little pleasure."

I have heard people ask whether Madame Récamier was a woman of intellect. But it seems to me we have the answer already. She had in the highest degree, not the type of mind which seeks to shine for itself, but that which recognizes the ability of others and brings it to the light. She wrote little: very early she had contracted the habit of writing the least possible; but this little was good and of a perfect turn. Her talk was simple, accurate, and pointed. In telling of the past, she liked best to choose something delicate or subtle, a lighthearted or amiable saying, a piquant situation, and she neglected the rest; she remembered with taste.

She was a seductive listener; nothing good that you might say passed by without her letting you know that she saw it. She questioned you with interest, and attended wholly to your answer. On leaving her, were it only for her smiles and her silences, you had a personal interest in thinking well of her mind.

As to the youthfulness, the beauty, of her heart, if it has been given to all to appreciate it, it is especialy for those some day to speak of it who have enjoyed it more intimately. After the death of M. Ballanche and M. de Châteaubriand, although she had still about her M. Ampère, the Duke de Noailles, and many other affectionate friends, she only languished and wore out her days. She died May 11, 1849, in her seventy-second year. This unique person, whose memory will live as long as French society, was very gracefully painted by Gérard, in the freshness of her youth. Her bust was sculptured by Canova in its ideal beauty. Achille Devéria made a faithful sketch of her on the day of her death, expressive of suffering and of repose.

# VIRGINIA WOOLF

## *Dr. Burney's Evening Party*

THE party was given either in 1777 or in 1778; on which day or month of the year is not known, but the night was cold. Fanny Burney, from whom we get much of our information, was accordingly either twenty-five or twenty-six, as we choose. But in order to enjoy the party to the full it is necessary to go back some years and to scrape acquaintance with the guests.

Fanny, from the earliest days, had always been fond of writing. There was a cabin at the end of her stepmother's garden at King's Lynn, where she used to sit and write of an afternoon till the oaths of the seamen sailing up and down the river drove her in. But it was only in the afternoon and in remote places that her half-suppressed, uneasy passion for writing had its way. Writing was held to be slightly ridiculous in a girl; rather unseemly in a woman. Besides, one never knew, if a girl kept a diary, whether she might not say something indiscreet—so Miss Dolly Young warned her; and Miss Dolly Young, though exceedingly plain, was esteemed as a woman of the highest character in King's Lynn. Fanny's stepmother also disapproved of writing. Yet so keen was the joy—"I cannot express the pleasure I have in writing down my thoughts at the very moment, and my opinion of people when I first see them," she wrote—that scribble she must. Loose sheets of paper fell from her pocket and were picked up and read by her father to her agony and shame; once she was forced to make a bonfire of all her papers in the back garden. At last some kind of compromise seems to have been arrived at. The morning was sacred to serious tasks like sewing; it was only in the afternoon that she allowed herself to scribble—letters, diaries, stories, verses in the look-out place which overhung the river, till the oaths of the sailors drove her in.

There was something strange in that, perhaps, for the eighteenth century was the age of oaths. Fanny's early diary is larded with them. "God help me." "Split me." "Stab my vitals," together with damned and devilishes dropped daily and hourly from the lips of her adored father and her venerated Daddy Crisp. Perhaps Fanny's attitude to language was altogether a little abnormal. She was immensely susceptible to the power of words, but not nervously or acutely as Jane Austen was. She adored fluency and the sound of language pouring warmly and copiously over the printed page. Directly she read *Rasselas*, enlarged and swollen sentences formed on the tip of her childish pen, in the manner of Dr. Johnson. Quite early in life she would go out of her way to avoid the plane name of Tomkins. Thus, whatever she heard from her Cabin at the end of the garden was sure to affect her more than most girls, and it is also clear that while her ears were sensitive to sound, her soul was sensitive to meaning. There was something a little prudish in her nature. Just as she avoided the name of Tomkins, so she avoided the roughnesses, the asperities, the plainnesses of daily life. The chief fault that mars the extreme vivacity and vividness of the early diary is that the profusion of words tends to soften the edges, and the sweetness of the sentiment to smooth out the outlines. Thus, when she heard the sailors swearing, though Maria Allen, her half-sister would, one believes, have liked to stay, and perhaps toss a kiss over the water—her future history allows us to take the liberty of thinking so—Fanny went indoors.

Fanny went indoors, but not to solitary meditation. The house, whether it was in Lynn or in London—and by far the greater part of the year was spent in Poland Street—hummed with activity. There was the sound of the harpsichord; the sound of singing; there was the sound—for such concentration seems to pervade a whole house with its murmur—of Dr. Burney writing furiously, surrounded by note-books in his study; and there were great bursts of chatter and laughter when, returning from their various occupations, the Burney children met together. Nobody enjoyed family life more than Fanny did. For there her shyness only served to fasten the nickname of Old Lady upon her; there she had a familiar audience for her humour; there she need not bother about her clothes; there—perhaps the fact that their mother had died when they were all young was partly the cause of it—was that intimacy which expresses itself in jokes and legends and a private language ("The wig is wet," they would say, winking at each other); there were endless confabulations, and confidences between sisters and brothers and brothers and sisters. Nor could there be any doubt that the Burneys—Susan and James and Charles and Fanny and Hetty and Charlotte—were a gifted race. Charles was a scholar; James was a humorist; Fanny was a writer; Susan was musical—each had some special gift or characteristic to add to the common stock. And besides their natural gifts they were happy in the fact that their father was a very popular man; a man, too, so admirably situated by his talents, which were social, and his birth, which was gentle, that they could mix without difficulty either with lords or with bood-binders, and had, in fact, as free a run of life as could be wished.

As for Dr. Burney himself, there are some points about which, at this distance of time, one may feel dubious. It is difficult to be sure what, had one met him now, one would have felt for him. One thing is certain—one would have met him everywhere. Hostesses would be competing to catch him. Notes would wait for him. Telephone bells would interrupt him. For he was the most sought-after, the most occupied of men. He was always dashing in and dashing off. Sometimes he dined off a box of sandwiches in his carriage. Sometimes he went out at seven in the morning, and was not back from his round of music lessons till eleven at night. And when he was not teaching he was writing. The "habitual softness of his manners," his great social charm, his haphazard untidy ways; everything, notes, money, manuscripts, was tossed into a drawer, and he was robbed of all his savings once, but his friends were delighted to make it up for him; his odd adventures—did he not fall asleep after a bad crossing at Dover, and so return to France and so have to cross the Channel again?—endeared him to everybody. It is, perhaps, his diffuseness that makes him a trifle nebulous. He seems to be for ever writing and then re-writing, and requiring his daughters to write for him, endless books and articles, while over him unchecked, unfiled, unread, perhaps, pour down notes, letters, invitations to dinner which he cannot destroy and means some day to annotate and collect, until he seems to melt away at last in a cloud of words. When he died at the age of eighty-eight, there was nothing to be done by the most devoted of daughters but to burn the whole accumulation entire. Even Fanny's love of language was suffocated. But if we fumble a little as to our feeling for Dr. Burney, Fanny certainly did not. She adored her father. She never minded how many times she had to lay aside her own writing in order to copy out his. And he returned her affection. Though his ambition for her success at Court was foolish, perhaps, and almost cost her her life, she had only to cry when a distasteful suitor was pressed on her, "Oh Sir, I wish for nothing! Only let me live with you!" for the emotional doctor to reply "My Life! Thou shalt live with me for ever if thou wilt. Thou canst not think I meant to get rid of thee?" And not only were his eyes full of tears, but, what was more remarkable, he never mentioned Mr. Barlow again. Indeed, the Burneys were a happy family; a mixed composite, oddly assorted family; for there were the Allens, too, and little half-brothers and half-sisters were being born and growing up.

So time passed, and the passage of the years made it impossible for the family to continue in Poland Street any longer. First they moved to Queen Square, and then, in 1774, to the house where Newton had lived, in St. Martin's Street, Leicester Fields; where his Observatory still stood, and his room with the painted panels was still to be seen. Here in a mean street, but in the centre of the town, the Burneys set up their establishment. Here Fanny went on scribbling, stealing to the Observatory as she had stolen to the Cabin at Lynn, for she exclaimed, "I cannot any longer resist what I find to be irresistible, the pleasure of popping down my thoughts from time to time upon paper." Here came so many famous people either to be closeted with the doctor, or, like Garrick, to sit with him while his fine head of natural hair was brushed, or to join the lively family dinner, or, more formally to gather together in a musical party, where all the Burney children played and their father "dashed away" on the harpsichord, and perhaps some foreign musician of distinction performed a solo—so many people came for one reason or another to the house in St. Martin's Street that it is only the eccentrics, the grotesques that catch the eye. One remembers, for instance, the Ajujari, the astonishing soprano, because she had been "mauled as an infant by a pig, in consequence of which she is reported to have a silver side." One remembers Bruce, the traveller, because he had a "most extraordinary complaint. When he attempted to speak, his whole stomach suddenly seemed to heave like an organ bellows. He did not wish to make any secret about it, but spoke of it as having originated in Abyssinia. However, one evening, when he appeared rather agitated, it lasted much longer than usual, and was so violent that it alarmed the company." One seems to remember, for she paints herself while she paints the others, Fanny herself slipping eagerly and lightly in and out of all this company, with her rather prominent gnat-like eyes, her shy, awkward manners that concealed the quickest observation, the most retentive memory, so that as soon as the company had gone, she stole to the Observatory and wrote down every word, every scene, in letters twelve pages long for her beloved Daddy Crisp at Chessington. For that old hermit—he had retired to a house in a field in dudgeon with society—though professing to be better pleased with a bottle of wine in his cellar and a horse in his stable, and a game of backgammon at night, than with all the fine company in the world, was always agog for news. He scolded his Fannikin if she did not tell him all about her fine goings-on. And he scolded her again if she did not write at full tilt exactly as the words came into her head.

Mr. Crisp wanted to know in particular "about Mr. Greville and his notions." For, indeed, Mr. Greville was a perpetual source of curiosity. It is a thousand pities that time with her poppy dust has covered Mr. Greville, who was once so eminent so that only his most prominent features, his birth, his person, and his nose emerge. Fulke Greville was the descendant—he must, one fancies, have emphasized the fact from the way in which it is repeated—of the friend of Sir Philip Sidney. A coronet, indeed, "hung almost suspended over his head." In person he was tall and well proportioned. "His face, features, and complexion were striking for masculine beauty." "His air and carriage were noble with conscious dignity"; his bearing was "lofty, yet graceful." But all these gifts and qualities, to which one must add that he rode and fenced and danced and played tennis to admiration, were marred by prodigious faults. He was supercilious in the extreme; he was selfish; he was fickle. He was a man of violent temper. His introduction to Dr. Burney in the first place was due to his doubt whether a musician could be fit company for a gentleman. When he found that young Burney not only played the harpsichord to perfection, but curved his finger and rounded his hand as he played; that he answered plain "Yes, Sir," or "No, Sir," being more interested in the music than in his patron; that it was only indeed when Greville himself thrummed pertinaciously from memory that he could stand it no longer, and broke into vivacious conversation—it was only when he found that young Burney was not only gifted but well bred into the bargain that, being himself a very clever man, he no longer stood upon his dignity. Burney became his friend and equal. Burney, indeed, almost became his victim. For if there was one thing that the descendant of the friend of Sir Philip Sidney detested it was what he called "fogrum." By that expressive word he seems to have meant the middle-class virtues of discretion and respectability, as opposed to the aristocratic virtues of what he called "*ton*." Life must be lived dashingly, daringly, with perpetual display, even if the display was extremely expensive, and, as seemed possible to those who trailed dismally round his grounds praising the improvements, as boring to the man who had made them as to the unfortunate guests whose admiration he insisted upon extorting. But Greville could not endure fogrum in himself or in his friends. He threw the obscure young musician into the fast life of White's and Newmarket, and watched with amusement to see if he sank or swam. Burney, most adroit of men, swam as if born to the water, and the descendant of the friend of Sir Philip Sidney was pleased. From being his protégé, Burney became his confidant. Indeed, the splendid gentleman, for all his high carriage, was in need of one. For Greville, could one wipe away the poppy dust that covers him, was one of those tortured and unhappy souls who find themselves torn asunder by opposite desires. On the one hand he was consumed with the wish to be in the first flight of fashion and to do "the thing," however costly or dreary "the thing" might be. On the other, he was secretly persuaded that "the proper bent of his mind and understanding was for metaphysics." Burney, perhaps, was a link between the world of *ton* and the world of fogrum. He was a man of breeding who could dice and bet with the bloods; he was also a musician who could talk of intellectual things and ask clever people to his house.

Thus Greville treated the Burneys as his equals, and came to their house, though his visits were often interrupted by the violent quarrels which he managed to pick even with the amiable Dr. Burney himself. Indeed, as time went on there was nobody with whom Greville did not quarrel. He had lost heavily at the gambling-tables. His prestige in society was sunk. His habits were driving his family from him. Even his wife, by nature gentle and conciliatory, though excessive thinness made her seem fitted to sit for a portrait "of a penetrating, puissant and sarcastic fairy queen," was wearied by his infidelities. Inspired by them she had suddenly produced that famous Ode to Indifference, "which had passed into every collection of fugitive pieces in the English language" and (it is Madam D'Arblay who speaks) "twined around her brow a garland of wide-spreading and unfading fragrance." Her fame, it may be, was another thorn in her husband's side, for he, too, was an author. He himself had produced a volume of Maxims and Characters; and having "waited for fame with dignity rather than anxiety, because with expectation unclogged with doubt," was beginning perhaps to become a little impatient. Fame held aloof. Meanwhile he was fond of the society of clever people, and it was largely at his desire that the famous party in St. Martin's Street met together that very cold night.

## II

In those days, when London was so small, it was easier than now for people to stand out on an eminence which they scarcely struggled to keep, but enjoyed by unanimous consent. Everybody knew and remembered when they saw her that Mrs. Greville had written an Ode to Indifference; everybody knew that Mr. Bruce had travelled in Abyssinia; so, too, everybody knew that there was a house at Streatham presided over by a lady called Mrs. Thrale. Without troubling to write an ode, without hazarding her life among savages, without possessing either high rank or vast wealth, Mrs. Thrale was a celebrity. By the exercise of powers difficult to define—for to feel them one must have sat at table and noticed a thousand audacities and deftnesses and skilful combinations which die with the moment—Mrs. Thrale had the reputation of a great hostess. Her fame spread far beyond her house. People who had never seen her discussed her. People wanted to know what she was like; whether she was really so witty and so well read; whether it was a pose; whether she had a heart; whether she loved her husband the brewer, who seemed a dull dog; why she had married him; whether Dr. Johnson was in love with her—what, in short, was the secret of her power. For power she had—that was indisputable.

Even then, perhaps, it would have been difficult to say in what it consisted. For she possessed the one quality which can never be named;

she enjoyed the one gift which never ceases to excite discussion. Somehow or other she was a personality. The young Burneys, for instance, had never seen Mrs. Thrale or been to Streatham, but the stir which she set going round her had reached them in St. Martin's Street. When their father came back from giving his first music lesson to Miss Thrale at Streatham they flocked about him to hear his account of her mother. Was she as brilliant as people made out? Was she kind? Was she cruel? Had he liked her? Dr. Burney was in high good temper—in itself a proof of his hostess's power—and he replied, not, we may be sure, as Fanny rendered it, that she was a "star of the first constellation of female wits: surpassing, rather than equalizing the reputation which her extraordinary endowments, and the splendid fortune which made them conspicuous, had blazoned abroad"—that was written when Fanny's style was odd and tarnished, and its leaves were fluttering and falling profusely to the ground; the doctor, we may suppose, answered briskly that he had enjoyed himself hugely; that the lady was a very clever lady; that she had interrupted the lesson all the time; that she had a very sharp tongue—there was no doubt of that; but he would go to the stake for it that she was a good-hearted woman at bottom. Then they must have pressed to know what she looked like. She looked younger than her age—which was about forty. She was rather plump, very small, fair with very blue eyes, and had a scar or cut on her lip. She painted her cheeks, which was unnecessary, because her complexion was rosy by nature. The whole impression she made on one was of bustle and gaiety and good temper. She was, he said, a woman "full of sport," whom nobody could have taken for a creature that the doctor could not bear, a learned lady. Less obviously, she was very observant, as her anecdotes were to prove; capable of passion, though that was not yet visible at Streatham; and, while curiously careless and good-tempered about her dues as a wit or a blue stocking, had an amusing pride in being descended from a long line of Welsh gentry (whereas the Thrales were obscure), and drew satisfaction now and then from the reflection that in her veins ran the blood, as the College of Heralds acknowledged, of Adam of Salzburg.

Many women might have possessed these qualities without being remembered for them. Mrs. Thrale possessed besides one that has given her immortality: the power of being the friend of Dr. Johnson. Without that addition, her life might have fizzled and flamed to extinction, leaving nothing behind it. But the combination of Dr. Johnson and Mrs. Thrale created something as solid, as lasting, as remarkable in its way as a work of art. And this was an achievement that called for much rarer powers on the part of Mrs. Thrale than the qualities of a good hostess. When the Thrales first met Johnson he was in a state of profound gloom, crying out such lost and terrible words that Mr. Thrale put his hand before his mouth to silence him. Physically, too, he was afflicted with asthma and dropsy; his manners were rough; his habits were gross; his clothes were dirty; his wig was singed; his linen was soiled; and he was the rudest of men. Yet Mrs. Thrale carried this monster off with her to Brighton and then domesticated him in her house at Streatham, where he was given a room to himself, and where he spent habitually some days in the middle of every week. This might have been on her part but the enthusiasm of a curiosity hunter, ready to put up with a host of disagreeables for the sake of having at her house the original Dr. Johnson, whom anybody in England would gladly pay to see. But it is clear that her connoisseurship was of a finer type. She understood—her anecdotes prove it—that Dr. Johnson was somehow a rare, an important, an impressive human being whose friendship might be a burden but was certainly an honour. And it was not by any means so easy to know this then as it is now. What one knew then was that Dr. Johnson was coming to dinner. Who would be there, one wondered with anxiety? For if it was a Cambridge man there might be an outburst. If it was a Whig there would certainly be a scene. If it was a Scotsman anything might happen. Such were his whims and prejudices. Next one would have to bethink one, what had one ordered for dinner? For the food never went uncriticized; and even when one had provided him with young peas from the garden, one must not praise them. Were not the young peas charming, Mrs. Thrale asked once? and he turned upon her, after gobbling down masses of pork and veal pie with lumps of sugar in it, and snapped "Perhaps they would be so—to a pig." And then what would the talk be about, one must have speculated? If it got upon painting or music he was apt to dismiss it with scorn, for both arts were indifferent to him. Then if a traveller told a tale he was sure to pooh-pooh it, because he believed nothing that he had not seen. Then if any one were to express sorrow in his presence it might well draw down upon one a rebuke for insincerity. "When, one day, I lamented the loss of a cousin killed in America: 'Prithee, my dear,' said he, 'have done with canting: how would the world be the worse for it, I may ask, if all your relations were at once spitted like larks, and roasted for Presto's supper?' In short, the meal would be strewn with difficulties; the whole affair might run upon the rocks at any moment."

Had Mrs. Thrale been a shallow curiosity hunter she would have shown him for a season or so and then let him drop. But Mrs. Thrale realized even at the moment that one must submit to be snubbed and bullied and irritated and offended by Dr. Johnson because—well, what was the force that sent an impudent and arrogant young man like

Boswell slinking back to his chair like a beaten boy when Johnson bade him? Why did she herself sit up till four in the morning pouring out tea for him? There was a force in him that awed even a competent woman of the world, that subdued even a thick-skinned, conceited boy. He had a right to scold Mrs. Thrale for inhumanity, when she knew that he spent only seventy pounds a year on himself and with the rest of his income supported a houseful of decrepit and ungrateful lodgers. If he gobbled at table and tore the peaches from the wall he went back punctually to London to see that his wretched inmates had their three good meals over the week-end. Moreover, he was a warehouse of knowledge. If the dancing-master talked about dancing, Johnson could out-talk him. He could keep one amused by the hour with his tales of the underworld, of the topers and scallywags who haunted his lodgings and claimed his bounty. He said things casually that one never forgot. But what was perhaps more engaging than all his learning and virtue, was his love of pleasure, his detestation of the hermit, of the mere book-worm, his passion for life and society. And then, as a woman would, Mrs. Thrale loved him for his courage—that he had separated two fierce dogs that were tearing each other to pieces in Mr. Beauclerc's sitting-room; that he had thrown a man, chair and all, into the pit of a theatre; that, blind and twitching as he was, he rode to hounds on Brightelmstone Downs, and followed the hunt as if he had been a gay dog instead of a huge and melancholy old man. Moreover, there was a natural affinity between them. She drew him out: she made him say what without her he would never have said; indeed, he had confessed to her some painful secret of his youth which she never revealed to anybody. Above all, they shared the same passion. Of talk they could neither of them ever have enough.

Thus Mrs. Thrale could always be counted on to produce Dr. Johnson; and it was, of course, Dr. Johnson whom Mr. Greville most particularly wished to meet. As it happened, Dr. Burney had renewed his acquaintance with Dr. Johnson after many years, when he went to Streatham to give his first music lesson. Dr. Johnson had been there, "wearing his mildest aspect." For he remembered Dr. Burney with kindness. He remembered a letter that Dr. Burney had written to him in praise of the dictionary. He remembered, too, that Dr. Burney having called upon him, years ago, and found him out, had dared to cut some bristles from the hearth broom to send to an admirer. When he met Dr. Burney again at Streatham, he had instantly taken a liking to him; soon he was brought by Mrs. Thrale to see Dr. Burney's books; it was quite easy, therefore, for Dr. Burney to arrange that on a certain night in the early spring of 1777 or 1778, Mr. Greville's great wish to meet Dr. Johnson and Mrs. Thrale should be gratified. A day was fixed and the engagement was made.

Nobody could fail to be aware that the meeting of so many marked and distinguished characters might be difficult. Dr. Johnson was, of course, notoriously formidable. But the danger was not confined to Dr. Johnson; Mr. Greville himself was domineering and exacting; his temper had grown still more uncertain since his gambling losses had made him of less account in the world of *ton*. Then Mrs. Greville was a poetess; it was likely enough that she would prove her right to the laurel by some contest with a lady whose fame was at the moment brighter than her own. Mrs. Thrale was good humour itself; still, it was likely that she would try for a tilt with Mrs. Greville; nor was she wholly dependable, for she had "sudden flashes of wit which she left to their own consequences." Besides, it was an occasion; everybody felt it to be so; wits would be on the strain; expectation on tiptoe. Dr. Burney, with the tact of a man of the world, foresaw these difficulties, and took steps to avert them. But there was, one vaguely feels, something a little obtuse about Dr. Burney. The eager, kind, busy man, with his head full of music and his desk stuffed with notes, lacked discrimination. He had not noticed that Dr. Johnson, when he visited them the other day, and found them at the harpsichord, had withdrawn to the bookcase and browsed upon a volume of the *British Encyclopædia*, till the music was over. He was not aware, in spite of the way in which Mrs. Thrale interrupted his lessons, that she did not know "a flat from a sharp." To his innocent mind, music was the universal specific. If there was going to be any difficulty music would solve it. He therefore asked Signor Piozzi to be of the party.

The night arrived. The fire was lit. The chairs were placed. The company arrived. As Dr. Burney had foreseen, the awkwardness was great. Things indeed seemed to go wrong from the start. Dr. Johnson had come in his worsted wig, very clean and prepared evidently for enjoyment. But after one look at him, Mr. Greville seemed to decide that there was something formidable about the old man; it would be better not to compete; it would be better to play the fine gentleman, and leave it to literature to make the first advances. Murmuring, apparently, something about having the toothache, Mr. Greville "assumed his most supercilious air of distant superiority and planted himself, immovable as a noble statue, upon the hearth." He said nothing. Mrs. Greville was longing to distinguish herself, but judging it proper for Dr. Johnson to begin, she said nothing. Mrs. Thrale, who might have been expected to break up the solemnity, felt, it seemed, that the party was not her party and, waiting for the principals to engage, resolved to say nothing. Mrs. Crewe, the Grevilles' daughter, lovely and vivacious as she was, had come to be entertained and instructed and therefore very naturally she, too, said nothing. Nobody said anything. Everybody waited. Here was the very moment for which Dr. Burney in his wisdom had prepared. He nodded to Signor Piozzi; and Signor Piozzi stepped to the instrument and began to sing. Accompanying himself on the pianoforte, he sang an *aria parlante*. He sang beautifully, he sang his best. But far from breaking the awkwardness and loosing the tongues, the music increased the constraint. Nobody spoke. Everybody waited for Dr. Johnson to begin. There, indeed, they showed their fatal ignorance, for if there was one thing that Dr. Johnson never did, it was to begin. Somebody had always to start a topic before he consented to pursue it or demolish it. Now he waited in silence to be challenged. But he waited in vain. Nobody dared. The roulades of Signor Piozzi continued uninterrupted. As he saw his chance of a pleasant evening of conversation diminish, Dr. Johnson sank into silent abstraction and sat with his back to the piano gazing at the fire. The *aria parlante* continued uninterrupted. At last the strain became unendurable. At last Mrs. Thrale could stand it no longer. It was the attitude of Mr. Greville, apparently, that roused her resentment. There he stood on the hearth in front of the fire "staring around him at the whole company in curious silence sardonically." What right had he, even if he were the descendant of the friend of Sir Philip Sidney, to despise the company and absorb the fire? Her own pride of ancestry suddenly asserted itself. Did not the blood of Adam of Salzburg run in her veins? Was it not as blue as that of the Grevilles and far more sparkling? Giving rein to the spirit of recklessness which sometimes bubbled in her, she rose, and stole on tiptoe to the pianoforte. Signor Piozzi was still singing and accompanying himself dramatically as he sang. She began a ludicrous mimicry of his gestures: she shrugged her shoulders, she cast up her eyes, she reclined her head on one side just as he did. At this singular display the company began to titter—indeed, it was a scene that was to be described "from coterie to coterie throughout London, with comments and sarcasms of endless variety." People who saw Mrs. Thrale at her mockery that night never forgot that this was the beginning of that criminal affair, the first scene of that "most extraordinary drama" which lost Mrs. Thrale the respect of friends and children, which drove her in ignominy from England, and scarcely allowed her to show herself in London again—this was the beginning of her most reprehensible, her most unnatural passion for one who was not only a musician but a foreigner. All this still lay on the laps of the gods. Nobody yet knew of what iniquity the vivacious lady was capable. She was still the respected wife of a wealthy brewer.

Happily, Dr. Johnson was staring at the fire, and knew nothing of the scene at the piano. But Dr. Burney put a stop to the laughter instantly. He was shocked that his guest, even if he were a foreigner and a musician, should be ridiculed behind his back, and stealing to Mrs. Thrale he whispered kindly but with authority in her ear that if she had no taste for music herself she should consider the feelings of those who had. Mrs. Thrale took the rebuke with admirable sweetness, nodded her acquiescence and returned to her chair. But she had done her part. After that nothing more could be expected from her. Let them now do what they chose—she washed her hands of it, and seated herself "like a pretty little Miss," as she said afterwards, to endure what yet remained to be endured "of one of the most humdrum evenings that she had ever passed."

If no one had dared to tackle Dr. Johnson in the beginning it was scarcely likely that they would dare now. He had apparently decided that the evening was a failure so far as talk was concerned. If he had not come dressed in his best clothes he might have had a book in his pocket which he could have pulled out and read. As it was, nothing but the resources of his own mind were left him; but these were huge; and these he explored as he sat with his back to the piano, looking the very image of gravity, dignity and composure.

At last the *aria parlante* came to an end. Signor Piozzi indeed, finding nobody to talk to, fell asleep in his solitude. Even Dr. Burney by this time must have been aware that music is not an infallible specific; but there was nothing for it now. Since people would not talk, the music must continue. He called upon his daughters to sing a duet. And then, when that was over, there was nothing for it but that they must sing another. Signor Piozzi still slept, or still feigned sleep. Dr. Johnson explored still further the magnificent resources of his own mind. Mr. Greville still stood superciliously upon the hearth-rug. And the night was cold.

But it was a grave mistake to suppose that because Dr. Johnson was apparently lost in thought, and certainly almost blind, he was not aware of anything, particularly of anything reprehensible, that was taking place in the room. His "starts of vision" were always astonishing and almost always painful. So it was on the present occasion. He suddenly woke up, He suddenly roused himself. He suddenly uttered the words for which the company had been waiting all the evening.

"If it were not for depriving the ladies of the fire," he said, looking fixedly at Mr. Greville, "I should like to stand upon the hearth myself!" The effect of the outburst was prodigious. The Burney children said afterwards that it was as good as a comedy. The descendant of the friend of Sir Philip Sidney quailed before the Doctor's glance. All the blood of all the Brookes rallied itself to overcome the insult. The son of a bookseller should be taught his place. Greville did his best to smile —a faint, scoffing smile. He did his best to stand where he had stood the whole evening. He stood smiling, or trying to smile, for two or perhaps for three minutes more. But when he looked round the room and saw all eyes cast down, all faces twitching with amusement, all sympathies plainly on the side of the bookseller's son, he could stand there no longer. Fulke Greville slunk away, sloping even his proud shoulders, to a chair. But as he went, he rang the bell "with force." He demanded his carriage.

"The party then broke up; and no one from amongst it ever asked, or wished for its repetition."

## HENRY ADAMS

# *Letters from Japan*

1886

### *To John Hay*

SAN FRANCISCO, 11 June, 1886.

MY ship is in the bay, all ready at the quay, but before I wend my way, good-bye to thee John Hay; or words to that effect, for I have not my usual facility at verse today. San Francisco looks dusty, wintry and seedy, as I look over it at 8.30 P.M., from the fourth story of the Palace Hotel. Sea-sickness lies before, and the alkali desert behind this town. I have no choice between the two; but I find the town an unhappy medium.

Our journey was a glorious success. As I got into my train at Boston on Thursday the 3rd, to start for New York, my brother Charles came down to tell me that his directors' car had unexpectedly arrived at Boston that morning, and would return to Omaha the next day. So I went to New York rejoicing; passed a delightful day with King, St. Gaudens, etc., and at six P.M. dragged poor La Farge, in a dishevelled and desperate, but still determined mind, on board the Albany express. Never listen to the man who says that corporations have no souls! At Albany I tumbled into the U. P. car at eleven o'clock at night, and from that moment till we reached here yesterday, we had nothing to think about except to amuse ourselves. The U. P. fed, clothed and carried us, as affectionately as though we had money to lend; and landed us at last, not at Omaha, but in the court of this palace, just like two little Aladdins from school.

La Farge's delight with the landscape was the pleasantest thing on the journey. While I read Buddhism and slept, he tried to sketch from the moving car. His results were a sort of purple conglomerate, but the process amused him. On the Humboldt river our thermometer stood at 98° inside the car; but I am the creature of habit, and you will not be surprised that, even under these circumstances, I had Mme. Modjeska and her husband to twelve-o'clock breakfast. *C'est plus fort que moi!* Clearly I am a breakfasting animal.

Adventures we discard, for we are old and no longer vain; but La Farge makes a delicate humor glimmer about our path. Among other people whom he left in New York, likely to tear their hair on hearing of his departure, was the agent of Cassell, for he is illustrating Shelley's Sky Lark. To this unhappy man, La Farge telegraphed from Poughkeepsie: "The purple evening melts around my flight." I know not how meek the spirit of that man may be, but the evening of most men, under such conditions, would have been purple with oaths. At Omaha a young reporter got the better of us; for when in reply to his inquiry as to our purpose in visiting Japan, La Farge beamed through his spectacles the answer that we were in search of Nirvana, the youth looked up like a meteor, and rejoined: "It's out of season!"

We were yesterday afternoon to see our steamer. So far as we could learn, we were the only passengers. We were given the two best staterooms, with the promise of as many more as we might ask for. If you and King were with us, we would capture the ship, turn pirate, and run off to a cocoa-nut island. As it is, we shall be sea-sick without crime. If La Farge sees anything he wants, I will buy it for you, as it will probably be good. If not, I will spend it for myself, and send you whatever you don't want. . . .

## *To John Hay*

YOKOHAMA, 9 July, 1886.

We have been here a week. Between the wish that you were here with us, and the conviction that you would probably by this time be broken up if you had come, I am distraught. Amusing it certainly is—beyond an idea—but comfortable or easy it is not by any means—and I can honestly say that one works for what one gets.

We have devoted the week to Tokio, and you can judge what sort of a place it is from the fact that there is neither hotel nor house in it where we can be so nearly comfortable as we are in a third-rate hotel at Yokohama, twenty miles away. Here we have rooms directly on the bay, with air as fresh as the Japs make it; and here we return every evening to sleep. Sturgis Bigelow acts as our courier and master of ceremonies, but La Farge has mastered Mandarin Chinese, and hopes soon to be a fluent talker of Daimio Japanese. As for me, I admire.

Fenollosa and Bigelow are stern with us. Fenollosa is a tyrant who says we shall not like any work done under the Tokugawa Shoguns. As these gentlemen lived two hundred and fifty years or thereabouts, to 1860, and as there is nothing at Tokio except their work, La Farge and I are at a loss to understand why we came; but it seems we are to be taken to Nikko shortly and permitted to admire some temples there. On secret search in Murray, I ascertain that the temples at Nikko are the work of Tokugawa Shoguns. I have not yet dared to ask about this apparent inconsistency for fear of rousing a fresh anathema.

The temples and Tokugawas are, I admit, a trifle baroque. For sticking a decisive bit of infamous taste into the middle of a seriously planned, and minutely elaborated mass of refined magnificence, I have seen no people—except perhaps our own—to compare with the Japs. We have the future before us to prove our capacity, but they now stand far ahead. Some of the temples are worse than others, but I am inclined to let Fenollosa have his way with them, if he will only let me be amused by the humor. Positively everything in Japan laughs. The jinrickshaw men laugh while running at full speed five miles with a sun that visible sizzles their drenched clothes. The women all laugh, but they are obviously wooden dolls, badly made, and can only cackle, clatter in pattens over asphalt pavements in railway stations, and hop or slide in heedless straw sandals across floors. I have not yet seen a woman with any better mechanism than that of a five-dollar wax doll; but the amount of oil used in fixing and oiling and arranging their hair is worth the money alone. They can all laugh, so far. The shopkeepers laugh to excess when you say that their goods are forgeries and worthless. I believe the Mikado laughs when his ministers have a cabinet council. The gilt dragon-heads on the temples are in a broad grin. Everything laughs, until I expect to see even the severe bronze doors of the tombs, the finest serious work I know, open themselves with the same eternal and meaningless laughter, as though death were the pleasantest jest of all.

In one respect Japan has caused me a sensation of deep relief. In America I had troubled myself much because my sense of smell was gone. I thought I never should again be conscious that the rose or the new-mown hay had odor. How it may be about the rose or the hay I know not; but since my arrival here I perceive that I am not wholly without a nose. La Farge agrees with me that Japan possesses one pervasive, universal, substantive smell—an oily, sickish, slightly fetid odor—which underlies all things, and though infinitely varied, is always the same. The smell has a corresponding taste. The bread, the fruit, the tea, the women, and the water, the air and the gods, all smell or taste alike. This is monotonous but reassuring. I have reasoned much and tried many experiments to ascertain the cause of this phenomenon, but it seems to be a condition of existence, and the accompaniment of Japanese civilisation. Without the smell, Japan would fall into dissolution.

I am trying to spend your money. It is hard work, but I will do it, or succumb. Kaki-monos are not to be got. Porcelain worth buying is rare. Lacquer is the best and cheapest article. Bronzes are good and cheap. I want to bring back a dozen big bronze vases to put on the grass before our houses in summer, for palms or big plants, so as to give our houses the look of a cross between curio shops and florists. Tokio contains hardly anything worth getting except bronzes. A man at Osaka has sent up some two hundred and fifty dollars worth of lacquers, sword-hilts, inlaid work, and such stuff. As he has the best shop in Japan we took the whole lot, and have sent for more. Inros are from ten to fifteen dollars. I shall get a dozen for presents. Good cloisonné, either Chinese or Japanese, is most rare. Fine old porcelain is rare and dear. Embroideries are absolutely introuvable. Even books seem scarce. Japan has been cleaned out. My big bronze vases will cost from fifty to two hundred dollars apiece, but these will be good. . . .

I have not presented my Japanese letters of introduction, as I found it would imply a course of entertainments which I would rather avoid. Tokio is an impossible sort of place for seeing anyone. It is a bunch of towns, and the Europeans live all over it, so that one goes five miles or so to make a call or to see one's dearest friend for five minutes. The thermometer today is anywhere between 90° and 200° in the streets, and calling on formal ministers of state under such conditions is not amusing. . . .

I shall go to Osaka and Kioto in September, unless the country is absolutely closed by cholera. Indeed I should do many other things if I were not anxious to spare La Farge the risk of illness. He continues to be the most agreeable of companions, always cheerful, equable, sweet-tempered, and quite insensible to ideas of time, space, money or railway trains. To see him flying through the streets of Tokio on a jinrickshaw is a most genial vision. He peers out through his spectacles as though he felt the absurdity as well as the necessity of looking at the show as though it were real, but he enjoys it enormously, especially the smell, which quite fascinates him. He keeps me in perpetual good humor. . . . I am lost in wonder how he ever does work; but he can be energetic, and his charm is that whether energetic or lazy he has the neatest humor, the nicest observation, and the evenest temper you can imagine. When he loses the trains, I rather enjoy it. After all, who cares?

Of startling or wonderful experience we have had none. The only moral of Japan is that the children's story-books were good history. This is a child's country. Men, women and children are taken out of the fairy books. The whole show is of the nursery. Nothing is serious; nothing is taken seriously. All is toy; sometimes, as with the women, badly made and repulsive; sometimes laughable, as with the houses, gardens and children; but always taken from what La Farge declares to have been the papboats of his babyhood. I have wandered, so to express it, in all the soup-plates of forty-eight years' experience, during the last week, and have found them as natural as Alice found the Mock Turtle. Life is a dream, and in Japan one dreams of the nursery.

## *To John Hay*

NIKKO, 24 July, 1886.

Do you happen to know where Nikko is? If not, I cannot tell you. All I know is that it is in a valley among some green mountains in the insides of Japan; that it is pretty; that the hour is 8 A.M., of a sweet morning; that I am lying, in a Jap kimono on the upper verandah of the smallest doll house your children ever saw; that La Farge is below, in the bath-room, painting our toy garden, with its waterfall and miniature mountains; and that at nine o'clock we are to step down to the Fenollosas to breakfast.

Since Monday, July 12, we have been here, and here we are likely to stay. The shortest possible experience of Japanese travel in its most favorable form satisfied me that pleasure lay not there. We had but six or eight hours between Tokio and this place. Four hours were by rail, rather pleasant though hot. I enjoyed looking out at the ridiculous landscape, though it was mostly a rice field, where numerous Japs with immense round hats, and little else, paddled about, up to their knees and elbows in black dirt which I compliment in calling mud. Here and there were groves about temples, or bamboo thickets about cabins. As night came on, bonfires smoked, to keep away mosquitoes, and, by the shade of Yeyas, they were not built without reason; for, although I saw no other four-footed animal, except three pack-horses and three dogs, in fifty miles, the skeets restored a liberal average for beasts of prey. We reached at 9 P.M. a town called Utso-nomiya. So I was credibly informed, at least, and I believe it; for I know that we got into a wagon, and were driven two miles, at a full run, through a street thronged with infant children and paper lanterns. I know not how many we immolated; I soon wearied of counting; but I do know that our driver shouted, at intervals of flogging his brutes; that a devil at his side blew a penny trumpet; that another devil ran ahead and yelled; and that at last we were dropped not at a door, but, as usual, at a counter, and were told to take off our shoes. We were then led across a miniature court, past several open privies (which smelt), and an open bath-house where naked men and women were splashing, up a ladder staircase, to three rooms which were open to each other, and to the air and moon. We were pleased. La Farge and I gamboled in the sprightliness of our youth and spirits. The rooms were clean and adorned with kakimonos and bronzes. We lay on the floor and watched our neighbors below, while Bigelow concocted food out of a can of Mulligatawny soup and boiled rice. After eating this compound and smoking a cigar I would have wished to sleep a little, and in truth our beds and mosquito nets were built. At midnight I wooed slumber; but first the *amidos* or sliding shutters of the whole house below had to be slammed, for twenty minutes; then all the slammers had to take a last bath, with usual splashing and unutterable noises with their mouth and throat, which Bigelow assured us to be only their way of brushing their teeth. I have never known at what hour these noises ceased, but they ended at last, and we all fell asleep.

Presently I was waked by a curious noise in the court. It was a man, moving about, and stopping every few steps to rap two bits of wood together—clack-clack—like castanets. He interested me for twenty minutes. I understand he was the watchman on pattens, and that he thus notifies thieves to be on their guard. During this part of the entertainment I became aware that all was not well with myself; in short that I had an attack of cholera of the worst sort; a pain internal, passing into desperate nausea; then into drenching perspiration, and lastly into a violent diarrhoea. With these afflictions I struggled for an hour or two, and at last crept back to bed, weak as the moonlight which illuminated my sufferings, and hoping only for an hour of forgetfulness; when, long before daylight, the *amidos* began to slam again, the bath began to splash, the bathers choked and coughed, and chaos came.

Towards nine o'clock we consulted. Then it seemed that La Farge was suffering just as I did. Both of us were in a miserable state of weakness, trusting only that the end of our mortal career might arrive soon to bring repose. I was reduced to laughing at La Farge's comments to a point where exhaustion became humorous. Bigelow brewed for us some of my Chinese tea, for Japanese tea was nauseous. We managed to dress; and at half past eleven we were stuffed into a cart and rattled off over roads that we remember. That wagon understood jouncing. We hung on to any handy rail, and, when we could, we fell in the wagon rather than in the rice-fields. Ten miles of these gaieties brought us into a road between rows of huge cryptomerias, which seem to be a kind of giant pine; and when our horses struck this region, the ways being heavy with mud and mending, they refused to go at all. For ten miles they balked every hundred yards, and if an ascent intervened, they balked there besides. Changing horses made the matter worse; the fresher the horse, the more vigorously he balked; while our two drivers beat them over the head and withers with a heavy club. On experiment I found that I could stand—when not laughing—

and I thought walking less fatiguing than sitting to see the brutes beaten. I crawled up the hills, and perspired freely with a temperature of 90°, but in course of the day I had four cups of tea, and walked about as many miles. At six o'clock we reached Nikko; I climbed up a long stone stair to our small house; and went energetically to bed.

We have never found out what upset us, nor has Bigelow found out what poisoned his arm and laid him up for a week at the same time. All we know is that our drive to Nikko did us no harm, and in a few days we were all right again, with a fancy for staying quiet and not immediately indulging in the luxuries of Japanese hotels. Our small palace of two rooms, with paper windows and two hospitable shaven priests who say only *Ohio,* satisfy our yearnings. I have had cholera enough for the present. I admit that Mrs. Fenollosa's table had a share in our Sybaritism. The fact that, if we travel, we have nowhere to go where there is anything to see, except to Kioto and the south, is also an element. Kioto and Osaka are hotter than the future life; they are overrun with cholera; so is Yokohama where we had it common, and it has now extended to Tokio. No one seems ever to travel in the north and west, or to go to Kui-sui [1] even for Satsuma ware. Nikko is the prettiest part of Japan; here are the great temples of Yeyas (Iye-yasu) and Iye-mitsu, the first and third Shoguns; here, if it were not for show waterfalls, I can be content, and La Farge can sketch.

In truth the place is worth coming to see. Japan is not the last word of humanity, and Japanese art has a well-developed genius for annoying my prejudices; but Nikko is, after all, one of the sights of the world. I am not sure where it stands in order of rank, but after the pyramids, Rome, Mme. Tussaud's wax-works, and 800 16th Street, I am sure Nikko deserves a place. Without forgetting the fact that the temples are here and there rather cheap grotesque, the general result of temple and tomb, architecture, ornament, landscape and foliage, is very effective indeed. When you reflect that the old Shoguns spent twelve or fourteen millions of dollars on this remote mountain valley, you can understand that Louis Quatorze and Versailles are not much of a show compared with Nikko.

Photographers give no idea of the scale. They show here a gate and there a temple, but they cannot show twenty acres of ground, all ingeniously used to make a single composition. They give no idea of a mountain-flank, with its evergreens a hundred feet high, modelled into a royal, posthumous residence and deified abode. I admit to thinking it a bigger work than I should have thought possible for Japs. It is a sort of Egypt in lacquer and greenth. . . .

[1] Kiyosumi?

27 *July*. Yesterday arrived from Osaka a large lot of kakimonos, sent up by the great curio-dealer, Yamanaka. I gleaned about two dozen out of the lot. They are cheap enough, but I fear that Fenollosa, who is in Tokio, will say they are Tokugawa rot, and will bully me into letting them go. He is now trying to prevent my having a collection of Hokusai's books. He is a kind of St. Dominic, and holds himself responsible for the dissemination of useless knowledge by others. My historical indifference to everything but facts, and my delight at studying what is hopefully debased and degraded, shock his moral sense. I wish you were here to help us trample on him. He has joined a Buddhist sect; I was myself a Buddhist when I left America, but he has converted me to Calvinism with leanings towards the Methodists.

### *To Elizabeth Cameron*

NIKKO, 13 August, 1886.

Thanks for your kind little note which gave me real pleasure in my Japanese retreat. In return I can only tell you that Japan is a long way from America, but that it is not far enough to prevent my thinking too much about home matters. I have heard but once from there, since I sailed, and luckily all my news was pleasant. In six weeks more I shall be starting for home. . . .

La Farge and I have found shelter in the mountains from the heat and hotels of Japan. We have a little box of a Japanese house, where we look out on a Japanese temple-garden, and on Japanese mountains, all like the pictures that one sees on plates. We are princely in our style. The dealers in *curios* send us, from far and wide, whatever they can find that we like, and our rooms are full of such rubbish. La Farge sketches. I waste time as I can, sometimes walking, or going over the hills on rats of pack-horses; sometimes photographing in the temple grounds; sometimes sitting cross-legged, and looking at bales of stuffs or lacquers; sometimes at tea-houses, watching the sun when it kindly sets behind the big mountain Nan-tai-zan, and leaves us in a less perspiring condition than we are by day. The scenery is very pretty; not unlike that of the Virginia Springs; and the temperature much the same though very moist. Of interesting people I see nothing. I doubt whether there are any such. The Japanese women seem to me impossible. After careful inquiry I can hear of no specimen of your sex, in any class of society, whom I ought to look upon as other than a *curio*. They are all badly made, awkward in movement, and suggestive of monkeys. The children are rather pretty and quite amusing, but the mammas are the reverse; and one is well able to judge at least the types of popular beauty, seeing that there is little clothing to hide it, and that little is apt to be forgotten.

This branch of my historical inquiries has not proved rich; but, though the people are not a success in regard to personal attractions, they are very amusing indeed, and have given us infinite varieties of laughter ever since we saw our first fishing-boat. I do not advise you to allow yourself three months' leisure in order to get used to various pervasive smells, and to forget all your previous education in the matter of food, houses, drains, and vehicles. If you can live on boiled rice or stewed eels, or bad, oily, fresh tea; or in houses without partitions or walls except of paper; or in cities absolutely undrained, and with only surface wells for drinking water; or if you can sit on your heels all through five hours at the theatre, and can touch the floor with your forehead when I call upon you; and say *Hei* and *Ha* at stated intervals, you will do very well in Japan. I do all these things with less success than is to be desired, for I cannot sit on my heels at all, and I suffer to the extent of anguish even in sitting cross-legged; Japanese food makes me sea-sick, and the smell of Tokio seems to get into food, drink, and dreams; but I have not yet had my three months' education, and have even evaded it by flying to the mountains and by getting myself fed and protected after the American manner. After ten days of modified Japanese experiments I was content with what I had learned. Nothing but necessity would induce me to try another Japanese article of food or to pass another night in a Japanese inn, for the first experiment proved nearly fatal; and although I did not fear death, I shrank from dying of Japanese soup in a Japanese inn, with Japanese women to look at as my last association with earth. This weakness on my part shows the sad effects of too long life. One ought to enjoy poisonous mushrooms fried in bad oil, and to delight in looking at wooden women without any figures, waddling on wooden pattens.

Our faculty for laughing has been greatly increased, but we try in vain to acquire the courteous language of the country. No European can learn to track out the intricate holes and burrows in which Japanese courtesy hides itself. I wish I could master, in order to teach you, the ceremony of the *Ocha-no-yu*, or honorable five-o'clock tea. I declined to buy a book which contained paintings showing fifty arrangements of the charcoal to boil the kettle on this occasion; and as many more of the ways in which a single flower might be set in a porcelain stand. My friend Bigelow bought the pictures and is professor of the art. Simpler tasks satisfy me. Seeing the woman who has charge of our horses eating hard green plums, I requested Bigelow to tell her with my compliments that she would suffer from stomach-ache. Her reply, profoundly serious, was to the effect that my remark had truth; her stomach did respectfully ache. I learned much from this attitude of respect which even the digestive apparatus of a Japanese peasant woman assumes towards a stranger.

I have bought *curios* enough to fill a house, but nothing that I like, or want for myself. The stuffs are cheap and beautiful, but I have found no really fine embroidery. The lacquer is relatively cheap, but I do not care for it. I can find no good porcelain or bronze, and very few wall-pictures. Metal work is easy to get, and very choice, but what can one do with sword-guards and knife handles? I am puzzled to know what to bring home to please myself. If I knew what would please you, I would load the steamer with it. . . .

## *To John Hay*

NIKKO, 22 August, 1886.

I have still to report that purchases for you are going on, but more and more slowly, for I believe we have burst up all the pawn-brokers' shops in Japan. Even the cholera has shaken out the little that is worth getting. Bigelow and Fenollosa cling like misers to their miserable hoards. Not a kakimono is to be found, though plenty are brought. Every day new bales of rubbish come up from Tokio or elsewhere; mounds of books; tons of bad bronze; holocausts of lacquer; I buy literally everything that is merely possible; and yet I have got not a hundred dollars' worth of things I want for myself. You shall have some good small bits of lacquer, and any quantity of *duds* to encumber your tables and mantles, but nothing creditable to our joint genius. As for myself, I have only one *Yokomono*—or kakimono broader than it is long—and one small bronze, that I care to keep as the fruit of my summer's perspiration.

For Japan is the place to perspire. No one knows an ideal dogday who has not tried Japan in August. From noon to five o'clock I wilt. As for travelling, I would see the rice-fields dry first. I have often wondered what King would have done, had he come with us. I've no doubt he would have seen wonderful sights, but I should have paid his return passage on a corpse. For days together I make no attempt at an effort, while poor La Farge sketches madly and aimlessly.

By the bye, a curious coincidence happened. Bigelow announced one morning that King and Hay were coming from Tokio with loads of curios for us. La Farge and I stared and inquired. Then it appeared that Bigelow and Fenollosa employ two men—Kin, pronounced King, and Hei, pronounced Hay—to hunt curios for them, and had sent them word to bring up whatever they could find. I thought this one of the happiest accidents I ever heard, and I only wish that Messrs. King and Hay had brought better things, as their American namesakes expected. They meant well, but they lacked means. Nevertheless they brought a few nice bits, to sustain the credit of their names.

Fairly bored by sweltering in this moistness, I stirred up Mrs. Fenollosa to a little expedition last Tuesday. Fenollosa is unwell; La Farge is hard at work; but Mrs. Fenollosa, Bigelow and I, started to visit Yumoto, the Saratoga, or White Sulphur, of Japan. Yumoto lies just fourteen miles above us among the mountains, and with one of my saddle horses I could easy go there and return on the same day; but such a journey in Japan is serious. Only pedestrians, coolies, or Englishmen work hard. Mrs. Fenollosa summoned five pack-horses. All Japanese horses known to me are rats, and resemble their pictures, which I had supposed to be bad drawing; but these pack-horses are rats led by a man, or more often by a woman, at a very slow walk. Mrs. Fenollosa mounted one; Bigelow another; I ascended a third; a servant and baggage followed on a fourth; the fifth carried beds, blankets, linen, silver, eatables, and drinks. At half past eight the caravan started, and at half past ten it arrived at the foot of Chiu-zen-ji pass, where one climbs a more or less perpendicular mountain side for an hour. I preferred my own legs to the rat's, and walked up. So we arrived at Lake Chiu-zen-ji, a pretty sheet of water about seven miles long, at the foot of the sacred mountain Nan-tai-zan. On the shore of this lake is a temple, where pilgrims begin the ascent of the mountain, sacred to Sho-do Sho-nin, who devoted fifteen years of his valuable existence, in the eighth century, to the astounding feat of climbing it. As it is very accessible, and only eight thousand feet above the sea, Sho-do Sho-nin is a very popular and greatly admired saint, and some five thousand pilgrims come every August to follow his sainted steps. Next the temple are some inns, but not a farm or a human dwelling exists on the lake or among the mountains; for if the Japanese like one thing more than another it is filthy rice-fields, and if they care less for one thing than another, it is mountains. All this lovely country, from here to the sea of Japan, is practically a dense wilderness of monkeys, as naked as itself; but the monkeys never seem out of place as a variety, though I have not met them in society, and speak only from association. We stopped at an inn, and while lunch was making ready, Bigelow and I went out in a kind of frigate for a swim in the lake. After lunch, sending our beasts ahead, we sailed to the next starting-point, just the length of a cigar. Another two miles of rise brought us to a moor for all the world like Estes Park and the Rocky Mountains. Crossing this, we climbed another ascent, and came out on an exquisite little green lake with woody mountains reflected on its waters. Nothing could be prettier than the path along this shore, but it was not half so amusing to me as our entrance into the village of Yumoto, with its dozen inns and no villagers; for, by the roadside, at the very entrance, I saw at last the true Japan of my dreams, and broke out into carols of joy. In a wooden hut, open to all the winds, and public as the road, men, women and children, naked as the mother that bore them, were sitting, standing, soaking and drying themselves, as their ancestors had done a thousand years ago.

I had begun to fear that Japan was spoiled by Europe. At Tokio even the coolies wear something resembling a garment, and the sexes are obliged to bathe apart. As I came into the country I noticed first that the children were naked; that the men wore only a breech-clout; and that the women were apt to be stripped to the waist; but I had begun to disbelieve that this disregard of appearances went further. I was wrong. No sooner had we dismounted than we hurried off to visit the baths; and Mrs. Fenollosa will bear me witness that for ten minutes we stood at the entrance of the largest bath-house, and looked on at a dozen people of all ages, sexes and varieties of ugliness, who paid not the smallest regard to our presence. I should except one pretty girl of sixteen, with quite a round figure and white skin. I did notice that for the most part, while drying herself, she stood with her back to us.

When this exceptionally pleasing virgin walked away, I took no further interest in the proceedings, though I still regard them as primitive. Of the habits and manners of the Japanese in regard to the sexes, I see little, for I cannot conquer a feeling that Japs are monkeys, and the women very badly made monkeys; but from others I hear much on the subject, and what I hear is very far from appetising. In such an atmosphere one talks freely. I was a bit aghast when one young woman called my attention to a temple as a remains of phallic worship; but what can one do? Phallic worship is as universal here as that of trees, stones and the sun. I come across shrines of phallic symbols in my walks, as though I were an ancient Greek. One cannot quite ignore the foundations of society. . . .

25 *August*. I can't say, "let's return to our sheep," for there are no sheep in Japan, and I have eaten nothing but bad beef since landing. As for returning to my remarks on Yumoto as connected with the sexes, I decline to do it. In spite of King, I affirm that sex does not exist in Japan, except as a scientific classification. I would not affirm that there are no exceptions to my law; but the law itself I affirm as the foundation of archaic society. Sex begins with the Aryan race. I have seen a Japanese beauty, which has a husband, *Nabeshame*, if I hear right—a live Japanese Marquis, late Daimio of Hizo, or some other place; but though he owns potteries, he has, I am sure, no more suc-

cessful bit of bric-à-brac than his wife is; but as for being a woman, she is hardly the best Satsuma. . . .

## *To John Hay*

KIOTO, 9 September, 1886.

Kioto at last! La Farge and I made an impressive entry at nine o'clock last night, with our suite, by moonlight, and this morning—at half past six o'clock—we are sitting on our verandah, looking out over the big city, he sketching, and both of us incessantly wishing that you and King were with us, for there is no kind of doubt that Japan is *omoshirvi*, a word we pronounce *œmushrvi*, which means amusing, and is always in use. Kioto is *omoshirvi* as we look over it; a sort of Japanese Granada. For two months we have heard and talked of nothing but Kioto, and here we are! Think of it, dissolute man! It is being in the new Jerusalem with a special variety of Jews. You see at once why La Farge and I are up and active at SIX A.M. . . .

La Farge and I, after six days of boiled and furious activity at Yokohama, trying to get things done, which is something the Japanese never do, gave it up; but I would have given you a present if you could have seen us on our expedition last Friday to what the old books called the *Dye boots*.[1] This remnant of the vanished splendor of Kamakura is about twenty miles from Yokohama, and next to Kioto and Narra, we have damned it persistently for two months because of the heat. I bought—for you or others—various specimens of so-called Kamakura lacquer, the only instance in human history where *nacre* has been used with success; and every time I saw the stuff, I cursed it because I had not had energy to see the Dai Butsu. Last Friday we saw it, and as La Farge says, it is the most successful colossal figure in the world; he sketched it, and I, seizing the little priest's camera, mounted to the roof of his porch, and, standing on my head at an angle of impossibility, perpetrated a number of libels on Buddha and Buddhism without shame at the mild contempt of his blessed little moustache, which is ächt Japanesisch of today. This is not my story. I mention it in passing Kamakura, for we saw no more of the city which is no longer existing or visible; but having lunched at a tea-house, and watched a heavy shower make the roads hopeless, we were persuaded by the Ho—Houro, Japanese phœnix, an acute disease known as a travelling servant whose death in torture is a matter only of hours—to return by way of the beach of Enoshima. Although we knew that all view of Fuji—

[1] Daibutsu, or Great Buddha.

the only object of such a trip—was hopeless, we let ourselves in for what proved to be an hour's walk over a soft sand-beach in a steam-bath. In half the distance La Farge fell into his jinrickshaw exhausted, and I tumbled into the Pacific ocean and swam or waded to the next village. When I tried to come out of the water, the surf covered me with black sand; my clothes were so wet that I could not get them on, and my boots were full of water. So I put on my coat, tied a yellow oil-paper rain-cover round my waist, and seating myself in my kurama, stuck my naked legs over the footboard, and was whirled through the village like a wild Indian. The curious part of the matter was that in a mile of transit to the nearest tea-house, not even a child raised an eye-lid of surprise, whereas La Farge, who followed later, in complete European costume, was received with enthusiasm. Evidently my outfit is the one expected from Americans in this country. We drove back to Yokohama afterwards in the dark, and I could not wonder at the calmness with which my legs had been received. As we drove through mile after mile of village without front walls, every house offered a dimly lighted study of legs in every attitude. My eyes still whirl with the wild succession of men's legs, and of women's breasts, in every stage of development and decomposition, which danced through that obscurity.

On Sunday we took a French steamer for Kobe. . . . Kobe is only the European settlement for Osaka and Kioto, a kind of waiting-room, to Yamanaka's, towards whose shop I am leading you. . . . Only one lesson was impressed more deeply than ever on my heart; which was that if I want good things, I must buy Chinese. In porcelain there is no comparison; in embroidery, none; in kakimonos, not much. The best Chinese is always out of sight ahead, as in cloisonné, and, I think, even in bronze, though bronze is *the* Japanese metal. Only in gold lacquer and small metal work, like sword-guards, or perhaps small ivories, like netsukes, where Japanese humor and lightness have the field to themselves, the Japanese excel. They are quite aware of their own inferiority, and the prices they pay for good Chinese or Corean work are out of all proportion to their own. . . .

My trouble is in the temptation to buy masses of indifferent work, which is the best I can get. . . . None of the things are large. Except for temples or gardens the Japs make few large things for themselves. Their small houses and low rooms are not suited to big ornament. Everything you see of that sort, especially tall bronzes, porcelains and lacquers, unless it comes from temples or gardens, is made for export and is not true Japanese. Things like *Inros,* lacquer boxes a few inches long; *netsukes* of ivory or wood; *fukusas,* or embroidered and woven stuffs like my eagle-and-ocean screen; swords; small kakimonos; tea-jars from two to twelve inches high; flower vases, porcelain or bronze, from ten inches to eighteen in height; in short, anything that will go on a table, or is easily handled, is Japanese domestic decoration. The big vases, especially the big grotesque bird-flower-and-dragon vases, are *never* seen out of the shops in Yokohama. No Japanese ever dreamed of such decoration, except perhaps for a temple or some public place. All his best, choicest and Jap-sneeziest work is in little things to be worn, or to be shown to guests at his Cha-no-yu, or Tea-party, in a bare little room, about ten feet square, with walls of Chinese simplicity; white plaster and wood unplaned. . . .

*Sunday*, 12 *Septr.* This travelling is taking hold of my system. We cannot stand the pace. At our age occasional repose is a benefit. La Farge and I have jounced in kurumas, rattled through temples; asked questions, and talked Japanese, or listened to it, till we cower in fear before every new suggestion. We are nauseated by curios; I detest temples; he is persecuted by letters of introduction, and I, who have delivered only one of mine, pass all my time trying to escape hospitality. At last I understand the duties of life. Never be hospitable to a traveller. He is only happy in freedom. Damn him, and let him go.

One Japanese interior is highly amusing, but the joke is not rich enough for two. I find myself here with La Farge, T. Walsh, of Walsh, Hall & Co., two interpreters; a travelling servant; the Governor of Kioto's secretary; three Kioto merchants; and madness! The temples are ordered to produce their treasures for us; the houses drag out all their ancestral properties, and very curious they are; the artists in porcelain, the dealers in curios, and even the schools we are expected to inspect as connoisseurs. Today we had three hours at the house of Kassiobawara San, an elderly merchant here, who happens to live in the oldest house in the city; then at noon we started in kurumas, with a stewing heat, for a river twelve miles off; then we shot what the *Ho* calls "rabbits" for an hour, in a boat; we got through the rapids only to jounce for another hour or two in kurumas back to Kioto, where two makers of porcelain and a big curio dealer were sitting at the door of my room, and a Japanese gentleman was waiting to call on La Farge. The Japanese gentleman sat till half past eleven, thereby driving us to wish ourselves in bed or somewhere.

All the same, since leaving Nikko we have just piled in the impressions. If we do not soon become masters of the Japanese science, we shall at least learn something of our own to take its place. We will turn out a new Japan of our own. La Farge has bought materials enough—vast mounds of rubbish—to construct a world of decoration, paint forests of pictures, and exhaust the windows of Christianity. I have learned so many new facts of which I am ignorant, that I could fill winter evenings with my want of knowledge. The only branch we have not yet exhausted is that of the dances, and we intend to begin today on this sphere of usefulness. Geishas are ordered for this evening. If they please me as little as most of their Japanese sisters, I shall not want further acquaintance. I am in hot pursuit of the Butterfly Dance, and have started a chase through the temples in search of it. On the whole, Osaka and Kioto pan out well.

*Wednesday morning*, 15 *Septr*. I close this despatch by reporting that we had our Geisha ball, in all the forms, last night. No words can give you an idea of the drollness. I am lost in astonishment at this flower of eastern culture. I cannot quite say that it is like an imaginary theatre in a nursery of seven-year-old girls, or that it is absolutely and disgustingly proper, because all my Japanese friends got drunk on saki, and some of the singing women were highly trained; but for an exhibition of mechanical childishness I have seen nothing to equal it except a Japanese garden, or a batch of Japanese dolls. Absolutely the women's joints clacked audibly, and their voices were metallic.

I will tell you all about it when we meet; but La Farge is so much more amusing about it than I can be, that you had better wait till our book comes out, in which he will write the story, and I draw the pictures.

# DIDEROT

## *Rameau's Nephew*

*"Vertumnis, quotquot sunt, natus iniquis."* *
(Horat. Lib. II. Sat. VII.)

Be the day fair or foul, it is my custom, towards five in the evening, to walk in the Palais-Royal gardens. I am that man who may be seen, always alone, day-dreaming on d'Argenson's bench. I converse with myself on politics, love, taste, and philosophy. I give my mind full licence; I leave it free to follow the first notion, wise or foolish, that occurs to it, as one may see in the Allée de Foy our dissolute young gallants walk close on the heels of some courtesan with giddy air, laughing face, bright eye and pert nose, then leave her for some other, tackling them all and adhering to none. My thoughts are my wantons.

If the weather is too cold or too wet, I take refuge in the Café de la Régence; there I find entertainment in watching the chess-players. Paris is the place in all the world, and the Café de la Régence the place in all Paris, where this game is played best. It is at Rey's that Légal, the profound player, the subtle Philidor, and the sound Mayot are pitted against one another; that you will see the most astonishing play and hear the worst conversation; for, if one may be a man of sense and a great chess-player, like Légal, it is also possible to be a great chess-player and a fool, like Foubert and Mayot.

One afternoon I was there, watching a great deal, speaking little, listening as little as possible, when I was accosted by one of the queerest figures ever seen in this country where God has made no lack of them. He is a mixture of fineness and baseness, of good sense and folly. Ideas of right and wrong must be very strangely confused in his head; for he displays his natural good qualities without ostentation and his bad ones without shame. He is endowed, moreover, with a vigorous constitution, a rare imaginative fervour and an uncommonly powerful pair of lungs. If ever you meet him, and you are not stopped by his eccentricity, either you will put your fingers in your ears or you will run away. Heavens, what terrible lungs! Nothing can be more unlike him than he is himself at times. Sometimes he is thin and haggard, like a sick man in the last stages of consumption; you might count his teeth through his cheeks. You would say he had gone without food for several days, or had just come from a Trappist monastery. The month after, he

* Born with the enmity of all the gods.

is plump and stout, as if he had been a constant guest at a financier's dinner-table, or had been shut up in a Cistercian monastery. One day, with his linen soiled, his breeches torn, his clothes in rags and his shoes in pieces, he will go about hanging his head, avoiding people, and you feel inclined to call him and offer him alms. Next day, powdered and curled, well clad and shod, he holds his head high, shows himself off, and you would almost take him for a gentleman. He lives from day to day: sad or merry according to circumstances. His first care in the morning, as soon as he is up, is to find out where he is to dine; after dinner, he thinks where he will get supper. Night, too, brings its problem. Either he goes back on foot to the little attic where he lives, unless the landlady, tired of waiting for her rent, has asked to have the key back; or else he subsides in a tavern in the suburbs to wait for daylight with a hunk of bread and a pot of beer. When he has not six sous in his pocket, which sometimes happens, he has recourse either to a cabman of his acquaintance or to the coachman of some great noble who lets him sleep on the straw, beside the horses. In the morning he still has part of his mattress in his hair. If the weather is mild, he walks all night along the Cours or the Champs-Elysées. With daylight he reappears in town, still wearing the clothes he had on the night before, and wearing them sometimes for the rest of the week. I have no high opinion of such eccentrics. Some people accept them as familiar acquaintances, even as friends. Once a year they engage my interest when I meet them, because their character is in violent contrast with that of other people, and they break the tedious uniformity introduced by our education, our social conventions, our customary notions of propriety. If one such person appears in a gathering, he acts like a grain of yeast that starts a fermentation, and restores to everyone part of his natural individuality. He shakes and stirs up people; he calls forth approval or blame; he brings out the truth; he shows one which are honest folk, and unmasks rogues. It's then that a man of sense listens and learns to distinguish between people.

I had known this particular eccentric for a long time. He used to visit a household to which his gifts had won him an entry. There was an only daughter; he used to swear to the father and mother that he would marry their child. They would shrug their shoulders, laugh in his face, tell him he was mad; and I could foresee the thing being accomplished. He would borrow from me a few crowns which I would let him have. He had found his way, I don't know how, into certain respectable households, where his place was laid at table on condition that he did not speak unless he was given permission. He would keep silence, and eat in a fury. If, seized with a desire to break the contract, he opened his mouth, at the first word everyone at table cried out: "Oh,

Rameau!" Then, his eyes glittering with wrath, he would fall to eating again even more furiously. You were curious to know the man's name, and now you know it. He is the nephew of that celebrated musician, who has delivered us from the plainsong of Lulli which we had been droning out for over a hundred years; who has written so many unintelligible imaginings and apocalyptic truths on the theory of music, which neither he nor anyone else has ever understood, and who has given us a certain number of operas which contain harmony, fragments of song, disconnected ideas, clamour, flights, triumphs, spears, glories, murmurs, victories, in breathless succession; dance tunes that will last for ever; and who, having buried the Florentine, will himself be buried by the virtuosi of Italy, which he foresaw and which made him gloomy, sad and surly; for there is no one as peevish, not even a pretty woman who finds a pimple on her nose when she gets up, as an author in danger of outliving his reputation: witness Marivaux and the younger Crébillon.

He accosts me . . . "Aha! so here you are, master philosopher; and what are you doing among this gang of idlers? Do you, too, waste your time shoving the wood?" Thus the games of chess and draughts are contemptuously referred to.

*I*: No; but when I've nothing better to do, it amuses me to spend a moment watching those who do it well.

*He*: In that case, you're seldom amused; except Légal and Philidor, the rest don't know a thing about it.

*I*: What about M. de Bissy?

*He*: He stands, as a chess-player, where Mlle. Clairon stands as an actress. Both know all that can be learnt about these games.

*I*: You are hard to please: and I see that you only spare those who are really great.

*He*: Yes, in such trivialities as chess, draughts, poetry, eloquence, music; of what use is the second-rate in such matters?

*I*: Very little, I admit. But there must be a great number of men practising them in order that the man of genius may emerge. He is one out of a multitude. But let us leave that. I haven't seen you for an age; I never think of you when I don't see you, but I am always pleased to see you again. What have you been doing?

*He*: What you and I and all other men do: some good, some harm, sometimes nothing at all. And then I've been hungry, and eaten when I got the chance; and after eating I've been thirsty, and sometimes I've had a drink. Meanwhile my beard grew; and when it was grown I shaved it off.

*I*: That was a mistake; it's all you lacked to be a sage.

*He*: Yes, indeed. I've a high, wrinkled brow; a fiery eye; a prominent nose; broad cheeks; black bushy eyebrows; a big mouth, a curled lip and a square face. If this great chin were covered with a long beard, do you know, I should look very well in bronze or marble.

*I*: By the side of Caesar, Marcus Aurelius and Socrates?

*He*: No, I'd be better between Diogenes and Phryne. I have the effrontery of the one, and I'm a frequent visitor of the other.

*I*: Have you kept well?

*He*: Yes, usually; but not wonderfully well to-day.

*I*: What! here you are with the belly of a Silenus and a face. . . .

*He*: A face that might belong to his antagonist. Well, it seems that the ill-humour that dries up my dear uncle makes his dear nephew grow fat.

*I*: Speaking of that uncle, do you sometimes see him?

*He*: Yes, passing in the street.

*I*: Does he never do you a kindness?

*He*: If he ever does to anyone, it's by mistake. He is a philosopher after his kind. He thinks only of himself; the rest of the universe doesn't exist for him. His wife and daughter can die whenever they choose; so long as the church bells that toll for them always sound a twelfth and a seventeenth, all will be well. He's lucky in that respect. And that is what I value particularly in people of genius. They are good at one thing only. Beyond that, nothing. They don't know what it means to be citizens, fathers, mothers, relatives, friends. Between you and me, one ought to resemble them in every respect; but one must not wish their seed to be common. Men are necessary, but not men of genius. No, on my word, they are not wanted at all! It is they who change the face of the globe; and stupidity about the smallest things is so common and so powerful that it cannot be reformed without an uproar. Part of what they plan gets established; part remains as it was; hence two gospels, a harlequin's coat. The wisdom of Rabelais' monk is the true wisdom, for his own peace of mind and that of others: to do one's duty more or less, always speak well of the reverend prior, and let the world go as it will. It goes all right, since the majority is satisfied with it. If I knew any history, I would demonstrate to you that harm has always come, here below, through some man of genius. But I know no history, because I know nothing at all. Devil take me if ever I learnt anything; and if I am any the worse for having learnt nothing. One day I was having dinner with a minister of the King of France, as clever as they're made; well, he proved to us, as clear as one and one make two, that nothing was more useful to nations than falsehood; nothing more harmful than the truth. I don't remember his proofs very well, but the evident conclusion was that men of genius are detestable, and that if a child, at birth, bore on its brow the mark of this dangerous gift of nature, it should either be smothered or thrown in the river.

*I*: And yet these people who are so hostile to genius all claim to possess it.

*He*: I really think they do in their hearts; but I don't think they would dare to confess as much.

*I*: That is through modesty. So you conceived a fearful hatred for genius there?

*He*: One which I shall never get over.

*I*: But I have seen the times when you were in despair at being only a common man. You will never be happy, if the two sides of an argument distress you equally. You must make your decision and keep to it. While agreeing with you that men of genius are usually peculiar, or that, as the proverb says, there is no great wit without a grain of madness, we can't help admiring them, and we shall always despise the centuries that have produced none. They will still be the glory of the nations among whom they have lived; sooner or later, statues are erected to them, and they are regarded as benefactors of the human race. With all due respect to that wonderful minister whom you quoted to me, I believe that, if falsehood may be useful for a moment, it is inevitably harmful in the long run; and that, on the contrary, truth is inevitably useful in the long run, though it may do harm for the moment. From which I am inclined to conclude that the man of genius who condemns some general error, or who wins credit for some great truth, is always a being worthy of our reverence. It may so happen that this being falls a victim to prejudice and to law; but laws are of two kinds; some are of absolute justice and universality, others are peculiar, and only owe their sanction to human blindness or to the necessity of circumstances. These cast only a passing shame on the man who is guilty of infringing them; a shame which in course of time is reversed and falls irrevocably on the judges and nations. Who is the dishonoured man to-day, Socrates or the judge who made him drink hemlock?

*He*: And is Socrates any the better off for that? Does it alter the fact that he was condemned, that he was put to death, that he was an unruly citizen? By despising a bad law, did he any the less encourage the foolish to despise good laws? Was he any the less a bold, eccentric individual? You just now came near admitting something not very favourable to men of genius.

*I*: Listen to me, my dear fellow. A society should have no bad laws; and if it had only good ones, it would never have occasion to persecute a genius. I did not say that genius was inseparably attached to perverseness, nor perverseness to genius. A fool is more likely to be bad than a man of intelligence. If a genius should usually be an ill-mannered fellow, difficult to deal with, cantankerous, unbearable, if he should even be evil-natured, what would you conclude therefrom?

*He*: That he ought to be drowned.

*I*: Gently, my dear fellow. Here now, tell me; I won't take your uncle for an example; he is a hard man, brutal and inhuman, miserly, a bad father, a bad husband, a bad uncle; but it is not really certain whether he is a genius, whether he has greatly furthered the progress of his art and whether his works will be talked of in ten years' time. But take Racine; there's an unquestioned genius for you, and one who was not considered exactly a good man. Take Voltaire. . . .

*He*: Don't press me too closely; I am logical.

*I*: Which would you rather, that he should have been a good man, sticking to his counter like Briasson, or to his yard-measure like Barbier; a good husband, getting a legitimate child regularly every year from his wife; a good father, a good uncle, a good neighbour, an honest tradesman, but nothing more; or that he should have been a knave, treacherous, ambitious, envious, evil-natured; and yet the author of *Andromaque*, *Britannicus*, *Iphigénie*, *Phèdre*, *Athalie?*

*He*: Why, for his own sake, perhaps, it would have been better if he had been the first of these two men.

*I*: Indeed, that's infinitely truer than you think.

*He*: Oh, that's just like you people! If we say anything sensible, it's bound to be by chance, like madmen or men inspired; you are the only people who know what you are saying. Yes, master philosopher, I know what I'm saying, just as much as you know what you're saying.

*I*: Well, then, why—"for his own sake"?

*He*: Because all those fine works of his didn't bring him in twenty thousand francs; whereas if he had been some worthy silk merchant of the rue St.-Denis or St.-Honoré, some worthy wholesale grocer, some apothecary doing good business, he would have collected a huge fortune, and, by collecting it, there's no sort of pleasure he could not have enjoyed; he would have given a guinea from time to time to some poor devil of a buffoon, like myself, who would have made him laugh, and who would have procured him on occasions a young girl to relieve him from the tedium of eternal cohabitation with his wife; we should have had excellent meals at his house and played for high stakes, drunk excellent wines, excellent liqueurs, excellent coffee, gone on pleasure-parties; and so you see I knew what I was saying. You laugh. But let me have my say. He would have been better towards those around him.

*I*: Undoubtedly; provided that he did not use in some dishonourable fashion the wealth he gained through legitimate trade; that he turned out of his house all those gamblers, parasites, insipid flatterers, idlers, perverse hangers-on; and that he set his shop-assistants to flog soundly the meddler who offers to relieve husbands, by variety, from the boredom of habitual cohabitation with their wives.

*He*: Flog him, monsieur! flog him? In a well-regulated town nobody gets flogged. And it's an honest profession; many people, even titled people, practise it. And what the devil do you want a man to spend his money on, if not on enjoying good food, good company, good wine, fine women, pleasures of every description, amusements of all sorts? I'd as soon be a beggar as possess a great fortune and enjoy none of these things. But let us get back to Racine. There's a man who was good only for those who never knew him, when he was no longer alive.

*I*: Granted. But weigh up the good and the bad. A thousand years hence, he will still cause tears to flow; he will awaken men's admiration in all the countries of the earth; he will inspire compassion, pity, tenderness. Men will ask who he was, of what country, and they will envy France for him. He caused pain to a few beings who are no more, who scarcely interest us to-day; we have nothing to fear from his vices or his faults. No doubt it would have been better if he had received from nature a good man's virtue, together with a great man's talents. He was like a tree that withers up a few trees planted in its neighbourhood, that chokes the plants growing at its feet, but that lifts its crest into the clouds, and widely spreads its branches; that grants shade to those who have come, who come still, and who will yet come to rest around its majestic trunk; that yields fruits of an exquisite savour, which continually renew themselves. One might wish that de Voltaire were also as gentle as Duclos, as ingenuous as the abbé Trublet, as upright as the abbé d'Olivet; but since that is impossible, let us look at the question from its really significant side; let us forget for a moment the position we occupy in space and time; and take a long view over the centuries to come, the remotest regions and peoples yet unborn. Let us consider the good of our species. If we are not generous enough, let us at least forgive nature for having been wiser than ourselves. If you throw cold water over the head of Greuze, you may extinguish his talent at the same time as his vanity. If you render de Voltaire less sensitive to criticism, he will no longer be able to penetrate the soul of Mérope. He will cease to move you.

*He*: But if nature were as powerful as she is wise, why did she not make them as good as she made them great?

*I*: But don't you see that with that line of reasoning you upset the general order of things, and that if all were excellent here on earth nothing would be excellent?

*He*: You are right. The important point is that you and I should exist and that we should be you and I. Apart from that, let all go as best it can. The best possible order of things, to my mind, is that which requires that I should exist; and a fig for the most perfect of worlds, if it doesn't include me. I'd rather exist, and even be an extravagant reasoner, than not exist at all.

*I*: There is no one who doesn't think as you do, and who nevertheless doesn't condemn the existing order of things, without seeing that he repudiates his own existence.

*He*: True.

*I*: Then let us accept things as they are. Let us see what they cost us and what they bring us in; and let us leave out of account all that we don't understand well enough to praise or blame, and which is perhaps neither good nor evil, so long as it be necessary, as many honest folk imagine it to be.

*He*: I don't understand much of this harangue of yours. It appears to be philosophy; and I warn you that I'll have nothing to do with that. All I know is, that I'd like to be someone different, on the chance of being a man of genius, a great man. Yes, I must admit it, there is something within me that tells me so. I've never heard anyone praised without being secretly infuriated at their praise. I am envious. When I'm told something discreditable about their private life, I listen to it with pleasure; it puts us more on a level. It makes my mediocrity easier to bear. I say to myself: "Assuredly you could never have written *Mahomet;* but neither could you have praised Maupeou." So then, I have been, I still am, resentful of my mediocrity. Yes, yes, I am mediocre and I resent it. I have never heard the overture to *Indes galantes* played, never heard anyone sing the *Profondes abîmes du Ténare*, or *Nuit, eternelle nuit*, without saying to myself with sorrow, there's something you'll never do. So then, I am jealous of my uncle; and if there were at his death a few fine pieces for the harpsichord in his portfolio, I shouldn't hesitate between remaining myself and being him.

*I*: If that's all that distresses you, it's hardly worth it.

*He*: It's nothing. These moments are soon over.

Then he began to sing once more the overture of *Indes galantes* and the air *Profondes abîmes*, and added:

"The something within that speaks to me says: 'Rameau, you'd be very glad to have written those two pieces; if you had written those two, you could certainly have written two others; and when you had written a certain number, you'd be played and sung everywhere; when you walked, you'd hold your head high; your conscience would bear witness to you of your own merit; others would point you out. They would say: 'that's the man who wrote those pretty gavottes.'" And he sang the gavottes. Then, with the air of a man who is moved, who is overjoyed, who has tears of joy in his eyes, he added, rubbing his hands together: "You'd have a good house (he seemed to be measuring its span with his arms), a good bed (he was stretching himself out in it nonchalantly), good wines (and he smacked his tongue as he tasted them), a fine carriage (he lifted his foot to climb into it), pretty women (already he seemed to stroke their bosoms and gaze at them voluptuously), a hundred little snobs would come to flatter me every day" and he imagined them around him; he saw Palissot, Poinsinet, the Frérons, father and son, La Porte; he listened to them, swelled with pride, approved them, smiled at them, disdained them, scorned them, dismissed them, recalled them; when he went on:

"And so you'd be told in the morning that you were a great man; you'd read in the *History of Three Centuries* that you were a great man; you'd be convinced, by evening, that you were a great man; and that great man, Rameau the nephew, would fall asleep to the sweet murmur of the praises echoing in his ear; even as he slept he would have a satisfied air; his chest would expand, would rise and fall easily; he would snore like a great man."

And, as he spoke, he let himself sink lazily onto a bench; he closed his eyes and mimed the happy sleep he was imagining. Having enjoyed for some minutes the sweetness of this rest, he woke up, stretched his arms and yawned, rubbed his eyes and seemed to be still looking around him for his insipid flatterers.

*I*: Do you believe then that a happy man sleeps in a special way?

*He*: Do I not believe it! I, poor wretch, when at night I have gone back to my attic and crawled on to my pallet, I crouch under my blanket; my chest is constricted, I breathe with difficulty—just a sort of feeble murmur that can scarcely be heard; whereas a financier makes his whole lodging resound and astounds the whole street. But what distresses me to-day is not that I snore and sleep so meanly, like a pauper.

*I*: It's sad, all the same.

*He*: What has happened to me is far sadder.

*I*: What's that?

*He*: You've always taken some interest in me because I'm a good fellow whom you despise at heart, but who amuses you.

*I*: That is the truth.

*He*: And so I'll tell you.

Before beginning, he heaved a deep sigh and clasped his head in his hands. Then, resuming an air of calm, he said:

"You know that I'm ignorant, foolish, mad, impertinent, idle, an arrant rogue, as they say in Burgundy, a thief, a glutton. . . ."

*I*: What a panegyric!

*He*: It's true in every respect. Not a word to be left out. No discussion on that point, if you please; no one knows me better than I know myself; and I'm not saying all there is to say.

*I*: I don't want to vex you; and I'll accept everything.

*He*: Well! I was living with some people who'd taken a fancy to me just because I was endowed to an uncommon degree with all these qualities.

*I*: That is odd. Up till now I had believed that one either concealed them from oneself, or that one excused them in oneself and despised them in others.

*He*: How can one conceal them from oneself? You may be sure that when Palissot is alone and examines himself, he has plenty to say then. You may be sure that when he's alone with his colleague, they frankly confess they're a pair of notorious rascals. As for despising them in others, my folk were too fair for that, their own character made me a wonderful success with them. I was in clover. They made a fuss of me; they couldn't lose sight of me for a moment without missing me. I was their little Rameau, their pretty Rameau, their crazy, impertinent, ignorant, lazy, greedy Rameau, their buffoon, their great big fool of a Rameau. And every one of these familiar epithets brought with it a smile or a caress for me, a little tap on the shoulder, a box on the ear, a kick, at table a dainty morsel flung on my plate, away from table some liberty at which I took no offence. For I never take offence. People can do what they like to me, with me and in front of me, and I'll not take exception. And how little presents rained on me! Great ass that I am, I've lost everything! I've lost everything, through having had some common sense, for the first, the only time, in my life. Ah! if ever that happens again!

*I*: What was it all about?

*He*: An incomparable, incomprehensible, unpardonable piece of stupidity.

*I*: But what was the stupidity?

*He*: Rameau, Rameau, had you been taken on for that? The stupidity of having had a little taste, a little wit, a little sense. Rameau, my friend, that will teach you to stay as God made you and as your patrons desired you. And so they took you by the shoulders; they led you to the door; they said to you: "Knave, be off with you; never show yourself again. The creature wants to show sense and reason, it seems! Be off! We've enough and to spare of these qualities." You went away biting your fingers; it's your cursed tongue you should have bitten before. Just for lack of forethought, here you are on the pavement, penniless, not knowing where to bestow yourself. You were fed like a king and you're going back to the garbage-pail; you had a good home, and now you'll be only too glad if you can have your attic again; you had a good bed, and now the straw awaits you, between M. de Soubise's coachman and friend Robbé. Instead of that sweet peaceful sleep you've been enjoying, you will hear with one ear the neighing and trampling of horses, with the other the far more intolerable sound of dry, hard, barbarous verses. Oh thoughtless wretch, possessed of a million devils!

*I*: But mightn't there be some way of getting back? Is the fault you have committed so unpardonable? In your place I would go and see these people again; they need you more than you think.

*He*: Oh, I am sure that now they haven't got me to make them laugh they are as dull as ditchwater.

*I*: I should go and seek them out, then. I should not leave them time to get on without me, to turn to some respectable amusement; for who knows what may happen?

*He*: That is not what I'm afraid of. That won't happen.

*I*: Sublime though you may be, another can take your place.

*He*: Hardly.

*I*: Granted. Nevertheless I should go, with that distracted countenance, those wild eyes, your shirt all gaping at the neck, your hair dishevelled, in that truly tragic state you are in now. I should throw myself at the feet of the goddess; I should press my face to the ground, and without getting up I should say in a low, sobbing voice: "Forgive me, madame! I am unworthy and infamous; it was just an unfortunate moment; for you know that I am not subject to having common sense, and I promise never to have any again in my life."

To my amusement, as I was holding forth to him, he mimed my words. He fell prostrate; he pressed his face against the earth; he seemed to be holding between his hands the tip of a slipper; he wept, he sobbed, and said: "Yes, my little queen; yes, I promise, I'll never have any again in all my life." Then getting up suddenly, he added in a grave, reflective tone:

*He*: Yes, you are right. I think that is the best thing. She is good. M. Vieillard says she is so good. And I know a bit about that too. But still, to go and humiliate oneself before a she-ape! To beg for mercy at the feet of a little second-rate actress who's followed everywhere by the hisses of the pit! I, Rameau! son of M. Rameau, apothecary, of Dijon, a worthy man who has never bent the knee before anyone! I, Rameau, nephew of him whom they call the great Rameau, who may be seen walking about the Palais-Royal, upright, his arms in the air ever since M. Carmontelle sketched him stooping with his hands under his coat-tails! I who have composed pieces for the harpsichord that no one plays, but which will perhaps be the only ones to go down to posterity, which will play them; that I, I should go. . . . I tell you, monsieur, it is impossible. (And, clapping his right hand to his breast, he added:) I feel here something rising up and saying: Rameau, you shall do no such thing. There must be a certain dignity inherent in man's nature, that nothing can suppress. It is aroused for no apparent reason; yes, for no reason, for on certain other days it would cost me nothing to be as base as you like; on such days, for a farthing, I'd kiss the arse of little Mlle. Hus.

*I*: Well, but, my friend, she's white and pretty, young, soft and plump; and that's an act of humility to which one more fastidious than yourself might sometimes be willing to abase himself.

*He*: Let us be clear; there's a literal arse-kissing and a figurative arse-kissing. Ask fat Bergier, who kisses Mme. de la Marque's arse both literally and figuratively; and I declare, in that particular case, the literal and the figurative would displease me equally.

*I*: If the expedient I have suggested does not suit you, then have courage enough to be a penniless beggar.

*He*: It's hard to be penniless while there are so many wealthy fools at whose expense one might live. And then, self-contempt is so unbearable.

*I*: Is that a feeling you've experienced?

*He*: Have I experienced it! How many times have I said to myself: What, Rameau, there are ten thousand good tables in Paris, each laid for fifteen or twenty, and of all those places not one is for you! There are purses full of gold being shed right and left, and not one coin falls to you! A thousand petty wits, without talent or merit; a thousand little wenches, without any charms; a thousand dull intriguers go well-clad, and shall you go naked? Must you be foolish to that extent? Couldn't you flatter as well as anyone? Couldn't you lie, swear, perjure yourself, make promises, keep or break them as well as anyone? Couldn't you crawl on all fours as well as anyone? Couldn't you assist Madame's intrigue and carry Monsieur's *billet-doux*, as well as anyone? Couldn't you encourage this young man to speak to Mademoiselle, and persuade Mademoiselle to listen to him, as well as anyone? Couldn't you indicate to the daughter of some bourgeois that she is ill-dressed, that fine earrings, a little rouge, some lace and a gown *à la polonaise* would suit her to perfection? That those little feet were not made for walking in the streets? That a fine gentleman, young and rich, who has a gold-laced coat, a superb carriage and six great footmen, has seen her as he passed by, and been charmed by her, and in consequence from that day on has ceased to touch food and drink, can't sleep, and may die?—"But my papa?"—Well, well, your papa may be just a bit angry at first.—"And mamma, who's always exhorting me to be a good girl? who tells me that honour is all that matters in this world?"—Old-fashioned talk that means nothing.—"And my confessor?"—You need not see him any more; or if you persist in the whim of going to relate all your pastimes to him, it may cost you a few pounds of sugar and coffee.—"He's a strict man, and has already refused me absolution on account of that song, '*Come into my cell.*'" That's because you had nothing to give him. . . . But when you appear before him with all your lace. . . . "Shall I have lace then?"—Of course, and of every sort. With your fine diamond earrings. . . . "Shall I have fine diamond earrings?"—Yes.—"Like those of the marquise who sometimes comes to buy gloves in our shop?"—Exactly. In a fine carriage, with dapple-grey horses, two great footmen, a little negro, and the groom going in front; with rogue and patches, and your train carried.—"Going to the ball?"—Yes, to the ball, to the opera, to the play. . . . Already her heart leaps for joy. You play with a scrap of paper you hold between your fingers.—"What's that?"—Oh, nothing.—"I think it is something."—It's a note.—"And for whom?"—For you, if you had a little curiosity.—"Curiosity, I've plenty of that. Let me see."—She reads. "An interview? that is impossible."—On your way to Mass.—"Mamma is always with me; but if he were to come here, rather early in the morning; I get up first, and I am at the counter before they're up. . . ."—He comes; he pleases; and one fine day, at dusk, the pretty ones disappears, and my two thousand crowns are handed over. . . . What! possessing that talent, you lack bread? Aren't you ashamed, you wretch? I remembered a crowd of rascals, who didn't come up to my ankle, and who were overflowing with riches. I wore a coat of coarse cloth, and they were clad in velvet; they leaned on sticks with golden knobs and curved handles; and they had Aristotle and Plato engraved on the signet-rings they had on their fingers. And yet what used they to be? Wretched tenth-rate musicians for the most part; now they're as good as lords. Then I felt brave, high-hearted, keen-minded, capable of anything. But it seems that this happy condition did not endure; for up till now, I've not succeeded in making any real progress. However that may be, that is the text of my frequent soliloquies, which you may paraphrase as you please—provided that you conclude therefrom that I do know self-contempt, that torment of the conscience which springs from the uselessness of the gifts that Heaven has allotted to us; it is the most cruel of all torments. A man might almost as well not have been born.

I listened to him, and while he was acting the scene between the procurer and the young girl whom he seduces, my soul was disturbed by two contrary impulses; I did not know whether to give way to a longing to laugh or to a fit of indignation. I was in distress. A score of times a burst of laughter would prevent my anger from breaking out; a score of times the anger rising within my heart ended in a burst of laughter. I was astounded at such shrewdness allied with such baseness; such sound ideas alternating with such falseness; such a general perversity of feeling, such utter corruption, together with such uncommon frankness. He noticed the struggle that was going on within me and said: "What is the matter?"

*I*: Nothing.

*He*: You seem distressed.

*I*: So I am.

*He*: But tell me, what do you advise me to do?

*I*: To change the subject. Unfortunate creature, to what an abject state you have fallen!

*He*: I admit it. Nevertheless don't be too much upset about my state. I did not intend, when I confided in you, to distress you. I saved some money at these people's; remember that I needed nothing, absolutely nothing, and that I was allowed so much for pocket money.

(Then he began once more to beat his brow with his fist, to bite his lip, and to roll his eyes wildly to the ceiling, adding:)

But it's all over and done with. I have set something aside. Time has passed; and that's always something saved.

*I*: You mean something lost.

*He*: No, no, saved. Every instant one grows rich. One day less to live, or one crown to the good, it comes to the same thing. The important point is to go easily, freely, pleasantly, copiously, to the closet every evening: *O stercum pretiosum!* * That is the great end of life, for all conditions of men. At the last moment, we are all equally rich; Samuel Bernard who by dint of thefts, plunder, and bankruptcies leaves twenty-seven million in gold, and Rameau who leaves nothing at all, Rameau for whom charity will provide a bit of packing cloth for a shroud. The dead man hears no bells tolling. In vain do a hundred priests sing themselves hoarse for him; in vain does a long procession

* O precious excrement.

of burning torches go before and behind him; his soul it not walking beside the master of ceremonies. Whether you rot under marble or under the earth, you still rot. Whether you have round your coffin children in red and children in blue, or no one at all, it makes no difference. And then, just look at this wrist of mine; it used to be stiff as the devil. These ten fingers were so many sticks fixed in a wooden metacarpal; and these tendons were like old strings of cat-gut, drier, stiffer and less flexible than those that have been used on a turner's wheel. But I worried them, broke them, shattered them so; you won't give way, and I, damn it, I say you shall; and it's going to be so.

And as he said this, with his right hand he seized the fingers and wrist of his left hand; and he twisted them over and under till the tips of his fingers touched his arm; his joints were cracking; I was afraid the bones would be dislocated.

*I*: Take care (I told him) you'll injure yourself.

*He*: Don't be afraid. They are used to it; for ten years I've been treating them worse than this. And against their will, the b–s had to get accustomed to it, and learn to place themselves on the keys and fly over the strings. And so, now, it's all right; yes, it's all right.

At the same time he assumed the pose of a fiddler; he hummed an allegro by Locatelli; his right arm imitated the movement of the bow; his left hand and fingers seemed to move up and down the neck; if he played a note out of tune, he would stop, tune the string up or down, pluck it with his nail to make sure it was in tune, take up the music again where he had left off; beat time with his feet, throwing about his head, his feet, hands, arms, and whole body. Just as you have sometimes seen, at the Sacred Concert, Ferrari or Chiabran, or some other virtuoso, undergoing the same convulsions, appearing to suffer the same torments, and causing one about the same distress, for is it not a painful thing to behold a man in agony when he is engaged in representing pleasure? Draw a curtain to hide that man from me, if he must show me a victim on the rack. In the midst of his convulsions and his cries, there would occur a holding-note, one of those passages of harmony in which the bow moves slowly over several strings at once; then his face would take on an ecstatic look, his voice softened, he listened to himself with delight. There is no question but the chords were sounding in his ears and in mine. Then, putting his instrument back under his left arm, with the same hand with which he was holding it, and letting drop his right hand with the bow: "Well," he said, "what do you think of that?"

*I*: Wonderful.

*He*: It seems to me to be all right; it sounds about as good as other people. . . .

(And immediately he crouches down like a musician sitting at the harpsichord.)

*I*: I ask mercy, for your sake and my own!

*He*: No, no, since I've got you, you shall listen to me. I don't want anyone's approval given in ignorance. You will praise me in a more confident tone, and that may get me a pupil.

*I*: I mix with so few people; and you'll tire yourself in vain.

*He*: I never get tired.

As I saw that it was useless for me to try and take pity on the fellow, the violin sonata having put him all in a lather, I decided to let him have his own way. Behold him then sitting at the harpsichord; his legs bent, his head lifted towards the ceiling where you would think he saw a musical score set down; singing, trying out his fingers, performing a piece by Alberti or Galuppi, I don't know which. His voice went like the wind, and his fingers flew over the notes; now leaving the treble to take up the bass, now dropping the accompaniment to return to the treble. His face expressed various emotions in turn; you could distinguish tenderness, anger, delight and pain; you could feel the soft and the loud passages. And I am sure one more skilled than I could have recognized the piece through its movement and character, through his varied expressions and through some fragments of song which he uttered at intervals. But the oddest thing was, that he fumbled from time to time; he corrected himself as though he had made some mistake, and grew vexed at no longer having the piece at his fingers' ends.

"So now you see," he said, standing up again and wiping the drops of sweat that ran down his cheeks, "that we too know how to place an augmented fourth or a superfluous fifth, and are familiar with the sequence of dominants. Those chromatic passages about which dear uncle makes so much ado, they're nothing so tremendous, we can deal with them."

*I*: You've given yourself a great deal of trouble to show me how very clever you are; I was willing to take your word for it.

*He*: Very clever? oh, no; I know my job more or less, and that's more than enough. For in this country is one obliged to know what one teaches?

*I*: Not more than to know what one learns.

*He*: That is true, damn it, very true. Come, now, master philosopher, speak honestly, with your hand on your heart. Wasn't there a time when you weren't as well-off as you are to-day?

*I*: I'm none too well off even yet.

*He*: But now you wouldn't go to the Luxembourg in summer, don't you remember. . . .

*I*: Don't talk of that; yes, I remember.

*He*: Dressed in a grey plush coat. . . .

*I*: Yes, yes.

*He*: All worn out on one side; with torn cuffs, and black woollen stockings sewn up behind with white thread.

*I*: Oh, yes, all right, just as you please.

*He*: What did you do then in the Allée des Soupirs?

*I*: I cut a sorry figure.

*He*: When you left there you'd pace the pavement.

*I*: That's so.

*He*: You taught mathematics.

*I*: Without knowing the first thing about it; isn't that what you were coming to?

*He*: Exactly.

*I*: I learnt while teaching others, and I made a few good students.

*He*: That may be, but music isn't the same as algebra or geometry. Now that you've become a fine gentleman. . . .

*I*: Not so fine!

*He*: That your pockets are well-lined. . . .

*I*: Not so well!

*He*: You have masters for your daughter.

*I*: Not yet. Her mother sees to her education, since one needs peace in the home.

*He*: Peace in the home? Good Lord, one only has that when one is the servant or the master; and master is what one should be. I've had a wife, God rest her soul; but when at times she happened to answer back, I'd get on my high horse; I'd wield my thunder; I'd say, like God, "Let there be light," and there was light. And so, in four years, we never once had to raise our voices against each other! How old is your child?

*I*: That has nothing to do with it.

*He*: How old is your child?

*I*: What the devil, let's leave my child and her age out of it, and get back to the teachers she will have.

*He*: On my oath, I know nothing so obstinate as a philosopher. If one were to beg very humbly, could one find out from my lord philosopher, about what age is mademoiselle his daughter?

*I*: You may assume she is eight.

*He*: Eight! She should have had her fingers on the keyboard four years ago.

*I*: But perhaps I was none too anxious to include in the plans for her education a study that takes up so much time and serves so little purpose.

*He*: And what will you teach her then, if you please?

*I*: To reason correctly, if I can; a very uncommon thing among men and rarer still among women.

*He*: Oh! let her talk nonsense as much as she likes, provided she be pretty, amusing and a flirt.

*I*: Since nature has been so unkind to her as to give her a delicate constitution together with a sensitive spirit, and to expose her to the same troubles in life as if she had a strong constitution and a heart of bronze, I will teach her, if I can, to bear them with courage.

*He*: Eh! Let her weep and suffer, make a fuss and have her nerves on edge like all of them, provided she be pretty and amusing and a flirt. What, no dancing?

*I*: No more than is necessary to make a curtsey, to have a decent carriage and presence, and to know how to walk gracefully.

*He*: No singing?

*I*: No more than is necessary to pronounce correctly.

*He*: No music?

*I*: If there were a good teacher of harmony, I'd willingly put her in his charge, for two hours a day during a year or two; no more.

*He*: And in the place of the essential things you are suppressing?

*I*: I put some grammar, fables, history, geography, a little drawing and a good deal of moral instruction.

*He*: How easy it would be for me to prove to you the uselessness of all such learning in a world such as ours; uselessness, nay, perhaps even danger. But for the moment I'll restrict myself to one question; won't she need one or two teachers?

*I*: No doubt.

*He*: Ah, now we're back again. And these teachers, do you expect they will know the grammar, the fables, the history, the geography, the morality about which they will give her lessons? Nonsense, my dear sir, nonsense. If they knew these things well enough to teach them, they would not be teaching them.

*I*: And why so?

*He*: Because they would have spent their whole lives studying them. One needs a profound knowledge of art or science in order to have a good grasp of their elements. Works of classic rank can only be produced by those who have grown grey in harness. The middle and the end illuminate the obscurity of the beginnings. Ask your friend M. d'Alembert, who leads the chorus in mathematical science, if he is too good to deal with its elements. It was only after thirty or forty years of practice that my uncle perceived the first glimmerings of musical theory.

*I*: O madman! archmadman! (I cried), how comes it that in your wild head there should be so many sound ideas mingled with so many extravagant ones?

*He*: Who the devil can tell? Chance flings them to you, and they stick. The fact remains, that as long as one doesn't know everything, one knows nothing well. One cannot tell whither one thing goes, whence another comes, where each of them should be put, which should go first, which would be better second. Can one teach well without method? And how does method come? I tell you, my dear philosopher, I have a conviction that physics will always be a wretched science; a drop of water taken up on a needle's point out of the vast ocean, a grain of sand detached from the chain of the Alps. And what about the causes of phenomena? Truly it would be better to know nothing than to know so little, and that so ill; and that is precisely where I'd got to, when I became a teacher of accompaniment and composition. What are you thinking about?

*I*: I am thinking that all you have just said to me is specious rather than sound. But let us leave that. You say you have taught accompaniment and composition?

*He*: Yes.

*I*: And you knew nothing at all about them?

*He*: No, on my word; and that is why there were others who were worse than I—those who thought they knew something. At least I spoilt neither the taste nor the hands of the children. When they passed from me to a good teacher, as they had learnt nothing, at any rate they had nothing to unlearn; and that was always so much money and time saved.

*I*: How did you set about it?

*He*: Like everyone else. I would arrive, throw myself into a chair: "What dreadful weather! How tiring the pavements are!" I would chatter and gossip a little: "Mlle. Lemierre was to have played the part of a vestal in the new opera, but she's pregnant for the second time. It's not known who is to understudy her. Mlle. Arnould has just left her little count. They say she's begun to negotiate with Bertin. Still, the little count found M. de Montamy's porcelain. At the last amateur concert there was an Italian woman who sang like an angel. That Préville is a remarkable creature. You should see him in the *Mercure galant;* the riddle scene is priceless. Poor Dumesnil, she's no longer responsible for her words and actions. Come, Mademoiselle, take your book." While Mademoiselle, without hurrying, looks for her book which she has mislaid, while a maid is sent for and scolded, I go on: "Really there's no understanding la Clairon. I've heard talk of a most absurd marriage, that of Mademoiselle what d'you call her, a little creature that he kept, by whom he'd had two or three children, and who had been kept by so many others." "Come, Rameau, that's impossible, you're talking nonsense." "I'm not talking nonsense. They even say that the thing is done. There's a rumour that Voltaire is dead; all the better. . . ." "Why all the better?" "Because it means he's going to produce some good joke. He usually dies a fortnight before." What else shall I tell you? I would repeat a few low stories, that I'd picked up in the houses I had been in; for we are all great tale-bearers. I would play the fool. They would listen, they would laugh, they'd exclaim: "He is always delightful." Meanwhile Mademoiselle's book would at last be found under an arm-chair where it had been dragged about, chewed and torn by a young puppy or kitten. She would sit down to her harpsichord. At first she'd make a noise on it by herself. Then I would draw near, after making some sign of approval to the mother. The mother: "It's not going too badly: if we'd only try, but we won't try. We prefer to waste our time chattering, prinking, running around and Heaven knows what. No sooner are you gone than the book is shut, not to be opened till you return. But then you never scold her. . . ." Meanwhile as something had to be done, I would take her hands and place them differently. I would lose my temper, I'd cry "G, G, Mademoiselle, it's a G." The mother: "Mademoiselle, have you no ear? Without being at the harpsichord, or seeing your book, I can tell that it should be a G. You give Monsieur an infinite amount of trouble. I cannot think why he is so patient. You don't remember anything he tells you. You make no progress. . . ."

Then I would abate the violence of my attack somewhat, and shaking my head, say: "Forgive me, Madame; it would go better if Mademoiselle would try, if she would study a little; but it's not going badly." The mother: "In your place, I'd keep her a year at the same piece." "Oh, for that matter, she's not going to leave it until she has mastered all the difficulties; and that won't be as long as Madame thinks." The mother: "Monsieur Rameau, you flatter her; you are too good. That's the only thing she'll remember from her lesson, and she'll certainly be able to repeat it to me when the opportunity arises." The hour would pass, my pupil would offer me the fee for the lesson with the graceful gesture of the arm and the curtsy that she had learnt from the dancing-master. I'd put it in my pocket, while the mother said: "Very nice, Mademoiselle. If Javilliar were there he'd applaud you." I would gossip for a moment longer, out of politeness; then I'd disappear, and that's what used to be called a lesson in accompaniment.

*I*: And are things different to-day?

*He*: Good heavens, I should think so. I arrive. I look grave. I hastily remove my muff. I open the harpsichord. I try the keys. I am always in a hurry; if I'm kept waiting one minute, I yell as though I'd had five shillings stolen. In an hour's time I have to be at such and such a place; in two hours, at the house of the Duchess of so and so. A beautiful marquise expects me to dinner; and after that there's a concert at the Baron de Bagge's in the rue Neuve-des-Petits-Champs.

*I*: And yet you're not expected anywhere?

*He*: True.

*I*: And why use all these base little tricks?

*He*: Base! Why base, if you please? They are customary among people in my condition. I don't abase myself by doing as everyone else does. I didn't invent them; and it would be queer and clumsy of me not to conform with them. Of course, I know that if you are going to apply in this case certain general principles of Lord knows what morality, which everyone talks about and no one practises, what's white will appear black and what's black will appear white. But, master philosopher, there is a general conscience just as there is a general grammar; and then in every language there are exceptions, which you scholars, I believe, call . . . help me out. . . .

*I*: Idioms.

*He*: Exactly. Well, then, each condition has its exceptions to the general conscience; I'd like to describe them as professional idioms.

*I*: I understand. Fontenelle speaks well, writes well, although his style abounds in French idioms.

*He*: And the sovereign, the minister, the financier, the magistrate, the soldier, the writer, the lawyer, the attorney, the merchant, the banker, the artisan, the singing-master and the dancing-master are all highly respectable people, although their conduct deviates on several points from the general conscience, and is full of moral idioms. The older established things are, the more idioms there are; the worse times are, the more the idioms multiply. The trade is as good as the man; and contrariwise, in the long run, a man is as good as his trade. So a man must make the most of his trade.

*I*: All that I can understand clearly from this tangled argument is that few trades are practised honestly, or else few men are honest in their trade.

*He*: Well, none of them are; but, on the other hand, few men are rogues outside their shop; and all would go fairly well, but for a certain number of people who are said to be assiduous, precise, exact in the fulfilment of their duties, strict, that is to say, always inside their shops, following their trade from morning till night and doing nothing else. And so they are the only people who get rich and who are respected.

*I*: Thanks to idioms.

*He*: Just so; I see you have understood me. Now then, one idiom that belongs to all conditions, since certain idioms are common to all countries and all times just as certain follies are, one common idiom is to procure for oneself the widest possible custom, and one common folly is to believe that the man with the widest custom is the cleverest. There are two exceptions to the general conscience to which one is obliged to conform. It is a kind of credit; a thing worth nothing in itself, but which takes its value from public opinion. They say that "Good fame is better than a belt of gold"; and yet he who has good fame hasn't got a golden belt, and from what I can see these days, he who has a golden belt is never without fame. As far as possible one should have both fame and the belt. And that is my object when I make the most of myself by what you describe as base tricks and mean little ruses. I give my lesson and I give it well; there's the general rule. I create the impression that I have more lessons to give than the day has hours, there's the idiom.

*I*: And do you give the lessons well?

*He*: Yes, not badly, tolerably well. Dear uncle's fundamental bass has made all that much simpler. Formerly I used to steal my pupil's money; yes, I stole it, that's certain. To-day I earn it, at least as much as anyone else.

*I*: And used you to steal it without remorse?

*He*: Oh, without any remorse. They say that "when one thief robs another, the devil laughs." The parents were bursting with wealth, acquired God knows how; they were courtiers, financiers, big merchants, bankers, business-men. I helped them to make restitution, I and a crowd of others whom they employed like myself. In nature, all species devour one another, in society all conditions of men devour one another. We mete our justice to one another, without interference from the law. Formerly through la Deschamps, to-day through la Guimard, the prince gets his revenge on the financiers; and through the dressmaker, the jeweller, the upholsterer, the sempstress, the swindler, the ladies'-maid, the cook, and the harness-maker, the financier has his revenge on la Deschamps. In the midst of all this, only the imbecile or the idler is injured, without having offended anyone; and serve him right. Whence you see that these exceptions to the common conscience, these moral idioms about which so much fuss is made, and which are described as "jugglers' tricks," are nothing at all, and that, on the whole, all that is needed is to have good sight.

*I*: I admire yours.

*He*: And then, there's poverty. The voice of conscience and honour is very weak when the bowels are crying out. It's enough that if I ever grow rich I shall certainly have to make restitution, and that I'm firmly resolved to do so in every possible way, through good fare, gaming, wine and women.

*I*: But I fear you'll never grow rich.

*He*: I suspect as much.

*I*: However, if things should turn out otherwise, what would you do?

*He*: I should believe as all re-clad beggars do; I should be the most insolent rascal ever seen. It's then that I should remember all they made me suffer; and I should pay them back for all the outrages they inflicted on me. I love to give orders, and I shall give them. I love to be praised, and people shall praise me. I shall have the whole of Vilmorien's gang in my service, and I shall say to them, as they said to me, "Now then, rogues, amuse me," and they will amuse me. "Get your claws into honest folks," and the honest folks, if there are any left, will be torn to shreds. And then we shall have women; we'll call each other "thou" when we are drunk; we shall get drunk; we'll tell tall stories; we'll have all sorts of perversions and vices. It will be delicious. We shall prove that Voltaire has no genius; that Buffon, always mounted on stilts, is just an inflated ranter; that Montesquieu is nothing but a society wit; we shall pack d'Alembert back to his mathematics; we shall rain blows on all you little Catos who despise us out of envy, in whom modesty is the cloak of pride, and who are sober from sheer necessity. And as for music, then's the time we shall make music!

*I*: From the noble use you'd make of your riches, I can see what a pity it is that you should be a beggar. Such a way of living would contribute greatly to the honour of the human race, to the benefit of your fellow-citizens, and to your own glory!

*He*: I believe you are laughing at me, master philosopher. You don't know with whom you are dealing; you don't suspect that I represent the most important section of society, in town and at court. All our rich folks, in every profession, may or may not have said to themselves just what I've been telling you in confidence; but the fact is that the life which I should lead, were I in their shoes, is exactly the life they do lead. I'll tell you what you're like, you fellows, you think that the same happiness suits everyone. What a strange fantasy! Your sort of happiness presupposes a certain romantic turn of mind which we haven't got, an unusual temperament, peculiar tastes. You decorate this eccentricity with the name of virtue; you call it philosophy. But do virtue and philosophy suit everyone? He has them who can, and maintains them if he can. Imagine the universe grown wise and philosophical; admit that it would be devilish dull! Look here, long live philosophy, long live the wisdom of Solomon: to drink good wine, to guzzle delicate food, tumble pretty women and rest on soft beds! Except for this, all is vanity.

*I*: Ah! but to defend one's country?

*He*: Vanity. There's no longer any such thing as one's country. From one pole to the other I can see only tyrants and slaves.

*I*: To help one's friends?

*He*: Vanity. Does one have friends? And if one had them, ought one to make them guilty of ingratitude? For, look at it closely, you'll see that is all one's reward for services rendered. Gratitude is a burden; and all burdens are meant to be shaken off.

*I*: To have some position in society and fulfil the duties thereof?

*He*: Vanity. What does it matter whether or not one has a position, so long as one is rich; since one only takes up the position in order to become rich? And where does fulfilling one's duties lead to? To jealousy, trouble, persecution. Is that how one gets on in the world? No, good heavens, but by playing the courtier, frequenting great folks, studying their tastes, humouring their whims, pandering to their vices, subscribing to their unjust actions; there's the secret.

*I*: To attend to the education of one's children?

*He*: Vanity. That's the business of a tutor.

*I*: But if that tutor, steeped in your principles, neglects his duties; who will be the sufferer?

*He*: Well, not I, but perhaps some day my daughter's husband or my son's wife.

*I*: But if both of them rush headlong into debauchery and vice?

*He*: That befits their social position.

*I*: If they forfeit their honour?

*He*: Whatever one does, one can't forfeit one's honour when one is rich.

*I*: If they are ruined?

*He*: So much the worse for them.

*I*: I see that if you dispense with attending to the conduct of your wife, your children and your servants, you are quite liable to neglect your business affairs.

*He*: Excuse me; it is sometimes hard to find money; and it is prudent to set about that well in advance.

*I*: You won't take much care of your wife?

*He*: None at all, please. The best way of dealing with one's beloved mate, to my mind, is to do just what suits one. Don't you think society would be most amusing if everyone followed his own bent?

*I*: Why not? The evening is always most beautiful to me when I am pleased with the way I've spent the morning.

*He*: And to me too.

*I*: It is their utter idleness that makes society people so fastidious about their pleasures.

*He*: Don't you believe that; they are constantly on the go.

*I*: As they never weary themselves they never find relief from weariness.

*He*: Don't you believe that; they are always exhausted.

*I*: Pleasure is always a business for them, never a need.

*He*: All the better; a need is always disagreeable.

*I*: They wear out everything. Their souls grow stupefied, boredom overtakes them. Surrounded as they are by an abundance that oppresses them, they would be grateful to anyone who took their life from them. For all they know of happiness is that part that is soonest dulled. I do not despise the pleasures of the senses. I have a palate too, and it can savour a delicate dish, a fragrant wine; I have a heart and eyes, and I like to see a pretty woman. I love to feel beneath my hand her firm round breast, to press my lips to hers, to drink delight in her glances and to die of it in her arms. I can enjoy an occasional wild party with my friends, even if it be somewhat riotous. But I won't conceal the fact that it is infinitely sweeter to me to have been of help to someone in distress, to have concluded some difficult piece of business, or given wholesome advice; to have read a pleasant book, walked awhile with a man or woman who is dear to me; spent a few hours teaching my children, written a good page, fulfilled the duties of my profession; or said to her whom I love a few tender affectionate words that make her clasp her arms around my neck. I know of certain deeds to have done which I'd give all I possess. *Mahomet* is a noble work; I'd rather have rehabilitated the memory of the Calas family. A man I know had taken refuge at Carthagena. He was a younger son of a family, in a land where custom bequeaths the whole of a fortune to the eldest. There he learnt that his elder brother, a spoilt child, after robbing his over-indulgent father and mother of all their goods, had driven them from their country home, and that the poor old folks were pining away in poverty in some small provincial town. What did he do then, this younger son, whom his parents' harsh treatment had driven to seek his fortune in a far country? He sent them help; he hastily settled up his business. He came home, a rich man; he brought back his father and mother to their house. He married his sisters. Ah, my dear Rameau, this man considered this period as the happiest of all his life. Tears stood in eyes as he told me of it; and I myself, as I tell you the story, feel my heart stirred with joy, and delight interrupts my words.

*He*: What extraordinary creatures you are!

*I*: What unfortunate creatures you are, if you cannot conceive that a man may rise superior to his fate, and that it is impossible to be unhappy under the aegis of two such noble deeds.

*He*: That's a species of happiness with which I shall not easily become familiar, for one meets it very seldom. But according to you, then, people ought to behave decently?

*I*: In order to be happy? Most certainly!

*He*: Yet I see an infinite number of decent folk who are not happy, and an infinite number who are happy without being decent folk.

*I*: So it seems to you.

*He*: And isn't it all through being sensible and sincere for one minute that I've nowhere to go for supper to-night?

*I*: Why no, it's through not being so always. It's through not realizing early enough that one should first provide oneself with some means of livelihood independent of servitude.

*He*: Independent or not, what I've provided for myself is at least the most comfortable.

*I*: And the least certain, and the least decent.

*He*: But best suited to my character, which is that of an idler, a fool, and a worthless blackguard.

*I*: No doubt.

*He*: And, since I can be happy through vices that are natural to me, acquired without labour and maintained without effort, vices that fit in with the customs of my fellow-countrymen, that please the taste of my patrons and suit their petty personal requirements better than virtues, which would embarrass them by accusing them from morning till night; it would be most odd for me to go torturing myself like a lost soul, in order to distort myself and make myself other than I am; to take on a character that's foreign to my own; worthy qualities, I grant you, we won't quarrel about that; but qualities which it would cost me much to acquire and to practise, which would lead to nothing or maybe worse than nothing, by exposing me to the continual satire of the rich folk among whom beggars like myself have to make a living. Virtue is highly praised, but she is hated and shunned; she is cold as ice, and in this world we must keep our feet warm. And then, it would inevitably make me bad-tempered; for why are pious people so often hard, disagreeable, unsociable? Because they have imposed on themselves a task that's not natural to them. They suffer, and when one suffers one makes others suffer. That doesn't suit me, nor my patrons either; I have to be gay, pliable, amusing, comic, absurd. Virtue commands respect; and respect is uncomfortable. Virtue commands admiration; and admiration is not amusing. I'm dealing with people who are bored, and I have to make them laugh. Now absurdity and craziness arouse laughter, so I have to be crazy and absurd; and if nature had not made me so, the quickest way would be to pretend to be so. Luckily I've no need to be a hypocrite; there are so many already of every variety, not counting those who are hypocritical with themselves. That Chevalier de La Morlière who cocks his hat over his ear, bears his head so bravely, looks down over his shoulder at passers-by, wears a long sword dangling on his thigh, has an insult all ready for anyone that goes swordless, and seems to challenge all comers, what's he doing? Trying his utmost to persuade himself that he's a brave man; but he is a coward. If you offer him a fillip on the nose, he'll receive it meekly. If you want to make him talk less loudly, raise your own voice. Show him your stick, or kick his behind; astonished to discover himself a coward, he will ask you who told you he was? how you found it out? He didn't know it himself, a minute ago; a long habit of aping bravery had taken him in. He had assumed the airs of it so much that he believed in its reality. And that woman who mortifies her flesh and visits prisons, who is present at all meetings in aid of charity, who goes about with downcast eyes and would not dare look a man in the face, always on her guard against the seductions of the senses; in spite of all this, her heart throbs, she heaves sighs, her passions are awakened, desires obsess her, and her imagination calls up, night and day, scenes from the *Portier des Chartreux*, postures from Aretino. What happens to her then? What does her chambermaid think when she gets up in her nightgown and flies to the help of her dying mistress? Go back to bed, Justine; it's not you that your mistress was calling in her delirium. And as for friend Rameau, if one day he began to show contempt for wealth, women, good fare and idleness, to be censorious, what would he be? A hypocrite. Rameau must stay what he is; a happy robber among rich robbers; and not a braggart of virtue or even a virtuous man, gnawing his crust of bread alone or among beggars. And, to speak plainly, I've no use for your sort of felicity, for the happiness that suits a few visionaries like yourself.

*I*: I see, my dear fellow, that you don't know what that happiness is, and that you're not even capable of learning.

*He*: All the better, good God, all the better. It would make me die of hunger, boredom, and maybe remorse.

*I*: Accordingly the only advice I have to give you is to get back quickly into the house from which you rashly let yourself be turned out.

*He*: And to do what you don't disapprove of in the literal sense, and what rather repels me in the figurative sense?

*I*: That's what I think.

*He*: Apart from this metaphor, what I dislike at the present moment, and what I shan't mind the next.

*I*: How very peculiar!

*He*: There's nothing peculiar about that. I'm quite willing to be abject, but it must not be under constraint. I'm willing to lower my dignity—you're laughing?

*I*: Yes, "your dignity" makes me laugh.

*He*: Every man has his own; I'm willing to forget mine, but at my own discretion, and not at anyone else's orders. Have I got to crawl when they say "crawl" to me? That's the worm's way of moving, and it's mine; we both assume it when we're allowed to go as we like; but we rise up when our tails are trodden on. My tail has been trodden on, and I shall rise up. And then you've no conception of what a bedlam the place is. Imagine a sullen, melancholy person, a prey to nerves, swathed in a dressing-gown that goes two or three times round him; who's disgusted with himself and everything else; whom you can hardly get to smile, though you contort yourself, body and mind, in a hundred different ways; who watches coldly while I twist my face into quaint grimaces, and my wit into even quainter ones; for, between ourselves, Father Noel, that unpleasant Benedictine whose grimaces are so famous, is, despite his success at Court, a mere wooden puppet compared to me—and I'm not flattering myself nor him either. In vain do I torture myself—striving to reach the sublime heights of bedlam; it's no use. Will he laugh or won't he? That's what I have to keep saying to myself, in the midst of my contortions; and you can see how much all this uncertainty hinders one's talent. My hypochondriac, his face buried in a nightcap that comes down over his eyes, looks like a motionless Chinese puppet that has a string fastened to its chin, the end of which hangs down below its chair. You wait for the string to be pulled; and it isn't pulled; or if it happens that the jaw gapes a little, it is to utter some distressing word, some word that tells you that you haven't been noticed, that all your monkey-tricks are wasted. That word is in answer to a question you put to him four days ago; once it's said, the mastoid muscle relaxes, and the jaw closes again.

(Then he began to imitate the man in question; he sat in a chair, his head rigid, his hat pulled down to his eyelids, his eyes half closed, his arms dangling, moving his jaw like an automaton and saying:)

"Yes, you are right, Mademoiselle. Delicacy is needed there." And that is decisive; always and irrevocably, evening and morning, when he's dressing or dining, at the café or the card-table, at the theatre or at supper, in bed, and, God forgive me, I believe in his mistress's arms. I'm never within earshot in the last-named circumstances, to hear him make his decisions; but I'm devilish tired of all the others. Gloomy, obscure and peremptory, like fate: such is our patron.

On the other hand, there's a prude who puts on airs of importance; one could submit to telling her she's pretty, because she still is, although she has a few scabs here and there on her face, and is emulating the bulk of Madame Bouvillon. I like flesh when it's handsome flesh, but then, too much is too much, and movement is so essential to matter! *Item*, she's prouder, stupider, and more ill-humoured than a goose. *Item*, she has pretensions to wit. *Item*, one has to persuade her that one thinks her wittier than anyone else. *Item*, she knows nothing, and yet her word has to be decisive too. *Item*, one has to applaud her decisions, clap hands and stamp feet, jump for joy, be in ecstasies of admiration: "How fine, how delicate, how well expressed, what subtlety of observation, what originality of feeling! How do women do it? Without study, through sheer instinct, by the light of nature; the thing's miraculous. And then people want you to believe that experience, study, reflection and education have something to do with it!" And such like nonsense; and one weeps for joy. Ten times a day one must bow down, one knee bent forward, the other leg drawn back, arms stretched out towards the goddess, one must try to read her wish in her eyes, hang on her lips, await her orders, and then be off like a flash. Who can submit to playing such a part, except the wretch who finds thereby, twice or thrice a week, the wherewithal to quieten the affliction of his intestines? What is one to think of the others, like Palissot, Fréron, Poinsinet, Baculard and company, who haven't the rumble of a hungry belly to excuse their servility?

*I*: I'd never have thought you were so fastidious.

*He*: I'm not. To begin with I saw what others did, and I did the same, even rather better because I am more frankly impudent, a better play-actor, hungrier and stronger in the lung. I seem to be a direct descendant of the famous Stentor.

And to give me a correct notion of the strength of that organ, he began to cough with enough violence to shake the windows of the café and attract the attention of the chess-players.

*I*: But what use is that talent?

*He*: Can't you guess?

*I*: No, I am a bit stupid.

*He*: Suppose a quarrel has begun and its outcome is uncertain; I get up, and loosing my thunder, I say: "That is so, as Mademoiselle declares. That's what I call good judgment. I defy all our wits to equal it. It's expressed with real genius." But one must not always show approval in the same way. That would be monotonous, and seem insincere. One would become tedious. It takes tact and resourcefulness to save one from that; one must know how to prepare and where to place such major tones, such peremptory utterances, how to seize the right occasion and the right moment. When, for example, feelings are divided; when the quarrel has reached its peak of violence; when no one listens to anyone else, and everyone is speaking at once; one should be standing aloof, in the corner of the room furthest from the battlefield, and having prepared for one's explosion by a long silence, fall suddenly like a bomb into the midst of the combatants. No one has that art to the same degree as I. But where I really excel is in the opposite direction; I can produce gentle noises accompanied by a smile, an infinite variety of facial expressions marking approval; nose, mouth, forehead, eyes come into play; I have such supple loins, a way of twisting my spine, of lifting and dropping my shoulders, of spreading out my fingers, bending my head, closing my eyes, showing as much bewilderment as though I had heard the voices of angels and divinities speaking from heaven. That's real flattering. I don't know if you grasp the full force of that particular pose. I didn't invent it, but no one has surpassed me in performance. Just look.

*I*: It's unique, that is true.

*He*: Do you think any tolerably vain woman has a head to withstand that?

*I*: No. It must be admitted that you have carried the art of making fools and behaving basely as far as it can be carried.

*He*: Try as they will, the whole lot of them, they'll never get so far. The best of them, Palissot for instance, will never be more than a good scholar at it. But, though it's amusing at first to play such a part, and though one gets a certain enjoyment from laughing inwardly at the stupidity of those whom one's making drunk, the pleasure palls in the long run; and then, after a certain number of discoveries, one is obliged to repeat oneself. Wit and art have their limits; only God and a few rare geniuses find their road grow wider, the further they go. Bouret may be one of these. Certain inventions of his strike me, even me, as truly sublime. The little dog, the *Book of Happiness*, the torches on the Versailles road, are things that amaze and humiliate me. It's enough to make one throw up one's job in disgust.

*I*: What do you mean by "the little dog"?

*He*: Where do you come from? What, seriously, don't you know how that remarkable man managed to divert the affection of a small dog from himself to the Lord Chancellor, who had taken a liking to it?

*I*: I confess I don't know.

*He*: All the better. It's one of the most beautiful things ever thought of; all Europe was astonished at it, and it aroused the envy of every courtier. Let's see how you, who aren't lacking in shrewdness, would have set about it in his place. Remember that the dog loved Bouret. Remember that the minister's strange garments frightened the little creature. Remember that there was only a week in which to overcome all the difficulties. One needs to know all the conditions of the problem in order to appreciate fully the beauty of its solution. Well?

*I*: Well, I must confess that I should find the simplest things of that sort perplexing.

*He*: Listen, (he said to me, with a little tap on the shoulder, for he takes these liberties), listen and admire. He gets a mask made in the likeness of the Lord Chancellor; he borrows the voluminous robe from a valet. He covers his face with the mask, he puts on the robe. He calls his dog. He gives it biscuits. Then suddenly, changing his attire, he is no longer the Lord Chancellor, he is Bouret, calling his dog and beating it. By repeating this exercise from morning till night, before two or three days were up he's taught the dog to fly from Bouret, the Farmer-General and to run to Bouret the Lord Chancellor. But I'm too kind; you are un unbeliever and don't deserve to learn of the miracles that are performed around you.

*I*: In spite of that, I beg of you, what about the book and the torches?

*He*: No, no. Ask the pavements, and they'll tell you about those things; and take advantage of the circumstance that has brought us together to learn things that are known only to me.

*I*: You're right.

*He*: To have borrowed the robe and the wig—I'd forgotten about the wig!—of the Lord Chancellor! To have had a mask made in his likeness! That mask, particularly, leaves me dizzy. And, in consequence, this man enjoys the highest respect; he owns millions. There are some who've won the Cross of St. Louis, but who have no bread; so why run after the Cross, at the risk of getting one's neck broken, instead of turning to an occupation that involves no danger and never fails to bring its reward? That's what I call doing things on the grand scale. Such models are discouraging; one pities oneself, and one gets bored. That mask, that mask! I'd give one of my fingers to have thought of the mask.

*I*: But with such enthusiasm for fine things, and such a fertile genius as you possess, have you invented nothing?

*He*: Oh, excuse me, yes; for example, that admiring attitude of the back, of which I spoke to you; I consider that as my own, although the envious might perhaps dispute my claim to it. I believe, indeed, that it has been used before; but who else has realized how convenient it is for laughing up one's sleeve at the vain fellow one is admiring? I've over a hundred ways of embarking on the seduction of a young girl, by her mother's side, without the latter noticing, and even of involving her as an accomplice. While I was still a beginner in this career, I rejected with scorn all the vulgar methods of passing a *billet-doux.* I've ten ways of getting it snatched from me; and among these ways I dare flatter myself some are original. Above all, I have the gift of encouraging a timid young man; I've made some succeed, who had neither wit nor presence. If all this were written down, I think I should be granted some measure of genius.

*I*: Would you be singled out for praise?

*He*: I don't doubt it.

*I*: In your place, I should set down these things on paper. It would be a pity to lose them.

*He*: True, but you don't guess how low an opinion I have of method and precept. The man who needs a textbook will never go far. Men of genius read little, practise much and are self-made. Look at Caesar, Turenne, Vauban, the Marquise de Tencin, her brother the cardinal and his secretary, the abbé Trublet. And Bouret? Who gave Bouret lessons? No one. Such rare men as these are formed by nature. Do you think the story of the dog and the mask is written down anywhere?

*I*: But in your idle hours, when the gnawing of your empty stomach or the exhaustion of your overloaded stomach prevents you from sleeping. . . .

*He*: I'll think it over; it's better to write great things than to perform trivial ones. Then one's soul is uplifted; one's imagination is excited, inflamed and expanded; whereas it merely shrinks when used to convey to the little Hus woman one's astonishment at the applause the foolish public persists in lavishing on that simpering Dangeville, whose acting is so dull, who walks almost bent double on the stage, who's always gazing affectedly into the eyes of the person to whom she's speaking, and acting in a sly manner, and who mistakes her own grimaces for subtlety, her mincing walk for grace; and on that declamatory Clairon, who is leaner, stiffer, more affected, more artificial than you'd think possible. The idiotic audience claps them with wild enthusiasm, and never notices that we are a little bundle of charms;—it's true that the bundle is getting a bit plump, but what matter?—that we have the loveliest skin, the loveliest eyes, the sweetest mouth; not much passion, it's true, and a walk that's certainly not light, though it isn't so clumsy as they make out. On the other hand, there's no one to come near us on the matter of feeling.

*I*: What do you mean by all this? Are you speaking sincerely or ironically?

*He*: The trouble is that this confounded feeling is all within, and that not a glimpse of it can be caught from outside. But I who am talking to you, I know she's got it, and I know it well. If it's not feeling exactly, it's something like it. You ought to see, when the temper takes us, how we treat our valets, how we box our chambermaids' ears, what great kicks we deal out to the Treasurer of the *Parties Casuelles* * if he fails in the slightest degree to pay us the respect that's due to us. I tell you she's a little imp packed with feeling and dignity. . . . Why, you're bewildered, aren't you?

*I*: I admit that I can't make out whether you are speaking sincerely or maliciously. I'm a simple fellow; be good enough to deal more frankly with me, and leave aside your art.

*He*: Well, that's how we hold forth to the little Hus, on the subject of la Clairon and la Dangeville, with just a few words interspersed to put you on your guard. I'll allow you take me for a knave, but not for a fool; and only a fool, or a man crazy with love, would say such ridiculous things seriously.

*I*: But how can one bring oneself to say them at all?

*He*: It can't be accomplished suddenly; but little by little, one reaches the point. *Ingenii largitor venter.*†

*I*: One needs to be driven by a very cruel hunger.

*He*: Maybe. Yet, exaggerated as they seem to you, believe me, those to whom these phrases are addressed are more accustomed to hear them than we are to venture on saying them.

*I*: Is there anyone amongst you brave enough to share your opinion?

*He*: Anyone, you say? It's the way the whole group thinks and speaks.

*I*: Those of you who aren't great knaves must be great fools.

*He*: Fools, amongst us? I swear there's only one; the man who makes much of us, in order that we may deceive him.

*I*: But how can anyone let himself be so grossly deceived? For, after all, the superior talent of Dangeville and Clairon is an unquestioned fact.

*He*: A lie that flatters is swallowed whole; truth, if it tastes bitter, is only sipped little by little. And then, we wear such an air of conviction and sincerity!

*I*: Yet you must at some time have infringed the principles of art, and let slip by mistake one of those bitter truths that hurt; for, despite the wretched, abject, base and abominable role you have assumed, I believe you have a sensitive soul at bottom.

*He*: I? Not at all. Devil take me if I know what I am at bottom. On the whole, I'm plain-minded and frank-natured; never dishonest, if there's anything to gain by being honest; never honest, if there's anything to gain by dishonesty. I say things just as they occur to me; if

* Bertin was "*Trésorier des Parties Casuelles.*"

† The belly is the dispenser of wit.

they're sensible so much the better; if they're absurd, no one heeds them. I make full use of my freedom of speech. I've never in my life taken thought before speaking, while speaking or after speaking. And thus I offend nobody.

*I*: And yet you did happen to offend those good folks amongst whom you were living and who had been so exceedingly kind to you.

*He*: Ah, well, it can't be helped; it's a misfortune, such as one expects in life. There's no such thing as continual happiness; I was too well off, it could not last. As you know, we are a large and well-chosen band. You can get your training in humanity there; the antique tradition of hospitality is renewed. We pick up all poets who fall flat; we got Palissot after his *Zarès*, Bret after the *Faux Généreux;* all unpopular musicians; all unread authors; all actresses that get hissed; all actors that get hooted at; a gang of shame-faced wretches, of mean parasites, at whose head I have the honour to be, the gallant leader of a timid band. I'm the person who urges them to eat, the first time they come; who calls for drinks for them. They take up so little room! A few ragged youths who don't know which way to turn, but who've got a good appearance; others, scoundrels who wheedle the patron and send him to sleep, so as to enjoy after him the favours of the patroness. We seem gay, but at bottom we're all bad-tempered and hungry. Wolves are not more ravenous, nor tigers more cruel. We devour like wolves when the ground has long been covered with snow; like so many tigers, we tear up everyone who is successful. Sometimes Bertin's mob, and Monsauge's and Vilmorien's get together; and then there's a fine din in the menagerie. Never before were seen in one place so many sullen, peevish, mischievous and angry animals. You hear nothing but the names of Buffon, Duclos, Montesquieu, Rousseau, Voltaire, d'Alembert, Diderot; and God knows with what epithets they're accompanied. We won't credit anyone with intelligence who's not as stupid as ourselves. The comedy of the *Philosophes* was first planned here; the scene of the pedlar was supplied by me, from out of the *Théologie en quenouille*. You're not spared in it, any more than the others.

*I*: All the better. Perhaps that does me more honour than I deserve. I should feel humiliated if those who speak ill of so many clever and decent folk should venture to speak well of me.

*He*: There are many of us, and every one must contribute his share. After the larger animals have been sacrificed, we slaughter the others.

*I*: You earn your bread dearly if you insult science and virtue for a living.

*He*: I've already told you that we don't count. We abuse everyone and we hurt nobody. Sometimes the ponderous abbé d'Olivet is one of us, or the fat abbé LeBlanc, or Batteux the hypocrite. The fat abbé is only spiteful before dinner. When he's had his coffee he flings himself into an arm-chair, propping his feet against the mantelpiece, and goes to sleep like an old parrot on its perch. If the din becomes violent, he yawns, stretches his arms, rubs his eyes and says, "Well, what's the matter?" "We're arguing as to whether Piron has more wit than Voltaire." "Let's get this clear. Wit, you said? You're not discussing taste? for, as regards taste, your Piron has no notion of it." "Has no notion?" "No." And there we are embarked on a dissertation about taste. Then the patron raises his hand to show that we must listen to him, for taste is what he particularly prides himself upon. "Taste," says he, "taste is a thing. . . ." I declare I don't know what sort of thing he said it was, and neither did he.

Sometimes friend Robbé is with us. He entertains us with his cynical stories, with descriptions of the miracles worked among the convulsionaries of St. Médard, of which he was an eye-witness; and with some cantos of his poem on a subject with which he is saturated. I hate his verse, but I love to hear him recite. He looks like a fanatic. Everyone round him exclaims: "There's a real poet for you." Between you and me, such poetry is a mere medley of noises of all sorts, the barbaric clamour of the Tower of Babel. And sometimes, too, there comes one who looks a dull and stupid fool, but who's as witty as the devil and more cunning than an old monkey. One of those faces that calls for jokes and jeers and that God made to teach a lesson to those who judge by appearances, when their mirror should have taught them that it's as easy for a clever man to look a fool, as for a fool to be concealed behind a clever face. It's a very common weakness to sacrifice a good man for the sake of amusing the others; and this fellow is always made a victim of it. We lay this trap for all new-comers, and I've hardly ever seen one avoid it.

(I was sometimes surprised by the exactness with which this madman observed men and characters; and I told him so. He answered me:)

*He*: One can profit by bad company, you see, just as by licentiousness. The loss of one's prejudices compensates for the loss of one's innocence. In the company of bad men, where vices appear unmasked, one gets to learn all about them. And then I've read a bit.

*I*: What have you read?

*He*: I've read, and I read and re-read constantly, Theophrastus, La Bruyère and Molière.

*I*: Those are excellent books.

*He*: They are far better than people think; but who knows how to read them?

*I*: Everyone, according to his degree of intelligence.

*He*: Scarcely anyone. Can you tell me what people look for in these books?

*I*: Amusement and instruction.

*He*: But what sort of instruction? That's the important point.

*I*: To know one's duties, to love virtue and to hate vice.

*He*: Whereas I learn from them all that one should do and all that one shouldn't. Thus when I read *L'Avare* I say to myself: Be a miser if you like; but take care not to speak like a miser. When I read *Tartuffe* I say: Be a hypocrite if you like, but don't talk like a hypocrite. Keep vices that are useful to you, but avoid the manner and appearance that express them, for these would make you ridiculous. To preserve oneself from that manner and those appearances one needs to be familiar with them; now these authors have drawn excellent portraits of them. I am myself and I remain as I am: but I act and speak as it suits me. I'm not one of those people who despise moralists. There's much to be gained from them, especially from those who have put their morality into practice. Vice only hurts men at intervals; the outward signs of vice hurt them from morning till night. Perhaps it is better to be insolent than to look insolent; if you've an insolent character, you only insult people from time to time; if you've an insolent face, you insult them all the time. For that matter, you mustn't suppose that I am the only reader of this kind. My only merit here lies in doing systematically, intelligently, from a reasonable and correct view of things, what most others do from instinct. As a result, their reading does not make them better than me, but they remain ridiculous against their will, whereas I am so only when I please, and then I leave them far behind me; for that same art that teaches me to avoid being ridiculous on some occasions, also teaches me to be ridiculous in masterly fashion on other occasions. Then I remember all that others have said, all that I've read, and I add all I can of my own invention, which is astonishingly fertile in that kind of style.

*I*: It's a good thing you have revealed these secrets to me, otherwise I might have thought you inconsistent.

*He*: I'm not that at all; for luckily, if there's one occasion on which one must avoid being ridiculous, there are a hundred on which one needs to play the fool. It's the best role to assume in the company of the great. For a long time there was an official king's fool; there has never been an official king's wise man. I'm the fool of Bertin and of many others, perhaps yours at this moment; or perhaps you are mine. A really wise man would have no fool. So then, he who has a fool is not wise; if he is not wise, he is a fool; and perhaps, were he the king himself, his fool's fool. Moreover, you must remember that, where something as variable as morality is concerned, nothing is absolutely, essentially, generally true or false, except that one must be as it is to one's interest to be: good or bad, wise or foolish, respectable or ridiculous, honest or vicious. If by any chance virtue had led to fortune, either I should have been virtuous, or I should have pretended to be, like anyone else. I was asked to be ridiculous, and I made myself so; as for vice, nature had seen to that by herself. I say vice, because I'm speaking your language; for if we were to have it out, we might find that you call vice what I call virtue, and virtue what I call vice.

Then we have the authors of the *Opéra Comique*, their actors and actresses; and often their producers, Corby, Moette—all people of great resourcefulness and merit! And I was forgetting the great literary critics: the *Fore-Runner*, the *Little Notices*, the *Literary Year*, the *Literary Observer*, the *Weekly Censor*, the whole clique of pamphleteers.

*I*: The *Literary Year*, the *Literary Observer?* That isn't possible. They detest one another.

*He*: True; but all beggars make friends over the platter. That damned *Literary Observer!* I wish the devil had carried him off with all his leaflets! That dog of a little priest, that miserly stinking usurer was the cause of my disaster. He appeared on our horizon yesterday, for the first time. He arrived at the hour that drives us all from our lairs, the dinner-hour. When the weather's bad, he's a lucky one amongst us who has a florin in his pocket to pay for a cab! The man who has sneered at his colleague for arriving in the morning muddied up to the backbone and wet to the skin, may be in the same plight himself when he gets home at night. One of us, I don't remember who, had a violent quarrel a few months ago with the Savoyard sweeper who had installed himself outside the door. They had a current account; the creditor wanted his debtor to settle up, and the debtor had no money and yet couldn't avoid his creditor if he wanted to go upstairs.

Well, dinner was served; the abbé was in the place of honour, near the head of the table. I came in and noticed him. "How's this, abbé," said I, "you're presiding? That's all very well for to-day, but to-morrow you will please go down one place, the next day one more place, and so on from one place to another, either to the right or to the left, from the seat that I occupied once before you, Fréron once after me, Dorat once after Fréron, Palissot once after Dorat, until you come to a halt beside me, who am a poor wretched b— like yourself, *qui siedo sempre come un maestoso cazzo fra duoi coglioni.*" The abbé, who's a good-natured fellow and takes everything in good part, began to laugh. Mademoiselle, impressed with the truth of my remark and the exactness of my comparison, began to laugh; all those who were sitting to the right and left of the abbé, and who'd been sent down one place by him, began to laugh; everyone laughed except Monsieur, who grew angry and spoke to me in terms that would have meant nothing if we had been alone. "Rameau, you are an impertinent fellow." "I know that well; it was on that condition that you took me up." "A scoundrel." "No more than another." "A beggarly wretch." "Should I be here otherwise?" "I'll have you kicked out." "After dinner I'll go of my own accord." "You had better." We had dinner; I didn't miss a single bite. After eating well and drinking freely, since after all that made no difference, and Sir Belly is a gentleman to whom I've never borne ill-will, I made up my mind and got ready to go. I had given my word in presence of so many people that I was bound to keep it. I took a considerable time prowling about the room looking for my stick and my hat where they were not, and all the time expecting that the patron would let loose a fresh flood of insults, that someone would step in, and that, after getting really angry, we should end by making it up. I roamed round and round, for I myself wasn't in the least upset; but as for the patron, he strode up and down, his fist under his chin, his cap pulled down even lower than usual, gloomier and blacker than Homer's Apollo letting fly his arrows over the Grecian army. Mademoiselle came up to me. "But, Mademoiselle, what is it that's so unusual? Have I been unlike myself to-day?" "I insist on his going." "I'll go . . . I've not been wanting in respect to him." "Excuse me; Monsieur l'abbé was invited and. . . ." "He has been lacking in respect to himself, by inviting the abbé, and by receiving me and other rascals like me." "Come now, Rameau dear, you must beg Monsieur l'abbé's pardon." "I don't want his pardon." "Come, come, it'll all blow over." I was taken by the hand and led to the abbé's chair; I stretched out my arms and gazed at the abbé with a sort of admiration, for who has ever begged the abbé's pardon? "Abbé, abbé," I said to him, "all this is very silly, isn't it?" And then I burst out laughing, and so did the abbé. Thus I was forgiven in this quarter; but now I must approach the other, and what I had to say to him was quite a different matter. I can't really remember how I worded my apology. . . "Monsieur here's this madman." "He's been vexing me for too long; I never want to hear of him again." "He's very sorry he annoyed you." "Yes, he annoyed me very much." "It won't happen to him any more. . . ." "Nor to any other rascal."

I don't know if it was one of his bad-tempered days, when Mademoiselle is afraid to go near him and daren't touch him except with velvet gloves on, or if he couldn't hear what I said, or if I said the wrong thing; but it was worse than before. What the devil, doesn't he know me? Doesn't he know that I'm a child and on some occasions let loose everything under me? And then I believe, God forgive me, that they wouldn't let me have a moment's respite. It would wear out a steel puppet to have its strings pulled from morning till night and from night till morning. I've got to distract them, that's the condition; but I've got to amuse myself sometimes. In the middle of this confusion, a fatal thought came into my head, a thought that gave me arrogance, a thought that inspired me with pride and insolence; namely, that they couldn't get on without me, that I was an essential person.

*I*: Yes, I believe you are very useful to them, but that they are still more so to you. You won't find such a good house again for the asking; but they'll find a hundred fools for one that fails them.

*He*: A hundred fools like me! Master philosopher, they're not so common. Dull fools, yes. People are harder to please in the matter of folly than in the matter of talent or virtue. I am rare in my kind, yes, very rare. Now that they haven't got me, what's happened to them? They are as dull as ditchwater. I'm an inexhaustible treasury of impertinence. I had a sally for every moment, which would make them laugh till they cried, I was a complete madhouse for them.

*I*: And for your part you had board and bed, coat, waistcoat and breeches, shoes and a guinea a month.

*He*: That was the good side of it. That was the profit; but you don't mention the costs. To begin with, if there was a rumour of any new play, whatever the weather I had to ferret about all the attics in Paris until I'd found the author of it; I had to get leave to read the work, and I had to insinuate adroitly that there was one part in it which would be admirably played by someone of my acquaintance. "And by whom, if you please?" "By whom? What a question! By the most gracious, charming, delicate . . ." "You mean Mademoiselle Dangeville? Do you know her, by any chance?" "Yes, a little; but she's not the person." "Who then?" I'd murmur the name. "She!" "Yes, she," I'd repeat it, somewhat embarrassed; for I have a certain shame, and when this name is repeated, you should see what a long face the poet pulls or how, at other times, he bursts out laughing in my face. Nevertheless, I had to bring my man along to dinner, whether he liked or no; and he, afraid of committing himself, would make excuses, proffer thanks. You should have seen how I was treated when I didn't succeed in my negotiation; I was a clumsy brute, a fool, a dolt, I was good for nothing; I wasn't worth the glass of water I was given to drink. It was far worse when a play was on, and I must go fearlessly, amidst the hoots of an audience which, whatever they say, is a good judge, and clap my solitary pair of hands; draw all eyes towards me; sometimes draw on to myself the hisses that were meant for the actress; and hear whispered beside me: "That's one of her lover's valets in disguise; won't the rascal be quiet?" People don't know what drives one to such conduct, they think it's sheer idiocy, whereas there is a motive that excuses everything.

*I*: Even the violation of civil laws.

*He*: In the end, however, people got to know me, and they'd say: "Oh, it's Rameau." My expedient was to fling out a few ironical words that saved my solitary applause from appearing ridiculous, by inviting a contrary interpretation. You must admit that it needed a powerful interest to make one brave the assembled audience in this fashion, and that each of these labours was worth more than half-a-crown.

*I*: Why didn't you get some assistance?

*He*: That happened sometimes, and I made a little profit over that. Before going to the scene of my torture, I must load my memory with the purple passages, where I should have to give the lead. If I chanced to forget them and make a mistake, I was all trembling when I went home; you've no conception what an uproar there'd be. And then, there was a pack of dogs to look after in the house; it's true that I'd stupidly imposed this task on myself; cats that I had to superintend; and it was lucky for me if Micou did me the favour of tearing my cuff or my hand with his claws. Criquette was a victim to colic, and I had to rub her belly. Formerly Mademoiselle used to suffer from the vapours; to-day she calls it nerves. I won't mention other trifling disorders which she discusses freely in front of me. Let that pass; I've never attempted to restrain anyone. I've read somewhere or other that a certain monarch, surnamed the Great, would sometimes stand leaning against the back of his mistress's commode. One behaves without restraint with one's intimates, and I was that, more than anyone, in those days. I'm the apostle of familiarity and ease. I preached them there by my example, and nobody took offence; they had only to leave me alone. I've sketched the patron for you. Mademoiselle is beginning to grow heavy; you should hear the good stories they tell on that subject.

*I*: You're not one of those people?

*He*: Why not?

*I*: Because it is unseemly, to say the least, to laugh at one's benefactors.

*He*: But is it not worse still to assume that one's benefactions give one the right to debase one's protégé?

*I*: But if that protégé were not base in himself, nothing would give the protector such a right.

*He*: But if the people in question were not ridiculous in themselves, there'd be no good stories told about them. And then, is it my fault if they keep low company? Is it my fault if, when they keep low company, they are betrayed and made fools of? A man who can bring himself to live with the likes of us, if he has common sense, must be prepared for any amount of wickedness. When they take us up, don't they know us for what we are, for self-seeking, vile, perfidious souls? If they know us it's all right. There's a tacit agreement that they'll do good towards us, and that sooner or later we shall repay that good with evil. Does not such an agreement exist between a man and his monkey or his parrot? Brun cries out in horror because Palissot, his friend and his guest, has written verses against him. Palissot had to write the verses and it's Brun who is wrong. Poinsinet cries out in horror because Palissot has attributed to him the verses he wrote against Brun. Palissot had to attribute the verses to Poinsinet; and Poinsinet is in the wrong. Little abbé Rey cries out in horror because his mistress was stolen by his friend Palissot to whom he'd introduced her. But either he should never have introduced her to a man like Palissot, or else he should have resigned himself to losing her. Palissot did his duty; and the abbé Rey is in the wrong. The bookseller David cries out in horror because his colleague Palissot slept or wanted to sleep with his wife; the wife of the bookseller David cries out in horror because Palissot has let it be understood by anyone who wanted to listen that he'd slept with her; whether or not Palissot did sleep with the bookseller's wife is a difficult question to settle, because the wife was bound to deny what may have happened, and Palissot may have given us to believe something that didn't happen. However that may be, Palissot played his part, and David and his wife are in the wrong. Let Helvétius cry out in horror because Palissot represents him on the stage as a dishonest man, Palissot who still owes him the money he lent him for treatment of his ill-health, for food and clothing; what other conduct could he have expected from a man stained with every kind of infamy, who just to amuse himself induces his friend to abjure religion, who embezzles the fortune of his associates, who knows no loyalty, no law, no feeling; who seeks after wealth *per fas et nefas;** who measures his days by his misdeeds; and who has represented himself on the stage as one of the most dangerous of rascals, a stroke of impudence unprecedented, surely, in the past, and unrepeatable in the future. No; it's not Palissot but Helvétius who is in the wrong. If a young provincial is taken to the menagerie at Versailles, and out of stupidity ventures to thrust his hand through the bars of the tiger's cage, or the panther's; if that young man leaves his arm between the jaws of the savage beast, which is in the wrong? All that is written down in the tacit agreement. So much the worse for whoever doesn't know it or forgets it. By reference to that universal, sacred agreement, I could justify any number

* By fair means or foul.

of people whom we accuse of wickedness, when we should rather accuse ourselves of stupidity! Yes, fat Countess, it's you who are in the wrong when you gather around you what people of your sort call "creatures," and these creatures act basely towards you, make you act basely yourselves, and expose you to the indignation of decent folk. Decent folk do their duty, and these creatures do theirs; it's yourselves who are in the wrong to take them up. If Bertinhus * lived quietly and calmly with his mistress, if through the honesty of their characters they had won the acquaintance of honest folk, if they had drawn around them men of talent, men known in society for their virtue; if they had devoted to a small, well-chosen and enlightened group such leisure hours as they could spare from the pleasure of each other's company, of mutual love confessed in the silence of seclusion; do you think there would be any stories, good or bad, told about them? What, then, has happened to them? Just what they deserved. Their imprudence has been punished; and we were destined by Providence, from all eternity, to deal justice to the Bertins of our day; and our fellows among posterity are destined to deal justice to the Bertins and Monsauges to come. But while we carry out her just decrees against these fools, you, who depict us as we are, you carry out her just decrees against ourselves. What would you think of us if, with our immoral ways, we aspired to enjoy the respect of the public?—that we were crazy. And those who expect decent conduct from men born vicious, men of vile degraded character, are they wise? Everything has its right price in this world. There are two public prosecutors; one, at your door, chastizes crimes against society. Nature is the other. She takes cognizance of all vices that the law lets slip. You are given to sexual excesses; very well, you shall have the dropsy. You indulge in debauchery; you shall have consumption. You open wide your doors to scoundrels, and live amongst them; you shall be betrayed, made mock of, despised. The best thing is to be resigned to the fairness of these sentences, and to say to oneself "you deserved that"; to shake one's ears and either correct one's faults or remain as one is, but on the aforesaid conditions.

*I*: You are right.

*He*: And besides, I don't invent any of those unkind stories; I stick to the role of tale-bearer. They say that some days ago, about five in the morning, a fearful uproar was heard; all the bells were ringing; cries sounded, the broken, indistinct cries of a man who's being smothered: "Help, help, I'm choking, I'm dying." These cries issued from the patron's room. They went to his rescue. Our stout lady, who'd quite lost her head, who'd lost her sight, who had passed out, as one

* Nickname of Bertin, whose mistress was Mlle. Hus.

does at such times, went on speeding up her movements, lifting herself up on both hands as high as she could and then letting fall onto the Treasurer of the *Parties Casuelles* her full weight of two or three hundred pounds, with all the velocity imparted to it by the frenzy of pleasure. It was a hard job getting him free. A queer fancy that, for a little hammer to put itself underneath a heavy anvil!

*I*: You're a filthy fellow. Let's speak of something else. Since we've been talking I've had one question on the tip of my tongue.

*He*: Why did you keep it there so long?

*I*: Because I feared it might be indiscreet.

*He*: After what I've just disclosed to you, I don't know what I could keep secret from you.

*I*: You are well aware of my opinion of your character?

*He*: Perfectly. I'm an abject, despicable wretch in your eyes, and sometimes in my own too; but not often. I congratulate myself on my vices more often than I blame myself for them. You are more constant in your contempt.

*I*: That's true; but why reveal your full villainy to me?

*He*: First, because you were already acquainted with a good part of it, and I saw there was more to be gained than lost by confessing the remainder to you.

*I*: How's that, if you please?

*He*: If there's one quality in which it's essential to attain sublimity, it is wickedness. A petty thief gets spat upon; but a great criminal can't be refused some sort of admiration. His courage astonishes you. His cruelty makes you shudder. Consistency of character is always appreciated.

*I*: But you haven't got it yet, this desirable consistency of character. From time to time, you seem to me to vacillate in your principles. It's not clear whether you owe your wickedness to nature or to study, and whether study has carried you as far as it might.

*He*: I agree with you; but I've done my best. Have I not been modest enough to recognize more perfect beings than myself? Have I not spoken of Bouret with the deepest admiration? Bouret is the world's greatest man, to my mind.

*I*: But you come next, immediately after Bouret.

*He*: No.

*I*: Palissot, then?

*He*: Palissot, but not Palissot alone.

*I*: And who can be found worthy to share the second rank with him?

*He*: The renegade of Avignon.

*I*: I've never heard tell of this renegade of Avignon; but he must be a most astonishing man.

*He*: So he is.

*I*: The history of great men has always interested me.

*He*: I can well believe it. This man used to live with a good, honest descendant of Abraham, one of those who were promised to the Father of all believers in number as many as the stars.

*I*: With a Jew?

*He*: With a Jew. He had won first the Jew's pity, then his goodwill, finally his whole-hearted trust. For that's the way it always is. We rely so much on our good deeds, that we seldom withhold our confidence from the man on whom we have showered kindnesses. How can we expect men not to be ungrateful, when we offer them the opportunity to be so without punishment? This is a wise thought which did not occur to our Jew. So he confided to the renegade that his conscience would not allow him to eat pork. You shall see how a fertile mind took advantage of this confession. A few months went by, during which our renegade displayed an ever-increasing attachment. When his Jew seemed to him thoroughly touched, thoroughly captivated, and thoroughly convinced, by his attentions, that he had no better friend among all the tribes of Israel . . . admire the circumspection of this man. He made no haste. He allowed the pear to ripen before he shook the branch. Too much enthusiasm might ruin his plan. You see, it is generally the case that greatness of character is due to a natural balance between several contrary qualities.

*I*: Oh, let your reflections alone, and go on with your story.

*He*: That cannot be. There are certain days when I have to reflect. It's a disease that must run its course. Where had I got to?

*I*: To a well-established intimacy between the Jew and the renegade.

*He*: Then the pear had ripened. . . . But you're not listening to me. What are you thinking about.

*I*: I'm thinking about the unevenness of your tone, sometimes lofty, sometimes base.

*He*: How can a vicious man maintain an even tone? . . . Well, one evening he came up to his kind friend, looking terrified, his voice broken, his face pale as death, trembling in every limb. "What is the matter?" "We are lost." "Lost? How is that?" "Lost, I tell you, hopelessly lost." "What do you mean?" "One moment, let me recover from my terror." "Come, come, be calm," said the Jew to him, instead of saying, "You're an arrant knave; I don't know what you have to tell me, but you're an arrant knave; you're acting terror."

*I*: And why ought he to have spoken thus to him?

*He*: Because the man was deceiving him, and had gone too far. That's quite clear to me, so don't interrupt me any more. "We are lost, hopelessly lost." Don't you feel the affectation of the repeated "lost"?

"A traitor has denounced us to the Holy Inquisition, you as a Jew, me as a renegade, an infamous renegade." Notice how the traitor unblushingly used the most odious terms. It takes more courage than you'd think to call oneself by one's right name. You don't know what it costs to reach that point.

*I*: I certainly don't. But this infamous renegade? . . .

*He*: Was a deceiver; but a very skilful one. The Jew takes fright, begins tearing his beard, rolls on the ground. He sees the police-spies at his door; he sees himself arrayed in the *sanbenito;* and sees his *auto-da-fé* being made ready. "My friend, my dear friend, my only friend, what are we to do?" "To do? Why, let ourselves be seen about, assume an air of complete security, behave just as usual. This tribunal proceeds secretly, but slowly. We must take advantage of its delays to sell everything. I'll go and hire a boat, or get someone else to hire it; yes, someone else will be best. We'll deposit your fortune in it, for it's your fortune they're after; and we will go, you and I, to seek beneath another sky the freedom to serve our God and to follow unmolested the law of Abraham and of our conscience. In the dangerous situation we are in, the important point is to do nothing rash." No sooner said than done. The boat is hired, and provided with foodstuffs and with sailors. The Jew's fortune is put on board. Next day at dawn they are to set sail. They may sup cheerfully and sleep in safety. Next day they are to escape from their persecutors. During the night the renegade gets up, robs the Jew of his pocket-book, his purse and his jewels; goes on board and makes off. And do you think that's all? Well, you're quite wrong. When I was told this story, I guessed what I've concealed from you to test your shrewdness. It's just as well you are an honest man; you'd have made a very poor rogue. Up till now, that's all the renegade was—a wretched knave whom nobody would want to resemble. But he achieved sublimity in his wickedness by himself informing against his good friend the Israelite, who was seized by the Holy Inquisition when he awoke, and of whom a fine bonfire was made a few days later. And thus it came about that the renegade enjoyed untroubled possession of the fortune of that accursed descendant of those who crucified Our Lord.

*I*: I don't know which I think more horrible—the villainy of your renegade or the tone in which you speak of it.

*He*: That's just what I was telling you. You cannot be merely contemptuous of a deed of such atrocity; and that's the reason for my sincerity. I wanted to show you the high degree of excellence I'd attained in my art; to compel you to confess that I was at least original in my degradation, to take up my place, in your mind, in the rank of great rascals, and then to cry: *Vivat Mascarillus, fourbum Imperator!* Come on, then, master philosopher, join in the chorus: *Vivat Mascarillus, fourbum Imperator.*

And with that he began to sing a most remarkable fugue. The melody was now grave and majestic, now light and playful; one moment he would imitate the bass; the next, one of the treble parts; he suggested the sustained passages by stretching out his arm and his neck; and thus he made and played for himself a triumphal song, which clearly showed that he knew more about good music than about good morals. As for myself, I did not know whether to run or to stay, whether to laugh or to be revolted. I stayed, intending to turn the talk on to some topic that might drive from my mind the horror that possessed it. I began to find intolerable the presence of a man who discussed a horrible deed, a loathsome crime, as a connoisseur of painting or poetry would examine the beauties of a work of art; or as a moralist or a historian might pick out and praise the details of a heroic action. I grew gloomy, in spite of myself. He noticed it, and said:

*He*: What's the matter with you; are you feeling ill?

*I*: Yes, somewhat: but it will pass.

*He*: You have the anxious look of a man who is haunted by an unpleasant thought.

*I*: That's just it.

After a moment's silence on his part and on mine, during which he walked up and down whistling and singing, I said, to bring him back to where his talent lay:

*I*: What are you composing nowadays?

*He*: Nothing.

*I*: That must be tedious.

*He*: I was stupid enough already. I went to hear that music of Duni's and our other young composers, and that was the end of me.

*I*: You admire that style, then?

*He*: Of course.

*I*: And you find beauty in these new songs?

*He*: Beauty? I should say so! What recitative! How true, how expressive!

*I*: Every imitative art has its model in nature. What model does the musician take when he writes a song?

*He*: Why not start further back? What is a song?

*I*: I must confess that question is beyond my powers. That's the way we all are; we retain in our memories only terms that we think we understand, through using them frequently and perhaps applying them correctly; we have in our minds only vague conceptions of their meaning. When I utter the word "song," I have no clear conception, any more than you and most of your fellows have when you say reputation, blame, honour, vice, virtue, modesty, decency, shame, absurdity.

*He*: Song is an imitation of the sounds of the physical world or of the accents of passion, by means of the notes of a scale invented by art or inspired by nature, as you please, and rendered either by the voice or by an instrument; and you see that, if certain terms are changed, the definition holds good for painting, rhetoric, sculpture and poetry. Now, to come to your question: what is the model for the musician or his song? Speech, if the model is a living thinking being; sound, if the model is inanimate. Speech must be considered as one line, and song as another which twines itself about the first. The stronger and truer the speech, which is the basis of the song, and the greater the number of points at which the intertwining song touches it, the more convincing and beautiful will the song be. And that is what our young musicians have grasped very well. When you hear: *Je suis un pauvre diable* you fancy you hear a miser complaining; if he did not sing, he would speak in the same tones to the earth when he entrusts his gold to it and says *O terre, reçois mon trésor*. And the little girl who feels her heart throb, who blushes and is distressed and begs his lordship to let her go, would she express herself otherwise? These compositions include every sort of character, an infinite variety of speech. It's sublime, you may take my word for it. You should go and hear the piece where the young man who feels himself dying cries: *Mon coeur s'en va*. Listen to the song: listen to the symphony, and then you shall tell me what difference there is between the true voice of a dying man and the phrases of this song. You will see if the line of the melody doesn't entirely coincide with the line of the speech. I haven't mentioned rhythm, which is yet another of the conditions of song; I've confined myself to expression; and nothing is truer than this saying, which I've read somewhere: *Musices seminarium accentus;* accent is the nursery of melody. You may judge from this how difficult and important it is to be able to write good recitative. There's no fine tune from which a fine recitative cannot be made, and no fine recitative from which a clever man could not extract a fine tune. I wouldn't like to affirm that whoever recites well will sing well; but I'd be much surprised if a man who sang well could not recite well. And you may believe all that I'm telling you; for it is true.

*I*: I'd ask nothing better than to believe you, if there were not one little obstacle that prevents me.

*He*: And that is?

*I*: That if this music is sublime, then that of the divine Lulli, of Campra, Destouches and Mouret, and even, between ourselves, that of your dear uncle, must be a little dull.

Whispering in my ear, he answered me:

*He*: I don't want to be overheard, for there are many people here who know me; but that's just what it is. I don't care about my dear uncle, since that's what you call him—he's a man of stone; if he saw me with my tongue hanging out a foot, he wouldn't offer me a glass of water; but let him go on making the devil's own din with his *hon-hon, hin-hin, tu-tu-tu, turelu-tutu* in octaves and sevenths; those who are beginning to know something about it and who don't any longer mistake mere noise for music, will never put up with that. There ought to be a police regulation forbidding anyone, whatever his rank or position, to perform Pergolesi's *Stabat*. That *Stabat* should have been burnt by the public executioner. Good Lord, those damned Bouffons with their *Servante Maîtresse* and their *Tracollo* have given us a good kick in the backside. Formerly such things as *Tancrède, Issé, Europe galante, les Indes, Castor, les Talents Lyriques*, would play for four, five, six months. There was no end to the performances of *Armide*. And now they're toppling over like card castles. And so Rebel and Francœur are in the wildest rage. They say that all's lost, that they are ruined; that if we put up with this low market-place music any longer, the nation's music is done for; and that the Royal Academy of the blind-alley will have to shut up shop. There's certainly some truth in that. The old fogies who have gone there every Friday for thirty or forty years, instead of enjoying themselves as they used to, are bored and yawn without quite knowing why. They ask themselves why, and can't answer. Why don't they ask me? Duni's prophecy will be fulfilled; and at the rate things are going, I'll stake my life that in four or five years from the *Peintre amoureux de son modèle* there won't be a cat left in the famous blind-alley. Those worthy folks! They gave up their own symphonies in order to play Italian symphonies; they thought their ears would grow accustomed to these and yet their vocal music remain unaffected; as though symphony did not bear to song the same relation—except for a certain freedom engendered by the range of the instrument and the mobility of the player's fingers—as song to real speech. As though the violin did not ape the singer, who may one day, when the beautiful has given place to the difficult, ape the violin; the first man who played Locatelli was the apostle of the new music. Let them tell their tale to somebody else! What, once we've become accustomed to the imitation of the accents of passion or of natural phenomena—for that is the whole scope of music's objective—shall we retain our liking for flights, lances, glories, triumphs, victories? "*Va t'en voir s'ils viennent, Jean.*" They imagined that they could weep and laugh at scenes of tragedy and comedy set to music, that they could listen to the accents of fury, hatred, jealousy, the true lamentations of love, the ironies and witticisms of the French or Italian theatre, and yet remain admirers of *Ragonde* and *Platée*. Stuff and nonsense, I'd say!—that they could continually experience with what facility, flexibility, and softness the harmony, prosody, ellipses and inversions of the Italian tongue lend themselves to the art of song, to its movement, its expression, its phrases, and to the measured value of sounds, and that they could still remain unaware how stiff, dead, clumsy, heavy, pedantic and monotonous is their own. Well, well! They persuaded themselves that after mingling their tears with those of a mother mourning her son's death, after shuddering to hear a tyrant give orders for a murder, they would not find tedious their fairy tales, their insipid mythology, their little sugary madrigals, that are not more indicative of the poet's bad taste than of the wretched state of an art that puts up with them. Worthy folks! It is not so, and it never can be. The true, the good and the beautiful have their rights. These may be contested, but they will be admired in the end. Anything which does not bear this stamp, though it may be admired for a while, will set you yawning in the end. Yawn, then, gentlemen, yawn as much as you please. Don't hesitate to yawn. The rule of nature, and of my trinity, against which the gates of hell will never prevail—the true which is the father, and which engenders the good which is the son, whence proceeds the beautiful which is the Holy Spirit—is being quietly established. The strange god takes his place humbly on the altar, beside the national idol; little by little he becomes more firmly settled there; one fine day, he gives his neighbour a shove with his elbow, and crash, there goes the idol. They say that's the way the Jesuits implanted Christianity in China and in India. And in spite of all the Jansenists say, this political method that goes towards its goal, without noise or bloodshed, with no martyrs made and not a single tuft of hair torn out, seems to me the best.

*I*: All this you've been saying is fairly reasonable.

*He*: Reasonable? All the better. Devil take me if I'm trying to be! It just comes as it pleases. I'm like those musicians in the blind-alley were when my uncle appeared; if I make a lucky hit, it's because a charcoal-burner's apprentice will always speak better about his trade than a whole academy and all the Duhamels in the world.

And then he began to walk about, humming in his throat some of the airs from the *Ile des fous*, the *Peintre amoureux de son modèle*, the *Maréchal ferrant*, the *Plaideuse*, and from time to time he exclaimed, raising his hands and eyes to heaven: "And isn't that beautiful? Good God, can a man have ears in his head and yet ask such a question?" He began to get excited and to sing to himself. As his passion grew he raised his voice; then came gestures, facial grimaces and bodily contortions; and I said, "Good, now he's losing his head and we shall have some fresh scene"; and so it was; he burst forth, "*Je suis un pauvre misérable. . . . Monseigneur, monseigneur, laissez-moi partir. . . . O terre, reçois mon or: conserve bien mon trésor. . . . Mon âme, mon âme, ma vie! O terre. . . . Le voilà le petit ami; le voilà . . . le petit ami! . . . Aspettare e non venire. . . . A Zerbina penserete. . . . Sempre in contrasti con te si sta. . . .*"

He mixed up in confusion thirty tunes, Italian, French, tragic, comic, of every sort and character; now in a bass voice he sank down to the underworld, now he screamed shrilly; and mimicked the walk, carriage and gestures of the different characters singing; by turns furious, pacified, imperious, sneering. Now he plays a young girl in tears, and reproduces all her mincing airs; now he becomes a priest, a king, a tyrant, threatening, commanding, flying into a rage; now he is a slave and obeys. He grows calm, he laments, he complains, he laughs; never out of tune or time, never losing the sense of the words nor the character of the air. All the chess-players had left their boards and gathered round him. The windows of the café were filled outside by the passers-by who had stopped to hear the noise. There were shouts of laughter fit to raise the roof. But he noticed nothing; he went on, in a state of mental aberration and ecstasy so near to madness, that it seemed doubtful whether he would recover, whether he should not be hastily put into a carriage and taken straight to the asylum. Singing a fragment of Jomelli's *Lamentations* he repeated the finest passages of each piece with incredible precision, truth and fire; during that fine accompanied recitative in which the prophet paints the desolation of Jerusalem he shed a torrent of tears that set us all weeping. Everything was in it, refinement of singing, expressive power, and grief. He stressed the passages which revealed particularly the composer's greatness; he would leave the vocal score to take up the instrumental part, which he would suddenly abandon in order to return to the voice; intermingling one with the other so as to preserve the connections and the unity of the whole; seizing hold of our souls, and holding them in suspense, in the most extraordinary situation I have ever known. . . . Was it admiration I felt? yes, it was admiration; was it pity? yes, it was pity; but a certain tinge of absurdity was fused with these feelings and changed their nature. But you would have burst out laughing at the way he mimicked the various instruments. With his cheeks puffed out and swollen, on a harsh gloomy note, he reproduced the horns and bassoons; he assumed a shrill nasal tone for the oboes; hurrying his voice at an incredible speed, for the stringed instruments, whose smallest intervals he sought to render; he whistled for the piccolo, he cooed for the flutes; shouting, singing, flinging himself about like a madman;

playing all by himself the parts of dancers and singers, male and female, of a whole orchestra and a whole operatic company, dividing himself into twenty different roles, running, stopping short, with the look of one possessed, his eyes flashing, foaming at the mouth. It was terribly hot; and the sweat that ran in the furrows of his brow and along his cheeks, mingled with the powder from his hair, streamed down and streaked the top of his coat. What did I not see him do? He wept, he laughed, he sighed, he gazed; now tender, now tranquil, now furious; he was a woman swooning from grief; an unfortunate wretch a prey to despair; a towering temple; birds hushing their song at sunset; waters murmuring in a cool and lonely spot, or falling in torrents from a high mountain; now a storm, a tempest, where the cry of those about to perish mingles with the whistling of the wind and the crash of thunder. Now he was night with its gloom, now darkness and silence, for even silence may be painted with sounds. He had gone quite out of his mind. . . . Tired out, like a man emerging from a deep sleep or a prolonged fit of abstraction, he stayed motionless, stupefied, bewildered. He gazed around him, like one who has lost his way and tries to recognize the place where he is. He was waiting to recover his strength and his wits; mechanically he wiped his face. Like a man waking up to see a crowd of people round his bed; forgetting entirely, or completely unaware of what he had done, he cried out at first: "Why, gentlemen, what is the matter? What's the reason for your laughter and astonishment? What is the matter?" Then he added: "There's real music for you, and a real musician. And yet, gentlemen, certain pieces by Lulli are not to be despised. I defy anyone to improve on the scene beginning '*Ah, j'attendrai*' without altering the words. Certain passages of Campra are not to be despised, nor my uncle's airs for the violin, nor his gavottes, his entries of priests, soldiers, and sacrificers. . . . *Pâles flambeaux, nuit plus affreux que les ténèbres. . . . Dieu du Tartare, Dieu de l'Oubli. . . .*" Here he swelled his voice and sustained his notes; the neighbours came to their windows; we thrust our fingers into our ears. He added: "That's where lungs are needed, a powerful organ, a great volume of breath. But soon we shall be greeting the Assumption; Lent and the Epiphany are over. They don't yet know what should be set to music, nor consequently, what suits a musician. Lyric poetry is not born yet. But they'll come to it; by dint of hearing Pergolesi, the Saxon, Terradeglias, Traetta, and the others; by dint of reading Metastasio, they'll have to come to it."

*I*: What? So Quinault, La Motte and Fontenelle didn't know their business?

*He*: Not the new style. There are not six consecutive lines in all their charming poems that could be set to music. There are ingenious maxims, light, tender, delicate love-poems; but if you would know how useless all that is for our art, the most violent of all, not excepting that of Demosthenes, let these verses be recited to you and see how cold, how languid, how monotonous they seem. There's nothing in them you see, that can serve as a model for song. I'd as soon have to set to music La Rochefoucauld's *Maxims* or the *Pensées* of Pascal. The line that's to suit us must be dictated by the animal cry of passion. We need expressions hurrying after one another; the short phrase, its sense broken, suspended; the musician must have the whole and each of its parts at his disposal, must be able to omit or repeat a word, add one that's lacking, turn the phrase round and round without destroying it, like a polypus; all of which makes it far harder to write lyric poetry in French than in languages that allow inversions, and that actually present all these advantages. . . . *Barbare, cruel, plonge ton poignard dans mon sein. Me voilà prête à recevoir le coup fatal. Frappe. Ose. . . . Ah! je languis, je meurs. . . . Un feu secret s'allume dans mes sens. . . . Cruel amour, que veux-tu de moi? . . . Laisse-moi la douce paix dont j'ai joui. . . . Rends-moi la raison . . .** We need strong passions; the tenderness of the musician and the lyric poet must be exaggerated. The aria almost always winds up the scene. We need exclamations, interjections, pauses, interruptions, affirmations, denials; we call, invoke, cry, moan, weep and laugh frankly. No wit, no epigrams; none of your pretty thoughts. All that is too far from plain nature. Don't go and think, now, that the acting and declamation of stage-players can serve as models for us. No, no. We need something more vigorous, less mannered, more sincere. The more monotonous and unaccented our language, the more essential to us are the plain speech and common utterances of passion. The cry of animal impulse or of human emotion provides the accent that is lacking.

While he spoke thus, the crowd that surrounded us, either failing to understand or taking no interest in what he was saying, had drawn back, since generally children, like men, and men, like children, would rather be amused than instructed; each had gone back to his game; and we remained alone, in our corner. Sitting on a bench, leaning his head against the wall, his arms dangling, his eyes half shut, he said: "I don't know what's the matter with me; when I came here, I was fresh and

* "Ah, cruel barbarian, plunge thy dagger into my breast. See I am ready to receive the fatal blow. . . . Strike. . . . Dare. . . . Ah! I am falling, I am dying. . . . A hidden fire enflames my senses. . . . Cruel love, what do you demand of me? Leave me the quiet peace which I have enjoyed. . . . Let me be sane once more. . . ."

lively; now I'm beaten, broken, as though I'd walked ten leagues. It's come over me all of a sudden."

*I*: Would you like to drink something?

*He*: With pleasure. I feel hoarse and weak, and my chest is sore. This happens almost every day, I don't know why.

*I*: What would you like?

*He*: Whatever you please. I'm not particular. Poverty has taught me to like anything.

We were served with beer and lemonade. He filled a great glass and emptied it twice or thrice in succession. Then, like a man revived, he coughed loudly, began to throw himself about and to speak once more:

*He*: But in your opinion, my lord philosopher, is it not a very queer thing that a foreigner, an Italian, like Duni, should come and teach us how to accent our music, how to make our song comply with every sort of movement, of rhythm, of interval, of speech, without offending prosody? It wasn't such a formidable task, after all. Anyone who had listened to a beggar asking for alms in the street, or a man in a fit of anger, a jealous woman raging, a lover in despair, or a flatterer, yes, a flatterer softening his tone, drawling his syllables, speaking in a honeyed voice; in a word, to any passion, no matter what, provided that by its energy it is worthy to serve as model for a musician—must have noticed two things; first, that there is no fixed length for syllables, long or short, nor even any fixed proportion between their lengths; next, that passion deals with prosody almost as it pleases, that it can compass the widest intervals, and that the man who exclaims at the climax of his distress, "Ah, unfortunate wretch that I am," rises on the interjectory syllable to the highest and shrillest note, and sinks on the others to the deepest and gravest notes, compassing an octave or an even greater interval, and giving to each sound the quantity that suits the turn of the melody, without offending the ear, although neither the long nor the short syllables will keep the length or brevity they had in unimpassioned speech. What a long way we have travelled since the days when we cited as prodigies of musical declamation the parentheses from *Armide*: "*Le vainqueur de Renaud* (*si quelqu'un le peut être*)" and the "*Obéissons sans balancer*" from the *Indes galantes!* To-day such prodigies make me shrug my shoulders in pity. At the pace art is progressing, I don't know where it will end up. Meanwhile let's have a drink.

He had two or three without knowing what he was doing. He would have drowned himself, as he had exhausted himself, without noticing, if I had not shifted the position of the bottle for which he was groping absent-mindedly. Then I said:

*I*: How comes it that with such fine judgment and great sensitiveness in regard to the beauties of the art of music, you should be so blind to what is beautiful in moral matters, and so insensitive to the charms of virtue?

*He*: Because, apparently, these require a sense that I don't possess; a fibre that has not been granted me, a slack string that is plucked in vain, that won't vibrate; or perhaps because I have always lived among good musicians who were bad men; whence it happens that my ear has become very sensitive and my heart deaf. And then there's something hereditary in it. My father's blood and my uncle's are the same blood. The paternal molecule was hard and obtuse; and that cursed paternal molecule has assimilated all the rest.

*I*: Do you love your child?

*He*: Do I love him, the little rascal? I'm mad about him.

*I*: Won't you seriously endeavour to check the effect of that cursed molecule in him?

*He*: I think such an endeavour would be quite useless. If he is destined to be a good man, I shall not prevent him. But if the molecule has determined that he is to be a rogue like his father, the trouble I should have taken to make a decent man of him would do him a great deal of harm; his education continually thwarting the tendency of the molecule, he would be pulled by two contrary forces, and would walk all awry along the path of life, as I see an infinite number of men doing, equally at sea in right and wrong; they are what we call "creatures," which is the most to be dreaded of all epithets, since it indicates mediocrity, and the utmost degree of disdain. A great rogue is a great rogue, but is not a "creature." Before the paternal molecule had gained the upper hand again, and had brought him to the state of perfect baseness which I have reached, an infinite time would have passed; he would waste his best years. I'm doing nothing about it just now. I let him grow; I examine him. He is already greedy, artful, a thief, an idler, a liar. I'm very much afraid he's a chip off the old block.

*I*: And you'll make a musician of him, so that nothing shall be lacking in the resemblance?

*He*: A musician! a musician! sometimes I look at him, grinding my teeth, and say: "If you ever get to know a single note, I think I'll wring your neck."

*I*: And pray, why?

*He*: It leads to nothing.

*I*: It leads to everything.

*He*: Yes, when one excels at it; but who can promise himself that his child will excel? There are ten thousand chances to one that he'd never be more than a wretched string-scraper like myslef. Do you know that it might well be easier to find a child fit to govern a kingdom, to become a great king, than a great fiddler?

*I*: It seems to me that pleasing talents, even though second-rate, amid a people without morals and sunk in debauchery and luxury, carry a man quickly forward in the path of fortune. I myself have heard the following conversation between a sort of patron and a sort of protégé. The latter had been advised to apply to the former, as being an obliging man who might help him. "Monsieur, what do you know?"—"I know mathematics tolerably well."—"Well, then, teach mathematics; after you've covered yourself with mud on the pavements of Paris for ten or twelve years, you'll have three or four hundred *livres* a year."—"I've studied law, and I am well-versed in jurisprudence."—"If Puffendorf and Grotius came back into the world they would die of hunger, propped up against a milestone."—"I have a good knowledge of history and geography."—"If there were any parents who took their children's education seriously, your fortune would be made, but there aren't any."—"I'm a fairly good musician."—"Well! Why didn't you say that at first? And to show you what profit can be got from that talent, I have a daughter. Come every day, from half-past seven till nine in the evening; you shall give her lessons, and I will give you twenty-five *louis* a year. You shall breakfast, dine, lunch and sup with us. The rest of your day will be your own; you may dispose of it to your own advantage."

*He*: And what became of this man?

*I*: If he had been wise, he'd have made his fortune, which apparently is the only thing you have eyes for.

*He*: Undoubtedly. Gold, gold. Gold is everything, and all the rest, without gold, is nothing. And so, instead of stuffing his head with fine maxims, which he'd have to forget on pain of being nothing but a beggar, when I possess a sovereign, which doesn't happen often, I stand in front of him. I pull the sovereign from my pocket, I show it to him with admiration. I raise my eyes to heaven. I kiss the sovereign in front of him. And to make him understand still better the importance of the sacred coin, I speak to him in a lisping voice, I point out with my finger all that one can buy with it, a pretty frock, a pretty cap, a nice cake. Then I put the sovereign in my pocket. I walk about proudly; I lift up the flap of my waistcoat; I pat my pocket with my hand; and that's how I make him understand that the self-confidence he sees in me springs from the sovereign that's in there.

*I*: Nothing could be better. But if it should happen that, deeply impressed with the value of the sovereign, one day. . . .

*He*: I follow you. One must shut one's eyes to that possibility. There's no moral principle but has its disadvantage. At the worst, it means a bad quarter of an hour and then all's over.

*I*: Even from your point of view, so wise and courageous, I persist in believing that it would be a good thing to make a musician of him. I know no quicker method of getting into touch with those in power, of serving their vices and putting one's own to profit.

*He*: True; but I have schemes for a swifter and surer success. Ah! if only he were a girl! But just as one doesn't do what one pleases, so one has to accept what comes; to profit by it as much as possible; and to that end one should not be so foolish as to give a spartan education to a child destined to live in Paris, like so many fathers, who could do nothing worse if they planned disaster for their children. If my child's education is bad, that is the fault of my country's morals, and not mine. Let who can be responsible. I want my son to be happy; or, what comes to the same thing, to be honoured, rich and powerful. I have some knowledge of the easiest ways to attain this end; and I'll teach him these early. If you blame me, all you wise men, the crowd and my success will absolve me. He will have gold, you may take my word for it. If he has enough of it, he'll lack nothing, not even your esteem and your respect.

*I*: Maybe you're wrong.

*He*: Or else he'll do without them, like many others.

In all this, there were a great many of those things that people think, and according to which they act, but which they never say. To tell the truth, that was the most marked difference between this fellow and most of those around us. He admitted the vices that he had, and that others have; but he was no hypocrite. He was neither less nor more abominable than they; he was only franker and more consistent, and sometimes profound in his depravity. I shuddered to think what his child would become, under such a teacher. It is certain that, brought up according to ideas so strictly modelled on our morality, he was bound to go far, unless something checked his progress prematurely.

*He*: Oh, you needn't be afraid. The important and difficult point to which a good father must pay particular attention is, not so much to give his child vices that will make him rich, ridiculous ways that will win him the favour of great folks—every one does that, if not systematically like myself, at all events in practice and by precept—but to indicate to him just how far to go, the art of avoiding shame, dishonour and the penalty of the law; such discords in the social harmony need careful placing, preparing and resolving. There's nothing so dull as a series of perfect harmonies. Something is needed to add savour, to divide up the beam and scatter its rays.

*I*: Very good. By this comparison, you bring me back from morals to music, which I had left against my will; and I thank you for that, since, to be honest with you, I like you better as a musician than as a moralist.

*He*: And yet I'm quite an inferior musician, and quite a superior moralist.

*I*: I have my doubts about that; but even if it were so, I am a decent man, and my principles are not yours.

*He*: So much the worse for you. Ah! if only I had your talents!

*I*: Leave my talents out of it; and let's get back to yours.

*He*: If only I could express myself like you! But I talk a damned ludicrous jargon, belonging half to society and literary folk and half to the market-place.

*I*: I speak badly. I can only tell the truth; and that doesn't always succeed, as you know.

*He*: But it's not in order to tell the truth, it's in order to tell lies well that I covet your talents. If only I knew how to write, how to fling a book together, write a dedication, make a fool drunk with his own merit, wheedle my way into women's favour!

*I*: And you can do all that a thousand times better than I can. I should not be worthy even to take lessons from you.

*He*: So many great qualities wasted, and their value unsuspected by you!

*I*: I get back to the full such value as I set on them.

*He*: If that were so, you would not be wearing that rough coat, that waistcoat of coarse cloth, those woollen stockings, those thick shoes, that ancient wig.

*I*: Quite so. A man must be most unskilful, if he doesn't get rich though he goes to any length to become so. But, you see, there are people like myself who don't consider wealth as the most precious thing on earth; queer people.

*He*: Most queer. One can't be born with that turn of mind. One acquires it; for it's not found in nature.

*I*: Not in human nature?

*He*: Not in human nature. Everything that lives, without exception, seeks its own well-being at another's expense; and I'm certain that if I left my little rascal to grow up, without telling him about anything, he would want to be richly clad, a favourite among men, beloved by women, and to grasp to himself all the joys of life.

*I*: If the little savage were left to himself, if he preserved all his foolishness and combined the violent passions of a man of thirty with the lack of reason of a child in the cradle, he'd wring his father's neck and go to bed with his mother.

*He*: That proves the necessity of a good education, and who disputes that? And what is a good education, if not that which leads to every sort of pleasure, without danger and without difficulty?

*I*: I'm not far from agreeing with you; but let us avoid making ourselves plain.

*He*: Why?

*I*: Because I fear our agreement is only apparent, and that, if once we embarked on a discussion of the dangers and difficulties to be avoided, we should no longer understand one another.

*He*: And what does that matter?

*I*: Let's leave that alone, I tell you. I could not teach you what I know on that subject; and you will find it easier to teach me what you do know, and I do not, about music. Dear Rameau, let us talk about music, and you tell me how it happens that with such a gift for appreciating, remembering and reproducing the finest passages from great masters, with all the enthusiasm that they inspire in you and that you communicate to others, you have composed nothing worthwhile.

Instead of answering me, he began to shake his head, and pointing his finger to the sky, exclaimed: "What about the stars? When nature created Leo, Vinci, Pergolesi, Duni, she smiled. She assumed a solemn and imposing air when she created my dear uncle Rameau, who'll be known as the great Rameau for about ten years, and then will be heard of no more. When she threw together his nephew, she made a grimace, and then another, and then yet another." And as he said these words he was making all sorts of faces, expressive of contempt, disdain and irony; and he seemed to be kneading a lump of dough between his fingers and laughing at the absurd shapes he gave it. When he had done this, he threw the grotesque image away and said:

"That's how she made me and flung me beside other grotesques, some apopletic, with great wrinkled bellies, short necks, great eyes starting out from their heads; others with crooked necks; some dried-up, bright-eyed, hook-nosed; all began to burst with laughter when they saw me; and I put my hands on my ribs and burst with laughter on seeing them; for fools and lunatics are amused by one another; they seek out and attract each other. If, once I'd got there, I hadn't found ready to hand the proverb that says "a fool's money is a clever man's heritage," I'd have invented it. I felt that nature had put my birthright in the purse of those grotesque puppets and I thought up a thousand ways of regaining possession of it."

*I*: I know those ways; you've told me of them and I have much admired them. But amongst so many expedients, why did you not try that of a fine work of art?

*He*: That's what a man of the world said to the abbé LeBlanc. . . . The abbé said: "The Marquise de Pompadour takes me up in her hand, carries me to the threshold of the Academy, and there withdraws her hand, and I tumble down and break both my legs." The man of the world replied: "Well, abbé, you must get up again and burst open the door with your head." The abbé retorted: "That's what I tried to do; and do you know what I got from it? A bump on the forehead."

After this little tale, my friend began to walk about with his head bent, with a pensive and downcast air; he sighed, wept, lamented, raised his hands and his eyes, beat his head with his fist till he almost broke his brow or his fingers, and added: "And yet it seems to me there's something inside there; but I knock it and shake it in vain, nothing comes out." Then he began to shake his head and beat his brow harder than ever, and said: "Either there's no one in, or they won't answer." The next moment he assumed a haughty air, lifted his head, laid his right hand on his heart, and walked about saying:

"I can feel, yes, I can feel." He imitated a man growing angry, growing indignant, moved to tenderness, commanding, beseeching, and improvised speeches expressing wrath, commiseration, hatred and love; he sketched the character of these passions with surprising subtlety and truth. Then he added: "That's it, I think. Now it's coming; that's what comes of finding a midwife who knows how to stimulate and hasten the birthpangs, and to bring forth the child. When I'm alone, I take up my pen, I want to write, I bite my nails, I scratch my forehead. Nothing doing, the god is not at home. I had persuaded myself that I had genius; and at the finish of my line I read that I'm a fool, a fool, a fool. But how is one to feel, to be uplifted, to paint with power, when one frequents such people as those whom one has to see in order to live; with the kind of talk one makes and listens to going on all around, and such gossip as: 'To-day the boulevard was delightful. Have you heard the "little monkey"? She acts enchantingly. Monsieur So-and-So has the finest dapple-grey carriage-horses you can imagine. Beautiful Madame What-not is beginning to fade. At forty, fancy doing one's hair that way! Young Miss What's-her-name is covered with diamonds which cost her hardly. . . . You mean that cost her dear? . . . No, no. . . . Where did you see her? . . . At *L'Enfant d'Arlequin perdu et retrouvé*. The scene of despair is played as it never was before. The Punchinello at the *Foire* theatre has a voice, but no subtlety, no soul. Madame So-and-so has given birth to two children at once. Each father can have his own. . . .' And do you think that this, said again and again and listened to every day, can fire one and lead one to great things?"

*I*: No. It would be better to shut oneself up in one's attic, drink water, eat dry bread, and search one's own soul.

*He*: Possibly; but I haven't the courage for that; and then, why sacrifice one's happiness to an uncertain success? And think of the name I bear! Rameau! It's embarrassing to be called Rameau. Talent is not like nobility, which is transmitted and which grows more illustrious as it passes from grandfather to father, from father to son, from son to grandson, without any merit being required on the descendant's part! The old stock branches out into an enormous collection of fools; but what matter? It's not the same with talent. To win merely the same fame as one's father, one must be cleverer than he. One must inherit something of his fibre. That fibre was lacking in me; but my wrist has got supple, the bow is plied and the pot boils. There's soup, if there's no glory.

*I*: In your place, I wouldn't take it for granted; I should try.

*He*: And do you think I haven't tried? I wasn't fifteen when I said to myself for the first time: "What's the matter with you, Rameau? You're dreaming. And what are you dreaming about? That you'd like to have done, or to do, something that excites the admiration of the universe. Well! it's as easy as winking! Just whistle and snap your fingers and they'll come to you!" At a later age I repeated what I'd said as a child. To-day I still repeat it; and yet I remain beside the statue of Memnon.

*I*: What do you mean by the statue of Memnon?

*He*: Surely that's quite plain. Around the statue of Memnon there were an infinite number of others, on which the sun's rays fell equally; but his was the only one that uttered sounds. There's one poet, Voltaire, and who else? Voltaire; and the third, Voltaire; and the fourth, Voltaire. There's one musician, Rinaldo da Capua; there's Hasse; there's Pergolesi; there's Alberti; there's Tartini; there's Locatelli; there's Terradeglias; there's my uncle; there's that little Duni who has neither looks nor presence, but who has feeling, good God, who has the gift of song and of expression. The rest, beside these few Memnons, are like so many pairs of ears stuck on the end of a stick. And so we're beggars, too wretched for any words. Ah, master philosopher, poverty's a terrible thing. I see it crouching down with its mouth agape to catch a few drops of the icy water that escapes from the barrel of the Danaïdes. I don't know if it quickens the wit of the philosopher; but it chills the poet's head confoundedly. You can't sing well underneath that barrel. Even so, he's a lucky man who can get there at all; I've been there, and I wasn't able to stay there. I'd been guilty of that folly once before. I've travelled in Bohemia, in Germany, in Switzerland, in Holland, a devil of a long way.

*I*: Underneath the leaking barrel?

*He*: Underneath the leaking barrel; there was a wealthy and extravagant Jew who loved music and my crazy ways. I made music to have pleased the gods. I played the fool; I lacked nothing. My Jew was a man who knew his law, and who observed it with the utmost rigidity, sometimes amongst friends, always amongst strangers. He got himself into a tiresome scrape that I must tell you about, for it's amusing. There was at Utrecht a charming courtesan. He desired this Christian; he dispatched a secret agent to her, with a bill of exchange for a considerable sum. The queer creature refused his offer. The Jew was in despair about it. The agent said to him: "Why distress yourself thus? You want to go to bed with a pretty woman? Nothing is easier, and even to go to bed with one who's prettier than the one you're after—with my wife, whom I'll let you have at the same price." No sooner said than done. The agent keeps the bill of exchange and the Jew goes to bed with the agent's wife. The bill falls due. The Jew lets it be claimed and disputes its validity. There is a lawsuit. The Jew said to himself: "This man will never dare say on what conditions he has my bill, and I shan't pay it." In court he cross-questions the agent. "From whom did you get this bill?"—"From yourself."—"Was it for money lent?"—"No."—"For merchandise provided?"—"No."—"For services rendered?"—"No, but that's nothing to do with the matter. I have got it. You signed it, and you shall pay it."—"I did not sign it."—"Am I a forger then?"—"You, or some other whose agent you are."—"I am base, but you are a knave. I tell you you'd better not drive me too far. I shall tell everything. I shall dishonour myself, but I shall ruin you." The Jew made light of the threat; and the agent revealed the whole affair at the next session. Both of them were found guilty; and the Jew was condemned to pay the bill of exchange, the value of which was spent on the relief of the poor. Then I parted company with him. I came back here. What was I to do? for I must either die of poverty or do something. All sorts of schemes then passed through my head. One day I was on the point of going off to join some provincial company of actors, where I'd be equally good or bad on the stage or in the orchestra; next day, I contemplated getting one of those pictures painted that they fix on the end of a pole and stick up at a street crossing, and standing there shouting at the top of my voice: "This is the town where he was born: here he is taking leave of his father the apothecary; here he is arriving at the capital, seeking his uncle's house; here he is at the feet of his uncle, who drives him away: here he is with a Jew, etc.,

etc." Next day, I was fully determined to throw in my lot with street-singers; that might not have been a bad thing to do; we'd have given a concert under my dear uncle's windows, and he'd have died of rage. I took another course.

Here he stopped, and assumed, first, the attitude of a man holding a violin, tuning the strings with a twist of his arm, and next, that of a poor wretch worn out with fatigue, whose strength fails him, whose legs are shaking, who'll die unless someone gives him a bit of bread; he indicated his dire need by pointing his finger at his half-opened mouth; then he added: "You understand. They'd throw me a morsel. We'd fight for it, three or four of us, starving creatures. And now, think your great thoughts, create your beautiful works in the midst of such distress!"

*I*: It would be difficult.

*He*: Tossed hither and thither, I'd landed yonder at last. I was in clover there. I'm out of it. Now I shall have to saw cat-gut once more, and start pointing my finger at my gaping mouth again, There's nothing stable in this world. To-day we're on the top, to-morrow at the bottom of the wheel. We're led by cursed circumstance, and led very badly.

Then, drinking a draught that was left at the bottom of the bottle, and addressing his neighbour: "For pity's sake, Sir, a small pinch. That's a fine snuffbox you have. You don't happen to be a musician? . . .—No. . . .—All the better for you; for they're a most unfortunate set of wretches. Fate decreed that I should be one; whereas perhaps, at Montmartre, there is in a mill, a miller or a miller's boy who'll never hear any other sound than that of his clapper, and who might have invented the finest songs. To the mill, Rameau! to the mill, that's where you belong."

*I*: Whatever man undertakes, he was destined to it by nature.

*He*: She makes some strange blunders. For my part I don't see things from that height at which the man who prunes a tree with shears is indistinguishable from the caterpillar that nibbles its leaves, and whence you only see two different animals each fulfilling its duty. Take up your perch on the epicycle of Mercury; and from there, if you like, imitate Réaumur, and as he divides the genus of flies into those that sow, those that roam, and those that scythe, you may divide the human species into joiners, carpenters, couriers, dancers and singers. That's your own business. I won't meddle with it. I'm in this world, and I mean to stop here. But if it's natural to have an appetite—for I always find myself coming back to appetite, to the sensation that's ever-present with me—I think things are ordered very badly if one sometimes has nothing to eat. What a devil of a system! Some men enjoying a super-abundance of everything, while others have a stomach as insistent as theirs, a hunger that renews itself like theirs, and nothing to get their teeth into. Worst of all is the constrained attitude that want imposes on us. The needy man doesn't walk straight like his fellows; he jumps, he crawls, wriggles, creeps along; he spends his life taking and holding poses.

*I*: What are poses?

*He*: Go and ask Noverre. The world provides far more than his art can imitate.

*I*: And so you, also, to use your own expression or Montaigne's, have taken up your 'perch on the epicycle of Mercury,' and contemplate the varied pantomime of the human race?

*He*: No, no, I tell you. I'm too heavy to rise so high. I leave to the cranes their home in the clouds. I stick to the earth. I look around me; and I take up my poses, or I amuse myself watching the poses others take up. I'm an excellent mime, as you shall judge.

Then he began to smile, and to imitate the sycophant, the suppliant, the time-server; with his right foot forward, his left drawn back, his back bent, his head raised, his eyes apparently fixed on other eyes, his mouth a little open, his arms stretched out towards some object; he awaits an order, he receives it; he is off like a dart, he comes back, he has done his errand and gives his account of it. He attends to everything; he picks up things that fall; he puts a cushion or a footstool under someone's feet; he holds a saucer; he draws up a chair; he opens a door; he shuts a window, draws curtains; he watches the master and mistress; he stands motionless, arms dangling, legs together; he listens; he seeks to read faces; and then adds: "That's my pantomime, and it's about the same as and that of all flatterers, courtiers, lackeys and beggars."

This man's crazy tricks, the tales of the abbé Galiani and the extravagant fantasies of Rabelais have sometimes set me musing deeply. These three storehouses have furnished me with ludicrous masks which I put on the faces of the grave personages; and I see a prelate as Pantaloon, a president as a satyr, a monk as a hog, a minister as an ostrich and his chief secretary as a goose.

*I*: But, according to you (I said to him), there are many beggars in this world; and I know no one who is not acquainted with some steps of your dance.

*He*: You are right. There is in the whole kingdom only one man who walks straight, that's the Sovereign. All the others take up poses.

*I*: The Sovereign? You can't be too sure about that; don't you think he sometimes has by his side some little foot, some little cluster of curls, some little nose that compels him to do a bit of play-acting? Whoever needs somebody else, is poor and takes up a pose. The king takes a pose before his mistress, and before God; he performs his pantomime steps. The minister performs as courtier, flatterer, lackey or beggar before his king. The crowd of climbers assume your poses as they perform before the minister, in a hundred ways, each one viler than the other; so does the abbé in his bands and long gown, once a week at least, before the official who controls the list of livings. I tell you, what you call the beggars' pantomime is the way the whole world goes. Every one has his little Hus and his Bertin.

*He*: That comforts me.

But while I was speaking, he was mimicking the poses of the people I mentioned, in the most comical fashion; for instance, for the little abbé, he held his hat under his arm, and his breviary in the left hand; with the right, he lifted up the tail of his coat; he walked with his head slightly bent over one shoulder, his eyes downcast, playing the hypocrite so perfectly that I seemed to see the author of the *Réfutations* before the Bishop of Orléans. When I spoke of flatterers and climbers he fell prostrate; behold Bouret at the Comptroller-general's!

*I*: That's a fine performance (I said), but yet there is one being who has no need to play your pantomime. That is the philosopher, who has nothing and who asks for nothing.

*He*: And where is such a creature to be found? If he has nothing, he must suffer; if he begs for nothing, he'll get nothing, and he'll go on suffering.

*I*: No. Diogenes laughed at wants.

*He*: But he had to be clothed.

*I*: No; he went naked.

*He*: Sometimes it was cold in Athens.

*I*: Less so than here.

*He*: But people ate there.

*I*: Of course.

*He*: At whose expense?

*I*: At nature's. Who provides for the savage? Why, the earth, the animals, fishes, trees, herbs, roots and streams.

*He*: That's a poor dinner-table.

*I*: It's a large one.

*He*: It is badly served.

*I*: Yet we despoil it to supply our own tables.

*He*: But you'll admit that the industry of our cooks, pastry-cooks, chefs, restaurant-keepers and confectioners contributes something! On so austere a diet, your Diogenes cannot have had very rebellious organs.

*I*: You're wrong there. In those days the Cynic's robe was the same as our monk's gown, and its virtue was much the same. The Cynics were the Carmelites and Franciscans of Athens.

*He*: I've got you there. Diogenes must therefore have played the pantomime too; if not before Pericles, at least before Laïs and Phryne.

*I*: You're wrong again. Though others paid a high price for the courtesan she'd give herself to him for pleasure.

*He*: But if it happened that the courtesan was busy and the Cynic in a hurry. . . .

*I*: He went back to his tub and did without her.

*He*: And you'd advise me to imitate him?

*I*: On my life, it would be better than to cringe, to degrade and prostitute oneself.

*He*: But I need a good bed, good food, warm clothes in winter, cool clothes in summer; rest and money and many other things; and I'd rather owe them to someone's kindness than acquire them by hard work.

*I*: That's because you are an idler, a glutton, a base and grovelling soul.

*He*: I think I told you as much.

*I*: The good things in life have their price, no doubt; but you don't know the price of what you are sacrificing in order to obtain them. You play your base pantomime, as you always have done and as you always will do.

*He*: It's true. But that has cost me little, and now costs me nothing. And that's why I'd be wrong to assume a different demeanour, which would be uncomfortable for me and which I should not keep up. But I see from what you tell me that my poor little wife was a sort of philosopher. She was as brave as a lion. Sometimes we went without bread and hadn't a penny. We'd sold almost all our clothes. I would fling myself across the foot of the bed and there rack my brains trying to find someone who'd lend me a crown, which I should not pay back; while she, merry as a grig, would sit down to her harpsichord, and sing to her own accompaniment. She had a voice like a nightingale; I'm sorry you never heard her. When I was to perform at any concert I'd take her along with me. On the way I'd say: "Come on, madame, make them admire you; display your talent and your charms; carry them away, bowl them over." We'd arrive; she'd sing, she'd carry them all away, bowl them over. Alas, I've lost her, poor darling! Besides her talent, she had a mouth so small you could hardly put your little finger in it; teeth like a row of pearls; such eyes, such feet; such a skin, such cheeks, such breasts, such slim legs like a gazelle, and thighs and buttocks fit for a sculptor's model. Sooner or later she'd have the Farmer-General at least. What a walk, what buttocks, oh, my goodness, what buttocks!

Then he began to imitate his wife's walk; he tripped along, carrying his head high, flirting with a fan, waggling his backside; it was the funniest and most absurd caricature of our little coquettes.

Then resuming the thread of his discourse, he added: "I took her walking everywhere, in the Tuileries, in the Palais-Royal. I could never have kept her. When she crossed the street of a morning, bareheaded, in her short jacket, you'd have stopped to watch her, and you might have encircled her with four fingers without squeezing her. Those who followed her, who watched her tripping along on her little feet, and studied that plump bottom outlined under her light petticoats, quickened their steps; she'd let them catch her up; then she'd swiftly turn on them those two great brilliant black eyes of hers; that made them stop short. The front of the medal was as good as the back. But alas, I've lost her, and all my hopes of fortune have vanished with her. I'd taken her with that sole end in view, I'd confided all my schemes to her; and she had too much shrewdness not to see their certainty of success, and too much wisdom not to approve of them."

And then he began to sob and weep, saying:

"No, no, I shall never get over her loss. Since then I've taken to a priest's skull-cap and bands."

*I*: Out of grief?

*He*: If you like. But really to carry my bowl about on my head. . . . But do look what time it is, for I must go to the opera.

*I*: What's being played?

*He*: Something of Dauvergne's. There are quite good things in his music; it's a pity he wasn't the first to say them. Among the dead, there are always some who distress the living. It can't be helped. *Quisque suos* [*non*] *patimur manes*.* But it's half-past five. I hear the bell ringing vespers for the abbé of Canaye and for myself. Good-bye, master philosopher. Isn't it true that I am always the same?

*I*: Alas, yes, unfortunately.

*He*: May that misfortune last another forty years. He laughs best who laughs last.

(1762–1773)

* "Each of us suffers his appropriate punishment in the next world."

# APHORISMS

## IV

Samuel Butler:

All progress is based upon a universal innate desire on the part of every organism to live beyond its income.

From a worldly point of view there is no mistake so great as that of being always right.

An apology for the Devil: It must be remembered that we have only heard one side of the case. God has written all the books.

Oscar Wilde:

Experience is the name every one gives to his mistakes.

The Peerage . . . is the best thing in fiction that the English have ever done.

She tried to found a salon, but only succeeded in opening a restaurant.

The greatest tyranny in the world is the tyranny of the weak over the strong.

If others had not been foolish, we should be.

Blake

The more things a man is ashamed of, the more respectable he is.

G. B. Shaw

Every hero becomes a bore at last.

Emerson

Those who cannot remember the past are condemned to repeat it.

Santayana

It is not to be imagined by how many different ways vanity defeats its own purposes.

CHESTERFIELD

Most people enjoy the inferiority of their best friends.

CHESTERFIELD

Men who do not make advances to women are apt to become victims to women who make advances to them.

BAGEROT

One's eyes are what one is; one's mouth what one becomes.

GALSWORTHY

## BYRON

# *Don Juan,* Canto I

I

I WANT a hero: an uncommon want,
  When every year and month sends forth a new one,
Till, after cloying the gazettes with cant,
  The age discovers he is not the true one:
Of such as these I should not care to vaunt,
  I'll therefore take our ancient friend Don Juan–
We all have seen him, in the pantomime,
Sent to the devil somewhat ere his time.

II

Vernon, the butcher Cumberland, Wolfe, Hawke,
  Prince Ferdinand, Granby, Burgoyne, Keppel, Howe,
Evil and good, have had their tithe of talk,
  And fill'd their sign-posts then, like Wellesley now;
Each in their turn like Banquo's monarchs stalk,
  Followers of fame, 'nine farrow' of that sow:
France, too, had Buonaparté and Dumourier
Recorded in the Moniteur and Courier.

III

Barnave, Brissot, Condorcet, Mirabeau,
  Petion, Clootz, Danton, Marat, La Fayette,
Were French, and famous people, as we know;
  And there were others, scarce forgotten yet,
Joubert, Hoche, Marceau, Lannes, Dessaix, Moreau,
  With many of the military set,
Exceedingly remarkable at times,
But not at all adapted to my rhymes.

IV

Nelson was once Britannia's god of war,
  And still should be so, but the tide is turn'd:
There's no more to be said of Trafalgar,
  'Tis with our hero quietly inurn'd;

Because the army's grown more popular,
  At which the naval people are concern'd:
Besides, the prince is all for the land service,
Forgetting Duncan, Nelson, Howe, and Jervis.

V

Brave men were living before Agamemnon,*
  And since, exceeding valorous and sage,
A good deal like him too, though quite the same none;
  But then they shone not on the poet's page,
And so have been forgotten;—I condemn none,
  But can't find any in the present age
Fit for my poem (that is, for my new one);
So, as I said, I'll take my friend Don Juan.

VI

Most epic poems plunge *in medias res*
  (Horace makes this the heroic turnpike road),
And then your hero tells, whene'er you please,
  What went before—by way of episode,
While seated after dinner at his ease,
  Beside his mistress in some soft abode,
Palace, or garden, paradise, or cavern,
Which serves the happy couple for a tavern.

VII

That is the usual method, but not mine—
  My way is to begin with the beginning;
The regularity of my design
  Forbids all wandering as the worst of sinning,
And therefore I shall open with a line
  (Although it cost me half an hour in spinning)
Narrating somewhat of Don Juan's father,
And also of his mother, if you'd rather.

VIII

In Seville was he born, a pleasant city,
  Famous for oranges and women: he
Who has not seen it will be much to pity,
  So says the proverb †—and I quite agree;
Of all the Spanish towns is none more pretty,
  Cadiz, perhaps—but that you soon may see—

* "Vixere fortes ante Agamemnona," &c.—HORACE.
† [Quien no ha visto Sevilla no ha visto maravilla.]

Don Juan's parents lived beside the river,
A noble stream, and call'd the Guadalquivir.

IX

His father's name was Jóse—*Don,* of course,
  A true Hidalgo, free from every stain
Of Moor or Hebrew blood, he traced his source
  Through the most Gothic gentlemen of Spain;
A better cavalier ne'er mounted horse,
  Or, being mounted, e'er got down again,
Than Jóse, who begot our hero, who
Begot—but that's to come—Well, to renew

X

His mother was a learned lady, famed
  For every branch of every science known—
In every Christian language ever named,
  With virtues equall'd by her wit alone.
She made the cleverest people quite ashamed;
  And even the good with inward envy groan,
Finding themselves so very much exceeded
In their own way, by all the things that she did.

XI

Her memory was a mine; she knew by heart
  All Calderon and greater part of Lopé,
So that if any actor miss'd his part,
  She could have served him for the prompter's copy;
For her Feinagle's were an useless art,*
  And he himself obliged to shut up shop—he
Could never make a memory so fine as
That which adorned the brain of Donna Inez.

XII

Her favourite science was the mathematical,
  Her noblest virtue was her magnanimity;
Her wit (she sometimes tried at wit) was Attic all,
  Her serious sayings darken'd to sublimity;
In short, in all things she was fairly what I call
  A prodigy: her morning dress was dimity,
Her evening silk, or, in the summer, muslin,
And other stuffs, with which I won't stay puzzling.

* Professor Feinagle in 1812 gave lectures at the Royal Institution on Mnemonics.

XIII

She knew the Latin—that is, 'the Lord's prayer,'
  And Greek—the alphabet—I'm nearly sure;
She read some French romances here and there,
  Although her mode of speaking was not pure;
For native Spanish she had no great care,
  At least her conversation was obscure;
Her thoughts were theorems, her words a problem,
As if she deem'd that mystery would ennoble 'em.

XIV

She liked the English and the Hebrew tongue,
  And said there was analogy between 'em;
She proved it somehow out of sacred song,
  But I must leave the proofs to those who've seen 'em,
But this I heard her say, and can't be wrong,
  And all may think which way their judgments lean 'em,
'Tis strange—the Hebrew noun which means 'I am,'
The English always use to govern d—n.'

XV

Some women use their tongues—she *look'd* a lecture,
  Each eye a sermon, and her brow a homily,
An all-in-all sufficient self-director,
  Like the lamented late Sir Samuel Romilly,
The Law's expounder, and the State's corrector,
  Whose suicide was almost an anomaly—
One sad example more, that 'All is vanity'
(The jury brought their verdict in 'Insanity').

XVI

In short, she was a walking calculation,
  Miss Edgeworth's novels stepping from their covers,
Or Mrs Trimmer's books on education,
  Or 'Cœlebs' Wife' set out in quest of lovers;
Morality's prim personification,
  In which not Envy's self a flaw discovers;
To others' share let 'female errors fall,'
For she had not even one—the worst of all.

XVII

Oh! she was perfect, past all parallel—
  Of any modern female saint's comparison;

So far above the cunning powers of hell,
  Her guardian angel had given up his garrison:
Even her minutest motions went as well
  As those of the best time-piece made by Harrison.
In virtues nothing earthly could surpass her,
Save thine 'incomparable oil,' Macassar! *

XVIII

Perfect she was; but as perfection is
  Insipid in this naughty world of ours,
Where our first parents never learn'd to kiss
  Till they were exiled from their earlier bowers,
Where all was peace, and innocence, and bliss,
  (I wonder how they got through the twelve hours),
Don Jóse, like a lineal son of Eve,
Went plucking various fruit without her leave.

XIX

He was a mortal of the careless kind,
  With no great love for learning or the learn'd,
Who chose to go where'er he had a mind,
  And never dream'd his lady was concern'd;
The world, as usual, wickedly inclined
  To see a kingdom or a house o'erturn'd,
Whisper'd he had a mistress, some said *two,*
But for domestic quarrels *one* will do.

XX

Now Donna Inez had, with all her merit,
  A great opinion of her own good qualities;
Neglect, indeed, requires a saint to bear it,
  And such, indeed, she was in her moralities:
But then she had a devil of a spirit,
  And sometimes mix'd up fancies with realities,
And let few opportunities escape
Of getting her liege lord into a scrape.

XXI

This was an easy matter with a man
  Oft in the wrong, and never on his guard,

* 'Description des *vertus incomparables* de l nuile Macassar.'—See the Advertisement.

And even the wisest, do the best they can,
  Have moments, hours, and days, so unprepared,
That you might 'brain them with their lady's fan;'
  And sometimes ladies hit exceeding hard,
And fans turn into falchions in fair hands,
And why and wherefore no one understands.

XXII

'Tis pity learned virgins ever wed
  With persons of no sort of education,
Or gentlemen who, though well-born and bred,
  Grow tired of scientific conversation:
I don't choose to say much upon this head,
  I'm a plain man, and in a single station;
But–Oh! ye lords of ladies intellectual,
Inform us truly, have they not henpeck'd you all?

XXIII

Don Jóse and his lady quarrell'd–*why*,
  Not any of the many could divine,
Though several thousand people chose to try;
  'Twas surely no concern of theirs nor mine;
I loathe that low vice–curiosity;
  But if there's anything in which I shine,
'Tis in arranging all my friends' affairs,
Not having, of my own, domestic cares.

XXIV

And so I interfered, and with the best
  Intentions; but their treatment was not kind;
I think the foolish people were possess'd,
  For neither of them could I ever find,
Although their porter afterwards confess'd–
  But that's no matter, and the worst's behind,
For little Juan o'er me threw, down stairs,
A pail of housemaid's water unawares.

XXV

A little curly-headed, good-for-nothing,
  And mischief-making monkey from his birth;
His parents ne'er agreed except in doting
  Upon the most unquiet imp on earth:

Instead of quarrelling, had they been both in
  Their senses, they'd have sent young master forth
To school, or had him soundly whipp'd at home,
To teach him manners for the time to come.

XXVI

Don Jóse and the Donna Inez led
  For some time an unhappy sort of life,
Wishing each other, not divorced, but dead.
  They lived respectably as man and wife;
Their conduct was exceedingly well-bred,
  And gave no outward signs of inward strife,
Until at length the smother'd fire broke out,
And put the business past all kind of doubt.

XXVII

For Inez call'd some druggists and physicians,
  And tried to prove her loving lord was *mad;*
But as he had some lucid intermissions,
  She next decided he was only *bad;*
Yet when they ask'd her for her depositions,
  No sort of explanation could be had,
Save that her duty both to man and God
Required this conduct—which seem'd very odd.

XXVIII

She kept a journal, where his faults were noted,
  And open'd certain trunks of books and letters,
All which might, if occasion served, be quoted;
  And then she had all Seville for abettors,
Besides her good old grandmother (who doted):
  The hearers of her case became repeaters,
Then advocates, inquisitors, and judges,
Some for amusement, others for old grudges.

XXIX

And then this best and meekest woman bore
  With such serenity her husband's woes,
Just as the Spartan ladies did of yore,
  Who saw their spouses kill'd and nobly chose
Never to say a word about them more—
  Calmly she heard each calumny that rose,

And saw *his* agonies with such sublimity,
That all the world exclaim'd, 'What magnanimity!'

XXX

No doubt this patience, when the world is damning us,
Is philosophic in our former friends;
'Tis also pleasant to be deem'd magnanimous.
The more so in obtaining our own ends;
And what the lawyers call a '*malus animus*,'
Conduct like this by no means comprehends:
Revenge in person's certainly no virtue,
But then 'tis not *my* fault if *others* hurt you.

XXXI

And if our quarrels should rip up old stories
And help them with a lie or two additional,
*I'm* not to blame, as you well know—no more is
Any one else—they were become traditional:
Besides, their resurrection aids our glories
By contrast, which is what we just were wishing all:
And science profits by this resurrection—
Dead scandals form good subjects for dissection.

XXXII

Their friends had tried at reconciliation,
Then their relations, who made matters worse,
('Twere hard to tell upon a like occasion
To whom it may be best to have recourse—
I can't say much for friend or yet relation):
The lawyers did their utmost for divorce,
But scarce a fee was paid on either side,
Before, unluckily, Don Jóse died.

XXXIII

He died: and most unluckily, because
According to all hints I could collect
From counsel learned in those kinds of laws
(Although their talk's obscure and circumspect),
His death contrived to spoil a charming cause:
A thousand pities also with respect
To public feeling, which on this occasion
Was manifested in a great sensation.

XXXIV

But ah! he died; and buried with him lay
  The public feeling and the lawyers' fees:
His house was sold, his servants sent away,
  A Jew took one of his two mistresses,
A priest the other—at least so they say:
  I ask'd the doctors after his decease—
He died of the slow fever call'd the tertian,
And left his widow to her own aversion.

XXXV

Yet Jóse was an honourable man;
  That I must say, who knew him very well:
Therefore his frailties I'll no further scan.
  Indeed, there were not many more to tell;
And if his passions now and then outran
  Discretion, and were not so peaceable
As Numa's (who was also named Pompilius),*
He had been ill brought up, and was born bilious.

XXXVI

Whate'er might be his worthlessness or worth,
  Poor fellow! he had many things to wound him,
Let's own—since it can do no good on earth—
  It was a trying moment that which found him
Standing alone beside his desolate hearth,
  Where all his household gods lay shiver'd round him:
No choice was left his feelings or his pride,
Save death, or Doctors' Commons—so he died.

XXXVII

Dying intestate, Juan was sole heir
  To a Chancery suit, and messuages, and lands,
Which, with a long minority and care,
  Promised to turn out well in proper hands:
Inez became sole guardian, which was fair,
  And answer'd but to nature's just demands;
An only son left with an only mother,
Is brought up much more wisely than another.

* —'primus qui legibus urbem
Fundabit, Curibus parvis et paupere terrâ
Missus in imperium magnum.'—VIRG.

XXXVIII

Sagest of women, even of widows, she
  Resolved that Juan should be quite a paragon,
And worthy of the noblest pedigree
  (His sire was of Castile, his dam from Arragon):
Then for accomplishments of chivalry,
  In case our lord the king should go to war again,
He learn'd the arts of riding, fencing, gunnery,
And how to scale a fortress—or a nunnery.

XXXIX

But that which Donna Inez most desired,
  And saw into herself, each day, before all
The learned tutors whom for him she hired,
  Was, that his breeding should be strictly moral.
Much into all his studies she inquired,
  And so they were submitted first to her, all,
Arts, sciences, no branch was made a mystery
To Juan's eyes, excepting natural history.

XL

The languages, especially the dead;
  The sciences, and most of all the abstruse;
The arts, at least all such as could be said
  To be the most remote from common use;
In all these he was much and deeply read;
  But not a page of anything that's loose,
Or hints continuation of the species,
Was ever suffer'd, lest he should grow vicious.

XLI

His classic studies made a little puzzle,
  Because of filthy loves of gods and goddesses,
Who in the earlier ages raised a bustle,
  But never put on pantaloons or boddices.
His reverend tutors had at times a tussle,
  And for their Æneids, Iliads, and Odysseys,
Were forced to make an odd sort of apology,
For Donna Inez dreaded the mythology.

XLII

Ovid's a rake, as half his verses show him,
  Anacreon's morals are a still worse sample,

Catullus scarcely had a decent poem,
  I don't think Sappho's Ode a good example,
Although Longinus * tells us there is no hymn
  Where the sublime soars forth on wings more ample;
But Virgil's songs are pure, except that horrid one
Beginning with '*Formosum Pastor Corydon.*'

XLIII

Lucretius' irreligion is too strong
  For early stomachs to prove wholesome food;
I can't help thinking Juvenal was wrong,
  Although no doubt his real intent was good,
For speaking out so plainly in his song,
  So much, indeed, as to be downright rude;
And then what proper person can be partial
To all those nauseous epigrams of Martial?

XLIV

Juan was taught from out the best edition,
  Expurgated by learned men, who place,
Judiciously, from out the schoolboy's vision,
  The grosser parts; but fearful to deface
Too much their modest bard by this omission,
  And pitying sore his mutilated case,
They only add them all in an appendix,†
Which saves in fact the trouble of an index:

XLV

For there we have them all 'at one fell swoop,
  Instead of being scatter'd through the pages;
They stand forth marshall'd in a handsome troop,
  To meet the ingenuous youth of future ages,
Till some less rigid editor shall stoop
  To call them back into their separate cages,
Instead of standing staring all together,
Like garden-gods—and not so decent either.

XLVI

The Missal, too (it was the family Missal),
  Was ornamented in a sort of way

* See Longinus, Section 10, 'ἵνα μὴ ἓν τι περὶ αὐτην πάθος φαίνηται, παθων δὲ σύνοδος'.

† Fact. There is, or was, such an edition, with all the obnoxious epigrams of Martial placed by themselves at the end.

Which ancient mass-books often are, and this all
  Kinds of grotesques illumined; and how they,
Who saw those figures on the margin kiss all,
  Could turn their optics to the text and pray,
Is more than I know—but Don Juan's mother
Kept this herself, and gave her son another.

XLVII

Sermons he read, and lectures he endured,
  And homilies, and lives of all the saints;
To Jerome and to Chrysostom inured,
  He did not take such studies for restraints:
But how faith is acquired, and then ensured,
  So well not one of the aforesaid paints
As Saint Augustine in his fine confessions,
Which make the reader envy his transgressions.*

XLVIII

This, too, was a seal'd book to little Juan—
  I can't but say that his mamma was right,
If such an education was the true one.
  She scarcely trusted him from out her sight;
Her maids were old; and if she took a new one,
  You might be sure she was a perfect fright.
She did this during even her husband's life—
I recommend as much to every wife.

XLIX

Young Juan wax'd in goodliness and grace;
  At six a charming child, and at eleven
With all the promise of as fine a face
  As e'er to man's maturer growth was given.
He studied steadily, and grew apace,
  And seem'd at last in the right road to heaven,
For half his days were pass'd at church, the other
Between his tutors, confessor, and mother.

* See his Confessions, l, i, c. ix. By the representation which Saint Augustine gives of himself in his youth, it is easy to see that he was what we should call a rake. He avoided the school as the plague; he loved nothing but gaming and public shows; he robbed his father of everything he could find; he invented a thousand lies to escape the rod, which they were obliged to make use of to punish his irregularities.

L

At six, I said, he was a charming child,
  At twelve he was a fine but quiet boy;
Although in infancy a little wild,
  They tamed him down amongst them; to destroy
His natural spirit not in vain they toil'd.
  At least it seem'd so; and his mother's joy
Was to declare how sage, and still, and steady,
Her young philosopher was grown already.

LI

I had my doubts, perhaps I have them still,
  But what I say is neither here nor there;
I knew his father well, and have some skill
  In character—but it would not be fair
From sire to son to augur good or ill:
  He and his wife were an ill-sorted pair—
But Scandal's my aversion—I protest
Against all evil-speaking, even in jest.

LII

For my part I say nothing—nothing—but
  *This* I will say—my reasons are my own—
That if I had an only son to put
  To school (as God be praised that I have none),
'Tis not with Donna Inez I would shut
  Him up to learn his catechism alone:
No—no—I'd send him out betimes to college
For there it was I pick'd up my own knowledge.

LIII

For there one learns—'tis not for me to boast,
  Though I acquired—but I pass over *that*,
As well as all the Greek I since have lost:
  I say that there's the place—but '*Verbum sat.*'
I think I pick'd up too, as well as most,
  Knowledge of matters—but no matter *what*:
I never married—but I think, I know
That sons should not be educated so.

LIV

Young Juan now was sixteen years of age,
  Tall, handsome, slender, but well knit: he seem'd

Active, though not so sprightly, as a page;
And everybody but his mother deem'd
Him almost man; but she flew in a rage
And bit her lips (for else she might have scream'd)
If any said so, for to be precocious
Was in her eyes a thing the most atrocious.

LV

Amongst her numerous acquaintance, all
Selected for discretion and devotion,
There was the Donna Julia, whom to call
Pretty were but to give a feeble notion
Of many charms in her as natural
As sweetness to the flower, or salt to ocean,
Her zone to Venus, or his bow to Cupid
(But this last simile is trite and stupid).

LVI

The darkness of her Oriental eye
Accorded with her Moorish origin;
(Her blood was not all Spanish, by the by.
In Spain, you know, this is a sort of sin).
When proud Granada fell, and, forced to fly,
Boabdil wept, of Donna Julia's kin
Some went to Africa, some stay'd in Spain,
Her great-great-grandmamma chose to remain.

LVII

She married (I forget the pedigree)
With an Hidalgo, who transmitted down
His blood less noble than such blood should be;
At such alliances his sires would frown,
In that point so precise in each degree
That they bred *in and in*, as might be shown,
Marrying their cousins—nay, their aunts and nieces,
Which always spoils the breed, if it increases.

LVIII

This heathenish cross restored the breed again,
Ruin'd its blood, but much improved its flesh;
For from a root the ugliest in Old Spain
Sprung up a branch as beautiful as fresh:

The sons no more were short, the daughters plain.
  But there's a rumour which I fain would hush,
'Tis said that Donna Julia's grandmamma
Produced her Don more heirs at love than law.

LIX

However this might be, the race went on
  Improving still through every generation,
Until it centered in an only son,
  Who left an only daughter: my narration
May have suggested that this single one
  Could be but Julia (whom on this occasion
I shall have much to speak about), and she
Was married, charming, chaste, and twenty-three.

LX

Her eye (I'm very fond of handsome eyes)
  Was large and dark, suppressing half its fire
Until she spoke, then through its soft disguise
  Flash'd an expression more of pride than ire,
And love than either; and there would arise,
  A something in them which was not desire,
But would have been, perhaps, but for the soul
Which struggled through and chasten'd down the whole.

LXI

Her glossy hair was cluster'd o'er a brow
  Bright with intelligence, and fair and smooth;
Her eyebrow's shape was like the aërial bow,
  Her cheek all purple with the beam of youth,
Mounting at times to a transparent glow,
  As if her veins ran lightning: she, in sooth,
Possess'd an air and grace by no means common;
Her stature tall—I hate a dumpy woman.

LXII

Wedded she was some years, and to a man
  Of fifty, and such husbands are in plenty;
And yet, I think, instead of such a ONE,
  'Twere better to have TWO of five-and-twenty,
Especially in countries near the sun,
  And now I think on't, 'mi vien in mente,'

Ladies even of the most uneasy virtue
Prefer a spouse whose age is short of thirty.

LXIII

'Tis a sad thing, I cannot choose but say,
  And all the fault of that indecent sun,
Who cannot leave alone our helpless clay,
  But will keep baking, broiling, burning on,
That howsoever people fast and pray,
  The flesh is frail, and so the soul undone:
What men call gallantry, and gods adultery,
Is much more common where the climate's sultry.

LXIV

Happy the nations of the moral North!
  Where all is virtue, and the winter season
Sends sin, without a rag on, shivering forth
  ('Twas snow that brought St Anthony to reason); *
Where juries cast up what a wife is worth,
  By laying whate'er sum, in mulct, they please on
The lover, who must pay a handsome price,
Because it is a marketable vice.

LXV

Alfonso was the name of Julia's lord,
  A man well looking for his years, and who
Was neither much beloved, nor yet abhorr'd:
  They lived together as most people do,
Suffering each other's foibles by accord,
  And not exactly either *one* or *two;*
Yet he was jealous, though he did not show it,
For jealousy dislikes the world to know it.

LXVI

Julia was—yet I never could see why—
  With Donna Inez quite a favourite friend;
Between their tastes there was small sympathy,
  For not a line had Julia ever penn'd:
Some people whisper (but no doubt they lie,
  For malice still imputes some private end)
That Inez had, ere Don Alfonso's marriage,
Forgot with him her very prudent carriage;

* For the particulars of St Anthony's recipe for hot blood in cold weather, see Mr Alban Butler's 'Lives of the Saints.'

LXVII

And that, still keeping up the old connection,
Which time had lately render'd much more chaste,
She took his lady also in affection,
And certainly this course was much the best.
She flatter'd Julia with her sage protection,
And complimented Don Alfonso's taste:
And if she could not (who can?) silence scandal,
At least she left it a more slender handle.

LXVIII

I can't tell whether Julia saw the affair
With other people's eyes, or if her own
Discoveries made, but none could be aware
Of this, at least no symptom e'er was shown,
Perhaps she did not know, or did not care,
Indifferent from the first, or callous grown;
I'm really puzzled what to think or say,
She kept her counsel in so close a way.

LXIX

Juan she saw, and, as a pretty child,
Caress'd him often—such a thing might be
Quite innocently done, and harmless styled,
When she had twenty years, and thirteen he;
But I am not so sure I should have smiled
When he was sixteen, Julia twenty-three:
These few short years make wondrous alterations,
Particularly amongst sunburnt nations.

LXX

Whate'er the cause might be, they had become
Changed; for the dame grew distant, the youth shy,
Their looks cast down, their greetings almost dumb.
And much embarrassment in either eye:
There surely will be little doubt with some
That Donna Julia knew the reason why;
But as for Juan, he had no more notion
Then he who never saw the sea or ocean.

LXXI

Yet Julia's very coldness still was kind,
And tremulously gentle her small hand

Withdrew itself from his, but left behind
  A little pressure, thrilling, and so bland,
And slight, so very slight, that to the mind
  'Twas but a doubt; but ne'er magician's wand
Wrought change with all Armida's fairy art
Like what this light touch left on Juan's heart.

LXXII

And if she met him, though she smiled no more,
  She look'd a sadness sweeter than her smile,
As if her heart had deeper thoughts in store
  She must not own, but cherish'd more the while
For that compression, in its burning core:
  Even innocence itself has many a wile,
And will not dare to trust itself with truth,
And love is taught hypocrisy from youth.

LXXIII

But passion most dissembles, yet betrays
  Even by its darkness; as the blackest sky
Foretells the heaviest tempest, it displays
  Its workings through the vainly guarded eye,
And in whatever aspect it arrays
  Itself, 'tis still the same hypocrisy.
Coldness or anger, even disdain or hate,
Are masks it often wears, and still too late.

LXXIV

Then there were sighs, the deeper for suppression,
  And stolen glances sweeter for the theft,
And burning blushes, though for no transgression,
  Tremblings when met, and restlessness when left;
All these little preludes to possession,
  Of which young passion cannot be bereft,
And merely tend to show how greatly love is
Embarrass'd at first starting with a novice.

LXXV

Poor Julia's heart was in an awkward state;
  She felt it going, and resolved to make
The noblest efforts for herself and mate,
  For honour's, pride's, religion's, virtue's sake:
Her resolutions were most truly great,
  And almost might have made a Tarquin quake;

She pray'd the Virgin Mary for her grace,
As being the best judge of a lady's case.

LXXVI

She vow'd she never would see Juan more,
  And next day paid a visit to his mother,
And look'd extremely at the opening door,
  Which, by the Virgin's grace, let in another;
Grateful she was, and yet a little sore—
  Again it opens, it can be no other:
'Tis surely Juan now—No! I'm afraid
That night the Virgin was no further pray'd.

LXXVII

She now determined that a virtuous woman
  Should rather face and overcome temptation,
That flight was base and dastardly, and no man
  Should ever give her heart the least sensation;
That is to say, a thought beyond the common
  Preference, that we must feel upon occasion,
For people who are pleasanter than others,
But then they only seem so many brothers.

LXXVIII

And even if by chance—and who can tell?
  The devil's so very sly—she should discover
That all within was not so very well,
  And, if still free, that such or such a lover
Might please perhaps, a virtuous wife can quell
  Such thoughts, and be the better when they're over;
And if the man should ask, 'tis but denial:
I recommend young ladies to make trial.

LXXIX

And then there are such things as love divine,
  Bright and immaculate, unmix'd and pure,
Such as the angels think so very fine,
  And matrons, who would be no less secure,
Platonic, perfect, 'just such love as mine:'
  Thus Julia said—and thought so, to be sure;
And so I'd have her think, were I the man
On whom her reveries celestial ran.

LXXX

Such love is innocent, and may exist
  Between young persons without any danger.
A hand may first, and then a lip, be kiss'd;
  For my part, to such doings I'm a stranger,
But *here* these freedoms form the utmost list
  Of all o'er which such love may be a ranger.
If people go beyond, 'tis quite a crime,
But not my fault—I tell them all in time.

LXXXI

Love, then, but love within its proper limits,
  Was Julia's innocent determination
In young Don Juan's favour, and to him its
  Exertion might be useful on occasion;
And, lighted at too pure a shrine to dim its
  Ethereal lustre, with what sweet persuasion
He might be taught, by love and her together—
I really don't know what, nor Julia either.

LXXXII

Fraught with this fine intention, and well fenced
  In mail of proof—her purity of soul,
She, for the future, of her strength convinced,
  And that her honour was a rock or mole,
Exceeding sagely from that hour dispensed
  With any kind of troublesome control;
But whether Julia to the task was equal
Is that which must be mention'd in the sequel.

LXXXIII

Her plan she deem'd both innocent and feasible;
  And surely, with a stripling of sixteen,
Not scandal's fangs could fix on much that's seizable,
  Or if they did so, satisfied to mean
Nothing but what was good, her breast was peaceable—
  A quiet conscience makes one so serene!
Christians have burnt each other, quite persuaded
That all the Apostles would have done as they did.

LXXXIV

And if in the mean time her husband died
  But Heaven forbid that such a thought should cross

Her brain, though in a dream! (and then she sigh'd,)
  Never could she survive that common loss;
But just suppose that moment should betide,
  I only say suppose it—*inter nos.*
(This should be *entre nous*, for Julia thought
In French, but then the rhyme would go for nought.)

LXXXV

I only say, suppose this supposition:
  Juan being then grown up to man's estate
Would fully suit a widow of condition;
  Even seven years hence it would not be too late;
And in the interim (to pursue this vision),
  The mischief, after all, could not be great,
For he would learn the rudiments of love,
I mean the seraph way of those above.

LXXXVI

So much for Julia. Now we'll turn to Juan.
  Poor little fellow! he had no idea
Of his own case, and never hit the true one:
  In feelings quick, as Ovid's Miss Medea,
He puzzled over what he found a new one,
  But not as yet imagined it could be a
Thing quite in course, and not at all alarming,
Which, with a little patience, might grow charming.

LXXXVII

Silent and pensive, idle, restless, slow,
  His home deserted for the lonely wood,
Tormented with a wound he could not know,
  His, like all deep grief, plunged in solitude:
I'm fond myself of solitude or so,
  But then I beg it may be understood,
By solitude I mean a sultan's, not
A hermit's, with a harem for a grot.

LXXXVIII

'Oh Love! in such a wilderness as this,
  Where transport and security entwine,
Here is the empire of thy perfect bliss,
  And here thou art a god indeed divine.' *

* Campbell's *Gertrude of Wyoming*. I think the opening of Canto II., but quote from memory.

The bard I quote from does not sing amiss,
  With the exception of the second line,
For that same twining 'transport and security
Are twisted to a phrase of some obscurity.

LXXXIX

The poet meant, no doubt, and thus appeals
  To the good sense and senses of mankind,
The very thing which everybody feels,
  As all have found on trial, or may find,
  That no one likes to be disturb'd at meals
  Or love.—I won't say more about 'entwined
Or 'transport,' as we knew all that before,
But beg 'Security' will bolt the door.

XC

Young Juan wander'd by the glassy brooks,
  Thinking unutterable things: he threw
Himself at length within the leafy nooks
  Where the wild branch of the cork forest grew;
There poets find materials for their books,
  And every now and then we read them through,
So that their plan and prosody are eligible,
Unless, like Wordsworth, they prove unintelligible.

XCI

He, Juan (and not Wordsworth) so pursued
  His self-communion with his own high soul
Until his mighty heart, in its great mood,
  Had mitigated part, though not the whole
Of its disease: he did the best he could
  With things not very subject to control,
And turn'd, without perceiving his condition,
Like Coleridge, into a metaphysician.

XCII

He thought about himself, and the whole earth,
  Of man the wonderful, and of the stars,
And how the deuce they ever could have birth;
  And then he thought of earthquakes and of wars,
How many miles the moon might have in girth,
  Of air-balloons, and of the many bars

To perfect knowledge of the boundless skies;—
And then he thought of Donna Julia's eyes.

XCIII

In thoughts like these true wisdom may discern
  Longings sublime, and aspirations high,
Which some are born with, but the most part learn
  To plague themselves withal, they know not why:
'Twas strange that one so young should thus concern
  His brain about the action of the sky:
If *you* think 'twas philosophy that this did,
I can't help thinking puberty assisted.

XCIV

He pored upon the leaves, and on the flowers,
  And heard a voice in all the winds; and then
He thought of wood-nymphs and immortal bowers,
  And how the goddesses came down to men.
He miss'd the pathway, he forgot the hours,
  And when he look'd upon his watch again,
He found how much old Time had been a winner;
He also found that he had lost his dinner.

XCV

Sometimes he turn'd to gaze upon his book,
  Boscan, or Garcillasso * :—by the wind
Even as the page is rustled while we look,
  So by the poesy of his own mind
Over the mystic leaf his soul was shook,
  As if 'twere one whereon magicians bind
Their spells, and give them to the passing gale,
According to some good old woman's tale.

XCVI

Thus would he while his lonely hours away,
  Dissatisfied, nor knowing what he wanted;
Nor glowing reverie, nor poet's lay,
  Could yield his spirit that for which it panted,
A bosom whereon he his head might lay,
  And hear the heart beat with the love it granted;
With—several other things which I forget,
Or which, at least, I need not mention yet.

* Spanish poets.

XCVII

Those lonely walks and lengthening reveries
  Could not escape the gentle Julia's eyes;
She saw that Juan was not at his ease;
  But that which chiefly may, and must, surprise,
Is, that the Donna Inez did not tease
  Her only son with question or surmise:
Whether it was she did not see, or would not,
Or, like all very clever people, could not.

XCVIII

This may seem strange, but yet 'tis very common;
  For instance—gentlemen, whose ladies take
Leave to o'erstep the written rights of woman,
  And break the—Which commandment is't they break?
(I have forgot the number, and think no man
  Should rashly quote for fear of a mistake.)
I say when these same gentlemen are jealous,
They make some blunder, which their ladies tell us.

XCIX

A real husband always is suspicious,
  But still no less suspects in the wrong place;
Jealous of some one who had no such wishes,
  Or pandering blindly to his own disgrace,
By harbouring some dear friend extremely vicious;
  The last indeed's infallibly the case:
And when the spouse and friend are gone off wholly,
He wonders at their vice, and not his folly.

C

Thus parents also are at times short-sighted;
  Though watchful as the lynx, they ne'er discover,
The while the wicked world beholds, delighted,
  Young Hopeful's mistress, or Miss Fanny's lover,
Till some confounded escapade has blighted
  The plan of twenty years, and all is over;
And then the mother cries, the father swears,
And wonders why the devil he got heirs.

CI

But Inez was so anxious, and so clear
  Of sight, that I must think, on this occasion

She had some other motive much more near,
For leaving Juan to this new temptation;
But what that motive was, I shan't say here;
Perhaps to finish Juan's education,
Perhaps to open Don Alfonso's eyes,
In case he thought his wife too great a prize.

CII

It was upon a day, a summer's day;—
Summer's indeed a very dangerous season,
And so is spring, about the end of May:
The sun no doubt is the prevailing reason;
But whatsoe'er the cause is, one may say,
And stand convicted of more truth than treason,
That there are months which nature grows more merry in—
March has its hares, and May must have its heroine.

CIII

'Twas on a summer's day—the sixth of June:
I like to be particular in dates,
Not only of the age and year, but moon:
They are a sort of post-house, where the Fates
Change horses, making history change its tune,
Then spur away o'er empires and o'er states,
Leaving at last not much besides chronology,
Excepting the post-obits of theology.

CIV

'Twas on the sixth of June, about the hour
Of half-past six—perhaps still nearer seven—
When Julia sate within as pretty a bower
As e'er held houri in that heathenish heaven
Described by Mahomet, and Anacreon Moore,
To whom the lyre and laurels have been given,
With all the trophies of triumphant song—
He won them well, and may he wear them long!

CV

She sate, but not alone; I know not well
How this same interview had taken place,
And even if I knew, I should not tell—
People should hold their tongues in any case:

No matter how or why the thing befell,
  But there were she and Juan, face to face—
When two such faces are so, 'twould be wise,
But very difficult, to shut their eyes.

CVI

How beautiful she look'd! her conscious heart
  Glow'd in her cheek, and yet she felt no wrong.
O Love! how perfect is thy mystic art,
  Strengthening the weak, and trampling on the strong!
How self-deceitful is the sagest part
  Of mortals whom thy lure hath led along—
The precipice she stood on was immense,
So was her creed in her own innocence.

CVII

She thought of her own strength and Juan's youth,
  And of the folly of all prudish fears,
Victorious virtue, and domestic truth,
  And then of Don Alfonso's fifty years:
I wish these last had not occurr'd, in sooth,
  Because that number rarely much endears,
And through all climes, the snowy and the sunny,
Sounds ill in love, whate'er it may in money.

CVIII

When people say, 'I've told you *fifty* times,'
  They mean to scold, and very often do;
When poets say, 'I've written *fifty* rhymes,'
  They make you dread that they'll recite them too;
In gangs of *fifty*, thieves commit their crimes;
  At *fifty*, love for love is rare, 'tis true:
But then, no doubt, it equally as true is,
A good deal may be bought for *fifty* louis.

CIX

Julia had honour, virtue, truth, and love
  For Don Alfonso; and she inly swore,
By all the vows below to powers above,
  She never would disgrace the ring she wore,
Nor leave a wish which wisdom might reprove;
  And while she ponder'd this, besides much more,

One hand on Juan's carelessly was thrown,
Quite by mistake—she thought it was her own.

CX

Unconsciously, she lean'd upon the other,
  Which play'd within the tangles of her hair;
And to contend with thoughts she could not smother,
  She seem'd, by the distraction of her air.
'Twas surely very wrong in Juan's mother
  To leave together this imprudent pair:
She who for many years had watch'd her son so;
I'm very certain *mine* would not have done so.

CXI

The hand which still held Juan's, by degrees
  Gently, but palpably, confirm'd its grasp,
As if it said, 'Detain me, if you please:'
  Yet there's no doubt she only meant to clasp
His fingers with a pure Platonic squeeze;
  She would have shrunk as from a toad, or asp,
Had she imagined such a thing could rouse
A feeling dangerous to a prudent spouse.

CXII

I cannot know what Juan thought of this,
  But what he did is much what you would do;
His young lip thank'd it with a grateful kiss,
  And then, abash'd at its own joy, withdrew
In deep despair, lest he had done amiss,
  Love is so very timid when 'tis new:
She blush'd and frown'd not, but she strove to speak,
And held her tongue, her voice was grown so weak.

CXIII

The sun set, and up rose the yellow moon:
  The devil's in the moon for mischief; they
Who call'd her *chaste*, methinks began too soon
  Their nomenclature; there is not a day,
The longest, not the twenty-first of June,
  Sees half the business in a wicked way
On which three single hours of moonshine smile—
And then she looks so modest all the while.

CXIV

There is a dangerous silence in that hour,
  A stillness which leaves room for the full soul
To open all itself, without the power
  Of calling wholly back its self-control;
The silver light which, hallowing tree and tower,
  Sheds beauty and deep softness o'er the whole
Breathes also to the heart, and o'er it throws
A loving languor, which is not repose.

CXV

And Julia sate with Juan, half embraced,
  And half retiring from the glowing arm,
Which trembled like the bosom where 'twas placed:
  Yet still she must have thought there was no harm,
Or else 'twere easy to withdraw her waist;
  But then the situation had its charm,
And then—God knows what next—I can't go on:
I'm almost sorry that I e'er begun.

CXVI

O Plato! Plato! you have paved the way,
  With your confounded fantasies, to more
Immoral conduct, by the fancied sway
  Your system feigns o'er the controlless core
Of human hearts, than all the long array
  Of poets and romancers:—You're a bore,
A charlatan, a coxcomb—and have been,
At best, no better than a go-between.

CXVII

And Julia's voice was lost, except in sighs,
  Until too late for useful conversation;
The tears were gushing from her gentle eyes,
  I wish, indeed, they had not had occasion:
But who, alas, can love, and then be wise?
  Not that remorse did not oppose temptation:
A little still she strove, and much repented,
And whispering 'I will ne'er consent'—consented.

CXVIII

'Tis said that Xerxes offer'd a reward
  To those who could invent him a new pleasure;

Methinks the requisition's rather hard,
  And must have cost his majesty a treasure:
For my part, I'm a moderate-minded bard,
  Fond of a little love (which I call leisure):
I care not for new pleasures, as the old
Are quite enough for me, so they but hold.

CXIX

O pleasure! you're indeed a pleasant thing,
  Although one must be damn'd for you, no doubt:
I make a resolution every spring,
  Of reformation ere the year run out;
But somehow this my vestal vow takes wing,
  Yet still, I trust, it may be kept throughout:
I'm very sorry, very much ashamed,
And mean next winter to be quite reclaim'd.

CXX

Here my chaste muse a liberty must take—
  Start not, still chaster reader—she'll be nice hence-
Forward, and there is no great cause to quake:
  This liberty is a poetic licence,
Which some irregularity may make
  In the design: and as I have a high sense
Or Aristotle and the Rules, 'tis fit
To beg his pardon when I err a bit.

CXXI

This licence is to hope the reader will
  Suppose from June the sixth (the fatal day,
Without whose epoch my poetic skill,
  For want of facts, would all be thrown away),
But keeping Julia and Don Juan still
  In sight, that several months have pass'd; we'll say
'Twas in November, but I'm not so sure
About the day—the era's more obscure.

CXXII

We'll talk of that anon.—'Tis sweet to hear,
  At midnight on the blue and moonlit deep,
The song and oar of Adria's gondolier,
  By distance mellow'd, o'er the waters sweep;

'Tis sweet to see the evening star appear;
'Tis sweet to listen as the night-winds creep
From leaf to leaf; 'tis sweet to view on high
The rainbow, based on ocean, span the sky.

CXXIII

'Tis sweet to hear the watch-dog's honest bark
Bay deep-mouth'd welcome as we draw near home;
'Tis sweet to know there is an eye will mark
Our coming, and look brighter when we come;
'Tis sweet to be awaken'd by the lark,
Or lull'd by falling waters; sweet the hum
Of bees, the voice of girls, the song of birds,
The lisp of children, and their earliest words.

CXXIV

Sweet is the vintage, when the showering grapes
In Bacchanal profusion reel to earth,
Purple and gushing: sweet are our escapes
From civic revelry to rural mirth:
Sweet to the miser are his glittering heaps;
Sweet to the father is his first-born's birth;
Sweet is revenge—especially to women,
Pillage to soldiers, prize-money to seamen.

CXXV

Sweet is a legacy, and passing sweet
The unexpected death of some old lady
Or gentleman of seventy years complete,
Who've made 'us youth' wait too—too long already
For an estate, or cash, or country-seat,
Still breaking, but with stamina so steady,
That all the Israelites are fit to mob its
Next owner for their double-damn'd post-obits.

CXXVI

'Tis sweet to win, no matter how, one's laurels,
By blood or ink; 'tis sweet to put an end
To strife; 'tis sometimes sweet to have our quarrels,
Particularly with a tiresome friend:
Sweet is old wine in bottles, ale in barrels;
Dear is the helpless creature we defend
Against the world: and dear the schoolboy spot
We ne'er forget, though there we are forgot.

CXXVII

But sweeter still than this, than these, than all,
  Is first and passionate love—it stands alone,
Like Adam's recollection of his fall:
  The tree of knowledge has been pluck'd, all's known—
And life yields nothing further to recall
  Worthy of this ambrosial sin, so shown,
No doubt in fable, as the unforgiven
Fire which Prometheus filch'd for us from heaven.

CXXVIII

Man's a strange animal, and makes strange use
  Of his own nature, and the various arts,
And likes particularly to produce
  Some new experiment to show his parts;
This is the age of oddities let loose,
  Where different talents find their different marts:
You'd best begin with truth; and when you've lost your
Labour, there's a sure market for imposture.

CXXIX

What opposite discoveries we have seen!
  (Signs of true genius and of empty pockets:)
One makes new noses, one a guillotine,
  One breaks your bones, one sets them in their sockets;
But vaccination certainly has been
  A kind antithesis to Congreve's rockets,
With which the doctor paid off an old pox,
By borrowing a new one from an ox.

CXXX

Bread has been made (indifferent) from potatoes,
  And galvanism has set some corpses grinning,
But has not answer'd like the apparatus
  Of the Humane Society's beginning,
By which men are unsuffocated gratis:
  What wondrous new machines have late been spinning!
I said the small-pox has gone out of late,
Perhaps it may be follow'd by the great.

CXXXI

'Tis said the great came from America;
  Perhaps it may set out on its return,—

The population there so spreads, they say
'Tis grown high time to thin it in its turn,
With war, or plague, or famine, any way,
So that civilization they may learn;
And which in ravage the more loathsome evil is—
Their real lues, or our pseudo-syphilis?

CXXXII

This is the patent age of new inventions
For killing bodies, and for saving souls,
All propagated with the best intentions;
Sir Humphry Davy's lantern, by which coals
Are safely mined for in the mode he mentions,
Timbuctoo travels, voyages to the Poles,
Are ways to benefit mankind, as true,
Perhaps, as shooting them at Waterloo.

CXXXIII

Man's a phenomenon, one knows not what,
And wonderful beyond all wondrous measure;
'Tis pity though, in this sublime world, that
Pleasure's a sin, and sometimes sin's a pleasure;
Few mortals know what end they would be at,
But whether glory, power, or love, or treasure,
The path is through perplexing ways, and when
The goal is gain'd, we die, you know—and then—

CXXXIV

What then?—I do not know, no more do you—
And so good-night.—Return we to our story:
'Twas in November, when fine days are few,
And the far mountains wax a little hoary,
And clap a white cape on their mantles blue;
And the sea dashes round the promontory,
And the loud breaker boils against the rock,
And sober suns must set at five o'clock.

CXXXV

Twas, as the watchmen say, a cloudy night:
No moon, no stars, the wind was low or loud
By gusts, and many a sparkling hearth was bright
With the piled wood, round which the family crowd;

There's something cheerful in that sort of light,
  Even as a summer sky's without a cloud:
I'm fond of fire, and crickets, and all that,
A lobster salad, and champagne, and chat.

CXXXVI

'Twas midnight—Donna Julia was in bed,
  Sleeping, most probably,—when at her door
Arose a clatter might awake the dead,
  If they had never been awoke before;
And that they have been so, we all have read,
  And are to be so, at the least, one more:
The door was fasten'd, but with voice and fist
First knocks were heard, then 'Madam—madam—hist!

CXXXVII

'For God's sake, Madam—Madam—here's my master,
  With more than half the city at his back—
Was ever heard of such a curst disaster!
  'Tis not my fault—I kept good watch—Alack!
Do pray undo the bolt a little faster—
  They're on the stair just now, and in a crack
Will all be here; perhaps he yet may fly—
Surely the window's not so *very* high!'

CXXXVIII

By this time Don Alfonso was arrived,
  With torches, friends and servants in great number;
The major part of them had long been wived,
  And therefore paused not to disturb the slumber
Of any wicked woman, who contrived
  By stealth her husband's temples to encumber:
Examples of this kind are so contagious,
Were *one* not punish'd, *all* would be outrageous.

CXXXIX

I can't tell how, or why, or what suspicion
  Could enter into Don Alfonso's head;
But for a cavalier of his condition
  It surely was exceedingly ill-bred,
Without a word of previous admonition,
  To hold a levée round his lady's bed,

And summon lackeys, arm'd with fire and sword,
To prove himself the thing he most abhorr'd.

CXL

Poor Donna Julia! starting as from sleep
(Mind—that I do not say—she had not slept),
Began at once to scream, and yawn, and weep;
Her maid Antonio, who was an adept,
Contrived to fling the bed-clothes in a heap,
As if she had just now from out them crept:
I can't tell why she should take all this trouble
To prove her mistress had been sleeping double.

CXLI

But Julia mistress, and Antonia maid,
Appear'd like two poor harmless women, who
Of goblins, but still more of men, afraid,
Had thought one man might be deterr'd by two,
And therefore side by side were gently laid,
Until the hours of absence should run through,
And truant husband should return, and say,
'My dear, I was the first who came away.'

CXLII

Now Julia found at length a voice, and cried,
'In heaven's name, Don Alfonso, what d'ye mean?
Has madness seized you? Would that I had died
Ere such a monster's victim I had been!
What may this midnight violence betide?
A sudden fit of drunkenness or spleen?
Dare you suspect me, when the thought would kill?
Search, then, the room!'—Alfonso said, 'I will.'

CXLIII

*He* search'd, *they* search'd, and rummaged everywhere,
Closet and clothes-press, chest, and window-seat,
And found much linen, lace, and several pair
Of stockings, slippers, brushes, combs, complete,
With other articles of ladies fair,
To keep them beautiful, or leave them neat;
Arras they prick'd and curtains with their swords,
And wounded several shutters and some boards.

CXLIV

Under the bed they search'd, and there they found—
  No matter what—it was not that they sought;
They open'd windows, gazing if the ground
  Had signs or footmarks, but the earth said nought;
And then they stared each other's faces round:
  'Tis odd, not one of all these seekers thought,
And seems to me almost a sort of blunder,
Of looking *in* the bed as well as under.

CXLV

During this inquisition, Julia's tongue
  Was not asleep—'Yes, search and search,' she cried,
'Insult on insult heap, and wrong on wrong!
  It was for this that I became a bride!
For this in silence I have suffer'd long
  A husband like Alfonso at my side:
But now I'll bear no more, nor here remain,
If there be law or lawyers in all Spain.

CXLVI

'Yes, Don Alfonso! husband now no more,
  If ever you indeed deserved the name,
Is't worthy of your years? you have three-score—
  Fifty, or sixty, it is all the same—
Is't wise or fitting, causeless to explore
  For facts against a virtuous woman's fame?
Ungrateful, perjured, barbarous Don Alfonso,
How dare you think your lady would go on so?

CXLVII

'Is it for this I have disdain't to hold
  The common privileges of my sex?
That I have chosen a confessor so old
  And deaf, that any other it would vex,
And never once he has had cause to scold,
  But found my very innocence perplex
So much, he always doubted I was married—
How sorry you will be when I've miscarried!

CXLVIII

'Was it for this that no Cortejo e'er
  I yet have chosen from out the youth of Seville?

Is it for this I scarce went anywhere,
  Except to bull-fights, mass, play, rout, and revel
Is it for this, whate'er my suitors were,
  I favour'd none—nay, was almost uncivil?
Is it for this that General Count O'Reilly,
Who took Algiers, declares I used him vilely?

CXLIX

'Did not the Italian Musico Cazzani
  Sing at my heart six months at least in vain?
Did not his countryman, Count Corniani,
  Call me the only virtuous wife in Spain?
Were there not also Russians, English, many?
  The Count Strongstroganoff I put in pain,
And Lord Mount Coffeehouse, the Irish peer,
Who kill'd himself for love (with wine) last year.

CL

'Have I not had two bishops at my feet?
  The Duke of Ichar, and Don Fernan Nunez;
And is it thus a faithful wife you treat?
  I wonder in what quarter now the moon is:
I praise your vast forbearance not to beat
  Me also, since the time so opportune is—
Oh, valiant man! with sword drawn and cock'd trigger,
Now, tell me, don't you cut a pretty figure?

CLI

'Was it for this you took your sudden journey,
  Under pretence of business indispensable,
With that sublime of rascals, your attorney,
  Whom I see standing there, and looking sensible
Of having play'd the fool? Though both I spurn, he
  Deserves the worst: his conduct's less defensible,
Because, no doubt, 'twas for his dirty fee,
And not from any love to you nor me.

CLII

'If he comes here to take a deposition,
  By all means let the gentleman proceed;
You've made the apartment in a fit condition:
  There's pen and ink for you, sir, when you need—

Let everything be noted with precision,
  I would not you for nothing should be fee'd—
But, as my maid's undrest, pray turn your spies out.'
'Oh!' sobb'd Antonia, 'I could tear their eyes out.'

CLIII

There is the closet, there the toilet, there
  The antechamber—search them under, over;
There is the sofa, there the great arm-chair,
  The chimney—which would really hold a lover.
I wish to sleep, and beg you will take care
  And make no further noise, till you discover
The secret cavern of this lurking treasure;
And when 'tis found, let me, too, have that pleasure.

CLIV

'And now, Hidalgo! now that you have thrown
  Doubt upon me, confusion over all,
Pray have the courtesy to make it known
  *Who* is the man you search for? how d'ye call
Him? what's his lineage? let him but be shown:
  I hope he's young and handsome—is he tall?
Tell me; and be assured that, since you stain
My honour thus, it shall not be in vain.

CLV

At least, perhaps, he is not sixty years,
  At that age he would be too old for slaughter,
Or for so young a husband's jealous fears—
  Antonia! let me have a glass of water.
I am ashamed of having shed these tears,
  They are unworthy of my father's daughter;
My mother dream'd not, in my natal hour,
That I should fall into a monster's power.

CLVI

'Perhaps 'tis of Antonia you are jealous;
  You saw that she was sleeping by my side,
When you broke in upon us with your fellows:
  Look where you please—we've nothing, sir, to hide;
Only another time, I trust, you'll tell us,
  Or for the sake of decency abide

A moment at the door, that we may be
Drest to receive so much good company.

CLVII

'And now, sir, I have done, and say no more;
  The little I have said may serve to show
The guileless heart in silence may grieve o'er
  The wrongs to whose exposure it is slow—
I leave you to your conscience as before,
  'Twill one day ask you *why* you used me so.
God grant you feel not then the bitterest grief!
Antonia! where's my pocket handkerchief?'

CLVIII

She ceased, and turn'd upon her pillow; pale
  She lay, her dark eyes flashing through their tears,
Like skies that rain and lighten; as a veil,
  Waved and o'ershading her wan cheek, appears
Her streaming hair: the black curls strive, but fail,
  To hide the glossy shoulder, which uprears
Its snow through all; her soft lips lie apart,
And louder than her breathing beats her heart.

CLIX

The Senhor Don Alfonso stood confused;
  Antonia bustled round the ransack'd room,
And, turning up her nose, with looks abused
  Her master and his myrmidons, of whom
Not one, except the attorney, was amused:
  He, like Achates, faithful to the tomb,
So there were quarrels, cared not for the cause
Knowing they must be settled by the laws.

CLX

With prying snub-nose and small eyes, he stood,
  Following Antonia's motions here and there,
With much suspicion in his attitude.
  For reputations he had little care;
So that a suit or action were made good,
  Small pity had he for the young and fair;
And ne'er believ'd in negatives, till these
Were proved by competent false witnesses.

CLXI

But Don Alfonso stood with downcast looks,
  And, truth to say, he made a foolish figure;
When, after searching in five hundred nooks,
  And treating a young wife with so much rigour,
He gain'd no point, except some self-rebukes,
  Added to those his lady with such vigour
Had pour'd upon him for the last half-hour,
Quick, thick, and heavy—as a thunder-shower.

CLXII

At first he tried to hammer an excuse,
  To which the sole reply was tears and sobs,
And indications of hysterics, whose
  Prologue is always certain throes, and throbs,
Gasps, and whatever else the owners choose:
  Alfonso saw his wife, and thought of Job's;
He saw too, in perspective, her relations,
And then he tried to muster all his patience.

CLXIII

He stood in act to speak, or rather stammer,
  But sage Antonia cut him short before
The anvil of his speech received the hammer,
  With, 'Pray, sir, leave the room, and say no more,
Or madam dies.'—Alfonso mutter'd, 'D—n her,'
  But nothing else—the time of words was o'er;
He cast a rueful look or two, and did,
He knew not wherefore, that which he was bid.

CLXIV

With him retired his '*posse comitatus*,'
  The attorney last, who linger'd near the door
Reluctantly, still tarrying there as late as
  Antonia let him—not a little sore
At this most strange and unexplain'd '*hiatus*'
  In Don Alfonso's facts, which just now wore
An awkward look; as he revolved the case,
The door was fasten'd in his legal face.

CLXV

No sooner was it bolted than—Oh shame!
  Oh sin! Oh sorrow! and Oh womankind!

How can you do such things and keep your fame,
   Unless this world, and t'other too, be blind?
Nothing so dear as an unfilch'd good name!
   But to proceed—for there is more behind:
With much heartfelt reluctance be it said,
Young Juan slipp'd, half-smother'd, from the bed.

CLXVI

He had been hid—I don't pretend to say
   How, nor can I indeed describe the where—
Young, slender, and pack'd easily, he lay,
   No doubt, in little compass, round or square;
But pity him I neither must nor may
   His suffocation by that pretty pair:
'Twere better, sure, to die so, than be shut
With maudlin Clarence in his Malmsey butt.

CLXVII

And, secondly, I pity not, because
   He had no business to commit a sin,
Forbid by heavenly, fined by human, laws,
   At least 'twas rather early to begin;
But at sixteen the conscience rarely gnaws
   So much as when we call our old debts in
At sixty years, and draw the accompts of evil,
And find a deuced balance with the devil.

CLXVIII

Of his position I can give no notion
   'Tis written in the Hebrew Chronicle,
How the physicians, leaving pill and potion,
   Prescribed by way of blister, a young belle,
When old King David's blood grew dull in motion,
   And that the medicine answer'd very well:
Perhaps 'twas in a different way applied,
For David lived, but Juan nearly died.

CLXIX

What's to be done? Alfonso will be back
   The moment he has sent his fools away.
Antonia's skill was put upon the rack,
   But no device could be brought into play.

And how to parry the renew'd attack?
  Besides, it wanted but few hours of day:
Antonia puzzled; Julia did not speak,
But press'd her bloodless lip to Juan's cheek.

CLXX

He turn'd his lip to hers, and with his hand
  Call'd back the tangles of her wandering hair;
Even then their love they could not all command,
  And half forgot their danger and despair.
Antonia's patience now was at a stand—
  'Come, come, 'tis no time now for fooling there,'
She whisper'd, in great wrath; 'I must deposit
This pretty gentleman within the closet.'

CLXXI

'Pray keep your nonsense for some luckier night—
  *Who* can have put my master in this mood?
What will become on't?—I'm in such a fright.
  The devil's in the urchin, and no good—
Is this a time for giggling? this a plight?
  Why, don't you know that it may end in blood
You'll lose your life, and I shall lose my place
My mistress, all, for that half-girlish face.

CLXXII

'Had it but been for a stout cavalier
  Of twenty-five or thirty—(Come, make haste)—
But for a child, what piece of work is here!
  I really, madam, wonder at your taste—
(Come, sir, get in)—my master must be near:
  There for the present, at the least, he's fast,
And if we can but till the morning keep
Our counsel—(Juan, mind, you must not sleep).'

CLXXIII

Now Don Alfonso, entering, but alone,
  Closed the oration of the trusty maid:
She loiter'd, and he told her to be gone,
  An order somewhat sullenly obey'd;
However, present remedy was none,
  And no great good seem'd answer'd if she stay'd.

Regarding both with slow and sidelong view,
She snuff'd the candle, curtsied, and withdrew.

CLXXIV

Alfonso paused a minute–then begun
  Some strange excuses for his late proceeding:
He would not justify what he had done;
  To say the best, it was extreme ill-breeding;
But there were ample reasons for it, none
  Of which he specified in this his pleading:
His speech was a fine sample, on the whole,
Of rhetoric, which the learn'd call '*rigmarole*.

CLXXV

Julia said nought; though all the while there rose
  A ready answer, which at once enables
A matron, who her husband's foible knows,
  By a few timely words to turn the tables,
Which, if it does not silence, still must pose–
  Even if it should comprise a pack of fables.
'Tis to retort with firmness, and when he
Suspects with *one*, do you reproach with *three*.

CLXXVI

Julia, in fact, had tolerable grounds–
  Alfonso's loves with Inez were well known;
But whether 'twas that one's own guilt confounds–
  But that can't be, as has been often shown,
A lady with apologies abounds;–
  It might be that her silence sprang alone
From delicacy to Don Juan's ear,
To whom she knew his mother's fame was dear.

CLXXVII

There might be one more motive, which makes two,
  Alfonso ne'er to Juan had alluded–
Mention'd his jealousy, but never who
  Had been the happy lover, he concluded,
Conceal'd amongst his premises; 'tis true,
  His mind the more o'er this its mystery brooded:
To speak of Inez now were, one may say,
Like throwing Juan in Alfonso's way.

CLXXVIII

A hint, in tender cases, is enough;
  Silence is best; besides, there is a *tact*—
(That modern phrase appears to me sad stuff,
  But it will serve to keep my verse compact)—
Which keeps, when push'd by questions rather rough,
  A lady always distant from the fact:
The charming creatures lie with such a grace,
There's nothing so becoming to the face.

CLXXIX

They blush, and we believe them; at least I
  Have always done so; 'tis of no great use,
In any case attempting a reply,
  For then their eloquence grows quite profuse;
And when at length they're out of breath, they sigh,
  And cast their languid eyes down, and let loose
A tear or two, and then we make it up;
And then—and then—and then—sit down and sup.

CLXXX

Alfonso closed his speech, and begg'd her pardon,
  Which Julia half withheld and then half granted,
And laid conditions he thought very hard on,
  Denying several little things he wanted:
He stood like Adam lingering near his garden,
  With useless penitence perplex'd and haunted,
Beseeching she no further would refuse,
When, lo! he stumbled o'er a pair of shoes.

CLXXXI

A pair of shoes!—what then? not much, if they
  Are such as fit with ladies' feet; but these
(No one can tell how much I grieve to say)
  Were masculine: to see them, and to seize,
Was but a moment's act.—Ah! well-a-day!
  My teeth begin to chatter, my veins freeze—
Alfonso first examined well their fashion,
And then flew out into another passion.

CLXXXII

He left the room for his relinquish'd sword,
  And Julia instant to the closet flew.

Fly, Juan, fly! for heaven's sake—not a word—
  The door is open—you may yet slip through
The passage you so often have explored—
  Here is the garden-key. Fly—fly—Adieu!
Haste—haste! I hear Alfonso's hurrying feet—
Day has not broke—there's no one in the street.'

CLXXXIII

None can say that this was not good advice;
  The only mischief was, it came too late:
Of all experience 'tis the usual price,
  A sort of income-tax laid on by fate:
Juan had reach'd the room-door in a trice,
  And might have done so by the garden-gate,
But met Alfonso in his dressing gown,
Who threaten'd death—so Juan knock'd him down.

CLXXXIV

Dire was the scuffle, and out went the light;
  Antonia cried out 'Rape!' and Julia 'Fire!'
But not a servant stirr'd to aid the fight.
  Alfonso, pommell'd to his heart's desire,
Swore lustily he'd be revenged this night:
  And Juan, too, blasphemed an octave higher;
His blood was up; though young, he was a Tartar,
And not at all disposed to prove a martyr.

CLXXXV

Alfonso's sword had dropp'd ere he could draw it,
  And they continued battling hand to hand,
For Juan very luckily ne'er saw it;
  His temper not being under great command,
If at that moment he had chanced to claw it,
  Alfonso's days had not been in the land
Much longer.—Think of husbands', lovers' lives!
And how ye may be doubly widows—wives!

CLXXXVI

Alfonso grappled to detain the foe,
  And Juan throttled him to get away,
And blood ('twas from the nose) began to flow;
  At last, as they more faintly wrestling lay,

Juan contrived to give an awkward blow,
  And then his only garment quite gave way:
He fled, like Joseph, leaving it; but there,
I doubt, all likeness ends between the pair.

CLXXXVII

Lights came at length, and men, and maids, who found
  An awkward spectacle their eyes before;
Antonio in hysterics, Julia swoon'd,
  Alfonso leaning breathless by the door;
Some half-torn drapery scatter'd on the ground,
  Some blood and several footsteps, but no more;
Juan the gate gain'd, turn'd the key about,
And liking not the inside, lock'd the out.

CLXXXVIII

Here ends this canto. Need I sing, or say,
  How Juan naked, favour'd by the night,
Who favours what she should not, found his way,
  And reach'd his home in an unseemly plight?
The pleasant scandal which arose next day,
  The nine days' wonder which was brought to light,
And how Alfonso sued for a divorce,
Were in the English newspapers, of course.

CLXXXIX

If you would like to see the whole proceedings,
  The depositions and the cause at full,
The names of all the witnesses, the pleadings
  Of counsel to nonsuit, or to annul,
There's more than one edition, and the readings
  Are various, but they none of them are dull:
The best is that in shorthand, ta'en by Gurney,
Who to Madrid on purpose made a journey.

CXC

But Donna Inez, to divert the train
  Of one of the most circulating scandals
That had for centuries been known in Spain,
  At least since the retirement of the Vandals,
First vow'd (and never had she vow'd in vain)
  To Virgin Mary several pounds of candles;

And then, by the advice of some old ladies,
She sent her son to be shipp'd off from Cadiz.

CXCI

She had resolved that he should travel through
  All European climes by land or sea,
To mend his former morals, and get new,
  Especially in France and Italy
(At least this is the thing most people do).
  Julia was sent into a convent: she
Grieved, but perhaps her feelings may be better
Shown in the following copy of her letter:—

CXCII

'They tell me 'tis decided, you depart:
  'Tis wise—'tis well, but not the less a pain
I have no further claim on your young heart,
  Mine is the victim, and would be again;
To love too much has been the only art
  I used;—I write in haste, and if a stain
Be on this sheet, 'tis not what it appears:
My eyeballs burn and throb, but have no tears.

CXCIII

'I loved, I love you, for this love have lost
  State, station, heaven, mankind's, my own esteem;
And yet cannot regret what it hath cost,
  So dear is still the memory of that dream;
Yet if I name my guilt, 'tis not to boast,
  None can deem harshlier of me than I deem:
I trace this scrawl because I cannot rest—
I've nothing to reproach, or to request.

CXCIV

'Man's love is of man's life a thing apart,
  'Tis woman's whole existence; man may range
The court, camp, church, the vessel, and the mart,
  Sword, gown, gain, glory, offer in exchange
Pride, fame, ambition, to fill up his heart,
  And few there are whom these cannot estrange:
Men have all these resources, we but one,
To love again, and be again undone.

CXCV

'You will proceed in pleasure, and in pride,
  Beloved and loving many; all is o'er
For me on earth, except some years to hide
  My shame and sorrow deep in my heart's core,
These I could bear, but cannot cast aside
  The passion which still rages as before—
And so farewell—forgive me, love me—No;
That word is idle now—but let it go.

CXCVI

'My breast has been all weakness, is so yet;
  But still I think I can collect my mind;
My blood still rushes where my spirits set,
  As roll the waves before the settled wind;
My heart is feminine, nor can forget—
  To all, except one image, madly blind:
So shakes the needle, and so stands the pole,
As vibrates my fond heart to my fix'd soul.

CXCVII

'I have no more to say, but linger still,
  And dare not set my seal upon this sheet;
And yet I may as well the task fulfil,
  My misery can scarce be more complete:
I had not lived till now, could sorrow kill;
  Death shuns the wretch who fain the blow would meet;
And I must even survive this last adieu,
And bear with life, to love and pray for you.'

CXCVIII

This note was written upon gilt-edged paper,
  With a neat little crow-quill, slight and new;
Her small white hand could hardly reach the taper,
  It trembled as magnetic needles do,
And yet she did not let one tear escape her;
  The seal a sunflower; '*Elle vous suit partout*,'
The motto cut upon a white cornelian;
The wax was superfine, its hue vermilion.

CXCIX

This was Don Juan's earliest scrape; but whether
  I shall proceed with his adventures is

Dependent on the public altogether:
  We'll see, however, what they say to this,
Their favour in an author's cap's a feather,
  And no great mischief's done by their caprice;
And if their approbation we experience,
Perhaps they'll have some more about a year hence.

CC

My poem's epic, and is meant to be
  Divided in twelve books; each book containing,
With love, and war, a heavy gale at sea,
  A list of ships, and captains, and kings reigning,
New characters; the episodes are three:
  A panoramic view of hell's in training,
After the style of Virgil and of Homer,
So that my name of epic's no misnomer.

CCI

All these things will be specified in time,
  With strict regard to Aristotle's rules,
The *Vade Mecum* of the true sublime,
  Which makes so many poets and some fools:
Prose poets like blank verse, I'm fond of rhyme,
  Good workmen never quarrel with their tools;
I've got new mythological machinery,
And very handsome supernatural scenery.

CCII

There's only one slight difference between
  Me and my epic brethren gone before;
And here the advantage is my own, I ween
  (Not that I have not several merits more,
But this will more peculiarly be seen):
  They so embellish, that 'tis quite a bore
Their labyrinth of fables to thread through,
Whereas this story's actually true.

CCIII

If any person doubt it, I appeal
  To history, tradition, and to facts,
To newspapers, whose truth all know and feel,
  To plays in five, and operas in three, acts;

All these confirm my statement a good deal,
  But that which more completely faith exacts
Is that myself, and several now in Seville,
  *Saw* Juan's last elopement with the devil.

CCIV

If ever I should condescend to prose,
  I'll write poetical commandment, which
Shall supersede beyond all doubt all those
  That went before; in these I shall enrich
My text with many things that no one knows,
  And carry precept to the highest pitch:
I'll call the work 'Longinus o'er a Bottle;
Or, Every Poet his *own* Aristotle.'

CCV

Thou shalt believe in Milton, Dryden, Pope;
  Thou shalt not set up Wordsworth, Coleridge, Southey;
Because the first is crazed beyond all hope,
  The second drunk, the third so quaint and mouthey:
With Crabbe it may be difficult to cope,
  And Campbell's Hippocrene is somewhat drouthy:
Thou shalt not steal from Samuel Rogers, nor
Commit–flirtation with the muse of Moore.

CCVI

Thou shalt not covet Mr Sotheby's muse,
  His Pegasus, nor anything that's his;
Thou shalt not bear false witness like 'the Blues'–
  (There's one, at least, is very fond of this);
Thou shalt not write, in short, but what I choose;
  This is true criticism, and you may kiss–
Exactly as you please, or not–the rod;
But if you don't, I'll lay it on, by G–d!

CCVII

If any person should presume to assert
  This story is not moral, first, I pray
That they will not cry out before they're hurt,
  Then that they'll read it o'er again, and say
(But doubtless nobody will be so pert)
  That this is not a moral tale, though gay;

Besides, in Canto Twelfth, I mean to show
The very place where wicked people go.

CCVIII

If, after all, there should be some so blind
  To their own good, this warning to despise,
Led by some tortuosity of mind,
  Not to believe my verse and their own eyes,
And cry that they the moral cannot find,
  I tell him, if a clergyman, he lies;
Should captains the remark, or critics, make,
They also lie, too—under a mistake.

CCIX

The public approbation I expect,
  And beg they'll take my word about the moral,
Which I with their amusement will connect
  (So children cutting teeth receive a coral);
Meantime they'll doubtless please to recollect
  My epical pretensions to the laurel;
For fear some prudish readers should grow skittish,
I've bribed my grandmother's review—the *British*.

CCX

I sent it in a letter to the Editor,
  Who thank'd me duly by return of post—
I'm for a handsome article his creditor;
  Yet, if my gentle Muse he please to roast,
And break a promise after having made it her,
  Denying the receipt of what it cost,
And smear his page with gall instead of honey,
All I can say is—that he had the money.

CCXI

I think that, with this holy new alliance,
  I may ensure the public, and defy
All other magazines of art or science,
  Daily, or monthly, or three-monthly; I
Have not essay'd to multiply their clients,
  Because they tell me 'twere in vain to try,
And that the *Edinburgh Review* and *Quarterly*
Treat a dissenting author very martyrly.

CCXII

'*Non ego hoc ferrem calida juventa*
  *Consule Planco,*' Horace said, and so
Say I; by which quotation there is meant a
  Hint that, some six or seven good years ago
(Long ere I dreamt of dating from the Brenta),
  I was most ready to return a blow,
And would not brook at all this sort of thing
In my hot youth—when George the Third was king.

CCXIII

But now, at thirty years, my hair is grey—
  (I wonder what it will be like at forty?
I thought of a peruke the other day)—
  My heart is not much greener; and, in short, I
Have squander'd my whole summer while 'twas May,
  And feel no more the spirit to retort: I
Have spent my life, both interest and principal,
And deem not, what I deem'd, my soul invincible.

CCXIV

No more—no more—Oh! never more on me
  The freshness of the heart can fall like dew,
Which out of all the lovely things we see
  Extracts emotions beautiful and new,
Hived in our bosoms like the bag o' the bee:
  Think'st thou the honey with those objects grew?
Alas! 'twas not in them, but in thy power
To double even the sweetness of a flower.

CCXV

No more—no more—Oh! never more, my heart,
  Canst thou be my sole world, my universe!
Once all in all, but now a thing apart,
  Thou canst not be my blessing or my curse:
The illusion's gone for ever, and thou art
  Insensible, I trust, but none the worse,
And in thy stead I've got a deal of judgment,
Though Heaven knows how it ever found a lodgment.

CCXVI

My days of love are over; me no more
  The charms of maid, wife, and still less of widow,

Can make the fool of which they made before:
  In short, I must not lead the life I did do;
The credulous hope of mutual minds is o'er,
  The copious use of claret is forbid, too:
So for a good old-gentlemanly vice,
I think I must take up with avarice.

CCXVII

Ambition was my idol, which was broken
  Before the shrines of Sorrow and of Pleasure;
And the two last have left me many a token,
  O'er which reflection may be made at leisure:
Now, like Friar Bacon's brazen head, I've spoken,
  'Time is, Time was, Time's past;'—a chymic treasure
Is glittering youth, which I have spent betimes—
My heart in passion, and my head on rhymes.

CCXVIII

What is the end of Fame? 'tis but to fill
  A certain portion of uncertain paper:
Some liken it to climbing up a hill,
  Whose summit, like all hills, is lost in vapour:
For this men write, speak, preach, and heroes kill,
  And bards burn what they call their 'midnight taper.'
To have, when the original is dust,
A name, a wretched picture, and worse bust.

CCXIX

What are the hopes of man? Old Egypt's king
  Cheops erected the first pyramid,
And largest, thinking it was just the thing
  To keep his memory whole, and mummy hid;
But somebody or other, rummaging,
  Burglariously broke his coffin's lid:
Let not a monument give you or me hopes,
Since not a pinch of dust remains of Cheops.

CCXX

But I, being fond of true philosophy,
  Say very often to myself, 'Alas!
All things that have been born were born to die,
  And flesh (which Death mows down to hay) is grass;

You've pass'd your youth not so unpleasantly,
  And if you had it o'er again—'twould pass—
So thank your stars that matters are no worse,
And read your Bible, sir, and mind your purse.'

CCXXI

But for the present, gentle reader! and
  Still gentler purchaser! the bard—that's I—
Must, with permission, shake you by the hand,
  And so your humble servant, and good-bye!
We meet again if we should understand
  Each other; and if not, I shall not try
Your patience further than by this short sample—
'Twere well if others follow'd my example.

CCXXII

'Go, little book, from this my solitude!
  I cast thee on the waters—go thy ways!
And if, as I believe, thy vein be good,
  The world will find thee after many days.'
When Southey's read, and Wordsworth understood,
  I can't help putting in my claim to praise—
The four first rhymes are Southey's, every line;
For God's sake, reader! take them not for mine.

# FORSTER

## *My Own Centenary*

(FROM "THE TIMES" OF A.D. 2027)

It is a hundred years ago today since Forster died; we celebrate his centenary indeed within a few months of the bicentenary of Beethoven, within a few weeks of that of Blake. What special tribute shall we bring him? The question is not easy to answer, and were he himself still alive he would no doubt reply, "My work is my truest memorial." It is the reply that a great artist can always be trusted to make. Conscious of his lofty mission, endowed with the divine gift of self-expression, he may rest content, he is at peace, doubly at peace. But we, we who are not great artists, only the recipients of their bounty—what shall we say about Forster? What can we say that has not already been said about Beethoven, about Blake? Whatever shall we say?

The Dean of Dulborough, preaching last Sunday in his own beautiful cathedral, struck perhaps the truest note. Taking as his text that profound verse in Ecclesiasticus, "Let us now praise famous men," he took it word by word, paused when he came to the word "famous," and, slowly raising his voice, said: "He whose hundredth anniversary we celebrate on Thursday next is famous, and why?" No answer was needed, none came. The lofty Gothic nave, the great western windows, the silent congregation—they gave answer sufficient, and passing on to the final word of his text, "men," the Dean expatiated upon what is perhaps the most mysterious characteristic of genius, its tendency to appear among members of the human race. Why this is, why, since it is, it is not accompanied by some definite outward sign through which it might be recognized easily, are questions not lightly to be raised. There can be no doubt that his contemporaries did not recognize the greatness of Forster. Immersed in their own little affairs, they either ignored him, or forgot him, or confused him, or, strangest of all, discussed him as if he was their equal. We may smile at their blindness, but for him it can have been no laughing matter, he must have had much to bear, and indeed he could scarcely have endured to put forth masterpiece after masterpiece had he not felt assured of the verdict of posterity.

Sir Vincent Edwards, when broadcasting last night, voiced that verdict not uncertainly, and was fortunately able to employ more wealth of illustration than had been appropriate in Dulborough Minster for the Dean. The point he very properly stressed was our writer's loftiness of aim. "It would be impossible," he said, "to quote a single sentence that was not written from the very loftiest motive," and he drew from this a sharp and salutary lesson for the so-called writers of today. As permanent head of the Ministry of Edification, Sir Vincent has, we believe, frequently come into contact with the younger generation, and has checked with the kindliness of which he is a past master their self-styled individualism—an individualism which is the precise antithesis of true genius. They confuse violence with strength, cynicism with open-mindedness, frivolity with joyousness—mistakes never made by Forster who was never gay until he had earned a right to be so, and only criticized the religious and social institutions of his time because they were notoriously corrupt. We know what the twentieth century was. We know the sort of men who were in power under George V. We know what the State was, what were the churches. We can as easily conceive of Beethoven as a Privy Councillor or of Blake as, forsooth, an Archbishop as of this burning and sensitive soul acquiescing in the deadening conditions of his age. What he worked for—what all great men work for—was for a New Jerusalem, a vitalized State, a purified Church; and the offertory at Dulborough last Sunday, like the success of Sir Edward's appeal for voluntary workers under the Ministry, show that he did not labour in vain.

The official ceremony is for this morning. This afternoon Lady Turton will unveil Mr. Boston Jack's charming statue in Kensington Gardens, and so illustrate another aspect of our national hero: his love of little children. It had originally been Mr. Boston Jack's intention to represent him as pursuing an ideal. Since, however, the Gardens are largely frequented by the young and their immediate supervisors, it was felt that something more whimsical would be in place, and a butterfly was substituted. The change is certainly for the better. It is true that we cannot have too many ideals. On the other hand, we must not have too much of them too soon, nor, attached as it will be to a long copper wire, can the butterfly be confused with any existing species and regarded as an incentive to immature collectors. Lady Turton will couple her remarks with an appeal for the Imperial Daisy Chain, of which she is the energetic Vice-President, and simultaneously there will be a flag collection throughout the provinces.

Dulborough, the Ministry of Edification, the official ceremony, Kensington Gardens! What more could be said? Not a little. Yet enough has been said to remind the public of its heritage, and to emphasize and define the central essence of these immortal works. And what is that essence? Need we say? Not their greatness—they are obviously great.

*The Pleasure of Their Company*

Not their profundity—they are admittedly profound. It is something more precious than either: their nobility. Noble works, nobly conceived, nobly executed, nobler than the Ninth Symphony or the *Songs of Innocence*. Here is no small praise, yet it can be given, we are in the presence of the very loftiest, we need not spare or mince our words, nay, we will add one more word, a word that has been implicit in all that have gone before: like Beethoven, like Blake, Forster was essentially English, and in commemorating him we can yet again celebrate what is best and most permanent in ourselves.

# ERASMUS

## From *The Praise of Folly*

*Folly speaks*: You have my name, gentlemen . . . gentlemen . . . what shall I add by way of an epithet? What but "most foolish"? For by what more honorable style could the Goddess of Folly address her devotees? But since it is not known to very many from what stock I have sprung, I shall now attempt, with the Muses' kind help, to set this forth. Not Chaos, or Orcus, or Saturn, or Iapetus, or any other of that old-fashioned and musty set of gods, was my father at all. It was Plutus, who only, in spite of Hesiod, Homer, and Jove himself to boot, is "the father of gods and men." At a single nod of Plutus, as of old so nowadays, all things sacred and profane are turned topsy-turvy. At his pleasure, all war, peace, empires, plans, judgments, assemblies, marriages, treaties, pacts, laws, arts, sports, weighty matters (my breath is giving out)—in short, all public and private affairs of mortal men, are governed. Without his help all that population of deities of the poets' making—nay, I speak very boldly, even those top gods—either would not exist at all or would be "diners at home," keeping house very meagrely. To the person who rouses Plutus's anger Pallas herself cannot bring help enough; on the other hand, whoever possesses his favor can bid great Jove and his thunder go hang themselves. "I glory to have such a father." And he did not procreate me out of his head, as Jupiter did that austere and homely Pallas; but rather out of Youth, the loveliest nymph of all, and the jolliest as well. Nor did he do this confined in the irksome marriage-bond—the way that blacksmith was born lame!—but indeed he did it in a much pleasanter manner, "mingled in love," as our father Homer puts it. Yet, make no mistake, it was not the Plutus of Aristophanes, already decrepit and weak in the eyes, that engendered me, but the same god healthy and as yet heated by his youth; nor by youth only, but also by nectar, which he had chanced to drink rather copiously and rather straight at a banquet of the gods.

If you are also wanting to know the place of my nativity (seeing that in these days it is accounted a prime point of nobility, in what place you uttered your first cries), I was not brought forth in floating Delos, or on the foaming sea, or "in hollow caverns," but right in the Fortunate Isles, where all things grow "without ploughing or planting." In those islands is no drudgery or old age, nor is there any sickness. In the fields one never sees a daffodil, mallow, leek, bean, or any of such kind of trash; but one's eyes and nose are enchanted at the same time by moly, panacea, nepenthes, sweet marjoram, ambrosia, lotus, rose, violet, hyacinth, and the gardens of Adonis. And being born among these delights, I did not enter upon life with weeping, but right off I laughed sweetly at my mother. Nor indeed do I envy great Jupiter his nurse, a she-goat, since two charming nymphs nourished me at their breasts—Drunkenness, offspring of Bacchus, and Ignorance, Pan's daughter.

These two you see here in the company of my other attendants and followers. If you wish to know all their names, you will not hear them from me, so help me, except in Greek. This one whom you observe here, with the eyebrows haughtily raised, is Philautia. She with the smiling eyes, so to speak, whom you see clapping her hands, is named Kolakia. The one who is half asleep, and like a drowsy person, is called Lethe. She that leans on her elbows, with her hands folded, is Misoponia. Hedone is the one wearing the rosy wreath and smelling of perfumes. The lady with the uncertain eyes rolling here and there is called Anoia; and she with the glistening skin and body in good point is Tryphe. You see also two male gods among the girls, one of whom they call Comus, the other Negretos Hypnos. These, I say, are my household servants, with whose faithful help I bring every sort of thing under my rule, maintaining my empire even over emperors.

You have learned of my family, upbringing, and companions. Now, that it may not look as if I have usurped the name of goddess for myself without good grounds, please give closest attention while I tell how many advantages I bestow on both gods and men, and how broadly my power is displayed. For if, as some one has judiciously observed, this only is to be a god, to help men, and if deservedly they have been admitted to the rank of gods who have shown to mortals the use of wine, or grain, or any other such commodity, why am not I of right named and venerated as the *alpha* of all gods, who single-handed bestow all things on all men?

In the first place, what can be dearer or more precious than life? And the beginning and first principle of life is owed to whom else but me? Not the spear of "potent-fathered" Pallas, not the shield of "cloud-compelling" Jove, procreates the children of men or multiplies their race. Even he, the father of gods and king of men, who shakes all heaven by a nod, is obliged to lay aside his three-pronged thunder and that Titanic aspect by which, when he pleases, he scares all the gods, and assume another character in the slavish manner of an actor, if he wishes to do what he never refrains from doing, that is to say, to beget children. Now the Stoics believe that they are next-door neighbors to gods. But give me a triple Stoic, or a quadruple one, or, if you will, a

Stoic multiplied by six hundred; if for this purpose he will not put off his beard, the ensign of wisdom (though displayed also by goats), yet he will certainly lay by his gravity, smooth his brow, renounce his rock-bound principles, and for a few minutes toy and talk nonsense. In fine, the wise man must send for me, I repeat, if he ever wishes to become a father. And why not speak to you still more frankly, as is my fashion? I beg to inquire whether the head, whether the face, the breast, the hand, or the ear—all of them accounted honorable members—generates gods and men? I judge not; nay, rather that foolish, even silly, part which cannot be named without laughter, is the propagator of the human race. This is at last that sacred spring from which all things derive existence, more truly than from the elemental tetrad of Pythagoras.

Now tell me, what man, by heaven, could wish to stick his head into the halter of marriage if, as your wiseacres have the habit of doing, he first weighed with himself the inconveniences of wedded life? Or what woman would ever admit her husband to her person, if she had heard or thought about the dangerous pains of child-birth and the irksomeness of bringing up a child? But since you owe your existence to the marriage-bed, and marriage is owing to Anoia, a servant of mine, you can see how vastly indebted you are to me! Then, too, would a woman who has gone through all this, wish to make a second venture, if the power and influence of my Lethe did not attend her? And in spite of what Lucretius claims, Venus herself would not deny that without the addition of my presence her strength would be enfeebled and ineffectual. So it is that from this brisk and silly little game of mine come forth the haughty philosophers (to whose places those who are vulgarly called monks have now succeeded), and kings in their scarlet, pious priests, and triply most holy popes; also, finally, that assembly of the gods of the poets, so numerous that Olympus, spacious as it is, can hardly accommodate the crowd.

But let it be accounted a little thing that the seed-plot and source of existence are mine, if I do not show that whatever is profitable in any life is also of my giving. For what about it? Can life be called life at all if you take away pleasure? . . . You applaud! I knew that none of you is so wise—or rather so foolish—no, I prefer to say so wise—as to err on that point. Even the famous Stoics do not really scorn pleasure, but they studiously dissemble and attack it in public with a thousand reproaches, only to the end that, with other people scared off, they may enjoy it more liberally. But let them tell me, by Jove, what part of life is not sad, unpleasant, graceless, flat, and burdensome, unless you have pleasure added to it, that is, a seasoning of folly? As proof of this, there is extant that lovely tribute to me by Sophocles, who can never be sufficiently praised, "To know nothing affords the happiest life"; and he would be authority enough, but come, I will open the whole matter, step by step.

First of all, who does not know that the earliest period of a man's life is by far the happiest for him and by far the most pleasant for all about him? What is it in children, that we should kiss them the way we do, and cuddle them, and fondle them—so that even an enemy would give aid to one of that age—except this enchantment of folly, which prudent nature carefully bestows on the newly born; so that by this pleasure, as a sort of prepayment, they win the favor of their nurses and parents and make these forget the pains of bringing them up. After this comes adolescence. How welcome it is in every home! How well everyone wishes it! How studiously does everyone promote it, how officiously they lend it the helping hand! But, I ask, whence comes this grace of youth? Whence but from me, by whose favor the young know so little—and how lightly worn is that little! And presently when lads grown larger begin, through experience and discipline, to have some smack of manhood, I am a liar if by the same token the brightness of their beauty does not fade, their quickness diminish, their wit lose its edge, their vigor slacken. The farther one gets from me, then, the less and less he lives, until *molesta senectus* (that is, irksome old age) arrives, hateful to others, to be sure, but also and more so to itself.

Old age would not be tolerable to any mortal at all, were it not that I, out of pity for its troubles, stand once more at its right hand; and just as the gods of the poets customarily save, by some metamorphosis or other, those who are dying, in like manner I bring those who have one foot in the grave back to their infancy again, for as long as possible; so that the folk are not far off in speaking of them as "in their second childhood." If anyone would like to know the method of bringing about this alteration, I shall not conceal it. I lead them to my spring of Lethe—for that stream rises in the Fortunate Isles, and only a little rivulet of it flows in the underworld—so that then and there they may drink draughts of forgetfulness. With their cares of mind purged away, by gentle stages they become young again. But now, you say, they merely dote, and play the fool. Yes, quite so. But precisely this it is to renew one's infancy. Is to be childish anything other than to dote and play the fool? As if in that age the greatest joy were not this, that one knows nothing! For who does not dread and shun as a prodigy the boy who has a man's wisdom? As the proverb current among the folk has it, "I hate a boy of premature wisdom." Who could bear to converse or transact business with an old man who should join to his long experience of things, an equal vigor of mind and sharpness of judgment? Hence it is that an old man dotes, thanks to me.

Yet this dotard of mind, meanwhile, is exempt from those carking cares by which your wise man is distracted. My dotard, too, is still an acceptable pot-companion. He does not feel life's tedium, which a younger constitution can scarce abide. Occasionally, like the old gentleman in Plautus, he goes back to conning those three letters, *a, m, o*—the unhappiest man in the world if he had his wits about him; but meanwhile happy, through my grace, a source of pleasure to his friends, a hail-fellow-well-met. Thus it is that, in Homer, speech sweeter than honey flows from the lips of Nestor, while that of Achilles is bitter; and in the same author the old men sitting on the wall utter gracious and elegant discourse. On this one score, indeed, the old even have an advantage over real childhood, which is sweet but tongue-tied, and lacks the chief solace of life, uninhibited garrulousness. Add to this that the old take great pleasure in children, and children in turn are delighted with the old. "God ever brings like to like." For wherein do they differ, except that age is more wrinkled and has counted more birthdays? Otherwise, their whitish hair, mouth without teeth, shortened body, appetite for milk, babbling, chatter, toying, shortness of memory, heedlessness, and all their other traits, agree exactly. And the farther the old proceed in age, the nearer they come back to the semblance of childhood; until like children indeed, having no weariness of life or sense of death, they take leave of the world.

Now let anyone that will compare this boon of mine with the metamorphoses produced by other gods. Those which they worked when angry it is not well to mention; but take the stories of people toward whom they were especially friendly. They would transform somebody into a tree, or a bird, or a cicada, or even into a snake; as if this were not to perish indeed—to be made into something else! But I restore the very same man to the best and happiest part of his life. And if mortals would abstain utterly from any contact with wisdom, and live out their span continuously in my company, there would not be any such thing as old age, but in happiness they would enjoy perpetual youth. For do you not see that the austere fellows who are buried in the study of philosophy, or condemned to difficult and wracking business, grow old even before they have been young—and this because by cares and continual hard driving of their brains they insensibly exhaust their spirits and dry up their radical moisture? On the contrary, my morons are as plump and sleek as the hogs of Acarnania (as the saying is), with complexions well cared for, never feeling the touch of old age; unless, as rarely happens, they catch something by contagion from the wise—so true is it that the life of man is not destined to be in every respect happy.

These arguments have the strong support of a proverb current among the folk; as they often say, "Folly is the one thing that makes fleeting youth linger and keeps ugly old age away." And rightly do they bruit it about concerning the people of Brabant, that although time brings prudence to others, the older Brabanters grow, the more foolish they are. Yet no other race is more genial than theirs in the ordinary converse of life, and no other race feels so little the misery of old age. Neighbors to the Brabanters, by affinity of temperament as much as by geography, are my Hollanders—for why should I not call mine those who are such eager amateurs of folly that they have won a proverbial name for it, a name they are not ashamed of, but bandy back and forth among themselves?

Go, foolish mortals, and vainly seek for your Medeas and Circes and Venuses and Auroras, and the unknown fountain in which you may restore your youth! When all the time I alone have that power; I alone use it. In my shop is that miraculous juice with which the daughter of Memnon lengthened the days of her grandfather Tithonus. I am that Venus by whose favor Phaon grew young again so that he might be loved so much by Sappho. Mine are those herbs (if they exist), mine that fountain, mine the spells which not only bring back departed youth but, still better, preserve it in perpetuity. If, then, all of you subscribe to this sentiment, that nothing is better than adolescence or more undesirable than age, I think you must see how much you owe to me, who conserve so great a good and fend off so great an evil.

But what am I doing, talking about mortal men? Survey the universal sky, and you may cast my name in my teeth if you can find anyone at all among the gods who is not foul and despicable except so far as he is graced by my divine power. For why is Bacchus always young and curly-haired? Simply because, frantic and giddy, he passes his life in feasts, routs, dances, and games, and has no tittle of converse with Pallas. So far is he from wanting to be accounted wise, in brief, that it tickles him to be worshipped in gambols and sport; nor is he offended by the proverb which gave him the nickname of fool, as thus: "More foolish than Morychus." For as time went on they changed his name to Morychus, because the wanton countryfolk used to smear his statue, placed before the gates of his temple, with new wine and fresh figs. And then what scoffs the Old Comedy throws at him! "O stupid god," they say, "and worthy to be born from a thigh!" But who would not choose to be stupid and foolish Bacchus, always festive, always downy of cheek, always bringing gaiety and delight to all, rather than to be "deep-counselled" Jove, who frightens everybody, or Pan in his peevishness, infecting all things with his disorders, or Vulcan, full of cinders and foul from the labors of his shop, or even Pallas herself, "always peering grimly," with her Gorgon's head and fearful spear? Why is Cupid forever a boy? Why, but because he is a trifler, and cannot do or even consider anything at all sane. Why does the beauty of the aureate Venus keep an eternal spring? Surely because she is related to me; whence also she bears in her face my father's color, and for that reason in Homer she is "golden Aphrodite." Lastly, she laughs perpetually, if we can in anything believe the poets or their rivals, the sculptors. What divinity did the Romans ever worship more devoutly than Flora, that breeder of all delights? Nay, if one faithfully seeks in Homer to learn the story of the austere gods, he will find it replete with folly. But why stop to record the doings of the others, when you know so well the loves and pastimes of Jove the Thunderer himself? When the chaste Diana, forgetting her sex, does nothing but hunt, being all the time desperately in love with Endymion? . . .

But now the time has come when, following the pattern of Homer, we should turn our backs on the heavens and travel down again to earth, where likewise we shall perceive nothing joyous or fortunate except by my favor. First of all, you see with what foresight nature, the source and artificer of the human race, has made provision that this race shall never lack its seasoning of folly. For since, by the Stoic definitions, wisdom is no other than to be governed by reason, while folly is to be moved at the whim of the passions, Jupiter, to the end, obviously, that the life of mankind should not be sad and harsh, put in—how much more of passions than of reason? Well, the proportions run about one pound to half an ounce. Besides, he imprisoned reason in a cramped corner of the head, and turned over all the rest of the body to the emotions. After that he instated two most violent tyrants, as it were, in opposition to reason: anger, which holds the citadel of the breast, and consequently the very spring of life, the heart; and lust, which rules a broad empire lower down, even to the privy parts. How much reason is good for, against these twin forces, the ordinary life of men sufficiently reveals when reason—and it is all she can do—shouts out her prohibitions until she is hoarse and dictates formulas of virtue. But the passions simply bid their so-called king go hang himself, and more brazenly roar down the opposition, until the man, tired out as well, willingly yields and knuckles under.

But a tiny bit more than a grain of reason is vouchsafed to the male, born as he is for handling affairs; and in order that he might give and take counsel in manly fashion, he brought me into the council chamber, as everywhere else. Right off I gave him advice worthy of myself: namely, that he should form an alliance with woman—a stupid animal, God wot, and a giddy one, yet funny and sweet—so that in domestic familiarity her folly might leaven the lumpishness of the male temperament. When Plato shows himself in doubt whether to place woman in the class of rational creatures or in that of brutes, he only wishes to point out how flagrant is the folly of the sex. For if by chance some woman wishes to be thought of as wise, she does nothing but show herself twice a fool. It is as if one took a bull to the masseuse, a thing quite "against the grain," as the phrase is. It is doubly a fault, you know, when against nature one assumes the color of a virtue, warping one's character in a direction not its own. Just as, according to the proverb of the Greeks, "an ape is always an ape, though dressed in scarlet," so a woman is always a woman—that is, a fool—whatever part she may have chosen to play.

And yet I do not suppose the female sex is so foolish as to become incensed at me for this, that I, a woman and Folly as well, attribute folly to women. For if they rightly consider the matter, they are bound to score up a credit to Folly for this, that in many respects they are better off than men. For one thing, they have the gift of beauty, which with good reason they prefer above all things else. Assisted by it, they wield a tyranny over tyrants themselves. Whence but from the malady of prudence comes that horrendous visage, rough as to skin, with an undergrowth of beard and a suggestion of senility, in men? Whereas the cheeks of women are always bare and smooth, their voice gentle, their skin soft, as if presenting a picture of perpetual youth. Furthermore, what else do they want in life but to be as attractive as possible to men? Do not all their trimmings and cosmetics have this end in view, and all their baths, fittings, creams, scents, as well—and all those arts of making up, painting, and fashioning the face, eyes, and skin? Just so. And by what other sponsor are they better recommended to men than by folly? What is there that men will not permit to women? But for what consideration, except pleasure? And women please by no other thing than their folly. The truth of this no one will deny who has considered what nonsense a man talks with a woman, and what quaint tricks he plays, as often as he has a mind to enjoy the delights of feminine society.

You have heard, then, about the source whence flows the first and sovereign solace of life. But there are some men, principally old ones, who are topers rather than womanizers, and decree that the highest pleasure lies in bouts of drinking. Whether there can be any genteel entertainment with no woman present, let others decide. This remains certain: without some relish of folly, no banquet is pleasing. Hence if someone is not present who creates laughter by his real or simulated folly, the revellers send out and get a comedian for hire, or bring in some other silly parasite, who by his jests—that is, foolish gibes—will drive silence and moroseness away from the company. For what avails it to load the belly with all those fine wines, savory dishes, and rare meats, if similarly our eyes and ears, our whole souls, do not batten on laughter, jests, and witticisms? I am the only confectioner of these desserts. Yes, and those other ceremonies of banquets, such as choosing a king by lot, playing at dice, drinking healths, sending the cups around, singing in rounds and relays, dancing, mimicking—the Seven Sages of Greece did not discover these for the solace of mankind; I did. The nature of all this sort of thing is such that the more of folly it has in it, the more it advantages the life of men, which surely ought not to be called life at all if it is unhappy. Yet unhappy it must needs be, unless by diversions of this kind you chase away ennui, the brother of unhappiness.

Yet there are others, perhaps, who do not care for this department of pleasure either, but find satisfaction in the love and familiar society of friends, letting it be known that friendship uniquely deserves to be preferred above all else; as being so necessary a thing that not air, fire, or water is more so; and so delightful that he who would take it from the world would take the sun from the sky; and lastly so honorable (as if honor had something to do with the subject) that the philosophers themselves have not hesitated to name it among the greatest goods. But what if I demonstrate that I am both the stem and the stern of this admired good also? And I shall not demonstrate it by ambiguous syllogisms, sorites, horned dilemmas, or any other sophistical subtleties of that sort; but by crude common sense, as the phrase is, I shall point it out as plainly as if with my finger. Go to! Conniving at your friends' vices, passing them over, being blind to them and deceived by them, even loving and admiring your friends' egregious faults as if they were virtues—does not this seem pretty close to folly? Think a moment of the fellow who kisses the mole on his mistress's neck, or of the other who is delighted by the growth on his little lady's nose, or of the father who says of his cross-eyed son that his eyes twinkle? What is all this, I ask you, but sheer folly? Ay, you all vote—triple and quadruple foolishness! Yet this same foolishness both joins friends and, after joining them, keeps their friendship alive. . . .

What has been said of friendship applies even better to marriage, which is an indivisible bond of life. Good Lord, what divorces, or worse things, would not happen all over the place, were not the domestic association of man and woman propped up and fostered by flattery, by jesting, by pliableness, ignorance, dissimulation—satellites of mine, remember! Mercy me, how few marriages would come off, if the husband prudently inquired what tricks his seemingly coy and modest little lady had played long before the wedding! And still fewer, though entered upon, would last, did not most of the wife's doings escape her husband's knowledge, through his negligence or stupidity. But these blessings are owed to Folly. She brings it about that the wife pleases the husband, the husband pleases the wife, the household is tranquil, the alliance holds. A husband is laughed at, called cuckoo, cuckold, or what not, when he kisses away the tears of his whorish wife; but how much happier thus to be deceived than to harass himself by an unresting jealousy and to spoil everything with distressing brawls.

In sum, no society, no union in life, could be either pleasant or lasting without me. A people does not for long tolerate its prince, or a master tolerate his servant, a handmaiden her mistress, a teacher his student, a friend his friend, a wife her husband, a landlord his tenant, a partner his partner, or a boarder his fellow-boarder, except as they mutually or by turns are mistaken, on occasion flatter, on occasion wisely wink, and otherwise soothe themselves with the sweetness of folly.

Now I am aware that this seems the most that can be said, but you are going to hear what is greater. I ask you: will he who hates himself love anyone? Will he who does not get along with himself agree with another? Or will he who is disagreeable and irksome to himself bring pleasure to any? No one would say so, unless he were himself more foolish than Folly. But were you to bar me out, each man would be so incapable of getting along with any other that he would become a stench in his own nostrils, his possessions would be filthy rags, and he would be hateful to himself. The reason for this is that nature, in many respects a stepmother rather than a mother, has sowed some seed of evil in the breasts of mortal men, and particularly of men somewhat judicious, which makes them dissatisfied with what is their own, while admiring what belongs to another. Thus it comes about that every endowment, every grace and elegance of life, suffers taint and is lost. For what avails beauty, chiefest gift of the immortal gods, if it is touched by the malady of decay? What price youth, if it is infected by the germs of age? And finally, what in the whole business of life, whether private or public, can you carry through with grace—for not only in art but in every action the great thing is to do whatever you do in a seemly way—except as this lady, Philautia, stands at your right hand, she who by merit takes the place of sister to me, and everywhere plays my part with fidelity?

For what is so foolish as to be satisfied with yourself? Or to admire yourself? Yet on the other hand, if you are displeased with yourself, what can you do that is pleasing or graceful or seemly? Take this ingredient from life, and at once the orator, like his style, will be flat and cold, the musician will be as sour as his notes, the actor, with all his mimicry, will be hissed from the stage, the painter as well as his pictures will be cheap, and the poor doctor will famish among his poor medicines. Without self-love, though you may be a handsome Nireus, you will appear like Thersites; you will seem a Nestor, though a Phaon; a sow instead of Minerva, tongue-tied instead of eloquent, a gawk instead of a man of the world. That is how necessary it is to capture your own fancy, and to appreciate your own value by a bit of self-applause, before you can be held in price by others. Finally, since the better part of happiness is to wish to be what you are, why certainly my Philautia reaches that end by a short cut; so that no one is ashamed of his own looks, no one regrets his own temperament, or feels shame for his race, his locality, his profession, or his fatherland. An Irishman does not want to change places with an Italian, or a Thracian with an Athenian, or a Scythian with a dweller in the Fortunate Isles. Oh, the singular foresight of nature, who, in spite of such differences of condition, equalizes all things! Where she has withheld some of her bounties, there she is wont to add a little more self-love; but I have made a foolish saying, for self-love is itself the greatest bounty of nature.

# ALDOUS HUXLEY

## *The Tillotson Banquet*

### I

YOUNG Spode was not a snob; he was too intelligent for that, too fundamentally decent. Not a snob; but all the same he could not help feeling very well pleased at the thought that he was dining, alone and intimately, with Lord Badgery. It was a definite event in his life, a step forward, he felt, towards that final success, social, material, and literary, which he had come to London with the fixed intention of making. The conquest and capture of Badgery was an almost essential strategical move in the campaign.

Edmund, forty-seventh Baron Badgery, was a lineal descendant of that Edmund, surnamed Le Blayreau, who landed on English soil in the train of William the Conqueror. Ennobled by William Rufus, the Badgerys had been one of the very few baronial families to survive the Wars of the Roses and all the other changes and chances of English history. They were a sensible and philoprogenitive race. No Badgery had ever fought in any war, no Badgery had ever engaged in any kind of politics. They had been content to live and quietly to propagate their species in a huge machicolated Norman castle, surrounded by a triple moat, only sallying forth to cultivate their property and to collect their rents. In the eighteenth century, when life had become relatively secure, the Badgerys began to venture forth into civilised society. From boorish squires they blossomed into *grands seigneurs*, patrons of the arts, virtuosi. Their property was large, they were rich; and with the growth of industrialism their riches also grew. Villages on their estate turned into manufacturing towns, unsuspected coal was discovered beneath the surface of their barren moorlands. By the middle of the nineteenth century the Badgerys were among the richest of English noble families. The forty-seventh baron disposed of an income of at least two hundred thousand pounds a year. Following the great Badgery tradition, he had refused to have anything to do with politics or war. He occupied himself by collecting pictures; he took an interest in theatrical productions; he was the friend and patron of men of letters, of painters, and musicians. A personage, in a word, of considerable consequence in that particular world in which young Spode had elected to make his success.

Spode had only recently left the university. Simon Gollamy, the editor of the *World's Review* (the "Best of all possible Worlds"), had got to know him—he was always on the look out for youthful talent—had seen possibilities in the young man, and appointed him art critic of his paper. Gollamy liked to have young and teachable people about him. The possession of disciples flattered his vanity, and he found it easier, moreover, to run his paper with docile collaborators than with men grown obstinate and case-hardened with age. Spode had not done badly at his new job. At any rate, his articles had been intelligent enough to arouse the interest of Lord Badgery. It was, ultimately, to them that he owed the honour of sitting to-night in the dining-room of Badgery House.

Fortified by several varieties of wine and a glass of aged brandy, Spode felt more confident and at ease than he had done the whole evening. Badgery was rather a disquieting host. He had an alarming habit of changing the subject of any conversation that had lasted for more than two minutes. Spode had found it, for example, horribly mortifying when his host, cutting across what was, he prided himself, a particularly subtle and illuminating disquisition on baroque art, had turned a wandering eye about the room and asked him abruptly whether he liked parrots. He had flushed and glanced suspiciously towards him, fancying that the man was trying to be offensive. But no; Badgery's white, fleshy, Hanoverian face wore an expression of perfect good faith. There was no malice in his small greenish eyes. He evidently did genuinely want to know if Spode liked parrots. The young man swallowed his irritation and replied that he did. Badgery then told a good story about parrots. Spode was on the point of capping it with a better story, when his host began to talk about Beethoven. And so the game went on. Spode cut his conversation to suit his host's requirements. In the course of ten minutes he had made a more or less witty epigram on Benvenuto Cellini, Queen Victoria, sport, God, Stephen Phillips, and Moorish architecture. Lord Badgery thought him the most charming young man, and so intelligent.

"If you've quite finished your coffee," he said, rising to his feet as he spoke, "we'll go and look at the pictures."

Spode jumped up with alacrity, and only then realised that he had drunk just ever so little too much. He would have to be careful, talk deliberately, plant his feet consciously, one after the other.

"This house is quite cluttered up with pictures," Lord Badgery complained. "I had a whole wagon-load taken away to the country last week; but there are still far too many. My ancestors would have their portraits painted by Romney. Such a shocking artist, don't you think? Why couldn't they have chosen Gainsborough, or even Reynolds? I've had all the Romneys hung in the servants' hall now. It's such a comfort to know that one can never possibly see them again. I suppose you know all about the ancient Hittites?"

"Well . . ." the young man replied, with befitting modesty.

"Look at that, then." He indicated a large stone head which stood in a case near the dining-room door. "It's not Greek, or Egyptian, or Persian, or anything else; so if it isn't ancient Hittite, I don't know what it is. And that reminds me of that story about Lord George Sanger, the Circus King . . ." and, without giving Spode time to examine the Hittite relic, he led the way up the huge staircase, pausing every now and then in his anecdote to point out some new object of curiosity or beauty.

"I suppose you know Deburau's pantomimes?" Spode rapped out as soon as the story was over. He was in an itch to let out his information about Deburau. Badgery had given him a perfect opening with his ridiculous Sanger. "What a perfect man, isn't he? He used to . . ."

"This is my main gallery," said Lord Badgery, throwing open one leaf of a tall folding door. "I must apologise for it. It looks like a roller-skating rink." He fumbled with the electric switches and there was suddenly light—light that revealed an enormous gallery, duly receding into distance according to all the laws of perspective. "I dare say you've heard of my poor father," Lord Badgery continued. "A little insane, you know; sort of mechanical genius with a screw loose. He used to have a toy railway in this room. No end of fun he had, crawling about the floor after his trains. And all the pictures were stacked in the cellars. I can't tell you what they were like when I found them: mushrooms growing out of the Botticellis. Now I'm rather proud of this Poussin; he painted it for Scarron."

"Exquisite!" Spode exclaimed, making with his hand a gesture as though he were modelling a pure form in the air. "How splendid the onrush of those trees and leaning figures is! And the way they're caught up, as it were, and stemmed by that single godlike form opposing them with his contrary movement! And the draperies . . ."

But Lord Badgery had moved on, and was standing in front of a little fifteenth-century Virgin of carved wood.

"School of Rheims," he explained.

They "did" the gallery at high speed. Badgery never permitted his guest to halt for more than forty seconds before any work of art. Spode would have liked to spend a few moments of recollection and tranquillity in front of some of these lovely things. But it was not permitted.

The gallery done, they passed into a little room leading out of it. At the sight of what the lights revealed, Spode gasped.

"It's like something out of Balzac," he exclaimed. "Un de ces salons dorés où se déploie un luxe insolent. You know."

"My nineteenth-century chamber," Badgery explained. "The best thing of its kind, I flatter myself, outside the State Apartments at Windsor."

Spode tiptoed round the room, peering with astonishment at all the objects in glass, in gilded bronze, in china, in feathers, in embroidered and painted silk, in beads, in wax, objects of the most fantastic shapes and colours, all the queer products of a decadent tradition, with which the room was crowded. There were paintings on the walls—a Martin, a Wilkie, an early Landseer, several Ettys, a big Haydon, a slight pretty water-colour of a girl by Wainewright, the pupil of Blake and arsenic poisoner, a score of others. But the picture which arrested Spode's attention was a medium sized canvas representing Troilus riding into Troy among the flowers and plaudits of an admiring crowd, and oblivious (you could see from his expression) of everything but the eyes of Cressida, who looked down at him from a window, with Pandarus smiling over her shoulder.

"What an absurd and enchanting picture!" Spode exclaimed.

"Ah, you've spotted my Troilus." Lord Badgery was pleased.

"What bright harmonious colours! Like Etty's, only stronger, not so obviously pretty. And there's an energy about it that reminds one of Haydon. Only Haydon could never have done anything so impeccable in taste. Who is it by?" Spode turned to his host inquiringly.

"You were right in detecting Haydon." Lord Badgery answered. "It's by his pupil, Tillotson. I wish I could get hold of more of his work. But nobody seems to know anything about him. And he seems to have done so little."

This time it was the younger man who interrupted.

"Tillotson, Tillotson . . ." He put his hand to his forehead. A frown incongruously distorted his round, floridly curved face. "No . . . yes, I have it." He looked up triumphantly with serene and childish brows. "Tillotson, Walter Tillotson—the man's still alive."

Badgery smiled. "This picture was painted in 1846, you know."

"Well, that's all right. Say he was born in 1820, painted his masterpiece when he was twenty-six, and it's 1913 now; that's to say he's only ninety-three. Not as old as Titian yet."

"But he's not been heard of since 1860," Lord Badgery protested.

"Precisely. Your mention of his name reminded me of the discovery I made the other day when I was looking through the obituary notices in the archives of the *World's Review*. (One has to bring them up to date every year or so for fear of being caught napping if one of these old birds chooses to shuffle off suddenly.) Well, there, among them—I remember my astonishment at the time—there I found Walter Tillotson's biography. Pretty full to 1860, and then a blank, except for a pencil note in the early nineteen hundreds to the effect that he had returned from the East. The obituary has never been used or added to. I draw the obvious conclusion: the old chap isn't dead yet. He's just been overlooked somehow."

"But this is extraordinary," Lord Badgery exclaimed. "You must find him, Spode—you must find him. I'll commission him to paint frescoes round this room. It's just what I've always vainly longed for—a real nineteenth-century artist to decorate this place for me. Oh, we must find him at once—at once."

Lord Badgery strode up and down in a state of great excitement.

"I can see how this room could be made quite perfect," he went on. "We'd clear away all these cases and have the whole of that wall filled by a heroic fresco of Hector and Andromache, or 'Distraining for Rent,' or Fanny Kemble as Belvidera in 'Venice Preserved'—anything like that, provided it's in the grand manner of the 'thirties and 'forties. And here I'd have a landscape with lovely receding perspectives, or else something architectural and grand in the style of Belshazzar's feast. Then we'll have this Adam fireplace taken down and replaced by something Mauro-Gothic. And on these walls I'll have mirrors, or no! let me see . . ."

He sank into meditative silence, from which he finally roused himself to shout:

"The old man, the old man! Spode, we must find this astonishing old creature. And don't breathe a word to anybody. Tillotson shall be our secret. Oh, it's too perfect, it's incredible! Think of the frescoes."

Lord Badgery's face had become positively animated. He had talked of a single subject for nearly a quarter of an hour.

## II

Three weeks later Lord Badgery was aroused from his usual after-luncheon somnolence by the arrival of a telegram. The message was a short one. "Found.—SPODE." A look of pleasure and intelligence made human Lord Badgery's clayey face of surfeit. "No answer," he said. The footman padded away on noiseless feet.

Lord Badgery closed his eyes and began to contemplate. Found! What a room he would have! There would be nothing like it in the world. The frescoes, the fireplace, the mirrors, the ceiling. . . . And a small, shrivelled old man clambering about the scaffolding, agile and quick like one of those whiskered little monkeys at the Zoo, painting away, painting away. . . . Fanny Kemble as Belvidera, Hector and Andromache, or why not the Duke of Clarence in the Butt, the Duke of Malmsey, the Butt of Clarence. . . . Lord Badgery was asleep.

Spode did not lag long behind his telegram. He was at Badgery House by six o'clock. His lordship was in the nineteenth-century chamber, engaged in clearing away with his own hands the bric-à-brac. Spode found him looking hot and out of breath.

"Ah, there you are," said Lord Badgery. "You see me already preparing for the great man's coming. Now you must tell me all about him."

"He's older even than I thought," said Spode. "He's ninety-seven this year. Born in 1816. Incredible, isn't it! There, I'm beginning at the wrong end."

"Begin where you like," said Badgery genially.

"I won't tell you all the incidents of the hunt. You've no idea what a job I had to run him to earth. It was like a Sherlock Holmes story, immensely elaborate, too elaborate. I shall write a book about it some day. At any rate, I found him at last."

"Where?"

"In a sort of respectable slum in Holloway, older and poorer and lonelier than you could have believed possible. I found out how it was he came to be forgotten, how he came to drop out of life in the way he did. He took it into his head, somewhere about the 'sixties, to go to Palestine to get local colour for his religious pictures—scapegoats and things, you know. Well, he went to Jerusalem and then on to Mount Lebanon and on and on, and then, somewhere in the middle of Asia Minor, he got stuck. He got stuck for about forty years."

"But what did he do all that time?"

"Oh, he painted, and started a mission, and converted three Turks, and taught the local Pashas the rudiments of English, Latin, and perspective, and God knows what else. Then, in about 1904, it seems to have occurred to him that he was getting rather old and had been away from home for rather a long time. So he made his way back to England, only to find that everyone he had known was dead, that the dealers had never heard of him and wouldn't buy his pictures, that he was simply a ridiculous old figure of fun. So he got a job as a drawing-master in a girls' school in Holloway, and there he's been ever since, growing older and older, and feebler and feebler, and blinder and deafer, and generally more gaga, until finally the school has given him the sack. He had about ten pounds in the world when I found him. He lives in a kind of black hole in a basement full of beetles. When his ten pounds are spent, I suppose he'll just quietly die there."

Badgery held up a white hand. "No more, no more. I find literature quite depressing enough. I insist that life at least shall be a little gayer. Did you tell him I wanted him to paint my room?"

"But he can't paint. He's too blind and palsied."

"Can't paint?" Badgery exclaimed in horror. "Then what's the good of the old creature?"

"Well, if you put it like that . . ." Spode began.

"I shall never have my frescoes. Ring the bell, will you?"

Spode rang.

"What right has Tillotson to go on existing if he can't paint?" went on Lord Badgery petulantly. "After all, that was his only justification for occupying a place in the sun."

"He doesn't have much sun in his basement."

The footman appeared at the door.

"Get someone to put all these things back in their places," Lord Badgery commanded, indicating with a wave of the hand the ravaged cases, the confusion of glass and china with which he had littered the floor, the pictures unhooked. "We'll go to the library, Spode; it's more comfortable there."

He led the way through the long gallery and down the stairs.

"I'm sorry old Tillotson has been such a disappointment," said Spode sympathetically.

"Let us talk about something else; he ceases to interest me."

"But don't you think we ought to do something about him? He's only got ten pounds between him and the workhouse. And if you'd seen the blackbeetles in his basement!"

"Enough—enough. I'll do everything you think fitting."

"I thought we might get up a subscription amongst lovers of the arts."

"There aren't any," said Badgery.

"No; but there are plenty of people who will subscribe out of snobbism."

"Not unless you give them something for their money."

"That's true. I hadn't thought of that." Spode was silent for a moment. "We might have a dinner in his honour. The Great Tillotson Banquet. Doyen of the British Art. A Link with the Past. Can't you see it in the papers? I'd make a stunt of it in the *World's Review*. That ought to bring in the snobs."

"And we'll invite a lot of artists and critics—all the ones who can't stand one another. It will be fun to see them squabbling." Badgery laughed. Then his face darkened once again. "Still," he added, "it'll be a very poor second best to my frescoes. You'll stay to dinner, of course."

"Well, since you suggest it. Thanks very much."

## III

The Tillotson Banquet was fixed to take place about three weeks later. Spode, who had charge of the arrangements, proved himself an excellent organiser. He secured the big banqueting-room at the Café Bomba, and was successful in bullying and cajoling the manager into giving fifty persons dinner at twelve shillings a head, including wine. He sent out invitations and collected subscriptions. He wrote an article on Tillotson in the *World's Review*—one of those charming, witty articles couched in the tone of amused patronage and contempt with which one speaks of the great men of 1840. Nor did he neglect Tillotson himself. He used to go to Holloway almost every day to listen to the old man's endless stories about Asia Minor and the Great Exhibition of '51 and Benjamin Robert Haydon. He was sincerely sorry for this relic of another age.

Mr. Tillotson's room was about ten feet below the level of the soil of South Holloway. A little grey light percolated through the area bars, forced a difficult passage through panes opaque with dirt, and spent itself, like a drop of milk that falls into an inkpot, among the inveterate shadows of the dungeon. The place was haunted by the sour smell of damp plaster and of woodwork that has begun to moulder secretly at the heart. A little miscellaneous furniture, including a bed, a washstand and chest of drawers, a table and one or two chairs, lurked in the obscure corners of the den or ventured furtively out into the open. Hither Spode now came almost every day, bringing the old man news of the progress of the banquet scheme. Every day he found Mr. Tillotson sitting in the same place under the window, bathing, as it were, in his tiny puddle of light. "The oldest man that ever wore grey hairs," Spode reflected as he looked at him. Only there were very few hairs left on that bald, unpolished head. At the sound of the visitor's knock Mr. Tillotson would turn in his chair, stare in the direction of the door with blinking, uncertain eyes. He was always full of apologies for being so slow in recognising who was there.

"No discourtesy meant," he would say, after asking. "It's not as if I had forgotten who you were. Only it's so dark and my sight isn't what it was."

After that he never failed to give a little laugh, and, pointing out of the window at the area railings, would say:

"Ah, this is the place for somebody with good sight. It's the place for looking at ankles. It's the grand stand."

It was the day before the great event. Spode came as usual, and Mr. Tillotson punctually made his little joke about the ankles, and Spode, as punctually, laughed.

"Well, Mr. Tillotson," he said, after the reverberation of the joke had died away, "to-morrow you make your re-entry into the world of art and fashion. You'll find some changes."

"I've always had such extraordinary luck," said Mr. Tillotson, and Spode could see by his expression that he genuinely believed it, that he had forgotten the black hole and the blackbeetles and the almost exhausted ten pounds that stood between him and the workhouse. "What an amazing piece of good fortune, for instance, that you should have found me just when you did. Now, this dinner will bring me back to my place in the world. I shall have money, and in a little while—who knows?—I shall be able to see well enough to paint again. I believe my eyes are getting better, you know. Ah, the future is very rosy."

Mr. Tillotson looked up, his face puckered into a smile, and nodded his head in affirmation of his words.

"You believe in the life to come?" said Spode, and immediately flushed for shame at the cruelty of the words.

But Mr. Tillotson was in far too cheerful a mood to have caught their significance.

"Life to come," he repeated. "No, I don't believe in any of that stuff—not since 1859. The 'Origin of Species' changed my views, you know. No life to come for me, thank you! You don't remember the excitement of course. You're very young, Mr. Spode."

"Well, I'm not so old as I was," Spode replied. "You know how middle-aged one is as a schoolboy and undergraduate. Now I'm old enough to know I'm young."

Spode was about to develop this little paradox further, but he noticed that Mr. Tillotson had not been listening. He made a note of the gambit for use in companies that were more appreciative of the subtleties.

"You were talking about the 'Origin of Species,'" he said.

"Was I?" said Mr. Tillotson, waking from reverie.

"About its effect on your faith, Mr. Tillotson."

"To be sure, yes. It shattered my faith. But I remember a fine thing by the Poet Laureate, something about there being more faith in honest doubt, believe me, than in all the . . . all the . . . I forget exactly what; but you see the train of thought. Oh, it was a bad time for religion. I am glad my master Haydon never lived to see it. He was a man of fervour. I remember him pacing up and down his studio in Lisson Grove, singing and shouting and praying all at once. It used almost to frighten me. Oh, but he was a wonderful man, a great man. Take him for all in all, we shall not look upon his like again. As usual, the Bard is right. But it was all very long ago, before your time, Mr. Spode."

"Well, I'm not as old as I was," said Spode, in the hope of having his paradox appreciated this time. But Mr. Tillotson went on without noticing the interruption.

"It's a very, very long time. And yet, when I look back on it, it all seems but a day or two ago. Strange that each day should seem so long and that many days added together should be less than an hour. How clearly I can see old Haydon pacing up and down! Much more clearly, indeed, than I see you, Mr. Spode. The eyes of memory don't grow dim. But my sight is improving, I assure you; it's improving daily. I shall soon be able to see those ankles." He laughed, like a cracked bell —one of those little old bells, Spode fancied, that ring, with much rattling of wires, in the far-off servants' quarters of ancient houses. "And very soon," Mr. Tillotson went on, "I shall be painting again. Ah, Mr. Spode, my luck is extraordinary. I believe in it, I trust in it. And after all, what is luck? Simply another name for Providence, in spite of the 'Origin of Species' and the rest of it. How right the Laureate was when he said that there was more faith in honest doubt, believe me, than in all the . . . er, the . . . er . . . well, you know. I regard you, Mr. Spode, as the emissary of Providence. Your coming marked a turning-point in my life, and the beginning, for me, of happier days. Do you know, one of the first things I shall do when my fortunes are restored will be to buy a hedgehog."

"A hedgehog, Mr. Tillotson?"

"For the blackbeetles. There's nothing like a hedgehog for beetles. It will eat blackbettles till it's sick, till it dies of surfeit. That reminds me of the time when I told my poor great master Haydon—in joke, of course—that he ought to send in a cartoon of King John dying of a surfeit of lampreys for the frescoes in the new Houses of Parliament. As I told him, it's a most notable event in the annals of British liberty—the providential and exemplary removal of a tyrant."

Mr. Tillotson laughed again—the little bell in the deserted house; a ghostly hand pulling the cord in the drawing-room, and phantom footmen responding to the thin, flawed note.

"I remember he laughed, laughed like a bull in his old grand manner. But oh, it was a terrible blow when they rejected his design, a terrible blow! It was the first and fundamental cause of his suicide."

Mr. Tillotson paused. There was a long silence. Spode felt strangely moved, he hardly knew why, in the presence of this man, so frail, so ancient, in body three parts dead, in the spirit so full of life and hopeful patience. He felt ashamed. What was the use of his own youth and cleverness? He saw himself suddenly as a boy with a rattle scaring birds —rattling his noisy cleverness, waving his arms in ceaseless and futile activity, never resting in his efforts to scare away the birds that were always trying to settle in his mind. And what birds! wide-winged and beautiful, all those serene thoughts and faiths and emotions that only visit minds that have humbled themselves to quiet. Those gracious visitants he was for ever using all his energies to drive away. But this old man, with his hedgehogs and his honest doubts and all the rest of it —his mind was like a field made beautiful by the free coming and going, the unafraid alightings of a multitude of white, bright-winged creatures. He felt ashamed. But then, was it possible to alter one's life? Wasn't it a little absurd to risk a conversion? Spode shrugged his shoulders.

"I'll get you a hedgehog at once," he said. "They're sure to have some at Whiteley's."

Before he left that evening Spode made an alarming discovery. Mr. Tillotson did not possess a dress-suit. It was hopless to think of getting one made at this short notice, and, besides, what an unnecessary expense!

"We shall have to borrow a suit, Mr. Tillotson. I ought to have thought of that before."

"Dear me, dear me." Mr. Tillotson was a little chagrined by this unlucky discovery. "Borrow a suit?"

Spode hurried away for counsel to Badgery House. Lord Badgery surprisingly rose to the occasion. "Ask Boreham to come and see me," he told the footman who answered his ring.

Boreham was one of those immemorial butlers who linger on, generation after generation, in the houses of the great. He was over eighty now, bent, dried up, shrivelled with age.

"All old men are about the same size," said Lord Badgery. It was a comforting theory. "Ah, here he is. Have you got a spare suit of evening clothes, Boreham?"

"I have an old suit, my lord, that I stopped wearing in—let me see—was it nineteen seven or eight?"

"That's the very thing. I should be most grateful, Boreham, if you could lend it to me for Mr. Spode here for a day."

The old man went out, and soon reappeared carrying over his arm a very old black suit. He held up the coat and trousers for inspection. In the light of day they were deplorable.

"You've no idea, sir," said Boreham deprecatingly to Spode—"you've no idea how easy things get stained with grease and gravy and what not. However careful you are, sir—however careful."

"I should imagine so." Spode was sympathetic.

"However careful, sir."

"But in artificial light they'll look all right."

"Perfectly all right," Lord Badgery repeated. "Thank you, Boreham; you shall have them back on Thursday."

"You're welcome, my lord, I'm sure." And the old man bowed and disappeared.

On the afternoon of the great day Spode carried up to Holloway a parcel containing Boreham's retired evening-suit and all the necessary appurtenances in the way of shirts and collars. Owing to the darkness and his own feeble sight Mr. Tillotson was happily unaware of the defects in the suit. He was in a state of extreme nervous agitation. It was with some difficulty that Spode could prevent him, although it was only three o'clock, from starting his toilet on the spot.

"Take it easy, Mr. Tillotson, take it easy. We needn't start till half-past seven, you know."

Spode left an hour later, and as soon as he was safely out of the room Mr. Tillotson began to prepare himself for the banquet. He lighted the gas and a couple of candles, and, blinking myopically at the image that fronted him in the tiny looking-glass that stood on his chest of drawers, he set to work, with all the ardour of a young girl preparing for her first ball. At six o'clock, when the last touches had been given, he was not unsatisfied.

He marched up and down his cellar, humming to himself the gay song which had been so popular in his middle years:

*Oh, oh, Anna Maria Jones!*
*Queen of the tambourine, the cymbals, and the bones!*

Spode arrived an hour later in Lord Badgery's second Rolls-Royce. Opening the door of the old man's dungeon, he stood for a moment, wide-eyed with astonishment, on the threshold. Mr. Tillotson was standing by the empty grate, one elbow resting on the mantelpiece, one leg crossed over the other in a jaunty and gentlemanly attitude. The effect of the candlelight shining on his face was to deepen every line and wrinkle with intense black shadow; he looked immeasurably old. It was a noble and pathetic head. On the other hand, Boreham's outworn evening-suit was simply buffoonish. The coat was too long in the sleeves and the tail; the trousers bagged in elephantine creases about his ankles. Some of the grease-spots were visible even in candlelight. The white tie, over which Mr. Tillotson had taken infinite pains and which he believed in his purblindness to be perfect, was fantastically lop-sided. He had buttoned up his waistcoat in such a fashion that one button was widowed of its hole and one hole of its button. Across his shirt front lay the broad green ribbon of some unknown Order.

"Queen of the tambourine, the cymbals, and the bones," Mr. Tillotson concluded in a gnat-like voice before welcoming his visitor.

"Well, Spode, here you are. I'm dressed already, you see. The suit, I flatter myself, fits very well, almost as though it had been made for me. I am all gratitude to the gentleman who was kind enough to lend it to me; I shall take the greatest care of it. It's a dangerous thing to lend clothes. For loan oft loseth both itself and friend. The Bard is always right."

"Just one thing," said Spode. "A touch to your waistcoat." He unbuttoned the dissipated garment and did it up again more symmetrically.

Mr. Tillotson was a little piqued at being found so absurdly in the wrong.

"Thanks, thanks," he said, protestingly, trying to edge away from his valet. "It's all right, you know; I can do it myself. Foolish oversight. I flatter myself the suit fits very well."

"And perhaps the tie might . . ." Spode began tentatively. But the old man would not hear of it.

"No, no. The tie's all right. I can tie a tie, Mr. Spode. The tie's all right. Leave it as it is, I beg."

"I like your Order."

Mr. Tillotson looked down complacently at his shirt front. "Ah, you've noticed my Order. It's a long time since I wore that. It was given me by the Grand Porte, you know, for services rendered in the Russo-Turkish War. It's the Order of Chastity, the second class. They only give the first class to crowned heads, you know—crowned heads and ambassadors. And only Pashas of the highest rank get the second. Mine's the second. They only give the first class to crowned heads . . ."

"Of course, of course," said Spode.

"Do you think I look all right, Mr. Spode?" Mr. Tillotson asked, a little anxiously.

"Splendid, Mr. Tillotson—splendid. The Order's magnificent."

The old man's face brightened once more. "I flatter myself," he said, "that this borrowed suit fits me very well. But I don't like borrowing clothes. For loan oft loseth both itself and friend, you know. And the Bard is always right."

"Ugh, there's one of those horrible beetles!" Spode exclaimed.

Mr. Tillotson bent down and stared at the floor. "I see it," he said, and stamped on a small piece of coal, which crunched to powder under his foot. "I shall certainly buy a hedgehog."

It was time for them to start. A crowd of little boys and girls had collected round Lord Badgery's enormous car. The chauffeur, who felt that honour and dignity were at stake, pretended not to notice the children, but sat gazing, like a statue, into eternity. At the sight of Spode and Mr. Tillotson emerging from the house a yell of mingled awe and derision went up. It subsided to an astonished silence as they climbed into the car. "Bomba's," Spode directed. The Rolls-Royce gave a faintly stertorous sigh and began to move. The children yelled again, and ran along beside the car, waving their arms in a frenzy of excitement. It was then that Mr. Tillotson, with an incomparably noble gesture, leaned forward and tossed among the seething crowd of urchins his three last coppers.

## IV

In Bomba's big room the company was assembling. The long gilt-edged mirrors reflected a singular collection of people. Middle-aged Academicians shot suspicious glances at youths whom they suspected, only too correctly, of being iconoclasts, organisers of Post-Impressionist Exhibitions. Rival art critics, brought suddenly face to face, quivered with restrained hatred. Mrs. Nobes, Mrs. Cayman, and Mrs. Mandragore, those indefatigable hunters of artistic big game, came on one another all unawares in this well-stored menagerie, where each had expected to hunt alone, and were filled with rage. Through this crowd of mutually repellent vanities Lord Badgery moved with a suavity that seemed unconscious of all the feuds and hatreds. He was enjoying himself immensely. Behind the heavy waxen mask of his face, ambushed behind the Hanoverian nose, the little lustreless pig's eyes, the pale thick lips, there lurked a small devil of happy malice that rocked with laughter.

"So nice of you to have come, Mrs. Mandragore, to do honour to England's artistic past. And I'm so glad to see you've brought dear Mrs. Cayman. And is that Mrs. Nobes, too? So it is! I hadn't noticed her before. How delightful! I knew we could depend on your love of art."

And he hurried away to seize the opportunity of introducing that eminent sculptor, Sir Herbert Herne, to the bright young critic who had called him, in the public prints, a monumental mason.

A moment later the Maître d'Hôtel came to the door of the gilded saloon and announced, loudly and impressively, "Mr. Walter Tillotson." Guided from behind by young Spode, Mr. Tillotson came into the room slowly and hesitatingly. In the glare of the lights his eyelids beat heavily, painfully, like the wings of an imprisoned moth, over his filmy eyes. Once inside the door he halted and drew himself up with a conscious assumption of dignity. Lord Badgery hurried forward and seized his hand.

"Welcome, Mr. Tillotson—welcome in the name of English art!"

Mr. Tillotson inclined his head in silence. He was too full of emotion to be able to reply.

"I should like to introduce you to a few of your younger colleagues, who have assembled here to do you honour."

Lord Badgery presented everyone in the room to the old painter, who bowed, shook hands, made little noises in his throat, but still found himself unable to speak. Mrs. Nobes, Mrs. Cayman, and Mrs. Mandragore all said charming things.

Dinner was served; the party took their places. Lord Badgery sat at the head of the table, with Mr. Tillotson on his right hand and Sir Herbert Herne on his left. Confronted with Bomba's succulent cooking and Bomba's wines, Mr. Tillotson ate and drank a good deal. He had the appetite of one who has lived on greens and potatoes for ten years among the blackbeetles. After the second glass of wine he began to talk, suddenly and in a flood, as though a sluice had been pulled up.

"In Asia Minor," he began, "it is the custom when one goes to dinner, to hiccough as a sign of appreciative fullness. *Eructavit cor meum,* as the Psalmist has it; he was an Oriental himself."

Spode had arranged to sit next to Mrs. Cayman; he had designs upon her. She was an impossible woman, of course, but rich and useful; he wanted to bamboozle her into buying some of his young firends' pictures.

"In a cellar?" Mrs. Cayman was saying, "with blackbeetles? Oh, how dreadful! Poor old man! And he's ninety-seven, didn't you say? Isn't that shocking! I only hope the subscription will be a large one. Of course, one wishes one could have given more oneself. But then, you know, one has so many expenses, and things are so difficult now."

"I know, I know," said Spode, with feeling.

"It's all because of Labour," Mrs. Cayman explained. "Of course, I should simply love to have him in to dinner sometimes. But, then, I feel he's really too old, too *farouche* and *gâteux;* it would not be doing a kindness to him, would it? And so you are working with Mr. Gollamy now? What a charming man, so talented, such conversation . . ."

"*Eructavit cor meum,*" said Mr. Tillotson for the third time. Lord Badgery tried to head him off the subject of Turkish etiquette, but in vain.

By half-past nine a kinder vinolent atmosphere had put to sleep the hatreds and suspicions of before dinner. Sir Herbert Herne had discovered that the young Cubist sitting next him was not insane and actually knew a surprising amount about the Old Masters. For their part these young men had realised that their elders were not at all malignant; they were just very stupid and pathetic. It was only in the bosoms of Mrs. Nobes, Mrs. Cayman, and Mrs. Mandragore that hatred still reigned undiminished. Being ladies and old-fashioned, they had drunk almost no wine.

The moment for speech-making arrived. Lord Badgery rose to his feet, said what was expected of him, and called upon Sir Herbert to propose the toast of the evening. Sir Herbert coughed, smiled and began. In the course of a speech that lasted twenty minutes he told anecdotes of Mr. Gladstone, Lord Leighton, Sir Alma Tadema, and the late Bishop of Bombay; he made three puns, he quoted Shakespeare and Whittier, he was playful, he was eloquent, he was grave. . . . At the end of his harangue Sir Herbert handed to Mr. Tillotson a silk purse containing fifty-eight pounds ten shillings, the total amount of the subscription. The old man's health was drunk with acclamation.

Mr. Tillotson rose with difficulty to his feet. The dry, snakelike skin of his face was flushed; his tie was more crooked than ever; the green ribbon of the Order of Chastity of the second class had somehow climbed up his crumpled and maculate shirt front.

"My lords, ladies, and gentlemen," he began in a choking voice, and then broke down completely. It was a very painful and pathetic spectacle. A feeling of intense discomfort afflicted the minds of all who looked upon that trembling relic of a man, as he stood there weeping and stammering. It was as though a breath of the wind of death had blown suddenly through the room, lifting the vapours of wine and tobacco-smoke, quenching the laughter and the candle flames. Eyes floated uneasily, not knowing where to look. Lord Badgery, with great presence of mind, offered the old man a glass of wine. Mr. Tillotson began to recover. The guests heard him murmur a few disconnected words.

"This great honour . . . overwhelmed with kindness . . . this magnificent banquet . . . not used to it . . . in Asia Minor . . . *eructavit cor meum.*"

At this point Lord Badgery plucked sharply at one of his long coat tails. Mr. Tillotson paused, took another sip of wine, and then went on with a newly won coherence and energy.

"The life of the artist is a hard one. His work is unlike other men's work, which may be done mechanically, by rote and almost, as it were, in sleep. It demands from him a constant expense of spirit. He gives continually of his best life, and in return he receives much joy, it is true—much fame, it may be—but of material blessings, very few. It is eighty years since first I devoted my life to the service of art; eighty years, and almost every one of those years has brought me fresh and painful proof of what I have been saying: the artist's life is a hard one."

This unexpected deviation into sense increased the general feeling of discomfort. It became necessary to take the old man seriously, to regard him as a human being. Up till then he had been no more than an object of curiosity, a mummy in an absurd suit of evening-clothes with a green ribbon across the shirt front. People could not help wishing that they had subscribed a little more. Fifty-eight pounds ten—it wasn't enormous. But happily for the peace of mind of the company, Mr. Tillotson paused again, took another sip of wine, and began to live up to his proper character by talking absurdly.

"When I consider the life of that great man, Benjamin Robert Haydon, one of the greatest men England has ever produced . . ." The audience heaved a sigh of relief; this was all as it should be. There was a burst of loud bravoing and clapping. Mr. Tillotson turned his dim eyes round the room, and smiled gratefully at the misty figures he beheld. "That great man, Benjamin Robert Haydon," he continued, "whom I am proud to call my master and who, it rejoices my heart to see, still lives in your memory and esteem,—that great man, one of the greatest that England has ever produced, led a life so deplorable that I cannot think of it without a tear."

And with infinite repetitions and divagations, Mr. Tillotson related the history of B. R. Haydon, his imprisonments for debt, his battle with the Academy, his triumphs, his failures, his despair, his suicide. Half-past ten struck. Mr. Tillotson was declaiming against the stupid and prejudiced judges who had rejected Haydon's designs for the decoration of the new Houses of Parliament in favour of the paltriest German scribblings.

"That great man, one of the greatest England has ever produced, that great Benjamin Robert Haydon, whom I am proud to call my master and who, it rejoices me to see, still lives on in your memory and esteem—at that affront his great heart burst; it was the unkindest cut of all. He who had worked all his life for the recognition of the artist by the State, he who had petitioned every Prime Minister, including the Duke of Wellington, for thirty years, begging them to employ artists to decorate public buildings, he to whom the scheme for decorating the Houses of Parliament was undeniably due . . ." Mr. Tillotson lost a grip on his syntax and began a new sentence. "It was the unkindest cut of all, it was the last straw. The artist's life is a hard one."

At eleven Mr. Tillotson was talking about the pre-Raphaelites. At a quarter past he had begun to tell the story of B. R. Haydon all over again. At twenty-five minutes to twelve he collapsed quite speechless into his chair. Most of the guests had already gone away; the few who remained made haste to depart. Lord Badgery led the old man to the door and packed him into the second Roll-Royce. The Tillotson Banquet was over; it had been a pleasant evening, but a little too long.

Spode walked back to his rooms in Bloomsbury, whistling as he went.

The arc lamps of Oxford Street reflected in the polished surface of the road; canals of dark bronze. He would have to bring that into an article some time. The Cayman woman had been very successfully nobbled. "Voi che sapete," he whistled—somewhat out of tune, but he could not hear that.

When Mr. Tillotson's landlady came in to call him on the following morning, she found the old man lying fully dressed on his bed. He looked very ill and very, very old; Boreham's dress-suit was in a terrible state, and the green ribbon of the Order of Chastity was ruined. Mr. Tillotson lay very still, but he was not asleep. Hearing the sound of footsteps, he opened his eyes a little and faintly groaned. His landlady looked down at him menacingly.

"Disgusting!" she said; "disgusting, I call it. At your age."

Mr. Tillotson groaned again. Making a great effort, he drew out of his trouser pocket a large silk purse, opened it, and extracted a sovereign.

"The artist's life is a hard one, Mrs. Green," he said, handing her the coin. "Would you mind sending for the doctor? I don't feel very well. And oh, what shall I do about these clothes? What shall I say to the gentleman who was kind enough to lend them to me? Loan oft loseth both itself and friend. The Bard is always right."

# MONTAIGNE

## *Of Anger*

PLUTARCH is admirable throughout, but especially where he judges of human actions. What fine things does he say in the comparison of Lycurgus and Numa upon the subject of our great folly in abandoning children to the care and government of their fathers? The most of our civil governments, as Aristotle says,[1] leave, after the manner of the Cyclops, to every one the ordering of their wives and children, according to their own foolish and indiscreet fancy; and the Lacedæmonian and Cretan are almost the only governments that have committed the education of children to the laws. Who does not see that in a state all depends upon their nurture and bringing up? and yet they are left to the mercy of parents, let them be as foolish and ill-conditioned as they may, without any manner of discretion.

Amongst other things, how often have I, as I have passed along our streets, had a good mind to get up a farce, to revenge the poor boys whom I have seen flayed, knocked down, and miserably beaten by some father or mother, when in their fury, and mad with rage? You shall see them come out with fire and fury sparkling in their eyes.

Rabie jecur incendente, feruntur,
Præcipites; ut saxa jugis abrupta, quibus mons
Subtrahitur, clivoque latus pendente recedit,[2]

(and according to Hippocrates, the most dangerous maladies are they that disfigure the countenance), with a roaring and terrible voice, very often against those that are but newly come from nurse, and there they are lamed and spoiled with blows, whilst our justice takes no cognisance of it, as if these maims and dislocations were not executed upon members of our commonwealth:

Gratum est, quod patriæ civem populoque dedisti,
Si facis, ut patriæ sit idoneus, utilis agris,
Utilis et bellorum et pacis rebus agendis.[3]

[1] Moral. ad Nicom., x. 9.

[2] "They are headlong borne with burning fury as great stones torn from the mountains, by which the steep sides are left naked and bare."—JUVENAL, *Sat.* vi. 647.

[3] "It is well when to thy country and the people thou hast given a citizen, provided thou make him fit for his country's service; useful to till the earth, useful in affairs of war and peace."—*Idem, ibid.*, xiv. 70.

There is no passion that so much transports men from their right judgment as anger. No one would demur upon punishing a judge with death who should condemn a criminal on the account of his own choler; why, then, should fathers and pedagogues be any more allowed to whip and chastise children in their anger? 'Tis then no longer correction, but revenge. Chastisement is instead of physic to children; and should we endure a physician who should be animated against and enraged at his patient?

We ourselves, to do well, should never lay a hand upon our servants whilst our anger lasts. When the pulse beats, and we feel emotion in ourselves, let us defer the business; things will indeed appear otherwise to us when we are calm and cool. 'Tis passion that then commands, 'tis passion that speaks, and not we. Faults seen through passion appear much greater to us than they really are, as bodies do when seen through a mist.[1] He who is hungry uses meat; but he who will make use of chastisement should have neither hunger nor thirst to it. And moreover, chastisements that are inflicted with weight and discretion, are much better received and with greater benefit by him who suffers; otherwise, he will not think himself justly condemned by a man transported with anger and fury, and will allege his master's excessive passion, his inflamed countenance, his unwonted oaths, his emotion and precipitous rashness, for his own justification:

> Ora tument ira, nigrescunt sanguine venæ,
> Lumina Gorgoneo sævius igne micant.[2]

Suetonius reports[3] that Caius Rabirius having been condemned by Cæsar, the thing that most prevailed upon the people (to whom he had appealed) to determine the cause in his favour, was the animosity and vehemence that Cæsar had manifested in that sentence.

Saying is one thing and doing is another; we are to consider the sermon and the preacher distinctly and apart. These men, though they had a pretty business in hand, who in our times have attempted to shake the truth of our Church by the vices of her ministers; she extracts her testimony elsewhere; 'tis a foolish way of arguing and that would throw all things into confusion. A man, whose morals are good, may have false opinions, and a wicked man may preach truth, even though he believe it not himself. 'Tis doubtless a fine harmony when doing and saying go together; and I will not deny but that saying, when the actions follow, is not of greater authority and efficacy, as Eudamidas

[1] Plutarch, That we should Restrain Anger, c. 11.

[2] "Their faces swell, their veins grow black with rage, and their eyes sparkle with Gorgonian fire."—OVID, *De Art. Amandi*, iii. 503.

[3] Life of Cæsar, c. 12

said,[1] hearing a philosopher talk of military affairs: "These things are finely said, but he who speaks them is not to be believed, for his ears have never been used to the sound of the trumphet." And Cleomenes,[2] hearing an orator declaiming upon valour, burst out into laughter, at which the other being angry; "I should," said he to him, "do the same if it were a swallow that spoke of this subject; but if it were an eagle I should willingly hear him." I perceive, methinks, in the writings of the ancients, that he who speaks what he thinks, strikes much more home than he who only feigns. Hear Cicero speak of the love of liberty: hear Brutus speak of it, the mere written words of this man sound as if he would purchase it at the price of his life. Let Cicero, the father of eloquence, treat of the contempt of death; let Seneca do the same: the first languishingly drawls it out, so that you perceive he would make you resolve upon a thing on which he is not resolved himself; he inspires you not with courage, for he himself has none; the other animates and inflames you. I never read an author, even of those who treat of virtue and of actions, that I do not curiously inquire what kind of a man he was himself; for the Ephori at Sparta, seeing a dissolute fellow propose a wholesome advice to the people, commanded him to hold his peace, and entreated a virtuous man to attribute to himself the invention, and to propose it.[3] Plutarch's writings, if well understood, sufficiently bespeak their author, and so that I think I know him even into his soul; and yet I could wish that we had some fuller account of his life. And I am thus far wandered from my subject, upon the account of the obligation I have to Aulus Gellius, for having left us in writing [4] this story of his manners, that brings me back to my subject of anger. A slave of his, a vicious, ill-conditioned fellow, but who had the precepts of philosophy often ringing in his ears, having for some offence of his been stript by Pultarch's command, whilst he was being whipped, muttered at first, that it was without cause and that he had done nothing to deserve it; but at last falling in good earnest to exclaim against and rail at his master, he reproached him that he was no philosopher, as he had boasted himself to be: that he had often heard him say it was indecent to be angry, nay, had written a book to that purpose; and that the causing him to be so cruelly beaten, in the height of his rage, totally gave the lie to all his writings, to which Plutarch calmly and coldly answered, "How, ruffian," said he, "by what dost thou judge that I am now angry? Does either my face, my colour, or my voice give any manifestation of my being moved? I do not think my eyes look fierce, that my countenance appears

[1] Plutarch, Apothegms of the Lacedæmonians.

[2] *Idem, ibid.*

[3] Aulus Gellius, xviii. 3.

[4] *Idem*, i. 26.

troubled, or that my voice is dreadful; am I red, do I foam, does any word escape my lips I ought to repent? Do I start? Do I tremble with fury? For those, I tell thee, are the true signs of anger." And so, turning to the fellow that was whipping him, "Ply on thy work," said he, "whilst this gentleman and I dispute." This is the story.

Archytas Tarentinus, returning from a war wherein he had been captain-general, found all things in his house in very great disorder, and his lands quite out of tillage, through the ill husbandry of his receiver, and having caused him to be called to him; "Go," said he, "if I were not in anger I would soundly drub your sides." [1] Plato likewise, being highly offended with one of his slaves, gave Speusippus order to chastise him, excusing himself from doing it because he was in anger.[2] And Carillus, a Lacedæmonian, to a Helot, who carried himself insolently towards him: "By the Gods," said he, "if I was not angry, I would immediately cause thee to be put to death." [3]

'Tis a passion that is pleased with and flatters itself. How often, being moved under a false cause, if the person offending makes a good defence and presents us with a just excuse, are we angry against truth and innocence itself? In proof of which, I remember a marvellous example of antiquity.

Piso, otherwise a man of very eminent virtue, being moved against a soldier of his, for that returning alone from forage he could give him no account where he had left a companion of his, took it for granted that he had killed him, and presently condemned him to death. He was no sooner mounted upon the gibbet, but behold his wandering companion arrives, at which all the army were exceedingly glad, and after many embraces of the two comrades, the hangman carried both the one and the other into Piso's presence, all those present believing it would be a great pleasure even to himself; but it proved quite contrary; for through shame and spite, his fury, which was not yet cool, redoubled; and by a subtlety which his passion suddenly suggested to him, he made three criminal for having found one innocent, and caused them all to be despatched: the first soldier, because sentence had passed upon him; the second, who had lost his way, because he was the cause of his companion's death; and the hangman, for not having obeyed the order which had been given him.

Such as have had to do with testy and obstinate women, may have experimented into what a rage it puts them, to oppose silence and coldness to their fury, and that a man disdains to nourish their anger. The orator Celius was wonderfully choleric by nature; and to one who supped in his company, a man of a gentle and sweet conversation, and

[1] Cicero, Tusc. Quæs., iv. 36.
[2] Seneca, De Ira, iii. 12.
[3] Plutarch, Apothegms.

who, that he might not move him, approved and consented to all he said; he, impatient that his ill humour should thus spend itself without aliment: "For the love of the gods deny me something," said he, "that we may be two." [1] Women, in like manner, are only angry, that others may be angry again, in imitation of the laws of love. Phocion, to one who interrupted his speaking by injurious and very opprobrious words, made no other return than silence, and to give him full liberty and leisure to vent his spleen; which he having accordingly done, and the storm blown over, without any mention of this disturbance, he proceeded in his discourse where he had left off before.[2] No answer can nettle a man like such a contempt.

Of the most choleric man in France (anger is always an imperfection, but more excusable in a soldier, for in that trade it cannot sometimes be avoided) I often say, that he is the most patient man that I know, and the most discreet in bridling his passions; which rise in him with so great violence and fury,

> Magno veluti cum flamma sonore
> Virgea suggeritur costis undantis aheni
> Exsultantque æstu latices, furit intus aquai
> Fumidus atque altè spumis exuberat amnis,
> Nec jam se capit unda; volat vapor ater ad auras.[3]

that he must of necessity cruelly constrain himself to moderate it. And for my part, I know no passion which I could with so much violence to myself attempt to cover and conceal: I would not set wisdom at so high a price; and do not so much consider what a man does, as how much it costs him to do no worse.

Another boasted himself to me of the regularity and sweetness of his manners, which are in truth, very singular; to whom I replied, that it was indeed something, especially in persons of so eminent a quality as himself, upon whom every one had their eyes, to present himself always well-tempered to the world; but that the principal thing was to make provision for within and for himself; and that it was not, in my opinion, very well to order his business inwardly to grate himself, which I as afraid he did, in putting on and outwardly maintaining this visor and regular appearance.

A man incorporates anger by concealing it, as Diogenes told Demosthenes, who, for fear of being seen in a tavern, withdrew himself the more retiredly into it: "The more you retire, the farther you enter

[1] Seneca, De Ira, iii. 8.

[2] Plutarch, Instructions for those who manage State Affairs, c. 10.

[3] "When with loud crackling noise, a fire of sticks is applied to the boiling caldron's side, by the heat in frisky bells the liquor dances; but within the water rages, and high the smoky fluid in foam overflows. Nor can the wave now contain itself: in pitchy steam it flies all abroad."—*Æneid*, vii. 462.

in."[1] I would rather advise that a man should give his servant a box of the ear a little unseasonably, than rack his fancy to present this grave and composed countenance; and had rather discover my passions than brood over them at my own expense; they grow less in venting and manifesting themselves; and 'tis much better their point should wound others without, than be turned towards ourselves within. "Omnia vitia in aperto leviora sunt: et tunc perniciosissima, quum, simulata sanitate, subsidunt."[2] I admonish all those who have authority to be angry in my family, in the first place to manage their anger and not to lavish it upon every occasion, for that both lessens the value and hinders the effect: rash and incessant scolding runs into custom, and renders itself despised; and what you lay out upon a servant for a theft, is not felt, because it is the same he has seen you a hundred times employ against him for having ill washed a glass, or set a stool out of place. Secondly, that they be not angry to no purpose, but make sure that their reprehension reach him with whom they are offended; for, ordinarily, they rail and bawl before he comes into their presence, and continue scolding an age after he is gone;

Et secum petulans amentia certat:"[3]

they attack his shadow, and drive the storm in a place where no one is either chastised or concerned, but in the clamour of their voice. I likewise in quarrels condemn those who huff and vapour without an enemy: those rodomontades should be reserved to discharge upon the offending party:

Mugitus veluti cum prima in prælia tauris
Terrificos ciet, atque irasci in cornua tentat,
Arboris obnixus trunco, ventosque lacessit
Ictibus, et sparsa ad pugnam proludit arena.[4]

When I am angry, my anger is very sharp but withal very short, and as private as I can; I lose myself indeed in promptness and violence, but not in trouble; so that I throw out all sorts of injurious words at random, and without choice, and never consider pertinently to dart my language where I think it will deepest wound, for I commonly make use of no other weapon in my anger than my tongue. My servants have a better bargain of me in great occasions than in little; the light

[1] Diogenes Laertius, Life of Diogenes the Cynic, vi. 34.

[2] "All vices are less dangerous when open to be seen, and then most pernicious when they lurk under a dissembled good nature."—SENECA, *Ep.*, 56.

[3] "And petulant madness contends with itself."—CLAUDIAN, in *Eutrop.*, i. 237.

[4] "As when a bull to usher in the fight makes dreadful bellowings, and whets his horns against the trunk of a tree; with blows he beats the air, and preludes to the fight by spurning the sand."—*Æneid*, xii. 103.

ones surprise me; and the mischief on't is, that when you are once upon the precipice, 'tis no matter who gave you the push, for you always go to the bottom; the fall urges, moves, and makes haste of itself. In great occasions this satisfies me, that they are so just every one expects a reasonable indignation, and then I glorify myself in deceiving their expectation; against these, I fortify and prepare myself; they disturb my head, and threaten to transport me very far, should I follow them. I can easily contain myself from entering into one of these passions, and am strong enough, when I expect them, to repel their violence, be the cause never so great; but if a passion once prepossess and seize me, it carries me away, be the cause never so small. I bargain thus with those who may contend with me; when you see me moved first, let me alone, right or wrong; I'll do the same for you. The storm is only begot by a concurrence of angers, which easily spring from one another, and are not born together. Let every one have his own way, and we shall be always at peace. A profitable advice, but hard to execute. Sometimes also it falls out that I put on a seeming anger, for the better governing of my house, without any real emotion. As age renders my humours more sharp, I study to oppose them, and will, if I can, order it so, that for the future I may be so much the less peevish and hard to please, as I have more excuse and inclination to be so, although I have heretofore been reckoned amongst those who have the greatest patience.

A word more to conclude this chapter. Aristotle says,[1] that anger sometimes serves for arms to virtue and valour. 'Tis likely it may be so, nevertheless, they who contradict him[2] pleasantly answer, that 'tis a weapon of novel use, for we move all other arms, this moves us; our hands guide it not, 'tis it that guides our hands; it holds us, we hold not it.

[1] Moral. ad Nicom., iii. 8.
[2] Seneca, De Ira, i. 16.

# GIBBON

## From the *Autobiography*

In the fifty-second year of my age, after the completion of an arduous and successful work, I now propose to employ some moments of my leisure in reviewing the simple transactions of a private and literary life. Truth, naked, unblushing truth, the first virtue of more serious history, must be the sole recommendation of this personal narrative. The style shall be simple and familiar: but style is the image of character; and the habits of correct writing may produce, without labour or design, the appearance of art and study. My own amusement is my motive, and will be my reward: and if these sheets are communicated to some discreet and indulgent friends, they will be secreted from the public eye till the author shall be removed beyond the reach of criticism or ridicule.

A lively desire of knowing and of recording our ancestors so generally prevails, that it must depend on the influence of some common principle in the minds of men. We seem to have lived in the persons of our forefathers; it is the labour and reward of vanity to extend the term of this ideal longevity. Our imagination is always active to enlarge the narrow circle in which nature has confined us. Fifty or a hundred years may be allotted to an individual; but we step forward beyond death with such hopes as religion and philosophy will suggest; and we fill up the silent vacancy that precedes our birth, by associating ourselves to the authors of our existence. Our calmer judgment will rather tend to moderate, than to suppress, the pride of an ancient and worthy race. The satirist may laugh, the philosopher may preach, but Reason herself will respect the prejudices and habits which have been consecrated by the experience of mankind. Few there are who can sincerely despise in others an advantage of which they are secretly ambitious to partake. The knowledge of our own family from a remote period will be always esteemed as an abstract pre-eminence, since it can never be promiscuously enjoyed; but the longest series of peasants and mechanics would not afford much gratification to the pride of their descendant. We wish to discover our ancestors, but we wish to discover them possessed of ample fortunes, adorned with honourable titles, and holding an eminent rank in the class of hereditary nobles, which has been maintained for the wisest and most beneficial purposes, in almost every climate of the globe, and in almost every modification of political society.

Wherever the distinction of birth is allowed to form a superior order in the state, education and example should always, and will often, produce among them a dignity of sentiment and propriety of conduct, which is guarded from dishonour by their own and the public esteem. If we read of some illustrious line, so ancient that it has no beginning, so worthy that it ought to have no end, we sympathise in its various fortunes; nor can we blame the generous enthusiasm, or even the harmless vanity, of those who are allied to the honours of its name. For my own part, could I draw my pedigree from a general, a statesman, or a celebrated author, I should study their lives with the diligence of filial love. In the investigation of past events our curiosity is stimulated by the immediate or indirect reference to ourselves; but in the estimate of honour we should learn to value the gifts of nature above those of fortune; to esteem in our ancestors the qualities that best promote the interests of society; and to pronounce the descendant of a king less truly noble than the offspring of a man of genius, whose writings will instruct or delight the latest posterity. The family of Confucius is, in my opinion, the most illustrious in the world. After a painful ascent of eight or ten centuries, our barons and princes of Europe are lost in the darkness of the middle ages; but, in the vast equality of the empire of China, the posterity of Confucius have maintained, above two thousand two hundred years, their peaceful honours and perpetual succession. The chief of the family is still revered, by the sovereign and the people, as the lively image of the wisest of mankind. The nobility of the Spencers has been illustrated and enriched by the trophies of Marlborough; but I exhort them to consider the *Fairy Queen* as the most precious jewel of their coronet. Our immortal Fielding was of the younger branch of the Earls of Denbigh, who draw their origin from the Counts of Habsburg, the lineal descendants of Eltrico,[1] in the seventh century Duke of Alsace. Far different have been the fortunes of the English and German divisions of the family of Habsburg: [2] the former, the knights and sheriffs of Leicestershire, have slowly risen to the dignity of a peerage; the latter, the Emperors of Germany and Kings of Spain, have threatened the liberty of the old, and invaded the treasures of the new world. The successors of Charles the Fifth may disdain their brethren of England; but the romance of *Tom Jones*, that exquisite picture of human manners, will outlive the palace of the Escurial, and the imperial eagle of the house of Austria.

That these sentiments are just, or at least natural, I am the more in-

[1] Or Ethics of Alamania.

[2] The descent of the Fieldings from the Hapsburg family has been proved to be an error by Mr. J. H. Round.

clined to believe, as I am not myself interested in the cause; for I can derive from my ancestors neither glory nor shame. Yet a sincere and simple narrative of my own life may amuse some of my leisure hours; but it will subject me, and perhaps with justice, to the imputation of vanity. I may judge, however, from the experience both of past and of the present times, that the public are always curious to know the men who have left behind them any image of their minds: the most scanty accounts of such men are compiled with diligence, and perused with eagerness; and the student of every class may derive a lesson, or an example, from the lives most similar to his own. My name may hereafter be placed among the thousand articles of a Biographia Britannica; and I must be conscious that no one is so well qualified as myself to describe the series of my thoughts and actions. The authority of my masters, of the grave Thuanus, and the philosophic Hume, might be sufficient to justify my design; but it would not be difficult to produce a long list of ancients and moderns, who, in various forms, have exhibited their own portraits. Such portraits are often the most interesting, and sometimes the only interesting parts of their writings; and, if they be sincere, we seldom complain of the minuteness or prolixity of these personal memorials. The lives of the younger Pliny, of Petrarch, and of Erasmus are expressed in the epistles which they themselves have given to the world. The essays of Montaigne and Sir William Temple bring us home to the houses and bosoms of the authors: we smile without contempt at the headstrong passions of Benvenuto Cellini, and the gay follies of Colley Cibber. The confessions of St. Austin and Rousseau disclose the secrets of the human heart; the commentaries of the learned Huet[1] have survived his evangelical demonstration; and the memoirs of Goldoni are more truly dramatic than his Italian comedies. The heretic and the churchman are strongly marked in the characters and fortunes of Whiston and Bishop Newton; and even the dulness of Michael de Marolles and Anthony Wood acquires some value from the faithful representation of men and manners. That I am equal or superior to some of these, the effects of modesty or affectation cannot force me to dissemble.

My family is originally derived from the county of Kent. The southern district, which borders on Sussex and the sea, was formerly overspread with the great forest Anderida, and even now retains the denomination of the *Weald*, or Woodland. In this district, and in the hundred and parish of Rolvenden, the Gibbons were possessed of lands in the year one thousand three hundred and twenty-six; and the elder branch of the family, without much increase or diminution of prop-

[1] The "Confessions" of Augustine and Rousseau may easily be secured, but the "Commentaries" of Huet, Bishop of Avranches, are scarce.

erty, still adheres to its native soil. Fourteen years after the first appearance of his name, John Gibbon is recorded as the Marmorarius or architect of King Edward the Third: the strong and stately castle of Queensborough, which guarded the entrance of the Medway, was a monument of his skill; and the grant of an hereditary toll on the passage from Sandwich to Stonar, in the Isle of Thanet, is the reward of no vulgar artist. In the visitations of the heralds the Gibbons are frequently mentioned: they held the rank of Esquire in an age when that title was less promiscuously assumed: one of them, in the reign of Queen Elizabeth, was captain of the militia of Kent; and a free school, in the neighbouring town of Benenden, proclaims the charity and opulence of its founder. But time, or their own obscurity, has cast a veil of oblivion over the virtues and vices of my Kentish ancestors; their character or station confined them to the labours and pleasures of a rural life: nor is it in my power to follow the advice of the poet, in an inquiry after a name—

> Go! search it there, where to be born, and die
> Of rich and poor makes all the history—

so recent is the institution of our parish registers. In the beginning of the seventeenth century a younger branch of the Gibbons of Rolvenden migrated from the country to the city; and from this branch I do not blush to descend. The law requires some abilities; the church imposes some restraints; and before our army and navy, our civil establishments, and India empire, had opened so many paths of fortune, the mercantile profession was more frequently chosen by youths of a liberal race and education, who aspired to create their own independence. Our most respectable families have not disdained the counting-house, or even the shop; their names are inrolled in the Livery and Companies of London; and in England, as well as in the Italian commonwealths, heralds have been compelled to declare that gentility is not degraded by the exercise of trade. . . .

I was born at Putney, in the county of Surrey, the 27th of April, O.S., in the year one thousand seven hundred and thirty-seven; the first child of the marriage of Edward Gibbon, Esq., and of Judith Porten.[1] My lot might have been that of a slave, a savage, or a peasant;

[1] The union to which I owe my birth was a marriage of inclination and esteem. Mr. James Porten, a merchant of London, resided with his family at Putney, in a house adjoining to the bridge and churchyard, where I have passed many happy hours of my childhood. He left one son (the late Sir Stanier Porten) and three daughters: Catherine, who preserved her maiden name, and of whom I shall hereafter speak; another daughter married Mr. Darrel, of Richmond, and left two sons, Edward and Robert; the youngest of the three sisters was Judith, my mother.

nor can I reflect without pleasure on the bounty of nature, which cast my birth in a free and civilised country, in an age of science and philosophy, in a family of honourable rank, and decently endowed with the gifts of fortune. From my birth I have enjoyed the right of primogeniture; but I was succeeded by five brothers and one sister, all of whom were snatched away in their infancy. My five brothers, whose names may be found in the parish register of Putney, I shall not pretend to lament: but from my childhood to the present hour I have deeply and sincerely regretted my sister, whose life was somewhat prolonged, and whom I remember to have been an amiable infant. The relation of a brother and a sister, especially if they do not marry, appears to me of a very singular nature. It is a familiar and tender friendship with a female, much about our own age; an affection perhaps softened by the secret influence of sex, but pure from any mixture of sensual desire, the sole species of platonic love that can be indulged with truth, and without danger.

At the general election of 1741 Mr. Gibbon and Mr. Delmé stood an expensive and successful contest at Southampton, against Mr. Dummer and Mr. Henly, afterwards Lord Chancellor and Earl of Northington. The Whig candidates had a majority of the resident voters; but the corporation was firm in the Tory interest: a sudden creation of one hundred and seventy new freemen turned the scale; and a supply was readily obtained of respectable volunteers, who flocked from all parts of England to support the cause of their political friends. The new parliament opened with the victory of an opposition which was fortified by strong clamour and strange coalitions. From the event of the first divisions, Sir Robert Walpole perceived that he could no longer lead a majority in the House of Commons, and prudently resigned (after a dominion of one and twenty years) the guidance of the state (1742). But the fall of an unpopular minister was not succeeded, according to general expectation, by a millennium of happiness and virtue: some courtiers lost their places, some patriots lost their characters, Lord Orford's offences vanished with his power; and after a short vibration, the Pelham government was fixed on the old basis of the Whig aristocracy. In the year 1745 the throne and the constitution were attacked by a rebellion which does not reflect much honour on the national spirit; since the English friends of the Pretender wanted courage to join his standard, and his enemies (the bulk of the people) allowed him to advance into the heart of the kingdom. Without daring, perhaps without desiring, to aid the rebels, my father invariably adhered to the Tory opposition. In the most critical season he accepted, for the service of the party, the office of alderman in the city of London: but the duties were so repugnant to his inclination and habits, that he resigned his gown at the end of a few months. The second parliament in which he sate was prematurely dissolved (1747): and as he was unable or unwilling to maintain a second contest for Southampton, the life of the senator expired in that dissolution.

The death of a new-born child before that of its parents may seem an unnatural, but it is strictly a probable event: since of any given number the greater part are extinguished before their ninth year, before they possess the faculties of the mind or body. Without accusing the profuse waste or imperfect workmanship of nature, I shall only observe that this unfavourable chance was multiplied against my infant existence. So feeble was my constitution, so precarious my life, that, in the baptism of my brothers, my father's prudence successively repeated my christian name of Edward, that, in case of the departure of the eldest son, this patronymic appellation might be still perpetuated in the family.

—Uno avulso non deficit alter.[1]

To preserve and to rear so frail a being, the most tender assiduity was scarcely sufficient; and my mother's attention was somewhat diverted by her frequent pregnancies, by an exclusive passion for her husband, and by the dissipation of the world, in which his taste and authority obliged her to mingle. But the maternal office was supplied by my aunt, Mrs. Catherine Porten; at whose name I feel a tear of gratitude trickling down my cheek. A life of celibacy transferred her vacant affection to her sister's first child: my weakness excited her pity; her attachment was fortified by labour and success: and if there be any, as I trust there are some, who rejoice that I live, to that dear and excellent woman they must hold themselves indebted. Many anxious and solitary days did she consume in the patient trial of every mode of relief and amusement. Many wakeful nights did she sit by my bedside in trembling expectation that each hour would be my last. Of the various and frequent disorders of my childhood my own recollection is dark; nor do I wish to expatiate on so disgusting a topic. Suffice it to say, that while every practitioner, from Sloane and Ward to the Chevalier Taylor, was successively summoned to torture or relieve me, the care of my mind was too frequently neglected for that of my health: compassion always suggested an excuse for the indulgence of the master, or the idleness of the pupil; and the chain of my education was broken as often as I was recalled from the school of learning to the bed of sickness.

As soon as the use of speech had prepared my infant reason for the admission of knowledge, I was taught the arts of reading, writing, and

[1] One torn off, a second will not be lacking.—*Æneid* vi. 143.

arithmetic. So remote is the date, so vague is the memory of their origin in myself, that, were not the error corrected by analogy, I should be tempted to conceive them as innate. In my childhood I was praised for the readiness with which I could multiply and divide, by memory alone, two sums of several figures: such praise encouraged my growing talent; and had I persevered in this line of application, I might have acquired some fame in mathematical studies.

After this previous institution at home, or at a day-school, at Putney, I was delivered at the age of seven into the hands of Mr. John Kirkby, who exercised about eighteen months the office of my domestic tutor. His own words, which I shall here transcribe, inspire in his favour a sentiment of pity and esteem—"During my abode in my native county of Cumberland, in quality of an indigent curate, I used now and then in a summer, when the pleasantness of the season invited, to take a solitary walk to the sea-shore, which lies about two miles from the town where I lived. Here I would amuse myself, one while in viewing at large the agreeable prospect which surrounded me, and another while (confining my sight to nearer objects) in admiring the vast variety of beautiful shells thrown upon the beach; some of the choicest of which I always picked up, to divert my little ones upon my return. One time among the rest, taking such a journey in my head, I sat down upon the declivity of the beach with my face to the sea, which was now come up within a few yards of my feet; when immediately the sad thought of the wretched condition of my family, and the unsuccessfulness of all endeavours to amend it, came crowding into my mind, which drove me into a deep melancholy, and ever and anon forced tears from my eyes." [1] Distress at last forced him to leave the country. His learning and virtue introduced him to my father; and at Putney he might have found at least a temporary shelter, had not an act of indiscretion again driven him into the world. One day, reading prayers in the parish church, he most unluckily forgot the name of King George: his patron, a loyal subject, dismissed him with some reluctance and a decent reward; and *how* the poor man ended his days I have never been able to learn. Mr. John Kirkby is the author of two small volumes; the *Life of Automathes* (London, 1745), and an *English and Latin Grammar* (London, 1746), which, as a testimony of gratitude, he dedicated (November 5th, 1745) to my father. The books are before me: from them the pupil may judge the preceptor; and, upon the whole, his judgment will not be unfavourable. The grammar is executed with accuracy and skill, and I know not whether any better existed at the time in our language: but the *Life of Automathes* aspires to the honours of a philosophical fiction. It is the story of a

[1] From Kirkby's *Automathes*.

youth, the son of a shipwrecked exile, who lives alone on a desert island from infancy to the age of manhood. A hind is his nurse; he inherits a cottage, with many useful and curious instruments; some ideas remain of the education of his two first years; some arts are borrowed from the beavers of a neighbouring lake; some truths are revealed in supernatural visions. With these helps, and his own industry, Automathes becomes a self-taught though speechless philosopher, who had investigated with success his own mind, the natural world, the abstract sciences, and the great principles of morality and religion. The author is not entitled to the merit of invention, since he has blended the English story of *Robinson Crusoe* with the Arabian romance of *Hai Ebn Yokhdan*, which he might have read in the Latin version of Pocock. In the *Automathes* I cannot praise either the depth of thought or elegance of style; but the book is not devoid of entertainment or instruction; and among several interesting passages, I would select the discovery of fire, which produces by accidental mischief the discovery of conscience. A man who had thought so much on the subjects of language and education was surely no ordinary preceptor: my childish years, and his hasty departure, prevented me from enjoying the full benefit of his lessons; but they enlarged my knowledge of arithmetic, and left me a clear impression of the English and Latin rudiments.

In my ninth year (January 1746), in a lucid interval of comparative health, my father adopted the convenient and customary mode of English education; and I was sent to Kingston-upon-Thames, to a school of about seventy boys, which was kept by Dr. Wooddeson and his assistants. Every time I have since passed over Putney Common, I have always noticed the spot where my mother, as we drove along in the coach, admonished me that I was now going into the world, and must learn to think and act for myself. The expression may appear ludicrous; yet there is not, in the course of life, a more remarkable change than the removal of a child from the luxury and freedom of a wealthy house to the frugal diet and strict subordination of a school; from the tenderness of parents, and the obsequiousness of servants, to the rude familiarity of his equals, the insolent tyranny of his seniors, and the rod, perhaps, of a cruel and capricious pedagogue. Such hardships may steel the mind and body against the injuries of fortune; but my timid reserve was astonished by the crowd and tumult of the school; the want of strength and activity disqualified me for the sports of the play-field; nor have I forgotten how often in the year forty-six I was reviled and buffeted for the sins of my Tory ancestors. By the common methods of discipline, at the expense of many tears and some blood, I purchased the knowledge of the Latin syntax: and not long since I was possessed of the dirty volumes of Phædrus and Cornelius

Nepos, which I painfully construed and darkly understood. The choice of these authors is not injudicious. The *Lives* of Cornelius Nepos, the friend of Atticus and Cicero, are composed in the style of the purest age: his simplicity is elegant, his brevity copious: he exhibits a series of men and manners; and with such illustrations as every pedant is not indeed qualified to give, this classic biographer may initiate a young student in the history of Greece and Rome. The use of fables or apologues has been approved in every age from ancient India to modern Europe. They convey in familiar images the truths of morality and prudence; and the most childish understanding (I advert to the scruples of Rousseau) will not suppose either that beasts *do* speak, or that men *may* lie. A fable represents the genuine characters of animals; and a skilful master might extract from Pliny and Buffon some pleasing lessons of natural history, a science well adapted to the taste and capacity of children. The Latinity of Phædrus is not exempt from an alloy of the silver age; but his manner is concise, terse, and sententious: the Thracian slave discreetly breathes the spirit of a freeman; and when the text is sound, the style is perspicuous. But his fables, after a long oblivion, were first published by Peter Pithou, from a corrupt manuscript. The labours of fifty editors confess the defects of the copy, as well as the value of the original; and the schoolboy may have been whipped for misapprehending a passage which Bentley could not restore, and which Burman could not explain.

My studies were too frequently interrupted by sickness; and after a real or nominal residence at Kingston school of near two years, I was finally recalled (December 1747) by my mother's death, which was occasioned, in her thirty-eighth year, by the consequences of her last labour. I was too young to feel the importance of my loss; and the image of her person and conversation is faintly imprinted in my memory. The affectionate heart of my aunt, Catherine Porten, bewailed a sister and a friend; but my poor father was inconsolable, and the transport of grief seemed to threaten his life or his reason. I can never forget the scene of our first interview, some weeks after the fatal event; the awful silence, the room hung with black, the mid-day tapers, his sighs and tears; his praises of my mother, a saint in heaven; his solemn adjuration that I would cherish her memory and imitate her virtues; and the fervour with which he kissed and blessed me as the sole surviving pledge of their loves. The storm of passion insensibly subsided into calmer melancholy. At a convivial meeting of his friends, Mr. Gibbon might affect or enjoy a gleam of cheerfulness; but his plan of happiness was for ever destroyed: and after the loss of his companion he was left alone in a world, of which the business and pleasures were to him irksome or insipid. After some unsuccessful trials he renounced the tumult of London and the hospitality of Putney, and buried himself in the rural or rather rustic solitude of Buriton; from which, during several years, he seldom emerged.

As far back as I can remember, the house, near Putney Bridge and churchyard, of my maternal grandfather, appears in the light of my proper and native home. It was there that I was allowed to spend the greatest part of my time, in sickness or in health, during my school vacations and my parents' residence in London, and finally after my mother's death. Three months after that event, in the spring of 1748, the commercial ruin of her father, Mr. James Porten, was accomplished and declared. As his effects were not sold, nor the house evacuated, till the Christmas following, I enjoyed during the whole year the society of my aunt, without much consciousness of her impending fate. I feel a melancholy pleasure in repeating my obligations to that excellent woman, Mrs. Catherine Porten, the true mother of my mind as well as of my health. Her natural good sense was improved by the perusal of the best books in the English language; and if her reason was sometimes clouded by prejudice, her sentiments were never disguised by hypocrisy or affectation. Her indulgent tenderness, the frankness of her temper, and my innate rising curiosity, soon removed all distance between us: like friends of an equal age, we freely conversed on every topic, familiar or abstruse; and it was her delight and reward to observe the first shoots of my young ideas.[1] Pain and languor were often soothed by the voice of instruction and amusement; and to her kind lessons I ascribe my early and invincible love of reading, which I would not exchange for the treasures of India. I should perhaps be astonished, were it possible to ascertain the date at which a favourite tale was engraved, by frequent repetition, in my memory: the Cavern of the Winds; the Palace of Felicity; and the fatal moment, at the end of three months or centuries, when Prince Adolphus is overtaken by Time, who had worn out so many pair of wings in the pursuit. Before I left Kingston school I was well acquainted with Pope's Homer and the *Arabian Nights' Entertainments,* two books which will always please by the moving picture of human manners and specious miracles: nor was I then capable of discerning that Pope's translation is a portrait endowed with every merit excepting that of likeness to the original. The verses of Pope accustomed my ear to the sound of poetic harmony: in the death of Hector, and the shipwreck of Ulysses, I tasted the new emotions of terror and pity; and seriously disputed with my

[1] Gibbon evidently has in his mind the well-known lines in Thomson's *Seasons* ("Spring," l. 1149)—

"Delightful task to rear the tender thoughts
To teach the young idea how to shoot."

aunt on the vices and virtues of the heroes of the Trojan war. From Pope's Homer to Dryden's Virgil was an easy transition; but I know not how, from some fault in the author, the translator, or the reader, the pious Æneas did not so forcibly seize on my imagination; and I derived more pleasure from Ovid's *Metamorphoses*, especially in the fall of Phaeton, and the speeches of Ajax and Ulysses. My grandfather's flight unlocked the door of a tolerable library; and I turned over many English pages of poetry and romance, of history and travels. Where a title attracted my eye, without fear or awe I snatched the volume from the shelf; and Mrs. Porten, who indulged herself in moral and religious speculations, was more prone to encourage than to check a curiosity above the strength of a boy. This year (1748), the twelfth of my age, I shall note as the most propitious to the growth of my intellectual stature.

The relics of my grandfather's fortune afforded a bare annuity for his own maintenance; and his daughter, my worthy aunt, who had already passed her fortieth year, was left destitute. Her noble spirit scorned a life of obligation and dependence; and after revolving several schemes, she preferred the humble industry of keeping a boarding-house for Westminster School, where she laboriously earned a competence for her old age. This singular opportunity of blending the advantages of private and public education decided my father. After the Christmas holidays, in January 1749, I accompanied Mrs. Porten to her new house in College Street; and was immediately entered in the school, of which Dr. John Nicoll was at that time head-master. At first I was alone: but my aunt's resolution was praised; her character was esteemed; her friends were numerous and active: in the course of some years she became the mother of forty or fifty boys, for the most part of family and fortune; and as her primitive habitation was too narrow, she built and occupied a spacious mansion in Dean's Yard. I shall always be ready to join in the common opinion, that our public schools, which have produced so many eminent characters, are the best adapted to the genius and constitution of the English people. A boy of spirit may acquire a previous and practical experience of the world; and his playfellows may be the future friends of his heart or his interest. In a free intercourse with his equals, the habits of truth, fortitude, and prudence will insensibly be matured. Birth and riches are measured by the standard of personal merit; and the mimic scene of a rebellion has displayed in their true colours the ministers and patriots of the rising generation. Our seminaries of learning do not exactly correspond with the precept of a Spartan king,[1] "that the child should be instructed in the arts which will be useful to the man;" since a finished scholar may

[1] Agesilaus.

emerge from the head of Westminster or Eton in total ignorance of the business and conversation of English gentlemen in the latter end of the eighteenth century. But these schools may assume the merit of teaching all that they pretend to teach, the Latin and Greek languages: they deposit in the hands of a disciple the keys of two valuable chests; nor can he complain if they are afterwards lost or neglected by his own fault. The necessity of leading in equal ranks so many unequal powers of capacity and application will prolong to eight or ten years the juvenile studies which might be dispatched in half that time by the skilful master of a single pupil. Yet even the repetition of exercise and discipline contributes to fix in a vacant mind the verbal science of grammar and prosody; and the private or voluntary student, who possesses the sense and spirit of the classics, may offend, by a false quantity, the scrupulous ear of a well-flogged critic. For myself, I must be content with a very small share of the civil and literary fruits of a public school. In the space of two years (1749, 1750), interrupted by danger and debility, I painfully climbed into the third form; and my riper age was left to acquire the beauties of the Latin, and the rudiments of the Greek tongue. Instead of audaciously mingling in the sports, the quarrels, and the connections of our little world, I was still cherished at home under the maternal wing of my aunt; and my removal from Westminster long preceded the approach of manhood.

The violence and variety of my complaints, which had excused my frequent absence from Westminster School, at length engaged Mrs. Porten, with the advice of physicians, to conduct me to Bath: at the end of the Michaelmas vacation (1750) she quitted me with reluctance, and I remained several months under the care of a trusty maid-servant. A strange nervous affection, which alternately contracted my legs, and produced, without any visible symptoms, the most excruciating pain, was ineffectually opposed by the various methods of bathing and pumping. From Bath I was transported to Winchester, to the house of a physician; and after the failure of his medical skill, we had again recourse to the virtues of the Bath waters. During the intervals of these fits I moved with my father to Buriton and Putney; and a short unsuccessful trial was attempted to renew my attendance at Westminster School. But my infirmities could not be reconciled with the hours and discipline of a public seminary; and instead of a domestic tutor, who might have watched the favourable moments, and gently advanced the progress of my learning, my father was too easily content with such occasional teachers as the different places of my residence could supply. I was never forced, and seldom was I persuaded, to admit these lessons: yet I read with a clergyman at Bath some odes of Horace, and several episodes of Virgil, which gave me an imperfect and transient enjoyment of the Latin poets. It might now be apprehended that I should continue for life an illiterate cripple: but, as I approached my sixteenth year, nature displayed in my favour her mysterious energies: my constitution was fortified and fixed; and my disorders, instead of growing with my growth and strengthening with my strength, most wonderfully vanished. I have never possessed or abused the insolence of health: but since that time few persons have been more exempt from real or imaginary ills; and, till I am admonished by the gout, the reader will no more be troubled with the history of my bodily complaints. My unexpected recovery again encouraged the hope of my education; and I was placed at Esher, in Surrey, in the house of the Reverend Mr. Philip Francis, in a pleasant spot, which promised to unite the various benefits of air, exercise, and study (January 1752). The translator of Horace might have taught me to relish the Latin poets, had not my friends discovered in a few weeks that he preferred the pleasures of London to the instruction of his pupils. My father's perplexity at this time, rather than his prudence, was urged to embrace a singular and desperate measure. Without preparation or delay he carried me to Oxford; and I was matriculated in the university as a gentleman-commoner of Magdalen College before I had accomplished the fifteenth year of my age (April 3, 1752). . . .

A traveller who visits Oxford or Cambridge is surprised and edified by the apparent order and tranquillity that prevail in the seats of the English muses. In the most celebrated universities of Holland, Germany, and Italy, the students, who swarm from different countries, are loosely dispersed in private lodgings at the houses of the burghers: they dress according to their fancy and fortune; and in the intemperate quarrels of youth and wine, their *swords*, though less frequently than of old, are sometimes stained with each other's blood. The use of arms is banished from our English universities; the uniform habit of the academics, the square cap and black gown, is adapted to the civil and even clerical profession; and from the doctor in divinity to the undergraduate, the degrees of learning and age are externally distinguished. Instead of being scattered in a town, the students of Oxford and Cambridge are united in colleges; their maintenance is provided at their own expense, or that of the founders; and the stated hours of the hall and chapel represent the discipline of a regular, and, as it were, a religious community. The eyes of the traveller are attracted by the size or beauty of the public edifices: and the principal colleges appear to be so many palaces, which a liberal nation has erected and endowed for the habitation of science. My own introduction to the university of Oxford forms a new æra in my life; and at the distance of forty years

I still remember my first emotions of surprise and satisfaction. In my fifteenth year I felt myself suddenly raised from a boy to a man: the persons whom I respected as my superiors in age and academical rank entertained me with every mark of attention and civility; and my vanity was flattered by the velvet cap and silk gown which distinguish a gentleman-commoner from a plebian student. A decent allowance, more money than a schoolboy had ever seen, was at my own disposal; and I might command, among the tradesmen of Oxford, an indefinite and dangerous latitude of credit. A key was delivered into my hands, which gave me the free use of a numerous and learned library: my apartment consisted of three elegant and well-furnished rooms in the new building, a stately pile, of Magdalen College; and the adjacent walks, had they been frequented by Plato's disciples, might have been compared to the Attic shade on the banks of the Ilissus. Such was the fair prospect of my entrance (April 3, 1752) into the university of Oxford.

A venerable prelate, whose taste and erudition must reflect honour on the society in which they were formed, has drawn a very interesting picture of his academical life. "I was educated (says Bishop Lowth) in the UNIVERSITY OF OXFORD. I enjoyed all the advantages, both public and private, which that famous seat of learning so largely affords. I spent many years in that illustrious society, in a well-regulated course of useful discipline and studies, and in the agreeable and improving commerce of gentlemen and of scholars; in a society where emulation without envy, ambition without jealousy, contention without animosity, incited industry, and awakened genius; where a liberal pursuit of knowledge, and a genuine freedom of thought, was raised, encouraged, and pushed forward by example, by commendation, and by authority. I breathed the same atmosphere that the HOOKERS, the CHILLINGWORTHS, and the LOCKES had breathed before; whose benevolence and humanity were as extensive as their vast genius and comprehensive knowledge; who always treated their adversaries with civility and respect; who made candour, moderation, and liberal judgment as much the rule and law as the subject of their discourse. And do you reproach me with my education in this place, and with my relation to this most respectable body, which I shall always esteem my greatest advantage and my highest honour?" I transcribe with pleasure this eloquent passage, without examining what benefits or what rewards were derived by Hooker, or Chillingworth, or Locke, from their academical institution; without inquiring whether in this angry controversy the spirit of Lowth himself is purified from the intolerant zeal which Warburton had ascribed to the genius of the place. It may indeed be observed that the atmosphere of Oxford did not agree with Mr. Locke's constitution, and that the philosopher justly despised the academical bigots who expelled his person and condemned his principles. The expression of gratitude is a virtue and a pleasure: a liberal mind will delight to cherish and celebrate the memory of its parents; and the teachers of science are the parents of the mind. I applaud the filial piety which it is impossible for me to imitate; since I must not confess an imaginary debt, to assume the merit of a just or generous retribution. To the university of Oxford *I* acknowledge no obligation; and she will as cheerfully renounce me for a son, as I am willing to disclaim her for a mother. I spent fourteen months at Magdalen College; they proved the fourteen months the most idle and unprofitable of my whole life: the reader will pronounce between the school and the scholar, but I cannot affect to believe that nature had disqualified me for all literary pursuits. The specious and ready excuse of my tender age, imperfect preparation, and hasty departure, may doubtless be alleged; nor do I wish to defraud such excuses of their proper weight. Yet in my sixteenth year I was not devoid of capacity or application; even my childish reading had displayed an early though blind propensity for books; and the shallow flood might have been taught to flow in a deep channel and a clear stream. In the discipline of a well-constituted academy, under the guidance of skilful and vigilant professors, I should gradually have risen from translations to originals, from the Latin to the Greek classics, from dead languages to living science: my hours would have been occupied by useful and agreeable studies, the wanderings of fancy would have been restrained, and I should have escaped the temptations of idleness, which finally precipitated my departure from Oxford.

Perhaps in a separate annotation I may coolly examine the fabulous and real antiquities of our sister universities, a question which has kindled such fierce and foolish disputes among their fanatic sons. In the meanwhile it will be acknowledged that these venerable bodies are sufficiently old to partake of all the prejudices and infirmities of age. The schools of Oxford and Cambridge were founded in a dark age of false and barbarous science; and they are still tainted with the vices of their origin. Their primitive discipline was adapted to the education of priests and monks; and the government still remains in the hands of the clergy, an order of men whose manners are remote from the present world, and whose eyes are dazzled by the light of philosophy. The legal incorporation of these societies by the charters of popes and kings had given them a monopoly of the public instruction; and the spirit of monopolists is narrow, lazy, and oppressive; their work is more costly and less productive than that of independent artists; and the new improvements so eagerly grasped by the competition of freedom are admitted with slow and sullen reluctance in those proud corporations, above the fear of a rival, and below the confession of an error. We may scarcely hope that any reformation will be a voluntary act; and so deeply are they rooted in law and prejudice, that even the omnipotence of parliament would shrink from an inquiry into the state and abuses of the two universities.

The use of academical degrees, as old as the thirteenth century, is visibly borrowed from the mechanic corporations; in which an apprentice, after serving his time, obtains a testimonial of his skill, and a licence to practise his trade and mystery. It is not my design to depreciate those honours, which could never gratify or disappoint my ambition; and I should applaud the institution, if the degrees of bachelor or licentiate were bestowed as the reward of manly and successful study: if the name and rank of doctor or master were strictly reserved for the professors of science who have approved their title to the public esteem.

In all the universities of Europe, excepting our own, the languages and sciences are distributed among a numerous list of effective professors; the students, according to their taste, their calling, and their diligence, apply themselves to the proper masters; and in the annual repetition of public and private lectures, these masters are assiduously employed. Our curiosity may inquire what number of professors has been instituted at Oxford? (for I shall now confine myself to my own university); by whom are they appointed, and what may be the probable chances of merit or incapacity? how many are stationed to the three faculties, and how many are left for the liberal arts? what is the form, and what the substance, of their lessons? But all these questions are silenced by one short and singular answer, "That in the university of Oxford the greater part of the public professors have for these many years given up altogether even the pretence of teaching." Incredible as the fact may appear, I must rest my belief on the positive and impartial evidence of a master of moral and political wisdom, who had himself resided at Oxford. Dr. Adam Smith assigns as the cause of their indolence, that, instead of being paid by voluntary contributions, which would urge them to increase the number, and to deserve the gratitude of their pupils, the Oxford professors are secure in the enjoyment of a fixed stipend, without the necessity of labour, or the apprehension of control. It has indeed been observed, nor is the observation absurd, that, excepting in experimental sciences, which demand a costly apparatus and a dexterous hand, the many valuable treatises that have been published on every subject of learning may now supersede the ancient mode of oral instruction. Were this principle true in its utmost latitude, I should only infer that the offices and salaries which are become useless ought without delay to be abolished. But there still remains a material difference between a book and a professor; the hour of the lecture enforces attendance; attention is fixed by the presence, the voice, and the occasional questions of the teacher; the most idle will carry something away; and the more diligent will compare the instructions which they have heard in the school with the volumes which they peruse in their chamber. The advice of a skilful professor will adapt a course of reading to every mind and every situation; his authority will discover, admonish, and at last chastise the negligence of his disciples; and his vigilant inquiries will ascertain the steps of their literary progress. Whatever science he professes he may illustrate in a series of discourses, composed in the leisure of his closet, pronounced on public occasions, and finally delivered to the press. I observe with pleasure, that in the university of Oxford Dr. Lowth, with equal eloquence and erudition, has executed this task in his incomparable *Prælectiones* on the Poetry of the Hebrews.

The college of St. Mary Magdalen was founded in the fifteenth century by Wainfleet, Bishop of Winchester; and now consists of a president, forty fellows, and a number of inferior students. It is esteemed one of the largest and most wealthy of our academical corporations, which may be compared to the Benedictine abbeys of catholic countries; and I have loosely heard that the estates belonging to Magdalen College, which are leased by those indulgent landlords at small quit-rents and occasional fines, might be raised, in the hands of private avarice, to an annual revenue of nearly thirty thousand pounds. Our colleges are supposed to be schools of science, as well as of education; nor is it unreasonable to expect that a body of literary men, devoted to a life of celibacy, exempt from the care of their own subsistence, and amply provided with books, should devote their leisure to the prosecution of study, and that some effects of their studies should be manifested to the world. The shelves of their library groan under the weight of the Benedictine folios, of the editions of the fathers, and the collections of the middle ages, which have issued from the single abbey of St. Germain de Préz at Paris. A composition of genius must be the offspring of one mind; but such works of industry as may be divided among many hands, and must be continued during many years, are the peculiar province of a laborious community. If I inquire into the manufactures of the monks of Magdalen, if I extend the inquiry to the other colleges of Oxford and Cambridge, a silent blush, or a scornful frown, will be the only reply. The fellows or monks of my time were decent easy men, who supinely enjoyed the gifts of the founder: their days were filled by a series of uniform employments; the chapel and the hall, the coffee-house and the common room, till they retired, weary and well satisfied, to a long slumber. From the toil of reading, or thinking, or writing, they had absolved their conscience; and the first shoots of learning and ingenuity withered on the ground, without yielding any fruits to the owners or the public. As a gentleman-commoner, I was admitted to the society of the fellows, and fondly expected that some questions of literature would be the amusing and instructive topics of their discourse. Their conversation stagnated in a round of college business, Tory politics, personal anecdotes, and private scandal: their dull and deep potations excused the brisk intemperance of youth: and their constitutional toasts were not expressive of the most lively loyalty for the house of Hanover. A general election was now approaching: the great Oxfordshire contest already blazed with all the malevolence of party zeal. Magdalen College was devoutly attached to the old interest! and the names of Wenman and Dashwood were more frequently pronounced than those of Cicero and Chrysostom. The example of the senior fellows could not inspire the undergraduates with a liberal spirit or studious emulation; and I cannot describe, as I never knew, the discipline of college. Some duties may possibly have been imposed on the poor scholars, whose ambition aspired to the peaceful honours of a fellowship (*ascribi quietis ordinibus . . . Deorum*); [1] but no independent members were admitted below the rank of a gentleman-commoner, and our velvet cap was the cap of liberty. A tradition prevailed that some of our predecessors had spoken Latin declamations in the hall; but of this ancient custom no vestige remained: the obvious methods of public exercises and examinations were totally unknown; and I have never heard that either the president or the society interfered in the private economy of the tutors and their pupils.

The silence of the Oxford professors, which deprives the youth of public instruction, is imperfectly supplied by the tutors, as they are styled, of the several colleges. Instead of confining themselves to a single science, which had satisfied the ambition of Burman or Bernouilli, they teach, or promise to teach, either history, or mathematics, or ancient literature, or moral philosophy; and as it is possible that they may be defective in all, it is highly probable that of some they will be ignorant. They are paid, indeed, by private contributions; but their appointment depends on the head of the house: their diligence is voluntary, and will consequently be languid, while the pupils themselves, or their parents, are not indulged in the liberty of choice or change. The first tutor into whose hands I was resigned appears to have been one of the best of the tribe: Dr. Waldegrave was a learned and pious man, of a mild disposition, strict morals, and abstemious life, who seldom mingled in the politics or the jollity of the college. But his knowledge of

[1] To be admitted into the dignified assembly of the Gods.—Horace, *Odes*, III. iii. l. 35.

the world was confined to the university; his learning was of the last, rather than of the present age; his temper was indolent; his faculties, which were not of the first rate, had been relaxed by the climate, and he was satisfied, like his fellows, with the slight and superficial discharge of an important trust. As soon as my tutor had sounded the insufficiency of his disciple in school-learning, he proposed that we should read every morning, from ten to eleven, the comedies of Terence. The sum of my improvement in the university of Oxford is confined to three or four Latin plays; and even the study of an elegant classic, which might have been illustrated by a comparison of ancient and modern theatres, was reduced to a dry and literal interpretation of the author's text. During the first weeks I constantly attended these lessons in my tutor's room; but as they appeared equally devoid of profit and pleasure, I was once tempted to try the experiment of a formal apology. The apology was accepted with a smile. I repeated the offence with less ceremony; the excuse was admitted with the same indulgence: the slightest motive of laziness or indisposition, the most trifling avocation at home or abroad, was allowed as a worthy impediment; nor did my tutor appear conscious of my absence or neglect. Had the hour of lecture been constantly filled, a single hour was a small portion of my academic leisure. No plan of study was recommended for my use; no exercises were prescribed for his inspection; and, at the most precious season of youth, whole days and weeks were suffered to elapse without labour or amusement, without advice or account. I should have listened to the voice of reason and of my tutor; his mild behaviour had gained my confidence. I preferred his society to that of the younger students; and in our evening walks to the top of Heddington Hill we freely conversed on a variety of subjects. Since the days of Pocock and Hyde, Oriental learning has always been the pride of Oxford, and I once expressed an inclination to study Arabic. His prudence discouraged this childish fancy; but he neglected the fair occasion of directing the ardour of a curious mind. During my absence in the summer vacation Dr. Waldegrave accepted a college living at Washington in Sussex, and on my return I no longer found him at Oxford. From that time I have lost sight of my first tutor; but at the end of thirty years (1781) he was sill alive; and the practice of exercise and temperance had entitled him to a healthy old age. . . .

After the departure of Dr. Waldegrave I was transferred, with his other pupils, to his academical heir, whose literary character did not command the respect of the college. Dr. – well remembered that he had a salary to receive, and only forgot that he had a duty to perform. Instead of guiding the studies, and watching over the behaviour of his disciple, I was never summoned to attend even the ceremony of a lecture; and, excepting one voluntary visit to his rooms, during the eight months of his titular office the tutor and pupil lived in the same college as strangers to each other. The want of experience, of advice, and of occupation soon betrayed me into some improprieties of conduct, ill-chosen company, late hours, and inconsiderate expense. My growing debts might be secret; but my frequent absence was visible and scandalous: and a tour to Bath, a visit into Buckinghamshire, and four excursions to London in the same winter, were costly and dangerous frolics. They were indeed without a meaning, as without an excuse. The irksomeness of a cloistered life repeatedly tempted me to wander; but my chief pleasure was that of travelling; and I was too young and bashful to enjoy, like a Manly Oxonian in Town, the pleasures of London. In all these excursions I eloped from Oxford; I returned to college; in a few days I eloped again, as if I had been an independent stranger in a hired lodging, without once hearing the voice of admonition, without once feeling the hand of control. Yet my time was lost, my expenses were multiplied, my behaviour abroad was unknown; folly as well as vice should have awakened the attention of my superiors, and my tender years would have justified a more than ordinary degree of restraint and discipline.

It might at least be expected that an ecclesiastical school should inculcate the orthodox principles of religion. But our venerable mother had contrived to unite the opposite extremes of bigotry and indifference; an heretic, or unbeliever, was a monster in her eyes; but she was always, or often, or sometimes, remiss in the spiritual education of her own children. According to the statutes of the university, every student, before he is matriculated, must subscribe his assent to the Thirty-nine Articles of the Church of England, which are signed by more than read, and read by more than believe them. My insufficient age excused me, however, from the immediate performance of this legal ceremony; and the vice-chancellor directed me to return as soon as I should have accomplished my fifteenth year; recommending me, in the meanwhile, to the instruction of my college. My college forgot to instruct; I forgot to return, and was myself forgotten by the first magistrate of the university. Without a single lecture, either public or private, either Christian or Protestant, without any academical subscription, without any episcopal confirmation, I was left by the dim light of my catechism to grope my way to the chapel and communion-table, where I was admitted, without a question how far, or by what means, I might be qualified to receive the sacrament. Such almost incredible neglect was productive of the worst mischiefs. From my childhood I had been fond of religious disputation: my poor aunt has been often puzzled by the mysteries which she strove to believe; nor had the elastic spring been totally broken by the weight of the atmosphere of Oxford. The blind activity of idleness urged me to advance without armour into the dangerous mazes of controversy; and, at the age of sixteen, I bewildered myself in the errors of the Church of Rome.

The progress of my conversion may tend to illustrate at least the history of my own mind. It was not long since Dr. Middleton's free inquiry had sounded an alarm in the theological world: much ink and much gall had been spilt in the defence of the primitive miracles; and the two dullest of their champions were crowned with academic honours by the university of Oxford. The name of Middleton was unpopular; and his proscription very naturally led me to peruse his writings, and those of his antagonists. His bold criticism, which approaches the precipice of infidelity, produced on my mind a singular effect; and had I persevered in the communion of Rome, I should now apply to my own fortune the prediction of the Sibyl,

—Via prima salutis,
Quod minimè reris, Graiâ pandetur ab urbe.[1]

The elegance of style and freedom of argument were repelled by a shield of prejudice. I still revered the character, or rather the names, of the saints and fathers whom Dr. Middleton exposes; nor could he destroy my implicit belief that the gift of miraculous powers was continued in the church during the first four or five centuries of Christianity. But I was unable to resist the weight of historical evidence, that within the same period most of the leading doctrines of popery were already introduced in theory and practice: nor was my conclusion absurd, that miracles are the test of truth, and that the church must be orthodox and pure which was so often approved by the visible interposition of the Deity. The marvellous tales which are so boldly attested by the Basils and Chrysostoms, the Austins and Jeroms, compelled me to embrace the superior merits of celibacy, the institution of the monastic life, the use of the sign of the cross, of holy oil, and even of images, the invocation of saints, the worship of relics, the rudiments of purgatory in prayers for the dead, and the tremendous mystery of the sacrifice of the body and blood of Christ, which insensibly swelled into the prodigy of transubstantiation. In these dispositions, and already more than half a convert, I formed an unlucky intimacy with a young gentleman of our college. With a character less resolute, Mr. Molesworth had imbibed the same religious opinions; and some popish

[1] "Hope, where unlooked for, comes thy toils to crown
Thy road to safety from a Grecian town."
*Æneid* B. vi. l. 96 (Fairfax Taylor).

books, I know not through what channel, were conveyed into his possession. I read, I applauded, I believed: the English translations of two famous works of Bossuet, Bishop of Meaux, the *Exposition of the Catholic Doctrine*, and the *History of the Protestant Variations*, achieved my conversion, and I surely fell by a noble hand. I have since examined the originals with a more discerning eye, and shall not hesitate to pronounce that Bossuet is indeed a master of all the weapons of controversy. In the *Exposition*, a specious apology, the orator assumes, with consummate art, the tone of candour and simplicity; and the ten-horned monster is transformed, at his magic touch, into the milk-white hind, who must be loved as soon as she is seen. In the *History*, a bold and well-aimed attack, he displays, with a happy mixture of narrative and argument, the faults and follies, the changes and contradictions of our first reformers; whose variations (as he dexterously contends) are the mark of historical error, while the perpetual unity of the Catholic Church is the sign and test of infallible truth. To my present feelings it seems incredible that I should ever believe that I believed in transubstantiation. But my conqueror oppressed me with the sacramental words, "Hoc est corpus meum," and dashed against each other the figurative half-meanings of the Protestant sects: every objection was resolved into omnipotence; and after repeating at St. Mary's the Athanasian Creed, I humbly acquiesced in the mystery of the real presence.

To take up half on trust, and half to try,
Name it not faith, but bungling bigotry.
Both knave and fool the merchant we may call,
To pay great sums, and to compound the small,
For who would break with Heaven, and would not break for all? [1]

No sooner had I settled my new religion than I resolved to profess myself a Catholic. Youth is sincere and impetuous; and a momentary glow of enthusiasm had raised me above all temporal considerations.

By the keen Protestants, who would gladly retaliate the example of persecution, a clamour is raised of the increase of popery: and they are always loud to declaim against the toleration of priests and Jesuits who pervert so many of his majesty's subjects from their religion and allegiance. On the present occasion, the fall of one or more of her sons directed this clamour against the university; and it was confidently affirmed that popish missionaries were suffered, under various disguises, to introduce themselves into the colleges of Oxford. But justice obliges me to declare that, as far as relates to myself, this assertion is false; and that I never conversed with a priest, or even with a Papist, till my resolution from books was absolutely fixed. In my last excursion to Lon-

[1] Dryden's *The Hind and the Panther*, l. 141.

don I addressed myself to Mr. Lewis, a Roman Catholic bookseller in Russell Street, Covent Garden, who recommended me to a priest, of whose name and order I am at present ignorant. In our first interview he soon discovered that persuasion was needless. After sounding the motives and merits of my conversion, he consented to admit me into the pale of the church; and at his feet on the 8th of June 1753, I solemnly, though privately, abjured the errors of heresy. The seduction of an English youth of family and fortune was an act of as much danger as glory; but he bravely overlooked the danger, of which I was not then sufficiently informed. "Where a person is reconciled to the see of Rome, or procures others to be reconciled, the offence (says Blackstone) amounts to high treason." And if the humanity of the age would prevent the execution of this sanguinary statute, there were other laws of a less odious cast, which condemned the priest to perpetual imprisonment, and transferred the proselyte's estate to his nearest relation. An elaborate controversial epistle, approved by my director, and addressed to my father, announced and justified the step which I had taken. My father was neither a bigot nor a philosopher; but his affection deplored the loss of an only son; and his good sense was astonished at my strange departure from the religion of my country. In the first sally of passion he divulged a secret which prudence might have suppressed, and the gates of Magdalen College were for ever shut against my return. . . .

After carrying me to Putney, to the house of his friend Mr. Mallet, by whose philosophy I was rather scandalised than reclaimed, it was necessary for my father to form a new plan of education, and to devise some method which, if possible, might effect the cure of my spiritual malady. After much debate it was determined, from the advice and personal experience of Mr. Eliot (now Lord Eliot), to fix me, during some years, at Lausanne in Switzerland. Mr. Frey, a Swiss gentleman of Basil, undertook the conduct of the journey: we left London the 19th of June, crossed the sea from Dover to Calais, travelled post through several provinces of France, by the direct road of St. Quentin, Rheims, Langres, and Besançon, and arrived the 30th of June at Lausanne, where I was immediately settled under the roof and tuition of Mr. Pavilliard, a Calvinist minister.

The first marks of my father's displeasure rather astonished than afflicted me: when he threatened to banish, and disown, and disinherit a rebellious son, I cherished a secret hope that he would not be able or willing to effect his menaces; and the pride of conscience encouraged me to sustain the honourable and important part which I was now acting. My spirits were raised and kept alive by the rapid motion of my journey, the new and various scenes of the Continent, and the civility of Mr. Frey, a man of sense, who was not ignorant of books or the world. But after he had resigned me into Pavilliard's hands, and I was fixed in my new habitation, I had leisure to contemplate the strange and melancholy prospect before me. My first complaint arose from my ignorance of the language. In my childhood I had once studied the French grammar, and I could imperfectly understand the easy prose of a familiar subject. But when I was thus suddenly cast on a foreign land, I found myself deprived of the use of speech and of hearing; and, during some weeks, incapable not only of enjoying the pleasures of conversation, but even of asking or answering a question in the common intercourse of life. To a home-bred Englishman every object, every custom was offensive; but the native of any country might have been disgusted with the general aspect of his lodging and entertainment. I had now exchanged my elegant apartment in Magdalen College, for a narrow, gloomy street, the most unfrequented of an unhandsome town, for an old inconvenient house, and for a small chamber ill contrived and ill furnished, which on the approach of winter, instead of a companionable fire, must be warmed by the dull invisible heat of a stove. From a man I was again degraded to the dependence of a schoolboy. Mr. Pavilliard managed my expenses, which had been reduced to a diminutive state: I received a small monthly allowance for my pocket-money; and, helpless and awkward as I have ever been, I no longer enjoyed the indispensable comfort of a servant. My condition seemed as destitute of hope as it was devoid of pleasure: I was separated for an indefinite, which appeared an infinite term, from my native country; and I had lost all connection with my Catholic friends. I have since reflected with surprise, that, as the Romish clergy of every part of Europe maintain a close correspondence with each other, they never attempted, by letters or messages, to rescue me from the hands of the heretics, or at least to confirm my zeal and constancy in the profession of the faith. Such was my first introduction to Lausanne; a place where I spent nearly five years with pleasure and profit, which I afterwards revisited without compulsion, and which I have finally selected as the most grateful retreat for the decline of my life.

But it is the peculiar felicity of youth that the most unpleasing objects and events seldom make a deep or lasting impression; it forgets the past, enjoys the present, and anticipates the future. At the flexible age of sixteen I soon learned to endure, and gradually to adopt, the new forms of arbitrary manners: the real hardships of my situations were alienated by time. Had I been sent abroad in a more splendid style, such as the fortune and bounty of my father might have supplied, I might have returned home with the same stock of language and science which our countrymen usually import from the Continent. An exile and a prisoner as I was, their example betrayed me into some irregularities of wine, of play, and of idle excursions: but I soon felt the impossibility of associating with them on equal terms; and after the departure of my first acquaintance, I held a cold and civil correspondence with their successors. This seclusion from English society was attended with the most solid benefits. In the Pays de Vaud the French language is used with less imperfection than in most of the distant provinces of France: in Pavilliard's family necessity compelled me to listen and to speak; and if I was at first disheartened by the apparent slowness, in a few months I was astonished by the rapidity of my progress. My pronunciation was formed by the constant repetition of the same sounds; the variety of words and idioms, the rules of grammar, and distinctions of genders, were impressed in my memory: ease and freedom were obtained by practice; correctness and elegance by labour; and before I was recalled home, French, in which I spontaneously thought, was more familiar than English to my ear, my tongue, and my pen. The first effect of this opening knowledge was the revival of my love of reading, which had been chilled at Oxford; and I soon turned over, without much choice, almost all the French books in my tutor's library. Even these amusements were productive of real advantage: my taste and judgment were now somewhat riper. I was introduced to a new mode of style and literature; by the comparison of manners and opinions, my views were enlarged, my prejudices were corrected, and a copious voluntary abstract of the *Histoire de l'Eglise et de l'Empire*, by le Sueur, may be placed in a middle line between my childish and my manly studies. As soon as I was able to converse with the natives, I began to feel some satisfaction in their company: my awkward timidity was polished and emboldened; and I frequented for the first time assemblies of men and women. The acquaintance of the Pavilliards prepared me by degrees for more elegant society. I was received with kindness and indulgence in the best families of Lausanne; and it was in one of these that I formed an intimate and lasting connection with Mr. Deyverdun, a young man of an amiable temper and excellent understanding. In the arts of fencing and dancing, small indeed was my proficiency; and some months were idly wasted in the riding-school. My unfitness to bodily exercise reconciled me to a sedentary life, and the horse, the favourite of my countrymen, never contributed to the pleasures of my youth.

My obligations to the lessons of Mr. Pavilliard gratitude will not suffer me to forget: he was endowed with a clear head and a warm heart; his innate benevolence had assuaged the spirit of the church; he was rational, because he was moderate: in the course of his studies he had acquired a just though superficial knowledge of most branches of literature; by long practice he was skilled in the arts of teaching; and he laboured with assiduous patience to know the character, gain the affection, and open the mind of his English pupil. As soon as we began to understand each other, he gently led me, from a blind and undistinguishing love of reading, into the path of instruction. I consented with pleasure that a portion of the morning hours should be consecrated to a plan of modern history and geography, and to the critical perusal of the French and Latin classics: and at each step I felt myself invigorated by the habits of application and method. His prudence repressed and dissembled some youthful sallies; and as soon as I was confirmed in the habits of industry and temperance, he gave the reins into my own hands. His favorable report of my behaviour and progress gradually obtained some latitude of action and expense; and he wished to alleviate the hardships of my lodging and entertainment. The principles of philosophy were associated with the examples of taste; and by a singular chance, the book, as well as the man, which contributed the most effectually to my education, has a stronger claim on my gratitude than on my admiration. Mr. De Crousaz, the adversary of Bayle and Pope, is not distinguished by lively fancy or profound reflection; and even in his own country, at the end of a few years, his name and writings are almost obliterated. But his philosophy had been formed in the school of Locke, his divinity in that of Limborch and Le Clerc; in a long and laborious life, several generations of pupils were taught to think, and even to write; his lessons rescued the academy of Lausanne from Calvinistic prejudice; and he had the rare merit of diffusing a more liberal spirit among the clergy and people of the Pays de Vaud. His system of logic, which in the last editions has swelled to six tedious and prolix volumes, may be praised as a clear and methodical abridgment of the art of reasoning, from our simple ideas to the most complex operations of the human understanding. This system I studied, and meditated, and abstracted, till I obtained the free command of a universal instrument, which I soon presumed to exercise on my catholic opinions. Pavilliard was not unmindful that his first task, his most important duty, was to reclaim me from the errors of popery. The intermixture of sects has rendered the Swiss clergy acute and learned on the topics of controversy; and I have some of his letters in which he celebrates the dexterity of his attack, and my gradual concessions, after a firm and well-managed defence. I was willing, and I am now willing, to allow him a handsome share of the honour of my conversion: yet I must observe that it was principally effected by my private reflections; and I still remember my solitary transport at the discovery of a philosophical argument against the doctrine of transubstantiation: *that* the text of scripture, which seems to inculcate the real presence, is attested only by a single sense—our sight; while the real presence itself is disproved by three of our senses—the sight, the touch, and the taste. The various articles of the Romish creed disappeared like a dream; and after a full conviction, on Christmas Day 1754, I received the sacrament in the church of Lausanne. It was here that I suspended my religious inquiries, acquiescing with implicit belief in the tenets and mysteries which are adopted by the general consent of Catholics and Protestants.

Such, from my arrival at Lausanne, during the first eighteen or twenty months (July 1753—March 1755), were my useful studies, the foundation of all my future improvements. But every man who rises above the common level has received two educations: the first from his teachers; the second, more personal and important, from himself. He will not, like the fanatics of the last age, define the moment of grace; but he cannot forget the era of his life in which his mind has expanded to its proper form and dimensions. My worthy tutor had the good sense and modesty to discern how far he could be useful: as soon as he felt that I advanced beyond his speed and measure, he wisely left me to my genius; and the hours of lesson were soon lost in the voluntary labour of the whole morning, and sometimes of the whole day. The desire of prolonging my time gradually confirmed the salutary habit of early rising, to which I have always adhered, with some regard to seasons and situations: but it is happy for my eyes and my health that my temperate ardour has never been seduced to trespass on the hours of the night. During the last three years of my residence at Lausanne I may assume the merit of serious and solid application; but I am tempted to distinguish the last eight months of the year 1755 as the period of the most extraordinary diligence and rapid progress. In my French and Latin translations I adopted an excellent method, which, from my own success, I would recommend to the imitation of students. I chose some classic writer, such as Cicero and Vertot, the most approved for purity and elegance of style. I translated, for instance, an epistle of Cicero into French; and, after throwing it aside till the words and phrases were obliterated from my memory, I re-translated my French into such Latin as I could find; and then compared each sentence of my imperfect version with the ease, the grace, the propriety of the Roman orator. A similar experiment was made on several pages of the Revolutions of Vertot; I turned them into Latin, returned them after a sufficient interval into my own French, and again scrutinised the resemblance or dissimilitude of the copy and the original. By degrees I was less ashamed, by degrees I was more satisfied with myself; and I persevered in the practice of these double translations, which filled several books, till I had acquired the knowledge of both idioms, and the command at least of a correct style. This useful exercise of writing was accompanied and succeeded by the more pleasing occupation of reading the best authors. The perusal of the Roman classics was at once my exercise and reward. Dr. Middleton's History, which I then appreciated above its true value, naturally directed me to the writings of Cicero. The most perfect editions, that of Olivet, which may adorn the shelves of the rich, that of Ernesti, which should lie on the table of the learned, were not within my reach. For the familiar epistles I used the text and English commentary of Bishop Ross; but my general edition was that of Verburgius, published at Amsterdam in two large volumes in folio, with an indifferent choice of various notes. I read, with application and pleasure, *all* the epistles, *all* the orations, and the most important treatises of rhetoric and philosophy; and as I read, I applauded the observation of Quintilian, that every student may judge of his own proficiency by the satisfaction which he receives from the Roman orator. I tasted the beauties of language, I breathed the spirit of freedom, and I imbibed from his precepts and examples the public and private sense of a man. Cicero in Latin, and Xenophon in Greek, are indeed the two ancients whom I would first propose to a liberal scholar; not only for the merit of their style and sentiments, but for the admirable lessons, which may be applied almost to every situation of public and private life. Cicero's *Epistles* may in particular afford the models of every form of correspondence, from the careless effusions of tenderness and friendship, to the well-guarded declaration of discreet and dignified resentment. After finishing this great author, a library of eloquence and reason, I formed a more extensive plan of reviewing the Latin classics, under the four divisions of, 1, historians; 2, poets; 3, orators; and 4, philosophers, in a chronological series, from the days of Plautus and Sallust to the decline of the language and empire of Rome: and this plan, in the last twenty-seven months of my residence at Lausanne (January 1756–April 1758), I *nearly* accomplished. Nor was this review, however rapid, either hasty or superficial. I indulged myself in a second and even a third persual of Terence, Virgil, Horace, Tacitus, etc., and studied to imbibe the sense and spirit most congenial to my own. I never suffered a difficult or corrupt passage to escape, till I had viewed it in every light of which it was susceptible: though often disappointed, I always consulted the most learned or ingenious commentators, Torrentius and Dacier on Horace, Catrou and Servius on Virgil, Lipsius on Tacitus, Meziriac on Ovid, etc.; and in the ardour of my inquiries I embraced a large circle of historical and critical erudition. My abstracts of each book were made in the French language: my observations often branched into particular essays; and I can still read, without contempt, a dissertation of eight folio pages on eight lines (287–294) of the fourth *Georgic* of Virgil. Mr. Deyverdun, my friend, whose name will be frequently repeated, had joined with equal zeal, though not with equal perseverance, in the same undertaking. To him every thought, every composition, was instantly communicated; with him I enjoyed the benefits of a free conversation on the topics of our common studies.

But it is scarcely possible for a mind endowed with an active curiosity to be long conversant with the Latin classics without aspiring to know the Greek originals, whom they celebrate as their masters, and of whom they so warmly recommend the study and imitation;

—Vos exemplaria Græca
Nocturnâ versate manu, versate diurnâ.

It was now that I regretted the early years which had been wasted in sickness or idleness, or mere idle reading; that I condemned the perverse method of our schoolmasters, who, by first teaching the mother language, might descend with so much ease and perspicuity to the origin and etymology of a derivative idiom. In the nineteenth year of my age I determined to supply this defect; and the lessons of Pavilliard again contributed to smooth the entrance of the way, the Greek alphabet, the grammar, and the pronunciation according to the French accent. At my earnest request we presumed to open the *Iliad*; and I had the pleasure of beholding, though darkly and through a glass, the true image of Homer, whom I had long since admired in an English dress. After my tutor had left me to myself, I worked my way through about half the *Iliad*, and afterwards interpreted alone a large portion of Xenophon and Herodotus. But my ardour, destitute of aid and emulation, was gradually cooled, and, from the barren task of searching words in a lexicon, I withdrew to the free and familiar conversation of Virgil and Tacitus. Yet in my residence at Lausanne I had laid a solid foundation, which enabled me, in a more propitious season, to prosecute the study of Grecian literature.

From a blind idea of the usefulness of such abstract science, my father had been desirous, and even pressing, that I should devote some time to the mathematics; nor could I refuse to comply with so reasonable a wish. During two winters I attended the private lectures of Monsieur de Traytorrens, who explained the elements of algebra and geometry, as far as the conic sections of the Marquis de l'Hôpital, and appeared satisfied with my diligence and improvement.[1] But as my childish propensity for

[1] JOURNAL, January 1757.—I began to study algebra under M. de Traytorrens, went through the elements of algebra and geometry and the three first books of the Marquis de l'Hôpital's *Conic Sections*. I also read Tibullus, Catullus, Propertius, Horace (with Dacier's and Torrentius's notes), Virgil, Ovid's *Epistles*, with Meziriac's *Commentary*, the *Ars Amandi*, and the *Elegies;* like-

numbers and calculations was totally extinct, I was content to receive the passive impression of my professor's lectures, without any active exercise of my own powers. As soon as I understood the principles I relinquished for ever the pursuit of the mathematics; nor can I lament that I desisted before my mind was hardened by the habit of rigid demonstration, so destructive of the finer feelings of moral evidence, which must, however, determine the actions and opinions of our lives. I listened with more pleasure to the proposal of studying the law of nature and nations, which was taught in the academy of Lausanne by Mr. Vicat, a professor of some learning and reputation. But, instead of attending his public or private course, I preferred in my closet the lessons of his masters, and my own reason. Without being disgusted by Grotius or Puffendorf, I studied in their writings the duties of a man, the rights of a citizen, the theory of justice (it is, alas! a theory), and the laws of peace and war, which have had some influence on the practice of modern Europe. My fatigues were alleviated by the good sense of their commentator Barbeyrac. Locke's *Treatise of Government* instructed me in the knowledge of Whig principles, which are rather founded in reason than experience; but my delight was in the frequent perusal of Montesquieu, whose energy of style, and boldness of hypothesis, were powerful to awaken and stimulate the genius of the age. The logic of De Crousaz had prepared me to engage with his master Locke, and his antagonist Bayle; of whom the former may be used as a bridle, and the latter as a spur, to the curiosity of a young philosopher. According to the nature of their respective works, the schools of argument and objection, I carefully went through the *Essay on Human Understanding*, and occasionally consulted the most interesting articles of the *Philosophic Dictionary*. In the infancy of my reason I turned over, as an idle amusement, the most serious and important treatise: in its maturity the most trifling performance could exercise my taste or judgment; and more than once I have been led by a novel into a deep and instructive train of thinking. But I cannot forbear to mention three particular books, since they may have remotely contributed to form the historian of the Roman empire. 1. From the *Provincial Letters of Pascal*, which almost every year I have perused with new pleasure, I learned to manage the weapon of grave

wise the *Augustus* and *Tiberius* of Suetonius, and a Latin translation of Dion Cassius, from the death of Julius Cæsar to the death of Augustus. I also continued my correspondence, begun last year, with M. Allamand of Bex, and the Professor Breitinger of Zurich; and opened a new one with the Professor Gesner of Gottingen.

*N.B.*—Last year and this I read St. John's Gospel, with part of Xenophon's *Cyropædia;* the *Iliad*, and Herodotus: but, upon the whole, I rather neglected my Greek.

and temperate irony, even on subjects of ecclesiastical solemnity. 2. *The Life of Julian*, by the Abbé de la Bleterie, first introduced me to the man and the times; and I should be glad to recover my first essay on the truth of the miracle which stopped the rebuilding of the Temple of Jerusalem. 3. In Giannone's *Civil History of Naples* I observed with a critical eye the progress and abuse of sacerdotal power, and the revolutions of Italy in the darker ages. This various reading, which I now conducted with discretion, was digested, according to the precept and model of Mr. Locke, into a large common-place-book; a practice, however, which I do not strenuously recommend. The action of the pen will doubtless imprint an idea on the mind as well as on the paper; but I must question whether the benefits of this laborious method are adequate to the waste of time; and I must agree with Dr. Johnson (*Idler*, No. 74), "that what is twice read is commonly better remembered than what is transcribed."

During two years, if I forget some boyish excursions of a day or a week, I was fixed at Lausanne; but at the end of the third summer my father consented that I should make the tour of Switzerland with Pavilliard: and our short absence of one month (September 21–October 20, 1755) was a reward and relaxation of my assiduous studies. The fashion of climbing the mountains and reviewing the *glaciers* had not yet been introduced by foreign travellers, who seek the sublime beauties of nature. But the political face of the country is not less diversified by the forms and spirit of so many various republics, from the jealous government of the *few* to the licentious freedom of the *many*. I contemplated with pleasure the new prospects of men and manners; though my conversation with the natives would have been more free and instructive had I possessed the German as well as the French language. We passed through most of the principal towns in Switzerland; Neufchâtel, Bienne, Soleurre, Arau, Baden, Zurich, Basil, and Bern. In every place we visited the churches, arsenals, libraries, and all the most eminent persons; and after my return I digested my notes in fourteen or fifteen sheets of a French journal, which I despatched to my father, as a proof that my time and his money had not been misspent. Had I found this journal among his papers I might be tempted to select some passages; but I will not transcribe the printed accounts, and it may be sufficient to notice a remarkable spot, which left a deep and lasting impression on my memory. From Zurich we proceeded to the Benedictine Abbey of Einsiedlen, more commonly styled Our Lady of the Hermits. I was astonished by the profuse ostentation of riches in the poorest corner of Europe; amidst a savage scene of woods and mountains, a palace appears to have been erected by magic; and it was erected by the potent magic of religion. A crowd of palmers and votaries was prostrate before the altar. The title and worship of the Mother of God provoked my indignation; and the lively naked image of superstition suggested to me, as in the same place it had done to Zuinglius, the most pressing argument for the reformation of the church. About two years after this tour I passed at Geneva a useful and agreeable month; but this excursion and some short visits in the Pays de Vaud did not materially interrupt my studious and sedentary life ot Lausanne.

My thirst of improvement, and the languid state of science at Lausanne, soon prompted me to solicit a literary correspondence with several men of learning, whom I had not an opportunity of personally consulting. 1. In the perusal of Livy (xxx. 44) I had been stopped by a sentence in a speech of Hannibal, which cannot be reconciled by any torture with his character or argument. The commentators dissemble or confess their perplexity. It occurred to me that the change of a single letter, by substituting *otio* instead of *odio*, might restore a clear and consistent sense; but I wished to weigh my emendation in scales less partial than my own. I addressed myself to M. Crevier, the successor of Rollin, and a professor in the University of Paris, who had published a large and valuable edition of Livy. His answer was speedy and polite; he praised my ingenuity, and adopted my conjecture. 2. I maintained a Latin correspondence, at first anonymous, and afterwards in my own name, with Professor Breitinger of Zurich, the learned editor of a Septuagint Bible. In our frequent letters we discussed many questions of antiquity, many passages of the Latin classics. I proposed my interpretations and amendments. His censures, for he did not spare my boldness of conjecture, were sharp and strong; and I was encouraged by the consciousness of my strength, when I could stand in free debate against a critic of such eminence and erudition. 3. I corresponded on similiar topics with the celebrated Professor Matthew Gesner, of the University of Gottingen; and he accepted as courteously as the two former the invitation of an unknown youth. But his abilities might possibly be decayed; his elaborate letters were feeble and prolix; and when I asked his proper direction, the vain old man covered half a sheet of paper with the foolish enumeration of his titles and offices. 4. These professors of Paris, Zurich, and Gottingen were strangers whom I presumed to address on the credit of their name; but Mr. Allamand, minister at Bex, was my personal friend, with whom I maintained a more free and interesting correspondence. He was a master of language, of science, and, above all, of dispute; and his acute and flexible logic could support, with equal address, and perhaps with equal indifference, the adverse sides of every possible question. . . .

Before I was recalled from Switzerland I had the satisfaction of seeing the most extraordinary man of the age; a poet, an historian, a philosopher, who has filled thirty quartos, of prose and verse, with his various productions, often excellent, and always entertaining. Need I add the name of Voltaire? After forfeiting, by his own misconduct, the friendship of the first of kings, he retired, at the age of sixty, with a plentiful fortune, to a free and beautiful country, and resided two winters (1757 and 1758) in the town or neighbourhood of Lausanne. My desire of beholding Voltaire, whom I then rated above his real magnitude, was easily gratified. He received me with civility as an English youth; but I cannot boast of any peculiar notice or distinction, *Virgilium vidi tantum.*

The ode which he composed on his first arrival on the banks of the Leman Lake, *O Maison d' Aristippe! O Jardin d' Epicure*, etc., had been imparted as a secret to the gentleman by whom I was introduced. He allowed me to read it twice; I knew it by heart; and, as my discretion was not equal to my memory, the author was soon displeased by the circulation of a copy. In writing this trivial anecdote, I wished to observe whether my memory was impaired, and I have the comfort of finding that every line of the poem is still engraved in fresh and indelible characters. The highest gratification which I derived from Voltaire's residence at Lausanne was the uncommon circumstance of hearing a great poet declaim his own productions on the stage. He had formed a company of gentlemen and ladies, some of whom were not destitute of talents. A decent theatre was framed at Monrepos, a country-house at the end of a suburb; dresses and scenes were provided at the expense of the actors; and the author directed the rehearsals with the zeal and attention of paternal love. In two successive winters his tragedies of *Zayre*, *Alzire*, *Zulime*, and his sentimental comedy of the *Enfant Prodigue*, were played at the theatre of Monrepos. Voltaire represented the characters best adapted to his years, Lusignan, Alvaréz, Benassar, Euphemon. His declamation was fashioned to the pomp and cadence of the old stage; and he expressed the enthusiasm of poetry rather than the feelings of nature. My ardour, which soon became conspicuous, seldom failed of procuring me a ticket. The habits of pleasure fortified my taste for the French theatre, and that taste has perhaps abated my idolatry for the gigantic genius of Shakespeare, which is inculcated from our infancy as the first duty of an Englishman. The wit and philosophy of Voltaire, his table and theatre, refined, in a visible degree, the manners of Lausanne; and, however addicted to study, I enjoyed my share of the amusements of society. After the representation of Monrepos I sometimes supped with the actors. I was now familiar in some, and acquainted in many, houses; and my evenings were generally devoted to cards and conversation, either in private parties or numerous assemblies.

I hesitate, from the apprehension of ridicule, when I approach the delicate subject of my early love. By this word I do not mean the polite attention, the gallantry, without hope or design, which has originated in the spirit of chivalry, and is interwoven with the texture of French manners. I understand by this passion the union of desire, friendship, and tenderness, which is inflamed by a single female, which prefers her to the rest of her sex, and which seeks her possession as the supreme or the sole happiness of our being. I need not blush at recollecting the object of my choice; and though my love was disappointed of success, I am rather proud that I was once capable of feeling such a pure and exalted sentiment. The personal attractions of Mademoiselle Susan Curchod were embellished by the virtues and talents of the mind. Her fortune was humble, but her family was respectable. Her mother, a native of France, had preferred her religion to her country. The profession of her father did not extinguish the moderation and philosophy of his temper, and he lived content with a small salary and laborious duty in the obscure lot of minister of Crassy, in the mountains that separate the Pays de Vaud from the county of Burgundy. In the solitude of a sequestered village he bestowed a liberal, and even learned, education on his only daughter. She surpassed his hopes by her proficiency in the sciences and languages; and in her short visits to some relations at Lausanne, the wit, the beauty, and erudition of Mademoiselle Curchod were the theme of universal applause. The report of such a prodigy awakened my curiosity; I saw and loved. I found her learned without pedantry, lively in conversation, pure in sentiment, and elegant in manners; and the first sudden emotion was fortified by the habits and knowledge of a more familiar acquaintance. She permitted me to make her two or three visits at her father's house. I passed some happy days there, in the mountains of Burgundy, and her parents honourably encouraged the connection. In a calm retirement the gay vanity of youth no longer fluttered in her bosom; she listened to the voice of truth and passion, and I might presume to hope that I had made some impression on a virtuous heart. At Crassy and Lausanne I indulged my dream of felicity: but on my return to England, I soon discovered that my father would not hear of this strange alliance, and that, without his consent, I was myself destitute and helpless. After a painful struggle I yielded to my fate; I sighed as a lover, I obeyed as a son; my wound was insensibly healed by time, absence, and the habits of a new life. My cure was accelerated by a faithful report of the tranquillity and cheerfulness of the lady herself, and my love subsided in friendship and esteem. The minister of Crassy soon afterwards died;

his stipend died with him: his daughter retired to Geneva, where, by teaching young ladies, she earned a hard subsistence for herself and her mother; but in her lowest distress she maintained a spotless reputation and a dignified behaviour. A rich banker of Paris, a citizen of Geneva, had the good fortune and good sense to discover and possess this inestimable treasure; and in the capital of taste and luxury she resisted the temptations of wealth, as she had sustained the hardships of indigence. The genius of her husband has exalted him to the most conspicuous station in Europe. In every change of prosperity and disgrace he has reclined on the bosom of a faithful friend; and Mademoiselle Curchod is now the wife of M. Necker, the minister, and perhaps the legislator, of the French monarchy.

Whatsoever have been the fruits of my education, they must be ascribed to the fortunate banishment which placed me at Lausanne. I have sometimes applied to my own fate the verses of Pindar, which remind an Olympic champion that his victory was the consequence of his exile; and that at home, like a domestic fowl, his days might have rolled away inactive or inglorious.

If my childish revolt against the religion of my country had not stripped me in time of my academic gown, the five important years, so liberally improved in the studies and conversation of Lausanne, would have been steeped in port and prejudice among the monks of Oxford. Had the fatigue of idleness compelled me to read, the path of learning would not have been enlightened by a ray of philosophic freedom. I should have grown to manhood ignorant of the life and language of Europe, and my knowledge of the world would have been confined to an English cloister. But my religious error fixed me at Lausanne, in a state of banishment and disgrace. The rigid course of discipline and abstinence to which I was condemned invigorated the constitution of my mind and body; poverty and pride estranged me from my countrymen. One mischief, however, and in their eyes a serious and irreparable mischief, was derived from the success of my Swiss education: I had ceased to be an Englishman. At the flexible period of youth, from the age of sixteen to twenty-one, my opinions, habits, and sentiments were cast in a foreign mould; the faint and distant remembrance of England was almost obliterated; my native language was grown less familiar; and I should have cheerfully accepted the offer of a moderate independence on the terms of perpetual exile. By the good sense and temper of Pavilliard my yoke was insensibly lightened: he left me master of my time and actions; but he could neither change my situation nor increase my allowance, and with the progress of my years and reason I impatiently sighed for the moment of my deliverance. At length, in the spring of the year one thousand seven hundred and fifty-eight, my father signified his permission and his pleasure that I should immediately return home. We were then in the midst of a war: the resentment of the French at our taking their ships without a declaration had rendered that polite nation somewhat peevish and difficult. They denied a passage to English travellers, and the road through Germany was circuitous, toilsome, and perhaps, in the neighbourhood of the armies, exposed to some danger. In this perplexity, two Swiss officers of my acquaintance in the Dutch service, who were returning to their garrisons, offered to conduct me through France as one of their companions; nor did we sufficiently reflect that my borrowed name and regimentals might have been considered, in case of a discovery, in a very serious light. I took my leave of Lausanne on the 11th of April 1758, with a mixture of joy and regret, in the firm resolution of revisiting, as a man, the persons and places which had been so dear to my youth. We travelled slowly, but pleasantly, in a hired coach, over the hills of Franche-compté and the fertile province of Lorraine, and passed, without accident or inquiry, through several fortified towns of the French frontier: from thence we entered the wild Ardennes of the Austrian duchy of Luxemburg; and after crossing the Meuse at Liége, we traversed the heaths of Brabant, and reached, on the fifteenth day, our Dutch garrison of Bois le Duc. In our passage through Nancy my eye was gratified by the aspect of a regular and beautiful city, the work of Stanislaus, who, after the storms of Polish royalty, reposed in the love and gratitude of his new subjects of Lorraine. In our halt at Maestricht I visited Mr. De Beaufort, a learned critic, who was known to me by his specious arguments against the five first centuries of the Roman History. After dropping my regimental companions I stepped aside to visit Rotterdam and the Hague. I wished to have observed a country, the monument of freedom and industry; but my days were numbered, and a longer delay would have been ungraceful. I hastened to embark at the Brill, landed the next day at Harwich, and proceeded to London, where my father awaited my arrival. The whole term of my first absence from England was four years, ten months, and fifteen days.

. . . The only person in England whom I was impatient to see was my aunt Porten, the affectionate guardian of my tender years. I hastened to her house in College Street, Westminster; and the evening was spent in the effusions of joy and confidence. It was not without some awe and apprehension that I approached the presence of my father. My infancy, to speak the truth, had been neglected at home; the severity of his look and language at our last parting still dwelt on my memory; nor could I form any notion of his character, or my probable reception. They were both more agreeable than I could expect. The domestic discipline of our ancestors has been relaxed by the philosophy and softness of the age; and if my father remembered that he had trembled before a stern parent, it was only to adopt with his own son an opposite mode of behaviour. He received me as a man and a friend; all constraint was banished at our first interview, and we ever afterwards continued on the same terms of easy and equal politeness. He applauded the success of my education; every word and action was expressive of the most cordial affection; and our lives would have passed without a cloud, if his economy had been equal to his fortune, or if his fortune had been equal to his desires. During my absence he had married his second wife, Miss Dorothea Patton, who was introduced to me with the most unfavourable prejudice. I considered his second marriage as an act of displeasure, and I was disposed to hate the rival of my mother. But the injustice was in my own fancy, and the imaginary monster was an amiable and deserving woman. I could not be mistaken in the first view of her understanding, her knowledge, and the elegant spirit of her conversation: her polite welcome, and her assiduous care to study and gratify my wishes, announced at least that the surface would be smooth; and my suspicions of art and falsehood were gradually dispelled by the full discovery of her warm and exquisite sensibility. After some reserve on my side, our minds associated in confidence and friendship; and as Mrs. Gibbon had neither children nor the hopes of children, we more easily adopted the tender names and genuine characters of mother and of son. By the indulgence of these parents, I was left at liberty to consult my taste or reason in the choice of place, of company, and of amusements; and my excursions were bounded only by the limits of the island and the measure of my income. Some faint efforts were made to procure me the employment of secretary to a foreign embassy; and I listened to a scheme which would again have transported me to the Continent. Mrs. Gibbon, with seeming wisdom, exhorted me to take chambers in the Temple, and devote my leisure to the study of the law. I cannot repent of having neglected her advice. Few men, without the spur of necessity, have resolution to force their way through the thorns and thickets of that gloomy labyrinth. Nature had not endowed me with the bold and ready eloquence which makes itself heard amidst the tumult of the bar; and I should probably have been diverted from the labours of literature, without acquiring the fame or fortune of a successful pleader. I had no need to call to my aid the regular duties of a profession; every day, every hour, was agreeably filled; nor have I known, like so many of my countrymen, the tediousness of an idle life.

Of the two years (May 1758–May 1760) between my return to

England and the embodying of the Hampshire militia, I passed about nine months in London, and the remainder in the country. The metropolis affords many amusements, which are open to all. It is itself an astonishing and perpetual spectacle to the curious eye; and each taste, each sense may be gratified by the variety of objects which will occur in the long circuit of a morning walk. I assiduously frequented the theatres at a very propitious era of the stage, when a constellation of excellent actors, both in tragedy and comedy, was eclipsed by the meridian brightness of Garrick in the maturity of his judgment and vigour of his performance. The pleasures of a town-life are within the reach of every man who is regardless of his health, his money, and his company. By the contagion of example I was sometimes seduced; but the better habits which I had formed at Lausanne induced me to seek a more elegant and rational society; and if my search was less easy and successful than I might have hoped, I shall at present impute the failure to the disadvantages of my situation and character. Had the rank and fortune of my parents given them an annual establishment in London, their own house would have introduced me to a numerous and polite circle of acquaintance. But my father's taste had always preferred the highest and the lowest company, for which he was equally qualified; and after a twelve years' retirement he was no longer in the memory of the great with whom he had associated. I found myself a stranger in the midst of a vast and unknown city; and at my entrance into life I was reduced to some dull family parties, and some scattered connections, which were not such as I should have chosen for myself. The most useful friends of my father were the Mallets: they received me with civility and kindness, at first on his account, and afterwards on my own; and (if I may use Lord Chesterfield's words) I was soon *domesticated* in their house. Mr. Mallet, a name among the English poets, is praised by an unforgiving enemy for the ease and elegance of his conversation, and his wife was not destitute of wit or learning. By his assistance I was introduced to Lady Hervey, the mother of the present Earl of Bristol. Her age and infirmities confined her at home; her dinners were select; in the evening her house was open to the best company of both sexes and all nations; nor was I displeased at her preference and affectation of the manners, the language, and the literature of France. But my progress in the English world was in general left to my own efforts, and those efforts were languid and slow. I had not been endowed by art or nature with those happy gifts of confidence and address which unlock every door and every bosom; nor would it be reasonable to complain of the just consequences of my sickly childhood, foreign education, and reserved temper. While coaches were rattling through Bond Street, I have passed many a solitary evening in my lodging with my books. My studies were sometimes interrupted by a sigh, which I breathed towards Lausanne; and on the approach of spring I withdrew without reluctance from the noisy and extensive scene of crowds without company, and dissipation without pleasure. . . .

I have already hinted that the publication of my *Essay* was delayed till I had embraced the military profession. I shall now amuse myself with the recollection of an active scene, which bears no affinity to any other period of my studious and social life.

In the outset of a glorious war the English people had been defended by the aid of German mercenaries. A national militia has been the cry of every patriot since the Revolution; and this measure, both in parliament and in the field, was supported by the country gentlemen or Tories, who insensibly transferred their loyalty to the House of Hanover: in the language of Mr. Burke, they have changed the idol, but they have preserved the idolatry. In the act of offering our names and receiving our commissions as major and captain in the Hampshire regiment (June 12, 1759), we had not supposed that we should be dragged away, my father from his farm, myself from my books, and condemned, during two years and a half (May 10, 1760–December 23, 1762), to a wandering life of military servitude. But a weekly or monthly exercise of thirty thousand provincials would have left them useless and ridiculous; and after the pretence of an invasion had vanished, the popularity of Mr. Pitt gave a sanction to the illegal step of keeping them till the end of the war under arms, in constant pay and duty, and at a distance from their respective homes. When the king's order for our embodying came down, it was too late to retreat, and too soon to repent. The South battalion of the Hampshire militia was a small independent corps of four hundred and seventy-six officers and men, commanded by Lieutenant-Colonel Sir Thomas Worsley, who, after a prolix and passionate contest, delivered us from the tyranny of the Lord Lieutenant, the Duke of Bolton. My proper station, as first captain, was at the head of my own, and afterwards of the grenadier company; but in the absence, or even in the presence, of the two field officers, I was entrusted by my friend and my father with the effective labour of dictating the orders, and exercising the battalion. With the help of an original journal, I could write the history of my bloodless and inglorious campaigns; but as these events have lost much of their importance in my own eyes, they shall be despatched in a few words. From Winchester, the first place of assembly (June 4, 1760), we were removed, at our own request, for the benefit of a foreign education. By the arbitrary, and often capricious, orders of the War Office, the battalion successively marched to the pleasant and hospitable Blandford (June 17); to Hilsea barracks, a seat of disease and discord (September 1); to Cranbrook in the Weald of Kent (December 11); to the sea-coast of Dover (December 27); to Winchester camp (June 25, 1761); to the populous and disorderly town of Devizes (October 23); to Salisbury (February 28, 1762); to our beloved Blandford a second time (March 9); and finally, to the fashionable resort of Southampton (June 2), where the colours were fixed till our final dissolution (December 23). On the beach at Dover we had exercised in sight of the Gallic shores. But the most splendid and useful scene of our life was a four months' encampment on Winchester Down, under the command of the Earl of Effingham. Our army consisted of the Thirty-fourth Regiment of Foot and six militia corps. The consciousness of defects was stimulated by friendly emulation. We improved our time and opportunities in morning and evening field-days; and in the general reviews the South Hampshire were rather a credit than a disgrace to the line. In our subsequent quarters of the Devizes and Blandford we advanced with a quick step in our military studies; the ballot of the ensuing summer renewed our vigour and youth; and had the militia subsisted another year, we might have contested the prize with the most perfect of our brethren.

The loss of so many busy and idle hours was not compensated by any elegant pleasure; and my temper was insensibly soured by the society of our rustic officers. In every state there exists, however, a balance of good and evil. The habits of a sedentary life were usefully broken by the duties of an active profession: in the healthful exercise of the field I hunted with a battalion, instead of a pack; and at that time I was ready, at any hour of the day or night, to fly from quarters to London, from London to quarters, on the slightest call of private or regimental business. But my principal obligation to the militia was the making me an Englishman and a soldier. After my foreign education, with my reserved temper, I should long have continued a stranger to my native country, had I not been shaken in this various scene of new faces and new friends; had not experience forced me to feel the characters of our leading men, the state of parties, the forms of office, and the operation of our civil and military system. In this peaceful service I imbibed the rudiments of the language and science of tactics, which opened a new field of study and observation. I diligently read and meditated the *Mémoires Militaires* of Quintus Icilius (Mr. Guichardt), the only writer who has united the merits of a professor and a veteran. The discipline and evolutions of a modern battalion gave me a clearer notion of the phalanx and the legion; and the captain of the Hampshire grenadiers (the reader may smile) has not been useless to the historian of the Roman Empire.

A youth of any spirit is fired even by the play of arms, and in the first sallies of my enthusiasm I had seriously attempted to embrace the regular profession of a soldier. But this military fever was cooled by the enjoyment of our mimic Bellona, who soon unveiled to my eyes her naked deformity. How often did I sigh for my proper station in society and letters! How often (a proud comparison) did I repeat the complaint of Cicero in the command of a provincial army! From a service without danger I might indeed have retired without disgrace; but as often as I hinted a wish of resigning, my fetters were riveted by the friendly entreaties of the colonel, the parental authority of the major, and my own regard for the honour and welfare of the battalion. When I felt that my personal escape was impracticable, I bowed my neck to the yoke: my servitude was protracted far beyond the annual patience of Cicero; and it was not till after the preliminaries of peace that I received my discharge, from the act of government which disembodied the militia. . . .

After his oracle Dr. Johnson, my friend Sir Joshua Reynolds denies all original genius, any natural propensity of the mind to one art or science rather than another. Without engaging in a metaphysical or rather verbal dispute, I *know*, by experience, that from my early youth I aspired to the character of an historian. While I served in the militia . . . this idea ripened in my mind; nor can I paint in more lively colours the feelings of the moment than by transcribing some passages, under their respective dates, from a journal which I kept at that time. . . .

BERITON, AUGUST 4, 1761.

(*In a week's excursion from Winchester camp.*)

"After having long revolved subjects for my intended historical essay, I renounced my first thought of the expedition of Charles VIII. as too remote from us, and rather an introduction to great events than great and important in itself. I successively chose and rejected the crusade of Richard I., the barons' wars against John and Henry III., the history of Edward the Black Prince, the lives and comparisons of Henry V. and the Emperor Titus, the life of Sir Philip Sidney, and that of the Marquis of Montrose. At length I have fixed on Sir Walter Raleigh for my hero. His eventful story is varied by the characters of the soldier and sailor, the courtier and historian; and it may afford such a fund of materials as I desire, which have not yet been properly manufactured. At present I cannot attempt the execution of this work. Free leisure, and the opportunity of consulting many books, both printed and manuscript, are as necessary as they are impossible to be attained in my present way of life. However, to acquire a general insight into my subject and resources, I read the *Life of Sir Walter Raleigh* by Dr. Birch, his copious article in the *General Dictionary* by the same hand, and the reigns of Queen Elizabeth and James I. in Hume's *History of England*."

Beriton, July 26, 1762.
(*During my summer residence.*)

. . . "I have another subject in view, which is the contrast of the former history: the one a poor, warlike, virtuous republic, which emerges into glory and freedom; the other a commonwealth, soft, opulent, and corrupt; which, by just degrees, is precipitated from the abuse to the loss of her liberty: both lessons are, perhaps, equally instructive. This second subject is, *The History of the Republic of Florence, under the House of Medicis*: a period of one hundred and fifty years, which rises or descends from the dregs of the Florentine democracy to the title and dominion of Cosmo de Medicis in the Grand Duchy of Tuscany. I might deduce a chain of revolutions not unworthy of the pen of Vertot; singular men, and singular events; the Medicis four times expelled, and as often recalled; and the Genius of Freedom reluctantly yielding to the arms of Charles V. and the policy of Cosmo. The character and fate of Savonarola, and the revival of arts and letters in Italy, will be essentially connected with the elevation of the family and the fall of the republic. The Medicis, stirps quasi fataliter nata ad instauranda vel fovenda studia (*Lipsius ad Germanos et Gallos*, Epist. viii.), were illustrated by the patronage of learning; and enthusiasm was the most formidable weapon of their adversaries. On this splendid subject I shall most probably fix; but *when*, or *where*, or *how* will it be executed? I behold in a dark and doubtful perspective

Res altâ terrâ, et coligine mersas."

The youthful habits of the language and manners of France had left in my mind an ardent desire of revisiting the Continent on a larger and more liberal plan. According to the law of custom, and perhaps of reason, foreign travel completes the education of an English gentleman: my father had consented to my wish, but I was detained above four years by my rash engagement in the militia. I eagerly grasped the first moments of freedom: three or four weeks in Hampshire and London were employed in the preparations of my journey, and the farewell visits of friendship and civility: my last act in town was to applaud

Mallet's new tragedy of *Elvira;* a post-chaise conveyed me to Dover, the packet to Boulogne, and such was my diligence that I reached Paris on the 28th of January 1763, only thirty-six days after the disbanding of the militia. Two or three years were loosely defined for the term of my absence; and I was left at liberty to spend that time in such places and in such a manner as was most agreeable to my taste and judgment.

In this first visit I passed three months and a half (January 28–May 9), and a much longer space might have been agreeably filled without any intercourse with the natives. At home we are content to move in the daily round of pleasure and business; and a scene which is always present is supposed to be within our knowledge, or at least within our power. But in a foreign country, curiosity is our business and our pleasure; and the traveller, conscious of his ignorance, and covetous of his time, is diligent in the search and the view of every object than can deserve his attention. I devoted many hours of the morning to the circuit of Paris and the neighbourhood, to the visit of churches and palaces conspicuous by their architecture, to the royal manufactures, collections of books and pictures, and all the various treasures of art, of learning, and of luxury. An Englishman may hear without reluctance that in these curious and costly articles Paris is superior to London; since the opulence of the French capital arises from the defects of its government and religion. In the absence of Louis XIV. and his successors, the Louvre has been left unfinished: but the millions which have been lavished on the sands of Versailles, and the morass of Marli, could not be supplied by the legal allowance of a British king. The splendour of the French nobles is confined to their town residence; that of the English is more usefully distributed in their country seats; and we should be astonished at our own riches, if the labours of architecture, the spoils of Italy and Greece, which are now scattered from Inverary to Wilton, were accumulated in a few streets between Marylebone and Westminster. All superfluous ornament is rejected by the cold frugality of the Protestants; but the Catholic superstition, which is always the enemy of reason, is often the parent of the arts. The wealthy communities of priests and monks expend their revenues in stately edifices; and the parish church of St. Sulpice, one of the noblest structures in Paris, was built and adorned by the private industry of a late curé. In this outset, and still more in the sequel of my tour, my eye was amused; but the pleasing vision cannot be fixed by the pen; the particular images are darkly seen through the medium of five-and-twenty years, and the narrative of my life must not degenerate into a book of travels.

But the principal end of my journey was to enjoy the society of a polished and amiable people, in whose favour I was strongly prejudiced, and to converse with some authors, whose conversation, as I fondly imagined, must be far more pleasing and instructive than their writings. The moment was happily chosen. At the close of a successful war the British name was respected on the Continent:

—Clarum et venerabile nomen
Gentibus.

Our opinions, our fashions, even our games, were adopted in France; a ray of national glory illuminated each individual, and every Englishman was supposed to be born a patriot and a philosopher. For myself, I carried a personal recommendation; my name and my *Essay* were already known; the compliment of having written in the French language entitled me to some returns of civility and gratitude. I was considered as a man of letters, who wrote for amusement. Before my departure I had obtained from the Duke de Nivernois, Lady Hervey, the Mallets, Mr. Walpole, etc., many letters of recommendation to their private or literary friends. Of these epistles the reception and success were determined by the character and situation of the persons by whom and to whom they were addressed: the seed was sometimes cast on a barren rock, and it sometimes multiplied a hundred fold in the production of new shoots, spreading branches, and exquisite fruit. But upon the whole, I had reason to praise the national urbanity, which from the court has diffused its gentle influence to the shop, the cottage, and the schools. Of the men of genius of the age, Montesquieu and Fontenelle were no more; Voltaire resided on his own estate near Geneva; Rousseau in the preceding year had been driven from his hermitage of Montmorency; and I blush at my having neglected to seek, in this journey, the acquaintance of Buffon. Among the men of letters whom I saw, d'Alembert and Diderot held the foremost rank in merit, or at least in fame. I shall content myself with enumerating the well-known names of the Count de Caylus, of the Abbé de la Bleterie, Barthelemy, Reynal, Arnaud, of Messieurs de la Condamine, du Clos, de Ste. Palayé, de Bougainville, Caperonnier, de Guignes, Suard, etc., without attempting to discriminate the shades of their characters, or the degrees of our connection. Alone, in a morning visit, I commonly found the artists and authors of Paris less vain, and more reasonable, than in the circles of their equals, with whom they mingle in the houses of the rich. Four days in a week I had a place, without invitation, at the hospitable tables of Mesdames Geoffrin and du Bocage, of the celebrated Helvetius, and of the Baron d'Olbach. In these symposia the pleasures of the table were improved by lively and liberal conversation; the company was select, though various and voluntary.

The society of Madame du Bocage was more soft and moderate than that of her rivals, and the evening conversations of M. de Foncemagne were supported by the good sense and learning of the principal members of the Academy of Inscriptions. The opera and the Italians I occasionally visited; but the French theatre, both in tragedy and comedy, was my daily and favourite amusement. Two famous actresses then divided the public applause. For my own part, I preferred the consummate art of the Clairon to the intemperate sallies of the Dumesnil, which were extolled by her admirers as the genuine voice of nature and passion. Fourteen weeks insensibly stole away; but had I been rich and independent, I should have prolonged, and perhaps have fixed, my residence at Paris.

Between the expensive style of Paris and of Italy it was prudent to interpose some months of tranquil simplicity, and at the thoughts of Lausanne I again lived in the pleasures and studies of my early youth. Shaping my course through Dijon and Besançon, in the last of which places I was kindly entertained by my cousin Acton, I arrived in the month of May 1763 on the banks of the Leman Lake. It had been my intention to pass the Alps in the autumn; but such are the simple attractions of the place, that the year had almost expired before my departure from Lausanne in the ensuing spring. An absence of five years had not made much alteration in manners, or even in persons. My old friends, of both sexes, hailed my voluntary return; the most genuine proof of my attachment. They had been flattered by the present of my book, the produce of their soil; and the good Pavilliard shed tears of joy as he embraced a pupil whose literary merit he might fairly impute to his own labours. To my old list I added some new acquaintance, and among the strangers I shall distinguish Prince Lewis of Wirtemberg, the brother of the reigning duke, at whose country-house, near Lausanne, I frequently dined: a wandering meteor, and at length a falling star, his light and ambitious spirit had successively dropped from the firmament of Prussia, of France, and of Austria; and his faults, which he styled his misfortunes, had driven him into philosophic exile in the Pays de Vaud. He could now moralise on the vanity of the world, the equality of mankind, and the happiness of a private station. His address was affable and polite, and, as he had shone in courts and armies, his memory could supply, and his eloquence could adorn, a copious fund of interesting anecdotes. His first enthusiasm was that of charity and agriculture; but the sage gradually lapsed in the saint, and Prince Lewis of Wirtemberg is now buried in a hermitage near Mayence, in the last stage of mystic devotion. By some ecclesiastical quarrel, Voltaire had been provoked to withdraw himself from Lausanne, and retire to his castle at Ferney, where I again visited the poet and the actor, without seeking his more intimate acquaintance, to which I might now have pleaded a better title. But the theatre which he had founded, the actors whom he had formed, survived the loss of their master; and recent from Paris, I attended with pleasure at the representation of several tragedies and comedies. I shall not descend to specify particular names and characters; but I cannot forget a private institution which will display the innocent freedom of Swiss manners. My favourite society had assumed, from the age of its members, the proud denomination of the spring (*la société du printems*). It consisted of fifteen or twenty young unmarried ladies, of genteel though not of the very first families; the eldest perhaps about twenty; all agreeable, several handsome, and two or three of exquisite beauty. At each other's houses they assembled almost every day, without the control, or even the presence, of a mother or an aunt; they were trusted to their own prudence among a crowd of young men of every nation in Europe. They laughed, they sung, they danced, they played at cards, they acted comedies; but in the midst of this careless gaiety they respected themselves, and were respected by the men; the invisible line between liberty and licentiousness was never transgressed by a gesture, a word, or a look, and their virgin chastity was never sullied by the breath of scandal or suspicion: a singular institution, expressive of the innocent simplicity of Swiss manners. After having tasted the luxury of England and Paris, I could not have returned with satisfaction to the coarse and homely table of Madame Pavilliard; nor was her husband offended that I now entered myself as a *pensionnaire*, or boarder, in the elegant house of Mr. de Mesery, which may be entitled to a short remembrance, as it has stood above twenty years, perhaps, without a parallel in Europe. The house in which we lodged was spacious and convenient, in the best street, and commanding from behind a noble prospect over the country and the lake. Our table was served with neatness and plenty; the boarders were select; we had the liberty of inviting any guests at a stated price; and in the summer the scene was occasionally transferred to a pleasant villa about a league from Lausanne. The characters of master and mistress were happily suited to each other, and to their situation. At the age of seventy-five, Madame de Mesery, who has survived her husband, is still a graceful, I had almost said a handsome woman. She was alike qualified to preside in her kitchen and her drawing-room; and such was the equal propriety of her conduct, that, of two or three hundred foreigners, none ever failed in respect, none could complain of her neglect, and none could ever boast of her favour. Mesery himself, of the noble family of De Cousaz, was a man of the world, a jovial companion, whose easy manners and natural sallies maintained the cheerfulness of his house. His wit could laugh at his own ignorance: he disguised, by an air of profusion, a strict attention to his interest; and in this situation he appeared like a nobleman who spent his fortune and entertained his friends. In this agreeable society I resided nearly eleven months (May 1763–April 1764); and in this second visit to Lausanne, among a crowd of my English companions, I knew and esteemed Mr. Holroyd (now Lord Sheffield); and our mutual attachment was renewed and fortified in the subsequent stages of our Italian journey. Our lives are in the power of chance, and a slight variation on either side, in time or place, might have deprived me of a friend whose activity in the ardour of youth was always prompted by a benevolent heart, and directed by a strong understanding. . . .

I shall advance with rapid brevity in the narrative of this tour, in which somewhat more than a year (April 1764–May 1765) was agreeably employed. Content with tracing my line of march, and slightly touching on my personal feelings, I shall waive the minute investigation of the scenes which have been viewed by thousands, and described by hundreds, of our modern travellers. ROME is the great object of our pilgrimage; and 1st, the journey; 2nd, the residence; and 3rd, the return, will form the most proper and perspicuous division. 1. I climbed Mount Cenis, and descended into the plain of Piedmont, not on the back of an elephant, but on a light osier seat, in the hands of the dexterous and intrepid chairmen of the Alps. The architecture and government of Turin presented the same aspect of tame and tiresome uniformity, but the court was regulated with decent and splendid economy; and I was introduced to his Sardinian majesty Charles Emanuel, who, after the incomparable Frederic, held the second rank (*proximus longo tamen intervallo*) among the kings of Europe. The size and populousness of Milan could not surprise an inhabitant of London; but the fancy is amused by a visit to the Boromean Islands, an enchanted palace, a work of the fairies in the midst of a lake encompassed with mountains, and far removed from the haunts of men. I was less amused by the marble palaces of Genoa than by the recent memorials of her deliverance (in December 1746) from the Austrian tyranny; and I took a military survey of every scene of action within the enclosure of her double walls. My steps were detained at Parma and Modena by the precious relics of the Farnese and Este collections; but, alas! the far greater part had been already transported, by inheritance or purchase, to Naples and Dresden. By the road of Bologna and the Apennine I at last reached Florence, where I reposed from June to September, during the heat of the summer months. In the Gallery, and especially in the Tribune, I first acknowledged, at the feet of the Venus of Medicis, that the chisel may dispute the pre-eminence with the pencil, a truth in the fine arts which cannot on this side of the Alps be felt or understood. At home I had taken some lessons of Italian; on the spot I read with a learned native the classics of the Tuscan idiom; but the shortness of my time, and the use of the French language, prevented my acquiring any facility of speaking; and I was a silent spectator in the conversations of our envoy, Sir Horace Mann, whose most serious business was that of entertaining the English at his hospitable table. After leaving Florence I compared the solitude of Pisa with the industry of Lucca and Leghorn, and continued my journey through Sienna to Rome, where I arrived in the beginning of October. 2. My temper is not very susceptible of enthusiasm, and the enthusiasm which I do not feel I have ever scorned to affect. But at the distance of twenty-five years I can neither forget nor express the strong emotions which agitated my mind as I first approached and entered the *eternal city*. After a sleepless night, I trod, with a lofty step, the ruins of the Forum; each memorable spot where Romulus *stood*, or Tully spoke, or Cæsar fell, was at once present to my eye; and several days of intoxication were lost or enjoyed before I could descend to a cool and minute investigation. My guide was Mr. Byers, a Scotch antiquary of experience and taste; but in the daily labour of eighteen weeks the powers of attention were sometimes fatigued, till I was myself qualified, in a last review, to select and study the capital works of ancient and modern art. Six weeks were borrowed for my tour of Naples, the most populous of cities relative to its size, whose luxurious inhabitants seem to dwell on the confines of paradise and hell-fire. I was presented to the boy-king by our new envoy, Sir William Hamilton; who, wisely diverting his correspondence from the Secretary of State to the Royal Society and British Museum, has elucidated a country of such inestimable value to the naturalist and antiquarian. On my return I fondly embraced, for the last time, the miracles of Rome; but I departed without kissing the foot of Rezzonico (Clement XIII.), who neither possessed the wit of his predecessor Lambertini, nor the virtues of his successor Ganganelli. 3. In my pilgrimage from Rome to Loretto I again crossed the Apennine: from the coast of the Adriatic I traversed a fruitful and populous country, which could alone disprove the paradox of Montesquieu, that modern Italy is a desert. Without adopting the exclusive prejudice of the natives, I sincerely admire the paintings of the Bologna school. I hastened to escape from the sad solitude of Ferrara, which in the age of Cæsar was still more desolate. The spectacle of Venice afforded some hours of astonishment; the university of Padua is a dying taper; but Verona still boasts her amphitheatre, and his native Vicenza is adorned by the classic architecture of Palladio: the road of Lombardy and Piedmont (did Montesquieu find them without inhabitants?) led me back to Milan, Turin, and the passage of Mount Cenis, where I again crossed the Alps in my way to Lyons.

The use of foreign travel has been often debated as a general question; but the conclusion must be finally applied to the character and circumstances of each individual. With the education of boys, *where* or *how* they may pass over some juvenile years with the least mischief to themselves or others, I have no concern. But after supposing the previous and indispensable requisities of age, judgment, a competent knowledge of men and books, and a freedom from domestic prejudices, I will briefly describe the qualifications which I deem most essential to a traveller. He should be endowed with an active, indefatigable vigour of mind and body, which can seize every mode of conveyance, and support, with a careless smile, every hardship of the road, the weather, or the inn. The benefits of foreign travel will correspond with the degrees of these qualifications; but, in this sketch, those to whom I am known will not accuse me of framing my own panegyric. It was at Rome, on the 15th of October 1764, as I sat musing amidst the ruins of the Capitol, while the barefooted friars were singing vespers in the temple of Jupiter, that the idea of writing the decline and fall of the city first started to my mind. But my original plan was circumscribed to the decay of the city rather than of the empire, and though my reading and reflections began to point towards the object, some years elapsed, and several avocations intervened, before I was seriously engaged in the execution of that laborious work.

I had not totally renounced the southern provinces of France, but the letters which I found at Lyons were expressive of some impatience. Rome and Italy had satiated my curious appetite, and I was now ready to return to the peaceful retreat of my family and books. After a happy fortnight I reluctantly left Paris, embarked at Calais, again landed at Dover, after an interval of two years and five months, and hastily drove through the summer dust and solitude of London.

. . . As soon as I had paid the last solemn duties to my father, and obtained, from time and reason, a tolerable composure of mind, I began to form a plan of an independent life, most adapted to my circumstances and inclination. Yet so intricate was the net, my efforts were so awkward and feeble, that nearly two years (November 1770–October 1772) were suffered to elapse before I could disentangle myself from the management of the farm, and transfer my residence from Beriton to a house in London. During this interval I continued to divide my year between town and the country; but my new situation was brightened by hope; my stay in London was prolonged into the summer; and the uniformity of the summer was occasionally broken by visits and excursions at a distance from home. The gratification of my desires (they were not immoderate) has been seldom disappointed by the want of money or credit; my pride was never insulted by the visit of an importunate tradesman; and my transient anxiety for the past or future has been dispelled by the studious or social occupation of the present hour. My conscience does not accuse me of any act of extravagance or injustice, and the remnant of my estate affords an ample and honourable provision for my declining age. I shall not expatiate on my economical affairs, which cannot be instructive or amusing to the reader. It is a rule of prudence, as well as of politeness, to reserve such confidence for the ear of a private friend, without exposing our situation to the envy or pity of strangers; for envy is productive of hatred, and pity borders too nearly on contempt. Yet I may believe, and even assert, that, in circumstances more indigent or more wealthy, I should never have accomplished the task, or acquired the fame, of an historian; that my spirit would have been broken by poverty and contempt; and that my industry might have been relaxed in the labour and luxury of a superfluous fortune.

I had now attained the first of earthly blessings, independence: I was the absolute master of my hours and actions: nor was I deceived in the hope that the establishment of my library in town would allow me to divide the day between study and society. Each year the circle of my acquaintance, the number of my dead and living companions, was enlarged. To a lover of books the shops and sales of London present irresistible temptations; and the manufacture of my history required a various and growing stock of materials. The militia, my travels, the House of Commons, the fame of an author, contributed to multiply my connections: I was chosen a member of the fashionable clubs; and, before I left England in 1783, there were few persons of any eminence in the literary or political world to whom I was a stranger.[1] It would most assuredly be in my power to amuse the reader with a gallery of portraits and a collection of anecdotes. But I have always condemned the practice of transforming a private memorial into a vehicle of satire or praise. By my own choice I passed in town the greatest part of the year; but whenever I was desirous of breathing the air of the country

[1] From the mixed, though polite, company of Boodle's, White's, and Brooks's, I must honourably distinguish a weekly society, which was instituted in the year 1764, and which still continues to flourish, under the title of the Literary Club. (Hawkins's *Life of Johnson*, p. 415; Boswell's *Tour to the Hebrides*, p. 97.) The names of Dr. Johnson, Mr. Burke, Mr. Topham Beauclerc, Mr. Garrick, Dr. Goldsmith, Sir Joshua Reynolds, Mr. Colman, Sir William Jones, Dr. Percy, Mr. Fox, Mr. Sheridan, Mr. Adam Smith, Mr. Steevens, Mr. Dunning, Sir Joseph Banks, Dr. Warton and his brother Mr. Thomas Warton, Dr. Burney, etc., form a large and luminous constellation of British stars.

I possessed an hospitable retreat at Sheffield Place in Sussex, in the family of my valuable friend Mr. Holroyd, whose character, under the name of Lord Sheffield, has since been more conspicuous to the public.

No sooner was I settled in my house and library than I undertook the composition of the first volume of my *History*. At the outset all was dark and doubtful; even the title of the work, the true era of the Decline and Fall of the Empire, the limits of the introduction, the division of the chapters, and the order of the narrative; and I was often tempted to cast away the labour of seven years. The style of an author should be the image of his mind, but the choice and command of language is the fruit of exercise. Many experiments were made before I could hit the middle tone between a dull chronicle and a rhetorical declamation: three times did I compose the first chapter, and twice the second and third, before I was tolerably satisfied with their effect. In the remainder of the way I advanced with a more equal and easy pace; but the fifteenth and sixteenth chapters have been reduced, by three successive revisals, from a large volume to their present size; and they might still be compressed, without any loss of facts or sentiments. An opposite fault may be imputed to the concise and superficial narrative of the first reigns from Commodus to Alexander; a fault of which I have never heard, except from Mr. Hume in his last journey to London. Such an oracle might have been consulted and obeyed with rational devotion; but I was soon disgusted with the modest practice of reading the manuscript to my friends. Of such friends some will praise from politeness, and some will criticise from vanity. The author himself is the best judge of his own performance; no one has so deeply meditated on the subject; no one is so sincerely interested in the event.

By the friendship of Mr. (now Lord) Eliot, who had married my first-cousin, I was returned at the general election for the borough of Liskeard. I took my seat at the beginning of the memorable contest between Great Britain and America, and supported, with many a sincere and silent vote, the rights, though not, perhaps, the interest, of the mother-country. After a fleeting illusive hope, prudence condemned me to acquiesce in the humble station of a mute. I was not armed by nature and education with the intrepid energy of mind and voice,

Vincentem strepitus, et natum rebus agendis.

Timidity was fortified by pride, and even the success of my pen discouraged the trial of my voice. But I assisted at the debates of a free assembly; I listened to the attack and defence of eloquence and reason; I had a near prospect of the characters, views, and passions of the first men of the age. The cause of government was ably vindicated by *Lord*

*North*, a statesman of spotless integrity, a consummate master of debate, who could wield with equal dexterity the arms of reason and of ridicule. He was seated on the Treasury Bench between his Attorney- and Solicitor-General, the two pillars of the law and state, *magis pares quam similes;* and the minister might indulge in a short slumber, whilst he was upholden on either hand by the majestic sense of *Thurlow*, and the skilful eloquence of *Wedderburne*. From the adverse side of the house an ardent and powerful opposition was supported by the lively declamation of *Barré*, the legal acuteness of *Dunning*, the profuse and philosophic fancy of *Burke*, and the argumentative vehemence of *Fox*, who, in the conduct of a party, approved himself equal to the conduct of an empire. By such men every operation of peace and war, every principle of justice or policy, every question of authority and freedom, was attacked and defended; and the subject of the momentous contest was the union or separation of Great Britain and America. The eight sessions that I sat in parliament were a school of civil prudence, the first and most essential virtue of an historian.

The volume of my *History*, which had been somewhat delayed by the novelty and tumult of a first session, was now ready for the press. After the perilous adventure had been declined by my friend Mr. Elmsley, I agreed, upon easy terms, with Mr. Thomas Cadell, a respectable bookseller, and Mr. William Strahan, an eminent printer; and they undertook the care and risk of the publication, which derived more credit from the name of the shop than from that of the author. The last revisal of the proofs was submitted to my vigilance; and many blemishes of style, which had been invisible in the manuscript, were discovered and corrected in the printed sheet. So moderate were our hopes, that the original impression had been stinted to five hundred, till the number was doubled by the prophetic taste of Mr. Strahan. During this awful interval I was neither elated by the ambition of fame, nor depressed by the apprehension of contempt. My diligence and accuracy were attested by my own conscience. History is the most popular species of writing, since it can adapt itself to the highest or the lowest capacity. I had chosen an illustrious subject. Rome is familiar to the schoolboy and the statesman; and my narrative was deduced from the last period of classical reading. I had likewise flattered myself that an age of light and liberty would receive, without scandal, an inquiry into the human *causes* of the progress and establishment of Christianity.

I am at a loss how to describe the success of the work without betraying the vanity of the writer. The first impression was exhausted in a few days; a second and third edition were scarcely adequate to the demand; and the bookseller's property was twice invaded by the pirates of Dublin. My book was on every table, and almost on every toilette;

the historian was crowned by the taste or fashion of the day; nor was the general voice disturbed by the barking of any *profane* critic. The favour of mankind is most freely bestowed on a new acquaintance of any original merit; and the mutual surprise of the public and their favourite is productive of those warm sensibilities which at a second meeting can no longer be rekindled. If I listened to the music of praise, I was more seriously satisfied with the approbation of my judges. The candour of Dr. Robertson embraced his disciple. A letter from Mr. Hume overpaid the labour of ten years; but I have never presumed to accept a place in the triumvirate of British historians. . . .

From my early acquaintance with Lausanne I had always cherished a secret wish that the school of my youth might become the retreat of my declining age. A moderate fortune would secure the blessings of ease, leisure, and independence: the country, the people, the manners, the language, were congenial to my taste; and I might indulge the hope of passing some years in the domestic society of a friend. After travelling with several English,[1] Mr. Deyverdun was now settled at home, in a pleasant habitation, the gift of his deceased aunt: we had long been separated, we had long been silent; yet in my first letter I exposed, with the most perfect confidence, my situation, my sentiments, and my designs. His immediate answer was a warm and joyful acceptance; the picture of our future life provoked my impatience; and the terms of arrangement were short and simple, as he possessed the property, and I undertook the expense of our common house. Before I could break my English chain it was incumbent on me to struggle with the feelings of my heart, the indolence of my temper, and the opinion of the world, which unanimously condemned this voluntary banishment. In the disposal of my effects, the library, a sacred deposit, was alone excepted. As my post-chaise moved over Westminster Bridge I bade a long farewell to the "fumum et opes strepitumque Romæ."[2] My journey, by the direct road through France, was not attended with any accident, and I arrived at Lausanne nearly twenty years after my second departure. Within less than three months the coalition struck on some hidden rocks: had I remained on board I should have perished in the general shipwreck.

Since my establishment at Lausanne more than seven years have elapsed; and if every day has not been equally soft and serene, not a day, not a moment, has occurred in which I have repented of my choice. During my absence, a long portion of human life, many

[1] Sir Richard Worsley, Lord Chesterfield, Broderick Lord Midleton, and Mr. Hume, brother to Sir Abraham.

[2] "The smoke, and the wealth, and the street-noise of Rome."—Horace, *Odes*, B. III., xxix. 12.

changes had happened: my elder acquaintance had left the stage; virgins were ripened into matrons, and children were grown to the age of manhood. But the same manners were transmitted from one generation to another: my friend alone was an inestimable treasure; my name was not totally forgotten, and all were ambitious to welcome the arrival of a stranger and the return of a fellow-citizen. The first winter was given to a general embrace, without any nice discrimination of persons and characters. After a more regular settlement, a more accurate survey, I discovered three solid and permanent benefits of my new situation. 1. My personal freedom had been somewhat impaired by the House of Commons and the Board of Trade; but I was now delivered from the chain of duty and dependence, from the hopes and fears of political adventure: my sober mind was no longer intoxicated by the fumes of party, and I rejoiced in my escape as often as I read of the midnight debates which preceded the dissolution of parliament. 2. My English economy had been that of a solitary bachelor, who might afford some occasional dinners. In Switzerland I enjoyed, at every meal, at every hour, the free and pleasant conversation of the friend of my youth; and my daily table was always provided for the reception of one or two extraordinary guests. Our importance in society is less a positive than a relative weight: in London I was lost in the crowd; I ranked with the first families of Lausanne, and my style of prudent expense enabled me to maintain a fair balance of reciprocal civilities. 3. Instead of a small house between a street and a stable-yard, I began to occupy a spacious and convenient mansion, connected on the north side with the city, and open on the south to a beautiful and boundless horizon. A garden of four acres had been laid out by the taste of Mr. Deyverdun: from the garden a rich scenery of meadows and vineyards descends to the Leman Lake, and the prospect far beyond the lake is crowned by the stupendous mountains of Savoy. My books and my acquaintance had been first united in London; but this happy position of my library in town and country was finally reserved for Lausanne. Possessed of every comfort in this triple alliance, I could not be tempted to change my habitation with the changes of the seasons.

My friends had been kindly apprehensive that I should not be able to exist in a Swiss town at the foot of the Alps, after having so long conversed with the first men of the first cities of the world. Such lofty connections may attract the curious, and gratify the vain; but I am too modest, or too proud, to rate my own value by that of my associates; and, whatsoever may be the fame of learning or genius, experience has shown me that the cheaper qualifications of politeness and good sense are of more useful currency in the commerce of life. By many, conversation is esteemed as a theatre or a school: but, after the morning has been occupied by the labours of the library, I wish to unbend rather than to exercise my mind; and in the interval between tea and supper I am far from disdaining the innocent amusement of a game at cards. Lausanne is peopled by a numerous gentry, whose companionable idleness is seldom disturbed by the pursuits of avarice or ambition: the women, though confined to a domestic education, are endowed for the most part with more taste and knowledge than their husbands and brothers: but the decent freedom of both sexes is equally remote from the extremes of simplicity and refinement. I shall add, as a misfortune rather than a merit, that the situation and beauty of the Pays de Vaud, the long habits of the English, the medical reputation of Dr. Tissot, and the fashion of viewing the mountains and glaciers, have opened us on all sides to the incursions of foreigners. The visits of Mr. and Madame Necker, of Prince Henry of Prussia, and of Mr. Fox, may form some pleasing exceptions; but, in general, Lausanne has appeared most agreeable in my eyes when we have been abandoned to our own society. I had frequently seen Mr. Necker, in the summer of 1784, at a country house near Lausanne, where he composed his *Treatise on the Administration of the Finances*. I have since, in October 1790, visited him in his present residence, the castle and barony of Copet, near Geneva. Of the merits and measures of that statesman various opinions may be entertained; but all impartial men must agree in their esteem of his integrity and patriotism.

In the month of August 1784, Prince Henry of Prussia, in his way to Paris, passed three days at Lausanne. His military conduct has been praised by professional men; his character has been vilified by the wit and malice of a demon; but I was flattered by his affability, and entertained by his conversation.

In his tour to Switzerland (September 1788) Mr. Fox gave me two days of free and private society. He seemed to feel, and even to envy, the happiness of my situation; while I admired the powers of a superior man, as they are blended in his attractive character with the softness and simplicity of a child. Perhaps no human being was ever more perfectly exempt from the taint of malevolence, vanity, or falsehood.

My transmigration from London to Lausanne could not be effected without interrupting the course of my historical labours. The hurry of my departure, the joy of my arrival, the delay of my tools, suspended their progress; and a full twelvemonth was lost before I could resume the thread of regular and daily industry. A number of books most requisite and least common had been previously selected; the academical library of Lausanne, which I could use as my own, contained at least the fathers and councils; and I have derived some occasional succour from the public collections of Berne and Geneva. The fourth volume was soon terminated, by an abstract of the controversies of the Incarnation, which the learned Dr. Prideaux was apprehensive of exposing to profane eyes. It had been the original design of the learned Dean Prideaux to write the history of the ruin of the Eastern Church. In this work it would have been necessary not only to unravel all those controversies which the Christians made about the hypostatical union, but also to unfold all the niceties and subtle notions which each sect entertained concerning it. The pious historian was apprehensive of exposing that incomprehensible mystery to the cavils and objections of unbelievers; and he durst not, "seeing the nature of this book, venture it abroad in so wanton and lewd an age."

In the fifth and sixth volumes the revolutions of the empire and the world are most rapid, various, and instructive; and the Greek or Roman historians are checked by the hostile narratives of the barbarians of the East and the West.

It was not till after many designs and many trials that I preferred, as I still prefer, the method of grouping my picture by nations; and the seeming neglect of chronological order is surely compensated by the superior merits of interest and perspicuity. The style of the first volume is, in my opinion, somewhat crude and elaborate; in the second and third it is ripened into ease, correctness, and numbers; but in the three last I may have been seduced by the facility of my pen, and the constant habit of speaking one language and writing another may have infused some mixture of Gallic idioms. Happily for my eyes, I have always closed my studies with the day, and commonly with the morning; and a long, but temperate, labour has been accomplished without fatiguing either the mind or body; but when I computed the remainder of my time and my task, it was apparent that, according to the season of publication, the delay of a month would be productive of that of a year. I was now straining for the goal, and in the last winter many evenings were borrowed from the social pleasures of Lausanne. I could now wish that a pause, an interval, had been allowed for a serious revisal.

I have presumed to mark the moment of conception: I shall now commemorate the hour of my final deliverance. It was on the day, or rather night, of the 27th of June 1787, between the hours of eleven and twelve, that I wrote the last lines of the last page, in a summer-house in my garden. After laying down my pen I took several turns in a *berceau*, or covered walk of acacias, which commands a prospect of the country, the lake, and the mountains. The air was temperate, the sky was serene, the silver orb of the moon was reflected from the waters, and all nature was silent. I will not dissemble the first emotions of joy on recovery of my freedom, and, perhaps, the establishment of my fame.

But my pride was soon humbled, and a sober melancholy was spread over my mind, by the idea that I had taken an everlasting leave of an old and agreeable companion, and that, whatsoever might be the future date of my *History*, the life of the historian must be short and precarious. . . .

When I contemplate the common lot of mortality, I must acknowledge that I have drawn a high prize in the lottery of life. The far greater part of the globe is overspread with barbarism or slavery; in the civilised world the most numerous class is condemned to ignorance and poverty; and the double fortune of my birth in a free and enlightened country, in an honourable and wealthy family, is the lucky chance of a unit against millions. The general probability is about three to one that a new-born infant will not live to complete his fiftieth year.[1] I have now passed that age, and may fairly estimate the present value of my existence in the three-fold division of mind, body, and estate.

1. The first and indispensable requisite of happiness is a clear conscience, unsullied by the reproach or remembrance of an unworthy action.

— Hic murus aheneus esto,
Nil conscire sibi, nullâ pallescere culpâ.[2]

I am endowed with a cheerful temper, a moderate sensibility, and a natural disposition to repose rather than to activity: some mischievous appetites and habits have perhaps been corrected by philosophy or time. The love of study, a passion which derives fresh vigour from enjoyment, supplies each day, each hour, with a perpetual source of independent and rational pleasure; and I am not sensible of any decay of the mental faculties. The original soil has been highly improved by cultivation; but it may be questioned whether some flowers of fancy, some grateful errors, have not been eradicated with the weeds of prejudice. 2. Since I have escaped from the long perils of my childhood, the serious advice of a physician has seldom been requisite. "The madness of superfluous health" I have never known, but my tender constitution has been fortified by time, and the inestimable gift of the sound and peaceful slumbers of infancy may be imputed both to the mind and body. 3. I have already described the merits of my society and situation; but these enjoyments would be tasteless or bitter if their pos-

[1] See Buffon, *Supplément à l'Histoire Naturelle*, tom. vii. p. 158–164: of a given number of new-born infants, one half, by the fault of nature or man, is extinguished before the age of puberty and reason.—A melancholy calculation!

[2] "Let this be to thee as it were a brazen wall of defence, to be conscious of no evil that will cause you to grow pale in the presence of others."—Horace, *Epistles*, B. I., i. l. 59.

session were not assured by an annual and adequate supply. According to the scale of Switzerland I am a rich man; and I am indeed rich, since my income is superior to my expense, and my expense is equal to my wishes. My friend Lord Sheffield has kindly relieved me from the cares to which my taste and temper are most adverse: shall I add that, since the failure of my first wishes, I have never entertained any serious thoughts of a matrimonial connection?

I am disgusted with the affectation of men of letters, who complain that they have renounced a substance for a shadow, and that their fame (which sometimes is no insupportable weight) affords a poor compensation for envy, censure, and persecution.[1] My own experience, at least, has taught me a very different lesson: twenty happy years have been animated by the labour of my *History*, and its success has given me a name, a rank, a character in the world to which I should not otherwise have been entitled. The freedom of my writings has indeed provoked an implacable tribe; but, as I was safe from the stings, I was soon accustomed to the buzzing of the hornets: my nerves are not tremblingly alive, and my literary temper is so happily framed that I am less sensible of pain than of pleasure. The rational pride of an author may be offended, rather than flattered, by vague indiscriminate praise; but he cannot, he should not, be indifferent to the fair testimonies of private and public esteem. Even his moral sympathy may be gratified by the idea that now, in the present hour, he is imparting some degree of amusement or knowledge to his friends in a distant land; that one day his mind will be familiar to the grandchildren of those who are yet unborn.[2] I cannot boast of the friendship or favour of princes; the patronage of English literature has long since been devolved on our booksellers, and the measure of their liberality is the least ambiguous test of our common success. Perhaps the golden mediocrity of my fortune has contributed to fortify my application.

[1] Mr. d'Alembert relates that, as he was walking in the gardens of Sans Souci with the King of Prussia, Frederic said to him, "Do you see that old woman, a poor weeder, asleep on that sunny bank? she is probably a more happy being than either of us." The king and the philosopher may speak for themselves; for my part, I do not envy the old woman.

[2] In the first of ancient or modern romances (*Tom Jones*) this proud sentiment, this feast of fancy, is enjoyed by the genius of Fielding—"Come, bright love of fame, etc., fill my ravished fancy with the hopes of charming ages yet to come. Foretell me that some tender maid, whose grandmother is yet unborn, hereafter, when, under the fictitious name of Sophia, she reads the real worth which once existed in my Charlotte, shall from her sympathetic breast send forth the heaving sigh. Do thou teach me not only to foresee but to enjoy, nay even to feed on, future praise. Comfort me by the solemn assurance that, when the little parlour in which I sit at this moment shall be reduced to a worse furnished box, I shall be read with honour by those who never knew nor saw me, and whom I shall neither know nor see."—Book xiii., chap. 1.

The present is a fleeting moment, the past is no more; and our prospect of futurity is dark and doubtful. This day may *possibly* be my last: but the laws of probability, so true in general, so fallacious in particular, still allow about fifteen years.[1] I shall soon enter into the period which, as the most agreeable of his long life, was selected by the judgment and experience of the sage Fontenelle. His choice is approved by the eloquent historian of nature, who fixes our moral happiness to the mature season, in which our passions are supposed to be calmed, our duties fulfilled, our ambition satisfied, our fame and fortune established on a solid basis.[2] In private conversation, that great and amiable man added the weight of his own experience; and this autumnal felicity might be exemplified in the lives of Voltaire, Hume, and many other men of letters. I am far more inclined to embrace than to dispute this comfortable doctrine. I will not suppose any premature decay of the mind or body; but I must reluctantly observe that two causes, the abbreviation of time, and the failure of hope, will always tinge with a browner shade the evening of life.[3]

[1] Mr. Buffon, from our disregard of the possibility of death within the four-and-twenty hours, concludes that a chance which falls below or rises above ten thousand to one will never affect the hopes or fears of a reasonable man. The fact is true, but our courage is the effect of thoughtlessness, rather than of reflection. If a public lottery were drawn for the choice of an immediate victim, and if our name were inscribed on one of the ten thousand tickets, should we be perfectly easy?

[2] See Buffon.

[3] The proportion of a part to the whole is the only standard by which we can measure the length of our existence. At the age of twenty, one year is a tenth, perhaps, of the time which has elapsed within our consciousness and memory: at the age of fifty it is no more than the fortieth, and this relative value continues to decrease till the last sands are shaken by the hand of death. This reasoning may seem metaphysical; but on a trial it will be found satisfactory and just. The warm desires, the long expectations of youth are founded on the ignorance of themselves and of the world: they are gradually damped by time and experience, by disappointment and possession; and after the middle season the crowd must be content to remain at the foot of the mountain; while the few who have climbed the summit aspire to descend or expect to fall. In old age the consolation of hope is reserved for the tenderness of parents, who commence a new life in their children; the faith of enthusiasts, who sing hallelujahs above the clouds; and the vanity of authors, who presume the immortality of their name and writings.

# ACKNOWLEDGMENTS

THE EDITOR gratefully acknowledges the kindness of authors, agents, and publishers in giving permission to reproduce copyright material in THE PLEASURE OF THEIR COMPANY.

THE BOBBS-MERRILL COMPANY: for Chapter I from *The Young Melbourne* by Lord David Cecil, copyright 1939. Used by special permission of the publishers, The Bobbs-Merrill Company.

BRANDT AND BRANDT: for "Maltby and Braxton" from *Seven Men* by Max Beerbohm, published by Alfred A. Knopf, Inc. Copyright 1920 by Max Beerbohm.

JONATHAN CAPE, LTD: for the three aphorisms from *The Notebooks of Samuel Butler*. Reprinted by permission of Jonathan Cape, Ltd.

CASSELL & COMPANY, LTD: for the selection from *The Goncourt Journals* by Edmund and Jules de Goncourt, translated by Lewis Galantière. Reprinted by permission of Cassell & Company, Ltd.

CHATTO & WINDUS: for "The Tillotson Banquet" from *Mortal Coils* by Aldous Huxley. Reprinted by permission of Chatto & Windus.

THE CLARENDON PRESS, OXFORD: for "Zeus Cross-Examined" from *The Works of Lucian*, translated by F. T. and H. W. Fowler. Reprinted by permission of the publishers, The Clarendon Press, Oxford.

CONSTABLE AND COMPANY LTD: for six aphorisms by Vauvenargues and one aphorism by La Bruyère, translated by Elizabeth Lee; and for Chapter I from *The Young Melbourne* by Lord David Cecil. Reprinted by permission of Constable and Company, Ltd.

J. M. DENT & SONS, LTD: for one aphorism from *Pensées* by Blaise Pascal, translated by Leon Brunschvicg. Reprinted by permission of J. M. Dent & Sons, Ltd.

DODD, MEAD & COMPANY: for one aphorism from *Penguin Island* by Anatole France; and for four aphorisms from *Plays* by Oscar Wilde. Reprinted by permission of the publishers, Dodd, Mead and Company.

# *Acknowledgments*

Doubleday, Doran & Company, inc: for the selection from *The Goncourt Journals* by Edmund and Jules de Goncourt, translated by Lewis Galantière. Copyright 1937, by Doubleday, Doran and Company, Inc.

E. P. Dutton & Company: for one aphorism from *Pensées* by Blaise Pascal, translated by Leon Brunschvicg; and for three aphorisms from the *Notebooks* of Samuel Butler. Reprinted by permission of E. P. Dutton & Company.

E. M. Forster: for "My Own Centenary" from his *Abinger Harvest*, copyright 1936 by E. M. Forster.

Harcourt, Brace & Company, inc: for "Dr. Burney's Evening Party" from *The Second Common Reader* by Virginia Woolf, copyright 1932, by Harcourt, Brace & Company, Inc.; and for "My Own Centenary" from *Abinger Harvest* by E. M. Forster, copyright 1936, by E. M. Forster. Reprinted by permission of Harcourt, Brace & Company, Inc.

Harper & Brothers: for "The Tillotson Banquet" from *Mortal Coils* by Aldous Huxley, copyright 1921, by Aldous Huxley; and for a selection from *Mme. Récamier* by Ste. Beauve, translated by Frederick A. Manchester. Reprinted by permission of the publishers, Harper & Brothers.

The Hogarth Press: for "Dr. Burney's Evening Party" from *The Second Common Reader* by Virginia Woolf. Reprinted by permission of The Hogarth Press.

Houghton Mifflin Company: for a selection from *Letters of Henry Adams*. Reprinted by permission of the publishers, Houghton Mifflin Company.

International Publishers: for *Rameau's Nephew* by Diderot, translated by Jean Stewart and Jonathan Kemp. Reprinted by permission of International Publishers.

Princeton University Press: for *Erasmus: The Praise of Folly*, translated by Hoyt H. Hudson. Reprinted by permission of the Princeton University Press.

George Routledge & Sons ltd: for *Rameau's Nephew* by Diderot, translated by Jean Stewart and Jonathan Kemp. Reprinted by permission of George Routledge & Sons, Ltd.

STACKPOLE SONS: for eight aphorisms by La Rochefoucauld, translated by Louis Kronenberger. Reprinted by permission of Stackpole Sons.

THE VIKING PRESS, INC: for "The Matron of Ephesus" by Petronius and "The Jewels" by Guy de Maupassant from *The Short Story's Mutations* by Frances Newman. Copyright 1924, by B. W. Huebsch, Inc. Reprinted by permission of The Viking Press, Inc.

CHARLES SCRIBNER'S SONS: for permission to reprint *Washington Square* by Henry James.

## *A Note* ON THE TYPE IN WHICH THIS BOOK IS SET

*This book was set on the Linotype in Janson, a recutting made direct from the type cast from matrices made by Anton Janson some time between 1660 and 1687.*

*Of Janson's origin nothing is known. He may have been a relative of Justus Janson, a printer of Danish birth who practised in Leipzig from 1614 to 1635. Some time between 1657 and 1668 Anton Janson, a punch-cutter and type-founder, bought from the Leipzig printer Johann Erich Hahn the type-foundry which had formerly been a part of the printing house of M. Friedrich Lankisch. Janson's types were first shown in a specimen sheet issued at Leipzig about 1675.*

*The typography and the binding design are by Warren Chappell*

*Composed, printed, and bound by Kingsport Press, Kingsport, Tenn.*